To: Miriam and Harry

McGraw-Hill
Irwin

ACCOUNTING FOR DECISION MAKING AND CONTROL
Published by McGraw-Hill/Irwin, a business unit of The McGraw-Hill Companies, Inc., 1221
Avenue of the Americas, New York, NY, 10020. Copyright © 2006, 2003, 2000, 1997, 1995 by
The McGraw-Hill Companies, Inc. All rights reserved. No part of this publication may be
reproduced or distributed in any form or by any means, or stored in a database or retrieval
system, without the prior written consent of The McGraw-Hill Companies, Inc., including, but
not limited to, in any network or other electronic storage or transmission, or broadcast for
distance learning.

Some ancillaries, including electronic and print components. may not be available to customers
outside the United States.

This book is printed on acid-free paper.

1 2 3 4 5 6 7 8 9 0 VNH/VNH 0 9 8 7 6 5

ISBN 0-07-297586-5

Editorial director: *Brent Gordon*
Publisher: *Stewart Mattson*
Sponsoring editor: *Steve DeLancey*
Editorial assistant: *Megan McFarlane*
Marketing manager: *Marc Chernoff*
Senior project manager: *Christine A. Vaughan*
Senior production supervisor: *Sesha Bolisetty*
Senior designer: *Adam Rooke*
Media producer: *Elizabeth Mavetz*
Senior media project manager: *Susan Lombardi*
Developer, media technology: *Brian Nacik*
Cover design: *Brian Perveneckis*
Typeface: *11/12 Goudy*
Compositor: *Cenveo*
Printer: *Von Hoffmann Corporation*

Library of Congress Cataloging-in-Publication Data

Zimmerman, Jerold L., 1947-
  Accounting for decision making and control / Jerold L. Zimmerman. — 5th ed.
      p. cm.
  Includes bibliographical references and index.
  ISBN 0-07-297586-5 (alk. paper)
  1. Managerial accounting. I. Title
HF5657.4.Z55 2006
658.15'11—dc22   2005041975

www.mhhe.com

About the Author

Jerold L. Zimmerman
Jerold Zimmerman is Ronald L. Bittner Professor at the William E. Simon Graduate School of Business, University of Rochester. He holds an undergraduate degree from the University of Colorado, Boulder, and a doctorate from the University of California, Berkeley.

While at Rochester, Dr. Zimmerman has taught a variety of courses spanning accounting, finance, and economics. Accounting courses include non-profit accounting, intermediate accounting, accounting theory, and managerial accounting. A deeper appreciation of the challenges of managing a complex organization was acquired by spending four years as Deputy Dean of the Simon School.

Professor Zimmerman publishes widely in accounting on topics as diverse as cost allocations, municipal accounting, budgeting, taxes, auditing, financial accounting theory, mergers and acquisitions, trade unions, capital markets, and executive compensation. His paper, "The Costs and Benefits of Cost Allocations," won the American Accounting Association's Competitive Manuscript Contest. He is recognized for developing Positive Accounting Theory. This work, co-authored with colleague Ross Watts, also at the University of Rochester, received the American Institute of Certified Public Accountants' Notable Contribution to the Accounting Literature Award for "Towards a Positive Theory of the Determination of Accounting Standards" and "The Demand for and Supply of Accounting Theories: The Market for Excuses." Both papers appeared in the *Accounting Review*. Professors Watts and Zimmerman are also co-authors of the highly cited textbook, *Positive Accounting Theory* (Prentice Hall, 1986). More recently, Professors Watts and Zimmerman received the 2004 American Accounting Association Seminal Contribution to the Literature award. Professor Zimmerman's textbooks also include: *Managerial Economics and Organizational Architecture* with Clifford Smith and James Brickley, 3rd ed. (McGraw-Hill/Irwin, 2004) and *Management Accounting: Analysis and Interpretation* with Cheryl McWatters and Dale Morse (McGraw-Hill/Irwin, 2001). He is a founding editor of the *Journal of Accounting and Economics*, published by North-Holland. This scientific journal is one of the most highly referenced accounting publications.

He and his wife Dodie have two daughters, Daneille and Amy. Jerry has been known to occasionally engage friends and colleagues in an amicable diversion on the links.

Preface

During their professional careers, managers in all organizations, profit and non-profit, interact with their accounting systems. Sometimes managers use the accounting system to acquire information for decision making. At other times, the accounting system measures performance and thereby influences their behavior. The accounting system is both a source of information for decision making and part of the organization's control mechanisms—thus, the title of the book, *Accounting for Decision Making and Control.*

The purpose of this book is to provide students and managers with an understanding and appreciation of the strengths and limitations of an organization's accounting system, thereby allowing them to be more intelligent users of these systems. This book provides a framework for thinking about accounting systems and a basis for analyzing proposed changes to these systems. The text demonstrates that managerial accounting is an integral part of the firm's organizational architecture, not just an isolated set of computational topics.

Distinguishing Features

Conceptual Framework

This book differs from other managerial accounting texts in several ways. The most important difference is that it offers a conceptual framework for the study of managerial accounting. This book relies on **opportunity cost** and **organizational architecture** as the underlying framework to organize the analysis. Opportunity cost is the conceptual foundation underlying decision making. While accounting-based costs are not opportunity costs, in some circumstances accounting costs provide a starting point to estimate opportunity costs. The organizational architecture provides the conceptual foundation to understand how accounting is employed as part of the organization's control mechanism. These two concepts, opportunity costs and organizational architecture, provide the framework and illustrate the trade-offs created when accounting systems serve both functions: decision making and control.

Trade-Offs

This text emphasizes that there is no "free lunch;" improving an accounting system's decision-making ability often reduces its effectiveness as a control device. Likewise, using an accounting system as a control mechanism usually comes at the expense of using the system for decision making. Most texts discuss the importance of deriving different estimates of costs for different purposes. Existing books do a good job illustrating how accounting costs developed for one purpose, such as inventory valuation, cannot be used without adjustment for other purposes, such as a make-or-buy decision. However, these books often leave the impression that one accounting system can be used for multiple purposes as long as the users make the appropriate adjustments in the data.

What existing texts do not emphasize is the trade-off between designing the accounting system for decision making and designing it for control. For example, activity-based costing presumably improves the accounting system's ability for decision making (pricing and product design), but existing texts do not address what activity-based costing gives up in terms of control. *Accounting for Decision Making and Control* emphasizes the trade-offs managers confront in an organization's accounting system.

Economic Darwinism

A central theme throughout this book is **economic Darwinism,** which simply implies that accounting systems that survive in competitive industries must be yielding benefits that are at least as large as their costs. While newer accounting innovations such as activity-based costing are described, the text also indicates through a series of company histories that many elements of today's modern costing systems can be traced back to much earlier times. It is useful to understand that today's managers are struggling with the same accounting issues as their predecessors, because today's students will also be struggling with the same problems. These problems continue to exist because they involve making trade-offs, usually between systems for decision making (e.g., product pricing and make-or-buy decisions) versus control (e.g., performance evaluation).

Accounting systems differ across firms and change as firms' circumstances change. Today's students will be making these trade-offs in the future. The current rage in managerial accounting texts is to present the latest, most up-to-date accounting system innovations. While recent innovations are important to discuss, they should be placed in their proper perspective. Traditional absorption costing systems have survived the test of time for over one hundred years. Accounting system innovations are new, not necessarily better. We certainly do not know if they will survive.

Logical Sequence

Another meaningful distinction between this text and other books in the field is that the chapters in this text build on one another. The first four chapters develop the opportunity cost and organization theory foundation for the course. The remaining chapters apply the foundation to analyzing specific topics such as budgets and standard costs. Most of the controversy in product costing involves apportioning overhead. Before absorption, variable, and activity-based costing are described, an earlier chapter provides a general analysis of cost allocation. This analysis is applied in later chapters as the analytic framework for choosing among the various product costing schemes. Other books emphasize a modular, flexible approach that allows instructors to devise their own sequence to the material, with the result that these courses often appear as a series of unrelated, disjointed topics without any underlying cohesive framework. This book has 14 chapters, compared with the usual 18–25. Instead of dividing a topic such as cost allocation into three small, disjointed chapters, most topics are covered in one or at most two unified chapters.

End-of-Chapter Material

The end-of-chapter problem material is an integral part of any text, and especially important in *Accounting for Decision Making and Control*. The problems and cases are drawn from actual company applications described by former students based on their work experience. Many problems require students to develop critical thinking skills and to write short essays after preparing their numerical analyses. Good problems get students excited about the material and generate lively class discussions. Some problems do not have a single correct answer. Rather, they contain multiple dimensions demanding a broad managerial perspective. Marketing, finance, and human resource aspects of the situation are frequently posed. Few problems focus exclusively on computations.

Changes in the Fifth Edition

Based on extensive feedback from instructors using the first four editions and from my own teaching experience, the fifth edition focuses on improving the book's readability and accessibility. In particular, the following changes have been made:

- Each chapter has been revised based on student and instructor feedback. More intuitive, easier-to-understand numerical examples have been added.
- Additional actual company practices have been integrated into the text.
- Fifty new problems and cases supplement the existing problems. Users were uniform in their praise of the problem material. They found it challenged their students to critically analyze multidimensional issues while still requiring numerical problem-solving skills. Further problems and cases to complement this selection have been added.
- Summaries of recent research articles have been incorporated throughout the text.

Overview of Content

Chapter 1 presents the book's conceptual framework by using a simple decision context regarding accepting an incremental order from a current customer. The chapter describes why firms use a single accounting system and the concept of economic Darwinism, among other important topics. This chapter is an integral part of the text.

Chapters 2, 4, and 5 present the underlying conceptual framework. The importance of opportunity costs in decision making, cost–volume–profit analysis, and the difference between accounting costs and opportunity costs are discussed in Chapter 2. Chapter 4 summarizes recent advances in the theory of organizations and Chapter 5 describes the crucial role of accounting as part of the firm's organizational architecture. Chapter 3 on capital budgeting extends opportunity costs to a multiperiod setting. This chapter can be skipped without affecting the flow of later material. Alternatively, Chapter 3 can be assigned at the end of the course.

Chapter 6 applies the conceptual framework and illustrates the trade-off managers often must make between decision making and control in a budgeting system. Budgets are a decision-making tool to coordinate activities within the firm and are a device to control behavior. This chapter provides an in-depth illustration of how budgets are a significant part of an organization's decision-making and control apparatus.

Chapter 7 presents a general analysis of why managers allocate certain costs and the behavioral implications of these allocations. Cost allocations affect both decision making and incentives. Thus, there is again the trade-off between decision making and control. Chapter 8 continues the cost allocation discussion by describing the "death spiral" that can occur when significant fixed costs exist and excess capacity arises. This leads to an analysis of how to treat capacity costs—a trade-off between underutilization and overinvestment. Finally, several specific cost allocation methods such as service department costs and joint costs are described.

Chapter 9 applies the general analysis of overhead allocation in Chapters 7 and 8 to the specific case of absorption costing in a manufacturing setting. The managerial implications of traditional absorption costing are provided in Chapters 10 and 11. Chapter 10 analyzes variable costing, and activity-based costing is the topic of Chapter 11. Variable costing is an interesting example of economic Darwinism. Proponents of variable costing argue that it does not distort decision making and therefore should be adopted. Nonetheless it is not widely practiced, probably because of tax, financial reporting, and control considerations.

Chapter 12 discusses the decision-making and control implications of standard labor and material costs. Chapter 13 extends the discussion to overhead and marketing variances. Chapter 13 can be omitted without interrupting the flow of later material. Finally, Chapter 14 synthesizes the course by reviewing the conceptual framework and applying it to three recent organizational innovations: Total Quality Management, just-in-time (JIT) production, and the balanced scorecard. All three provide an opportunity to apply the analytic framework underlying the text.

Overview of Table of Contents

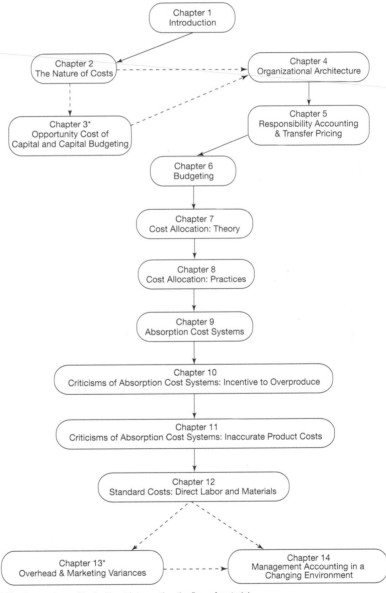

*Chapter can be omitted without interrupting the flow of material.

Using the Text

This book assumes that the student is familiar with introductory financial accounting. *Accounting for Decision Making and Control* can be used in advanced undergraduate, graduate, or executive programs. It is being used widely outside the United States. While the book relies on opportunity costs and concepts concerning organizations, much of the discussion is at an intuitive level. To focus on the managerial implications of the material, journal entries are deliberately de-emphasized.

The text is concise, which allows the instructor to supplement the course with additional outside readings or heavy problem assignments. The text has been used in a 10-week quarter course with few outside readings and two to three hours of homework assignments for every class period. MBA students find this challenging and rewarding. They report a better understanding of how to use accounting numbers, are more comfortable at preparing financial analyses, and are better able to take a set of facts and communicate a cogent analysis. Alternatively, the text can support a semester-length course. Executive MBA students praise the text's real-world applicability, readability, and the relevance of the problem material.

Some of the more challenging material is presented in appendixes following the chapters. The two appendixes to Chapter 2 describe the pricing decision and some of the difficulties encountered trying to estimate fixed and variable costs using regression analysis. Chapter 6's appendix contains a comprehensive master budget. Cost allocations as a tax system are presented in Chapter 7's appendix. The reciprocal method for allocating service department costs is described in the appendix to Chapter 8. The appendixes to Chapter 9 describe process costing and demand shifts, fixed costs, and pricing. Appendixes can be deleted without affecting future chapter discussions.

Supplements

Several important supplements accompany *Accounting for Decision Making and Control*. The Instructor's Resource Guide CD-ROM provides chapter-by-chapter teaching strategies, suggested problem assignments, recommended outside cases, lecture notes, sample syllabi, Chapter PowerPoint presentations, and, of course, complete solutions to all problem and case material within the text.

McGraw-Hill has also created a Web site to accompany the text, which can be found at *http://www.mhhe.com/business/accounting/zimmerman5e*. The Web site offers several useful features for students and instructors, including downloadable supplements, Chapter PowerPoint presentations, and Web site links. Professor Ronald S. Barden of Georgia State University has created the PowerPoint presentations for the professor and student, which add an important visual dimension to your lectures.

Acknowledgments

William Vatter and George Benston motivated my interest in managerial accounting. The genesis for this book and its approach reflect the oral tradition of my colleagues, past and present, at the University of Rochester. William Meckling and Michael Jensen stimulated my thinking and provided much of the theoretical structure underlying the book, as anyone familiar with their work will attest. My long and productive collaboration with Ross Watts sharpened my analytical skills and further refined the approach. He also furnished most of the intellectual capital for Chapter 3, including the problem material. Ray Ball has been a constant source of ideas and has contributed to my understanding of managerial accounting. Clifford Smith and James Brickley continue to enhance my economic education. Three colleagues, Andrew Christie, Dan Gode, and Scott Keating, supplied particularly insightful comments that enriched the analysis at critical junctions. Valuable comments from Anil Arya, Ron Dye, Kenneth Gartrell, Andy Leone, K. Ramesh, Shyam Sunder, and Joseph Weintrop are gratefully acknowledged.

This project benefited greatly from the honest and intelligent feedback of numerous instructors. I wish to thank Mahendra Gupta, Susan Hamlen, Badr Ismail, Charles Kile, Leslie Kren, Don May, William Mister, Mohamed Onsi, Ram Ramachandran, Stephen Ryan, Michael Sandretto, Deniz Saral, Gary Schneider, Joe Weber, and William Yancey. This book also benefited from two other projects with which I have been involved. Writing *Managerial Economics and Organizational Architecture* (McGraw-Hill/Irwin, 2004) with James Brickley and Clifford Smith and *Management Accounting: Analysis and Interpretation* (McGraw-Hill/Irwin, 2001) with Cheryl McWatters and Dale Morse helped me to better understand how to present certain topics.

To the numerous students who endured the development process, I owe an enormous debt of gratitude. I hope they learned as much from the material as I learned teaching them. Some were even kind enough to provide critiques and suggestions, in particular Jan Dick Eijkelboom. Others supplied, either directly or indirectly, the problem material in the text. The able research assistance of P. K. Madappa, Eamon Molloy, Dag Ozay, Jodi Parker, Steve Sanders, Richard Sloan, and especially Gary Hurst, contributed amply to the manuscript and problem material. Permission has been received from the Institute of Certified Management Accountants of the Institute of Management Accountants to use questions and/or unofficial answers from past CMA examinations. Financial support was received from the John M. Olin Foundation.

I learned how much a world-class publisher can enhance a textbook. Publishing textbooks requires a publisher with insight, dedication to detail, and patience. My colleagues at McGraw-Hill/Irwin have these qualities and made this book a reality. Janice Willett and Barbara Schnathorst did a superb job of editing the manuscript and problem material.

Besides providing editorial and production assistance, the publisher manages the outside review process. The very useful comments and suggestions from the following reviewers are greatly appreciated:

Urton Anderson	Linda Campbell	Bert Horwitz
Howard M. Armitage	William M. Cready	Steven Huddart
Ron Barden	James M. Emig	Robert Hurt
Kashi Balachandran	Gary Fane	Douglas A. Johnson
Da-Hsien Bao	Tahirih Foroughi	Lawrence A. Klein
Margaret Boldt	Ivar Fris	Thomas Krissek
David Borst	Jackson F. Gillespie	A. Ronald Kucic
Eric Bostwick	Irving Gleim	Chi-Wen Jevons Lee
Marvin L. Bouillon	Jon Glover	Suzanne Lowensohn
Wayne Bremser	Gus Gordon	James R. Martin
David Bukovinsky	Susan Haka	Alan H. McNamee

Marilyn Okleshen

Sam Phillips

Frank Probst

Ram Ramanar

William Rau

Jane Reimers

Thomas Ross

Harold P. Roth

P. N. Saksena

Donald Samaleson

Michael J. Sandretto

Arnold Schneider

Henry Schwarzbach

Norman Shultz

James C. Stallman

William Thomas
Stevens

Monte R. Swain

Paul F. Williams

Robert W. Williamson

Jeffrey A. Yost

S. Mark Young

Kathy Jones, my very able assistant, had the difficult and often impossible task of managing and editing the manuscript and instructor manual. She did a superb job. To my wife Dodie and daughters Daneille and Amy, thank you for setting the right priorities and for giving me the encouragement and environment to be productive. Finally, I wish to thank my parents for all their support.

Jerold L. Zimmerman
University of Rochester

Brief Contents

Contents

Chapter One

Introduction

Chapter Outline

TABLE 1–1   **Importance of Accounting Goals in Large Banks**

Goal of Cost Accounting Systems	Most Important	Second Most Important	Third Most Important	Fourth Most Important	Least Important	Total
Product development and pricing	61.2%	24.5%	14.3%	0.0%	0.0%	100%
Achieving cost reductions	22.4	42.9	26.5	8.2	0.0	100
Performance evaluation	14.6	27.1	35.4	18.7	4.2	100
Industry cost comparison	2.3	2.3	20.9	58.2	16.3	100

control use of accounting is to prevent fraud and embezzlement. Maintaining inventory records helps reduce employee theft. Accounting budgets, discussed more fully in Chapter 6, provide an example of both decision making and control. Asking each salesperson in the firm to forecast next year's sales in his or her territory and then aggregating across all salespeople produces an estimate of the firm's budgeted sales. This estimate is very useful for planning next year's most efficient production methods (decision making). Many firms also use the salespersons' forecasted sales amount to benchmark actual sales. Salespeople who beat their forecasts receive bonuses. Basing bonuses on beating budgeted sales targets is an example of using accounting numbers for control. Clearly, when salespeople know that their sales forecasts will be used in their compensation, they have strong incentives to underestimate their budget forecasts.

Using internal accounting systems for both decision making and control gives rise to the fundamental trade-off in these systems: A system cannot be designed to perform two tasks as well as a system that must perform only one task. Some ability to deliver knowledge for decision making is usually sacrificed to provide better motivation (control). The trade-off between providing knowledge for decision making and motivation/control arises continually throughout this text.

This book is applications oriented: It describes how the accounting system assembles knowledge necessary for implementing decisions using the theories from microeconomics, finance, operations management, and marketing. It also shows how the accounting system helps motivate employees to implement these decisions. Moreover, it stresses the continual trade-offs that must be made between the decision making and control functions of accounting.

A survey of the 49 largest banks and savings and loans in the United States asked managers to rank the importance of the various goals of their firm's accounting system. Table 1–1 indicates that product development and pricing was the most important goal and achieving cost reductions was the second most important goal. Performance evaluation was third most important—but it was ranked as the first or second most important goal by 41.7 percent of the bank executives. These results indicate that large banks use their accounting systems for decision making (product development, pricing, and cost control) and for controlling behavior (performance evaluation).[2]

---

[2] M Gardner and L Lammers, "Cost Accounting in Large Banks," *Management Accounting,* April 1988, pp. 34–39.

Alternative Approaches to Organizational Theory

This book uses an economic perspective to study how accounting can motivate and control behavior in organizations. Besides economics, a variety of other paradigms also are used to investigate organizations: scientific management (Taylor), the bureaucratic school (Weber), the human relations approach (Mayo), human resource theory (Maslow, Rickert, Argyris), the decision-making school (Simon), and the political science school (Selznick). For example, one branch of the human relations approach holds that "good leadership" generates greater productivity. A "good leader" is democratic rather than authoritarian, is employee-centered rather than production-centered, and cares about employees rather than bureaucratic rules.

Behavior is a complex topic. No single theory or approach is likely to capture all the elements. However, understanding managerial accounting requires addressing the behavioral and organizational issues. Economics offers one useful framework.

SOURCE: V Narayanan and R Nath, *Organization Theory: A Strategic Approach* (Burr Ridge, IL: Richard D. Irwin, 1993), pp. 28–47; and C Perrow, *Complex Organizations: A Critical Essay* (New York: Random House, 1986), p. 85.

The firm's accounting system is very much a part of the fabric that helps hold the organization together. It provides knowledge for decision making, and it provides information for evaluating and motivating the behavior of individuals within the firm. Being such an integral part of the organization, the accounting system cannot be studied in isolation from the other mechanisms used for decision making or for reducing organizational problems. A firm's internal accounting system should be examined from a broad perspective, as part of the larger organization design question facing managers.

B. Design and Use of Cost Systems

Managers make decisions and monitor subordinates who make decisions. Both managers and accountants must acquire sufficient familiarity with cost systems to perform their jobs. Accountants (often called *controllers*) are charged with designing, improving, and operating the firm's accounting system—an integral part of both the decision-making and performance evaluation systems. Both managers and accountants must understand the strengths and weaknesses of current accounting systems. Internal accounting systems, like all systems within the firm, are constantly being refined and modified. Accountants' responsibilities include making these changes.

An internal accounting system should have the following characteristics:

1. Provide the information necessary to identify the most profitable products and the pricing and marketing strategies to achieve the desired volume levels.
2. Provide information to detect production inefficiencies to ensure that the proposed products and volumes are produced at minimum cost.
3. When combined with the performance evaluation and reward systems, create incentives for managers to maximize firm value.

Management Innovations	**Activity-based cost (ABC) systems** first assign costs to activities in the production process and then either directly trace, or allocate, these costs to products using various methods that most accurately capture how the costs vary.

Activity-based cost (ABC) systems first assign costs to activities in the production process and then either directly trace, or allocate, these costs to products using various methods that most accurately capture how the costs vary.

Balanced score card provides a comprehensive framework that links a firm's strategic objectives to a coherent set of performance measures.

Benchmarking involves studying the best-performing organizations providing similar activities or products, thereby improving the operations of work processes.

Computer-aided manufacturing (CAM) uses programmable robots to perform functions such as welding car bodies and inserting electronic components in circuit boards. In addition to saving on some labor costs, robots have the advantage of being faster and more precise. CAM increases flexibility because manufacturing processes can be more quickly shifted from making one product to making another.

Electronic data interchange (EDI) is the direct exchange of data such as purchase orders and invoices between organizations via computer networks.

Enterprise resource planning (ERP) is an integrated, automated, computer-based system that tracks production by job, work center, and activity and then shares the information enterprisewide in real time.

Just-in-time (JIT) production is a manufacturing process designed to provide products as they are needed. Plants using JIT make a product when an order is received rather than making and holding it until it is sold or discarded. By making the product only when ordered, fewer units are wasted due to obsolescence. Organizations shift to JIT in part because of technological changes. For example, the advent of bar coding and the instant reporting of sales to suppliers allows customers to reduce inventory and allows suppliers to replenish inventory when needed.

Total quality management (TQM) is a philosophy of continually lowering costs and improving the provision of services and products to customers. Quality is defined by the customer and quality involves everyone within the organization. A shift to TQM means empowering employees to reduce costs and accommodate customer demands.

4. Support the financial accounting and tax accounting reporting functions. (In some instances, these latter considerations dominate the first three.)
5. Contribute more to firm value than it costs.

Figure 1–1 portrays the functions of the accounting system. In it, the accounting system supports both external and internal reporting systems. Examine the top half of Figure 1–1. The accounting procedures chosen for external reports to shareholders and taxing authorities are dictated in part by regulators. The **Securities and Exchange Commission (SEC)** and the **Financial Accounting Standards Board (FASB)** regulate the financial statements issued to shareholders. The **Internal Revenue Service (IRS)** regulates the accounting procedures used in calculating corporate income taxes. If the firm is involved in international trade, foreign tax authorities prescribe the accounting rules applied in calculating foreign

FIGURE 1–1

The multiple role of accounting systems

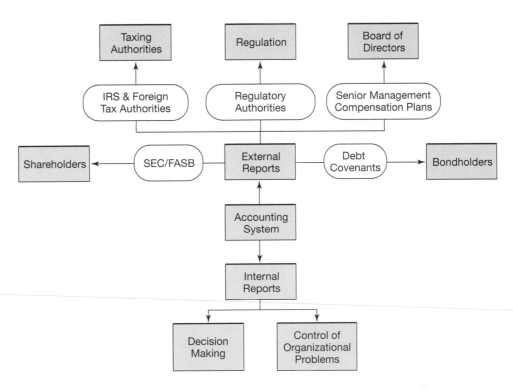

taxes. Regulatory agencies constrain public utilities' and financial institutions' accounting procedures.[3]

Management compensation plans and debt contracts often rely on external reports. Senior managers' bonuses are often based on accounting net income. Likewise, if the firm issues long-term bonds, it agrees in the debt covenants not to violate specified accounting-based constraints. For example, the bond contract might specify that the debt-to-equity ratio will not exceed some limit. Like taxes and regulation, compensation plans and debt covenants create incentives for managers to choose particular accounting procedures.[4]

As firms expand into international markets, external users of the firm's financial statements become global. No longer are the firm's shareholders, tax authorities, and regulators domestic. Rather, the firm's internal and external reports are used internationally in a variety of ways.

The bottom of Figure 1–1 illustrates that internal reports are used for decision making as well as control of organizational problems. As discussed earlier, managers use a variety of sources of data for making decisions. The internal accounting system provides one important source. These internal reports are also used to

---

[3] Tax laws can affect financial reporting and internal reporting. For example, a 1973 U.S. tax code change allowed firms to exclude manufacturing depreciation from inventories and write it off directly against taxable income of the period if the same method was used for external financial reporting. Such a provision reduces taxes for most firms, although few firms adopted the procedure. See E Noreen and R Bowen, "Tax Incentives and the Decision to Capitalize or Expense Manufacturing Overhead," *Accounting Horizons*, 1989.

[4] For further discussion of the incentives of managers to choose accounting methods, see R Watts and J Zimmerman, *Positive Accounting Theory* (Englewood Cliffs, NJ: Prentice Hall, 1986); and R Watts and J Zimmerman, "Positive Accounting Theory: A Ten-Year Perspective," *Accounting Review* 65 (January 1990), pp. 131–56.

Spaceship Lost Because Two Measures Used	Multiple accounting systems are confusing and can lead to errors. An extreme example of this occurred in 1999 when NASA lost its $125 million Mars spacecraft. Engineers at Lockheed Martin built the spacecraft and specified the spacecraft's thrust in English pounds. But NASA scientists, navigating the craft, assumed the information was in metric newtons. As a result, the spacecraft was off course by 60 miles as it approached Mars and crashed. Whenever two systems are being used to measure the same underlying event, people can forget which system is being used.

SOURCE: A Pollack, "Two Teams, Two Measures Equaled One Lost Spacecraft," *The New York Times*, October 1, 1999, p. 1.

evaluate and motivate (control) the behavior of managers in the firm. The internal accounting system reports on managers' performance and therefore provides incentives for them. Any changes to the internal accounting system can affect all the various uses of the resulting accounting numbers.

Because internal systems serve multiple users and have several purposes, the firm employs either multiple systems (one for each function) or one basic system that serves all three functions (decision making, performance evaluation, and external reporting). Firms can either maintain a single set of books and use the same accounting methods for both internal and external reports, or they can keep multiple sets of books. The decision depends on the costs of writing and maintaining contracts based on accounting numbers, the costs from the dysfunctional internal decisions made using a single system, the additional bookkeeping costs arising from the extra system, and the confusion of having to reconcile the different numbers arising from multiple accounting systems.

In some cases inexpensive accounting software packages and falling costs of computers have reduced the additional costs of maintaining multiple accounting systems. However, confusion arises when the systems report different numbers for the same concept. For example, when one system reports the manufacturing cost of a product as $12.56 and another system reports a unit cost of $17.19, managers wonder which system is producing the "right" number. Some managers may be using the $12.56 figure while others are using the $17.19 figure, causing inconsistency and uncertainty. Whenever two numbers for the same concept are produced, the natural tendency is to explain (i.e., reconcile) the differences. Managers involved in this reconciliation could have used this time in more productive ways. Also, using the same accounting system for multiple purposes increases the credibility of the financial reports for each purpose.[5] With only one accounting system, the external audit monitors the internal reporting system at little or no additional cost.

Interestingly, a survey of large U.S. firms found that managers typically use the same accounting procedures for both external and internal reporting. For example, the same accounting rules for leases are used for both internal and external reporting by 93 percent of the firms. Likewise, 79 percent of the firms use the same

---

[5]A Christie, "An Analysis of the Properties of Fair (Market) Value Accounting," *Modernizing U.S. Securities Regulation: Economic and Legal Perspectives*, K Lehn and R Kamphuis, eds. (Pittsburgh, PA: University of Pittsburgh, Joseph M. Katz Graduate School of Business, 1992).

| **Managers' Views on Their Accounting Systems** | A survey of 44 U.S. manufacturing plants found that plant managers overwhelmingly agreed that their accounting system fully meets the requirements for external reporting and cost control. However, when asked if their accounting system meets their requirements for making operating decisions, they gave significantly lower marks. In another survey, 261 plant managers were asked to identify the major problems with their current cost system. The following percentages show how many plant managers selected each item as a key problem. (Percentages add to more than 100 percent because plant managers could select more than one problem.) |

Provides inadequate information for product costing/pricing	53%
Lack of information for management decision making	52
Unsatisfactory operating performance measures	33
Lack of information for valid worker performance evaluation	30
Performance measures are not meaningful for competitive analysis	27
Performance measures are inconsistent with firm strategy	18
Other	17

Notice that operating managers (plant managers) are more likely to fault the accounting system for decision making than for motivation and control. These findings, and those of other researchers, indicate that internal accounting systems are less useful as a source of knowledge for decision making than for external reporting and control.

SOURCE: U Karmarkar, P Lederer, and J Zimmerman, "Choosing Manufacturing Production Control and Cost Accounting Systems," in *Measures for Manufacturing Excellence*, ed. R Kaplan (Boston: Harvard Business School, 1990); and A Sullivan and K Smith, "What Is Really Happening to Cost Management Systems in U.S. Manufacturing," *Review of Business Studies* 2 (1993), pp. 51–68.

| **Different Costs for Different Purposes** | "If there is a central thesis in this discussion it is this: that cost accounting has a number of functions, calling for different, if not inconsistent, information. As a result, if cost accounting sets out, determined to discover what the cost of everything is and convinced in advance that there is one figure which can be found and which will furnish exactly the information which is desired for every possible purpose, it will necessarily fail, because there is no such figure. If it finds a figure which is right for some purposes it must necessarily be wrong for others." |

SOURCE: J Clark, *Studies in the Economics of Overhead Costs* (Chicago: University of Chicago Press, 1923), p. 234.

procedures for inventory accounting and 92 percent use the same procedures for depreciation accounting.[6] Nothing prevents firms from using separate accounting systems for internal decision making and internal performance evaluation except the confusion generated and the extra data processing costs.

Probably the most important reason firms use a single accounting system is it allows reclassification of the data. An accounting system does not present a single,

---

[6] R Vancil, *Decentralization: Managerial Ambiguity by Design* (Burr Ridge, IL: Dow Jones-Irwin, 1979), p. 360.

bottom-line number, such as the "cost of publishing this textbook." Rather, the system reports the components of the total cost of this textbook: the costs of proofreading, typesetting, paper, binding, cover, and so on. Managers in the firm then reclassify the information on the basis of different attributes and derive different cost numbers for different decisions. For example, if the publisher is considering translating this book into Russian, not all the components used in calculating the U.S. costs are relevant. The Russian edition might be printed on different paper stock with a different cover. The point is, a single accounting system usually offers enough flexibility for managers to reclassify, recombine, and reorganize the data for multiple purposes.

A single internal accounting system requires the firm to make trade-offs. A system that is best for performance measurement and control is unlikely to be the best for decision making. It's like configuring a motorcycle for both off-road and on-road racing: Riders on bikes designed for both racing conditions probably won't beat riders on specialized bikes designed for just one type of racing surface. Wherever a single accounting system exists, additional analyses arise. Managers making decisions find the accounting system less useful and devise other systems to augment the accounting numbers for decision-making purposes.

Concept Questions		
	Q1–1	What causes the conflict between using internal accounting systems for decision making and control?
	Q1–2	Describe the different kinds of information provided by the internal accounting system.
	Q1–3	Give three examples of the uses of an accounting system.
	Q1–4	List the characteristics of an internal accounting system.
	Q1–5	Do firms have multiple accounting systems? Why or why not?

C. Marmots and Grizzly Bears

Economists and operating managers often criticize accounting data for decision making. Accounting data are often not in the form managers want for decision making. For example, the book value of a factory (historical cost less accumulated accounting depreciation) does not necessarily indicate the market or selling value of the factory, which is what a manager wants to know when contemplating shutting down the factory. Why do managers persist in using (presumably inferior) accounting information?

Before addressing this question, consider the parable of the marmots and the grizzly bears.[7] Marmots are small groundhogs that are a principal food source for certain bears. Zoologists studying the ecology of marmots and bears observed bears digging and moving rocks in the autumn in search of marmots. They estimated that the calories expended searching for marmots exceeded the calories obtained

---

[7] This example is suggested by J McGee, "Predatory Pricing Revisited," *Journal of Law & Economics* XXIII (October 1980), pp. 289–330.

Benchmarking and Economic Darwinism

Benchmarking is defined as "a . . . process of continuously comparing and measuring an organization's business processing against business leaders anywhere in the world to gain information which will help the organization take action to improve its performance."

Economic Darwinism predicts that successful firm practices will be imitated. Benchmarking is the practice of imitating successful business practices. The practice of benchmarking dates back to 607, when Japan sent teams to China to learn the best practices in business, government, and education. Today, most large firms routinely conduct benchmarking studies to discover the best business practices and then implement them in their own firms.

SOURCE: Society of Management Accountants of Canada, *Benchmarking: A Survey of Canadian Practice* (Hamilton, Ontario, Canada, 1994).

from their consumption. A zoologist relying on Darwin's theory of natural selection might conclude that searching for marmots is an inefficient use of the bear's limited resources and thus these bears should become extinct. But fossils of marmot bones near bear remains suggest that bears have been searching for marmots for a long time.

Since the bears survive, the benefits of consuming marmots must exceed the costs. Bears' claws might be sharpened as a by-product of the digging involved in hunting for marmots. Sharp claws are useful in searching for food under the ice after winter's hibernation. Therefore, the benefit of sharpened claws and the calories derived from the marmots offset the calories consumed gathering the marmots.

What does the marmot-and-bear parable say about why managers persist in using apparently inferior accounting data in their decision making? As it turns out, the marmot-and-bear parable is an extremely important proposition in the social sciences known as *economic Darwinism*. In a competitive world, if surviving organizations use some operating procedure (such as historical cost accounting) over long periods of time, then this procedure likely yields benefits in excess of its costs. Firms survive in competition by selling goods or services at lower prices than their competitors while still covering costs. Firms cannot survive by making more mistakes than their competitors.[8]

Economic Darwinism suggests that in successful (surviving) firms, things should not be fixed unless they are clearly broken. Currently, considerable attention is being directed at revising and updating firms' internal accounting systems because many managers believe their current accounting systems are "broken" and require major overhaul. Alternative internal accounting systems are being proposed, among them activity-based costing (ABC), balanced score cards, economic value added (EVA), and total quality management (TQM) accounting systems. These systems are discussed and analyzed later in terms of their ability to help managers make better decisions as well as to help provide better measures of performance for managers in organizations, thereby aligning managers' and owners' interests.

---

[8] See A Alchian, "Uncertainty, Evolution and Economic Theory," *Journal of Political Economy* 58 (June 1950), pp. 211–21.

Applying Economic Darwinism in Business

"My partner and I are succeeding in building our company largely because we apply the notion of *economic Darwinism* to our thinking about how to add value to our clients with our technology. The reason the marmots and grizzly bears parable seems to continually arise at work is precisely the 'Dumb Zoologist Hypothesis.' Except we call it the 'Dumb Venture Capitalist Hypothesis' or the 'Dumb Dot-com Founder Hypothesis.' We also are highly critical of the numerous companies that have been abundantly funded, only to fail because their 'brilliant ideas' ignored economic Darwinism. The marmot story seems to apply universally in these situations."

SOURCE: John Oliver, president, Digital Footbridge Inc. MBA, 1995 from Yale University.

Sixteenth-Century Cost Records

The well-known Italian Medici family had extensive banking interests and owned textile plants in the fifteenth and sixteenth centuries. They also used sophisticated cost records to maintain control of their cloth production. These cost reports contained detailed data on the costs of purchasing, washing, beating, spinning, and weaving the wool, of supplies, and of overhead (tools, rent, and administrative expenses). This evidence indicates that managers of these firms kept detailed records of their production costs.

SOURCE: P Garner, *Evolution of Cost Accounting to 1925* (Montgomery, AL: University of Alabama Press, 1954), pp. 12–13. Original source R de Roover, "A Florentine Firm of Cloth Manufacturers," *Speculum* XVI (January 1941), pp. 3–33.

Although internal accounting systems may appear to have certain inconsistencies with some particular theory, these systems (like the bears searching for marmots) have survived the test of time and therefore are likely to be yielding unobserved benefits (like claw sharpening). This book discusses these additional benefits. Two caveats must be raised concerning too strict an application of economic Darwinism:

1. Some surviving operating procedures can be neutral mutations. Just because a system survives does not mean that its benefits exceed its costs. Benefits less costs might be close to zero.
2. Just because a given system survives does not mean it is optimal. A better system might exist but has not yet been discovered.

The fact that most managers use their accounting system as the primary formal information system suggests that these accounting systems are yielding total benefits that exceed their total costs. These benefits include financial and tax reporting, providing information for decision making, and creating internal incentives. The proposition that surviving firms have efficient accounting systems does not imply that better systems do not exist, only that they have not yet been discovered. It is not necessarily the case that what is, is optimal. Economic Darwinism helps identify the costs and benefits of alternative internal accounting systems and is applied repeatedly throughout the book.

D. Management Accountant's Role in the Organization

To better understand internal accounting systems, it is useful to spend a moment considering how firms organize their accounting functions. No single organizational structure applies to all firms. Figure 1–2 presents one common organization chart. The design and operation of the internal and external accounting systems are the responsibility of the firm's chief financial officer (CFO). The firm's line-of-business or functional areas, such as marketing, manufacturing, and research and development, are shown under a single organization, operating divisions. The remaining staff and administrative functions include human resources, chief financial officer, legal, and other. In Figure 1–2, the chief financial officer oversees all the financial and accounting functions in the firm and reports directly to the president. The chief financial officer's three major functions include: controllership, treasury, and internal audit. Controllership involves tax administration, the internal and external accounting systems, and the planning and control systems (including budgeting and governmental reporting). Treasury involves short- and long-term financing, banking, credit and collections, investments, insurance, and capital budgeting. Depending on their size and structure, firms organize these functions differently. Figure 1–2 shows the internal audit group reporting directly to the chief financial officer. In other firms, internal audit reports to the controller, the chief executive officer, or the board of directors.[9]

The controller is the firm's chief management accountant and is responsible for data collection and reporting. The controller compiles the data for balance sheets and income statements and for preparing the firm's tax returns. In addition, this person prepares the internal reports for the various divisions and departments within the firm and helps the other managers by providing them with the data necessary to make decisions—as well as the data necessary to evaluate these managers' performance.

FIGURE 1–2

Organization chart for a typical corporation

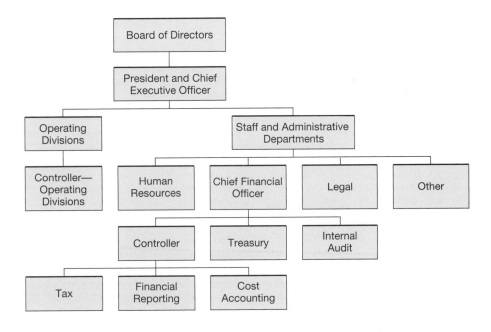

---

[9] J Schiff, *New Directions in Internal Auditing* (New York: Conference Board, 1990), p. 13.

The Controller's Job	Controllers' responsibilities are wide ranging:
	• "There is no business agenda the controller does not influence substantially."
	• "Their scope of responsibility touches every function of the company."
	• "[They] oversee the tidal wave of information that now floods into a company."
	• Controllers often oversee reengineering administrative functions, install new measurement metrics such as TQM, ABC, and EVA, and oversee the firm's employees' compensation, benefits, and retirement plans.
	• "Controllers are often asked to distill different information from different sources and then get a report into the hands of the CFO [chief financial officer]."
	• "You have to have a mastery of computer systems. . . . The controller is responsible for IS [information systems] these days."
	• "More time is spent wrestling with the steady stream of pronouncements from various accounting standard-setting bodies."
	SOURCE: J Goff, "Controller Burnout," *CFO*, September 1995, pp. 56–62.

Super CFOs (Chief Financial Officers)	*Fortune* magazine describes the new breed of CFOs as earning millions of dollars because they can create billions of dollars for the shareholders. Some even earn more than sports superstars. Top CFOs are described as "superb general managers who on top of strong financial and deal-making skills can often boast a grasp of operations or a keen sense of strategy. Instead of simply measuring value, today's CFOs create it." One of the best super CFOs is Judy Lewent of Merck, a large pharmaceutical company. She redesigned the way Merck estimated the profitability of new drugs. Instead of thinking it was losing money on R&D, Lewent devised a financial model that showed it was making money. This persuaded management to increase the R&D budget from $426 million in 1985 to $1.2 billion in 1995. Over the same time period, the stock price increased 39 percent as new, more profitable products came to market.
	SOURCE: *Fortune* (November 13, 1995), p. 162.

Usually, each operating division or department has its own controller. For example, if a firm has several manufacturing plants, each plant has its own plant controller, who reports to both the plant manager and the corporate controller. In Figure 1–2, the operating divisions have their own controllers. The plant controller provides the corporate controller with periodic reports on the plant's operations. The plant controller oversees the plant's budgets, payroll, inventory, and product costing system (which reports the cost of units manufactured at the plant). While most firms have plant-level controllers, some firms centralize these functions to reduce staff, so that all the plant-level controller functions are performed centrally out of corporate headquarters.

The "New Accounting"

A survey of 300 practicing U.S. accountants described the changing role of management accountants:

> Management accountants were not participants in the decision-making process. Instead, they functioned as support staff for the decision makers and were often informed of decisions after the fact. The bulk of their time was spent in the mechanical aspects of accounting . . . They were, in fact, the scorekeepers, the bean counters, the corporate cops.
>
> The role of management accountants is very different in 1999. Growing numbers of management accountants spend the bulk of their time as internal consultants or business analysts within their companies. Technological advances have liberated them from the mechanical aspects of accounting. They spend less time preparing standardized reports and more time analyzing and interpreting information. Management accountants work on cross-functional teams, have extensive face-to-face communications with people throughout their organizations, and are actively involved in decision making.
>
> The role of management accountants has evolved from serving internal customers into being a business partner. A business partner is an equal member of the decision-making team. As a business partner, a management accountant has the authority and responsibility to tell an operating executive why particular types of information may or may not be relevant to the business decision at hand, and is expected to suggest ways to improve the quality of the decision.

Notice that management accountants in this description perform both decision-making activities and control activities (corporate cop).

SOURCE: G Siegel, *Counting More, Counting Less, Transformations in the Management Accounting Profession: The 1999 Practice Analysis of Management Accounting* (Montvale, NJ: Institute of Management Accountants, 1999), pp. 4–5.

The controllership function at the corporate, division, and plant levels involves assisting decision making and control. The controller must balance providing information to other managers for decision making against providing monitoring information to top executives for use in controlling the behavior of lower-level managers.

We cannot stress the importance of the internal control system too much. Throughout this book, we use the term *control* to mean motivating employees to act in the owners' interests. The most basic conflict of interest between employees and owners is employee theft. To reduce the likelihood of embezzlement, firms install internal control systems, which are an integral part of the firm's control system. Internal and external auditors' first responsibility is to test the integrity of the firm's internal controls. Fraud and theft are prevented not just by having security guards and door locks but also by having procedures that require checks above a certain amount to be authorized by two people. Internal control systems include internal procedures, codes of conduct, and policies that prohibit corruption, bribery, and kickbacks. Finally, internal control systems should prevent intentional (or accidental) financial misrepresentation by managers.

Concept Questions	Q1–6	Define *economic Darwinism*.
	Q1–7	Describe the major functions of the chief financial officer.

E. Evolution of Management Accounting: A Framework for Change

Management accounting has evolved with the nature of organizations. Prior to 1800, most businesses were small, family-operated organizations. Management accounting was less important for these small firms. It was not critical for planning decisions and control reasons because the owner could directly observe the organization's entire environment. The owner, who made all of the decisions, delegated little decision-making authority and had no need to worry about motivation. Only as organizations grew larger would management accounting become more important.

Most of today's modern management accounting techniques were developed in the period from 1825 to 1925 with the growth of large organizations.[10] Textile mills in the early nineteenth century grew by combining the multiple processes (spinning the thread, dying, weaving, etc.) of making cloth. These large firms developed systems to measure the cost per yard or per pound for the separate manufacturing processes. The cost data allowed managers to compare the cost of conducting a process inside the firm versus purchasing the process from external vendors. Similarly, the railroads of the 1850s to 1870s developed cost systems that reported cost per ton-mile and operating expenses per dollar of revenue. These measures allowed managers to increase their operating efficiencies. In the early 1900s, Andrew Carnegie (at what was to become U.S. Steel) devised a cost system that reported detailed unit cost figures for material and labor on a daily and weekly basis. This system allowed senior managers to maintain very tight controls on operations and gave them accurate and timely information on marginal costs for pricing decisions. Merchandising firms such as Marshall Field's and Sears, Roebuck developed gross margin (revenues less cost of goods sold) and stock-turn ratios (sales divided by inventory) to measure and evaluate performance. Manufacturing companies such as Du Pont Powder Company and General Motors were also active in developing performance measures to control their growing organizations.

In the period from 1925 to 1975, management accounting was heavily influenced by external considerations. Income taxes and financial accounting requirements (e.g., those of the Financial Accounting Standards Board) were the major factors affecting management accounting.

Since 1975, two major environmental forces have changed organizations and caused managers to question whether traditional management accounting procedures (pre-1975) are still appropriate. These environmental forces are (1) factory automation and computer/information technology and (2) global competition. To adapt to these environmental forces, organizations must reconsider their organizational structure and their management accounting procedures.

Information technology advances such as the Internet, intranets, wireless communications, and faster microprocessors have had a big impact on internal accounting processes. More data are now available faster than ever before. Electronic data interchange, XTML, e-mail, B2B e-commerce, data warehousing, and online analytical processing (OLAP) are just a few examples of new technology impacting management accounting. For example, managers now have access to daily sales and operating costs in real time, as opposed to having to wait two weeks after the end

---

[10] P Garner, *Evolution of Cost Accounting to 1925* (Montgomery, AL: University of Alabama Press, 1954); and A Chandler, *The Visible Hand* (Cambridge, MA: Harvard University Press, 1977).

FIGURE 1–3

Framework for organizational change and management accounting

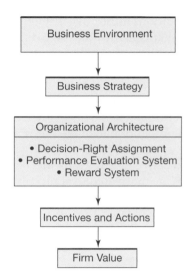

FIGURE 1–3

Framework for organizational change and management accounting

of the calendar quarter for this information. Firms have cut the time needed to prepare budgets for the next fiscal year by several months because the information is transmitted electronically in standardized electronic spreadsheets such as Excel.

The brief history of management accounting from 1825 to the present illustrates how management accounting has evolved in parallel with organizations' structure. Management accounting is used to provide information for planning decisions and control. It is useful for assigning decision-making authority, measuring performance, and determining rewards for individuals within the organization. Because management accounting is part of the organizational structure, the fact that management accounting evolves in a parallel and consistent fashion with other parts of the organizational structure is not surprising.

Figure 1–3 is a framework for understanding the role of accounting systems within firms and the forces that cause accounting systems to change. As described more fully in Chapter 14, environmental forces such as technological innovation and global competition change the organization's business strategies. For example, the Internet has allowed banks to offer electronic, online banking services. To implement these new strategies, organizations must adapt their organizational structure or architecture, which includes management accounting. An organization's architecture (the topic of Chapter 4) is composed of three related processes: (1) the assignment of decision-making responsibilities, (2) the measurement of performance, and (3) the rewarding of individuals within the organization.

The first component of the organizational architecture is the determination of the responsibilities of the different members of the organization. Decision rights define the duties each member of an organization is expected to perform. The decision rights of a particular individual within an organization are specified by that person's job description. Checkout clerks in grocery stores have the decision rights to collect cash from customers but don't have the decision rights to accept certain types of checks. A manager must be called for that decision. A division manager may have the right to set prices on products but not the right to borrow money by issuing debt. The president or the board of directors usually retains the right to issue debt.

The next two parts of the organizational architecture are the performance evaluation and reward systems. To motivate individuals within the organization, organizations must have a system for measuring their performance and rewarding them. Performance measures for a salesperson could include total sales and customer satisfaction based on a survey of customers. Performance measures for a manufacturing unit could include number of units produced, total costs, and percentage of defective units. The internal accounting system is often an important part of the performance evaluation system.

Performance measures are extremely important because rewards are generally based on performance measures. Rewards for individuals within organizations include wages and bonuses, prestige and greater decision rights, promotions, and job security. Because rewards are based on performance measures, individuals and groups are motivated to act to influence the performance measures. Therefore, the performance measures influence the direction of individual and group efforts within the organization. A poor choice of performance measures can lead to conflicts within the organization and derail efforts to achieve organizational goals. For example, measuring the performance of a college president based on the number of students attending the college encourages the president to allow ill-prepared students to enter the college and reduces the quality of the educational experience for other students.

As illustrated in Figure 1–3, changes in the business environment lead to new strategies and ultimately to changes in the firm's organizational architecture, including changes in the accounting system to better align the interests of the employees to the objectives of the organization. The new organizational architecture provides incentives for members of the organization to make decisions, which leads to a change in the value of the organization. The roles of accounting in this framework include assisting in the control of the organization through the organization's architecture and providing information for decision making. This framework for change will be referred to throughout the book.

F. Vortec Medical Probe Example

To illustrate some of the basic concepts developed in this text, suppose you have been asked to evaluate the following decision. Vortec Inc. manufactures a single product, a medical probe. Vortec sells the probes to wholesalers who then market them to physicians. Vortec has two divisions. The manufacturing division produces the probes; the marketing division sells them to wholesalers. The marketing division is rewarded on the basis of sales revenues. The manufacturing division is evaluated and rewarded on the basis of the average unit cost of making the probes. The plant's current volume is 100,000 probes per month. The following income statement summarizes last month's operating results.

VORTEC MANUFACTURING
Income Statement
Last Month

Sales revenue (100,000 units @ $5.00)	$500,000
Cost of sales (100,000 units @ $4.50)	450,000
Operating margin	$ 50,000
Less: Administrative expenses	27,500
Net income before taxes	$ 22,500

Medsupplies is one of Vortec's best customers. Vortec sells 10,000 probes per month to Medsupplies at $5 per unit. Last week Medsupplies asked Vortec's marketing division to increase its monthly shipment to 12,000 units, provided that Vortec would sell the additional 2,000 units at $4 each. Medsupplies would continue to pay $5 for the original 10,000 units. Medsupplies argued that because this would be extra business for Vortec, no overhead should be charged on the additional 2,000 units. In this case, a $4 price should be adequate.

Vortec's finance department estimates that with 102,000 probes the average cost is $4.47 per unit, and hence the $4 price offered by Medsupplies is too low. The current administrative expenses of $27,500 consist of office rent, property taxes, and interest and will not change if this special order is accepted. Should Vortec accept the Medsupplies offer?

Before examining whether the marketing and manufacturing divisions will accept the order, consider Medsupplies's offer from the perspective of Vortec's owners, who are interested in maximizing profits. The decision hinges on the cost to Vortec of selling an additional 2,000 units to Medsupplies. If the cost is more than $4 per unit, Vortec should reject the special order.

It is tempting to reject the offer because the $4 price does not cover the average total cost of $4.47. But will it cost Vortec $4.47 per unit for the 2,000-unit special order? Is $4.47 the cost per unit for each of the next 2,000 units?

To begin the analysis, two simplifying assumptions are made that are relaxed later:

- Vortec has excess capacity to produce the additional 2,000 probes.
- Past historical costs are unbiased estimates of the future cash flows for producing the special order.

Based on these assumptions, we can compare the incremental revenue from the additional 2,000 units with its incremental cost:

Incremental revenue (2,000 units × $4.00)		$8,000
Total cost @ 102,000 units (102,000 × $4.47)	$455,940	
Total cost @ 100,000 units (100,000 × $4.50)	450,000	
Incremental cost of 2,000 units		5,940
Incremental profit of 2,000 units		$2,060

The estimated incremental cost per unit of the 2,000 units is then

$$\frac{\text{Change in total cost}}{\text{Change in volume}} = \frac{\$455,940 - \$450,000}{2,000} = \$2.97$$

The estimated cost per incremental unit is $2.97. Therefore, $2.97 is the average per-unit cost of the extra 2,000 probes. The $4.47 cost is the average cost of producing 102,000 units, which is more than the $2.97 incremental cost per unit of producing the extra 2,000 probes.

Based on the $2.97 estimated cost, Vortec should take the order. Is this the right decision? Not necessarily. There are some other considerations:

1. Will these 2,000 additional units affect the $5 price of the 100,000 probes? Will Vortec's other customers continue to pay $5 if Medsupplies buys 2,000 units

at $4? What prevents Medsupplies from reselling the probes to Vortec's other customers at less than $5 per unit but above $4 per unit? Answering these questions requires management to acquire knowledge of the market for the probes.

2. What is the alternative use of the excess capacity consumed by the additional 2,000 probes? As plant utilization increases, congestion costs rise, production becomes less efficient, and the cost per unit rises. Congestion costs include the wages of the additional production employees and supervisors required to move, store, expedite, and rework products as plant volume increases. The $2.97 incremental cost computed from the average cost data on page 19 might not include the higher congestion costs as capacity is approached. This suggests that the $4.47 average cost estimate is wrong. Who provides this cost estimate and how accurate is it? Management must acquire knowledge of how costs behave at high volume. If Vortec accepts the Medsupplies offer, will Vortec be forced at some later date to forgo using this capacity for a more profitable project?

3. What costs will Vortec incur if the Medsupplies offer is rejected? Will Vortec lose the normal 10,000-unit Medsupplies order? If so, can this order be replaced?

4. Does the Robinson-Patman Act apply? The Robinson-Patman Act is a U.S. federal law prohibiting charging customers different prices if doing so is injurious to competition. Thus, it may be illegal to sell an additional 2,000 units to Medsupplies at less than $5 per unit. Knowledge of U.S. antitrust laws must be acquired. Moreover, if Vortec sells internationally, it will have to research the antitrust laws of the various jurisdictions that might review the Medsupplies transaction.

We have analyzed the question of whether Medsupplies's 2,000-unit order maximizes the owners' profit. The next question to address is whether the marketing and manufacturing divisions will accept Medsupplies's offer. Recall that marketing is evaluated based on total revenues and manufacturing is evaluated based on average unit costs. Therefore, marketing will want to accept the order as long as Medsupplies does not resell the probes to other Vortec customers and as long as other Vortec customers do not expect similar price concessions. Manufacturing will want to accept the order as long as it believes average unit costs will fall. Increasing production lowers average unit costs and makes it appear as though manufacturing has achieved cost reductions.

Suppose that accepting the Medsupplies offer will not adversely affect Vortec's other sales, but the incremental cost of producing the 2,000 extra probes is really $4.08, not $2.97, because there will be overtime charges and additional factory congestion costs. Under these conditions, both marketing and manufacturing will want to accept the offer. Marketing increases total revenue and thus appears to have improved its performance. Manufacturing still lowers average unit costs from $4.50 to $4.4918 per unit:

$$\$4.4918 = \frac{(\$4.50 \times 100,000) + (\$4.08 \times 2,000)}{102,000}$$

However, the shareholders are worse off. Vortec's cash flows are lower by $160 (or 2,000 units × [$4.00 − $4.08]). The problem is not that the marketing and manufacturing managers are "making a mistake." The problem is that the measures of performance are creating the wrong incentives. In particular, rewarding marketing for increasing total revenues and manufacturing for reducing average unit costs means there is no mechanism to ensure that the incremental revenues from the order ($8,000 = $4 × 2,000) are greater than the incremental costs ($8,160 = $4.08 × 2,000). Both marketing and manufacturing are doing what they were told to do (increase revenues and reduce average costs), but the value of the firm falls because the incentive systems are poorly designed.

Four key points emerge from this example:

1. *Beware of average costs.* The $4.50 unit cost tells us little about how costs will vary with changes in volume. Just because a cost is stated in dollars per unit does not mean that producing one more unit will add that amount of incremental cost.

2. *Use opportunity costs.* Opportunity costs measure what the firm forgoes when it chooses a specific action. The notion of opportunity cost is crucial in decision making. The opportunity cost of the Medsupplies order is what Vortec forgoes by accepting the special order. What is the best alternative use of the plant capacity consumed by the Medsupplies special order? (More on this in Chapter 2.)

3. *Supplement accounting data with other information.* The accounting system contains important data relevant for estimating the cost of this special order from Medsupplies. But other knowledge that the accounting system cannot capture must be assembled, such as what Medsupplies will do if Vortec rejects its offer. Managers usually augment accounting data with other knowledge such as customer demands, competitors' plans, future technology, and government regulations.

4. *Use accounting numbers as performance measures cautiously.* Accounting numbers such as revenues or average unit manufacturing costs are often used to evaluate managers' performance. Just because managers are maximizing particular performance measures tailored for each manager does not necessarily cause firm profits to be maximized.

The Vortec example illustrates the importance of understanding how accounting numbers are constructed, what they mean, and how they are used in decision making and control. The accounting system is a very important source of information to managers, but it is not the sole source of all knowledge. Also, in the overly simplified context of the Vortec example, the problems with the incentive systems and with using unit costs are easy to detect. In a complex company with hundreds or thousands of products, however, such errors are very difficult to detect. Finally, for the sake of simplicity, the Vortec illustration ignores the use of the accounting system for external reporting.

G. Outline of the Text

Internal accounting systems provide data for both decision making and control. The organization of this book follows this dichotomy. The first part of the text (Chapters 2 through 5) describes how accounting systems are used in decision making and providing incentives in organizations. These chapters provide the conceptual framework for the remainder of the book. The next set of chapters (Chapters 6 through 8) describes basic topics in managerial accounting, budgeting, and cost allocations. Budgets not only are a mechanism for communicating knowledge within the firm for decision making but also serve as a control device and as a way to partition decision-making responsibility among the managers. Likewise, cost allocations serve decision-making and control functions. In analyzing the role of budgeting and cost allocations, these chapters draw on the first part of the text.

The next section of the text (Chapters 9 through 13) describes the prevalent accounting system used in firms: absorption costing. Absorption cost systems are built around cost allocations. The systems used in manufacturing and service settings generate product costs built up from direct labor, direct material, and allocated overheads. After first describing these systems, we critically analyze them. A common criticism of absorption cost systems is that they produce inaccurate unit cost information, which can lead to dysfunctional decision making. Two alternative accounting systems (variable cost systems and activity-based cost systems) are compared and evaluated against a traditional absorption cost system. The conceptual framework in the first part of the text is used for this analysis. The next topic describes the use of standard costs as extensions of absorption cost systems. Standard costs provide benchmarks and are used to calculate accounting variances: the difference between the actual costs and standard costs. These variances are performance measures and thus are part of the firm's motivation and control system described earlier.

The last chapter (Chapter 14) expands the integrative approach summarized in section E of this chapter. This approach is then used to analyze three modifications of internal cost systems: quality measurement systems, just-in-time production, and balanced scorecards. These recent modifications are evaluated within a broad historical context. Just because these systems are new does not suggest they are better. They have not stood the test of time. Economic Darwinism, or competition from other systems, does not yet allow us to conclude that these new systems are better.

H. Summary

This book provides a framework for the analysis, use, and design of internal accounting systems. It explains how these systems are used for decision making and motivating people in organizations. Employees care about their self-interest, not the owners' self-interest. Hence, owners must devise incentive systems. Accounting numbers are used as measures of managers' performance and hence are part of the control system used to motivate managers. Most firms use a single internal accounting system as the primary data source for external reporting and internal uses. The fact that managers rely heavily on accounting numbers is not fully understood. Applying the economic Darwinism principle, the costs of multiple systems must outweigh the benefits for most firms. The costs are not only the direct costs of operating the system but also the indirect costs from dysfunctional decisions resulting from faulty information and poor performance evaluation systems. The remainder of this book addresses the costs and benefits of internal accounting systems.

Problems

P 1–1:   MBA Students

One MBA student was overheard saying to another, "Accounting is baloney. I worked for a genetic engineering company and we never looked at the accounting numbers and our stock price was always growing."

"I agree," said the other. "I worked in a rust bucket company that managed everything by the numbers and we never improved our stock price very much." Evaluate these comments.

SOURCE: K Gartrell.

P 1–2: One Cost System Isn't Enough

Robert S. Kaplan in "One Cost System Isn't Enough" (*Harvard Business Review*, January–February 1988, pp. 61–66) states,

> No single system can adequately answer the demands made by diverse functions of cost systems. While companies can use one method to capture all their detailed transactions data, the processing of this information for diverse purposes and audiences demands separate, customized development. Companies that try to satisfy all the needs for cost information with a single system have discovered they can't perform important managerial functions adequately. Moreover, systems that work well for one company may fail in a different environment. Each company has to design methods that make sense for its particular products and processes.
>
> Of course, an argument for expanding the number of cost systems conflicts with a strongly ingrained financial culture to have only one measurement system for everyone.

Critically evaluate the preceding quote.

P 1–3: U.S. and Japanese Tax Laws

Tax laws in Japan tie taxable income directly to the financial statements' reported income. That is, to compute a Japanese firm's tax liability, multiply the net income as reported to shareholders by the appropriate tax rate to derive the firm's tax liability. In contrast, U.S. firms typically have more discretion in choosing different accounting procedures for calculating net income for shareholders (financial reporting) and taxes.

What effect would you expect these institutional differences in tax laws between the United States and Japan to have on internal accounting and reporting?

P 1–4: Managers Need Accounting Information

The opening paragraph of an accounting textbook says, "Managers need accounting information and need to know how to use it."[11] Critically evaluate this statement.

P 1–5: Using Accounting for Planning

The owner of a small software company felt his accounting system was useless. He stated, "Accounting systems only generate historical costs. Historical costs are useless in my business because everything changes so rapidly."

a. Are historical costs useless in rapidly changing environments?

b. Should accounting systems be limited to historical costs?

P 1–6: Goals of a Corporation

A finance professor and a marketing professor were recently comparing notes on their perceptions of corporations. The finance professor claimed that the goal of a corporation should be to maximize the value to the shareholders. The marketing professor claimed that the goal of a corporation should be to satisfy customers.

What are the similarities and differences in these two goals?

---

[11] D Hansen and M Mowen, *Management Accounting*, 3rd ed. (Cincinnati: South-Western Publishing Co., 1994), p. 3.

P 1–7:   Budgeting

Salespeople at a particular firm forecast what they expect to sell next period. Their supervisors then review the forecasts and make revisions. These forecasts are used to set production and purchasing plans. In addition, salespeople receive a fixed bonus of 20 percent of their salary if they exceed their forecasts.

Discuss the incentives of the salespeople to forecast next-period sales accurately. Discuss the trade-off between using the budget for decision making versus using it as a control device.

P 1-8:   Golf Specialties

Golf Specialties (GS), a Belgian company, manufactures a variety of golf paraphernalia, such as head covers for woods, embroidered golf towels, and umbrellas. GS sells all its products exclusively in Europe through independent distributors. Given the popularity of Tiger Woods, one of GS's more popular items is a head cover in the shape of a tiger.

GS is currently making 500 tiger head covers a week at a per unit cost of 3.50 euros, which includes both variable costs and allocated fixed costs. GS sells the tiger head covers to distributors for 4.25 euros. A distributor in Japan, Kojo Imports, wants to purchase 100 tiger head covers per week from GS and sell them in Japan. Kojo offers to pay GS 2 euros per head cover. GS has enough capacity to produce the additional 100 tiger head covers and estimates that if it accepts Kojo's offer, the per unit cost of all 600 tiger head covers will be 3.10 euros. Assume the cost data provided (3.50 euros and 3.10 euros) are accurate estimates of GS's costs of producing the tiger head covers. Further assume that GS's variable cost per head cover does not vary with the number of head covers manufactured.

Required:

   a. To maximize firm value, should GS accept Kojo's offer? Explain why or why not.
   b. Given the data in the problem, what is GS's weekly fixed cost of producing the tiger head covers?
   c. Besides the data provided above, what other factors should GS consider before making a decision to accept Kojo's offer?

P 1–9:   Parkview Hospital

Parkview Hospital, a regional hospital, serves a population of 400,000 people. The next closest hospital is 50 miles away. Parkview's accounting system is adequate for patient billing. The system reports revenues generated per department but does not break down revenues by unit within departments. For example, Parkview knows patient revenue for the entire psychiatric department but does not know revenues in the child and adolescent unit, the chemical dependence unit, or the neuropsychiatric unit.

Parkview receives its revenues from three principal sources: the federal government (Medicare), the state government (Medicaid), and private insurance companies (Blue Cross–Blue Shield). Until recently, the private insurance companies continued to pay Parkview's increasing costs and passed these on to the firms through higher premiums for their employees' health insurance.

Last year Trans Insurance (TI) entered the market and began offering lower-cost health insurance to local firms. TI cut benefits offered and told Parkview that it would pay only a fixed dollar amount per patient. A typical firm could cut its health insurance premium 20 percent by switching to TI. TI was successful at taking 45 percent of the Blue Cross–Blue Shield customers. These firms faced stiff competition and sought to cut their health care costs.

Parkview management estimated that its revenues would fall 6 percent or $3.2 million next year because of TI's lower reimbursements. Struggling with how to cope with lower revenues, Parkview began the complex process of what programs to cut, how to shift the delivery of services from inpatient to outpatient clinics, and what programs to open to offset the revenue loss (for example, open an outpatient depression clinic). Management can forecast some of the costs of the proposed changes, but many of its costs and revenues (such as the cost of the admissions office) have never been tracked to the individual clinical unit.

Required:

    a. Was Parkview's accounting system adequate 10 years ago?

    b. Is Parkview's accounting system adequate today?

    c. What changes should Parkview make in its accounting system?

P 1–10: Montana Pen Company

Montana Pen Company manufactures a full line of premium writing instruments. It has 12 different styles and within each style, it offers ball point pens, fountain pens, mechanical pencils, and a roller ball pen. Most models also come in three finishes—gold, silver, and black matte. Montana Pen's Bangkok, Thailand, plant manufactures four of the styles. The plant is currently producing the gold clip for the top of one of its pen styles, no. 872. Current production is 1,200 gold no. 872 pens each month at an average cost of 185 baht per gold clip. (One U.S. dollar currently buys 35 baht.) A Chinese manufacturer has offered to produce the same gold clip for 136 baht. This manufacturer will sell Montana Pen 400 clips per month. If it accepts the Chinese offer and cuts the production of the clips from 1,200 to 800, Montana Pen estimates that the cost of each clip it continues to produce will rise from 185 baht to 212.5 baht per gold clip.

Required:

    a. Should Montana Pen outsource 400 gold clips for pen style no. 872 to the Chinese firm? Provide a written justification of your answer.

    b. Given your answer in part (*a*), what additional information would you seek before deciding to outsource 400 gold clips per month to the Chinese firm?

Chapter Two

The Nature of Costs

As described in Chapter 1, accounting systems measure costs, which managers use for external reports, decision making, and controlling the behavior of people in the organization. Understanding how accounting systems calculate costs requires a thorough understanding of what **cost** means. Unfortunately, that simple term has multiple meanings. Saying a product costs $3.12 does not reveal what the $3.12 measures. Additional explanation is often needed to clarify the assumptions that underlie the calculation of cost. A large vocabulary has arisen to communicate more clearly which cost meaning is being conveyed. Some examples include average cost, common cost, full cost, historical cost, joint cost, marginal cost, period cost, product cost, standard cost, fixed cost, opportunity cost, sunk cost, and variable cost, just to name a few.

We begin this chapter with the concept of opportunity cost, a powerful tool for understanding the myriad cost terms and for structuring managerial decisions. In addition, opportunity cost provides a benchmark against which accounting-based cost numbers can be compared and evaluated. Section B discusses how opportunity costs vary with changes in output. Section C extends this discussion to cost–volume–profit analysis. Section D compares and contrasts opportunity costs and accounting costs (which are very different). Section E describes some common methods for cost estimation.

A. Opportunity Costs

When you make a decision, you incur a cost. Nobel Prize–winning economist Ronald Coase noted, "The cost of doing anything consists of the receipts that could have been obtained if that particular decision had not been taken."[1] This notion is called **opportunity cost**—the benefit forgone as a result of choosing one course of action rather than another. Cost is a sacrifice of resources. Using a resource for one purpose prevents its use elsewhere. The return forgone from its use elsewhere is the opportunity cost of its current use. The opportunity cost of a particular decision depends on the other alternatives available.

The alternative actions comprise the *opportunity set*. Before making a decision and calculating opportunity cost, the opportunity set itself must be determined. Thus, it is important to remember that opportunity costs can be determined only within the context of a specific decision and only after specifying all the alternative actions. For example, the opportunity set for this Friday night includes the movies, a concert, staying home and studying, staying home and watching television, inviting friends over, and so forth.

The opportunity cost concept focuses managers' attention on the available alternative courses of action. Suppose you are considering three job offers. Job A pays a salary of $100,000, job B pays $102,000, and job C pays $106,000. In addition, you value each job differently in terms of career potential, developing your human capital, and the type of work. Suppose you value these nonpecuniary aspects of the three jobs at $8,000 for A, $5,000 for B, and only $500 for C. The following table summarizes the total value of each job offer. You decide to take job A because it has the highest total pecuniary and nonpecuniary compensation. The opportunity cost of job A is $107,000 (or $102,000 + $5,000), representing the amount forgone by not accepting job B, the next best alternative.

---

[1] R Coase, "Business Organization and the Accountant," originally published in *Accountant*, 1938. Reprinted in *L.S.E. Essays in Cost*, ed. J Buchanan and G Thirlby (New York University Press, 1981), p. 108.

Avoidable Costs and Opportunity Costs	Managers sometimes use the terms *avoidable* and *unavoidable costs*. *Avoidable costs* are those that will not be incurred if an existing operation is closed or changed. *Unavoidable costs* are those that will continue to be incurred regardless of which decision is made. For example, closing the painting department means laying off workers in that department; their salaries are avoidable costs. But the property taxes allocated to the painting department will still be incurred and are unavoidable costs. In general, avoidable costs are opportunity costs, while unavoidable costs are not opportunity costs.

replace it. The manager responsible for the failed software development will be held accountable for the failure and will have incentives to consume more firm resources trying to either fix it or cover up its failure before this knowledge becomes widely known.

The next example applies the opportunity cost concept to evaluating alternatives regarding labor.

Opportunity cost of labor

Suppose a firm's work force cannot be changed because of existing labor agreements. Employees are guaranteed 40 hours of pay per week. For the next three weeks only 35 hours of work per week per employee exists. What is the cost of taking a special order that will add five hours of work per employee? One is tempted to cost the five hours of labor in the special order at zero because these employees must be paid anyway. But the question remains, what will these employees do with the five hours if this special order is rejected? If they would do preventive maintenance on the machines or do general maintenance or improve their skills through training, then the opportunity cost of the labor for the special order is not zero but the value of the best forgone alternative use of the employees' time.

Public accounting firms confront this issue. The summer months tend to be low-demand periods relative to year-end. How the firm prices summer (off-peak) audits depends in part on the perceived opportunity cost of the staff's time.

If a firm owns fixed long-lived assets such as buildings and equipment, understanding their opportunity costs involves alternative uses of these assets. The next three examples describe the opportunity costs of capital assets.

Asset depreciation as an opportunity cost

Using assets can affect their value. Suppose a delivery van used four days a week can be sold next year for $14,000. If additional business is taken and the delivery van is used six days a week, its market value next year will be $8,000. Depreciation due to use for the additional business is $6,000 ($14,000 − $8,000). Additional labor for the driver's time, maintenance, gasoline, and oil are required.

The opportunity cost of using an asset is the decline in its value. Accounting depreciation (such as straight-line depreciation) is based on historical costs. Accounting depreciation does not necessarily reflect the opportunity cost of the van (its decline in value from use). However, accounting depreciation can be a reasonably accurate approximation of the decline in the market value of the asset. In any given year, accounting depreciation may not exactly capture the decline in the asset's market value. However, over the asset's economic life, accumulated accounting depreciation equals the decline in value. Holding managers responsi-

Relevant Costs and Opportunity Costs 	One often hears the term "relevant cost" being used to describe whether a particular cost should be considered in making a decision. Relevant costs are defined as "expected future costs that will differ under alternatives." Notice the close similarities between the definitions of relevant cost and opportunity cost ("the benefit forgone as a result of choosing one course of action rather than another"). Both relevant cost and opportunity cost require the decision maker to enumerate the set of alternatives being considered, to quantify the expected future resource flows for each alternative, and then to pick the alternative with the highest value. Opportunity cost is a well-defined, fundamental concept in economics that encompasses "relevant cost." While subtle differences exist between the two definitions, as a practical matter and to simplify the subsequent presentation, the remainder of the text uses the term "opportunity cost." SOURCE: C Horngren, *Cost Accounting: A Managerial Emphasis* (Englewood Cliffs, NJ: Prentice-Hall, 1977), p. 338.

ble for accounting depreciation commits them to recovering the historical cost of the asset in either additional revenues or cost savings.[3]

Interest on an asset as an opportunity cost
If the asset can be sold, then interest should be included as an opportunity cost. If the asset has no resale value, then obviously no interest is forgone. For example, a local area network and computers are purchased for $100,000. The interest rate is 8 percent. Should interest on the capital tied up in the hardware ($8,000) be included as a cost in the decision to continue to use the system? If the equipment has no market value, then interest is not a cost because the firm is not forgoing selling the hardware and earning interest on the proceeds. If the system can be sold, then the forgone interest on the proceeds is a cost. In the decision to close a factory or department, the interest on the scrap value of the assets is an opportunity cost. Chapter 3 presents an expanded discussion of the opportunity cost of a capital investment.

Opportunity cost of excess capacity
Suppose a plant operates at 75 percent capacity. Is the firm forgoing profits on the 25 percent of idle capacity? It is usually optimal to have some "excess" capacity in order to absorb random shocks to normal production, such as machine breakdowns and demand fluctuations, which increase production time and costs. When plants are built, rarely are they expected to run at 100 percent capacity. As plant utilization increases, per-unit costs increase as congestion rises.[4] The opportunity cost of increasing the plant's expected utilization, say from 75 percent to 85 percent of capacity, is the higher production cost imposed on the existing units that currently utilize 75 percent of the capacity.

---

[3]See R Ball, S Keating, and J Zimmerman, "Historical Costs as a Commitment Device," *Maandblad voor Accountancy en Bedrijfs economie* (Netherlands) (November 2000). Note that in computing the taxable gain or loss on the disposal of the asset, the accounting depreciation method used for taxes can affect the decision to retain or sell the asset.

[4]R Banker, S Datar, and S Kekre, "Relevant Costs, Congestion and Stochasticity in Production Environments," *Journal of Accounting & Economics* 10 (1988), pp. 171–97.

The Costs of the Sarbanes-Oxley Act

Following the accounting scandals at Enron, WorldCom, and Tyco and the demise of Arthur Andersen, the U.S. government enacted the Sarbanes-Oxley Act of 2002, the "Public Company Accounting Reform and Investor Protection Act." This law has many provisions, including the stipulation that audit committees of the board of directors have independent and "financially literate" outside directors; that independent auditors may not provide non-audit services to their clients; and that public companies and their auditors must report annually that management has "an adequate internal control structure and procedures for financial reporting." This last provision, known as section 404 of the act, is causing the greatest concern among publicly traded companies.

EMC Corporation, the $5 billion information-storage giant, estimates that it has spent more than $1 million and thousands of man-hours complying with Sarbanes-Oxley. In a survey of U.S. firms, CFO magazine reports that 48 percent of companies will spend at least $500,000 complying with the act, with 52 percent reporting that their compliance has yielded no benefits for their company. Digene Corp., a biotech firm, has seen its audit bill jump 72 percent.

Sarbanes-Oxley, by increasing both the duties and the liability of the officers and directors of public companies, has caused directors' fees and the insurance premiums of directors and officers to increase. Board-related costs, including director compensation and insurance, are expected to jump 50 percent.

In addition to the direct costs of complying with Sarbanes-Oxley, the act is imposing significant opportunity costs on companies. The CFO of the $5 billion Constellation Energy Group believes that the law makes the "fear of personal liability so great that managers are afraid to take risks on innovation." Some 33 percent of the CFO-surveyed companies have delayed or canceled other projects so they can comply with the law. Internal staff training has been reduced. Financial executives have less time to make strategic decisions as compliance efforts absorb 10 percent of a CFO's time in 40 percent of the companies. "Instead of being a business partner and doing all the positive things you'd like to do, you're triple-checking (SEC) filings." More small, publicly traded companies are going private because the cost of remaining public has increased. This deprives these companies of the benefits of being public, such as access to public equity markets and liquidity for equity investments.

But not everyone has been harmed by Sarbanes-Oxley. The law has been a windfall for auditors, lawyers, and software firms. A technology analyst at First Albany projects compliance-related technology will grow to $8 billion in 2005.

Source: A Nyberg, "Sticker Shock: The True Costs of Sarbanes-Oxley Compliance," CFO, September 2003, pp. 51-62.

Consider this illustration. The following table lists the output of a plant in units of production and the average cost per unit. Average costs rise as volume increases because congestion increases. This causes more machine breakdowns, and indirect labor (expediters, material handlers, production schedulers) must be hired to manage the increased congestion. The plant is currently operating at 75 percent capacity (150 units) and incurring average costs of $6.04 per unit.

Units	Capacity	Average Cost
130	65%	$6.00
140	70	6.02
150	75	6.04
160	80	6.06
170	85	6.08
180	90	6.11
190	95	6.15
200	100	6.20

Suppose production increases from 150 units (75 percent capacity) to 170 units (85 percent capacity). Increasing production by an extra 20 units causes the average cost of the base production of 150 units to rise from $6.04 to $6.08, or 4¢ per unit. The opportunity cost of producing 20 more units is not the average cost of $6.08 but the incremental cost of the last 20 units, $6.38 (or $[(170 \times \$6.08) - (150 \times \$6.04)] \div 20$ units). Another way of computing the opportunity cost of the last 20 units is

$$\$6.38 = \$6.08 + (4¢ \times 150) \div 20$$

Or the opportunity cost of producing 20 more units is composed of their average cost ($6.08) plus the cost increase that each of the 20 units imposes on the first 150 units ([4¢ $\times$ 150] $\div$ 20).

The final example describes how to evaluate the opportunity costs of introducing new products whose major competitors are the firm's existing products.

Opportunity cost of product line cannibalization
A company that produces personal computers (PCs) has 60 percent of a particular market niche, elementary school education. The company plans to introduce a new, high-end, faster computer with additional features. The major competition for the new PC is the firm's current high-end machine. In the first year, management projects sales of the new model to be 20,000 units. Sales of the existing machines are expected to fall by 7,000 units. Thus, the new PC "cannibalizes" the old PC's sales by 7,000 units. Are the forgone profits from the 7,000 units that could have been sold an opportunity cost of introducing the new computer? It depends on the opportunity set. If management expects competitors to introduce a machine that competes with the 7,000 units, meaning that the company is likely to have lost those units anyway, then the profits forgone on the 7,000 units are not an opportunity cost of introducing the new machine.

Concept Questions		
	Q2–1	Define *opportunity cost*.
	Q2–2	What are some characteristics of opportunity costs?
	Q2–3	A firm paid $8,325 last year for some raw material it planned to use in production. When is the $8,325 a good estimate of the opportunity cost of the material?
	Q2–4	Define *sunk cost* and give an example.
	Q2–5	What are avoidable and unavoidable costs? How are they related to opportunity costs?

FIGURE 2–1
Nonlinear cost curve

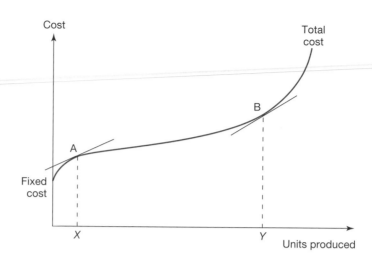

B. Cost Variation

Managers commonly decide how many units to produce or how much service to provide during a certain time period. Dell Computer must decide how many computers of a particular model to manufacture next quarter. United Airlines must decide whether to fly a 90-passenger jet or a 130-passenger jet between Denver and Palm Springs next month. Making these decisions requires an understanding of how costs change with volume—the topic of this section.

1. Fixed, Marginal, and Average Costs

Cost behavior is defined relative to some activity, such as the number of units produced, hours worked, pounds of ore mined, miles driven, or meals served. Usually, units produced is the measure of activity. For example, consider Figure 2–1, which illustrates the general relation between cost and units produced. Two important points emerge from Figure 2–1. First, even with no units produced, the firm still must incur some costs. The costs incurred when there is no production are called **fixed costs.** If the plant is idle, some costs such as property taxes, insurance, plant management, security, and so on must be incurred to provide production capacity. For example, Intel acquires land and builds a plant to manufacture a specific quantity of computer chips. It pays annual property taxes of $1.75 million on this land. The $1.75 million expenditure on property taxes is part of the cost Intel pays to have this manufacturing capacity at this plant.

Second, in general the cost curve is not a straight line as output expands, but rather is curvilinear. The particular shape of the curve arises because marginal cost varies with the level of production. **Marginal cost** is the cost of producing one more unit. In Figure 2–1, marginal cost is the slope of a line drawn tangent to the total cost curve. For the first few units, such as to the left of output level X, the slope of the tangent is quite steep. The marginal cost for the first few units is high because employees must be hired, suppliers must be found, and marketing channels must be opened. Therefore, the cost of starting operations and producing the first few units may be extremely high. Expanding output beyond the first few units allows the organization to achieve smooth, efficient production techniques. At normal production rates, the marginal cost of making additional units is relatively low. At high levels of output (output level Y), additional costs are incurred because of constraints on the use of space, machines, and employees. Machines are more likely to

Metro-Goldwyn-Mayer Inc.	MGM produces and distributes entertainment products worldwide, including motion pictures, television programming, home video, interactive media, music, and licensed merchandise. The company owns the largest modern film library in the world, consisting of approximately 4,000 titles. Its operating units include MGM Pictures, United Artists, MGM Television Entertainment, MGM Networks, MGM Distribution Co., and MGM Worldwide Television Distribution. MGM significantly improved its operating performance after a careful analysis of the fixed and variable costs of distributing movies to local cinemas. This analysis led MGM to convert a large fixed cost into a variable cost. It reduced head count 10 percent and stopped distributing independent films through United International Pictures. It now distributes these films itself.

SOURCE: L Calabro, "Everything in Moderation," *CFO*, February 2004, pp. 59-65.

fail when operating at or near capacity. Labor costs increase because employees are paid for overtime. Therefore, the marginal cost of making additional units when operating near capacity is higher than under normal operations.

By definition a fixed cost is not an opportunity cost of the decision to change the level of output. The decision to expand output usually does not affect property insurance premiums. Therefore, property insurance is a fixed cost with respect to volume and is not a cost when deciding to increase output. However, lower property insurance premiums are an important benefit when deciding to install smoke detectors. And an insurance premium is a cost of building and operating the plant.

The fact that a cost is fixed with respect to volume changes, however, does not mean that it cannot be managed or reduced. A firm can reduce insurance premiums by increasing deductibles or by lowering the risks being insured (installing fire alarms and sprinkler systems). Many fixed costs can be altered in the long run, in the sense that a particular plant can be closed. If a cost is fixed, this does not mean it is a constant and known with certainty. Fixed costs vary over time due to changes in prices. But fixed costs do not vary with changes in the number of units produced.

Another important cost term is **average cost.** Average cost per unit is calculated by dividing total cost by the number of units produced. Average cost is the slope of the line drawn from the origin to the total cost curve and is depicted in Figure 2–2 as the slope of the line from point O through point C.[5] The average cost at output level Z represents the cost *per unit* of producing Z units. For the pattern of costs in Figure 2–2, the average cost per unit is very high at low levels of output but declines as output increases. The average cost per unit only increases as output nears capacity. Notice that at Z units of production, the average cost is larger than the marginal cost. (The slope of OC is steeper than the slope of the tangent at point C.)

---

[5]Recall that the slope of a line is the ratio of the change in its vertical distance divided by the change in its horizontal distance. In Figure 2–2, the slope of the line OC is the distance CZ divided by the distance OZ. But CZ ÷ OZ is the total cost of producing Z units divided by Z units, which is the average cost of producing Z units.

FIGURE 2–2

Average and marginal cost

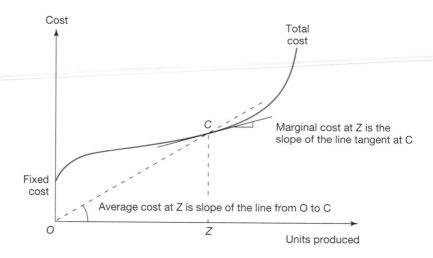

Exercise 1:

Suppose that a plant making steam boilers has the following costs per month:

Number of Boilers	Total Cost
1	$ 50,000
2	98,000
3	144,000
4	184,000
5	225,000
6	270,000
7	315,000
8	368,000
9	423,000
10	480,000

a. What are the marginal and average costs for each level of output?

b. The plant is currently making and selling eight boilers per month. The company can sell another steam boiler for $53,000. Should the company accept the offer?

Answer:

a.

Number of Boilers	Total Cost	Marginal Cost	Average Cost
1	$ 50,000	$50,000	$50,000
2	98,000	48,000	49,000
3	144,000	46,000	48,000
4	184,000	40,000	46,000
5	225,000	41,000	45,000
6	270,000	45,000	45,000
7	315,000	45,000	45,000
8	368,000	53,000	46,000
9	423,000	55,000	47,000
10	480,000	57,000	48,000

continued

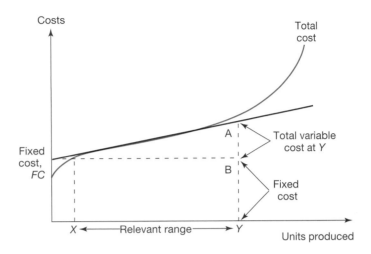

FIGURE 2–3

Linear approximation of total cost

> *b.* The company should reject the offer because the marginal cost of making the next boiler is $55,000, whereas the price is only $53,000. The average cost of $47,000 should not be used in this decision.

2. Linear Approximations

The cost of changing production levels is not always easy to estimate. Estimating the total cost curve in Figure 2–1 requires knowledge of both fixed cost and how consumption of facilities, labor, and materials varies as the rate of production increases. Such estimates are difficult to obtain, so managers often use approximations of these costs. One such approximation assumes the curve is linear instead of curvilinear.

An approximation of total cost in Figure 2–1 using a linear cost curve is provided in Figure 2–3. In this figure, estimating total cost requires an estimate of the y-axis intercept and the slope of the straight line. The intercept, FC, approximates the fixed costs. The slope of the line is the variable cost per unit. **Variable costs** are the additional costs incurred when output is expanded. When Chrysler expands the production of minivans at a particular plant from 200 to 250 vans per day, it must buy more parts, hire more employees, use more power, and so forth. All costs that increase when more vans are produced are variable costs.[6]

In Figure 2–3, the straight line is the sum of the fixed and variable cost approximations of total cost. The line is closest to the total cost in the range of normal operations. This range between output levels X and Y is called the *relevant range*. The **relevant range** encompasses the rates of output for which the sum of fixed and variable costs closely approximates total cost. Because the slopes of the total cost curve and the fixed and variable cost curve are about the same, the variable cost is a close approximation of the marginal cost. In the relevant range, variable cost can be used to estimate the cost of making additional units of output.

---

[6]While most managers understand intuitively the difference between fixed and variable costs, not everyone does. When asked the difference between a fixed cost and a variable cost, one employee replied, "A fixed cost? If it's broke, I fix it and it costs me." See R Suskind, "Guys Holding Axes and Chainsaws Get to Use Any Name They Like," *The Wall Street Journal*, February 26, 1992, p. B–1.

FIGURE 2–4

Step and mixed costs

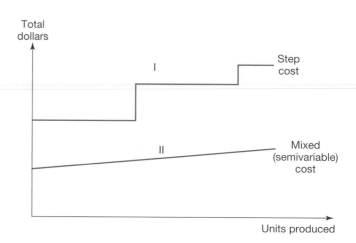

Notice that variable cost per unit approximates marginal cost per unit. The slope of the variable cost line is constant as the activity measure increases. Variable cost per unit is usually assumed to be constant. Later chapters relax this assumption. The terms *marginal cost* and *variable cost* are often used interchangeably, but the two are not necessarily the same. **Marginal cost** refers to the cost of the last unit produced and in most cases varies as volume changes. In some situations, marginal cost per unit does not vary with volume. Then marginal cost (per unit) and variable cost per unit are equal.

The straight-line approximation of total cost can be represented by the following equations:

$$\text{Total cost} = \text{Fixed cost} + \text{Variable cost}$$
$$\text{Total cost} = \text{Fixed cost} + (\text{Variable cost per unit})(\text{Units produced})$$
$$TC = FC + VC \times Q$$

where TC represents total cost, FC represents fixed cost, VC is variable cost per unit, and Q is the number of units. For example, suppose the fixed cost is $100,000 per month, the variable cost per unit is $3, and 15,000 units are to be manufactured. Total cost is calculated to be $145,000 (or $100,000 + $3 × 15,000 units). The total cost of $145,000 is an estimate of the cost of manufacturing 15,000 units.

3. Other Cost Behavior Patterns

Some costs vary with output (variable costs) and others do not (fixed costs). Between these two extreme cases are step costs and mixed (semivariable) costs. Each of these is described in turn and illustrated in Figure 2–4.

Step costs

One type of cost behavior involves **step costs,** expenditures fixed over a range of output levels (line I in Figure 2–4). For example, each supervisor can monitor a fixed number of employees. As output is expanded and the number of supervisors increases with the number of employees, the resulting increases in supervisory personnel expenditures are a step function. Likewise, once the number of transactions a computer system can process is exceeded, a larger machine is required. Expenditures on computers often behave as step costs.

Mixed (semivariable) costs

Many costs cannot be neatly categorized as purely fixed or variable. The cost of electricity used by a firm is a good example. Producing more output requires some

| Multiple Activity Measures in a Painting Department | Total cost in the painting department of a toy factory varies not only with the number of toys painted but also with the sizes of the toys, the types of surfaces painted, the kinds of paint applied, and so on. |

Paint costs $15 per gallon. To set up the painting machines to paint a part costs $500, which includes cleaning out the old color. Using the paint machine for one hour costs $70, which also includes the labor to operate it.

A particular part with 4,200 pieces in the batch requires 10 gallons of paint and eight hours of paint machine time. Using multiple activity bases, the cost of painting this part is calculated as

Setup cost	$ 500
Paint	150
Machine time	560
Total painting cost	$1,210

Notice that the cost of painting the parts includes a fixed setup cost of $500, which does not vary with the number of parts painted.

additional power. But some portion of the electric bill is just for turning on the lights and heating or cooling the plant whether the plant produces 1 unit or 50,000 units. Therefore, the cost of electricity is a mixture of fixed and variable costs. **Mixed** or **semivariable costs** are cost categories (such as electricity) that cannot be classified as being purely fixed or purely variable (line II in Figure 2–4).

4. Activity Measures

The discussion so far has focused on how total cost varies with changes in output (units produced). Output is the *measure of activity*. Consider a steel mill that makes 1 million tons of two-inch steel plate in one month and 1 million tons of one-inch steel plate in the next month. The cost of the one-inch steel plate will likely be higher because more work is required to roll out the thinner plate. In this factory, costs vary not only with weight of the output but also with its thickness. In general, costs vary based on units produced as well as on the size, weight, and complexity of the product.

In many costing situations, managers choose a single activity measure, such as the total number of toys painted or pounds of toys painted. This activity measure is then assumed to be the primary cost driver. The **cost driver** is that measure of physical activity most highly associated with variations in cost. For example, in the painting department, the quantity of paint used will be chosen as the cost driver if it has the highest association with total costs in the painting department.

An input measure, such as the number of labor hours spent painting, is often used as a single cost driver to capture the many factors and to simplify the process of estimating total cost. The choice of the activity/volume measure is often critical to the perceived variation of costs. This issue is discussed in greater detail in Chapter 11.

The problem with using a single activity measure is that it can be correct for one class of decisions but incorrect for others. Such categorizations indicate how costs vary but only for that particular decision. For example, expanding the

| Activity-Based Costing in Hospitals | Activity-based costing (ABC) seeks to derive more accurate cost information by identifying multiple activity measures (cost drivers). Activity-based costing suggests a hierarchy of cost drivers: **unit-level, batch-level, product-level,** and **facility-related.** Most costs can be categorized into one of these four classes. **Unit-level costs** vary with the number of units manufactured. **Batch-level costs,** such as the labor cost of setting up the machine to produce a batch, vary with the number of setups. **Product-level costs,** such as the cost of machines dedicated to manufacturing a particular product, vary with the number of products. And, **facility-related costs,** such as security and plant management, vary with the number of plants.* |

In hospitals, unit-level costs include those resources devoted to serving a patient for one day (patient-day). These include nursing, food, and linens. Batch-level costs include the admissions office. Admissions costs do not vary with patient-days but with the number of admissions. Product-level costs include the medical directors of specialty services such as pediatrics and orthopedics. These costs are generally fixed with respect to patient-days but vary with the number of medical services. Finally, facility-related costs include hospital administration.

*See R Cooper and R Kaplan, *The Design of Cost Management Systems* (Englewood Cliffs, NJ: Prentice Hall, 1991).

volume of an existing product in a given plant will cause a different set of costs to vary than will adding a new product line in the same plant or expanding the volume of a given product by building a new plant. Consider an automobile assembly line producing a single car model. Adding 125 cars per day of a second car model costs more than increasing production of the existing model by 125 cars. More labor is required to schedule, order parts, and store them for two different models than if just one model is produced. Thus, the variable costs of 125 cars depend on whether the additional cars are for an existing model or a new model.

Some costs are fixed with respect to some decisions but not others. Consider machine setups. Before a computer-controlled milling machine can begin milling parts, a technician must set up the machine by loading the proper computer program, loading the correct tools into the machine, adjusting the settings, making a few parts, and checking their tolerances. Once set up, the machine can produce a large number of parts without another machine setup. The cost of the setup is the cost of the technician's time, the material used to check the machine, and the forgone profits of not using the machine while it is being set up. This setup cost is independent of the number of units produced and thus is a fixed cost. However, if the machine produces 1,000 parts per batch, expanding volume from 1,000 parts to 2,000 parts doubles the number of setups and doubles the setup costs. On the other hand, if the plant increases volume to 2,000 parts by doubling batch size, setup costs remain fixed. Therefore, classifying setup costs as being either fixed or variable can be right for some decisions and wrong for others, depending on whether batch sizes change. If some decisions cause batch sizes to change and others do not, then any classification of setup costs as fixed or variable will be wrong for some decisions.

Most firms (82 percent) identify the fixed and variable components of their manufacturing costs.[7] But the particular expense classification varies widely. A

[7] W Cress and J Pettijohn, "A Survey of Budget-Related Planning and Control Policies and Procedures," *Journal of Accounting Education* 3 (Fall 1985), p. 73.

TABLE 2–1   Percentage of Variable, Semivariable, and Fixed Costs in Korea, Japan, and the United States

Types of Costs	Variable Cost			Semivariable Cost			Fixed Cost		
	Korea	*Japan*	*U.S.*	*Korea*	*Japan*	*U.S.*	*Korea*	*Japan*	*U.S.*
Production labor	41%	48%	71%	13%	5%	5%	27%	40%	7%
Setup labor	25	35	49	27	5	20	26	40	12
Repairs and maintenance	29	8	23	25	18	36	26	58	24
Tooling	22	28	24	26	23	27	32	38	25
Energy	40	38	21	20	28	36	15	25	23
Supervision	10	3	3	15	3	22	52	75	58
Depreciation	6	0	1	9	0	6	66	80	78

NOTE: Numbers do not add to 100 percent because some cost categories are classified into more than one type of cost.

SOURCE: I Kim and J Song, "U.S., Korea, & Japan Accounting: Practices in Three Countries," *Management Accounting*, August 1990, pp. 26–30.

study comparing the cost structures of Korean, Japanese, and U.S. firms reported the fraction of cost categories treated as variable, semivariable, or fixed. The results are shown in Table 2–1.

One interpretation of Table 2–1 is that the behavior of a particular cost, such as production labor, is fixed in some firms and variable in others. Production labor and energy are usually—but not always—variable or semivariable. Supervision and depreciation are usually fixed costs. It appears that in the United States, production labor is more often a variable cost, whereas in Korea and Japan it is more frequently semivariable or fixed. Prior to 1990, some Japanese firms had "lifetime" employment policies whereby employees are not laid off when the economy slumps. These lifetime employment policies cause labor to be a fixed cost because it does not vary with changes in output. However, the differences in the reported percentages in Table 2–1 might be a result of differences in survey methods used in the three countries. Also, these surveys invariably report accounting costs, not opportunity costs. As discussed in section D, the two can differ.

Concept Questions	Q2–6	Define *mixed cost* and give an example.
	Q2–7	Define *step cost* and give an example.
	Q2–8	Define *fixed cost*.
	Q2–9	Define *variable cost*. Is it the same as marginal cost? Explain.

C. Cost–Volume–Profit Analysis

1. Copier Example

Once costs are classified into fixed/variable categories, managers can perform cost–volume–profit analysis. The following example illustrates the essential features of this analysis. Suppose Xerox Corp. has a walk-up copy division that places coin-operated photocopying machines in public areas such as libraries, bookshops, and supermarkets. Customers pay 5¢ per copy and the store providing the space receives ½¢ per copy. Xerox provides the machine, paper, toner, and service. Machines are serviced every 30,000 copies at an average cost of $90 per service call. Paper and toner cost ½¢ per copy. The walk-up copy division is charged $185 per month per machine placed (the opportunity cost of the machine). The variable costs per copy are

Paper and toner	$0.005
Store owner	0.005
Service ($90 ÷ 30,000)	0.003
Variable costs	$0.013

The contribution margin is the difference between the price and the variable cost per copy. The contribution margin is the net receipts per copy that are contributed toward covering fixed costs and providing profits. In this example, the contribution margin is calculated as

Price	$0.050
Less variable costs	(0.013)
Contribution margin	$0.037

Given the contribution margin and monthly fixed costs, the number of copies each machine must sell monthly to recover costs is the ratio of fixed costs to the contribution margin. This quantity of copies is called the **break-even point** and is calculated as

$$\text{Break-even point} = \frac{\text{Fixed costs}}{\text{Contribution margin}} = \frac{\$185}{\$0.037} = 5,000 \text{ copies}$$

In other words, if the copier makes 5,000 copies each month, it produces net receipts (after variable costs) of $185 (or 5,000 × $0.037), which is just enough to recover the fixed costs.

The Xerox copier example illustrates that classifying costs into fixed and variable components provides a simple decision rule as to where to place copiers. If a store is expected to produce (or actually produces) fewer than 5,000 copies per month, a copier should not be located there. The break-even volume provides a useful management tool for where to place machines.

2. Calculating Break-Even and Target Profits

Let us study the cost–volume–profit analysis further. For simplicity, assume that production equals sales (to avoid inventory valuation issues such as the LIFO/FIFO choice). Also assume that the firm produces a single product. Figure 2–5 displays the total cost and revenue of producing various levels of output. The total revenue curve shows revenue when higher unit sales can be achieved only at lower prices. At high prices, volumes are low. As prices fall, volume increases and the slope of the total revenue curve becomes less steep. The total cost curve, also nonlinear, is the same cost curve depicted in Figure 2–1. Break-even occurs when total revenues equal costs. In Figure 2–5, two break-even volumes exist, labeled "Break-even point 1" and "Break-even point 2." The profit-maximizing point of output occurs when

FIGURE 2–5

*Total cost and
revenue curves*

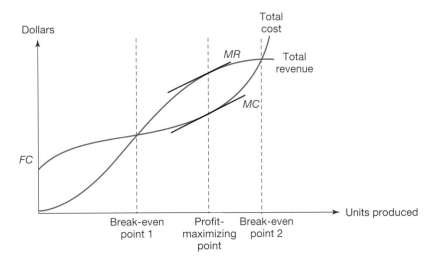

MC: Marginal cost is the slope of the total cost curve.
MR: Marginal revenue is the slope of the total revenue curve.
MC and MR are equal at the profit-maximizing point.

marginal revenue equals marginal cost (MC = MR). **Marginal revenue** refers to the receipts from the last unit sold. At any point, marginal revenue, like marginal cost, is the slope of the line just tangent to the total revenue curve.

As described in section B, it is difficult to estimate nonlinear functions. Linear approximations are often used. Figure 2–6 substitutes linear cost and linear revenue approximations for nonlinear curves. Instead of allowing price to vary with quantity, assume a constant price, P. The total revenue function, TR, is then

$$TR = P \times Q$$

where Q is output. If the firm can sell as much as it wants without affecting price, then assuming a linear revenue function, TR, does not distort the analysis. Likewise, total cost is assumed to follow a linear function of the form

$$TC = FC + VC \times Q$$

where FC is the fixed cost and VC is the variable cost per unit. For the moment, ignore income taxes.

Using linear functions allows managers to simplify analyzing how profits vary with output. In particular,

$$\text{Profit} = TR - TC = P \times Q - VC \times Q - FC \qquad (2.1)$$

$$\text{Profit} = (P - VC) \times Q - FC \qquad (2.2)$$

Break-even volume is the number of units sold that just covers fixed and variable costs. To find break-even volume, Q_{BE}, set equation (2.2) equal to zero and solve for Q.

$$\text{Profit} = 0 = (P - VC) \times Q_{BE} - FC \qquad (2.3)$$

$$Q_{BE} = \frac{FC}{P - VC} = \frac{FC}{\text{Contribution margin}} = \frac{FC}{CM}$$

Price minus variable costs ($P - VC$), the contribution margin per unit (CM), is the profit per unit sold that can be used to cover fixed costs (FC). Contribution

FIGURE 2–6

Linear approximations of cost and revenue curves and cost–volume–profit analysis

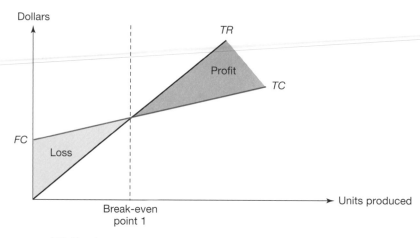

FC: Fixed cost
TR: Total revenue equals a constant price times total output ($P \times Q$)
TC: Total cost equals fixed costs plus the variable cost per unit times output ($FC + VC \times Q$)

margin is important because it measures the incremental net receipts of selling one more unit. Refer to Figure 2–6. If units produced is less than the break-even point, a loss occurs. If output exceeds break-even quantity, a profit is earned.

Note that the estimated break-even point, Q_{BE}, will not exactly correspond to the "real" break-even point, where total revenue equals total cost. The discrepancy occurs because *TR* and *TC* do not perfectly represent total revenue and opportunity costs, respectively.

Suppose we want to make a target after-tax profit of $Profit_T$ and the income tax rate is t. We can compute the number of units needed to make an after-tax profit by modifying equation (2.2) and solving for Q_T, target output:

$$Profit_T = [Q_T \times (P - VC) - FC] \times (1 - t) \tag{2.4}$$

$$Q_T = \frac{Profit_T}{(1 - t) \times CM} + \frac{FC}{CM} \tag{2.5}$$

Instead of memorizing this formula, it is better to start with equation (2.1) or (2.2) and make the necessary modifications to solve the particular problem at hand. Exercise 2 illustrates how to modify the formula.

Exercise 2:

DGA Tile manufactures ceramic flooring tiles. DGA's annual fixed costs are $740,000. The variable cost of each tile is $0.25, and tiles are sold for $6.50. DGA has a combined state and federal tax rate of 45 percent.

    a. How many tiles does DGA need to make and sell each year to earn an after-tax profit of $85,000?

    b. DGA must pay 10 percent of before-tax profits as a royalty payment to its founder. Now how many tiles must DGA make and sell to generate $85,000 after taxes? (Assume the royalty payment is not a tax-deductible expense.)

continued

Answer:

a. Let Q denote the number of tiles made and sold that generates $85,000 of after-tax profit. Given the above data, we can write

$$(\$6.50Q - \$0.25Q - \$740{,}000)(1 - 0.45) = \$85{,}000$$

$$(6.25Q - \$740{,}000) \times 0.55 = \$85{,}000$$

Solving for Q:

$$\$3.4375Q = \$85{,}000 + \$740{,}000 \times 0.55$$

$$Q = 143{,}127 \text{ tiles}$$

Therefore, to generate an after-tax profit of $85,000, about 143,000 tiles must be sold.

b. The formula with the royalty payment, R, is

$$(\$6.25Q - \$740{,}000) \times 0.55 - R = \$85{,}000$$

where

$$R = (\$6.25Q - \$740{,}000) \times 0.10$$

Substituting R into the earlier equation,

$$(\$6.25Q - \$740{,}000)(0.55 - 0.10) = \$85{,}000$$

$$Q = 148{,}622$$

The following exercise illustrates another use of contribution margins. It involves choosing the most profitable product to produce when capacity is constrained.

Exercise 3:

The Ralston Company produces three shirts. It only has 200 machine hours per day to produce shirts and has the following cost and production information:

	Basic	*Deluxe*	*Super*
Selling price	$7.50	$9	$13
Variable cost of production	$6.00	$7	$ 7
Machine hours to complete one shirt	0.6	2	3
Demand per day (shirts)	50	50	50

Ralston has fixed costs of $75 per day. How many shirts of each type should be produced?

Answer:

The opportunity cost of producing one type of shirt arises from not using those machine hours to produce another type of shirt. In this problem, to maximize firm profits in light

continued

of a capacity constraint, we must produce those products with the highest contribution margin *per unit of capacity*. First calculate the contribution margin per shirt and then convert this to the contribution margin per machine hour.

	Basic	Deluxe	Super
Selling price	$7.50	$9	$13
Variable cost of production	$6.00	$7	$7
Contribution margin per shirt	$1.50	$2	$6
Hours to complete one shirt	÷ 0.6	÷ 2	÷ 3
Contribution margin per machine hour	$2.50	$1	$2
Demand per day (shirts)	50	50	50
Production schedule (shirts)	50	10	50
× Hours to complete one shirt	0.6	2	3
Hours consumed	30	20	150

The decision rule to maximize profits is to produce the shirt(s) with the highest contribution margin per unit of scarce resource (machine hours). This is an application of the opportunity cost principle. Even though super has the highest contribution margin per unit, basic has the highest contribution margin per machine hour. Therefore, to maximize profits, produce 50 units of basic, which will consume 30 hours (or 50 units × 0.6 hours per unit). Next, produce 50 units of super, which consumes 150 hours of capacity. This leaves 20 hours of capacity to be used to produce 10 units of deluxe.

The preceding analysis suggests producing the market demand for basic and super but not for deluxe. Fixed costs never enter the analysis. By definition, fixed costs are fixed and cannot be relevant to the decision, which depends only on selling price, variable cost, and the capacity constraint.[*]

[*]One artificial aspect of this exercise is that the quantity demanded and the price are taken as constants. Clearly, at lower prices, more shirts will be demanded. Fixed demand is assumed merely to simplify the problem and focus on the cost behavior.

The Ralston Company example illustrates a very simple situation in which there is only one constraint. If there are multiple constraints, linear programming is a useful technique for identifying the profit-maximizing mix of products. The next section describes some of the shortcomings of cost–volume–profit analysis.

3. Limitations of Cost–Volume–Profit Analysis

Exercise 4:

Using equation (2.2), find the output, Q, that maximizes profits.

Answer:

Profits are maximized by setting output to infinity. That is, equation (2.2) cannot be used to maximize profits.

Exercise 4 illustrates that cost–volume–profit analysis is not useful for choosing the profit-maximizing output quantity when both revenues and costs are linear. Given this conclusion, what good is it? Cost–volume–profit analysis offers a useful place to start analyzing business problems. It gives managers an ability to do sensitivity analysis and ask simple what-if questions. And, as we saw in the copier example, break-even analysis can prove useful for certain types of decisions. However, there are several limitations of cost–volume–profit analysis:

1. Price and variable cost per unit must not vary with volume.
2. Cost–volume–profit is a single-period analysis. All revenues and costs occur in the same time period.
3. Cost–volume–profit analysis assumes a single-product firm. All fixed costs are incurred to produce a single product. If the firm produces multiple products, and fixed costs such as property taxes are incurred to produce all the products, then the break-even point or target profit for any one of the products depends on the volume of the other products. With multiple products and common fixed costs, it is not meaningful to discuss the break-even point for just one product.

Although these limitations are important, cost–volume–profit analysis forces managers to understand how costs and revenues vary with changes in output. In fact, 55 percent of 219 large U.S. firms surveyed use it.[8]

Notice in the earlier Xerox rental copier example that the assumptions underlying break-even analysis are not violated:

- Price does not vary with quantity.
- Variable cost per unit does not vary with quantity.
- Fixed costs are known.
- There is a single product (copies).
- All output is sold.

4. Multiple Products

As we saw above, one limitation of cost–volume–profit analysis is that it applies only to firms making a single product. One way to overcome this limitation is to assume a constant output mix of bundles with fixed proportions of the multiple products. Then a break-even or a target profit number of bundles can be calculated.

For example, suppose a winery produces two types of wine: merlot and chablis. The following table summarizes prices and variable costs of the winery, which has fixed costs of $500,000 per year.

	Merlot	*Chablis*
Price per case	$30	$20
Variable cost per case	20	15
Contribution margin per case	$10	$ 5

For every case of merlot produced, three cases of chablis are produced. Define a wine *bundle* to consist of four cases of which one is merlot and three are chablis.

---

[8]W Cress and J Pettijohn (1985), p. 68.

Each wine bundle has revenues of $90 (1 × $30 + 3 × $20), variable costs of $65 (1 × $20 + 3 × $15), and a contribution margin of $25 (1 × $10 + 3 × $5). The number of *bundles* required to break even is:

$$\frac{\text{Break-even number}}{\text{of bundles}} = \frac{\text{Fixed costs}}{\text{Contribution margin}} = \frac{\$500,000}{\$25} = 20,000 \text{ bundles}$$

Twenty thousand bundles needed to break even translate into 20,000 cases of merlot and 60,000 cases of chablis to break even. Hence, if a firm produces a variety of products in fixed proportions, then break-even analysis can be conducted by creating a standard bundle of products.

Exercise 5:

Using the winery example above, how many cases of merlot and chablis must be produced and sold to make an after-tax profit of $100,000 if the tax rate is 20 percent?

Answer:

The after-tax profit is calculated from the following equation:

After-tax profit = (1 − Tax rate) × (Revenues − Variable cost − Fixed costs)

$100,000 = (1 − 20%) × ($90B − $65B − $500,000)

where *B* is the number of bundles.
    Solving for *B* yields:

$$\$100,000 = .8 \times (\$25B - \$500,000)$$

$$\$100,000 = \$20B - \$400,000$$

$$B = \$500,000/\$20$$

$$B = 25,000 \text{ bundles}$$

In other words, 25,000 cases of merlot and 75,000 cases (3 × 25,000) of chablis must be sold to break even. At these production levels, $100,000 of after-tax profit is generated as demonstrated by the following income statement:

Revenue—Merlot	25,000 × $30	$ 750,000
Revenue—Chablis	75,000 × $20	1,500,000
Total revenue		$2,250,000
Less: Variable costs		
Merlot	25,000 × $20	$ 500,000
Chablis	75,000 × $15	1,125,000
Fixed costs		500,000
Total costs		$2,125,000
Income before taxes		$ 125,000
Taxes (20%)		25,000
Net income after taxes		$ 100,000

TABLE 2–2 **Operating Leverage**
(Production and Sales Are 10,000 Units)

		LoLev	HiLev
Revenue	10,000 units @ $8	$80,000	$80,000
Variable costs	10,000 units @ $4	40,000	
	10,000 units @ $2		20,000
Fixed costs		30,000	50,000
Net income		$10,000	$10,000

TABLE 2–3 **Operating Leverage**
(Production and Sales Are 7,500 Units)

		LoLev	HiLev
Revenue	7,500 units @ $8	$60,000	$60,000
Variable costs	7,500 units @ $4	30,000	
	7,500 units @ $2		15,000
Fixed costs		30,000	50,000
Net income (loss)		$ 0	$(5,000)

Concept Questions	Q2–10	What are the underlying assumptions in a cost–volume–profit analysis?
	Q2–11	What are the benefits and limitations of cost–volume–profit analysis?

5. Operating Leverage

Separating costs into fixed and variable components is useful for calculating break-even points. Estimating contribution margin is useful for pricing decisions and for deciding to take new orders. Understanding a product's fixed and variable costs is also useful for strategy reasons.

The higher a firm's fixed costs, the higher its operating leverage, which is the ratio of fixed costs to total costs. Operating leverage measures the sensitivity of profits to changes in sales. The higher the operating leverage, the greater the firm's risk. In firms with high operating leverage, small percentage changes in volume (i.e., sales) lead to large percentage changes in net cash flows (and profits). Therefore, firms with high operating leverage tend to have greater variability in cash flows and hence greater risk than firms with a lower ratio of fixed costs to total costs.

To illustrate the importance of operating leverage, consider the illustration in Table 2–2. Two companies, HiLev and LoLev, each sell 10,000 units of an identical product for $8 per unit. At that level of production, both companies have identical total costs of $70,000, and both companies are making $10,000 in profits. But three-sevenths of LoLev's costs are fixed, whereas five-sevenths of HiLev's costs are fixed. Therefore, HiLev has more operating leverage.

Suppose volume falls 25 percent. Table 2–3 indicates the impact on net income. In LoLev, net income falls to zero; in HiLev, a loss of $5,000 results.

TABLE 2–4   **Operating Leverage**
(Production and Sales Are 12,500 Units)

		LoLev	HiLev
Revenue	12,500 units @ $8	$100,000	$100,000
Variable costs	12,500 units @ $4	50,000	
	12,500 units @ $2		25,000
Fixed costs		30,000	50,000
Net income		$ 20,000	$ 25,000

Table 2–4 illustrates that when volume increases 25 percent, HiLev has a greater increase in profits than LoLev. Operating leverage amplifies the impact on earnings of a given percentage change in volume.

Firms with low variable costs per unit can sustain larger short-term price cuts when faced with increased competition. For example, a firm selling a product for $10 per unit that has a variable cost of $7 per unit can cut the price to just above $7 (for short periods of time) and still cover the variable costs of each unit. If that same firm has variable costs of $8 per unit, a price cut to below $8 causes a cash drain with each incremental unit. Knowledge of a competitor's cost structure is valuable strategic information in designing marketing campaigns. Estimating a firm's riskiness also requires knowledge of operating leverage.

Exercise 6:

Two Internet retailers have the following data:

(millions)	BuyEverything.com	SportsWhere.com
Sales	$120	$186
Variable costs	70	150
Fixed costs	40	24
Net income	$ 10	$ 12

a. Which retailer has more operating leverage?

b. Suppose the sales of each retailer double; which one's net income shows the greatest percentage increase?

c. Calculate the percentage change in each retailer's net income if sales fall 50 percent.

Answer:

a. BuyEverything.com's operating leverage (as measured by the ratio of fixed to total cost) is .36 ($40/$110) and SportsWhere.com's operating leverage is .14 ($24/$174). Hence, BuyEverything.com has more operating leverage.

continued

---

b. The following table calculates how net income changes with a doubling of sales:

(millions)	BuyEverything.com	SportsWhere.com
Sales	$240	$372
Variable costs	140	300
Fixed costs	40	24
Net income	$ 60	$ 48
Prior net income	$ 10	$ 12
% change	500%[*]	300%[†]

[*]($60 − $10)/$10
[†]($48 − $12)/$12

BuyEverything.com (which has more operating leverage from part *a*) shows the greatest percentage increase in net income.

c. The following table calculates how net income changes when sales fall 50 percent:

(millions)	BuyEverything.com	SportsWhere.com
Sales	$60	$93
Variable costs	35	75
Fixed costs	40	24
Net income	($15)	($ 6)
Prior net income	$10	$12
% change	− 250%[*]	− 150%[†]

[*](−$15 − $10)/$10
[†](−$6 − $12)/$12

BuyEverything.com (which has more operating leverage from part *a*) shows the greatest percentage decrease in net income.

D. Opportunity Costs versus Accounting Costs

The theoretically correct way to evaluate choices requires estimating opportunity costs. Estimating opportunity costs requires the decision maker to formulate all possible actions (the opportunity set) and the forgone net receipts from each of those alternatives so that the highest net cash flows from the set of actions not undertaken can be calculated. This yields the opportunity cost of the selected action. Such an exercise requires a special study for every decision, a time-consuming and costly activity. And after completing the study, the opportunity cost changes as the opportunity set changes. It is little wonder that managers devise shortcut

New Economy Firms and High Operating Leverage

Inktomi Corp. was a high-flying software company. It spent $10 million developing software to manage Web content. Once those fixed costs were incurred, each additional sale was almost pure profit. The president remarked, "You have no cost of goods. We don't even ship a physical diskette anymore. Next to the federal government, this is the only business that's allowed to print money." All this has changed.

Software development costs are up and sales have nosedived, causing Inktomi to report a loss of $58 million for the first quarter of 2001. Enormous fixed costs are required to research, develop, design, test, and market software. Intense competition and rapid obsolescence require high levels of spending each year. The result is a dramatic reversal of fortune leading to big swings in profits, stock prices, and hiring when sales sag. High operating leverage at Yahoo! caused its profits to plummet $87 million in the first quarter of 2001 to a loss of $33 million in the second quarter because sales fell 42 percent, yet expenses remained largely fixed.

High technology firms in the new economy incur large fixed costs and relatively low variable costs to produce intellectual property such as software and Web sites. This combination creates high operating leverage that causes these firms to be very risky. In good times they are flying high. In weak times, there is very little they can do to trim expenses.

SOURCE: G Ip, "Blame the Profit Dive on a Marked Change in Companies' Costs," *The Wall Street Journal*, May 16, 2001, p. A1.

---

approximations to estimating opportunity costs. Accounting-based costs are such a shortcut.

Accounting systems record "costs" after making the decisions. Accounting systems track asset conversions. When the firm acquires assets such as raw material, accountants record them in monetary terms (historical cost valuation). As the raw inputs are converted into intermediate products, accountants value the intermediate products at the historical costs of the raw inputs converted into the intermediate products. The in-process, partially completed units flowing through departments, are recorded in the accounts at historical costs. If an employee paid $12 per hour completes an intermediate product in two hours, the accounting system increases the cost of the intermediate product by $24. Completion and sale of the manufactured unit causes the historical costs attached to it to be transferred from the inventory accounts to the expense account "cost of goods sold." Accounting costs are not forward-looking opportunity costs; they look backward at the historical cost of the resources consumed to produce the product. Accounting systems produce accounting costs, not opportunity costs. However, accounting costs often provide a reasonable approximation of opportunity costs. Over short periods of time, prices and costs do not change very much. Thus, accounting costs can be reasonably accurate estimates of opportunity costs.

Besides providing data for decision making, internal accounting systems also provide data for controlling the behavior of people in organizations as well as the data for external financial reporting. The resources consumed to produce this textbook might differ from the opportunity cost of a new textbook. But the historical cost of this book provides information to senior managers as to how well the persons responsible for producing this book discharged their duties. Valuing the ending inventory of books, calculating taxes payable, and computing net income require the historical cost of this textbook.

Cost systems do not focus on opportunity costs, nor can they, since opportunity costs depend on the decision being contemplated. Accounting systems cannot anticipate all future decisions. They provide historical amounts useful for predicting the consequences of future actions. Thus, the term *cost* can refer to accounting cost (historical amounts) or to opportunity cost (the amount forgone by some decision), two very different concepts. In some cases, the user's meaning is obvious, but it is always important to question whether the term *cost* means opportunity cost or accounting cost.

1. Period versus Product Costs	To further understand how accounting costs differ from opportunity costs, we distinguish between product costs and period costs. **Product costs** include all those accounting costs incurred to manufacture a product. Product costs are inventoried and expensed only when the product is sold. **Period costs** are those costs that are expensed in the period in which they are incurred. They include all nonmanufacturing accounting costs incurred to sell the product. For example, administration, distribution, warehousing, selling, and advertising expenditures are period costs. Research and development is a period cost. Period costs are not part of the product's cost included in inventory.

Product costs include both fixed and variable manufacturing components. Likewise, period costs, the costs of distributing and selling the product, contain both fixed and variable components. Fixed period costs include salespersons' salaries, advertising, and marketing costs. Examples of variable period costs include distribution costs and sales commissions.

Accounting systems, even those used for internal purposes, distinguish between product and period costs. In most situations, unit cost figures refer to *product* costs excluding all *period* costs. Suppose that the unit manufacturing cost of a product is $23. Selling and distributing this product costs an additional $4 per unit. This $4 period cost includes both fixed and variable period costs. The total cost of manufacturing and selling each unit is $27. Many firms refer to the $23 product cost as a *unit manufacturing cost* (UMC). For decision-making purposes both period ($4) and product ($23) costs must be considered, so it is important to remember that a UMC usually excludes period costs.

Period costs and product costs are historical costs. They are not opportunity costs because they are the resources forgone from a past set of decisions. However, to the extent that the future looks a lot like the past, these historical costs can be useful predictors of opportunity costs.

2. Direct Costs, Overheads, and Opportunity Costs	The accounting concepts of direct costs versus overhead costs also illustrate the difference between opportunity and accounting costs. Direct costs and overhead costs form the core of this book, to which we will return in later chapters, particularly Chapters 9 through 13. But it is useful to introduce the terms now.

Direct costs of a product or service are those items that are easily traced to the product or service. Direct labor and direct material costs are direct costs. An employee producing a product is classified as direct labor. If this employee is idled by a machine breakdown, that idle time is classified as indirect labor. Indirect materials include those used in maintaining and testing machines as well as those lost in the machine during a breakdown. **Overhead** includes indirect labor and indirect material costs as well as other types of general manufacturing costs that cannot be directly traced, or are not worth tracing, to units being produced. Examples include the cost of the purchasing department, property taxes, maintenance, depreciation, insurance, security guards, and some engineering services. *Indirect cost* is another term for *overhead*.

Direct costs are usually variable. For example, to produce more copies of this book requires additional paper and ink (direct materials) and additional time by the person running the printing press (direct labor). But direct costs can be fixed. For example, the costs associated with a machine (depreciation, electricity, and routine maintenance) dedicated to one product are direct costs of that product and are largely fixed. Or, if the firm has a fixed labor force and does not adjust the quantity of labor as output changes, direct labor is a fixed cost. (This occurs when the firm has a "no-cut" labor agreement with its union.) If the firm has a material supply contract to purchase a fixed amount of noninventoriable input, then this direct material is a fixed cost over the life of the contract. For example, if a steel mill has a long-run supply contract to purchase a fixed amount of natural gas per year over the life of the contract, this direct material (natural gas) is largely a fixed cost. If the company can resell it, the natural gas is a variable cost. Overhead costs contain both fixed costs and variable costs.

The distinction between overhead and direct costs can be difficult to determine at times. For example, should the 3¢ worth of glue used in each bookcase containing $4 of wood and $12 of direct labor be treated as a direct or an indirect cost? To apply a cost–benefit criterion, we must decide what decisions will be affected if the glue is classified as direct versus indirect. In most cases, small dollar amounts of direct costs are treated as overhead because the costs of tracking and reporting them separately exceed the benefits. Never assume that all direct costs are variable and all overhead costs are fixed costs.

The following chart summarizes the relations among accounting cost terminology:

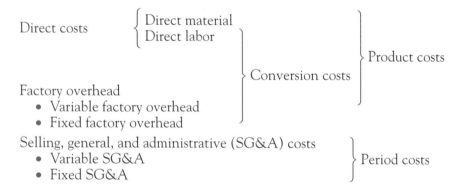

Product costs consist of direct material, direct labor, and overhead. The term **conversion costs** refers to direct labor and factory overhead. Period costs consist of selling, general, and administrative costs.

To illustrate these cost terms in a specific situation, consider the hot dog vendor Mary on the corner of 47th Street and Park Avenue in Manhattan. She sells hot dogs only. She leases her cart for $200 per day and pays a fee of $0.10

TABLE 2–5   Mary's Hot Dog Stand
Daily Income Statement

Revenues (1,000 @ $2)			$2,000
Direct costs			
Direct material			
Hot dogs (1,000 @ $0.70)	$700		
Buns (1,000 @ $0.15)	150		
Mustard (1,000 @ $0.035)	35		
Direct labor (10 hrs. @ $5)	50		
Direct costs		$935	
Overhead			
Variable overhead			
Lease on cart (1,000 @ $0.10)	$100		
Fixed overhead			
Cart rental	200		
Overhead		300	
Selling, general, and administrative expenses			
Variable SG&A			
Healthy Hot Dog fee (1,000 @ $0.18)	$180		
Fixed SG&A			
NYC license	125		
SG&A		305	
Total costs			1,540
Net income			$ 460

per hot dog sold. She works 10 hours and sells 1,000 hot dogs for $2.00 each. Her direct material costs per unit are $0.70 for hot dogs, $0.15 for buns, and $0.035 for mustard. She draws a salary of $5.00 per hour. She pays the Healthy Hot Dog Company $0.18 per hot dog sold to display a sign using the Healthy Hot Dog logo on her cart's umbrella, and she pays a New York City license fee of $125 per day. Table 2–5 presents her daily income statement.

By definition, overhead costs cannot be directly traced to products. Instead, they must be *allocated* to products. The most common allocation bases are direct labor hours, direct material, machine hours, and direct labor dollars. Managers usually choose the allocation basis that most closely approximates the factors that cause overhead to vary in the long run.

To illustrate the distinction between accounting and opportunity costs with respect to overheads, consider the following example: All expenses in a department containing 10 machines are allocated to the machines in the department. All 10 machines in the department are identical. Utilities, supervision, labor, depreciation, and engineering support are assigned to this department. The total cost divided by machine hours gives an hourly rate for allocating this department's costs to jobs. For example, suppose the total annual cost of this department is $525,000. Each machine normally operates 35 hours per week, 50 weeks per year, for 1,750 (or 35 × 50) hours per year. So the 10 machines normally operate

17,500 hours per year. This department thus has an overhead rate of $30 per machine hour ($525,000 ÷ 17,500 hours). If a particular job takes nine hours on the machines in this department, it is allocated $270 of "cost" (9 × $30). But did the firm actually incur $270 to process this job in the department? We don't know. The machine-hour rate ($30/hour) is an average accounting cost. It is a mixture of both fixed and variable costs, and it gives a false impression of variability. It does not tell us whether we made money on this job. In bidding for future jobs, the $30 per hour does not tell us what competitors will bid or what additional overhead costs will be incurred. Marginal overhead costs may be more or less than $30 per hour.

As plant volumes rise, congestion costs rise. Queues form. More expediters are hired to track inventory. Machine scheduling becomes more difficult. But the $30 per machine hour is not a function of plant utilization or the types of jobs in the plant.

In the long run, if the firm cannot charge prices (and generate sales) that cover all overhead costs (including depreciation of the assets), it will not be able to replace its assets. Of course, charging prices that cover overhead may price the firm out of the market completely. But by applying overhead costs (fixed and variable costs) to products, management can see whether the firm is viable under current conditions. The other reason for applying overhead costs to products is to control organizational problems. If the machine-hour rate is $30 this year and rises to $35 next year, senior managers are alerted that something has changed. By reporting the higher overhead cost, managers will investigate the reason for the change and presumably take corrective action.

Concept Questions	Q2–12	Why are opportunity costs costly to estimate?
	Q2–13	Define *direct costs*.
	Q2–14	Define *overhead costs*. How are they allocated?
	Q2–15	What are *period costs*?

E. Cost Estimation

Now that the important concepts of opportunity cost and how opportunity costs vary with changes in output have been introduced, they must be put into practice. Costs must be estimated, either from the accounting records or by some other method. This section describes two approaches to cost estimation: account classification and motion and time studies. The use of statistical regressions to estimate costs is described in Appendix B.

1. Account Classification

The simplest and the most common method of estimating fixed and variable costs is *account classification*. Each account in the accounting system is classified as being either fixed or variable. The sum of all the variable cost accounts, divided by a measure of volume (e.g., units produced), yields variable cost *per unit*. Likewise, the sum of all the accounts classified as fixed costs yields an estimate of the total fixed costs. While this method is quick and simple, it is not very precise. Its accuracy depends on the knowledge and intuition of the person classifying the accounts as fixed or variable.

Railroads Develop Unit Cost Data

In the 1870s, the railroads developed detailed and highly accurate cost estimates of hauling one ton of freight one mile. This has come to be known as the *cost per ton mile*. The calculation first involved separating the accounting records into four groups of accounts: costs that did not vary with the volume of traffic (general superintendence), costs that varied with the volume of freight but not the length of the haul (stations and agents), costs that varied with the number of trains run (conductors, engineers, and fuel), and interest on the capital investment. Each of these four costs was converted into a unit rate, and each freight shipment was costed based on its weight and how many miles it was carried.

These cost data allowed senior managers to monitor costs and to evaluate the performance of the managers responsible for the various segments of track. Cost per ton mile allowed subordinates' performance to be judged. By studying how the unit cost data varied over time and across various branches of the railroad, managers could evaluate the performance of the parts of the railroad and its managers. The railroads are an early but sophisticated example of using account classification as the basis of estimating unit costs.

SOURCE: A Chandler, *The Visible Hand* (Cambridge, MA: Harvard University Press, 1977), pp. 116–19.

2. Motion and Time Studies

In motion and time studies, industrial engineers estimate how much time a particular task or work activity requires with the goal of determining the optimal work method. Motion studies involve the systematic analysis of work methods considering the raw materials, the design of the product or process, the process or order of work, the tools, and the activity of each step. Besides estimating how long a particular activity should take, industrial engineers are often able to redesign the product or process to reduce the required time. Time studies employ a wide variety of techniques for determining the duration required for a particular activity under certain standard conditions. Work sampling (one type of time study) involves selecting a large number of observations taken at random intervals and observing how long employees take to perform various components of the job. It tells management how employees are currently spending their time, not how efficiently they could be spending their time. No benchmarks exist to judge performance. Work sampling tends to institutionalize existing inefficiencies. Motion and time studies are often expensive in terms of engineering time used in the studies. They also suffer from potential bias because of employees' incentives to underperform during the study period to set lower quotas.

Discussing some standard estimating techniques provides background for the methods available to derive cost information. Most of the problems presented in this and other books furnish the necessary cost data to solve the problem being posed. However, deriving the cost data is often more difficult than making a decision after securing the information. Besides engineering cost estimation techniques, accounting records are often the most prevalent source of cost data. Chapter 9 describes how accounting develops product costs.

| **Concept Question** | Q2–16 | What are motion and time studies? What are their objectives? |

F. Summary

This chapter emphasizes that decision making requires knowledge of opportunity costs, or the benefits forgone from actions precluded by the alternative selected. Opportunity costs can be determined only within a specific decision context by specifying all the alternative actions. While opportunity cost is the theoretically correct concept to use in decision making, it can be costly to estimate. Special studies are required to identify the alternative actions and forecast their likely consequences. Accounting costs often provide useful and less costly approximations for opportunity costs. However, costs reported by accounting systems are not opportunity costs. Opportunity costs are forward-looking and are usually not recorded by accounting systems.

Accounting costs measure the monetary resources expended for a particular activity. They provide a useful database to begin the process of estimating opportunity costs. Accounting costs also serve the important function of influencing the behavior of the firms' employees and managers. The accounting system reports the accounting cost of making the sofa this month and what the cost was last month to make the same sofa. Senior managers can then assess the performance of sofa production, providing incentives for the sofa-producing managers to pay attention to costs. If the accounting cost of the sofa is $208 this month, this number is not the opportunity cost of making the sofa. But if the same type of sofa had an accounting cost of $150 last month, something has happened that senior management will want to investigate. Chapter 4 explores these organizational control issues in more detail.

Managers must decide how many units of each product to manufacture. This decision also requires opportunity costs. One method of estimating opportunity costs for these decisions assumes that total costs are linear; hence, total costs are the fixed costs and variable costs per unit. A linear cost curve is also useful for cost–volume–profit analyses. These analyses focus managers' attention on how costs and profits vary with some volume measure. However, such analyses require assumptions to be made. These include assuming a single-period, single-product plant and linear cost and revenue curves.

When someone asks what something costs, the first reaction should be to find out for what purpose the cost number is to be used. If the cost number will be used for decision making, an opportunity cost must be generated for that decision context, which requires the decision maker to specify all the relevant alternative actions. If the number is to be used for financial reporting or taxes, a different cost number will be produced. If the cost number is being used to control behavior within the firm, probably a different number will be used. Cost numbers can vary significantly according to the purpose for which they are being produced.[9]

Appendix A: Costs and the Pricing Decision

One of the most important decisions managers make involves pricing the firm's goods and services. Clearly, the cost of producing the good or service is a crucial

---

[9]It has long been recognized that no single cost concept can serve all purposes. J Clark, writing in *Studies in the Economics of Overhead Costs* (Chicago: University of Chicago Press, 1923), p. 175, states, "We may start with the general proposition that the terminology of costs is in a state of much confusion and that it is impossible to solve this confusion by discovering and adopting the one correct usage, because there is no one correct usage, usage being governed by the varying needs of varying business situations and problems."

variable entering the pricing decision. This appendix discusses how managers use cost information in setting prices. There are two cases to consider: (1) the firm is a "price taker" and (2) the firm has "market power."

Price Takers

Some markets are very competitive. With many buyers and sellers of the same product, no single producer or consumer can influence the market price. For example, consider wheat farmers. With thousands of wheat farmers, no single farmer can affect the price of wheat by altering the amount of wheat the farmer produces. In this case, wheat farmers are price takers who do not set the price. They do, however, use cost information when deciding to grow (or not to grow) wheat.

While price takers understand that the price is given, they still must decide how much, if any, of the product to produce. Here cost data are extremely important. Suppose a wheat farmer leases land and equipment for $2,200,000 per year and expects to produce 1 million bushels of wheat. The variable cost per bushel is $1.60 and the market price of wheat is expected to be $3.90 per bushel when the wheat is harvested. The farmer expects to make $100,000 of profit (1 million bushels × ($3.90 − $1.60) − $2,200,000). If this is adequate compensation for the farmer's time and risk, she will lease the land and equipment and plant the wheat. So in this case, before the farmer decides to lease the land and plant wheat, she uses cost data to determine if the production decision (growing wheat) is worthwhile.

Suppose the land and equipment have been leased (and paid), but before the wheat is planted and the variable costs have been incurred, the price of wheat is expected to be only $3.65. Taking into account the fixed costs that have already been incurred, the farmer now expects to lose $150,000 (1 million bushels × ($3.65 − $1.60) − $2,200,000). However, the lease payments are sunk. The farmer still generates $2,050,000 of contribution margin, but not enough to recoup her fixed costs. She will still go ahead and plant the wheat. Not doing so will cost her the entire fixed cost of $2.2 million. If she thinks wheat prices next year will remain at $3.65 per bushel, she will not lease the land and equipment again.

To summarize, price takers use cost data to determine whether to undertake production, not to set prices. Fixed costs that have not yet been incurred are relevant in this production decision. Once incurred, the fixed costs are irrelevant in making production decisions.

Market Power

A more complicated pricing situation arises when producers have market power. Firms have market power if perfect substitutes do not exist for their products. This means that they can raise prices without losing all their customers to competitors. For instance, although Colgate and Crest compete directly, many customers do not view these toothpaste brands as perfect substitutes. Each company can raise their price and some consumers will not switch to the other toothpaste. But with higher prices, more customers will defect to competitors. This is not the situation with price takers. If a wheat farmer were to ask for a price above the prevailing market price, no one would pay this price because they can purchase identical wheat at a lower price.

When firms have market power, managers must decide not only whether to produce but also what price to charge. The next example illustrates how managers use cost data in the pricing decision.

TABLE 2–6   The Relation between the Price per Racket and the Quantity of
Rackets Sold at That Price

Price per Racket	Number of Rackets	Price per Racket	Number of Rackets
$1,050	500	$550	5,500
1,000	1,000	500	6,000
950	1,500	450	6,500
900	2,000	400	7,000
850	2,500	350	7,500
800	3,000	300	8,000
750	3,500	250	8,500
700	4,000	200	9,000
650	4,500	150	9,500
600	5,000	100	10,000

Consider a tennis racket company with a patent for a unique, high-performance tennis racket. The number of rackets sold depends on the price charged for the racket. At low prices, more rackets can be sold than at higher prices. After extensive study of competitors' prices for high-performance rackets, management expects the relation between price and quantity of rackets sold to be as depicted in Table 2–6. For example, at a price of $1,050 per racket, only 500 are sold, but if the price is dropped to $100 per racket, 10,000 can be sold.

The cost of producing the rackets consists of annual fixed costs of $1.9 million and variable costs of $100 per racket. The fixed costs include all fixed marketing, production, interest, and administration expenses, and the variable costs include all variable production and distribution expenses. Thus, total annual costs, TC, can be expressed as:

$$TC = \$1,900,000 + \$100Q \text{ (where } Q \text{ is the number of rackets)}$$

Notice that with this linear cost function, marginal cost (the cost of the last racket) and variable cost are both $100.

Given the data in Table 2–6 and the total cost curve, management can determine the profit-maximizing price to charge for tennis rackets. Table 2–7 provides the calculations.

As Table 2–7 shows, with a price per racket of $1,050, 500 rackets will be sold producing total revenues of $525,000 ($1,050 × 500), total cost of $1,950,000 ($1,900,000 + $100 × 500), and thus a loss of $1,425,000. Clearly, this is not the right price to charge. By calculating profits at all the other price-quantity combinations, we see that profits are maximized at $600,000 when price is set at $600 per racket and 5,000 rackets are sold. Total costs are $2.4 million ($1,900,000 + $100 × 5,000). Notice that profits are *not* maximized where revenues are maximized. Maximum revenues occur at a price-quantity combination of $550 per racket and 5,500 rackets, which is a lower-price–higher-quantity combination than the profit-maximizing combination.

Now let's study more closely how fixed and variable costs enter the profit maximizing pricing decision. We will examine two types of cost changes: an increase in fixed costs and an increase in variable costs.

TABLE 2–7   **Determining the Profit-Maximizing Price-Quantity Relation**

Price per Racket	Number of Rackets	Total Revenue	Total Cost	Total Profit (Loss)
$1,050	500	$ 525,000	$1,950,000	$(1,425,000)
1,000	1,000	1,000,000	2,000,000	(1,000,000)
950	1,500	1,425,000	2,050,000	(625,000)
900	2,000	1,800,000	2,100,000	(300,000)
850	2,500	2,125,000	2,150,000	(25,000)
800	3,000	2,400,000	2,200,000	200,000
750	3,500	2,625,000	2,250,000	375,000
700	4,000	2,800,000	2,300,000	500,000
650	4,500	2,925,000	2,350,000	575,000
600	5,000	3,000,000	2,400,000	600,000
550	5,500	3,025,000	2,450,000	575,000
500	6,000	3,000,000	2,500,000	500,000
450	6,500	2,925,000	2,550,000	375,000
400	7,000	2,800,000	2,600,000	200,000
350	7,500	2,625,000	2,650,000	(25,000)
300	8,000	2,400,000	2,700,000	(300,000)
250	8,500	2,125,000	2,750,000	(625,000)
200	9,000	1,800,000	2,800,000	(1,000,000)
150	9,500	1,425,000	2,850,000	(1,425,000)
100	10,000	1,000,000	2,900,000	(1,900,000)

Increase in fixed costs

Table 2–8 relects a rise in fixed costs from $1.9 million to $2.4 million, or a $500,000 increase. Suppose that the $2.4 million of fixed costs have not been incurred yet. Will the $500,000 increase in fixed costs change the pricing decision?

In Table 2–8 we see that a change in fixed costs does *not* alter the profit-maximizing pricing decision. Managers still set the price at $600 and expect to sell 5,000 rackets. In general, fixed costs do not enter the pricing decision. Fixed costs only determine whether the firm produces at all. If the contribution margin at the profit-maximizing price-quantity combination fails to cover the fixed costs (and the fixed costs have not yet been paid), the firm should not produce. For example, if fixed costs increased to $2.55 million, the profit-maximizing price-quantity combination would still be $600 and 5,000 rackets. But now the firm loses $50,000 at this price-quantity combination and it should not produce any rackets.

Increase in variable costs

We now consider how variable costs affect the pricing decision. Fixed costs are $1.9 million. If the variable cost of rackets increases from $100 to $200 per racket, the profit-maximizing price rises from $600 to $650 per racket and fewer rackets are sold (4,500 instead of 5,000). See Table 2–9. Notice that only $50 of the $100 variable cost increase is passed on to consumers. If the price were raised to $700 to recover all the $100 variable cost increase, even fewer rackets would be sold and the revenue decline would be greater than the cost increase.

Tables 2–7 to 2–9 illustrate a central point from economics: Only variable cost (which equals marginal cost in our linear cost function) affects the pricing decision. Fixed costs do not affect the pricing decision. Fixed costs only determine

TABLE 2–8   **Determining the Profit-Maximizing Price-Quantity Relation: Fixed Costs Increased by $500,000**

Price per Racket	Number of Rackets	Total Revenue	Total Cost	Total Profit (Loss)
$1,050	500	$ 525,000	$2,450,000	$(1,925,000)
1,000	1,000	1,000,000	2,500,000	(1,500,000)
950	1,500	1,425,000	2,550,000	(1,125,000)
900	2,000	1,800,000	2,600,000	(800,000)
850	2,500	2,125,000	2,650,000	(525,000)
800	3,000	2,400,000	2,700,000	(300,000)
750	3,500	2,625,000	2,750,000	(125,000)
700	4,000	2,800,000	2,800,000	0
650	4,500	2,925,000	2,850,000	75,000
600	5,000	3,000,000	2,900,000	100,000
550	5,500	3,025,000	2,950,000	75,000
500	6,000	3,000,000	3,000,000	0
450	6,500	2,925,000	3,050,000	(125,000)
400	7,000	2,800,000	3,100,000	(300,000)
350	7,500	2,625,000	3,150,000	(525,000)
300	8,000	2,400,000	3,200,000	(800,000)
250	8,500	2,125,000	3,250,000	(1,125,000)
200	9,000	1,800,000	3,200,000	(1,500,000)
150	9,500	1,425,000	3,350,000	(1,925,000)
100	10,000	1,000,000	3,400,000	(2,400,000)

TABLE 2–9   **Determining the Profit-Maximizing Price-Quantity Relation: Variable Costs Increased by $100 per Racket**

Price per Racket	Number of Rackets	Total Revenue	Total Cost	Total Profit (Loss)
$1,050	500	$ 525,000	$2,000,000	$(1,475,000)
1,000	1,000	1,000,000	2,100,000	(1,100,000)
950	1,500	1,425,000	2,200,000	(775,000)
900	2,000	1,800,000	2,300,000	(500,000)
850	2,500	2,125,000	2,400,000	(275,000)
800	3,000	2,400,000	2,500,000	(100,000)
750	3,500	2,625,000	2,600,000	25,000
700	4,000	2,800,000	2,700,000	100,000
650	4,500	2,925,000	2,800,000	125,000
600	5,000	3,000,000	2,900,000	100,000
550	5,500	3,025,000	3,000,000	25,000
500	6,000	3,000,000	3,100,000	(100,000)
450	6,500	2,925,000	3,200,000	(275,000)
400	7,000	2,800,000	3,300,000	(500,000)
350	7,500	2,625,000	3,400,000	(775,000)
300	8,000	2,400,000	3,500,000	(1,100,000)
250	8,500	2,125,000	3,600,000	(1,475,000)
200	9,000	1,800,000	3,700,000	(1,900,000)
150	9,500	1,425,000	3,800,000	(2,375,000)
100	10,000	1,000,000	3,900,000	(2,900,000)

whether the firm should produce the product. Economics texts demonstrate that the profit-maximizing price is determined where marginal (variable) cost equals marginal revenue.

Cost-Plus Pricing

One of the more common pricing methods used by firms is *cost-plus pricing*. Firms that use this technique calculate average total cost and mark up the cost to yield the selling price. Or,

$$\text{Selling price} = \text{Cost} + (\text{Markup percentage} \times \text{Cost})$$

To solve for the selling price, managers begin by calculating a *unit cost*:

$$\text{Unit cost} = \text{Variable cost} + (\text{Fixed costs/Unit sales})$$

Using our tennis racket example and 5,000 rackets,

$$\text{Unit cost} = \$100 + (\$1,900,000/5,000 \text{ rackets}) = \$480$$

Managers using a markup of 25 percent would set the price as:

$$\text{Selling price} = \$480 + (25 \text{ percent} \times \$480) = \$600$$

In this example, the formula yields the same price as our profit-maximizing price-quantity combination from Table 2–7. However, we started with the profit-maximizing quantity and markup. So by construction, we had to end up with the profit-maximizing price.

Suppose that fixed costs increase to $2 million and variable costs decrease to $80. Managers still expect to sell 5,000 rackets. Unit costs remain at $480 ($80 + $2,000,000/5,000). If managers maintain the same 25 percent markup, they will keep the price at $600. But this is no longer the profit-maximizing price. Variable costs have fallen, so managers should lower the price to $590 and sell 5,100 rackets.[10]

Profit-maximizing pricing considers only variable (marginal) costs and depends on the price sensitivity of customers. Cost-plus pricing appears to ignore both of these considerations. The cost-plus price marks up average total cost (both fixed and variable cost) and seems to ignore the demand for the product—just because managers target a 25 percent markup on average cost does not mean that customers will necessarily buy the product in the required quantities at the implied price.

Firms that consistently use bad pricing policies find themselves earning lower profits than they could with better pricing techniques and may even go out of business. If cost-plus pricing is so unsound, why is it so widely used? One explanation is that managers implicitly consider market demand in choosing the markup and unit sales in calculating the unit cost. If managers know that they face little competition, more units can be sold and higher markups will be chosen than when facing greater competition. Conceptually, there is always some target volume and markup that produces the profit-maximizing price.

The idea that managers choose markups and unit volumes based on market power when they use cost-plus price is supported empirically. Consider the price markups by a typical grocery store employing cost-plus pricing. One experienced

---

[10]To derive this new price-quantity combination, note that the price-quantity combinations in Table 2–6 are based on the following formula: Price = $1,100 − 0.1 × Quantity. This equation is used to calculate price-quantity combinations in 100 racket increments.

grocery store manager noted that "price sensitivity is the primary consideration in setting margins."[11] Staple products such as bread, hamburger, milk, and soup are relatively price sensitive and carry low margins (markups of under 10 percent above cost). Products with high margins (markups as high as 50 percent or more) tend to be those where consumers are less price sensitive, such as spices, seasonal fresh fruit, and nonprescription drugs.

Concept Question	Q2–17 How do fixed costs enter the pricing decision?

Appendix B: Estimating Fixed and Variable Costs

This chapter has discussed the importance of separating total costs into fixed and variable components. Clearly, management must have some way of estimating fixed and variable costs. Likewise, financial analysts would like to know how much of a firm's given costs are fixed and how much are variable. This appendix illustrates some of the practical considerations of estimating fixed and variable costs from actual company records using least squares regressions.

One might be tempted to think that a firm's fixed and variable costs can be easily estimated using accounting data. For example, consider the data plotted in Figure 2–7. The vertical axis represents total manufacturing cost for a given month, TC; the horizontal axis is the total units produced for the month, Q. The last 50 months of total cost and output are plotted as the points. Using these 50 data points, a regression line can be estimated and is shown as the straight line in Figure 2–7. That is, a regression of the following form is fitted to the data points:

$$TC_t = FC + VC \times Q_t + u_t \tag{2.6}$$

where

TC_t = Total cost in month t
FC = Estimated fixed cost
VC = Estimated variable cost per unit of output Q
Q_t = Output in units in month t
u_t = Ordinary least squares residual

Using data on the firm's total cost, TC, and output, Q, and estimating the regression in equation (2.6), the intercept, FC, is an estimate of the fixed cost, while the slope, VC, is an estimate of the variable cost per unit. In Figure 2–7, the estimated regression is

$$TC_t = \$53 + \$1.91Q_t \tag{2.7}$$

Fixed costs are estimated to be \$53 per month and variable costs are estimated to be \$1.91 per unit. The regression explains about 87 percent of the variance in total cost (i.e., the R^2 of the regression is 0.87).

The example in Figure 2–7 illustrates how regressions, in principle, can be used to estimate fixed and variable costs. To illustrate some of the difficulties in estimating fixed and variable costs using regression analysis on publicly available data, equation (2.6) is estimated using ordinary least squares (OLS) regression on

---

[11] J Pappas and M Hirschey, *Managerial Economics*, 6th ed. (Chicago: Dryden Press, 1990).

FIGURE 2–7

Estimating fixed and variable costs

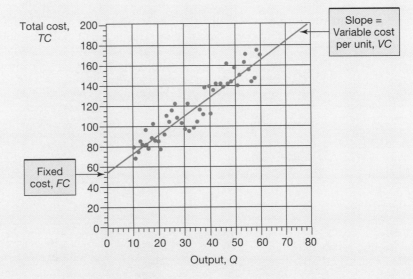

data from the steel industry from 1946 to 1997.[12] The 11 largest integrated steel companies, making up 81 percent of the steel industry capacity in 1978, are selected for analysis. Tons of steel shipped is the independent variable that measures output. The measure of total cost is cost of goods sold. Tons of steel shipped is published in firms' annual reports. Cost of goods sold comes from annual reports and is available in machine-readable form on the Standard & Poor's Compustat computer files.

In estimating equation (2.6) using steel company data, we must assume that the total cost curve for each firm is reasonably linear in volume. As discussed in section C on cost–volume–profit analysis, if costs are not linear, then the estimate of fixed costs—FC in equation (2.6)—is not an accurate estimate of the firm's actual fixed costs.

One problem with using data directly from Compustat is that annual reports are typically *consolidated* financial statements. Many steel companies in the late 1970s and 1980s launched major diversification programs to reduce their dependence on steel making. Steel companies were buying oil companies and mining companies. When such acquisitions are made, cost of goods sold contains a significant amount of nonsteel costs of operations. Thus, the dependent variable, TC_t, is measured with error, and this error tends to be correlated over time, causing the residuals to be "autocorrelated." That is, if the residual in year Y is high, it is likely that the residual in year $Y + 1$ is also high.

Beginning in the mid-1970s, firms were required to disclose information by major segments of their business. The segment data broke down cost of goods sold for steel operations. These data were collected from the annual reports and merged with the Compustat data. The results of estimating equation (2.6) are reported in Table 2–10.

Most of the steel companies do not have complete data for the entire 52 years. Some are missing steel production data, Q_t. Other firms have gone out of business (e.g., Kaiser and LTV), while others started reporting data after 1946 (e.g., McLouth). Six of the 11 estimated fixed costs and two of the estimated variable costs are negative. The amount of explained variation in cost of goods sold

[12] For a discussion of estimating cost functions, see D Besanko, D Dranove, and M Shanley, *The Economics of Strategy* (New York: John Wiley & Sons, 1996), pp. 510–22.

TABLE 2–10   Regressions of Steel Companies Estimating Fixed and Variable Costs
(Data from Compustat Using Cost of Goods Sold for Steel Operations Only, If Available)

$$TC_t = FC + VC \cdot Q_t + u_t, \; t = 1946, \ldots, 1997$$

Company	Fixed Costs (Billions)	Variable Costs/Ton	Number of Observations	R^2	Residual Autocorrelation
1. U.S. Steel	$ 6.0*	$ (91)	52	6%	0.85
2. Bethlehem	3.6*	(60)	52	0	0.92
3. National	0.8	175	34	6	0.95
4. Republic	(0.3)	277	37	7	0.89
5. LTV	(1.9)*	723*	52	68	0.81
6. McLouth	(0.2)	372	18	17	0.76
7. Armco	0.0	299*	48	33	0.94
8. Inland	(1.2)*	532*	49	53	0.87
9. Wheeling-Pittsburgh	(0.0)	323*	44	34	0.92
10. Kaiser	(0.2)	412*	28	28	0.56
11. CF&I	0.0	94*	19	36	0.83

*Statistically significant at the 0.01 level.

(R^2) is not high, ranging between 0 and 68 percent. The last column, residual autocorrelation, is quite high, indicating that the residuals are highly correlated over time. When the residuals are autocorrelated, the coefficients are estimated with error and the usual statistical significance tests are inappropriate. Computer programs are available to estimate equation (2.6) taking into account the residual autocorrelation.

Another issue that arises in Table 2–10 is stationarity. A model is said to be stationary if the underlying process that generated the data does not change over time. Up to 52 years of data are used to estimate the regressions. Employing such a long time series assumes that the cost structure is constant over time. If operating leverage is changing over time, then estimating a single equation assuming stationarity will lead to a misspecified model and (possibly) biased coefficients. There is good reason to believe that the steel industry has not had stationary operating leverage over the period 1946 to 1997. Following World War II, the open hearth furnace was used to produce most steel. This technology has been declining and now most steel is produced in basic oxygen or electric furnaces, which offer shorter heat times and therefore require less labor and capital per ton of steel.

This study of the steel companies' cost structures illustrates some of the practical difficulties in estimating fixed and variable costs. Often the underlying production processes are not stationary over time, which reduces the number of observations available for analysis. Using quarterly or even monthly observations introduces new problems. In particular, such interim data have seasonal patterns that must be removed with advanced econometric procedures. Moreover, interim data often contain cost allocations that distort the true underlying relations. For example, if supplies are purchased and expensed in one month but consumed over several months, the reported cost of goods sold contains measurement errors that make estimating fixed and variable costs problematic.

It is unlikely that financial analysts can use publicly available accounting data to generate useful firm-specific estimates of fixed and variable costs. Publicly traded companies are large heterogeneous combinations of many different production technologies and products. Product mixes and technologies are not stationary over long enough periods of time to generate enough observations to yield precise estimates of fixed and variable costs.

One reason for understanding the limitation of regression analysis for estimating fixed and variable costs is to avoid trying to apply this statistical procedure in areas in which it is unlikely to be useful. Regression analysis is a very powerful statistical procedure when applied in the appropriate circumstances. Accounting costs are probably not an appropriate application. On the other hand, carefully executed regression analyses can raise interesting questions and point to more refined studies of individual firms. A regression analysis might not give precise estimates of fixed and variable costs, but it might indicate relative differences.

Due to the practical difficulties in separating total costs into fixed and variable components, very few companies use regression analysis for this purpose. One study reports that 77 percent of the manufacturing sites surveyed divided costs into fixed and variable components, but fewer than 5 percent of these firms used statistical methods to accomplish this task.[13] The preceding study of steel companies illustrates some of the practical limitations of regression analysis and provides one possible reason that few firms use this statistical procedure. Generally, managers estimate fixed and variable costs by classifying individual accounts as being primarily fixed or primarily variable.

Concept Question	Q2–18	What are the major problems encountered in the use of public information and linear regression to estimate fixed and variable costs? Can these problems be overcome?

Self-Study Problems

Self-Study Problem 1: Exclusive Billiards

In each month, Exclusive Billiards produces between 4 and 10 pool tables. The plant operates one 40-hour shift to produce up to seven tables. Producing more than seven tables requires the craftsmen to work overtime. Overtime work is paid at a higher hourly wage. The plant can add overtime hours and produce up to 10 tables per month. The following table contains the total cost of producing between 4 and 10 pool tables.

Pool Tables	Total Cost
4	$62,800
5	66,000
6	69,200
7	72,400
8	75,800
9	79,200
10	82,600

---

[13]U Karmarkar, P Lederer, and J Zimmerman, "Choosing Manufacturing Production Control and Cost Accounting Systems," in *Measures for Manufacturing Excellence*, ed. R Kaplan (Boston: Harvard Business School, 1990).

As part of the franchise agreement, a Fast Oil franchisee must keep the business open 72 hours per week. Furthermore, the franchisee must lease all facilities and equipment on an annual basis as well as buy all supplies from the parent corporation. The parent company also requires that all franchises be capable of continually operating at full capacity. In the case of the Jefferson Road franchise, this requirement entails having two oil-change technicians and one oil-change manager at the facility at all times.

Fast Oil franchises offer only one service, oil change and lube, at one price, $22.95. Facilities and equipment are leased at $50,000 per year. Materials are sold to franchisees at the following prices: oil at $0.75 per quart, filters at $1 each, and lubrication material at $1 per 16 ounces. Each oil change and lube requires five quarts of oil, one filter, and four ounces of lubrication materials. Oil-change technicians are paid $8 per hour; managers earn $10 per hour. On average, an oil change and lube require one man-hour of work.

According to reliable studies, the number of customers at any given franchise is solely contingent upon the volume of drive-by traffic. On average, one out of every 1,723 cars that drive by a Fast Oil will stop in for an oil change. The Henrietta Chamber of Commerce knowledgeably states that 289,464 cars per week drive by the Jefferson Road franchise at a constant rate during its hours of business. If he keeps the franchise, Mike will work there 72 hours a week as the oil change manager. His sole compensation will be the profits of the business. This will be his only job. If he sells the franchise, Mike will invest the proceeds in Treasury bills that yield 7 percent per annum, with a time to maturity of one year.

Mike lives in a tax-free world and all cash flows are risk free. Assume a one-year time horizon, and assume exactly 52 weeks per year.

a. How many oil changes is the Jefferson Road franchise expected to perform in a year? Assuming that Mike keeps the franchise and ignoring opportunity costs of Mike's time and the interest on the proceeds from selling the franchise, what is the annual break-even point (in oil changes) for the franchise?

b. Define Mike's alternatives. If opportunity costs excluded in (a) are considered, calculate his break-even point (in number of oil changes).

c. If opportunity costs mentioned in (a) are *not* considered, calculate Mike's profit/loss. What would it be if opportunity costs were considered? What alternative should Mike choose?

Solution:

a. Given that 289,464 cars pass by weekly and one out of every 1,723 will stop in for an oil change and lube, the franchise is expected to perform 289,464/1,723 × 52 = 8,736 oil changes per year. The rest of the solution requires identification of the fixed and variable components of the franchise's costs.

The most obvious fixed cost is the annual lease cost of $50,000 per year. Since employee pay does not vary with output, labor costs are fixed. Employees must be paid simply for being at work, and the quantity of labor required is defined by the franchise agreement. (The time required to perform an oil change is relevant only as a capacity constraint; since there are 216 man-hours per week, 52 weeks per year, and each oil change requires one man-hour, total capacity for the facility is 11,232 changes per year.) Since Mike will work as oil-change manager, the labor cost will apply only to the two oil-change technicians (2 technicians × $8/hour × 72 hours/week × 52 weeks per year = $59,904 per year).

The only variable costs are materials costs. Cost per oil change is the most logical unit to consider, and one year is the obvious time horizon for consideration.

Variable Costs per Oil Change	
Oil costs:	
$0.75/quart × 5 quarts	$3.75
Lubrication costs:	
$1/pound × 4/16	0.25
Oil filter	1.00
	$5.00

The price of an oil change is $22.95. The accompanying table summarizes the break-even analysis:

Fixed costs (annual)		
Lease	$50,000	
Technicians	59,904	
Total fixed costs		$109,904
÷ **Contribution margin** (per unit)		
Price	$ 22.95	
Variable cost	5.00	
Contribution margin per unit		$ 17.95
Break-even (in oil changes)		6,123

b. Opportunity costs are defined as "the benefits forgone from actions that are precluded by the alternative selected." To assess the opportunity costs of a particular action, the set of mutually exclusive opportunities must be considered. Mike faces two choices:

- Quit his present job, work as oil-change manager, and keep the profits of the franchise.
- Keep his present job, sell the franchise to the parent company, and invest the proceeds in Treasury bills.

If Mike keeps the franchise, the following benefits are forgone:

- Income from the pet store job and value of free time given up. Mike earns $10 per hour. Therefore, the annual opportunity cost of the time he gives up to work at the oil-change franchise is $10 × 72 × 52 = $37,440 per year.
- Income lost from not selling the franchise and investing in Treasury bills. At 7 percent per year, $150,000 would provide income of $10,500.

The total opportunity cost of keeping the franchise is:

Opportunity cost of Mike's time	$37,440
Investment proceeds from sale of franchise	10,500
	$47,940

This cost should be considered a fixed cost, bringing break-even volume to 8,794 oil changes [($109,904 + $47,940) ÷ $17.95].

c. Ignoring Mike's opportunity costs, annual fixed costs for the business are covered at the 6,123rd oil change. The franchise "profit," therefore, is the contribution margin of all additional oil changes done during the year. For Mike, the profit is (8,736 − 6,123) × $17.95 = $46,907. Since $46,907 is far more than Mike could earn at the pet store, he might be tempted to keep and operate the oil-change franchise. However, when opportunity costs are considered, it would be better for Mike to sell the franchise back to the parent company. Since his opportunity costs are $47,940, Mike would in reality lose $1,033 by keeping the franchise.

This analysis ignores a number of additional factors that Mike should consider before making a final decision:

- How much growth is likely to occur in the oil-change business?
- What is the likelihood of losing the pet store job?
- Is it likely that technological or market changes will reduce the value of the franchise?
- How do the alternatives differ in risk?
- Does Mike like working in the pet store or would he prefer managing the oil-change franchise?

Problems

P 2–1:   Darien Industries

Darien Industries operates a cafeteria for its employees. The operation of the cafeteria requires fixed costs of $4,700 per month and variable costs of 40 percent of sales. Cafeteria sales are currently averaging $12,000 per month.

Darien has an opportunity to replace the cafeteria with vending machines. Gross customer spending at the vending machines is estimated to be 40 percent greater than current sales because the machines are available at all hours. By replacing the cafeteria with vending machines, Darien would receive 16 percent of the gross customer spending and avoid all cafeteria costs. How much does monthly operating income change if Darien Industries replaces the cafeteria with vending machines?

SOURCE: CMA adapted.

P 2–2:   Negative Opportunity Costs

Can opportunity costs be negative? Give an example.

P 2–3: NPR

In its radio fund-raising campaign, National Public Radio (NPR) stated, "On-air radio membership campaigns are the most cost-effective means we have for raising the funds necessary to bring you the type of programming you expect." NPR is commercial-free, member-supported radio. Most of its operating funds come from private individuals, corporations, and foundations. Twice a year it interrupts its regularly scheduled programming for fund-raising pledge campaigns where listeners are encouraged to call in and make pledges.

Critically evaluate the passage quoted above.

P 2–4: Silky Smooth Lotions

Silky Smooth lotions come in three sizes: 4, 8, and 12 ounces. The following table summarizes the selling prices and variable costs per case of each lotion size.

Per Case	4 Ounce	8 Ounce	12 Ounce
Price	$36.00	$66.00	$72.00
Variable cost	13.00	24.50	27.00

Fixed costs are $771,000. Current production and sales are 2,000 cases of 4-ounce bottles; 4,000 cases of 8-ounce bottles; and 1,000 cases of 12-ounce bottles. Silky Smooth typically sells the three lotion sizes in fixed proportions as represented by the preceding sales amounts.

Required:
How many cases of 4-, 8-, and 12-ounce lotion bottles must be produced and sold for Silky Smooth to break even, assuming that the three sizes are sold in fixed proportions?

P 2–5: J.P. Max Department Stores

J.P. Max is a department store carrying a large and varied stock of merchandise. Management is considering leasing part of its floor space for $72 per square foot per year to an outside jewelry company that would sell merchandise. Two areas currently in use are being considered: home appliances (1,000 square feet) and televisions (1,200 square feet). These departments had annual profits of $64,000 for appliances and $82,000 for televisions after allocated fixed occupancy costs of $7 per square foot were deducted. Allocated fixed occupancy costs include property taxes, mortgage interest, insurance, and exterior maintenance for the department store.

Required:
Considering all the relevant factors, which department should be leased and why?

P 2–6: Executive Stock Options

A large public accounting firm, reporting the findings of a survey on corporate directors' compensation, remarked, "Since there are usually greater growth rates in smaller companies, stock options offer directors a good chance at investment appreciation at no cost to the company."

A stock option has the following characteristic. Suppose one three-year stock option is granted to a director at today's stock price of $10. Then, at any time over the next three years, the director can buy one share of stock from the company at $10. If next year the stock rises to $14, the director can exercise the option by paying $10 to the company and receiving one share of stock, which can then be sold in the market for $14, thereby realizing a $4 gain.

What cost does the company incur by granting stock options to its directors?

P 2–7: Bidwell Company

Data for the Bidwell Company are as follows:

	Fixed	Variable	
Sales (100,000 units)			$1,000,000
Costs			
Raw material	$ 0	$300,000	
Direct labor	0	200,000	
Factory costs	100,000	150,000	
Selling and administrative costs	110,000	50,000	
Total costs	$210,000	$700,000	910,000
Operating income			$ 90,000

Required:

a. Based on the preceding data, calculate break-even sales in units.
b. If Bidwell Company is subject to an effective income tax rate of 40 percent, calculate the number of units Bidwell would have to sell to earn an after-tax profit of $90,000.
c. If fixed costs increase $31,500 with no other cost or revenue factors changing, calculate the break-even sales in units.

SOURCE: CMA adapted.

P 2–8: DisKing Company

DisKing Company is a retailer for video disks. The projected after-tax net income for the current year is $120,000 based on a sales volume of 200,000 video disks. DisKing has been selling the disks at $16 each. The variable costs consist of the $10 unit purchase price of the disks and a handling cost of $2 per disk. DisKing's annual fixed costs are $600,000, and DisKing is subject to a 40 percent income tax rate.

Management is planning for the coming year, when it expects that the unit purchase price of the video disks will increase 30 percent.

Required:

a. Calculate DisKing Company's break-even point for the current year in number of video disks.
b. Calculate the increased after-tax income for the current year from an increase of 10 percent in projected unit sales volume.
c. If the unit selling price remains at $16, calculate the volume of sales in dollars that DisKing Company must achieve in the coming year to maintain the same after-tax net income as projected for the current year.

SOURCE: CMA adapted.

P 2–9: Sunnybrook Farms

Sunnybrook Farms is a local grocery store that is currently open only Monday through Saturday. Sunnybrook is considering opening on Sundays. The annual incremental costs of Sunday openings are estimated at $24,960. Sunnybrook Farms's gross margin on sales is 20 percent. Sunnybrook estimates that 60 percent of its potential Sunday sales to customers are now made on other days. What one-day volume of Sunday sales would be necessary for Sunnybrook Farms to attain the same weekly operating income as in the current six-day week?

Source: CMA adapted.

P 2–10: Elly Industries

Elly Industries is a multiproduct company that currently manufactures 30,000 units of Part MR24 each month for use in production. The facilities now being used to produce Part MR24 have a fixed monthly cost of $150,000 and a capacity to produce 84,000 units per month. If Elly were to buy Part MR24 from an outside supplier, the facilities would be idle, but its fixed costs would continue at 40 percent of its present amount. The variable production costs of Part MR24 are $11 per unit.

Required:

a. If Elly Industries continues to use 30,000 units of Part MR24 each month, it would realize a net benefit by purchasing Part MR24 from an outside supplier only if the supplier's unit price is less than how much?

b. If Elly Industries can obtain Part MR24 from an outside supplier at a unit purchase price of $12.875, what is the monthly usage at which it will be indifferent between purchasing and making Part MR24?

Source: CMA adapted.

P 2–11: Emrich Processing

Emrich Processing is a small custom stainless steel parts processor. Customers send new and used stainless steel parts to Emrich for cleaning in various acid baths to remove small imperfections or films on the surface. These parts are used in a variety of applications, ranging from nuclear reactors to chemical and medical applications. Depending on the foreign substance to be removed, Emrich chooses the acid bath mixture and process.

Such chemical cleaning operations require highly skilled technicians to handle the dangerous acids. Environmental Protection Agency (EPA) and Occupational Safety and Health Administration (OSHA) regulations are closely followed. Once the part is treated in the proper chemical bath using other chemicals, a benign waste solution results that can be disposed of via the city sewer system.

On May 12, Emrich ordered a 50-gallon drum of a specialty acid known as GX-100 for use in a May 15 job. It used 25 of the 50 gallons in the drum. The 50 gallons cost $1,000. GX-100 has a shelf life of 30 days after the drum is opened before it becomes unstable and must be discarded. Because of the hazardous nature of GX-100 and the other chemicals Emrich uses, Emrich works closely with Environ Disposal, a company specializing in the disposal of hazardous wastes. At the time of ordering the GX-100, Emrich anticipated no other orders in the May–June time period that could use the remaining 25 gallons of GX-100. Knowing it would have 25 gallons remaining, it built $1,000 into the cost of the job to cover the cost of the GX-100 plus an additional $400 to cover the cost of having Environ dispose of the remaining 25 gallons.

released. For most movies, the audience demand is higher in the first two weeks than in the next two weeks.

American Cinema is evaluating two similar situation comedies. The first one, *Paris Is for Lovers*, is scheduled for release on October 1. The second comedy, *I Do*, is scheduled for release on October 14. American Cinema has decided to rent *Paris Is for Lovers* but must decide whether to run it for four weeks or to run it for two weeks and then replace it with *I Do*. Based on all the information about the stars in the movie, production costs, and prerelease publicity, management expects the two movies will have the same demand in the first two weeks and will have the same (lower) demand in weeks 3 and 4.

Required:

a. The only movie being released on October 14 is *I Do*. How should management go about deciding whether to rent *Paris* for four weeks or to rent it for two weeks and then replace it with *I Do*? In other words, provide American Cinema management with a decision-making rule to use in choosing between renting *Paris* for four weeks or just two weeks. American Cinema's tax rate is zero. Be sure to justify your advice with clearly described analysis.

b. How does your answer in part (*a*) change if American Cinema's income tax rate is 30 percent?

c. American Cinema's average movie patron purchases soda, popcorn, and candy that yields profits of $2 after supplies and labor. How does profit on these concession items affect your answer to part (*a*)? (Ignore taxes.)

P 2–17:   Home Auto Parts

Home Auto Parts is a large retail auto parts store selling the full range of auto parts and supplies for do-it-yourself auto repair enthusiasts. The store is arranged with three prime displays in the store: front door, checkout counters, and ends of aisles. These display areas receive the most customer traffic and contain special stands that display the merchandise with attractive eye-catching designs. Each display area is set up at the beginning of the week and runs for one week. Three items are scheduled next week for special display areas: Texcan Oil, windshield wiper blades, and floor mats. The accompanying table provides information for the three promotional areas scheduled to run next week:

Planned Displays for Next Week

Item	Ends of Aisles	Front Door	Checkout Counter
	Texcan Oil	Wiper blades	Floor mats
Sales price	69¢/can	$9.99	$22.99
Projected weekly volume	5,000	200	70
Unit cost	62¢	$7.99	$17.49

Based on past experience, management finds that virtually all display-area sales are made by impulse buyers. The display items are extra purchases by consumers attracted by the exhibits.

Before the store manager sets up the display areas, the distributor for Armadillo car wax visits the store. She says her firm wants its car wax in one of the three display areas and is prepared to offer the product at a unit cost of $2.50. At a retail price of $2.90, management expects to sell 800 units during the week if the wax is on special display.

Required:

a. Home Auto has not yet purchased any of the promotion items for next week. Should management substitute the Armadillo car wax for one of the three planned promotion displays? If so, which one?

b. A common practice in retailing is for the manufacturer to give free units to a retail store to secure desirable promotion space or shelf space. The Armadillo distributor decides to sweeten the offer by giving Home Auto 50 free units of car wax if it places the Armadillo wax on display. Does this change your answer to part (*a*)?

P 2–18:   Measer Enterprises

Measer Enterprises produces standardized telephone keypads and operates in a highly competitive market in which the keypads are sold for $4.50 each. Because of the nature of the production technology, the firm can produce only between 10,000 and 13,000 units per month, in fixed increments of 1,000 units. Measer has the following cost structure:

Production and Cost Data

	Units Produced			
	10,000	*11,000*	*12,000*	*13,000*
Factory cost, variable	$37,000	$40,800	$44,600	$48,400
Factory cost, fixed	9,000	9,000	9,000	9,000
Selling cost, variable	6,000	6,600	7,400	8,200
Administration, fixed	6,000	6,000	6,000	6,000
Total	$58,000	$62,400	$67,000	$71,600
Average unit cost	$5.80	$5.67	$5.58	$5.51

Required:
At what output level should the firm operate?

P 2–19:   Winter Company

Winter Company is a medium-size manufacturer of disk drives that are sold to computer manufacturers. At the beginning of 2003, Winter began shipping a much-improved disk drive, Model W899. The W899 was an immediate success and accounted for $5 million in revenues for Winter in 2003.

While the W899 was in the development stage, Winter planned to price it at $130. In preliminary discussions with customers about the W899 design, no resistance was detected to suggestions that the price might be $130. The $130 price was considerably higher than the estimated variable cost of $70 per unit to produce the W899, and it would provide Winter with ample profits.

Shortly before setting the price of the W899, Winter discovered that a competitor was readying a product very similar to the W899 and was no more than 60 days behind Winter's own schedule. No information could be obtained on the competitor's planned price, although it had a reputation for aggressive pricing. Worried about the competitor, and unsure of the market's size, Winter lowered the price of the W899 to $100. It maintained the price although, to Winter's surprise, the competitor announced a price of $130 for its product.

After reviewing the 2003 sales of the W899, Winter's management concluded that unit sales would have been the same if the product had been marketed at the original price of $130 each. Management has predicted that 2004 sales of the W899 would be either 85,000 units at $100 each or 60,000 units at $130 each. Winter has decided to raise the price of the disk drive to $130 effective immediately.

Having supported the higher price from the beginning, Sharon Daley, Winter's marketing director, believes that the opportunity cost of selling the W899 for $100 during 2003 should be reflected in the company's internal records and reports. In support of her recommendation, Daley explained that the company has booked these types of costs on other occasions when purchase discounts not taken for early payment have been recorded.

Required:

a. Define *opportunity cost* and explain why opportunity costs are not usually recorded.

b. Winter Company's management is considering Sharon Daley's recommendation to book the opportunity costs and have them reflected in its internal records and reports. If one were to record a nonzero opportunity cost, calculate the dollar amount of the opportunity cost that would be recorded by Winter Co. for 2003 and explain how this cost might be reflected on its internal reports.

c. Explain the impact of Winter Company's selection of the $130 selling price for the W899 on 2004 operating income. Support your answer with appropriate calculations.

SOURCE: CMA adapted.

P 2–20:   Leland Manufacturing

Leland Manufacturing uses 10 units of part KJ37 each month in the production of radar equipment. The cost to manufacture one unit of KJ37 is presented in the accompanying table.

Direct materials	$ 1,000
Materials handling (20% of direct material cost)	200
Direct labor	8,000
Manufacturing overhead	12,000
Total manufacturing cost	$21,200

Materials handling represents the direct variable costs of the receiving department and is applied to direct materials and purchased components on the basis of their cost. This is a separate charge in addition to manufacturing overhead. Leland's annual manufacturing overhead budget is one-third variable and two-third fixed. Scott Supply, one of Leland's reliable vendors, has offered to supply part KJ37 at a unit price of $15,000. The fixed cost of producing KJ37 is the cost of a special piece of testing equipment that ensures the quality of each part manufactured. This testing equipment is under a long-term, noncancelable lease. If Leland were to purchase part KJ37, materials handling costs would not be incurred.

Required:

a. If Leland purchases the KJ37 units from Scott, the capacity Leland was using to manufacture these parts would be idle. Should Leland purchase the parts from Scott? Make explicit any key assumptions.

b. Assume Leland Manufacturing is able to rent all idle capacity for $25,000 per month. Should Leland purchase from Scott Supply? Make explicit any key assumptions.

c. Assume that Leland Manufacturing does not wish to commit to a rental agreement but could use idle capacity to manufacture another product that would contribute $52,000 per month. Should Leland manufacture KJ37? Make explicit any key assumptions.

SOURCE: CMA adapted.

P 2–21: Fast Photo

Fast Photo operates four film developing labs in upstate New York. The four labs are identical: They employ the same production technology, process the same mix of films, and buy raw materials from the same companies at the same prices. Wage rates are also the same at the four plants. In reviewing operating results for November, the newly hired assistant controller, Matt Paige, became quite confused over the numbers:

	Plant A	Plant B	Plant C	Plant D
Number of rolls processed	50,000	55,000	60,000	65,000
Revenue ($000s)	$500	$550	$600	$650
Less:				
Variable costs	(195)	(242)	(298)	(352)
Fixed costs	(300)	(300)	(300)	(300)
Profit (loss)	$ 5	$ 8	$ 2	$ (2)

Upon further study, Matt learned that each plant had fixed overhead of $300,000. Matt remembered from his managerial accounting class that as volume increases, average fixed cost per unit falls. Because Plant D had much lower average fixed costs per roll than Plants A and B, Matt expected Plant D to be more profitable than Plants A and B. But the numbers show just the opposite. Write a concise but clear memo to Matt that will resolve his confusion.

P 2–22: Oil System

An industrial engineer has been studying the cost behavior of the automated oil cooling system in the numerically controlled cutting machine department. The oil cooling system circulates oil across the cutting tools as the machines make parts. Besides cooling the tools, the oil washes away cuttings. The oil system circulates the oil and separates out the cuttings, adds new oil as needed, and recycles the old oil. The system serves 10 machines.

Oil consumption has varied widely over the last few months, and management worries that the system is out of control. The industrial engineer has collected from the accounting reports monthly cost data on the oil used in the system over the last five years. The oil cost data represent monthly oil purchases. These cost data, combined with the number of machine cutting hours in the month (total number of machine hours spent cutting parts in the month), have led to the following regression results (both series were entered as positive numbers):

$$\begin{pmatrix} \text{Oil cost} \\ \text{in month } t \end{pmatrix} = -12{,}675 - 16.54 \times \begin{pmatrix} \text{Number of machine} \\ \text{cutting hours in month } t \end{pmatrix}$$

Based on the results of estimating this regression, the engineer concludes that the oil cooling system is out of control and a major engineering study of the system is warranted.

Interpret the regression results. Based on your interpretation, is an engineering study of the oil system warranted?

P 2–23:   MedView

The MedView brochure said, "Only 45 scans per month to cover the monthly equipment rental of $18,000."* The footnote at the bottom of the brochure read: *"Assumes a reimbursable fee of $475 per scan."

The MedView brochure refers to a new radiology imaging system that MedView rents for $18,000 per month. A "scan" refers to one imaging session that is billed at $475 per scan. Each scan involves giving the patient a chemical injection and requires exposing and developing an X-ray negative.

Required:

a. What variable cost per scan is MedView assuming in calculating the 45-scans-per-month amount?

b. Is the MedView brochure really telling the whole financial picture? What is it omitting?

2–24:   Manufacturing Cost Classification

A company makes DVD players and incurs a variety of different costs. Place a check in the appropriate column if the cost is a product cost or a period cost. Further, classify each product cost as direct materials, direct labor, or manufacturing overhead.

	Period Cost	Product Cost	Direct Labor	Direct Materials	Overhead
Advertising expenses for DVD					
Depreciation on PCs in marketing dept.					
Fire insurance on corporate headquarters					
Fire insurance on plant					
Leather carrying case for the DVD					
Motor drive (externally sourced)					
Overtime premium paid assembly workers					

continued

	Period Cost	Product Cost	Direct Labor	Direct Materials	Overhead
Factory building maintenance department					
Factory security guards					
Plastic case for the DVD					
Property taxes paid on corporate headquarters					
Salaries of public relations staff					
Salary of corporate controller					
Wages of engineers in quality control					
Wages paid assembly line employees					
Wages paid employees in finished goods warehouse					

2–25: Australian Shipping

In the 1800s Australia was a colony of England and most of its trade was with England. Australia primarily exported agricultural products such as wheat and imported manufactured goods such as steel, machinery, and textiles. The volume of trade measured in British pounds (£) was roughly equal in the sense that exports equaled imports. (Imports were slightly larger as there were net positive investments being made in Australia.) However, in cubic feet of cargo being shipped, exports to England exceeded imports. A British pound (£) of wheat required more cubic feet than £1 of manufactured goods. Hence, an imbalance of shipping existed. Numerous ships would carry agricultural products to England but return to Australia empty because no cargo of manufactured goods existed.

Large sail-powered ships required substantial ballast (weight) in the hold to keep the ship sailing properly, especially in rough seas. Before leaving England empty, the ships would purchase stone from local quarries for ballast. However, once in Australia, the stone had no market value, and in fact had to be hauled from the harbor area.

Consider the following facts for a particular ship in England with a shipment of Australian cargo for England.

1. The ship has contracted to sail to Australia and return with a cargo of Australian wheat. The ship has no cargo scheduled for London to Sydney.
2. The wheat-shipping contract calls for paying the captain and crew £4,900 for the round trip. The wheat seller will arrange for and pay Australian dock hands £250 to load the wheat in Sydney, and the wheat purchaser will arrange for and pay English dock hands to unload the wheat in London. The ship's crew does not load or unload the cargo.
3. To sail to Australia, the ship requires 10 tons of ballast. (1 ton = 2,000 pounds)
4. Stone can be quarried in England, transported to the docks, and loaded as ballast for £40 per ton. In Sydney, the stone can be unloaded and hauled away for £15 per ton.

5. Wrought iron bars of 10-foot lengths can also be used as ship ballast. Wrought iron bars can be purchased in England at £1.20 per bar. Each bar weighs 20 pounds. Wrought iron bars sell for £0.90 per bar in Sydney. The cost of loading the wrought iron in London is £15 per ton, and the cost of unloading it and transporting it to the Sydney market is £10 per ton.

Required:

a. Write a memo to the ship's captain describing what actions he should take with respect to using stone or wrought iron as ballast. Assume that interest rates are zero and all prices and quantities are known with certainty. Support your recommendation with a clearly labeled financial analysis.

b. Why do you think the price of wrought iron is lower in Sydney than in London?

P 2–26:   iGen3

The Xerox DocuColor iGen3 digital production press is a high volume, on-demand, full-color printer capable of producing up to 6,000 impressions (pages) per hour. It weighs nearly 3 tons, stretches 30 feet long, and holds more than 40 pounds of dry ink. It sells for over $500,000, and its principal market is print shops that produce mail order catalogs (e.g., L.L. Bean). Xerox offers two leasing options for the iGen3. Option A requires a three-year agreement with a monthly lease fee of $10,000 plus $0.01 per impression. Option B (also a three-year agreement) does not include a monthly lease fee but requires a charge of $0.03 per impression.

ColorGrafix is a print shop considering leasing the iGen3 to begin producing customized mail-order catalogs. Besides leasing the iGen3, ColorGrafix estimates that it will have to buy ink for the iGen3 at a cost of $0.02 per impression and hire an operator to run the iGen3 to produce the customized catalogs at a cost of $5,000 per month. ColorGrafix estimates that it can charge $0.08 per impression for customized color catalogs. (Note: the customer provides the paper stock on which the color impressions are printed.)

Required:

a. If ColorGrafix leases the iGen3 and chooses Option A, how many impressions per month will ColorGrafix have to sell and produce to break even?

b. If ColorGrafix leases the iGen3 and chooses Option B, how many impressions per month will ColorGrafix have to sell and produce to break even?

c. Should ColorGrafix choose Option A or Option B? Explain why.

d. ColorGrafix is a fairly new firm (only three years old) and has a substantial amount of debt that was used to help start the company. ColorGrafix has positive net cash flow after servicing the debt, but the owners of ColorGrafix have not felt it wise to withdraw any cash from the business since its inception, except for their salaries. ColorGrafix expects to sell and produce 520,000 impressions per month. Which lease option would you recommend ColorGrafix choose? Explain why.

P 2–27:   Adapt, Inc.

You work for the strategy group of Adapt Inc., a firm that designs and manufactures memory cards for digital cameras. Your task is to gather intelligence about Adapt's key competitor, DigiMem, a privately held company. Your boss has asked you to estimate DigiMem's fixed costs. Industry sources, such as trade associations, provide the following information on DigiMem:

DigiMem	Last Fiscal Year
Revenues (millions)	$6.200
Net income after taxes (millions)	$1.700
Income tax rate	40%
Operating margin*	70%

*Ratio of revenues less variable costs divided by revenues.

Required:

a. Using the preceding data, estimate DigiMem's annual fixed costs.

b. Why might your boss be interested in knowing DigiMem's fixed costs?

P 2–28:   Eastern University Parking

Eastern University faces a shortage of parking spaces and charges for parking. For nearby parking (e.g., behind the business school), faculty and staff pay $180 per year. Parking in lots Z and B, which are north and south of the campus and involve about a 10-minute walk to the business school, costs $124 per year. In setting these prices, the university seeks to recover the costs of parking and to manage the queue of people wishing to park on campus. The current $180 and $124 fees cover the costs of surface spaces. Lots Z and B have lower fees to compensate people for the longer walks and to encourage them to park in outlying lots. University officials say this fee structure, when multiplied by the number of parking stickers of each type sold, covers the cost of running the parking office and building new spaces.

The cost of providing a parking space consists of costs of construction of the space, maintenance, and security. The construction cost is the annual amount required to repay the cost of grading, draining, and asphalting the space. Maintenance includes snow removal, line painting, fixing the gates after the arms are broken by irate faculty members searching for a space, and patching the asphalt. Security costs include all costs of the parking officers who ticket the cars of staff and students parked illegally.

The university recently evaluated a proposal to construct an enclosed, multi-floor parking facility. Design estimates place the construction cost at $12,000 per enclosed space. The equivalent cost of a surface space is $900. The university uses a 10 percent cost of capital. (Assume that this is an appropriate interest rate.) To compensate the university for the cost of the capital involved in building parking garages, parking fees would have to be at least $1,200 per space per year, as opposed to $90 per space per year for the surface space. Because the university does not believe that faculty, staff, and students are willing to pay over $1,200 per year for a covered parking space, no plans exist to build a parking building.

Required:

Critically evaluate Eastern University's costing of parking permits. What do you think accounts for the university administration's reluctance to build a parking garage?

P 2–29: William Company

William Company owns and operates a nationwide chain of movie theaters. The 500 properties in the William chain vary from low-volume, small-town, single-screen theaters to high-volume, big-city, multiscreen theaters.

The management is considering installing machines that will make popcorn on the premises. These machines would allow the theaters to sell freshly popped popcorn rather than prepopped corn that is currently purchased in large bags. This new feature would be advertised and is intended to increase patronage at the company's theaters.

Annual rental costs and operating costs vary with the size of the machines. The machine capacities and costs are as follows:

	Economy	Regular	Super
Annual capacity (boxes)	50,000	120,000	300,000
Costs			
Annual machine rental	$8,000	$11,000	$20,000
Popcorn cost per box	13¢	13¢	13¢
Other costs per box	22¢	14¢	05¢
Cost of each box	08¢	08¢	08¢

Required:

   a. Calculate the volume level in boxes at which the economy popper and regular popper would earn the same profit (loss).
   b. Management can estimate the number of boxes to be sold at each of its theaters. Present a decision rule that would enable William's management to select the most profitable machine without having to make a separate cost calculation for each theater.
   c. Could management use the average number of boxes sold per seat for the entire chain and the capacity of each theater to develop this decision rule? Explain your answer.

SOURCE: CMA adapted.

P 2–30: Mastich Counters

Mastich Counters manufactures a material used to fabricate kitchen counters. It is a very durable, high-fashion, and expensive product that is installed in luxury homes. The manufacturing process is complicated and requires highly skilled employees, supervisors, and engineers. Mastich employs 450 people in its manufacturing operation. Most of the production employees are cross-functionally trained to perform several manufacturing tasks.

The firm's vacation policy gives employees three hours of paid vacation for every week of work. An employee who works 52 weeks accrues 156 hours or 3.9 weeks (156 ÷ 40) of paid vacation. In the past, Mastich allowed employees unlimited accumulation of vacation time. Some long-time employees had accumulated six months of vacation. When they retired from the firm, they continued to be paid for six months after leaving.

Management decided that allowing employees unlimited accumulation of vacation was costing the firm too much money when they left. Not only were the employees who left being paid, but so were their replacements. To correct this problem, management instituted a policy that an employee could not accumulate more than 156 hours of vacation. Once an employee's accumulated vacation exceeded 156 hours, these additional hours would not be added to his or her account. In addition, employees with more than 156 hours of accrued vacation had two years from the date of the policy change to bring their balance down to the maximum 156 hours. After the two-year phase-in period, the "take it or lose it" policy was strictly enforced.

While there was much grumbling about the "take it or lose it" policy, after the two-year phase-in period, the following comments were collected at a focus group held by the personnel department to assess the new policy:

- Manager A: "In some cases it has been very beneficial. Some of our people in high-stress positions were burned out. These people never took all their vacation. One woman took every Friday off for six months to use her excess vacation time. For the four days she worked, she was like a new person—refreshed, invigorated, and enthused."

- Manager B: "Well, that may be true, but this new policy, especially during the phase-in period, has been hell on our staffing. Some days, especially around weekends and holidays, we've had 30 percent of the plant on vacation. What impact do you think this has had on our production schedule and quality programs?"

- Manager C: "I have looked at the data and very few employees lose any accrued vacation. Fewer than 1 percent of the accrued vacation hours were lost last year after the phase-in period because employees did not use them."

Required:
Evaluate the costs and benefits of the new policy that limits accumulated vacation to 156 hours.

P 2–31: Optometry Practice

You are evaluating ways to expand an optometry practice and its earnings capacity. Optometrists perform eye exams, prescribe corrective lenses (eyeglasses and contact lenses), and sell corrective lenses. One way to expand the practice is to hire an additional optometrist. The annual cost of the optometrist, including salary, benefits, and payroll taxes, is $63,000. You estimate that this individual can conduct two exams per hour at an average price to the patient of $45 per exam. The new optometrist will work 40-hour weeks for 48 weeks per year. However, because of scheduling conflicts, patient no-shows, training, and other downtime, the new optometrist will not be able to conduct, bill, and collect 100 percent of his or her available examination time.

From past experience, you know that each eye exam drives additional product sales. Each exam will lead to either an eyeglass sale with a net profit (revenue less cost of sales) of $90 (not including the exam fee) or a contact lens sale with net profits of $65 (not including the exam fee). On average, 60 percent of the exams lead to eyeglass sales, 20 percent lead to contact lens sales, and 20 percent of the exams lead to no further sales.

Besides the salary of the optometrist, additional costs to support the new optometrist include:

Office occupancy costs	$1,200/year
Leased equipment	$330/year
Office staff	$23,000/year

Required:

In terms of the percentage of available time, what is the minimum level of examinations the new optometrist must perform to recover all the incremental costs of being hired?

P 2–32: JLE Electronics

JLE Electronics is an independent contract manufacturer of complex printed circuit board assemblies. Computer companies and other electronics firms engage JLE to assemble their boards. Utilizing computer-controlled manufacturing and test machinery and equipment, JLE provides manufacturing services employing surface mount technology (SMT) and pin-through-hole (PTH) interconnection technologies. The customer purchases the subcomponents and pays JLE a per-board fee to assemble the components.

JLE has a new one-of-a-kind, state-of-the-art board assembly line. The line can be operated 20 hours per day, seven days a week, in each three-week (21-day) period. Four customers have asked that their boards be manufactured on this line over the next three-week period. The following table summarizes the number of units of each board requested, the price JLE will charge for each board, JLE's variable and fixed cost per board, and the number of assembly line minutes each board requires. Fixed cost per board is the allocated cost of property taxes, fire insurance, accounting, depreciation, and so forth.

	Customers			
	A	B	C	D
Number of boards requested	2,500	2,300	1,800	1,400
Price	$38	$42	$45	$50
Variable cost/board*	23	25	27	30
Fixed cost/board	9	10	10	15
Number of machine minutes/board	3	4	5	6

*Allocated based on both machine minutes and direct labor cost.

Make the following assumptions:

- The four customer orders can be produced only on the new JLE line.
- If JLE rejects an order, future orders from that customer are not affected.
- There is no setup or downtime between orders.

- Customers are willing to have any number of boards produced by JLE up to the number of units specified above. For example, customer A has requested 2,500 boards in the 21-day period, but would accept a smaller number.
- The four customers comprise the entire set of potential customers who would want to use the new JLE line in the next 21-day period.

Required:

Which customer orders should be accepted? In other words, complete the following table:

		Customers		
	A	B	C	D
Number of boards requested to be produced in the next 21 days	2,500	2,300	1,800	1,400
Number of boards scheduled to be produced in the next 21 days	?	?	?	?

P 2–33: News.com

News.com is a Web site that offers users access to current national and international news stories. News.com does not charge users a fee for accessing the site, but rather charges advertisers $0.05 per hit to the Web site. A "hit" is a user that logs on the Web site.

News.com is considering two alternate ISPs that will link News.com's computer system to the World Wide Web—NetCom and Globalink. These firms are identical in access speeds and the number of users able to connect to the site per minute. Both ISPs are equally reliable. NetCom proposes to charge $3,000 per month plus $0.01 per hit to News.com. Globalink proposes to charge $2,000 per month plus $0.02 per hit. Assume that the only costs News.com incurs are the access fees charged by the ISP.

Required:

a. Calculate the number of hits to its Web site needed to break even if News.com uses NetCom.
b. Calculate the number of hits to its Web site needed to break even if News.com uses Globalink.
c. Which ISP do you recommend that News.com use? Explain why.
d. Monthly demand (in number of hits) for News.com is expected to be either 50,000 if the economy is slumping or 150,000 if the economy is booming, each equally probable. Which ISP should News.com choose and why?

P 2–34: Kinsley & Sons

Kinsley & Sons is a large, successful direct-mail catalog company in the highly competitive market for upscale men's conservative business and business-casual dress wear. On sales of $185 million they had earnings of $13 million. Most of the sales are from customers receiving the Kinsley catalog and placing orders through a toll-free (1-800) phone line. The remainder of their sales are from the *www.kinsley&sons.com* Web site, where customers place orders directly. Kinsley is organized into four departments: buying, catalog sales, Web sales, and distribution. Prices and margins are the same for catalog and Web sales.

The Web sales department is considering a major advertising and marketing campaign to drive additional sales to the Web site. Kinsley's market demographics, affluent professional males between 25 and 45, are very active Web buyers. The Web sales department expects the campaign to generate $56 million of additional Web site sales and profits of $4 million (before including the costs of the campaign). The annual cost of the advertising and marketing campaign is $2.8 million. The campaign also will have a favorable spillover effect on catalog sales through the 1-800 telephone line because the marketing for the Kinsley Web site will prompt additional catalog purchases. Additional profits of $600,000 are expected from catalog purchases resulting from the Web campaign.

In reviewing the proposal, the manager of catalog sales predicts that half of the additional Web sales and profits will come at the expense of catalog sales. That is, about $28 million of additional Web sales and $2 million of profits will come from Kinsley's existing catalog customers. Assume that all the data presented above are accurate, unbiased estimates.

Required:

    a. Should Kinsley & Sons undertake the additional advertising and marketing campaign for its Web site? Support your conclusion with data and/or figures.

    b. What critical/important assumptions underlie your recommendation in part (*a*)?

P 2–35: Littleton Imaging

Dr. Na Gu plans to open a radiology office that provides CAT scans. She can lease the CAT scanner for $1,200 per month plus $45 for each imaging session. In addition to the $45 lease cost per imaging session, Dr. Gu must purchase film for each session at a cost of $55. She plans to charge $250 for each session. Dr. Gu has identified a suitable office that she can rent for $1,400 per month. The monthly cost of a receptionist is $2,400 and two radiology technicians are $3,200 each per month. Office furnishings, phones, and office equipment cost $600 per month. She expects that her salary will be $15,000 per month.

Required:

    a. How many imaging sessions per month must Littleton Imaging conduct in order for the office to break even?

    b. How many imaging sessions per month must Littleton Imaging conduct in order for the office to yield an after-tax profit of $5,000 if the tax rate is 40 percent?

    c. Dr. Gu expects that the office will perform 200 imaging sessions per month. How much must she charge per session to break even?

P 2–36: Candice Company

Candice Company has decided to introduce a new product that can be manufactured by either of two methods. The manufacturing method will not affect the quality of the product. The estimated manufacturing costs of the two methods are as follows:

	Method A	*Method B*
Raw materials	$5.00	$5.60
Direct labor	6.00	7.20
Variable overhead	3.00	4.80
Directly traceable incremental fixed manufacturing costs per year	$2,440,000	$1,320,000

Candice's market research department has recommended an introductory unit sales price of $30. The incremental selling expenses are estimated to be $500,000 annually plus $2 for each unit sold, regardless of manufacturing method.

Required:

a. Calculate the estimated break-even point in annual unit sales of the new product if Candice Co. uses

(i) Manufacturing method A.

(ii) Manufacturing method B.

b. Which production technology should the firm use and why?

SOURCE: CMA adapted.

P 2–37: Mat Machinery

Mat Machinery has received an order from Dewey Sales Corp. for special machinery. Dewey pays Mat Machinery a deposit of 10 percent of the sales price for the order. Just before the order is completed, Dewey Sales Corp. declares bankruptcy. Details of the transaction from Mat's records show the following:

Sale price	$80,000
Cost incurred:	
Direct materials	15,000
Direct labor	25,000
Overhead applied	
Variable	12,500
Fixed	6,250
Fixed administration costs	5,875

Raytell Corp. offers to buy the machinery for $68,000 if it is reworked to its specifications. Additional costs for reworking are

Materials—$5,000   Labor—$6,000

A second alternative is to convert the machine to a standard model, which has a list price of $64,500. Converting the machine will require additional labor of $2,000 and materials of $6,500.

The third alternative is to sell the machine as-is for $55,000, net of discount. For commission purposes, this is treated as-a "standard" model.

Sales commissions are 2 percent on special orders and 1 percent on standard models. Raytell is considered a special order. All sales commissions are calculated on sales price, net of discount. A discount of 2 percent of the sales price is given on standard models.

Application rates for manufacturing overhead on all work, including rework and conversion, are

| Variable | 50 percent of direct labor cost |
| Fixed | 25 percent of direct labor cost |

Administration overheads are

| Fixed | 10 percent of direct labor, materials, and manufacturing overhead |

Required:

Which of the three alternatives should be chosen?

P 2–38:   Internal Support Services

T. Q. Jones is the manager of a machine design department in a large corporation. His engineers and designers charge their internal corporate clients on an hourly basis at $50 per hour. This represents the department's average cost for an hour's labor based on full capacity. Each engineer is assumed to have 1,800 billable hours per year. The $50 per hour is the sum of all the salaries and benefits divided by the product of 1,800 hours and the number of salaries in the numerator. The $50 per hour charged to users is the same regardless of the pay, position, or skill level of the engineer/designer assigned to the job. All large jobs (those in excess of $50,000) are estimated and contracted for up front, but in the past clients had no recourse except to continue paying if estimates were exceeded.

Recent competitive pressures on the entire corporation have caused many of T. Q.'s clients to seek competitive bids from outside the firm. T. Q.'s department has found itself sitting idle while outside design firms are awarded contracts.

T. Q. claims that he is being treated unfairly because he has no choice but to charge a higher price. Many times his most skilled and senior people spend their time assisting clients in establishing equipment requirements and investigating technology alternatives, only to find the bulk of the job farmed out to a small design firm that charges $30 per hour once critical design and technical decisions are made.

Required:

Critically evaluate this situation and list major issues as well as possible solutions.

SOURCE: L McGinn.

P 2–39:   G. Demopoulos & Son Inc.

G. Demopoulos & Son Inc. (GDS), a wholesale food distributor, is planning to expand its present operation by increasing its fleet of trucks. GDS now has eight trucks distributing products from a warehouse to various restaurants, hotels, and food markets.

Each truck driver is able to sell and distribute an average of 250 items per load once a day, five days a week. All trucks are operating at full capacity. GDS charges its customers $2 per item over the cost of goods for its service.

GDS is reviewing a plan to use an idle truck that is kept in case one of the other eight breaks down. If two or more trucks break down in any given day, the cost of renting a replacement truck is $90 per day. The company was offered $10,000 for the truck (estimated life of five years) and wants to know if it would be more profitable to use the truck to expand its existing business. The warehouse is at only 40 percent of capacity. The increase in administrative expenses from adding the route would be small. The company's current monthly costs for eight trucks are as follows:

Warehouse rental	$ 6,000
Utilities	325
Drivers' compensation	14,000
Insurance	200
G & A expenses	3,700
Gasoline expense	2,400
Truck maintenance	4,000

The new route will increase sales by 115 items per day and will be a wide-variety, low-volume route with a geographically dispersed customer base. If the new route is undertaken, the estimated salary expense of the driver will be $21,000 per year. Management is hesitant to use the idle truck because the existing fleet of trucks is getting old and each truck is expected to be inoperable an average of 20 days per year. If the truck is sold, the proceeds will be lent to a customer for five years at 12 percent interest.

Required:
Critically evaluate the alternatives facing GDS.

SOURCE: G Demopoulos, P Frocchi, S Koerner, N Marks.

P 2–40: Cost Behavior Patterns

For each of the following questions draw a graph that depicts how costs vary with volume. Completely label each graph and axis.

   a. Plant XXX works a 40-hour week. Management can vary the number of employees. Currently, 200 employees are being paid $10 per hour. The plant is near capacity. To increase output, a second 40-hour shift is being considered. To attract employees to the second shift, a 20 percent wage premium will be offered. Plot total labor costs as a function of labor hours per week.

   b. Plant YYY has a contract with the Texas Gas Company to purchase up to 150 million cubic feet of natural gas per month for a flat fee of $1.5 million. Additional gas can be purchased for $0.0175 per cubic foot. Plant YYY manufactures aluminum cans. One thousand cans require 10 cubic feet of gas. Plot total gas costs as a function of can production.

   c. Use the same facts as in (*b*), but plot the gas cost per can as a function of can production.

P 2–41: Royal Holland Line

Royal Holland is a cruise ship company. It currently has six ships and plans to add two more. It offers luxury passenger cruises in the Caribbean, Alaska, and the Far

East. Management is currently addressing what to do with an existing ship, the S.S. *Amsterdam*, when she is replaced by a new ship.

The S.S. *Amsterdam* was built 20 years ago for $100 million. For accounting purposes, she was assumed to have a 20-year life and hence is now fully depreciated. To replace the S.S. *Amsterdam* would cost $500 million, but her current market value is $371,250,000. The Holland Line can borrow or lend money at 10 percent.

The S.S. *Amsterdam* is now sailing the Caribbean and will be replaced next year by a new ship. The S.S. *Amsterdam* might be moved to the Mediterranean for a new seven-day Greek island tour. A seven-day cruise would depart Athens Sunday night, stop at four ports before returning to Athens Sunday morning, and prepare for a new cruise that afternoon. The S.S. *Amsterdam* can carry as many as 1,500 passengers.

The accompanying data summarize the operating cost for this seven-day cruise.

Estimated Operating Cost of Seven-Day Greek Island Cruise (S.S. *Amsterdam*)

	Variable Cost*	Fixed Cost†
Labor	$ 60,000	$ 80,000
Food	236,000	10,500
Fuel		177,000
Port fees and services		62,000
Marketing, advertising, promotion		240,000
Supplies	28,000	38,000
Totals	$324,000	$607,500

*Based on 1,200 passengers.

†Fixed costs per weekly cruise. Assume there are 50 weeks (and hence 50 cruises) in a year.

Required:

a. Assuming the seven-day Greek island cruise can be priced at an average of $1,620, calculate the break-even number of passengers per cruise using the data provided.

b. What major cost component is not included in management's estimates?

c. If you were to include the omitted cost component identified in (b), recalculate the break-even point for the S.S. *Amsterdam*'s Greek island cruise.

d. Passengers purchase beverages, souvenirs, and services while on the ship. The ship makes money on the purchases. If the ship line has a margin of 50 percent on all such on-board purchases, how much would the average passenger have to purchase for the break-even point to be 900 passengers?

P 2–42:   Cards Unlimited

Cards Unlimited buys trading cards of professional athletes (baseball, basketball, football, and hockey) from trading card manufacturers and then repackages and sells them to large retail chains. It has a contract with a card manufacturer called NBA Products. NBA Products is a wholly owned subsidiary of the National Basketball Association (NBA). NBA Products manufactures and distributes sports collectibles pertaining to the NBA. One NBA Products item is trading cards with NBA players' pictures on the cards.

Cards Unlimited buys the cards from NBA Products for $0.08 per card and then packages and sells them to Wal-Mart. Cards Unlimited's contract with Wal-Mart states that Cards Unlimited will sell only NBA cards within the United States to Wal-Mart.

Cards Unlimited promises to buy from NBA Products at least 750,000 cards and no more than 1 million cards per year. NBA Products promises to produce and sell no more than 1.5 million cards per year (to maintain the value of the cards). Wal-Mart has signed a three-year contract with Cards Unlimited to buy 900,000 NBA cards per year at a fixed price of $0.31 per card.

The variable costs of packaging the cards are $0.04, and the variable costs of selling and distributing them are $0.09 per card. Cards Unlimited's fixed costs are $1.2 million, including administrative overhead, plant and equipment overhead, and other manufacturing, administration, and distribution costs. Its plant is designed to process 14 million cards per year, but it is currently only processing 10 million cards.

Several foreign retail outlets have expressed interest in purchasing the remaining 100,000 cards Cards Unlimited can purchase from NBA Products. Negotiations have been held with retailers in Australia, England, and Italy.

- *Australia:* The Australian retailer would buy all 100,000 cards for $A0.43 (Australian dollars) per card. Cards Unlimited's variable selling and distribution costs are $A0.14 (instead of $0.09 for U.S. sales). The Australian–U.S. dollar exchange rate is 1.34 Australian dollars per U.S. dollar.
- *England:* The English retailer would buy all 100,000 cards for £0.21 (English pounds) per card. Cards Unlimited's variable selling and distribution costs are £0.06 (instead of $0.09 for U.S. sales). The pound–dollar exchange rate is 0.65 pounds per U.S. dollar.
- *Italy:* The Italian retailer would buy all 100,000 cards for 0.55 euros per card. Cards Unlimited's variable selling and distribution costs are 0.16 euros (instead of $0.09 for U.S. sales). The euro–dollar exchange rate is 1.60 euros per U.S. dollar.

Required:

a. Should Cards Unlimited purchase additional cards from NBA Products for international distribution and in which country should it sell them? Show your analysis and estimate the expected financial effect this will have on Cards Unlimited.

b. Cards Unlimited agrees to purchase an additional 100,000 cards from NBA Products for international distribution. After this decision is made and the international sale contract is signed, Wal-Mart threatens to cut its card purchases back to 800,000 cards unless Cards Unlimited agrees to reduce its price to $0.30 per card. What should Cards Unlimited do? Support your recommendation with a numerical analysis.

P 2–43: Roberts Machining

Roberts Machining specializes in fabricating metal racks that hold electronic equipment such as telephone switching units, power supplies, and so forth. Roberts designs and produces the metal stamping dies used to fabricate the racks. It is currently fabricating several racks for GTE. A new rack, the 1160, is scheduled to begin production. The die used to fabricate this rack cost Roberts $49,000 to design and build. This die was completed last week, and production of the 1160 is scheduled to begin next week. Rack 1160 is a specialized custom product only for GTE. GTE and Roberts have a one-year contract whereby Roberts agrees to manufacture and GTE agrees to purchase a fixed number of 1160 racks over the next 12 months for a fixed price per rack. The 1160 rack will not be produced beyond one year. This contract generates profits of $358,000 (after deducting the die's cost of $49,000). Roberts's accounting system recorded all expenditures for the 1160 die as a fixed asset with a one-year life. If this die is scrapped today or in one year's time, it has a scrap value of $6,800.

Easton, another metal fabricator, has offered to buy the 1160 die from Roberts for $588,000 and will supply 1160 racks to GTE. GTE has agreed to this supplier substitution. Roberts estimates that if it sells the 1160 tools and dies to Easton, it will lose a current cash equivalent of $192,000 of future profits that would have been generated from GTE and similar customers, but now this business will go to Easton. (Ignore all tax effects.)

Required:

a. List all the alternatives in Roberts's opportunity set with respect to the 1160 die.
b. Calculate the net cash flows associated with each alternative in Roberts's opportunity set listed in part (*a*).
c. What is the opportunity cost of each alternative in the opportunity set listed in part (*a*)?
d. What action should Roberts take with respect to the 1160 die?

P 2–44:   Doral Rentals

Amos Doral owns a small store that rents punchbowls, dishes, silverware, glassware, tables, and chairs to people having large parties. Amos runs the business by himself. He is considering adding power spray painters to his inventory of rentable items. A power spray painter is an electric air compressor and a paint sprayer used to paint or stain houses. Amos can lease the sprayers for $27 per week from a supplier. Amos expects he can rent the units for $38 per week. After each rental, Amos has to clean the sprayers with a solvent that costs $2 in materials per sprayer cleaned. Each customer is required to give Amos a credit card number for a deposit in case the sprayer is not returned or is damaged. Other rental companies report negligible losses due to theft or damage once the sprayer is secured with a credit card. Assume that sprayers are always rented for one-week periods and returned at the end of the week. (Note: Amos *leases* the sprayers and then *rents* them out.)

Required:

a. What fraction of the paint sprayers does Amos have to rent each week in order to break even?
b. Is Amos considering all the relevant factors if he just focuses on the lease cost of $27 and the cleaning costs of $2 per unit? What other costs and benefits should he consider in his analysis?
c. Before Amos signs the lease for the paint sprayers, he does some more research and discovers no other rental company in town rents sprayers. He decides to take out a yellow pages ad in the phone book for $25 per week and hire a part-time employee to clean the machines for $40 per

week. Amos expects 90 percent of the sprayers can be rented each week. How many machines must Amos lease to break even?

d. Being the sole supplier of power spray painters in town, Amos realizes he has market power. After talking to rental companies in other towns, he concludes that the following equation captures the relation between the market demand for sprayers rented per week and price:

$$\text{Rental price per sprayer} = \$69 - \text{Quantity of sprayers}$$

If Doral rents his sprayers using the above equation, he can rent all the sprayers that he leases. In other words, if Amos wants to rent 50 sprayers a week, he has to charge $19 per sprayer per week. Using the above price-quantity relation and the previous cost information ($27 weekly lease, $2 cleaning cost, and $65 per week for advertising and labor) AND assuming that all the sprayers he leases are rented each week, how many paint sprayers should Amos lease and what price should he charge?

P 2–45: Fuller Aerosols

Fuller Aerosols manufactures six different aerosol can products (room deodorants, hair sprays, furniture polish, and so forth) on its fill line. The fill line mixes the ingredients, adds the propellant, fills and seals the cans, and packs the cans in cases in a continuous production process. These aerosol products are then sold to distributors. The following table summarizes the weekly operating data for each product.

Fuller Aerosols
Weekly Operating Data

	AA143	AC747	CD887	FX881	HF324	KY662
Price/case	$37	$54	$62	$21	$34	$42
Fill time/case (minutes)	3	4	5	2	3	4
Fixed cost per product per week	$900	$240	$560	$600	$1800	$600
Cases ordered per week	300	100	50	200	400	200
Variable cost/case	$28	$50	$48	$17	$28	$40

Each product has fixed costs that pertain only to that product. If the product is discontinued for the week, the product's fixed costs are not incurred that week.

Required:

a. Calculate the break-even volume for each product.

b. Suppose the aerosol fill line can operate only 70 hours per week. Which products should be manufactured?

c. Suppose the aerosol fill line can operate only 50 hours per week. Which products should be manufactured?

P 2–46: Amy's Boards

Amy Laura is opening a snowboard rental store. She rents snowboards for skiing on a weekly basis for $75 per week including the boots. The skiing season is 20 weeks long. Laura can buy a snowboard and boots for $550, rent them for a season, and sell them for $250 at the end of the season.

The store rent is $7,200 per year. During the off-season, Laura sublets the store for $1,600. Salaries, advertising, and office expenses are $26,000 per year.

On average, 80 percent of the boards in any given week are rented. After each rental, the boards must be resurfaced and the boots deodorized. Labor (not included in the $26,000) and materials to prepare the board and boots to be rerented cost $7.

Required:

    a. How many boards must Laura purchase in order to break even?

    b. Suppose that Laura purchases 50 boards. What profit does she expect?

    c. Laura purchases 50 boards. What fraction of her boards must she rent each week to break even (including covering the cost of the boards)?

    d. Explain why the percentage utilization you calculated in part (*c*) differs from the expected rental rate of 80 percent.

P 2–47: Blue Sage Mountain

Blue Sage Mountain produces hinged snowboards. The price charged affects the quantity sold. The following equation captures the relation between price and quantity each month:

$$\text{Selling price} = \$530 - .2 \times \text{Quantity sold}$$

In other words, if they wish to sell 500 boards a month, the price must be $430 ($530 − .2 × 500). Fixed costs of producing the boards are $70,000 a month and the variable costs per board are $90.

Required:

    a. Prepare a table with quantities between 100 and 2,000 boards in increments of 100 that calculates the price, total revenue, total costs, and profits for each quantity-price combination.

    b. Determine the profit-maximizing quantity-price combination.

    c. Fixed costs fall from $70,000 a month to $50,000 a month. Should Blue Sage change its pricing decision?

    d. Variable costs fall from $90 per unit to $50 per unit. Should Blue Sage change its pricing decision?

P 2–48: Gold Mountain Ski Resort

You work for a venture capitalist and have been asked to analyze a proposal from a group of investors interested in building a new ski area in Colorado, the Gold Mountain Ski Resort. The demand for skiing is growing. Existing ski resorts have raised prices and reported record profits for the last two seasons. Gold Mountain's business strategy is to offer the ultimate ski experience—short lift lines, uncongested ski slopes, and spectacular scenery. With a 2,500-foot vertical drop, 10 trails and a single triple (three-person) ski lift, it can provide a very uncongested ski resort. The planned triple-person ski lift delivers a chair every 20 seconds, 180 chairs per hour (3 chairs per minute × 60 minutes per hour), or 540 skiers per hour (180 chairs per hour × 3 skiers per chair). This puts an average of only 54 skiers per hour on each of the 10 trails. Some trails will be more popular than others, but this average number of skiers per trail per hour is still below industry average.

The cost to build the ski runs, parking lots, and buildings and to erect the chair lift is $52 million. To raise this amount of capital requires an annual financing cost (debt service and dividends) of $8.3 million. The annual fixed operating cost (land lease, utilities, labor, taxes, insurance) of the ski resort is projected to be $4.1 million. For each 100 skiers per day, additional employees must be hired to staff the ticket office, ski patrol, parking lots, and so forth. The daily cost of the additional labor is $200 per 100 skiers per day.

The typical skier makes two ski runs per day (uses the lift twice). Ski resorts operate their lifts 8 hours per day, 120 days per year. Gold Mountain plans to sell one-day lift tickets for $60 per skier per day; no season passes will be offered.

Required:

a. Write a memo to the venture capital partner in charge of this account recommending one of three actions: aggressively pursue this investment, gather more information, or reject immediately. Justify your recommendation with a concise, well-reasoned, fact-based analysis.

b. After completing your analysis in (*a*), but before you submit it to your boss, Gold Mountain informs you that it is changing the triple-person chair lift to a four-person chair lift. This new chair will add an additional $75,000 per year to the annual financing cost, bringing the annual financing cost to $8.375 million. But instead of being able to lift 540 skiers per hour, the new chair can lift 720 skiers per hour. How do these new facts alter your conclusion in (*a*)?

Cases

Case 2–1: Old Turkey Mash

Old Turkey Mash is a whiskey manufactured by distilling grains and corn and then aging the mixture for five years in 50-gallon oak barrels. Distilling requires about a week and aging takes place in carefully controlled warehouses. Before it ages, the whiskey is too bitter to be consumed. Aging mellows the brew (and ultimately the consumer). The cost of the product prior to aging is $100 per barrel (direct plus indirect costs of distilling). In the aging process, each barrel must be inspected monthly and any leaks repaired. Every six months the barrels are rotated and sampled for quality. Costs of direct labor and materials in the aging process (excluding the cost of oak barrels) amount to $50 per barrel per year (all variable). As the whiskey ages, evaporation and leakage cause each 50-gallon barrel to produce only 40 gallons of bottled whiskey. New oak barrels cost $75 each and cannot be reused. After aging, they are cut in half and sold for flowerpots. The revenues generated from sales of the pots just cover the costs of disposing of the used barrels. As soon as the whiskey is aged five years, it is bottled and sold to wholesalers.

While domestic consumption of whiskey is falling, an aggressive international marketing campaign has opened up new international markets. The firm is in the third year of a five-year campaign to double production. Because it takes five years to increase production (an additional barrel of mash produced today does not emerge from the aging process for five years), the firm is adding 100,000 gallons of distilled product each year. Prior to the expansion, 500,000 distilled gallons were produced each year. Distilled output is being increased 100,000 gallons a year for five years until it reaches 1 million gallons. Distilled output is currently 800,000 gallons and is projected to rise to 900,000 gallons next year. The accompanying table describes production, sales, and inventory in the aging process.

	Base Year	Year 1	Year 2	Year 3
Production (distilled gallons)	500,000	600,000	700,000	800,000
Aged gallons sold	400,000	400,000	400,000	400,000
Warehouse Inventory at Beginning of Year				
4-year-old bbls	10,000	10,000	10,000	10,000
3-year-old bbls	10,000	10,000	10,000	10,000
2-year-old bbls	10,000	10,000	10,000	12,000
1-year-old bbls	10,000	10,000	12,000	14,000
New bbls added	10,000	12,000	14,000	16,000
Total bbls to be aged in year	50,000	52,000	56,000	62,000

(bbls = barrels)

Warehousing rental costs to age the base-year production of 10,000 barrels per year are $1 million per year. Additional warehouse rental cost of $40,000 per year must be incurred to age each additional 20,000 barrels (100,000 distilled gallons). All costs incurred in warehousing are treated as handling or carrying costs and are written off when incurred. Bottled Old Turkey is sold to distributors for $15 per gallon. These income statements summarize the firm's current operating performance:

	Base Year	Year 1	Year 2	Year 3
Revenues	$6,000,000	$6,000,000	$6,000,000	$6,000,000
Less:				
Cost of goods sold:				
10,000 bbls @ $100/ bbl	1,000,000	1,000,000	1,000,000	1,000,000
Oak barrels	750,000	900,000	1,050,000	1,200,000
Warehouse rental	1,000,000	1,040,000	1,120,000	1,240,000
Warehouse direct costs	2,500,000	2,600,000	2,800,000	3,100,000
Net income (loss)				
before taxes	$ 750,000	$ 460,000	$ 30,000	$ (540,000)
Income taxes (30%)	225,000	138,000	9,000	(162,000)
Net income after taxes	$ 525,000	$ 322,000	$ 21,000	$ (378,000)

Management is quite concerned about the loss that is projected for the third year of the expansion (the current year). The president has scheduled a meeting with the local bank to review the firm's current financial performance. This bank has been lending the firm the capital to finance the production expansion.

Required:

a. Instead of writing off all the warehousing and oak barrel costs, prepare revised income statements for years 1 through 3, treating the warehousing and barrel costs as product costs.

b. Which set of income statements (those given or the ones you prepared) should the president show the bank at the meeting? Justify your answer.

Case 2–2: Mowerson Division

The Mowerson Division of Brown Instruments manufactures testing equipment for the automobile industry. Mowerson's equipment is installed in several places along an automobile assembly line for component testing and is also used for recording and measurement purposes during track and road tests. Mowerson's sales have grown steadily, and revenue will exceed $200 million for the first time in 2001.

Mowerson designs and manufactures its own printed circuit boards (PCBs) for use in the test equipment. The PCBs are manually assembled in the Assembly Department, which employs 45 technicians. Because of a lack of plant capacity and a shortage of skilled labor, Mowerson is considering having the printed circuit boards manufactured by Tri-Star, a specialist in this field. Quality control restrictions and vendor requirements dictate that all PCBs be either manufactured by Mowerson or contracted to an outside vendor. The per-board cost of outside manufacture is higher than the in-house cost; however, management thinks that savings could also be realized from this change.

Jim Wright, a recently hired cost analyst, has been asked to prepare a financial analysis of the outside manufacturing proposal. Wright's report includes the assumptions he used in his analysis, along with his recommendation. His financial analysis appears below, and his notes and assumptions follow the analysis.

Required:

a. Discuss whether Jim Wright should have analyzed only the costs and savings that Mowerson will realize in 2002.

b. For each of the 10 items listed in Wright's financial analysis, indicate whether
   (i) The item is appropriate or inappropriate for inclusion in the report. If the item is inappropriate, explain why it should not be included in the report.
   (ii) The amount is correct or incorrect. If the amount is incorrect, state what the correct amount is.

c. What additional information about Tri-Star would be helpful to Mowerson in evaluating its manufacturing decision?

Annual Cost Savings Analysis for Tri-Star Contract

Savings	
1. Reduction in assembly technicians	
($28,500 × 40)	$1,140,000
2. Assembly supervisor transferred	35,000
3. Floor space savings	
[(1,000 × $9.50) + (8,000 × $6.00)]	57,500
4. Purchasing clerk, 1/2 time on special project	6,000
5. Purchase order reduction	
(2,000 orders @ $1.25 each)	2,500
6. Reduced freight expense	7,500
Total savings	$1,248,500

continued

Costs
7. Increased production cost

[($60.00 − 52.00) × 100,000 units]	$800,000	
8. Hire junior engineer	20,000	
9. Hire quality control inspector	22,000	
10. Increased storage cost for safety stock		
(Expected value of 4,200 units @ $2.00/unit)	8,400	
Total costs		850,400
Net annual savings		$ 398,100

Notes and assumptions

Personnel.   Assembly department technicians will be reduced by 40 at an annual savings (salary plus benefits) of $28,500 each. Five assemblers will remain to assist the field service department with repair work on the printed circuit boards; assemblers have always assisted in repair work. The supervisor of the assembly department will remain with Mowerson because he has only two years until retirement; a position will be created for him in the machining department, where he will serve as a special consultant.

Because of the elimination of purchasing and stocking of component parts required for PCB assembly, one purchasing clerk will be assigned half-time to a special project until his time can be more fully utilized.

A junior engineer will be hired to act as liaison between Mowerson and the manufacturer of the PCBs. In addition, a third quality control inspector will be needed to monitor the vendor's adherence to quality standards.

Floor space.   For the past two years, Mowerson has rented, on a month-to-month basis, 1,000 square feet of space for $9.50 per square foot in a neighboring building to accommodate the overflow of assembly work. The 8,000 square feet currently being used in Mowerson's main plant by the assembly department will be used for temporary stockroom storage. However, this space could be reclaimed for manufacturing use without overloading the stockroom facilities. This floor space is valued at $6 per square foot.

Production costs and volume.   Mowerson's cost for manufacturing printed circuit boards is as follows:

Direct material	$24.00
Direct labor	12.50
Variable overhead	6.25
Fixed overhead	9.25
Total cost	$52.00

The direct material cost includes normal scrap and other such material-related costs as incoming freight and issuing costs. Mowerson's annual cost for incoming freight attributed to PCBs is $7,500. Tri-Star will charge $60 per board, including the cost of delivery.

Mowerson's production volume of printed circuit boards for the past two years has been 80,000 and 90,000 boards, respectively. Projected production volumes for the next three years are:

2002	100,000
2003	120,000
2004	130,000

Storage costs.   Because Mowerson will not have direct control over the manufacture of the PCBs, the level of safety stock will be increased over the current level of 1,800 boards. The supervisor of the assembly department has provided the accompanying probabilities associated with reductions in Tri-Star's ability to produce and/or deliver PCBs.

Percentage of Time Tri-Star Deliveries Will Be Late	Probability (1)	Safety Stock of PCBs (2)	Expected Value (1) × (2)
4%	0.30	2,500	750
6	0.40	4,000	1,600
8	0.25	6,000	1,500
10	0.05	7,000	350
	New safety stock level		4,200

The variable cost to store the PCBs is $2 per board per year.

Other.   The variable cost of executing a purchase order at Mowerson is $1.25 for items such as postage, forms, and telephone. Since Mowerson will no longer have to purchase all the component parts required for the printed circuit boards, there will be a reduction of 2,000 purchase orders prepared annually.

Recommendation.   Based on the annual savings of $398,100 projected above, Mowerson should enter into an agreement with Tri-Star to manufacture the printed circuit boards.

SOURCE: CMA adapted.

Case 2–3:   Puttmaster

Innovative Sports sells a patented golf trainer called the Puttmaster. This device, which sells for $69.95, consists of a metal strip on the floor that is attached to the golfer's putter with elastic bands. By taking practice strokes with the putter attached to the Puttmaster, the golfer learns to feel how the putt should be stroked.

The Puttmaster is sold through a distributor who sells to retail stores (golf shops and sports outlets) and to the public through infomercials. The distributor pays Innovative Sports $30.85 for each Puttmaster. Innovative Sports also sells them through 30-minute television infomercials and on the Golf Channel (a cable TV channel) for $69.95 plus $15.95 for shipping and handling. Although each infomercial increases the public awareness of the product, thereby stimulating sales in the retail stores, infomercial sales also preempt retail sales. The distributor sells sufficiently large numbers of units that, for every 10 Puttmasters sold via the infomercial, two units will not be sold in a retail outlet.

For each unit sold on the infomercial, Innovative Sports pays $5.80 to the shipping company for mailing and $2.00 to the phone-answering company for providing the toll-free number and processing the order. Innovative Sports purchases

Puttmasters from the manufacturer, which produces them for $9.55. They are shipped directly to either the distributor or to the shipping company.

A 30-minute infomercial on the Golf Channel costs $845,000. Innovative Sports has already produced the taped show for the infomercial and is now deciding how many 30-minute infomercials to purchase over the next three months. The Golf Channel sells half-hour time slots 90 days in advance. From past experience, Innovative Sports estimates the first 30-minute infomercial will yield 22,000 unit sales. Each subsequent showing of the infomercial will yield only 90 percent of the units sold following the previous infomercial.

How many 30-minute infomercials should Innovative Sports purchase for the next 90 days?

Chapter Three

Opportunity Cost of Capital and Capital Budgeting

FIGURE 3–1

Future value of $10 invested at 5 percent

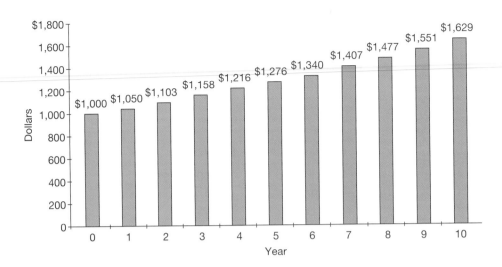

$$\$1,000 + 2(0.05 \times \$1,000) + [0.05 \times (0.05 \times \$1,000)]$$
$$= \$1,000 + \$100 + \$2.50$$
$$= \$1,102.50$$

The interest earned on the interest in the second year is called *compounding.* **Compound interest** describes the interest earned on the reinvested interest. To simplify the computations, Table 3–14 on page 153 contains compound interest factors. For example, the entry in Table 3–14 for 2 periods and 5 percent is 1.103. This 1.103 is the amount $1 will grow to in two years at 5 percent. One thousand dollars invested will grow to $1,103 (1.103 × $1,000).

We will now generalize the preceding illustration. Let PV represent the amount of money invested today at r percent per year and let FV represent the amount that will be available at the end of the two years. The general formula relating present dollars to dollars in two years at r percent per year is

$$PV(1 + r)^2 = PV(1 + 2r + r^2) = FV$$

The $2r$ term represents interest for two years on the original investment of PV, and r^2 is the interest on the interest (compound interest).

Figure 3–1 illustrates how $1,000 invested at 5 percent interest will increase in value. At the end of the first year, it has grown to $1,050 as we saw earlier. At the end of the second year, the $1,000 has grown to $1,103 (actually $1,102.50). By the end of the tenth year, the $1,000 amounts to $1,629. Notice that the values in Figure 3–1 correspond to the compound interest factors contained in Table 3–14 under the 5 percent column. The general formula for leaving money in the bank for n years and allowing the interest to accumulate and earn interest is

$$PV(1 + r)^n = FV \qquad \text{(Future value formula)}$$

All of the formulas of interest rate mathematics are just algebraic manipulations of this basic equation. The next formula derived is used to calculate **present values.**

2. Present Values   Suppose that instead of asking how much an investment will be worth at the end of n years, the question is how much money must be invested today at r percent per year to have *FV* tomorrow? For example, how much money must be invested today to be able to buy a $25,000 boat in six years? *FV* and *r* are known, but *PV* is unknown. This equation has three variables. For any two given variables, the equation can be solved for the third:

$$PV = \frac{FV}{(1 + r)^n} \qquad \text{(Present value formula)}$$

To solve for the boat example,

$$PV = \frac{\$25,000}{(1 + 0.05)^6}$$

$$= \frac{\$25,000}{1.3401}$$

$$= \$18,655.38$$

A deposit of $18,655.38 in the bank at 5 percent (allowing the principal and interest to compound) will grow to $25,000 at the end of six years. For the time being, we ignore the effects of taxes. Again, there is a table to help simplify the computation. Table 3–12 on page 151 contains the factor 0.746, which is what $1 received at the end of six years is worth today if the interest rate is 5 percent. Multiplying $25,000 by 0.746 yields $18,650, the same answer (except for rounding error).

3. Present Value of a Cash Flow Stream

So far, we have been dealing with just a single cash flow invested today or received in the future. Suppose there is a series of cash flows occurring at the end of each year for the next *n* years. That is, FV_1 is the cash received at the end of the first year, FV_2 is the cash received at the end of the second year, and FV_n is the cash received at the end of the *n*th year. What is the present value of this cash flow stream? We can apply the above *PV* formula to each cash flow:

$$PV = \frac{FV_1}{(1 + r)^1} + \frac{FV_2}{(1 + r)^2} + \frac{FV_3}{(1 + r)^3} + \ldots + \frac{FV_n}{(1 + r)^n}$$

For example, suppose an investor will receive payments of $500 at the end of the first year, $1,000 at the end of the second year, and $1,500 at the end of the third year. Figure 3–2 illustrates the stream of the three cash flows. How much is this stream of cash flows worth? Using the above formula

$$PV = \frac{\$500}{(1 + 0.05)^1} + \frac{\$1,000}{(1 + 0.05)^2} + \frac{\$1,500}{(1 + 0.05)^3}$$

$$= \$2,678.98$$

Therefore, receiving the cash flow stream illustrated in Figure 3–2 is the same as receiving $2,678.98 today if the interest rate is 5 percent.

The same answer can be found using Table 3–12. The first three numbers under the 5 percent column are 0.952, 0.907, and 0.864. These factors correspond to the numbers used in the preceding calculation of $2,678.98. The following illustrates how the factors in Table 3–12 can be used to compute the present value of the three cash flows described above:

Figure 3–2

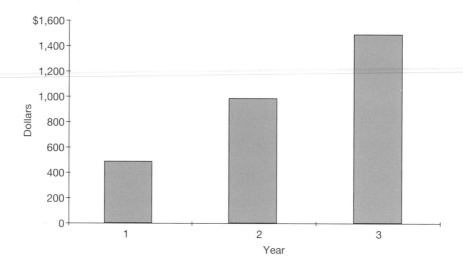

Year	Cash Flow	×	Table 3–12 Factor	=	Discounted Cash Flow
1	$ 500		0.952		$ 476
2	1,000		0.907		907
3	1,500		0.864		1,296
Total					$2,679

Each of the cash flows, FV_t, is said to be *discounted* (or divided) by $(1 + r)^t$ where t is the year in which the cash flow is received. Notice that $1 \div (1 + r)^t$ is always less than 1 for all positive interest rates. Therefore, a dollar received in the future is always worth less than a dollar today for positive interest rates. We will see that discounting is central to the concept of comparing alternatives involving cash flows received at different points of time. By discounting the future cash flows from each alternative to present values (or dollars today), we can compare which alternative is best.

The net present value of a stream of cash flows represents the increment to the value of the firm from accepting the investment. For example, suppose the current value of a firm is $400 million. This is the current market value of all the firm's outstanding debt and equity claims. If the firm makes an investment with a net present value of $17 million, then the value of all the outstanding debt and equity claims will rise to $417 million. The net present value of a cash flow stream is the change in the value of the firm from accepting the project. In perfectly competitive capital and product markets, the net present value of all investment projects should be zero. Under perfect competition, firms cannot earn abnormal profits; all investments return the market rate of interest. Therefore, investments can have a positive net present value only if the firm has some market power that allows it to charge prices that exceed long-run average cost; markets are not perfectly competitive. When analyzing investment projects with positive net present values, it is important to understand the source of the abnormal profits. (What factors are allowing the firm to earn a return more than its cost of capital?)

4. Perpetuities

We next consider **perpetuities,** or infinite streams of equal payments received each year. Some government bonds issued by the British government promise to pay a fixed amount of cash each year forever. How much would investors be willing to pay for such bonds? All of the future payments, $FV_1, FV_2, \ldots, FV_n$ are the same and equal to FV. Substituting FV into the general equation yields

$$PV = \frac{FV}{(1 + r)^1} + \frac{FV}{(1 + r)^2} + \frac{FV}{(1 + r)^3} + \ldots$$

Fortunately, using a bit of algebra, this expression simplifies to

$$PV + \frac{FV}{r} \qquad \text{(Perpetuity formula)}$$

This is the basic formula for a perpetuity, or an infinite cash flow stream, when the interest rate is r percent. If a bond pays \$100 per year in perpetuity and the interest rate is 5 percent, then investors would be willing to pay

$$PV = \frac{\$100}{0.05}$$
$$= \$2,000$$

5. Annuities

The next basic formula that is useful in many applications is the present value of an **annuity,** a stream of equal cash flows for a *fixed* number of years. Many financial instruments are annuities. For example, car loans and mortgage payments involve a fixed number of equal monthly payments. Corporate bonds pay a fixed amount twice a year over the term of the bond (usually 20 years). To derive the formula for an annuity, let FV again denote the annual cash flow received at the end of each of the next n years. The following diagram shows the timing of the n cash flows of each FV:

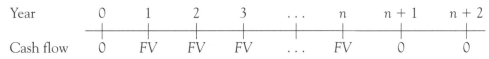

The formula for this annuity stream is

$$\frac{FV}{r} \left(1 - \frac{1}{(1 + r)^n} \right) \qquad \text{(Present value of annuity formula)}$$

To illustrate the application of the formula, suppose a prospective borrower can afford to pay \$1,000 per year for 10 years. How large a loan can be taken out today at an interest rate of 5 percent? Using our annuity formula, we get

$$PV = \frac{\$1,000}{0.05} \left(1 - \frac{1}{(1.05)^{10}} \right)$$
$$= \$20,000 \, (0.386087)$$
$$= \$7,721.73$$

Therefore, the bank will lend \$7,721.73 today, with payments of \$1,000 per year for 10 years. Instead of having to calculate a somewhat messy formula, let alone remember it, present value tables of annuity factors exist. Table 3–13 (on page 152) under the 5 percent column and 10 periods row contains the factor 7.722. This factor represents the present value of 10 annual cash flows discounted at 5 percent. If each annual cash flow is $1,000, then the present value of this cash flow stream is $7,722 (7.722 × $1,000). This is the same answer we got using the formula.

Another useful formula is the future value of an annuity. For example, how much will an investment of $1,000 a year for 18 years generate for a child's college education? Start with the present value of an annuity and then convert this amount to a future value by taking the present value formula for an annuity and multiplying it by $(1 + r)^n$. Or,

$$\frac{FV}{r}\left(1 - \frac{1}{(1 + r)^n}\right)(1 + r)^n$$

$$= FV\left(\frac{(1 + r)^n - 1}{r}\right) \quad \text{(Future value of annuity formula)}$$

To solve for how much money will be available for a child's education, substitute into the above equation:

$$\$1,000\left(\frac{(1.05)^{18} - 1)}{0.05}\right) = \$1,000\,(28.13238)$$

$$= \$28,132.38$$

Therefore, if interest is left to accumulate in the bank, an investment of $1,000 a year for 18 years at an interest rate of 5 percent will grow to over $28,000. Table 3–15 on page 154 simplifies the computation of future values of annuities. For the preceding example, the factor in Table 3–15 for 5 percent and 18 years is 28.132. This represents the future value of a stream of 18 annual payments of $1, discounted at 5 percent. Since $1,000 is received each year, the future value of this annuity stream at 5 percent is $28,132, as we computed using the future value of annuity formula.

6. Multiple Cash Flows per Year

So far we have considered only cash flows that occur once per year. How do we handle cash flows that occur more frequently, say, monthly? We could add up the monthly flows and treat them as a single annual cash flow on the last day of the year. But this ignores the interest we could earn on the monthly receipts. To illustrate, consider the difference between the following two alternatives: (1) receiving 12 monthly $1,000 payments or (2) receiving a single $12,000 payment at the end of the year. Before we can calculate which option is worth more, we first have to understand the relation between monthly and annual interest rates.

An annual interest rate involves only a single compounding interval. A monthly interest rate involves 12 compounding intervals. If the annual interest rate is 6 percent, what is the interest rate per month? It might be tempting to say $0.06 \div 12 = 0.005$, but this is wrong. To derive the monthly interest rate, recall the *law of one interest rate*. With no transactions costs and no risk, there can be only one interest rate in the market. The monthly and annual interest rates must be such that no one can earn more by investing at the monthly interest rate rather than the annual interest rate. A dollar invested at the monthly interest rate, r_m, must accumulate to the same amount at the end of the year as a dollar invested at the annual interest rate, r. The opportunity cost of investing at the monthly interest rate must be the same as the opportunity cost of investing at the annual interest rate or else a profit opportunity exists. Therefore, the following equation must hold:

$$(1 + r_m)^{12} = (1 + r)$$

$$(1 + r_m) = (1 + r)^{1/12}$$

$$r_m = (1 + r)^{1/12} - 1$$

$$= (1.06)^{1/12} - 1$$

$$= 0.004868$$

Now we can return to the original question and value the two alternatives. The monthly interest rate just derived is 0.004868, and the annual interest rate is 6 percent. Using the present value of the annuity formula to calculate the stream of 12 monthly $1,000 payments,

$$\frac{FV}{r}\left(1 - \frac{1}{(1 + r)^n}\right) = \frac{\$1,000}{0.004868}\left(1 - \frac{1}{(1.004868)^{12}}\right)$$

$$= \$205,423(0.056609)$$

$$= \$11,628.79$$

The present value of the single $12,000 payment is

$$\frac{FV}{(1 + r)^n} = \frac{\$12,000}{(1.06)^1} = \$11,320.75$$

Therefore, the 12 payments of $1,000 received at the end of each month are worth $308.04 more today than a single $12,000 payment received at the end of the year. The 12 monthly $1,000 payments are worth more than a single $12,000 payment at the end of the year because the monthly payments can earn interest during the year.

The preceding example illustrates that the earlier a payment is received, the more valuable is the payment. It also introduces the notion of the *compounding interval*. The key point is that the annual interest rate cannot be used to discount cash flows received more frequently than yearly. Some banks quote interest rates in annual terms, say 5 percent, but then compound the interest monthly. In this case, the *effective* annual interest is

$$\left(1 + \frac{r}{12}\right) - 1 = \left(1 + \frac{0.05}{12}\right)^{12} - 1$$

$$= (1.0041666667)^{12} - 1$$

$$= 0.05116$$

Therefore, if the bank has a stated annual interest rate of 5 percent but compounds monthly, the effective annual interest rate is 5.116 percent. If the bank's interest rate is 5 percent but it compounds interest *daily*, the effective annual rate is 5.127 percent.[1] Depositors wanting the highest *effective* interest rate will always choose the bank with the most frequent compounding interval, if the banks are all offering the same annual interest rate.

Besides using Tables 3–12 through 3–15 at the end of this chapter to simplify the computations, most computer spreadsheet programs and handheld calculators

---

[1] $0.05127 = \left(1 + \frac{0.05}{365}\right)^{365} - 1.$

TABLE 3–3   **Example Using Compound Interest Tables**
(Interest Rate = 5%)

	Cash Flow	Discount Factor	Source of Factor	Present Value
Years 1–20	$1,000	12.462	Table 3–13	$12,462
Years 1–10	1,000	7.722	Table 3–13	7,722
Year 21	3,000	0.359	Table 3–12	1,077
Total present value				$21,261

compute present values and future values. For example, Table 3–3 calculates the present value of the following cash flows (at $r = 5\%$): $2,000 for the first 10 years, $1,000 for the next 10 years, and $3,000 at the end of year 21.

Note how the calculations were simplified. In particular, the $2,000 stream for years 1 through 10 and the $1,000 stream for years 11 through 20 are equivalent to a $1,000 stream for the first 20 years and a $1,000 stream for the first 10 years. The discount factors for these two streams are taken from the annuity table (Table 3–13 on page 152). The single $3,000 payment in year 21 is discounted using the present value factor (Table 3–12 on page 151). Adding the three discounted cash flows together yields a present value of $21,261. As always, $21,261 represents the *opportunity cost* or the value of the cash flows when they are certain and the market rate of interest is 5 percent.

Concept Questions	Q3–3	Define the *present value of a future amount.*
	Q3–4	Define the *future value of a present amount.*
	Q3–5	Define *compound interest.*
	Q3–6	How do perpetuities differ from annuities?

C. Capital Budgeting: The Basics

Section A presented the concept of the opportunity cost of capital (a dollar today is not the same as a dollar tomorrow). Section B described how to convert dollars in different time periods into equivalent dollars. This section applies these concepts of opportunity cost to capital budgeting.

1. Decision to Acquire an MBA

Suppose Sue Koerner is considering returning to school to get an MBA degree. Her current wages are $35,000. Tuition, books, and fees cost $25,000 per year for two years. After earning her MBA, Sue's starting salary will be $65,000. Therefore, the MBA degree adds $30,000 per year to her salary. However, Sue must give up two years of current salary during graduate school plus pay tuition, books, and fees. At a current age of 31 and with an expected retirement age of 60, should Sue pursue the MBA? The market rate of interest is 5 percent. To illustrate the basic concepts, this example focuses on just the monetary aspects of the MBA and ignores the additional utility Sue receives from the prestige of earning an advanced

When Is a Fixed Cost an Opportunity Cost?	All costs are variable in the long run. When managers decide to build a plant of a given capacity, they commit the firm to making an investment. The amount invested in the plant becomes a sunk cost (assuming it has little resale value). The accountants then depreciate the investment over the life of the plant. These depreciated amounts are fixed costs in the accounting reports.
	Capital budgeting is the process of deciding how much to invest in projects that yield cash flows that span several periods. Prior to implementing a capital project, all the costs of the project are opportunity costs. Once the project is built, these opportunity costs become fixed costs to the extent that higher levels of output do not cause additional wear and tear on the facility.

TABLE 3–4   **The Decision to Get an MBA Degree**

		Net Cash Flow	Discount Factor	Present Value
Years 1–2	Forgone wages + Cost of school	$(60,000)	1.859	$(111,540)
Years 1–30	Additional wages with MBA	30,000	15.372	461,160
Years 1–2	Higher MBA wages not earned in first two years*	(30,000)	1.859	(55,770)
Total present value				$ 293,850

*The present value of $30,000 for two years is being deducted in this line because the line above includes the first two years. However, the higher salaries do not begin until year 3.

degree. Table 3–4 calculates the *net present value* of the MBA—the difference between the present value of the cash inflows and outflows.

In Table 3–4, the additional wages of $30,000 are treated as an annuity beginning in year 1, and then a two-year annuity of $30,000 beginning in year 1 is subtracted. This is the simplest way to perform the calculation. The computations in Table 3–4 assume that all cash flows occur at the end of the year. To keep the example simple, the additional wages from having the MBA degree are assumed to be constant at $30,000 per year over Sue's career. Given these assumptions, the decision to get an MBA is worth $293,850 in today's dollars. That is, the present value of the additional wages from receiving the MBA is greater than the amount forgone (two years' wages plus schooling costs) to acquire the degree.

The MBA degree example illustrates how to compare alternatives that have cash flows occurring at different points of time. The next example considers a slightly more complicated investment decision.

2. Decision to Open a Video Rental Store

Suppose Paul Woolf is considering opening a video rental store. The initial investment for videotapes, lease improvements, shelving, and equipment is $500,000. Suppose the store will be operated for four years and then sold at the end of the fourth year for $200,000 cash. Table 3–5 shows the projections of the store's annual operating profitability.

TABLE 3–5   Video Store Projected Profits, Years 1–4

	Year 1	Year 2	Year 3	Year 4
1. Sales (cash inflows)	$300,000	$450,000	$500,000	$500,000
2. Operating costs (cash outflows)	180,000	200,000	220,000	220,000
3. Depreciation	71,450	122,450	87,450	62,450
4. Pretax profit (1 − 2 − 3)	$ 48,550	$127,550	$192,550	$217,550
5. Tax at 34%	16,507	43,367	65,467	73,967
6. Net income after tax (4 − 5)	$ 32,043	$ 84,183	$127,083	$143,583

TABLE 3–6   Video Store Net Present Value, Years 1–4

	Initial Investment	Year 1	Year 2	Year 3	Year 4
1. Sales (cash inflows)		$300,000	$450,000	$500,000	$500,000
2. Operating costs (cash outflows)		180,000	200,000	220,000	220,000
3. Tax at 34% (cash outflows)		16,507	43,367	65,467	73,967
4. Cash flow from operations (1 − 2 − 3)		103,493	206,633	214,533	206,033
5. Cash flow from investment	$(500,000)				
6. Cash flow from disposal					185,108*
7. Net cash flow (4 + 5 + 6)	$(500,000)	$103,493	$206,633	$214,533	$391,141
8. Discount rate $1 \div (1.05)^n$	1.000	0.952	0.907	0.864	0.823
9. Present value at 5%	$(500,000)	$98,565	$187,422	$185,322	$321,793
10. Net present value					$293,102

*Cash flow from disposal = $200,000 less tax on excess of $200,000 over depreciated book value
= $200,000 − 0.34($200,000 − $156,200)
= $185,108

In this video store business, all the sales are for cash. Hence, all sales represent cash inflows. Depreciation amounts in Table 3–5 are based on accelerated depreciation tables allowed by the federal government in calculating taxable income. The after-tax profit in Table 3–5 is not the same as the net cash flow stream from the video store. The difference is the accounting accrual process of depreciation. The $500,000 initial investment is not written off in the first year but rather is capitalized and expensed via the accounting accrual of depreciation. In order to calculate the net present value of this investment, we must convert the accounting profit numbers in Table 3–5 into cash flows. The resulting cash flows and the net present value are presented in Table 3–6.

The net present value of the video store is $293,102. The net cash flows in each year (line 7) are composed of the cash flows from operations (line 4), the initial investment (line 5), and the cash flows from disposal (line 6). Cash flows from operations (line 4) are sales (line 1) less operating expenses (line 2) less taxes (line 3). At the end of the fourth year, the store is sold for $200,000. Under U.S. tax regulations, disposal values are ignored in calculating depreciation, and any gain on

TABLE 3–7   **Calculating Video Store Annual Cash Flows Starting with Net Income, Years 1–4**

	Initial Investment	Year 1	Year 2	Year 3	Year 4
1. Net income after tax (Table 3–5)		$32,043	$84,183	$127,083	$143,583
2. Depreciation (Table 3–5)		71,450	122,450	87,450	62,450
3. Cash flow from investment	$(500,000)				
4. Cash flow from disposal		0	0	0	185,108
5. Net cash flow (1 + 2 + 3 + 4)	$(500,000)	$103,493	$206,633	$214,533	$391,141

disposal is taxed as ordinary income when received. Thus, cash flow from disposal (line 6) is the disposal value less the 34 percent tax on the gain when the gain is the salvage value less book value. All of the initial cash outflow of $500,000 is assumed to occur immediately and therefore is discounted with a value of 1.000. The cash flows in years 1 through 4 are assumed to occur at the end of each year.

Instead of calculating the annual net cash flows as the sum of the component cash flows, as in Table 3–6, just add depreciation back to net income and subtract out new investments. Table 3–7 presents these calculations, which yield identical cash flows to those in Table 3–6.[2]

3. Essential Points about Capital Budgeting

Discount cash flows, not accounting earnings.
The important lesson in Table 3–6 is to discount cash flows, not accounting earnings. The reason for focusing on cash flows is that accounting earnings contain accounting accruals. The accounting process by its very nature keeps certain cash flows out of earnings. Investments are capitalized and then depreciated. Earnings do not contain amounts spent until the economic benefits of the investments are received. Likewise, sales are usually recorded when the legal liability arises, not when the cash is collected. Therefore, dollars earned, as computed by accounting earnings, do not reflect the dollars actually received. Table 3–7 illustrates that accounting income differs from cash flows due to the timing of depreciation and investment.

The reason we discount cash flows and not accounting earnings is because cash flows can be invested in the bank to generate interest. Accounting earnings, however, cannot be used to open a bank account. You cannot go to the store and buy soda and pretzels with accounting earnings.

Include working capital requirements.
The video store example is simple and does not include cash needed for working capital. However, many businesses carry significant accounts receivable and inventories. Such inventories represent cash tied up that could be earning interest if invested. Therefore, cash invested in such inventories should be included in the analysis. Likewise, many businesses allow customers to make purchases on credit. In these cases, additional cash must be invested to finance these accounts receivable. On the other hand, to the extent that the firm acquires goods and services on credit, the accounts payable offset the cash needed to finance current assets.

---

[2] In general, adding back to net income all non-cash flow expenses, such as depreciation, and subtracting from net income all non-cash flow revenues, such as accrued bond interest income, yields cash flow from operations.

Include opportunity costs but not sunk costs.

In the MBA example, the current wages forgone by attending graduate school are an opportunity cost of getting the MBA. They are included in the analysis and discounted as cash flows forgone. However, sunk costs are ignored. For example, the costs of acquiring the undergraduate degree (wages forgone, undergraduate tuition, and housing) necessary for admission into an MBA program are not included. The expenses incurred to receive the undergraduate degree are sunk costs because they were incurred prior to the decision to attend graduate school.

Exclude financing costs.

Do not include the interest charges on the debt used to finance the project. The costs of financing the project are implicitly included when future cash flows are discounted. If the project has a positive net present value, then its cash flows yield a return in excess of the firm's cost of capital, which more than compensates the firm for the financing costs.

    The discounted cash flow analyses of both the MBA and video store examples exclude all mention of how either of these projects would be financed. Were savings or student loans used to finance the MBA degree? Was the investment in the video store financed by a bank loan or by bringing in a partner who contributed cash? These considerations are excluded because the discount rate incorporates the cost of financing the project. Under the assumption of complete certainty and perfect capital markets, there can be only one interest rate in the market. Therefore, the firm can borrow all the necessary funds at this interest rate, and the financing of the project is irrelevant.

D. Capital Budgeting: Some Complexities

The preceding section presented two simplified capital budgeting examples: the MBA decision and the video store decision. These examples illustrate the basic mechanics of **discounted cash flow (DCF)** analysis. This section adds more complexities: risk, inflation, and depreciation tax shields.

1. Risk

One of our assumptions has been that all cash flows are riskless. This assumption, when coupled with the zero transactions-costs assumption, led to the result that there would be only one interest rate prevailing in the market and all future cash flows would be discounted at this riskless interest rate. But few cash flow streams are riskless, so we must have a way to deal with risky cash flows.

    Once we allow the possibility of risk, then the law of one interest rate no longer holds. Instead, we have the law of one interest rate for each risk class. Investments that have different risk will have different interest rates. In order to induce investments in higher-risk projects, a higher expected return is required. This is another law of finance: *A safe dollar is more valuable than a risky dollar.* Risky projects are discounted at a higher interest rate than safe projects.

    What we mean by risk, how it is measured, and how to choose risk-adjusted discount factors are the subject of corporate finance. We will not concern ourselves with deriving risk-adjusted discount rates. For any given risky cash flow stream, we assume that an equivalent risk-adjusted interest rate exists.

    Recall Paul Woolf's investment in a video retail store. One of Paul's alternatives is to invest at 5 percent in U.S. Treasury bonds, which are very unlikely to default. If the video store cash flows are risky, then 5 percent is not the opportunity cost of investing in the video store. Since a risky dollar is less valuable than a safe dollar, Paul must discount the video store cash flows using an interest rate from an investment with a comparable degree of risk. Suppose that the equity of a national chain of video stores returns 13 percent per year, and the stock in this company is comparable in risk to Paul's video store. Then 13 percent is the relevant, risk-adjusted interest rate to use in discounting the video store cash flows.[3]

Let r_i be the risk-adjusted discount rate for the ith investment project and let r_f be the risk-free rate of interest on government bonds. The following equation describes the relation between the risk-free rate and the riskless rate of interest:

$$r_i = r_f + \text{Risk premium}_i$$

This equation states that the required rate of return on an investment in risk class i is composed of two pieces. The first piece is the return that must be paid for investing in a riskless asset, r_f, and the second piece is a risk premium associated with risk class i. Thus, the first adjustment we must make when valuing risky cash flows is to choose a higher discount rate that corresponds to the risk inherent in the project's cash flows.

The second adjustment is to discount the expected cash flows. Since the cash flows are uncertain, one of several possible cash flows can result. Instead of discounting the highest or lowest cash flow that can occur, we discount the *expected* or average anticipated cash flow. For example, if the cash flows next year can be either $100 or $200 with equal probability, we would discount the expected cash flow of $150. The general formula for discounting risky cash flows is

$$PV = \sum_{t=0}^{n} \frac{E(\widetilde{CF}_t)}{(1 + r_t)^t}$$

$\widetilde{CF}_t$ is the risky cash flow in year t and $E(\widetilde{CF}_t)$ is the expected value of the uncertain cash flow. This formula says to discount expected cash flows using a risk-adjusted discount rate, r_i, appropriate for the risk inherent in the project. For example, if cash flows for the next five years will be either $100 or $200 per year with equal probability, the expected cash flows are $150. Suppose the discount rate for equivalent risk investments is 30 percent. Using Table 3–13 on page 152, the present value of this risky five-year annuity is $365.40 (or $150 × 2.436).

2. Inflation

So far we have ignored the effects of inflation. In fact, we have implicitly assumed there was no inflation. In the MBA example, the difference of $30,000 between Sue Koerner's current salary ($35,000) and her salary with the MBA ($65,000) was assumed to remain constant over time. However, even a small inflation rate of 3 percent per year can cause cash flows in 20 years to be very different from what they would be without inflation. At 3 percent inflation per year, a dollar will grow to about $1.81 in 20 years. Therefore, one should not ignore inflation in a DCF analysis.

Absent any inflation, people would still prefer a dollar today instead of a dollar tomorrow. In such an inflation-free world, the interest rate is the compensation paid to postpone consumption. Let r_{real} denote the **real interest rate,** or the rate of

---

[3]Note that the expected return on the stock of the video chain has comparable risk to the video store only if the chain has no debt. If the chain has debt, then the expected return on the stock is higher than the firm's cost of capital.

interest that would occur if there were no inflation. The real interest rate consists of the risk-free rate of return plus a risk premium. It is the market price that equates the supply and demand for capital for a given amount of risk.

If inflation is i percent per year, and $1 of consumption is delayed for one year, it will take $\$(1 + i)$ at the end of the year to buy the same $1 bundle of goods as could have been purchased at the beginning of the year. If inflation is 7 percent per year, buying the same $1 bundle costs $1.07 at the end of the year. To compensate for delaying consumption for one year when inflation is running at i percent, the **nominal interest rate** is

$$1 + r_{\text{nominal}} = (1 + r_{\text{real}})(1 + i)$$

The nominal interest rate is the interest rate observed in the market. It includes both the real component, r_{real}, and expected inflation. If the real interest rate is 3 percent and expected inflation is 7 percent, then the nominal interest rate is $(1.03)(1.07) - 1 = 0.1021 = 10.21\%$. A loan from a bank is repaid in future dollars whose purchasing power will be eroded by inflation. When lending money, the bank will impound the expected rate of inflation into the interest rate.

If discount rates are stated in nominal interest rates, then the cash flows being discounted should be stated in nominal terms. That is, they should be adjusted for inflation as well. If nominal interest rates are used in the denominator of the present value equation and the cash flows in the numerator are not adjusted, then inconsistent results are produced. To illustrate how to adjust cash flows for inflation, return to the video store example in Tables 3–5 and 3–6. There was no explicit statement about whether the cash flows in Table 3–6 were in real or nominal terms. Suppose the cash flows are real, meaning they do not account for inflation. Table 3–8 makes the following inflation assumptions: Price inflation for sales and disposal value will be 2 percent per year, and price inflation on operating costs will be 3 percent per year. First restate the cash flows into nominal dollars. Then discount these dollars using the nominal interest rate. Assume the nominal interest rate is 9 percent.

Sales (line 1) are restated at an inflation rate of 2 percent per year and operating costs (line 4) are restated at 3 percent per year. This produces inflation-adjusted sales (line 3) and inflation-adjusted operating costs (line 6). Depreciation is not adjusted because the tax laws do not allow historical cost depreciation to be adjusted for inflation. Nominal cash flows from operations are nominal sales less nominal operating costs less taxes. The remainder of Table 3–8 follows directly from Table 3–6, except the discount rate is 9 percent. The only other difference is that the disposal value of $200,000 is increased by a 2 percent inflation factor. After adjustment for inflation, the net present value of the video store is $234,585, compared with a net present value of $293,102 before. The net present value is lower because the future cash inflows, while increased by inflation, are being discounted at an even higher discount rate (9 percent versus the 5 percent in Table 3–6).

The important point to remember from this section is to discount nominal (inflation-adjusted) cash flows using nominal interest rates.

3. Taxes and Depreciation Tax Shields

Taxes are a very significant cash flow item in most discounted cash flow analyses. A corporate income tax rate of 34 percent implies that about a third of any project's profitability is taxed away. Therefore, taxes and how to minimize them become a very important element in capital budgets.

Accounting depreciation is an important device in minimizing taxes. The intuition is really quite simple. Suppose a company car costs $25,000 and taxable

TABLE 3–8 **Video Store Net Present Value, Years 1–4**
(Cash Flows Adjusted for Inflation)

	Initial Investment	Year 1	Year 2	Year 3	Year 4
1. Sales (real)		$300,000	$450,000	$500,000	$500,000
2. Inflation factor $(1.02)^n$		1.020	1.040	1.061	1.082
3. Sales (nominal) (1×2)		$306,000	$468,180	$530,604	$541,216
4. Operating costs (real)		180,000	200,000	220,000	220,000
5. Inflation factor $(1.03)^n$		1.030	1.061	1.093	1.126
6. Operating costs (nominal) (4×5)		$185,400	$212,180	$240,400	$247,612
7. Depreciation		71,450	122,450	87,450	62,450
8. Pretax profit $(3 - 6 - 7)$		$ 49,150	$133,550	$202,754	$231,154
9. Tax at 34% (8×0.34)		16,711	45,407	68,936	78,592
10. Cash flow from operations $(3 - 6 - 9)$		$103,889	$210,593	$221,268	$215,012
11. Cash flow from investment	$(500,000)				
12. Cash flow from disposal					195,989*
13. Net cash flow $(10 + 11 + 12)$	$(500,000)	$103,889	$210,593	$221,268	$411,001
14. Discount rate $1 \div (1.09)^n$	1.000	0.917	0.842	0.772	0.708
15. Present value at 9%	$(500,000)	$ 95,311	$177,252	$170,859	$291,163
16. Net present value					$234,585

*Cash flow from disposal = Nominal sales price less tax on excess of nominal sales price over depreciated book value
= $200,000(1.02)^4 − 0.34[$200,000(1.02)^4 − 156,200]
= $195,989

income will exceed $25,000 into the foreseeable future. For tax purposes, it would be highly preferable to reduce taxable income by expensing the entire $25,000 purchase price against this year's taxable income. However, the government will not permit this and insists that the car be depreciated over its useful life, say five years. The car has already been purchased, so the $25,000 is gone. The only question remaining is how quickly the cost of the car can be written off against taxable income. As long as the firm has taxable income, then accounting depreciation shields some portion of that income from taxes. And it is preferable to shield a dollar of taxable income today rather than tomorrow because a dollar saved today is worth more than a dollar saved tomorrow. Hence, a depreciation schedule for the car for the next five years of $10,000, $6,000, $3,600, $2,160, and $3,240 is preferable to a depreciation schedule of $5,000 per year for five years. Both schedules depreciate a total of $25,000, but the first recognizes the depreciation sooner, thereby reducing the present value of taxes paid.

Most firms use different depreciation methods for external reports to shareholders than for the Internal Revenue Service (IRS). The IRS allows firms to elect straight-line depreciation for shareholder reports and accelerated depreciation for tax returns. There are other accounting methods that can cause tax expense reported to shareholders to differ from the firm's actual tax bill. For example, the expected costs of product warranties are included in financial reports to shareholders when the product is sold. However, the cost of the warranty work is included for tax purposes only when actually incurred. When calculating a project's net present value, it is important to use the tax accounting rules rather than the accounting rules for shareholders. Taxes are a cash flow, and the accounting rules used to compute taxes affect the tax cash flows. The accounting methods used only for shareholder reports, however, do not affect tax cash flows.

As illustrated in the video store example, the treatment of accounting depreciation requires care. The following points should be noted:

- Depreciation is not a cash flow.
- Net income after deducting depreciation is not a cash flow.
- Depreciation is a tax-allowed expense.
- Depreciation affects taxes and therefore has an indirect effect on cash flows via taxes.
- When considering the cash flow effect of depreciation, use the depreciation method allowed for tax purposes.

Some simple algebra illustrates the indirect cash flow effect of depreciation. Let

τ = Tax rate
R = Revenue
E = All cash expenses (except depreciation)
D = Depreciation allowed for tax purposes

Using this notation, we can write down the following familiar formulas:

$$\text{Net income} = NI = (R - E - D)(1 - \tau)$$
$$\text{Taxes} = TAX = (R - E - D)\tau$$
$$\text{Cash flow} = CF = R - E - TAX$$
$$= R - E - (R - E - D)\tau$$
$$= (R - E)(1 - \tau) + D\tau$$

Notice the last term in the last cash flow equation, $D\tau$. This is the annual depreciation charge, D, times the tax rate, τ. The product of the two is *added* to the annual after-tax operating net cash flow, $(R - E)(1 - \tau)$, to arrive at the after-tax net cash flow as long as the firm has taxable income. From the last formula, we can clearly see that the larger the depreciation expense, the higher the firm's cash flow because the tax liability is lower. In this sense, depreciation is said to be a *tax shield* because it results in lower taxes and thus higher after-tax cash flow. The total amount of depreciation that can be deducted from taxes is limited to the original cost of the asset. Therefore, the sooner the depreciation is taken (assuming the firm has positive taxable income), the higher is the present value of the depreciation tax shield. Accelerated tax depreciation methods that allow earlier recognition of depreciation increase a project's net present value.

To illustrate the importance of early recognition of depreciation, consider the following example that captures the flavor of the tax code but avoids many of the technical complexities. An asset is purchased for $500,000. The asset has a five-year life and no salvage value. The tax rate is 34 percent. Table 3–9 lays out the calculation of the present value of the tax shields under the straight-line and double-declining-balance depreciation methods.

Double-declining-balance depreciation writes off the $500,000 original cost faster than straight-line depreciation. Therefore, its tax shield has a higher present value by $5,061. In other words, if double-declining-balance depreciation is used instead of straight-line depreciation for tax purposes (assuming the tax regulations allow this), the net present value of the project is increased by $5,061. This is about 1 percent of the asset's cost.

TABLE 3–9 **Net Present Value of Depreciation Tax Shields***

	Straight-Line Depreciation			Double-Declining-Balance Depreciation				
Year	Deprec. Expense	Tax Shield $(D\tau)$	PV of Tax Shield	DDB Rate[†]	Book Value at Beg. of Year	Deprec. Expense	Tax Shield $(D\tau)$	PV of Tax Shield
1	$100,000	$34,000	$32,381	0.4	$500,000	$200,000	$68,000	$ 64,762
2	100,000	34,000	30,839	0.4	300,000	120,000	40,800	37,007
3	100,000	34,000	29,370	0.4	180,000	72,000	24,480	21,147
4	100,000	34,000	27,972	0.4	108,000	43,200	14,688	12,084
5	100,000	34,000	26,640		64,800	64,800	22,032	17,213
	$500,000		$147,202			$500,000		$152,263

*$500,000 asset, no salvage, five-year life, 34% tax rate, 5% interest.
[†]DDB rate (double-declining-balance rate) is twice the straight-line rate; or, 40% = $2 \times \frac{1}{5}$.

Concept Questions		
	Q3–7	Define *net present value*.
	Q3–8	Explain why the interest rate on a one-year bank account paying interest monthly is not just one-twelfth the interest rate on a one-year bank account paying interest annually.
	Q3–9	What does it mean to say depreciation is a *tax shield* when evaluating capital projects?
	Q3–10	What are the components of the real interest rate?
	Q3–11	What are the components of the nominal interest rate?

E. Alternative Investment Criteria

Up to this point we have presented discounted cash flow (DCF) analysis, also called *net present value (NPV) analysis*, as the correct way to compare alternatives involving cash flows occurring at different points in time. Cash flows received or paid in different years cannot simply be added together, because a dollar today is worth more than a dollar tomorrow. Therefore, a future dollar must be discounted before it can be added to today's dollars. However, DCF analysis is not the only way to evaluate investment projects. Some firms use payback, accounting rates of return, or internal rates of return. These methods are first described and then critically evaluated. The last section presents survey data on how frequently they are used in practice.

1. Payback

A much simpler method of evaluating projects is the **payback method.** Payback is the number of years or months it takes to return the initial investment. Suppose a project's initial investment is $700,000 and subsequent yearly cash inflows are $200,000 for five years. This project has a payback of three and one-half years ($700,000 ÷ $200,000). In three and one-half years, the cash inflows just equal the initial investment of $700,000. The great advantage of payback is its simplicity. It is easy to compute and understand. No assumptions are required about the appropriate opportunity cost of capital for the particular project.

However, payback ignores the time value of money. Two projects are viewed as equally attractive if they have the same payback, even though all of the payback may occur in the payback year for one project but be spread out evenly over time for the other. For example, suppose two projects each require $300,000 investments but one pays $100,000 for three years and the other pays nothing for two years and $300,000 in the third year. Each has a three-year payback, but the first is more valuable because the $100,000 payments in years 1 and 2 can be earning interest.

Payback also ignores the cash flows beyond the payback period. Thus, payback ignores the "profitability" of the project. Two projects with the same investments and same cash flows per year up to the payback year have the same payback. But if one investment has no cash flows beyond the payback year and the other investment does, clearly the latter investment has a higher net present value.

Finally, payback lacks a benchmark for deciding which projects to accept and which to reject. What payback cutoff should the firm use as a criterion for project selection? Is a three-year payback good or bad? In contrast, the discounted cash flow method uses the opportunity cost of capital to discount the cash flows. If a project has a positive NPV using the opportunity cost of capital, the project is accepted. The benchmark in DCF analysis is the existence of a positive NPV. But no such benchmark exists for payback.

Advocates of payback argue that net present value, even after future cash flows are discounted, places too much emphasis on cash flows received in the future. Some managers believe that it is very difficult to forecast cash flows accurately beyond three or four years. Thus, they place very little weight on these cash flows. However, net present value mathematics automatically incorporates the higher uncertainty of the more distant cash flows. These inherently riskier future cash flows are discounted by larger discount factors. The cash flow in year t is discounted by $1/(1 + r)^t$ where r is the appropriate risk-adjusted discount rate. As t increases, the discount rate becomes smaller. The exclusive use of payback to evaluate investment projects tends to cause a firm to focus on short-term cash flows and ignore long-term rewards.

2. Accounting Rate of Return

Another method for project evaluation is the accounting rate of return. A project's accounting rate of return, also called **return on investment (ROI)**, is

$$ROI = \frac{\text{Average annual income from the project}}{\text{Average annual investment in the project}}$$

Consider the following investment of $10 million in a project that has a five-year life and no salvage value. The project's income in each of the next five years is

Operating income	$3,500,000
Depreciation (straight-line)	(2,000,000)
Net income before taxes	$1,500,000
Taxes (40%)	(600,000)
Net income	$ 900,000

The average net income and average investment are calculated in Table 3–10. Given the average net income and average investment, we can compute the project's ROI:

TABLE 3–10 **Average Net Income and Average Book Value of Investment**

Year	Net Income	Average Book Value of Investment
1	$900,000	$9,000,000
2	900,000	7,000,000
3	900,000	5,000,000
4	900,000	3,000,000
5	900,000	1,000,000
Average	$900,000	$5,000,000

$$ROI = \frac{\text{Average annual income from project}}{\text{Average annual investment in the project}}$$

$$= \frac{\$900,000}{\$5,000,000}$$

$$= 18\%$$

The accounting rate of return has the advantage of being easy to calculate, and it relates to the firm's accounting statements, which are familiar to managers. The problem is that it can lead to incorrect investment decisions. For example, suppose that a security purchased today for $100 pays $2,000 in 50 years. This security has the following ROI:

$$\text{Average annual cash inflow} = \frac{\$2,000}{50 \text{ years}}$$

$$= \$40$$

$$ROI = \frac{\$40}{\$100}$$

$$= 40\%$$

This security has a 40 percent accounting rate of return. Suppose the market rate of return is 10 percent. Using the accounting rate of return as our investment criterion, this investment appears quite attractive. But compute its net present value:

$$NPV = -\text{Initial investment} + \frac{FV}{(1 + r)^n}$$

$$= -\$100 + \frac{\$2,000}{(1 + 0.10)^{50}}$$

$$= -\$100 + \frac{\$2,000}{117.391}$$

$$= -\$100 + \$17.04$$

$$= -\$82.96$$

Actually, this investment has a negative net present value. Alternatively, investing the $100 at 10 percent would yield $11,739 in 50 years.

The accounting rate of return results in incorrect decisions because it ignores the time value of money. Calculating ROI involves computing the average annual income from the project. A dollar of income received today is treated the same as a dollar of income received in the future. The fact that these dollars are worth different amounts is ignored when accounting ROI is computed.

3. Internal Rate of Return (IRR)

The **internal rate of return (IRR)** method for comparing different projects appears on the surface to be very similar to the DCF method. The IRR method finds the interest rate that equates the initial outlay to the discounted future cash flows. If the project's internal rate of return exceeds a certain cutoff rate (e.g., the project's cost of capital), the project should be undertaken. For example, suppose an investment of $1,000 today generates $1,070 in a year. We can solve for the internal rate of return (*IRR*) or the interest rate that equates the two cash flows:

$$PV = \frac{FV}{(1 + IRR)}$$

$$\$1,000 = \frac{\$1,070}{(1 + IRR)}$$

$$(1 + IRR) = \frac{\$1,070}{\$1,000}$$

$$IRR = 0.07 = 7\%$$

In this very simple example, the internal rate of return on an investment of $1,000 today that generates a $1,070 payment in one year is 7 percent. If the cost of capital is 5 percent, then this investment offers a return in excess of its opportunity cost. The net present value of this investment is

$$NPV = -\$1,000 + \frac{\$1,070}{1.05}$$

$$= -\$1,000 + \$1,019.05$$

$$= \$19.05$$

Since the internal rate of return exceeds the cost of capital and the net present value is positive, both investment criteria give the same answer. The investment should be undertaken.

The advantage of IRR is that an investment project's return is stated as an interest rate. Some argue that it is easier to understand a project's return as 14 percent than to understand that it has a net present value of $628,623.

But the IRR and DCF (or net present value) methods do not always give consistent answers. Consider the following two *mutually exclusive* investments:

Investment 1: Invest $1,000 today and receive $1,070 in one year.
Investment 2: Invest $5,000 today and receive $5,300 in one year.

We know from the above that Investment 1 has an IRR of 7 percent and an NPV of $19.05. For Investment 2,

$$\$5,000 = \frac{\$5,300}{(1 + IRR)}$$

$$(1 + IRR) = \frac{\$5,300}{\$5,000}$$

$$IRR = 0.06 = 6\%$$

$$NPV = -\$5,000 + \frac{\$5,300}{1.05}$$

$$= -\$5,000 + \$5,047.62$$

$$= \$47.62$$

Which investment is better? The IRR criterion says Investment 1 is better because it has the higher IRR. But the net present value (DCF) criterion says Investment 2 is better because it has the higher NPV. Which is more valuable: a rate of return or cash? Net present value indicates how much cash in today's dollars an investment is worth, or the *magnitude* of the investment's return. The IRR indicates only the *relative* return on the investment. A 20 percent return on $1,000 ($20) is preferable to a 200 percent return on $1 ($2).

The fact that IRR and DCF can give inconsistent answers is not the only problem with the internal rate of return method. The IRR method also can give multiple rates for the same cash flows. Consider the following investment: $72,727 is received today in exchange for a promise to pay $170,909 next year; at the end of year 2, another $100,000 is received. To compute the IRR of this investment, solve the following equation:

$$PV = \$72,727 - \frac{\$170,909}{(1 + IRR)} + \frac{\$100,000}{(1 + IRR)^2} = 0$$

Let

$$x = \frac{1}{1 + IRR}$$

Then rewrite the formula as

$$PV = \$100,000x^2 - \$170,909x + \$72,727$$

Figure 3–3 plots the net present value of the preceding equation as a function of the discount rate. Notice that at discount rates of 10 percent and 25 percent, the net present value of the investment is zero; the curve crosses the *x*-axis in two places.[4] Thus, this particular investment has two discount rates that equate the investment cash inflows and outflows: 10 percent and 25 percent. Which is the right

---

[4]An exact numerical solution for the IRR can be found using the quadratic formula:

$$ax^2 + bx + c = 0$$

where

$$x = \frac{-b \pm \sqrt{b^2 - 4ac}}{2a}$$

$$a = \$100,000$$

$$b = -\$170,909$$

$$c = \$72,727$$

continued

FIGURE 3–3

The net present value of investment as a function of the internal rate of return (IRR). Investment: Receive $72,727 today and $100,000 in two years, but pay $170,909 next year.

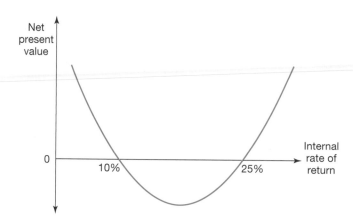

IRR for evaluating this project? As it turns out, if the cost of capital is less than 10 percent or greater than 25 percent, this project has a positive NPV and should be accepted. If the cost of capital is between 10 and 25 percent, the project has a negative NPV and should be rejected.

So far the examples have illustrated how internal rates of return are computed when there are two or three cash flows. With more than three cash flows, trial-and-error search is used to compute the IRR. Set up the problem as a standard discounted cash flow computation except you do not know the discount rate. Guess at a beginning discount rate (for example, 15 percent) and use this rate to compute the NPV. If the resulting NPV is positive, raise the discount rate (20 percent) and recompute the NPV. If the new NPV is now negative with the revised discount rate, try a lower discount rate (18 percent). Continue this trial-and-error procedure until the NPV of the project is very close to zero. The discount rate that causes the NPV to be zero is the IRR.

Figure 3–3 illustrates that in some cases the IRR method can yield multiple internal rates of return. In other cases, no internal rate of return can be computed even though the project has a positive NPV. These problems can make it difficult to implement the IRR method.

But perhaps the most serious problem with the internal rate of return method involves its reinvestment rate. The reinvestment rate is the interest rate used to compound cash flows received or paid over the life of the project. In the discounted cash flow method, each cash flow is discounted at the opportunity cost of

---

Substitute the values of a, b, and c into the quadratic formula and solve for x:

$$x = \frac{\$170,909 \pm \$10,913}{\$200,000}$$

or

$$x_1 = 0.90911 \text{ and}$$
$$x_2 = 0.79998$$

Since

$$x = \frac{1}{1 + IRR}$$

then

$$IRR = \frac{1}{x} - 1$$

and

$$IRR_1 = \frac{1}{0.90911} - 1 = 0.10 = 10\%$$

$$IRR_2 = \frac{1}{0.79998} - 1 = 0.25 = 25\%$$

TABLE 3–11   **Survey of Capital Budgeting Techniques Used in Practice**

	1988	*1980*	*1970*	*1965*
Expansion/New Operations				
Discounting	87%	71%	49%	31%
Accounting rate of return	4	10	25	33
Payback	4	5	16	19
Urgency	1	1	3	6
Other	4	13	7	11
Total	100%	100%	100%	100%
Replacement				
Discounting	60%	56%	35%	21%
Accounting rate of return	4	7	13	15
Payback	5	4	12	12
Urgency	23	23	32	40
Other	8	10	8	12
Total	100%	100%	100%	100%

SOURCE: Klammer, Koch, and Wilner (1991), Table 2.

capital. The implicit assumption in DCF is that intermediate cash flows are being reinvested at the market's rate of interest. If the market rate of interest is expected to be higher or lower in future years, nonconstant discount rates can be used. The IRR method assumes that all of the intermediate cash flows are being automatically reinvested at the project's constant internal rate of return. Thus, the IRR method implicitly assumes that the intermediate cash flows can be invested in a stock of projects identical to the one being considered and that the same internal rate of return can be achieved. If this is a one-time project, there are no projects like it in the future in which to reinvest the project's cash flows. Therefore, the internal rate of return method overstates a project's rate of return if other investments with the same reinvestment rate do not exist.

Based on the preceding discussions of internal rate of return, payback, and accounting rate of return, the theoretically correct method for comparing cash inflows and outflows that occur at different points of time is the discounted cash flow (net present value) method.

4. Methods Used in Practice

This section describes a survey of capital budgeting methods used in practice.[5] Five hundred large, publicly traded U.S. industrial firms were sampled and 100 usable responses were obtained. Many of these same firms had responded to similar surveys in the past, allowing the researchers to study how the frequency of use of a particular method changed over time. Table 3–11 reports the results of these surveys. Two types of capital projects were surveyed: expansion or new operations and replacement of existing assets. The following capital budgeting evaluation techniques were listed: discounting, accounting rate of return, payback, urgency, and other. *Discounting* includes both net present value and internal rate of return. *Urgency* means the managers accept a project if the consequences of rejecting it

---

[5] T Klammer, B Koch, and N Wilner, "Capital Budgeting Practices—A Survey of Corporate Use," *Journal of Management Accounting Research*, Fall 1991, pp. 113–30.

have an immediate adverse effect on the firm. For example, if the Environmental Protection Agency cites the firm for a pollution violation and warns that fines will begin accruing unless the firm complies, then the decision to install pollution abatement equipment is classified under "urgency."

The first thing to note from Table 3–11 is the relatively high usage of discounting methods. In 1988, in fact, 87 percent of expansion projects and 60 percent of replacement projects were evaluated using discounting methods. Urgency was the method used in 23 percent of the 1988 replacement projects. The second noteworthy fact is the dramatic increase, almost a tripling, in the use of discounting methods from 1965 to 1988. Some or all of the following reasons may account for this trend: Discounting methods are theoretically superior, they have been a mainstay in business school curriculums, and calculators and personal computers with programs that compute net present values and internal rates of return are now readily available. Finally, when interest rates are high, as they were in the 1980s, discounting methods produce fewer wrong decisions than do other methods.

Concept Questions		
	Q3–12	What are three problems with basing investment decisions on internal rate of return?
	Q3–13	Why is a dollar of initial investment in a building more valuable than a dollar of initial investment in land or working capital?
	Q3–14	Why are cash flows but not accounting earnings discounted in capital budgeting analyses?

F. Summary

Chapter 2 discussed opportunity cost as the benefit forgone from a specific decision. The benefit forgone by delaying a dollar today for a dollar in the future is the interest that could be earned on that dollar. A fundamental law of finance states that a dollar today is worth more than a dollar tomorrow. Making a decision that affects cash flows over time requires a mechanism for comparing current cash flows with future cash flows. This chapter demonstrates that discounted cash flow (net present value) analysis is the theoretically correct way to evaluate decisions that have multiperiod cash flow implications. Therefore, compound interest formulas are important mechanisms for comparing multiyear cash flow streams.

To simplify the presentation of concepts, the analysis initially assumed a zero-inflation, riskless world with no transactions costs. In such a world, a single risk-free rate of return would prevail; this riskless return is the opportunity cost of capital. All cash flow streams would be discounted at this riskless rate of return. If a cash flow stream's net present value is positive, then this stream should be accepted because its benefits exceed its opportunity cost.

But the world is not inflation-free and riskless. Therefore, the simple discounting mechanisms were modified in the following ways:

- Discount *expected* cash flows using the rate of return offered by an investment of comparable risk. The discount rate from an investment of comparable risk is the opportunity cost for bearing the risk in the project being evaluated.

- Discount *nominal* cash flows using nominal discount rates. Market interest rates are stated in nominal terms; they contain both a real interest rate and an inflation element. Therefore, in projecting cash flows, be sure to increase future cash flows by the amount of expected inflation when using nominal (market) discount rates. However, some future cash flows are contractually fixed, such as home or car loans or government and corporate bond repayments. These should not be increased for inflation.

Another very important consideration in valuing future cash flow streams is the effect of taxes, especially depreciation tax shields. Depreciation tax shields reduce future tax payments by the amount of the tax-allowed depreciation expense for initial capital investments. The tax-allowed depreciation methods should be used, not the depreciation methods used for external financial reports to shareholders.

It is important to realize that the value of the firm increases by the net present value of the investment project. For example, suppose the firm can invest $10 million in a project generating discounted cash flows of $13 million. This investment project with a net present value of $3 million increases the value of the firm by $3 million.

The final topic was alternative investment criteria: payback, accounting rate of return, and internal rate of return. Payback and accounting rate of return are simpler than net present value, but they can often lead to incorrect decisions because they do not incorporate the opportunity cost of capital. Internal rate of return is very similar to net present value, but it too has some problems. First, people want to maximize dollars in their pocket, not rates of return. Second, internal rate of return can yield multiple rates of return or no rates of return on projects, which is confusing and can lead to errors in accepting or rejecting projects. But the most serious problem is that IRR assumes there are other projects with the same rate of return as the project under consideration in which to invest the interim cash flows from the original project. This assumption can distort the project's profitability and lead to decision errors.

Managers can avoid all of these problems by following the net present value rule: Accept projects with positive expected nominal after-tax cash flows discounted using risk-adjusted nominal rates of return.

Self-Study Problems

Self-Study Problem 1: Avroland

Avroland is an amusement park in California. It currently uses a computer system to perform general accounting functions, including tracking ticket sales and payroll as well as employee and maintenance scheduling functions. The original system cost $300,000 when purchased two years ago. It has been depreciated for tax purposes using straight-line depreciation with an expected useful life of four more years and a zero salvage value. However, due to recent expansion, the computer system is no longer large enough. Upgrading the system to increase the storage capacity and processing speed to accommodate the extra data processing demands

If a farm has 100 acres, a total of $30,000 is to be repaid. No payments at all are to be made for the first five years. Then $1,000 is to be paid at the end of each year for 30 years to pay off the $30,000.

Is the farmer receiving a subsidy? Why? If the interest rate is 10 percent, what is the approximate capitalized value of the subsidy (if any)? Show all calculations.

P 3–18:   South American Mining

Suppose that a mining operation has spent $8 million developing an ore deposit in South America. Current expectations are that the deposit will require two years of development and will result in a realizable cash flow of $10 million at that time. The company engineer has discovered a new way of extracting the ore in only one year, but the procedure would necessitate an immediate outlay of $1 million.

Required:

a. Compute the IRR for the new outlay. (Note: There are two solutions! One is 787 percent. Find the other one.)

b. Based on your answer to (a), use the IRR criterion to determine if the company should make the outlay. Assume the market interest rate is 15 percent on one- and two-year bonds.

P 3–19:   House Mortgage

You have just purchased a house and have obtained a 30-year, $200,000 mortgage with an interest rate of 10 percent.

Required:

a. What is your annual payment?

b. Assuming you bought the house on January 1, what is the principal balance after one year? After 10 years?

c. After four years, mortgage rates drop to 8 percent for 30-year fixed-rate mortgages. You still have the old 10 percent mortgage you signed four years ago and you plan to live in the house for another five years. The total cost to refinance the mortgage is $3,000, including legal fees, closing costs, and points. The rate on a five-year CD is 6 percent. Should you refinance your mortgage or invest the $3,000 in a CD? The 6 percent CD rate is your opportunity cost of capital.

P 3–20:   Flower City Grocery

The Flower City Grocery is faced with the following capital budgeting decision. Its display freezer system must be repaired. The cost of this repair will be $1,000 and the system will be usable for another five years. Alternatively, the firm could purchase a new freezer system for $5,000 and sell the old one for $500. The new freezer system has more display space and will increase the profits attributable to frozen foods by 30 percent. Profits for that department were $5,000 in the last fiscal year. The company's cost of capital is 9 percent. Ignoring taxes, what should the firm do?

P 3–21:   Toledo Stadium

The city of Toledo has received a proposal to build a new multipurpose outdoor sports stadium. The expected life of the stadium is 20 years. It will be financed by a 20-year bond paying 8 percent interest annually. The stadium's primary tenant will be the city's Triple-A baseball team, the Red Hots. The plan's backers anticipate that the site also will be used for rock concerts and college and high school sports. The city does not pay any taxes. The city's cost of capital is 8 percent. The costs and estimated revenues are presented below.

Cash Outflows	
Construction costs	$12,000,000
General maintenance (including labor)	$250,000 per year
Cash Inflows	
Red Hots's lease payment	$650,000 per year
Concerts	$600,000 per year
College and high school sports	$50,000 per year

Required:

a. Should the city build the stadium? (Assume payments are made at the end of the year.)

b. The Red Hots have threatened to move out of Toledo if they do not get a new stadium. The city comptroller estimates that the move will cost the city $350,000 per year for 10 years in lost taxes, parking, and other fees. Should the city build the stadium now? State your reasoning.

P 3–22: PQR Coal Company

The PQR Coal Company has several conventional and strip mining operations. Recently, new legislation has made strip mining, which produces coal of high sulfur content, unprofitable, so those operations will be discontinued. Unfortunately, PQR purchased $1 million of earth-moving equipment for the strip mines two years ago and this equipment is not particularly well-suited to conventional mining.

Ms. Big, the president, suggests that since the equipment can be sold for $500,000, it should be scrapped. In her words, "I learned a long time ago that when you make mistakes it's best to admit them and take your lumps. By ignoring sunk costs you aren't tempted to throw good money after bad. The original value of the equipment is gone."

A new employee, Mr. Embeay, has suggested that the equipment should be adapted to the conventional operations. He argues, "We are about to spend $800,000 on some new conventional equipment. However, for a smaller expenditure of $250,000 we can adapt the old equipment to perform the same task. Of course, it will cost about $20,000 per year more to operate over the assumed 10-year lives of each alternative. But at an interest rate of 10 percent, the inclusion of the present value of $20,000 per year for 10 years and the initial $250,000 is still less than $800,000 for new equipment. While it's true that we should ignore sunk costs, at least this way we can cut our losses somewhat."

Who's correct? Why? What should PQR do? Why?

P 3–23: Student Loan Program

The National Direct Student Loan (NDSL) program allows college students to borrow funds from the federal government. The contract stipulates that the annual percentage rate of interest is 0 percent until 12 months after the student ceases his or her formal education (defined as at least half-time enrollment). At that time, interest becomes 4 percent per year. The maximum repayment period is

10 years. Assume that the student borrows $10,000 in the beginning of the first year of college and completes his or her education in four years. Loan repayments begin one year after graduation.

Required:

a. Assuming that the student elects the maximum payment period, what are the uniform annual loan repayments? (Assume all repayments occur at the end of the year.)

b. If the rate of interest on savings deposits is 6 percent, what is the minimum amount the student has to have in a bank account one year after graduation to make the loan payments calculated in (*a*)?

c. Are recipients of the NDSL program receiving a subsidy? If so, what is the present value of the subsidy when the loan is taken out?

P 3–24: Geico

Geico is considering expanding an existing plant on a piece of land it already owns. The land was purchased 15 years ago for $325,000 and its current market appraisal is $820,000. A capital budgeting analysis shows that the plant expansion has a net present value of $130,000. The expansion will cost $1.73 million, and the discounted cash inflows are $1.86 million. The expansion cost of $1.73 million does not include any provision for the cost of the land. The manager preparing the analysis argues that the historical cost of the land is a sunk cost, and, since the firm intends to keep the land whether or not the expansion project is accepted, the current appraisal value is irrelevant.

Should the land be included in the analysis? If so, how?

P 3–25: Cost-Saving Device

A proposed cost-saving device has an installed cost of $59,400. It will be depreciated for tax purposes on a straight-line basis over three years (zero salvage), although its actual life will be five years. The tax rate is 34 percent and the required rate of return on investments of this type is 10 percent.

What must be the pretax cost savings per year to favor the investment? Assume a zero salvage value for the device at the end of the five years.

Source: R. Watts.

P 3–26: Depreciation Tax Shield

An investment project involves the purchase of equipment at a cost of $100 million. For tax purposes, the equipment has a life of five years and will be depreciated on a straight-line basis. Inflation is expected to be 5 percent and the real interest rate is 5 percent. The tax rate is 40 percent.

What is the present value of the depreciation tax shield for the machine?

Source: R. Watts.

P 3–27: Housing Markets

A home identical to yours in your neighborhood sold last week for $150,000. Your home has a $120,000 assumable, 8 percent mortgage (compounded annually) with 30 years remaining. An assumable mortgage is one that the new buyer can assume at the old terms, continuing to make payments at the original interest rate. The house that recently sold did not have an assumable mortgage; that is, the buyers had to finance the house at the current market rate of interest, which is 15 percent. What price should you ask for your home?

A third home, again identical to the one that sold for $150,000, is also being offered for sale. The only difference between this third home and the $150,000 home is the property taxes. The $150,000 home's property taxes are $3,000 per year, while the third home's property taxes are $2,000 per year. The differences in the property taxes are due to vagaries in how the property tax assessors assessed the taxes when the homes were built. In this tax jurisdiction, once annual taxes are set, they are fixed for the life of the home. Assuming the market rate of interest is still 15 percent, what should be the price of this third home?

P 3–28: Mortgage Department

Suppose you are the manager of a mortgage department at a savings bank. Under the state usury law, the maximum interest rate allowed for mortgages is 10 percent compounded annually.

Required:

a. If you granted a $50,000 mortgage at the maximum rate for 30 years, what would be the equal annual payments?

b. If the current market internal rate on similar mortgages is 12 percent, how much money does the bank lose by issuing the mortgage described in (*a*)?

c. The usury law does not prohibit banks from charging points. One point means that the borrower pays 1 percent of the $50,000 loan back to the lending institution at the inception of the loan. That is, if one point is charged, the repayments are computed as in (*a*), but the borrower receives only $49,500. How many points must the bank charge to earn 12 percent on the 10 percent loan?

P 3–29: Electric Generator

A firm that purchases electric power from the local utility is considering the alternative of generating its own electricity. The current cost of obtaining the firm's electricity from its local utility is $42,000 per year. The cost of a steam generator (installed) is $140,000 and annual maintenance and fuel expenses are estimated at $22,000. The generator is expected to last for 10 years, at which time it will be worthless. The cost of capital is 10 percent and the firm pays no taxes.

Required:

a. Should the firm install the electric generator? Why or why not?

b. The engineers have calculated that with an additional investment of $40,000, the excess steam from the generator can be used to heat the firm's buildings. The current cost of heating the buildings with purchased steam is $21,000 per year. If the generator is to be used for heat as well as electricity, additional fuel and maintenance costs of $10,000 per year will be incurred. Should the firm invest in the generator and the heating system? Show all calculations.

P 3–30: Watson's Bay

Watson's Bay Co. is considering a contract to manufacture didgeridoos. Producing didgeridoos will require an investment in equipment of $100,000 and operating costs of $15 per didgeridoo produced. The contract calls for the company to deliver 3,000 didgeridoos a year for each of four years at a price of $30 per didgeridoo. At the end of four years the equipment is expected to be sold for $10,000. The equipment will be depreciated as follows:

Year	Depreciation Factor
1	0.3333
2	0.4445
3	0.1481
4	0.0741

The depreciation factor is applied to the full cost of the equipment (i.e., salvage value is not considered when depreciation is determined). The tax rate is 33 percent and the market rate of return for investments of this risk is 20 percent. Should Watson's Bay Co. take the contract to manufacture didgeridoos?

SOURCE: R. Watts.

P 3–31: Linda Lion Co.

The Linda Lion Co. has an investment opportunity that involves a current outlay of $1,000 for equipment. The investment will yield net cash inflows for four years. The net cash inflow at the end of the first year will be $400. Later years' cash inflows grow at the general rate of inflation. The equipment will be depreciated to zero on a straight-line basis, and there will be no salvage value at the end of four years. The tax rate is 40 percent, and the real rate of return required on investments of this risk is 10 percent.

Required:

    a. Should Linda Lion take the investment if the general rate of inflation is 5 percent?

    b. Is your answer different if the general rate of inflation is 15 percent? Explain why or why not.

SOURCE: R. Watts.

P 3–32: Dakota Mining

Dakota Mining is considering operating a strip mine, the cost of which is $4.4 million. Cash returns will be $27.7 million, all received at the end of the first year. The land must be returned to its natural state at a cost of $25 million, payable after two years. What is the project's internal rate of return?

Required:

    a. Should the project be accepted if the market rate of return is 8 percent?

    b. If the market rate of return is 14 percent?

Explain your reasoning.

SOURCE: R. Watts.

P 3–33: Overland Steel

Overland Steel operates a coal-burning steel mill in New York state. Changes in the state's air quality control laws will result in this mill's incurring a $1,000 per day fine (which will be paid at the end of the year) if it continues to operate. The mill currently operates every day of the year.

The mill was built 20 years ago at a cost of $15 million and has a remaining undepreciated book value of $3 million. The expected remaining useful life of the mill is 30 years.

The firm can sell the mill to a developer who wants to build a shopping center on the site. The buyer will pay $1 million for the site if the company demolishes the mill and prepares the site for the developer. Demolition and site preparation costs are estimated at $650,000.

Alternatively, the firm could install pollution control devices and other modernization devices at an initial outlay of $2.75 million. These improvements do not extend the useful life or salvage value of the plant, but they do reduce net operating costs by $25,000 per year in addition to eliminating the $1,000 per day fine. Currently, the net cash flows of operating the plant are $450,000 per year before any fines.

Assume

1. The market rate of interest is 14 percent.
2. There are no taxes.
3. The annual cash flow estimates given above are constant over the next 30 years.
4. At the end of the 30 years, the mill has an estimated salvage value of $2 million whether or not the pollution equipment has been installed.

Required:

Evaluate the various courses of action available to management and make a recommendation. Support your conclusions with neatly labeled calculations where possible.

P 3–34:   Black Feather Indian Nation

Black Feather Indian Nation is a 900 square-mile territory in North Dakota that has the legal right to sell gasoline without having to collect or pay state and federal taxes on it. Gasoline in North Dakota sells for $1.20 per gallon, which includes $0.50 of taxes. The reservation is in a rural part of North Dakota and is within 3–20 miles of five small cities, each with a population of between 20,000 and 60,000 people.

Black Feather Indian Nation asks your consulting firm to advise it about entering the retail gasoline business. It can buy gasoline at the wholesale delivered price of $0.65 per gallon. The Nation is considering building five stations on the perimeter of its territory to sell tax-free gasoline to non-Black Feather consumers for $0.70 per gallon. The total cost of the five stations, new road signs, and working capital is $4 million.

The consulting partner of your firm in charge of this assignment is preparing the firm's proposal to the Nation. He asks you to prepare a short memo outlining the analysis you think is necessary to answer this question: "Should the Black Feather Indian Nation invest $4 million and enter the retail gasoline business?"

Required:

Your memo should contain the following elements:

a. An outline of the general methodology (approach) you propose.

b. A detailed list of the data you propose to collect to implement the methodology suggested in (*a*). For each data item, describe how you plan to use the data.

P 3–35:   Scottie Corporation

a. Scottie Corporation has been offered a contract to produce 100 castings a year for five years at a price of $200 per casting. Producing the castings will require an investment in the plant of $35,000 and operating costs of $50 per casting produced. For tax purposes, depreciation will be on a straight-line basis over five years, with a full year's depreciation taken in both the beginning and ending years. The tax rate is 40 percent and the market's required rate of return on investments of this type is 10 percent. Assume cash flows except the initial investment occur at the end of the relevant years. Should Scottie accept the contract?

b. Suppose that the contract in (*a*) involves the use of some warehouse space that Scottie can neither use in the business nor rent out. Just before Scottie accepts or rejects the contract, Kampmeier Realty offers to rent the space for $3,000 a year for five years if Scottie renovates the space. The renovations would cost $10,000. The renovations also would be depreciated on a straight-line basis over five years, and the required return on the rental project is also 10 percent.

   (i) Does the rental offer change the net present value of the casting contract? Show all calculations.

   (ii) Is the annual rent for the space an opportunity cost of the casting order? Why or why not?

Source: R. Watts.

P 3–36:   Weil Inc.

Weil Inc. is examining a new project. Weil expects to sell 500 units per year at $20 net cash flow apiece for the next 10 years. In other words, the annual operating cash flow is projected to be $20 × 500 = $10,000 per year. The relevant discount rate is 20 percent, and the initial investment is $45,000.

Required:

a. What is the net present value?

b. Assume now that after the first year, the project can be dismantled and sold for $40,000. If the expected number of units sold in each of the remaining nine years is revised to equal the number of units sold in the first year, at what level of first-year sales would it make sense to abandon the project?

c. Now suppose that there are only two possible sales levels: 750 units and 250 units. If 750 units are sold in the first year, sales in years 2 through 10 will be 750 units. If 250 units are sold in the first year, sales in future years will be 250 units. If the two sales levels in year 1 are equally likely, what is the NPV of the project? Consider the possibility of abandonment (at a salvage value of $40,000) in answering the question.

d. What is the value of the option to abandon in (c)?

SOURCE: R. Watts.

P 3–37: Punch Press

A punch press currently in use has a book value of $1,800 and needs design modifications totaling $16,200, which would be capitalized at the present time and depreciated. The press can be sold for $2,600 now, but it could be used for three more years if the necessary modifications were made, at the end of which time it would have no salvage value.

A new punch press can be purchased at an invoice price of $26,900 to replace the present equipment. Freight-in will amount to $800, and installation will cost $500. These expenses will be depreciated, along with the invoice price, over the life of the machine. Because of the nature of the product manufactured, the new machine also will have an expected life of three years and will have no salvage value at the end of that time.

Using the old machine, operating profits before taxes and depreciation (revenues less costs) are $10,000 the first year and $8,000 in each of the next two years. Using the new machine, operating profits before taxes and depreciation (revenues less costs) are $18,000 in the first year and $14,000 in each of the next two years.

Corporate income taxes are 40 percent, and the same tax rate is applicable to gains or losses on sales of equipment. Both the present and proposed equipment would be depreciated on a straight-line basis over three years. Assuming the company wants to earn a 10 percent rate of return after taxes, should it modify the old machine or purchase the new one?

P 3–38: Apex Corporation

Two types of machine tools are available for performing a particular job in Apex Corporation. Tool A has an initial investment of $52,000, with operating costs of $26,000 per year, an economic service life of 12 years, and a salvage value of $6,000 at the end of that period. Tool B has an initial investment of $41,000, with operating costs of $32,000 per year, an economic service life of 12 years, and a salvage value of $4,500 at the end of that period. The tax rate is 40 percent, the depreciation method is sum of the years' digits, and the tax life for depreciation equals the economic service life.

Required:

a. Assuming the cost of capital is 8 percent, which tool should be purchased?

b. How would your answer to (*a*) change if double-declining-balance depreciation were used? (You may assume that you are allowed to switch to straight-line depreciation at any point during the asset's life.)

P 3–39: Eastern Educational Services

Eastern Educational Services is considering the following proposal to sell its teaching machine and purchase a new, improved machine. The following data are presented by the department head:

	Present Machine	New Machine
Purchase date	1/1/99	1/1/05
Original cost, installed	$100,000	$140,000
Salvage value	$20,000	$40,000
Useful life	10 years	4 years
Depreciation method	Straightline	Straightline
Present market value, net of disposal costs (book value $52,000)	$60,000	—
Property taxes and insurance	5% of original cost	5% of original cost
Annual maintenance costs and otherwise fixed costs (other than depreciation)	$10,000	$4,000
Variable production costs per unit	$5	$2

Additional information:

1. The company expects to produce 10,000 units a year selling at $10 each with either machine.
2. The company's tax rate is 40 percent on all income and expenses.
3. All annual income and expenses are assumed to occur at year-end.
4. The company's cost of capital is 12 percent after taxes.
5. The firm is located in a European country where capital gains are taxed at 40 percent. Capital gains are computed as the difference between the sales price and book value (original cost less accumulated depreciation).

Required:

a. Present a financial analysis in which you evaluate the proposal. A clear presentation is important.
b. Would you be more likely, less likely, or equally likely to recommend the purchase of the new machine given the following:
   (i) The company's discount rate is increased.
   (ii) The new machine can be depreciated by the double-declining-balance method.

TABLE 3-12   Present Value of $1 Received at the End of Period n at an Interest Rate of $i\%$

Periods	3%	4%	5%	6%	7%	8%	9%	10%	12%	14%	16%	18%	20%	25%	30%	35%	40%
1	0.971	0.962	0.952	0.943	0.935	0.926	0.917	0.909	0.893	0.877	0.862	0.847	0.833	0.800	0.769	0.741	0.714
2	0.943	0.925	0.907	0.890	0.873	0.857	0.842	0.826	0.797	0.769	0.743	0.718	0.694	0.640	0.592	0.549	0.510
3	0.915	0.889	0.864	0.840	0.816	0.794	0.772	0.751	0.712	0.675	0.641	0.609	0.579	0.512	0.455	0.406	0.364
4	0.888	0.855	0.823	0.792	0.763	0.735	0.708	0.683	0.636	0.592	0.552	0.516	0.482	0.410	0.350	0.301	0.260
5	0.863	0.822	0.784	0.747	0.713	0.681	0.650	0.621	0.567	0.519	0.476	0.437	0.402	0.328	0.269	0.223	0.186
6	0.837	0.790	0.746	0.705	0.666	0.630	0.596	0.564	0.507	0.456	0.410	0.370	0.335	0.262	0.207	0.165	0.133
7	0.813	0.760	0.711	0.655	0.623	0.583	0.547	0.513	0.452	0.400	0.354	0.314	0.279	0.210	0.159	0.122	0.095
8	0.789	0.731	0.677	0.627	0.582	0.540	0.502	0.467	0.404	0.351	0.305	0.266	0.233	0.168	0.123	0.091	0.068
9	0.766	0.703	0.645	0.592	0.544	0.500	0.460	0.424	0.361	0.308	0.263	0.225	0.194	0.134	0.094	0.067	0.048
10	0.744	0.676	0.614	0.558	0.508	0.463	0.422	0.386	0.322	0.270	0.227	0.191	0.162	0.107	0.073	0.050	0.035
11	0.722	0.650	0.585	0.527	0.475	0.429	0.388	0.350	0.287	0.237	0.195	0.162	0.135	0.086	0.056	0.037	0.025
12	0.701	0.625	0.557	0.497	0.444	0.397	0.356	0.319	0.257	0.208	0.168	0.137	0.112	0.069	0.043	0.027	0.018
13	0.681	0.601	0.530	0.469	0.415	0.368	0.326	0.290	0.229	0.182	0.145	0.116	0.093	0.055	0.033	0.020	0.013
14	0.661	0.577	0.505	0.442	0.388	0.340	0.299	0.263	0.205	0.160	0.125	0.099	0.078	0.044	0.025	0.015	0.009
15	0.642	0.555	0.481	0.417	0.362	0.315	0.275	0.239	0.183	0.140	0.108	0.084	0.065	0.035	0.020	0.011	0.006
16	0.623	0.534	0.458	0.394	0.339	0.292	0.252	0.218	0.163	0.123	0.093	0.071	0.054	0.028	0.015	0.008	0.005
17	0.605	0.513	0.436	0.371	0.317	0.270	0.231	0.198	0.146	0.108	0.080	0.060	0.045	0.023	0.012	0.006	0.003
18	0.587	0.494	0.416	0.350	0.296	0.250	0.212	0.180	0.130	0.095	0.069	0.051	0.038	0.018	0.009	0.005	0.002
19	0.570	0.475	0.396	0.331	0.277	0.232	0.194	0.164	0.116	0.083	0.060	0.043	0.031	0.014	0.007	0.003	0.002
20	0.554	0.456	0.377	0.312	0.258	0.215	0.178	0.149	0.104	0.073	0.051	0.037	0.026	0.012	0.005	0.002	0.001
21	0.538	0.439	0.359	0.294	0.242	0.199	0.164	0.135	0.093	0.064	0.044	0.031	0.022	0.009	0.004	0.002	0.001
22	0.522	0.422	0.342	0.278	0.226	0.184	0.150	0.123	0.083	0.056	0.038	0.026	0.018	0.007	0.003	0.001	0.001
23	0.507	0.406	0.326	0.262	0.211	0.170	0.138	0.112	0.074	0.049	0.033	0.022	0.015	0.006	0.002	0.001	0.000
24	0.492	0.390	0.310	0.247	0.197	0.158	0.126	0.102	0.066	0.043	0.028	0.019	0.013	0.005	0.002	0.001	0.000
25	0.478	0.375	0.295	0.233	0.184	0.146	0.116	0.092	0.059	0.038	0.024	0.016	0.010	0.004	0.001	0.001	0.000
26	0.464	0.361	0.281	0.220	0.172	0.135	0.106	0.084	0.053	0.033	0.021	0.014	0.009	0.003	0.001	0.000	0.000
27	0.450	0.347	0.268	0.207	0.161	0.125	0.098	0.076	0.047	0.029	0.018	0.011	0.007	0.002	0.001	0.000	0.000
28	0.437	0.333	0.255	0.196	0.150	0.116	0.090	0.069	0.042	0.026	0.016	0.010	0.006	0.002	0.001	0.000	0.000
29	0.424	0.321	0.243	0.185	0.141	0.107	0.082	0.063	0.037	0.022	0.014	0.008	0.005	0.002	0.000	0.000	0.000
30	0.412	0.308	0.231	0.174	0.131	0.099	0.075	0.057	0.033	0.020	0.012	0.007	0.004	0.001	0.000	0.000	0.000
35	0.355	0.253	0.181	0.130	0.094	0.068	0.049	0.036	0.019	0.010	0.006	0.003	0.002	0.000	0.000	0.000	0.000
40	0.307	0.208	0.142	0.097	0.067	0.046	0.032	0.022	0.011	0.005	0.003	0.001	0.001	0.000	0.000	0.000	0.000
60	0.170	0.095	0.054	0.030	0.017	0.010	0.006	0.003	0.001	0.000	0.000	0.000	0.000	0.000	0.000	0.000	0.000

TABLE 3–13 Present Value of an Annuity (A Stream of Dollars Received at the End of Each of the Next *n* Periods at an Interest Rate of *i*%)

Periods	3%	4%	5%	6%	7%	8%	9%	10%	12%	14%	16%	18%	20%	25%	30%	35%	40%
1	0.971	0.962	0.952	0.943	0.935	0.926	0.917	0.909	0.893	0.877	0.862	0.847	0.833	0.800	0.769	0.741	0.714
2	1.913	1.886	1.859	1.833	1.808	1.783	1.759	1.736	1.690	1.647	1.605	1.566	1.528	1.440	1.361	1.289	1.224
3	2.829	2.775	2.723	2.673	2.624	2.577	2.531	2.487	2.402	2.322	2.246	2.174	2.106	1.952	1.816	1.696	1.589
4	3.717	3.630	3.546	3.465	3.387	3.312	3.240	3.170	3.037	2.914	2.798	2.690	2.589	2.362	2.166	1.997	1.849
5	4.580	4.452	4.329	4.212	4.100	3.993	3.890	3.791	3.605	3.433	3.274	3.127	2.991	2.689	2.436	2.220	2.035
6	5.417	5.242	5.076	4.917	4.767	4.623	4.486	4.355	4.111	3.889	3.685	3.498	3.326	2.951	2.643	2.385	2.168
7	6.230	6.002	5.786	5.582	5.389	5.206	5.033	4.868	4.564	4.288	4.039	3.812	3.605	3.161	2.802	2.508	2.263
8	7.020	6.733	6.463	6.210	5.971	5.747	5.535	5.335	4.968	4.639	4.344	4.078	3.837	3.329	2.925	2.598	2.331
9	7.786	7.435	7.108	6.802	6.515	6.247	5.995	5.759	5.328	4.946	4.607	4.303	4.031	3.463	3.019	2.665	2.379
10	8.530	8.111	7.722	7.360	7.024	6.710	6.418	6.145	5.650	5.216	4.833	4.494	4.192	3.571	3.092	2.715	2.414
11	9.253	8.760	8.306	7.887	7.499	7.139	6.805	6.495	5.938	5.453	5.029	4.656	4.327	3.656	3.147	2.752	2.438
12	9.954	9.385	8.863	8.384	7.943	7.536	7.161	6.814	6.194	5.660	5.197	4.793	4.439	3.725	3.190	2.779	2.456
13	10.635	9.986	9.394	8.853	8.358	7.904	7.487	7.103	6.424	5.842	5.342	4.910	4.533	3.780	3.223	2.799	2.469
14	11.296	10.563	9.899	9.295	8.745	8.244	7.786	7.367	6.628	6.002	5.468	5.008	4.611	3.824	3.249	2.814	2.478
15	11.938	11.118	10.380	9.712	9.108	8.559	8.061	7.606	6.811	6.142	5.575	5.092	4.675	3.859	3.268	2.825	2.484
16	12.561	11.652	10.838	10.106	9.447	8.851	8.313	7.824	6.974	6.265	5.668	5.162	4.730	3.887	3.283	2.834	2.489
17	13.166	12.166	11.274	10.477	9.763	9.122	8.544	8.022	7.120	6.373	5.749	5.222	4.775	3.910	3.295	2.840	2.492
18	13.754	12.659	11.690	10.828	10.059	9.372	8.756	8.201	7.250	6.467	5.818	5.273	4.812	3.928	3.304	2.844	2.494
19	14.324	13.134	12.085	11.158	10.336	9.604	8.950	8.365	7.366	6.550	5.877	5.316	4.843	3.942	3.311	2.848	2.496
20	14.877	13.590	12.462	11.470	10.594	9.818	9.129	8.514	7.469	6.623	5.929	5.353	4.870	3.954	3.316	2.850	2.497
21	15.415	14.029	12.821	11.764	10.836	10.017	9.292	8.649	7.562	6.687	5.973	5.384	4.891	3.963	3.320	2.852	2.498
22	15.937	14.451	13.163	12.042	11.061	10.201	9.442	8.772	7.645	6.743	6.011	5.410	4.909	3.970	3.323	2.853	2.498
23	16.444	14.857	13.489	12.303	11.272	10.371	9.580	8.883	7.718	6.792	6.044	5.432	4.925	3.976	3.325	2.854	2.499
24	16.936	15.247	13.799	12.550	11.469	10.529	9.707	8.985	7.784	6.835	6.073	5.451	4.937	3.981	3.327	2.855	2.499
25	17.413	15.622	14.094	12.783	11.654	10.675	9.823	9.077	7.843	6.873	6.097	5.467	4.948	3.985	3.329	2.856	2.499
26	17.877	15.983	14.375	13.003	11.826	10.810	9.929	9.161	7.896	6.906	6.118	5.480	4.956	3.988	3.330	2.856	2.500
27	18.327	16.330	14.643	13.211	11.987	10.935	10.027	9.237	7.943	6.935	6.136	5.492	4.964	3.990	3.331	2.856	2.500
28	18.764	16.663	14.898	13.406	12.136	11.051	10.116	9.307	7.984	6.961	6.152	5.502	4.970	3.992	3.331	2.857	2.500
29	19.188	16.984	15.141	13.591	12.278	11.158	10.198	9.370	8.022	6.983	6.166	5.510	4.975	3.994	3.332	2.857	2.500
30	19.600	17.292	15.372	13.765	12.409	11.258	10.274	9.427	8.055	7.003	6.177	5.517	4.979	3.995	3.332	2.857	2.500
35	21.487	18.665	16.374	14.498	12.948	11.655	10.567	9.644	8.176	7.070	6.215	5.539	4.992	3.998	3.333	2.857	2.500
40	23.115	19.793	17.159	15.046	13.332	11.925	10.757	9.779	8.244	7.105	6.233	5.548	4.997	3.999	3.333	2.857	2.500
60	27.676	22.623	18.929	16.161	14.039	12.377	11.048	9.967	8.324	7.140	6.249	5.555	5.000	4.000	3.333	2.857	2.500
120	32.373	24.774	19.943	16.651	14.281	12.499	11.111	10.000	8.333	7.143	6.250	5.556	5.000	4.000	3.333	2.857	2.500
360	33.333	25.000	20.000	16.667	14.286	12.500	11.111	10.000	8.333	7.143	6.250	5.556	5.000	4.000	3.333	2.857	2.500

TABLE 3–14   Future Value of $1 Invested Today at i% Interest and Allowed to Compound for n Periods

Periods	3%	4%	5%	6%	7%	8%	9%	10%	12%	14%	16%	18%	20%	25%	30%	35%	40%
1	1.030	1.040	1.050	1.060	1.070	1.080	1.090	1.100	1.120	1.140	1.160	1.180	1.200	1.250	1.300	1.350	1.400
2	1.061	1.082	1.103	1.124	1.145	1.166	1.188	1.210	1.254	1.300	1.356	1.392	1.440	1.563	1.690	1.823	1.960
3	1.093	1.125	1.158	1.191	1.225	1.260	1.295	1.331	1.405	1.482	1.561	1.643	1.728	1.953	2.197	2.460	2.744
4	1.126	1.170	1.216	1.262	1.311	1.360	1.412	1.464	1.574	1.689	1.811	1.939	2.074	2.441	2.856	3.322	3.842
5	1.159	1.217	1.276	1.338	1.403	1.469	1.539	1.611	1.762	1.925	2.100	2.288	2.488	3.052	3.713	4.484	5.378
6	1.194	1.265	1.340	1.419	1.501	1.587	1.677	1.772	1.974	2.195	2.436	2.700	2.986	3.815	4.827	6.053	7.530
7	1.230	1.316	1.407	1.504	1.606	1.714	1.828	1.949	2.211	2.502	2.826	3.185	3.583	4.768	6.275	8.172	10.541
8	1.267	1.369	1.477	1.594	1.718	1.851	1.993	2.144	2.476	2.853	3.278	3.759	4.300	5.960	8.157	11.032	14.758
9	1.305	1.423	1.551	1.689	1.838	1.999	2.172	2.358	2.773	3.252	3.803	4.435	5.160	7.451	10.604	14.894	20.661
10	1.344	1.480	1.629	1.791	1.967	2.159	2.367	2.594	3.106	3.707	4.411	5.234	6.192	9.313	13.786	20.107	28.925
11	1.384	1.539	1.710	1.898	2.105	2.332	2.580	2.853	3.479	4.226	5.117	6.176	7.430	11.642	17.922	27.144	40.496
12	1.426	1.601	1.796	2.012	2.252	2.518	2.813	3.138	3.896	4.818	5.936	7.288	8.916	14.552	23.928	36.644	56.694
13	1.469	1.665	1.886	2.133	2.410	2.720	3.066	3.452	4.363	5.492	6.886	8.599	10.699	18.190	30.288	49.470	79.371
14	1.513	1.732	1.980	2.261	2.579	2.937	3.342	3.797	4.887	6.261	7.988	10.147	12.839	22.737	39.374	66.784	111.120
15	1.558	1.801	2.079	2.397	2.759	3.172	3.642	4.177	5.474	7.138	9.266	11.974	15.407	28.422	51.186	90.158	155.568
16	1.605	1.873	2.183	2.540	2.952	3.426	3.970	4.595	6.130	8.137	10.748	14.129	18.488	35.527	66.542	121.714	217.795
17	1.653	1.948	2.292	2.693	3.159	3.700	4.328	5.054	6.866	9.276	12.468	16.672	22.186	44.409	86.504	164.314	304.913
18	1.702	2.026	2.407	2.854	3.380	3.996	4.717	5.560	7.690	10.575	14.463	19.673	26.623	55.511	112.455	221.824	426.879
19	1.754	2.107	2.527	3.026	3.617	4.316	5.142	6.116	8.613	12.056	16.777	23.214	31.948	69.389	146.192	299.462	597.630
20	1.806	2.191	2.653	3.207	3.870	4.661	5.604	6.727	9.646	13.743	19.461	27.393	38.338	86.736	190.050	404.274	836.683
21	1.860	2.279	2.786	3.400	4.141	5.034	6.109	7.400	10.804	15.668	22.574	32.324	46.005	108.420	247.065	545.769	1,171.356
22	1.916	2.370	2.925	3.604	4.430	5.437	6.659	8.140	12.100	17.861	26.186	38.142	55.206	135.525	321.184	736.789	1,639.898
23	1.974	2.465	3.072	3.820	4.741	5.871	7.258	8.954	13.552	20.362	30.376	45.008	66.247	169.407	417.539	994.665	2,295.857
24	2.033	2.563	3.225	4.049	5.072	6.341	7.911	9.850	15.179	23.212	35.236	53.109	79.497	211.758	542.801	1,342.797	3,214.200
25	2.094	2.666	3.386	4.292	5.427	6.848	8.623	10.835	17.000	26.462	40.874	62.669	95.396	264.698	705.641	1,812.776	4,499.880
26	2.157	2.772	3.556	4.549	5.807	7.396	9.399	11.918	19.040	30.167	47.414	73.949	114.475	330.872	917.333	2,447.248	6,299.831
27	2.221	2.883	3.733	4.822	6.214	7.988	10.245	13.110	21.325	34.390	55.000	87.260	137.371	413.590	1,192.533	3,303.785	8,819.764
28	2.288	2.999	3.920	5.112	6.649	8.627	11.167	14.421	23.884	39.204	63.800	102.967	164.845	516.988	1,550.293	4,460.109	12,347.670
29	2.357	3.119	4.116	5.418	7.114	9.317	12.172	15.863	26.750	44.693	74.009	121.501	197.814	646.235	2,015.381	6,021.148	17,286.737
30	2.427	3.243	4.322	5.743	7.612	10.063	13.268	17.449	29.960	50.950	85.850	143.371	237.376	807.794	2,619.996	8,128.550	24,201.432
35	2.814	3.946	5.516	7.686	10.677	14.785	20.414	28.102	52.800	98.100	180.314	327.997	590.668	2,465.190	9,727.860	36,448.688	130,161.112
40	3.262	4.801	7.040	10.286	14.974	21.725	31.409	45.259	93.051	188.884	378.721	750.378	1,469.772	7,523.164	36,118.865	163,437.135	700,037.697

TABLE 3-15   Future Value of an Annuity (A Stream of n Dollars Invested Today at i% Interest and Allowed to Compound for n Periods)

Periods	3%	4%	5%	6%	7%	8%	9%	10%	12%	14%	16%	18%	20%	25%	30%	35%	40%
1	1.000	1.000	1.000	1.000	1.000	1.000	1.000	1.000	1.000	1.000	1.000	1.000	1.000	1.000	1.000	1.000	1.000
2	2.030	2.040	2.050	2.060	2.070	2.080	2.090	2.100	2.120	2.140	2.160	2.180	2.200	2.250	2.300	2.350	2.400
3	3.091	3.122	3.153	3.184	3.215	3.246	3.278	3.310	3.374	3.440	3.506	3.572	3.640	3.813	3.990	4.173	4.360
4	4.184	4.246	4.310	4.375	4.440	4.506	4.573	4.641	4.779	4.921	5.066	5.215	5.368	5.766	6.187	6.633	7.104
5	5.309	5.416	5.526	5.637	5.751	5.867	5.985	6.105	6.353	6.610	6.877	7.154	7.442	8.207	9.043	9.954	10.946
6	6.468	6.633	6.802	6.975	7.153	7.336	7.523	7.716	8.115	8.536	8.977	9.442	9.930	11.259	12.756	14.438	16.324
7	7.662	7.898	8.142	8.394	8.654	8.923	9.200	9.487	10.089	10.730	11.414	12.142	12.916	15.073	17.583	20.492	23.853
8	8.892	9.214	9.549	9.897	10.260	10.637	11.028	11.436	12.300	13.233	14.240	15.327	16.499	19.842	23.858	28.664	34.395
9	10.159	10.583	11.027	11.491	11.978	12.488	13.021	13.579	14.776	16.085	17.519	19.086	20.799	25.802	32.015	39.696	49.153
10	11.464	12.006	12.578	13.181	13.816	14.487	15.193	15.937	17.549	19.337	21.321	23.521	25.959	33.253	42.619	54.590	69.814
11	12.808	13.486	14.207	14.972	15.784	16.645	17.560	18.531	20.655	23.045	25.733	28.755	32.150	42.566	56.405	74.697	98.739
12	14.192	15.026	15.917	16.870	17.888	18.977	20.141	21.384	24.133	27.271	30.850	34.931	39.581	54.208	74.327	101.841	139.235
13	15.618	16.627	17.713	18.882	20.141	21.495	22.953	24.523	28.029	32.089	36.786	42.219	48.497	68.760	97.625	138.485	195.929
14	17.086	18.292	19.599	21.015	22.550	24.215	26.019	27.975	32.393	37.581	43.672	50.818	59.196	86.949	127.913	187.954	275.300
15	18.599	20.024	21.579	23.276	25.129	27.152	29.361	31.772	37.280	43.842	51.660	60.965	72.035	109.687	167.286	254.738	386.420
16	20.157	21.825	23.657	25.673	27.888	30.324	33.003	35.950	42.753	50.980	60.925	72.939	87.442	138.109	218.472	344.897	541.988
17	21.762	23.698	25.840	28.213	30.840	33.750	36.974	40.545	48.884	59.118	71.673	87.068	105.931	173.636	285.014	466.611	759.784
18	23.414	25.645	28.132	30.906	33.999	37.450	41.301	45.599	55.750	68.394	84.141	103.740	128.117	218.045	371.518	630.925	1,064.697
19	25.117	27.671	30.539	33.760	37.379	41.446	46.018	51.159	63.440	78.969	98.603	123.414	154.740	273.556	483.973	852.748	1,491.576
20	26.870	29.778	33.066	36.786	40.995	45.762	51.160	57.275	72.052	91.025	115.380	146.628	186.688	342.945	630.165	1,152.210	2,089.206
21	28.676	31.969	35.719	39.993	44.865	50.423	56.765	64.002	81.699	104.768	134.841	174.021	225.026	429.681	820.215	1,556.484	2,925.889
22	30.537	34.248	38.505	43.392	49.006	55.457	62.873	71.403	92.503	120.436	157.415	206.345	271.031	538.101	1,067.280	2,102.253	4,097.245
23	32.453	36.618	41.430	46.996	53.436	60.893	69.532	79.543	104.603	138.297	183.601	244.487	326.237	673.626	1,388.464	2,839.042	5,737.142
24	34.426	39.083	44.502	50.816	58.177	66.765	76.790	88.497	118.155	158.659	213.978	289.494	392.484	843.033	1,806.003	3,833.706	8,032.999
25	36.459	41.646	47.727	54.865	63.249	73.106	84.701	98.347	133.334	181.871	249.214	342.603	471.981	1,054.791	2,348.803	5,176.504	11,247.199
26	38.553	44.312	51.113	59.156	68.676	79.954	93.324	109.182	150.334	208.333	290.088	405.272	567.377	1,319.489	3,054.444	6,989.280	15,747.079
27	40.710	47.084	54.669	63.706	74.484	87.351	102.723	121.100	169.374	238.499	337.502	479.221	681.853	1,650.361	3,971.778	9,436.528	22,046.190
28	42.931	49.968	58.403	68.528	80.698	95.339	112.968	134.210	190.699	272.889	392.503	566.481	819.223	2,063.952	5,164.311	12,740.313	30,866.674
29	45.219	52.966	62.323	73.640	87.347	103.966	124.135	148.631	214.583	312.094	456.303	669.447	984.068	2,580.939	6,714.604	17,200.422	43,214.343
30	47.575	56.085	66.439	79.058	94.461	113.283	136.308	164.494	241.333	356.787	530.312	790.948	1,181.882	3,227.174	8,729.985	23,221.570	60,501.081
35	60.462	73.652	90.320	111.435	138.237	172.317	215.711	271.024	431.663	693.573	1,120.713	1,816.562	2,948.341	9,856.761	32,422.868	104,136.251	325,400.279
40	75.401	95.026	120.800	154.762	199.635	259.057	337.882	442.593	767.091	1,342.025	2,360.757	4,163.213	7,343.858	30,088.655	120,392.883	466,960.385	1,750,091.741

Chapter Four

Organizational Architecture

Chapter Outline

Chapter 2 described the important concept of opportunity cost and its relation to other costing terms. Understanding the nature of costs is critical to making decisions, including decisions about the design of cost systems. Internal accounting systems are used not only in decision making but also for influencing the behavior of individuals within organizations.

This chapter addresses the general problem of controlling behavior and describes how the firm's organizational architecture can influence behavior. Individuals working in firms will maximize their welfare, sometimes to the detriment of the organization's objectives, unless provided incentives to do otherwise. Accounting systems are often used to provide these incentives. For example, incentive bonuses are often based on accounting earnings. Section A presents some building blocks underlying the analysis. Section B describes how the firm's organizational architecture creates incentives for employees to maximize the organization's objectives. Sections C and D describe several ways accounting controls conflicts of interest inside the organization. The next chapter discusses two more accounting tools that are used to resolve organizational problems: responsibility accounting and transfer pricing.

A. Basic Building Blocks

Before describing the general problem of how to motivate and control behavior in organizations (the economics of organizations), this section first describes some underlying concepts:

1. Self-interested behavior, team production, and agency costs.
2. Decision rights and rights systems.
3. Role of knowledge and decision making.
4. Markets versus firms.
5. Influence costs.[1]

1. Self-Interested Behavior, Team Production, and Agency Costs

One of the fundamental tenets of economics is that individuals act in their self-interest to maximize their utility. Employees, managers, and owners are assumed to be rational, utility-maximizing people. Individuals have preferences for a wide variety of not only goods and services but also intangibles such as prestige, love, and respect, and they are willing to trade one thing they value for another. People evaluate the opportunities they face and select those that they perceive will make them better off. Moreover, individuals are not generally able to satisfy all their preferences. Limited resources (time, money, or skills) force people to make choices. When confronted with constraints or a limited set of alternatives, individuals will use their resourcefulness to relax the constraints and generate a larger opportunity set. For example, when the highway speed limit was reduced to 55 miles per hour, the CB radio and radar detector industries emerged to help resourceful, self-interested people circumvent the new law.[2]

---

[1] Much of the next two sections is based on M Jensen and W Meckling, "Specific and General Knowledge and Organizational Structure," *Contract Economics*, ed. L Werin and H Wijkander (Oxford: Blackwell, 1992), pp. 251–74. Also see J Brickley, C Smith, and J Zimmerman, *Managerial Economics and Organizational Architecture*, 3rd ed. (Boston: McGraw-Hill/Irwin, 2004).

[2] W Meckling, "Values and the Choice of the Model of the Individual in the Social Sciences," *Schweizerische Zeitschrift für Volkswirtschaft und Statistik*, December 1976.

Alternative Models of Behavior

Economists assume that individuals are self-interested and have preferences over a wide variety of things. This is not the only model of behavior. Psychologists offer another set of assumptions about how individuals make choices. Like economists, Maslow (1954) assumes that individuals are self-interested and have their own goals. He describes these goals in terms of satisfying different levels of needs. According to Maslow, an individual first seeks to satisfy physiological needs (food and shelter), followed by safety needs (security), love and belonging (a place within a group), esteem (self-respect), and self-actualization (creative expression).

No single model perfectly describes all behavior. Choosing among models involves trading off predictive ability and complexity. Usually, the more complex the model, the more it can explain. The advantage of using a very simple economic model as presented here is its ease of exposition. While it is not literally correct and ignores many important complicating issues, its simplicity allows the essential elements to be communicated easily.

SOURCE: A Maslow, *Motivation and Personality* (New York: Harper & Row, 1954). For an excellent review of alternative models of behavior, including a critique of the economic theories, see C Perrow, *Complex Organizations: A Critical Essay*, 3rd ed. (New York: Random House, 1986).

Individuals coalesce to form a firm because it can (1) presumably produce more goods or services collectively than individuals are capable of producing alone and (2) thus generate a larger opportunity set. Team production is the key reason that firms exist. Firms are contracting intermediaries. They facilitate exchanges among resource owners who voluntarily contract among themselves to benefit each party.[3] People choose to enter contracts because they are made better off by the exchange; there are gains to each party in contracting.

Team production implies that the productivity of any one resource owner is affected by the productivity of all the other team members, because output is a joint product of all the inputs. Suppose Sally Flax and Terry Green can produce more working together than working separately because they assist each other. Hence, Sally can increase Terry's output and vice versa. This interdependency has important implications for organizations and internal accounting. For one thing, measuring the productivity of one team member requires observing the inputs of all the other team members. However, inputs (such as effort) are typically difficult to observe. If two people are carrying a large, awkward box and it slips and falls, which employee do you blame? Did one of them let it go? Or did it slip out of one employee's hands because the other employee tripped?

In most cases, a resource owner's input cannot be directly observed. Hence, team members have incentives to shirk from their responsibilities. If it is difficult to observe Sally's effort, she has incentives when working with Terry to shirk. She can always blame either Terry or random uncontrollable events such as bad weather or missing parts as the reason for low joint output. If Sally and Terry are paid based on their joint output, each still has an incentive to shirk because each bears only half the cost of the reduced output. As the team size is increased, the

---

[3] C Barnard, *The Functions of the Executive* (Cambridge, MA: Harvard University Press, 1938), p. viii defines organizations as "a system of consciously coordinated activities or forces of two or more persons." See also M Jensen and W Meckling, "Theory of the Firm: Managerial Behavior, Agency Costs and Ownership Structure," *Journal of Financial Economics* 3 (1976), pp. 305–60.

Agency Problems at RJR–Nabisco	"It was no lie. RJR executives lived like kings. The top 31 executives were paid a total of $14.2 million, or an average of $458,000. Some of them became legends at the Waverly for dispensing $100 tips to the shoeshine girl. Johnson's two maids were on the company payroll. No expense was spared decorating the new headquarters, highlighted by the top-floor digs of the top executives. It was literally, the sweet life. A candy cart came around twice a day dropping off bowls of bonbons at each floor's reception areas. Not Baby Ruths but fine French confections. The minimum perks for even lowly middle managers was one club membership and one company car, worth $28,000. The maximum, as nearly as anyone could tell, was Johnson's two dozen club memberships and John Martin's $75,000 Mercedes."

SOURCE: B Burrough and J Helyar, *Barbarians at the Gate* (New York: Harper Perennial, 1990).

incentive to shirk becomes greater because the reduced output is spread over more team members. The incentive to shirk in team production is called the *free-rider problem*. Teams try to overcome the free-rider problem through the use of team loyalty—pressure from other team members—and through monitoring. Team production clearly has advantages, but it also causes a variety of organizational problems, in particular the free-rider problem.[4]

Another organizational problem arises when principals hire agents to perform tasks for them. For example, the chief executive officer (CEO) is the agent of the board of directors, who are in turn the elected agents of the shareholders. Vice presidents of the firm are agents of the president, managers are agents of vice presidents, and employees are agents of supervisors. Most employees in a chain of command are both principals to those who report to them and agents to those to whom they report. These principal-agent relationships pervade all organizations: profit and nonprofit firms, the military and other government units, and churches.

When hired to do a task, agents maximize their utility, which may or may not maximize the principal's utility. Agents' pursuit of their self-interest instead of the principal's is called the *principal-agent problem* or simply the *agency problem*.[5] The extreme example of an agency problem is employee theft of firm property. If undetected, such theft benefits the agent at the expense of the principal. The agent would prefer to see firm resources directed into activities that improve the agent's welfare even if these expenditures do not benefit the principal to the same degree. For example, agents prefer excessive perquisites such as gourmet company-provided lunches and on-the-job leisure. Differences among employees' risk tolerances, working horizons, and desired levels of job perks generate **agency costs**—the decline in firm value that results from agents pursuing their own interests to the detriment of the principal's interest. Agency costs can also arise when agents seek larger organizations to manage (empire building) for the sole purpose of increasing either their job security or their pay. (Many firms base pay on the number of employees reporting to the manager.)

---

[4] A Alchian and H Demsetz, "Production, Information Costs, and Economic Organization," *American Economic Review* 62 (1972), pp. 777–95.

[5] Jensen and Meckling (1976); H Simon, "A Formal Theory of the Employment Relationship," *Econometrica* 19 (1951), pp. 293–305; S Ross, "The Economic Theory of Agency: The Principal's Problem," *American Economic Review* 63 (1973), pp. 134–39; and O Williamson, *The Economic Institutions of Capitalism* (New York: The Free Press, 1985).

Agency Problems and the Failure of Barings Bank

Barings Bank of London, founded in 1762, was a gilt-edged institution that numbered Britain's Royal Family among its investors. In early 1995, the bank lost about $1.4 billion. One of its star traders, Nick Leeson in the Singapore office, was supposed to be arbitraging security prices between the Osaka Stock Exchange and the Singapore International Monetary Exchange (SIMEX).* In arbitraging, Leeson should have locked in a virtually riskless profit by selling the security on the exchange with the higher price while simultaneously buying it on the exchange with the lower price. There was supposed to be no net risk exposure to price changes.

However, Leeson was speculating. In effect, he bet that the security price would rise. But it fell, and Barings, Britain's oldest merchant bank, was sold to ING (the large Dutch financial institution) for £1. Barings's owners had lost their entire investment. Leeson was arrested and sentenced to six years in a Singapore jail for falsifying records and violating security laws.

How could this have happened? The bank's compensation system encouraged Leeson to speculate while providing senior managers with limited incentives to exercise tight control over their star trader. Barings traditionally paid out approximately 50 percent of gross earnings as annual bonuses. A system whereby managers participate in annual profits—but not losses—can encourage excessive risk taking. This incentive can be most pronounced when a small bet loses and the employee tries to make it up by doubling the bet. If this second bet also loses, there can be a strong incentive to double up again and "go for broke."

It appears that Leeson circumvented the bank's internal controls. The Singapore branch was small and Leeson had effective authority over trading as well as the bank's back office systems (bookkeeping, clearing, and settlement). He used that power to conceal losses and disguise the true nature of his activities—and thus he was able to "cook the books."

*The specific securities Leeson traded were futures contracts on the Nikkei 225—the main Japanese stock market index.

SOURCE: M Branchli, N Bray, and M Sesit, "Barings PLC Officials May Have Been Aware of Trading Position," *The Wall Street Journal*, March 6, 1995, p. 1.

In general, agency problems arise because of information asymmetries. The principal possesses less information than the agent. In the classic principal-agent problem, the principal hires the agent to perform some task, such as managing the principal's investment portfolio. If the agent works hard, the portfolio grows more than if the agent shirks. But the principal cannot observe how hard the agent is working (information asymmetry). Moreover, the investment portfolio's performance depends not just on how hard the agent works, but also on random events, such as general market movements or embezzlement by managers in a company in the investment portfolio. If the principal were able to observe the agent's effort, then a simple contract that pays the agent for effort expended could be used to force the agent to work hard. But since the agent's effort is not observable by the principal, the principal must contract on some other basis. One such contract could pay the agent a fraction of the portfolio's growth. But since part of the portfolio's performance depends on random factors, the agent could work hard, but adverse random events outside the agent's control could negate that hard work. While this contract induces hard work, it also imposes risk on the agent for which

TABLE 4–1   Example of the Horizon Problem

Year	Outlay	Cost Savings	Effect on Henry Metz's Bonus Compensation
1	$100,000	—	−$5,000
2	100,000	—	− 5,000
3	0	$150,000	+ 7,500
4	0	150,000	0
5	0	150,000	0
6	0	150,000	0

he or she must be compensated. Hence, most agency problems involve balancing stronger incentives for the agent to work hard against the higher risk premium required by the agent to compensate for the additional risk involved.

Consider another example of an agency problem, that of senior executives paid a fixed salary. Because executives have less incentive to maximize shareholder value than if they owned the entire firm themselves, incentive compensation plans are introduced to tie the executive's welfare more closely to shareholder welfare. The agent may have a lower tolerance for risk than the principal and therefore will choose more conservative actions. Principal–agent problems can also arise because most supervisors find it personally unpleasant to discipline or dismiss poorly performing subordinates. Instead of taking these unpopular actions, supervisors allow underperforming subordinates to remain in their positions, which reduces firm value. The difference between the value of the firm with and without the poorly performing subordinate is the agency cost imposed on the owners of the firm by the shirking supervisor.

If the agent expects to leave the organization before the principal, the agent will tend to focus on short-run actions. This leads to the *horizon problem:* Managers expecting to leave the firm in the near future place less weight than the principal on those consequences that may occur after they leave. As an example of the horizon problem, consider the case of a divisional manager, Henry Metz, who expects to retire in three years. Henry is paid a fixed salary plus 5 percent of his division's profits. To simplify the example, make the unrealistic assumption that Henry cares only about cash compensation. He can spend $100,000 on process improvements this year and next year that will yield $150,000 of cost savings for each of the following four years. Table 4–1 illustrates the cash flows.

The process improvements are clearly profitable, so they should be accepted.[6] But Henry, who has a three-year horizon, rejects the project because it reduces his total bonus. He bears much of the cost while his successor receives most of the benefits in years 4, 5, and 6. Nonpecuniary interests of the manager, such as peer pressure, tend to reduce the horizon problem. However, the basic point remains: Agents facing a known departure date place less weight on events that occur after they leave than on events that occur while they are still there; the long-term consequences of current decisions will matter far less to them than the short-term consequences.

---

[6] These process improvements have a positive net present value unless the discount rate is greater than 45 percent. Hence, under most market discount rates, they are profitable.

Agency Problems with Corporate Jet Pilots	Corporate jets often have to refuel on intercontinental flights, usually in Kansas or Nebraska. A typical refueling costs $1,800. Refuelers at the same airport compete by offering pilots frozen steaks, wine, or top-of-the-line golf gear. These freebies are usually offered only if the pilot forgoes discounts on fuel, and they are almost always given in a covert manner—so that the corporation owning the plane never knows why the pilot has chosen that particular refueler. Suppose the pilot chooses a refueler who charges $150 more than the least-cost option because the pilot gets $80 worth of gifts. This wealth transfer from the shareholders owning the jet to the pilot is an example of an agency problem. SOURCE: S McCartney, "We'll Be Landing So the Crew Can Grab a Steak," *The Wall Street Journal*, September 8, 1998, p. A1.

Adverse Selection and Moral Hazard Problems	Two types of agency problems have been given specific names. *Adverse selection* refers to the tendency of individuals with private information about something that benefits them to make offers that are detrimental to the trading partner. For example, individuals have more information regarding their health than do life insurance companies. If unconstrained, people who buy life insurance are likely to have more severe health problems than the average person assumed by the insurance company when setting its rates. After the insurance company sets its rates based on an average person, an adverse group of individuals will buy the insurance and the insurance company will lose money. To protect itself from adverse selection, insurance companies require medical exams and medical histories to exclude overly ill patients or to charge higher prices to riskier patients (e.g., smokers).
	Moral hazard problems arise when an individual has an incentive to deviate from the contract and take self-interested actions because the other party has insufficient information to know if the contract was honored. An example of a moral hazard problem often occurs in automobile accident claims. The insured may claim that the door was dented in the accident when in fact it was already dented and the accident only damaged the bumper. To reduce moral hazard problems a variety of solutions exist, including inspections and monitoring.

To reduce agency costs such as employee theft and the free-rider and horizon problems, firms incur costs.[7] These costs include hiring security guards to prevent theft, hiring supervisors to monitor employees, installing accounting and reporting systems to measure and reward output, and paying legal fees to enforce compliance with contracts. However, as long as it is costly to monitor agents' actions, some divergence between agents and principals will remain. It is usually not cost-efficient to eliminate all divergent acts.

Agency costs are also limited by the existence of a job market for managers, the market for corporate control, and competition from other firms. The job market for managers causes managers to limit their divergent actions to avoid being

---

[7] P Milgram and J Roberts, *Economics, Organizations & Management* (Englewood Cliffs, NJ: Prentice Hall, 1992); and Jensen and Meckling (1976).

| Assigning Decision Rights: The Zebra Team | Eastman Kodak manufactures a variety of black-and-white film products, such as X-ray film. Annual sales of these products are about $2 billion. Prior to 1989, Kodak used a very centralized decision-making process for manufacturing film. Manufacturing was divided into functions such as emulsion mixing (used for coating film), film coating, and film finishing.

In the late 1980s, poor performance motivated Kodak to reorganize the manufacturing of black-and-white film. Primary responsibility for the entire process was decentralized to a team of managers. A key feature of the new organization was the use of self-directed work teams. The results of this reorganization were impressive. The "Zebra Team" cut production costs by some $40 million and inventory by about $50 million.

A good example of employee empowerment is "Cholach's Chariot." Accumax is a film product used in manufacturing circuit boards. Any dust on the film translates into a broken wire on a circuit board and thus makes the film worthless. Accumax is finished and slit into final products in an ultraclean room. Unfortunately, the old supply cart used to transport the film to storage was not dust-free and thus much film was wasted. Bob Cholach was a slitter operator with specific knowledge about how the problem could be fixed by using an airtight transport cab. Through his efforts, such a cab was designed and built, resulting in significant benefits to the company. Comparing the new empowered work environment with the old system, Cholach noted, "In the old days I'd have been told, 'That's not your job so don't worry about it.' But here I was given the power and finances to design and build something that would help my teammates. It wasn't like dropping a piece of paper into a suggestion box, either. They let me run with it from start to finish."

SOURCE: S Frangos with S Bennett, *Team Zebra* (Essex Junction, VT: Oliver Wight Publications, 1993). |

replaced by other (outside) managers.[8] Replacements will occur if the board of directors has access to these job markets and incentives to replace the managers. If the board fails to reduce the firm's agency costs, the firm's stock price declines. Low stock prices encourage takeovers. The market for corporate control will then limit the agency costs of existing management via unfriendly takeovers. Finally, if both the job and corporate control markets fail, other firms in the same product market will supply better products at lower prices and eventually force firms with high agency costs out of business. However, to the extent that there are transactions costs in all these markets, it will not be cost-beneficial to drive agency costs to zero. For example, if the transaction costs of a corporate takeover, including legal, accounting, and underwriting fees, are 3 percent of the value of the firm, then it will not pay outsiders to acquire the firm if the magnitude of the agency costs they hope to eliminate are less than 3 percent. Thus, this level of agency costs will persist.

Agents maximize their utility, not the principal's. This problem is commonly referred to as **goal incongruence,** which simply means that individual agents have different goals from their principal. The term is misleading, because it suggests

[8] E Fama, "Agency Problems and the Theory of the Firm," *Journal of Political Economy*, April 1980, pp. 288–307.

<table>
<tr>
<td>

Use of Specific Knowledge at Apple Computer

</td>
<td>

Apple's PowerBook was among the first portable Macs. It had so many bells and whistles that it weighed 17 pounds. It did not do well in the market. In 1990, Apple began completely reworking the design of the computer from the consumer's viewpoint. The entire product-development team of software designers, industrial engineers, marketing people, and industrial designers was sent into the field to observe potential customers using other products. The team discovered that people used laptops on airplanes, in cars, and at home in bed. People wanted mobile computers, not just small computers. In response, Apple redesigned the PowerBook as a new product that was easy to use and distinctive. Sales improved.

The knowledge of what customers really wanted in a laptop computer was acquired by a team of employees who interacted closely with customers. The team members also had important knowledge that allowed them to take this information and use it to design a marketable product. Finally, they had the authority to modify the product based on their findings. It is less likely that this specific knowledge would have been incorporated in product design in a large centrally planned firm—in which a central office is in charge of making literally thousands of decisions.

SOURCE: "Hot Products, Smart Design Is the Common Thread," *BusinessWeek*, June 7, 1993, pp. 54–57.

</td>
</tr>
</table>

that the firm can secure congruence by changing personal preferences (i.e., utility functions) so that all individuals in the organization adopt the same goal. However, self-interested individuals' preferences are not easily altered. The firm can reduce the agency problem, if not goal incongruence, by structuring agents' incentives so that when agents maximize their utility (primarily incentive-based compensation), the principal's utility (or wealth) is also maximized. In other words, the agents' and principals' goals become congruent through the agents' incentive scheme, not through a change in the agents' underlying preferences.

2. Decision Rights and Rights Systems

All economic resources or assets are bundles of decision rights with respect to how they can or cannot be used. For example, ownership of a car includes a bundle of decision rights over its use, although not unrestricted use. The car owner can drive, sell, paint, or even destroy the car, but it is illegal to drive the car over the speed limit. The police powers of the state enforce private decision rights over assets; the threat of legal sanctions is brought to bear against someone interfering with another's rights. If someone prevents you from driving your car by stealing it, the thief can be imprisoned. Our system of private property rights, including the courts and the police, enforces and limits individual decision rights.

Management is the process by which the decision rights over the firm's assets are assigned to various people within the firm who are then held accountable for the results. If an individual is given decision-making authority over some decision (such as setting the price of a particular product), we say that person has the *decision right* for that product's price. Throughout the remainder of the book, we describe the importance of assigning decision rights to various individuals within the organization and the role of accounting in the assignment process. Who or what group of individuals has the decision rights to set the price, hire employees, accept a new order, or sell an asset? A key decision for many managers is whether to retain the right to make a particular decision or delegate the right to someone else. The question of whether the organization is centrally managed or decentralized is an issue of decision right assignment. **Employee empowerment** is a term that means assigning more decision rights to employees (i.e., decentralization). Accounting-based budgets assign decision rights to make expenditures to specific employees.

3. Role of Knowledge and Decision Making

Although they are rational and self-interested, individuals have limited capacities to gather and process knowledge. Since information (knowledge) is costly to acquire, store, and process, individual decision-making capacities are limited. Bill Gates cannot make all of the decisions at Microsoft because he lacks the time to acquire the knowledge necessary for decision making. The process of generating the knowledge necessary to make a decision and then transferring that knowledge within the firm drives the assignment of decision rights.[9]

Because knowledge is valuable in decision making, knowledge and decision making are generally linked; the right to make the decision and the knowledge to make it usually reside within the same person. In fact, a key organizational architecture issue is *whether and how to link knowledge and decision rights*. Some knowledge, such as price and quantity, is easy (inexpensive) to transfer. In these cases, the knowledge is transferred to the person with the right to make the decision. Other knowledge is more difficult and hence costlier to transfer. Technical knowledge, such as how to design a computer chip, is costly to transfer. Knowledge that changes quickly, such as whether a machine is idle for the next hour, is costly to transfer in time to be useful; therefore, the decision right to schedule the machine is transferred to the person with the knowledge.

Ideally, knowledge and decision rights are linked, but they do not always reside with the same person. Suppose it is very difficult to transfer knowledge and very difficult to monitor the person with the knowledge. Moreover, suppose large agency costs arise if the person with the knowledge has the decision rights. Firm value might be higher if another manager with less knowledge makes the decision. This will occur if the costs from the inferior decisions made by the manager with less knowledge are smaller than the agency costs that result from giving the decision rights to the person with the better knowledge. For example, in many firms, salespeople do not have the decision right to negotiate prices directly with the customer, even though they have specialized knowledge of the customer's demand curve. Pricing is determined centrally by managers with less information, perhaps to reduce the likelihood that the salesperson will offer a low price and receive a kickback from the customer.

Within all organizations, decision rights and knowledge must be linked. As we will see, accounting systems, especially budgets (Chapter 6) and standard costs (Chapter 12), are important devices for transferring knowledge to the individuals with the decision rights or giving the decision rights to individuals with the knowledge.

4. Markets versus Firms

Production occurs either within a firm or across markets. For example, some computer software is produced by computer hardware companies and bundled with the computer, while other software is produced and sold separately. As another example, stereos can be purchased as entire systems. Here, the manufacturer designs,

---

[9] M Jensen and W Meckling, *Contract Economics*, ed. L Werin and H Wijkander (Oxford: Blackwell, 1992), pp. 251–74.

Skoda	The large Czech automaker, Skoda, has some of its suppliers actually located physically inside Skoda's assembly plants. To improve quality and costs, an independent supplier that provides dashboards is in the Skoda assembly plant. While this is an example of two separate firms producing across markets, the two firms are closely linked physically.

SOURCE: J Perlez, "Skoda Gives Its Suppliers a Place in the Auto Plant," *The New York Times* (November 19, 1994), p. 41.

assembles, and ships complete units composed of a tuner-amplifier, CD player, speakers, and tape deck. Alternatively, the consumer can purchase the components separately and assemble a complete system.

Ronald Coase, the 1991 Nobel Prize winner in economics, argued that firms lower certain transactions costs below what it would cost to acquire equivalent goods or services in a series of market transactions.[10] He conjectured that firms exist when they have lower costs than markets. Team production, discussed earlier, is one way firms can have lower costs than markets. When a firm can substitute one transaction that occurs inside the firm for a series of external market contracts, total contracting costs usually are lower.

The longer the term of a contract, the more difficult and costly it is to negotiate and to specify the respective parties' tasks. Firms eliminate a series of short-term market contracts and replace them with a single long-term contract. For example, if the firm has a long-term project to develop a sophisticated piece of computer software, it is likely that such software will be developed inside the firm as opposed to being purchased from an outside programming firm.

The costs of acquiring knowledge and enforcing contracts drive some production to occur within firms and other production to occur in markets. If knowledge were costless to acquire and process and there were no transactions costs, there would be no multiperson firms. To purchase an automobile, the consumer would enter into thousands of separate contracts with individual assemblers. If knowledge were free, these contracts would be costless. But knowledge is not free; our ability to acquire and process it is limited. Firms emerge because they economize on repetitive contracting. For example, firms can hire and monitor employees more cheaply (including transactions costs) than individual consumers buying small amounts of labor services in markets.

Coase's analysis has led to an important proposition in economics. Firms that survive in competition must have a comparative advantage in constructing contracts for internal production. Surviving firms have lower transactions costs than the market. This is an application of economic Darwinism (discussed in Chapter 1).

Nonetheless, markets perform certain functions far better than firms. Ultimately, markets exist because of the right to transfer ownership of an asset and receive the proceeds. As noted earlier, individuals or firms have decision rights with respect to resources that they own, including the right to use those resources as they see fit (within the limits of the law), the right to sell the resources, and the right to

---

[10] R Coase, "The Nature of the Firm," *Economica* 4 (1937), pp. 386–405. Also, see R Watts, "Accounting Choice Theory and Market-Based Research in Accounting," *British Accounting Journal* 24 (1992), pp. 242–46 for a summary of the arguments for the types of costs that are lowered by firms. These arguments include economies of scale in contracting, team production and monitoring, postcontractual opportunism, and knowledge costs.

Firms versus Markets When Markets Ruled

Economic activities are organized in firms when the cost is lower than using markets and vice versa. Today much of the economic activity in the world is conducted within firms. In fact, it is hard to envision a world where large firms do not play an important role in the production and distribution of products. The importance of firms, however, is a relatively recent phenomenon. Indeed, prior to the middle of the nineteenth century, there were almost no large firms. Most production was conducted by small owner-managed operations. The activities of these operations were coordinated almost entirely through market transactions and prices. To quote Alfred Chandler in describing business organization before 1950,

> The traditional American business was a single-unit business enterprise. In such an enterprise an individual or a small number of owners operated a shop, factory, bank, or transportation line out of a single office. Normally, this type of firm handled only a single economic function, dealt in a single product line, and operated in one geographic area. Before the rise of the modern firm, the activities of one of these small personally owned and managed enterprises were coordinated and monitored by market and price mechanisms.

The large firm became feasible only with the development of improved energy sources, transportation, and communications. In particular, coal provided a source of energy that made it possible for the factory to replace artisans and small mill owners, while railroads enabled firms to ship production in large quantities to newly emerging urban centers. The telegraph allowed firms to coordinate activities of employees over larger geographic areas. These developments made it less expensive to coordinate production and distribution using administrative controls, rather than relying on numerous market transactions among numerous small firms.

SOURCE: A Chandler, *The Visible Hand: The Managerial Revolution in American Business* (Cambridge, MA: Harvard University Press, 1977).

Markets versus Firms: Taxicabs

To illustrate how markets help to control human behavior, consider the example of privately owned and operated cabs versus cabs owned by a taxi company and driven by different-salaried drivers. Which cabs will have a higher market value after being driven 50,000 miles? The owners of privately owned cabs have a greater incentive to maintain their cabs than the drivers of company-owned cabs. The resale price of each cab reflects wear and tear and maintenance. Since private cab drivers, as the sole drivers, bear all the financial consequences of their actions, they have an incentive to provide the correct amount of maintenance and generally drive the cab in such a way as to maximize the market value of the cab at resale. Drivers for the taxi company do not bear the consequences of any abusive driving and/or poor maintenance, unless the taxi company implements costly procedures to monitor the condition of the cabs after each driver's shift. To provide incentives for the cabbies not to damage the cabs, the taxi company must install monitoring devices, but it is prohibitively costly to detect all abuse (such as transmission damage).

the sales proceeds. Markets discipline those who have the resources to use them in their highest-valued way. If owners lower the value of their assets by not properly maintaining them, markets punish them by lowering the resale price. Thus, markets not only measure decision makers' performance but also reward or punish that behavior. In fact, markets do three things automatically that organizations (firms) can accomplish only through elaborate administrative devices: (1) measure performance, (2) reward performance, and (3) partition rights to their highest-valued use. When Adam Smith described the invisible hand of the market and how the market allocates resources to their most highly valued use, he was describing how the market influences behavior and assigns decision rights.[11]

Because an asset's current price reflects the future cash flows associated with it, decision rights over how assets will be used in the future tend to be assigned to those who value them the highest. In markets, decision rights are linked with knowledge. Individuals or firms with "better" knowledge in using the asset will be willing to pay a higher price for the asset, thereby linking knowledge with decision rights.

5. Influence Costs

To this point, we have assumed that when decision-making authority is granted to an individual or a team within the firm, that agent or team is then actively involved in decision making (subject to ratification and monitoring from others). Sometimes, however, firms use bureaucratic rules that purposely limit active decision making. For example, airlines allocate routes to flight attendants based on seniority—there is no supervisor deciding who gets which route. Similarly, some firms base promotions solely on years worked with the firm.

One potential benefit of limiting discretion in making decisions is that it reduces the resources consumed by individuals in trying to influence decisions. Employees are often very concerned about the personal effects of decisions made within the firm. For example, flight attendants care about which routes they fly. Employees are not indifferent to which colleagues are laid off in an economic downturn. These concerns motivate politicking and other potentially nonproductive activities. For instance, employees might waste valuable time trying to influence decision makers. In vying for promotions, employees might take dysfunctional actions to make other employees look bad.

By not assigning the decision right to a specific individual, influence costs are lowered because there is no one to lobby. This policy, however, can impose costs on an organization. For example, consider individuals who are competing for a promotion. Each of these individuals has an incentive to provide evidence to the supervisor that he or she is the most qualified person for the promotion. Such information is often useful in making better promotional decisions. However, the information comes at a cost—employees spend time trying to convince the supervisor that they are the most qualified candidate rather than performing some other activity such as selling products.

In some cases, the firm's profits are largely unaffected by decisions that greatly affect individual employee welfare. For example, firm profits might be invariant as to which flight attendant gets the Hawaii route versus the Sioux Falls route. It is in this setting that bureaucratic rules for decision making are most likely. The firm benefits from a reduction in influence costs but is little affected by the particular outcome of the decision process.

---

[11] A Smith, *The Wealth of Nations,* 1776, Cannan edition (New York: Modern Library, 1937).

Concept Questions		
	Q 4–1	What generates agency costs?
	Q 4–2	How are agency costs reduced, and what limits them?
	Q 4–3	Define *goal incongruence*.
	Q 4–4	How does one achieve goal congruence?
	Q 4–5	Why are knowledge and decision making linked within a firm?
	Q 4–6	Name three things markets do automatically that must be replaced with elaborate administrative systems in the firm.
	Q 4–7	What are influence costs?
	Q 4–8	Why do firms exist?

B. Organizational Architecture

When firms undertake certain repetitive transactions instead of contracting for them in outside markets, market prices for resources used inside the firm no longer exist. For example, the firm can be thought of as a bundle of resources used jointly to produce a product. Suppose one of the many jointly used resources is a punch press used in manufacturing. There is not a specific market price for the punch press used inside the firm. There is not a price for an hour of time on the punch press because the firm does not engage in selling time on this punch press piecemeal. There may be market prices for leasing time on other firms' punch presses, but if buying outside punch press services were cheaper than using the internal punch press, the punch press would not exist inside the firm.[12] The cost of buying outside services includes the external price and the transactions costs of using the market. Even if prices for seemingly equivalent transactions occurring in markets exist, they are unlikely to represent the opportunity cost for transactions within the firm. The transaction exists within the firm, not in the market, because the firm can perform the transaction more cheaply than the market. Hence, the external market price for the punch press, while indicative of what the firm can charge for time on its punch press, does not capture the opportunity cost of using the punch press inside the firm. The market price does not entirely capture the transactions cost savings of owning the punch press.[13]

1. Three-Legged Stool

The firm cannot always use the external market's price (even if available) to guide internal transactions. More important, in the absence of the discipline of the market, the parties to the firm must design administrative devices to (1) measure performance, (2) reward performance, and (3) partition decision rights. These three activities (called **organizational architecture**) are performed automatically by markets but must be performed by (costly) administrative devices inside the firm.[14]

---

[12] R Ball, "The Firm as a Specialist Contracting Intermediary: Applications to Accounting and Auditing," manuscript (Rochester, NY: William E. Simon Graduate School of Business Administration, University of Rochester, 1989).

[13] "Observed market prices cannot directly guide the owner of the input to perform in the same manner as if every activity he performs were measured and priced." S Cheung, "The Contractual Nature of the Firm," *Journal of Law & Economics* 26 (April 1983), p. 5.

[14] Jensen and Meckling (1992), p. 265.

Gaming Objective Performance- Evaluation Systems

This example illustrates how members of one local management team who did not want to lose their jobs successfully gamed the performance-evaluation system their company used in deciding when to close unprofitable mines.

> In this particular company, mines were shut down after the yield per ton of ore dropped below a certain level. One old marginal mine managed to stay open for several years because of the strategic behavior of its management. It happened that the mine contained one very rich pocket of ore. Instead of mining this all at once, the management used it as its reserve. Every time the yield of the ore it was mining fell below an acceptable level, it would mix in a little high-grade ore so the mine would remain open.

SOURCE: E Lawler and J Rhode, *Information and Control in Organizations* (Santa Monica, CA: Goodyear Publishing, 1976), 87–88.

Objective and Subjective Performance Criteria at Lincoln Electric Company

Lincoln Electric manufactures electric arc welding machines and welding disposables (electrodes). At the heart of Lincoln Electric's success is a strategy of building quality products at a lower cost than its competitors and passing the savings on to customers by continuously lowering prices. Lincoln has been able to implement this strategy, in part, through an employee incentive system that fosters labor-productivity increases arising from a pay-for-performance compensation plan.

The two components of Lincoln's performance evaluation scheme are pieces produced and merit rating. The first component is an objective, readily quantifiable performance measure for each production employee (i.e., the number of good units produced). The employee's wage is equal to the piece rate times the number of good units produced. (Employees are not paid for defects.) By working hard, in some cases even through lunch and breaks, employees can double and sometimes triple their pay.

The second component of Lincoln's evaluation scheme is the employee's merit rating. These ratings are used to determine the employee's share of the bonus pool. The size of the bonus pool approximately equals wages and is about twice Lincoln's net income after taxes, although there is substantial annual variation in the size of the pool. Each employee's merit evaluation is based on employee dependability, quality, output, and ideas and cooperation, assessed primarily by the employee's immediate supervisor.

Two important observations emerge from Lincoln Electric. First, the output from the performance evaluation system is used as an input by the performance reward system; the two systems are linked. Second, Lincoln uses highly objective, explicit measures of performance (piecework) as well as subjective measures (ideas and cooperation).

SOURCE: N Fast and N Berg, "The Lincoln Electric Company," Harvard Business School Case 376–028 (1975).

Performance evaluation can involve either objective or subjective performance measures or combinations of both. Objective criteria include explicit, verifiable measures such as paying employees on piece rates or sales. Subjective criteria focus on multiple hard-to-measure factors. For example, subjective performance measures of a manager include a variety of factors such as improving

**When the
Legs of the
Stool Don't
Balance**

Hammer and Champy describe a major airline in which the three legs of the
stool did not match. In this example, a plane was grounded for repairs at an airport. The nearest qualified mechanic was stationed at another airport. The decision right to allow the mechanic to work on the airplane was held by the
manager of the second airport. The manager's compensation, however, was tied
to meeting his own budget rather than to the profits of the overall organization.
The manager refused to send the mechanic to fix the plane immediately because the mechanic would have had to stay overnight and the hotel bill would
have been charged to the manager's budget. The mechanic was dispatched the
next morning so that he could return the same day. A multimillion-dollar aircraft was grounded, costing the airline thousands of dollars. The manager, however, avoided a $100 hotel bill. The mechanic would probably have been
dispatched immediately had the manager been rewarded on the overall profit of
the company or had the decision right been held by someone else with this
objective.

SOURCE: M Hammer and J Champy, *Reengineering the Corporation* (New York: Harper Business, 1993).

team spirit, getting along with peers, meeting budgets and schedules, and affirmative action hiring. Most firms use implicit, subjective performance measures
because jobs typically have multiple dimensions. If a few explicit characteristics
are chosen to reward performance, employees will ignore the hard-to-quantify aspects of their work. Although firms must measure and reward performance, the
performance measure need not be objective. Most firms that use objective performance measures supplement them with subjective measures to help ensure
that employees do not focus entirely on the objective criteria to the detriment of
their other responsibilities.

Besides measuring performance, organizations must reward favorable performance and in some cases punish unwanted behaviors (including firing employees). Agents meeting or exceeding performance expectations are rewarded with
pay increases, bonuses, promotions, and perquisites. Superior performance is rewarded with both monetary and nonmonetary compensation. Monetary rewards
involve salary, bonus, and retirement benefits. Nonmonetary rewards include prestigious job titles, better office location and furnishings, reserved parking spaces,
and country club memberships.

Another administrative device in firms is partitioning decision rights. Within
organizations, all decision rights initially reside with the board of directors. The
vast majority of these rights are assigned to the chief executive officer (CEO),
with the exception of the right to replace the CEO and set his or her pay. The
CEO retains some rights and reassigns the rest to subordinates. This downward
cascading of decision rights within an organization gives rise to the familiar pyra-
mid of hierarchies. Centralization and decentralization revolve around the issues
of partitioning decision rights between higher versus lower levels of the organization and linking knowledge and decision rights.

Ultimately, all organizations must construct three systems:

1. A system that measures performance.
2. A system that rewards and punishes performance.
3. A system that assigns decision rights.

<table>
<tr><td>

Decision Management and Decision Control at General Motors

</td><td>

General Motors was formed in 1908 when the Buick Motor Co. merged with a number of other firms. William Durant, the founder of General Motors, preferred buying other companies rather than building them from scratch. He also had little interest in bringing these many enterprises under central control. After much financial difficulty that extended through the 1920s, new managers, including Alfred P. Sloan, Jr., decided to reorganize the firm. They concluded that the company's activities were too varied and geographically dispersed to be controlled centrally. Instead, they organized the firm by the markets it served: cars, trucks, and parts. Each autonomous division contained manufacturing, distribution, and marketing, and each division integrated production and distribution by coordinating flows from suppliers to customers in their well-defined markets. The divisions were required to submit monthly and quarterly forecasts of sales and costs, which were approved by the central management and used to judge performance of the divisions.

In time, General Motors evolved as the modern multidivisional, decentralized firm. A corporate staff of financial and advisory experts assisted top management in evaluating the day-to-day operations of each division. The corporate office was able to concentrate on setting general policies for the entire firm and leave most of the operating decisions to the divisions. General policies were set by general executives "who had the time, information, and psychological commitment to the enterprise as a whole, rather than to one of its parts."

SOURCE: A Chandler, *The Visible Hand: The Managerial Revolution in American Business* (Cambridge, MA: Harvard University Press, 1977), pp. 457–63.

</td></tr>
</table>

<table>
<tr><td>

Use of Financial and Nonfinancial Performance Measures

</td><td>

One study found that nonfinancial physical measures such as labor headcounts, units of output, units in inventory, and units scrapped are used to run day-to-day operations. The nonfinancial data chosen are highly correlated with the financial reports of the manager's performance and are readily available on a daily or even hourly basis. Also, the nonfinancial data tend to be variables that the manager can control. Yet when asked about their "most valuable report in general," respondents said it was the monthly income or expense statement.

SOURCE: S McKinnon and W Bruns, *The Information Mosaic* (Boston: Harvard Business School Press, 1992).

</td></tr>
</table>

These three systems make up the firm's organizational architecture. They are like the legs of a three-legged stool. For the stool to remain level, all three legs must balance. Similarly, each of the three systems that compose the organization's architecture must be coordinated with the other two. The performance measurement system must measure the agent's performance in areas over which he or she has been assigned the decision rights. Likewise, the reward system must be matched to those areas over which performance is being measured. A person should not be assigned decision rights if the exercise of these rights cannot be measured and rewarded. Though this sounds obvious, changing one system often requires changing the other two systems.

The internal accounting system is a significant part of the performance measurement system. Changes are often made to this system without regard to their impact on the performance-reward and decision-assignment systems. Managers making changes to the accounting system are surprised when the stool is no longer level because one leg is now a different length than the other two.

Performance measurement systems generally use financial and nonfinancial measures of performance. Since this is an accounting text, we emphasize financial measures, although most companies also use nonfinancial metrics, including percentage of on-time deliveries, order completeness, factory ability to meet production schedules, excess inventory, employee turnover, manufacturing quality, percentage of defects and units of scrap, schedule performance, and customer complaints.

Financial indicators are collected and audited by the firm's accountants, whereas nonfinancial measures are more likely to be self-reported. Therefore, financial measures are usually more objective and less subject to managerial discretion. Nonfinancial indicators usually relate to important strategic factors. For example, airline profitability is very sensitive to the fraction of airline seats occupied. Thus, load factors are an important strategic measure in airlines. Nonfinancial measures provide information for decision making. Financial measures of performance tend to be for control.

One problem with using nonfinancial measures is that they tend to proliferate to the point that managers can no longer jointly maximize multiple measures. Numerous performance measures dilute attention. If several key indicators are used, senior managers must implicitly specify the relative weights for each indicator for performance evaluation. Which indicator is really the most important in assessing performance? If senior management does not specify the weights, subordinates are uncertain which specific goal should receive the most attention.

2. Decision Management versus Decision Control

Markets automatically control behavior and partition decision rights. The firm must design administrative devices to do what the market does. These administrative/management mechanisms include hierarchies to separate decision management from control, budgeting systems, periodic performance evaluation systems, standard operating rules and policy manuals, bonus plans and executive compensation schemes, and accounting systems. Some of these administrative devices, such as hierarchies and performance evaluation systems, are described in greater detail below. Budgeting systems and accounting systems are deferred to later chapters. (Standard operating rules and policy manuals are not addressed in this text.)

Perhaps the most important mechanism for resolving agency problems is a hierarchical structure that separates decision management from decision control.[15] All organizations have hierarchies with higher-level managers supervising lower-level employees. **Decision management** refers to those aspects of the decision process in which the manager either *initiates* or *implements* a decision. **Decision control** refers to those aspects of the decision process whereby managers either *ratify* or *monitor* decisions. See Figure 4–1. Managers rarely are given all the decision rights to make a particular decision. Rather, an elaborate system of approvals and monitoring exists. Consider a typical decision to hire a new employee. First, a

---

[15] See E Fama and M Jensen, "Separation of Ownership and Control," *Journal of Political Economy*, June 1983, pp. 301–25.

FIGURE 4–1

Steps in the decision-making process: Decision management versus decision control

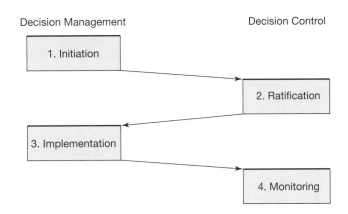

Decision Management   Decision Control

1. Initiation

2. Ratification

3. Implementation

4. Monitoring

manager requests authorization to add a new position. This request is reviewed by higher-level managers. Once the position is authorized, the manager making the request usually begins the recruiting and interviewing process. Eventually a new employee is hired. After a certain period, the employee's performance is evaluated. In general, the following steps in the decision process occur (categorized according to decision management or decision control): (1) initiation (management), (2) ratification (control), (3) implementation (management), and (4) monitoring (control). *Initiation* is the request to hire a new employee. *Ratification* is the approval of the request. *Implementation* is hiring the employee. *Monitoring* involves assessing the performance of the hired employee at periodic intervals to evaluate the person who hires the employee.

An individual manager typically does not have the authority to undertake all four steps in this decision process. The manager requesting a new position does not have the decision right to ratify (approve) the request. There is a *separation of decision management from control*. The same principle in the U.S. Constitution separates the powers of the various branches of government. The executive branch requests spending, which is approved by the legislature. The executive branch is

Capital Project Monitoring at Caterpillar 	Caterpillar Inc. monitors strategic capital projects such as a new plant over the life of each project. Once a capital project is approved and installed, a monitoring team reviews it every six months. Only large strategic projects (often composed of several individual capital assets), such as an axle factory or an assembly line, are evaluated. The project monitoring team consists of representatives from industrial engineering, manufacturing, materials acquisition, and cost accounting. They prepare a report that compares the actual results with the budgeted results. Reasons for any differences are listed, including a detailed report that reconciles why the project's current results differ from what was expected at the time the capital project was approved. In addition, the monitoring team issues a list of recommendations to improve the performance of the project. The monitoring team's findings are distributed to the manager of the project being evaluated, the building superintendent, the plant manager, the group presidents, and the corporate board of directors. SOURCE: J Hendricks, R Bastian, and T Sexton, "Bundle Monitoring of Strategic Projects," *Management Accounting*, February 1992, pp. 31–35.

then charged with making the expenditures. The judicial branch ultimately monitors both the executive and legislative branches.

As another example of how knowledge is linked with initiation rights and how hierarchies separate decision management from decision control, consider the decision to acquire capital assets. The decision to build a new plant usually begins with division managers who make a formal proposal to senior management. This is decision *initiation*. The initiating managers have specialized knowledge of their production process and product demand. The formal proposal usually takes the form of a capital budget request. Senior managers then ask the finance department to evaluate the discounted cash flow assumptions in the capital budget request. The finance department possesses specialized knowledge to judge risk-and-return assumptions in the discount rate and the analysis of the cash flows in the plan. Senior management assembles other knowledge from the human resource, real estate, and legal departments in the *ratification* process. Construction of the project—*implementation*—is the responsibility of the proposing managers or a separate facilities department within the firm. After construction is completed, accountants prepare monthly, quarterly, and annual reports on the division requesting and operating the capital project. This is part of the *monitoring* process.

Most organizations separate decision management from decision control. Before implementing a decision, someone higher up in the organization must ratify it. Management and control are not separated, however, when it is too costly to separate them. For example, managers are often assigned the decision rights to make small purchases (perhaps under $500) without ratification because the cost of separating management from control exceeds the benefits. Since it takes time to receive ratification, lost opportunities or other adverse consequences can occur. The most vivid illustration of delay costs is in the military. Fighter pilots flying in noncombat situations do not have the decision rights to fire at unauthorized or potential enemy planes. They first must notify their superiors and seek authority to shoot. But in combat situations, decision management and decision control are not separated because to do so would hamper the pilots' ability to respond in situations when delays can be catastrophic. Therefore, in combat situations pilots have the authority to fire at enemy aircraft. Another example where delays could be deadly: In some states paramedics can administer certain drugs in life-threatening situations without first getting a physician's approval.

Concept Questions	Q 4–9	Define *decision management* and *decision control* and give an example of each.
	Q 4–10	Describe the three systems all organizations must construct to control agency problems.
	Q 4–11	Describe the four major steps in the management decision process. How are agency problems reduced in this process?

C. Accounting's Role in the Organization's Architecture

The preceding section described the separation of decision management from decision control. One way to limit agency costs is to separate the decision rights to initiate and implement decisions (decision management) from the ratifying and monitoring functions (decision control). Accounting systems play a very important

Performance Measures in Retailing

Large department stores with multiple lines of goods such as clothing, furniture, jewelry, and glassware began to appear in the United States in the latter half of the 1800s (Lord & Taylor in 1858 and Macy's in 1870). These stores were in big cities that could support the large inventories they carried. These successful retailers had high volume and high inventory turnover by selling at low prices and low margins. They marked down slow-moving lines and did extensive local advertising.

In rural areas, mass marketing was done by mail-order houses. Montgomery Ward began in 1872; Sears and Roebuck began in 1887. The 1887 Montgomery Ward mail-order catalog was 540 pages long and contained 24,000 items. The success of the mail-order houses, like the department stores, was due to low prices and high volumes. Mail-order houses could process 100,000 orders per day.

At the heart of both the department stores and mail-order houses were the operating departments (such as women's and children's clothing, furniture, and housewares) and their buyers. The buyers had to acquire specialized knowledge of their customers' preferences. They committed their departments to purchase millions of dollars of goods before they knew whether the items could be sold.

Two types of information generated by the accounting department were used to evaluate the operating managers and their buyers: gross margin and stock turn. *Gross margin* is income (sales less cost of sales and operating expenses) divided by sales. *Stock turn* or *inventory turnover* is sales divided by average inventory; it measures the number of times stock on hand is sold and replaced during the year. Departments with higher stock turns are using their capital invested in inventories more efficiently. For example, the large Chicago merchandiser, Marshall Field's, had a stock turn of around five in the 1880s. The development of gross margin and stock turn illustrates how accounting-based performance-evaluation measures develop to match the decision rights partitioned to particular managers. Critical to the success of large mass distributors was partitioning decision rights to the buyers with the specialized knowledge and then evaluating and rewarding them based on their decision rights.

SOURCE: A Chandler, *The Visible Hand: The Managerial Revolution in American Business* (Cambridge, MA: Harvard University Press, 1977), pp. 223–36.

role in monitoring as part of the performance evaluation system. Accounting numbers are probably more useful in decision monitoring and often least useful in decision initiation and implementation. For decision management, managers want opportunity costs (described in Chapter 2). Accounting data are often criticized as not being useful for decision management, but their usefulness for decision control is frequently overlooked.

As a monitoring device, the accounting function is usually independent of operating managers whose performance the accounting report is measuring. The reason for this separation is obvious. Accounting, as part of the firm's monitoring technology, is designed to reduce agency costs, including theft and embezzlement. Since accounting reports bring subordinates' performance to the attention of their superiors, the reports should not be under the control of the subordinates. Internal accounting reports provide an overall review of subordinates' performance by giving senior managers reasonably objective and independent information. Shareholders and the board of directors use the accounting system to check on the performance of the chief executive officer (CEO) and senior managers. The CEO often has substantial influence over the accounting system since the corporate controller usually reports ultimately to the CEO. Some firms have the controller report to the independent audit committee of the board of directors. To use the accounting system for control of the CEO and senior management, the shareholders and outside directors on the board insist on an external, third-party audit of the financial results.[16]

To the extent financial measures are used for decision control and nonfinancial measures are used for decision management, the following implications arise:

1. Financial measures are not under the complete control of the people being monitored (i.e., the operating managers).
2. Nonaccounting measures, such as customer complaints and defect rates, are often more timely than accounting measures. Nonfinancial data can be reported more frequently than quarterly or monthly, as is usually the case for accounting data.
3. Not every decision requires ratification or monitoring. Decision control can be based on aggregate data to average out random fluctuations. Instead of monitoring every machine setup, it is usually cost-efficient to aggregate all setups occurring over the week and make sure the average setup time or cost is within acceptable levels.
4. Operating managers tend to be dissatisfied with financial measures for making operating decisions.[17] The accounting numbers are not especially timely for operating decisions. They often are at too aggregate a level and do not provide sufficient detail for the particular decision. In response, these operating managers develop their own, often nonfinancial, information systems to provide the more timely knowledge they require for decision management. But at the same time, they rely on accounting data to monitor the managers who report to them.

A number of specific internal accounting procedures, such as standard costs, budgeting, and cost allocations (described in later chapters), help reduce agency problems. Many accounting procedures are better understood as control mechanisms than as aids in decision management. For example, economists have long cautioned against using accountants' allocation of fixed costs to compute "average" unit costs in making short-term decisions. These unit costs bear little relation to short-term variable cost, which is necessary for determining the short-term profit-maximizing level of output.[18] However, average unit accounting costs can be useful as a control mechanism for detecting changes in a subunit's cost performance.

Applying the economic Darwinism principle (marmots and bears) suggests that these seemingly irrational accounting procedures must be yielding benefits in excess of their costs. Economists describe the dysfunctional output/pricing decision that can result when accounting average costs are used instead of variable costs.

---

[16] R Watts and J Zimmerman, "Agency Problems, Auditing and the Theory of the Firm: Some Evidence," *Journal of Law & Economics*, October 1983, pp. 613–33.

[17] Recall the box on page 9 in Chapter 1.

[18] Except when noted, throughout the book we assume that cost curves are linear and, hence, marginal and variable costs per unit are equal. This simplifies the terminology.

General Electric's Executive Compensation Contract	General Electric defines its 1997 bonus formula as follows:

General Electric defines its 1997 bonus formula as follows:

> The Plan Authorizes the Board of Directors to appropriate to an incentive compensation reserve each year up to 10% of the amount by which consolidated net earnings exceeds 5% of the Company's average consolidated capital investment.

In General Electric's plan, the executives do not receive a bonus unless the firm earns at least 5 percent on capital. This is a lower bound. Some businesses also place an upper bound on the bonus payout. A typical upper limit to a bonus payout might be stated as, "The incentive compensation reserve shall not exceed 10 percent of the total amount of the dividends paid on the corporation's stock." This upper bound, which is tied to dividends, helps reduce the overretention of cash in the firm. If the business is very profitable, the only way executives can increase their bonus payouts is by increasing dividends paid out to the shareholders.

SOURCE: General Electric Co. Proxy Statement (March 12, 1997).

These dysfunctional decisions are the indirect costs of using the accounting procedures. Reducing the firm's agency problems provides the necessary offsetting benefits to explain the preponderance of "irrational" accounting procedures. In addition to the benefits provided via organizational reasons, such procedures can provide benefits (or costs) via external reporting, tax reporting, and/or as a cost control device (see Figure 1–1).

The next section provides a specific example of how accounting earnings are used in executive compensation plans to better align managers' and shareholders' interests.

D. Example of Accounting's Role: Executive Compensation Contracts

Executive compensation contracts illustrate how accounting numbers help reduce agency costs. To better align the interests of shareholders and senior managers, most large U.S. corporations have incentive compensation contracts. This section briefly describes the design of these contracts and their reliance on accounting numbers. It illustrates how accounting performance measures are used to reduce agency problems.

Senior executives in the typical large U.S. firm are paid a salary plus an annual bonus; the bonus is, on average, 50 percent of the salary. The compensation committee of the board of directors, which usually consists of outside, nonmanagement directors, administers the annual bonus and the annual salary adjustment. The committee annually sets performance goals for each senior executive and establishes how large a bonus each will receive if he or she achieves the goals. The goals often consist of divisional earnings growth targets, market share, new product introduction schedules, affirmative action hiring targets, and other strategic measures appropriate for the particular manager. If managers meet their targets, they receive some combination of cash, stock options, restricted stock, or deferred compensation.

To protect shareholders from excessive payouts to senior executives and to give senior executives a sense of the whole organization rather than just their own part, the total bonus payout to all eligible managers is limited to some fraction of accounting earnings. Executive compensation contracts usually must be approved

	Total	
	2003	2002
Contributions:		
General contributions	$ 13,657,676	$ 13,642,476
Major gifts and bequests	4,712,032	4,751,059
Gifts in kind	804,247	637,977
Total contributions	$ 19,173,955	$ 19,031,512
Grants:		
Grants and contracts	$ 10,164,264	$ 7,768,755
Total public support	$140,614,355	$130,868,704
Revenue		
Investment and currency transactions	$ 264,893	$ 350,841
Service fees and other	1,636,717	1,522,652
Total revenue	$ 1,901,610	$ 1,873,493
Net Assets Released from Restrictions		
Satisfaction of program and time restrictions	—	—
Total public support and revenue	$142,515,965	$132,742,197
Expenses		
Program:		
Basic education	$ 41,263,708	$ 40,964,478
Health and sanitation	28,767,904	29,442,196
Nutrition	13,824,871	15,635,046
Early childhood development	11,850,954	10,717,133
Micro enterprise	14,555,029	9,183,004
Emergencies	2,802,575	2,861,528
Total program expenses	$113,032,041	$108,803,385
Supporting Services		
Fund raising	$ 16,777,149	$ 15,484,634
Management and general	12,651,014	11,156,134
Total supporting services	29,428,163	26,640,768
Total expenses from operations	142,493,204	135,444,153
Change in net assets from operations	$ 22,761	$ (2,701,956)
Non-Operating Revenues (Expenses)		
Realized (loss) gain on investments	$ (602,619)	$ 387,223
Unrealized gain (loss) on investments	696,584	(1,967,114)
Total non-operating revenues (expenses)	93,965	(1,579,891)
Change in net assets	$ 116,726	$ (4,281,847)

Case 4–2:   Woodhaven Service

Background

Woodhaven Service is a small, independent filling station located in the Woodhaven section of Queens. The station has three gasoline pumps and two service bays. The repair facility specializes in automotive maintenance (oil changes, tune-ups, etc.) and minor repairs (mufflers, shock absorbers, etc.). Woodhaven generally refers customers who require major work such as transmission rebuilds and electronics to shops that are better equipped to handle such repairs. Major repairs are done in-house only when both the customer and mechanic agree that this is the best course of action.

During the 20 years that he has owned Woodhaven Service, Harold Mateen's competence and fairness have built a loyal customer base of neighborhood residents. In fact, demand for his services has been more than he can reasonably meet, yet the repair end of his business is not especially profitable. Most of his competitors earn the lion's share of their profits through repairs, but Harold is making almost all of his money by selling gasoline. If he could make more money on repairs, Woodhaven would be the most successful service station in the area. Harold believes that Woodhaven's weakness in repair profitability is due to the inefficiency of his mechanics, who are paid the industry average of $500 per week. While Harold does not think he overpays them, he feels he is not getting his money's worth.

Harold's son, Andrew, is a student at the university, where he has learned the Socratic dictum, "To know the Good is to do the Good." Andrew provided his father with a classic text on employee morality, Dr. Weisbrotten's, *Work Hard and Follow the Righteous Way.* Every morning for two months, Harold, Andrew, and the mechanics devoted one hour to studying this text. Despite many lively and fascinating discussions on the rights and responsibilities of the employee, productivity did not improve one bit. Harold figured he would just have to go out and hire harder-working mechanics.

The failure of the Weisbrotten method did not surprise Lisa, Harold's daughter. She knew that Andrew's methods were bunk. As anyone serious about business knows, the true science of productivity and management of human resources resides in Professor von Drekken's masterful *Modifying Organizational Behavior through Employee Commitment.* Yes, employee commitment was the answer to everything! Harold followed the scientific methods to the letter. Yet, despite giving out gold stars, blowing up balloons, and wearing a smiley face button, he found Lisa's approach no more successful than Andrew's.

Compensation Plans

Harold thinks that his neighbor Jack Myers, owner of Honest Jack's Pre-Enjoyed Autorama, might be helpful. After all, one does not become as successful as Jack without a lot of practical knowledge. Or maybe it is Jack's great radio jingle that does it. Jack tells Harold,

> It's not the jingle, you idiot! It's the way I pay my guys. Your mechanics make $500 a week no matter what. Why should they put out for you? Because of those stupid buttons? My guys—my guys get paid straight commission and nothing more. They do good by me and I do good by them. Otherwise, let 'em starve.
>
> Look, it's real simple. Pay 'em a percent of the sales for the work they do. If you need to be a nice guy about it, make that percent so that if sales are average, then they make their usual $500. But if sales are better, they get that percent extra. This way they don't get hurt but got real reason to help you out.

This hurt Harold. He really liked those buttons. Still, Jack did have a point. Straight commission, however, seemed a little radical. What if sales were bad for a week? That would hurt the mechanics.

Harold figured that it would be better to pay each mechanic a guaranteed $300 a week plus a commission rate that would, given an average volume of business, pay them the extra $200 that would bring their wage back to $500. Under this system, the mechanics would be insulated from a bad week, would not be penalized for an average week, and would still have the incentive to attempt to improve sales. Yes, this seemed more fair.

On the other hand, maybe Jack knows only about the used car business, not about business in general. Harold figured that he should look for an incentive pay method more in line with the way things are done in the auto repair business. Perhaps he should pay his mechanics as he is paid by his customers—by the job. It is standard practice for service stations to charge customers a flat rate for the labor associated with any job. The number of labor hours for which the customer is charged is generally taken from a manual that outlines expected labor times for specific jobs on specific vehicles. The customer pays for these expected hours regardless of how many actual labor hours are expended on the job. Many shops also pay their mechanics by the job. Harold thinks that this approach makes sense because it links the mechanic's pay to the labor charges paid by the customer.

Required:

a. This case presents some popular approaches to alleviating agency costs. Although certain aspects of each of these methods are consistent with the views presented in the text, none of these methods is likely to succeed. Discuss the similarities and differences between the ideas of the chapter and

  (i) Dr. Weisbrotten's approach.

  (ii) Harold Mateen's idea of hiring "harder-working" mechanics.

b. Discuss the expected general effect on agency costs at Woodhaven Service of the new incentive compensation plans. How might they help Woodhaven? Assuming that Harold wants his business to be successful for a long time to come, what major divergent behaviors would be expected under the new compensation proposals? How damaging would you expect these new behaviors to be to a business such as Woodhaven Service? Also, present a defense of the following propositions:

  (i) Harold's plan offers less incentive for divergent behavior than Honest Jack's.

  (ii) Limiting a mechanic's pay by placing an upper bound of $750 per week on his or her earnings reduces the incentive for divergent behavior.

c. Suppose Harold owned a large auto repair franchise located in a department store in a popular suburban shopping mall. Suppose also that this department store is a heavily promoted, well-known national chain that is famous for its good values and easy credit. How should Harold's thinking on incentive compensation change? What if Harold did not own the franchise but was only the manager of a company-owned outlet?

d. In this problem, it is assumed that knowledge and decision rights are linked. The mechanic who services the car decides what services are warranted. Discuss the costs and benefits of this fact for Woodhaven Service and the independently owned chain-store repair shop.

e. Suppose that Woodhaven's problems are not due to agency costs. Briefly describe a likely problem that is apparent from the background description in this problem.

Chapter Five

Responsibility Accounting and Transfer Pricing

Chapter 4 described the general problem of motivating and thereby influencing individual behavior. This was called the *agency problem*. Chapter 4 also described how the organization's architecture can reduce this problem. The firm's organizational architecture consists of three interrelated systems: the performance evaluation system, the performance reward system, and the system that assigns decision rights. The accounting system plays an integral part in most firms' performance evaluation. This chapter discusses two additional examples of how accounting systems can be applied to reduce agency problems: responsibility accounting and transfer pricing.

A. Responsibility Accounting[1]

All but the smallest organizations are divided into subunits, each of which is granted decision rights and then evaluated based on performance objectives for that subunit. For example, the firm might be organized into marketing, manufacturing, and distribution departments. Manufacturing is further subdivided into parts manufacturing and assembly, and assembly is further organized by product assembled. These basic building blocks of the organization form the work groups that define and characterize what each part of the firm does. Assigning decision rights to the subunits is a critical part of solving the limited processing capacity of humans discussed in Chapter 4. **Responsibility accounting** begins with formal recognition of these subunits as responsibility centers. A responsibility accounting system is part of the performance evaluation system used to measure the operating results of the responsibility center.

The decision rights assigned to a subunit categorize the unit as a cost center, a profit center, or an investment center. The particular decision rights assigned to a

---

Responsibility Accounting Not New

In 1922, James O. McKinsey, founder of the consulting firm McKinsey & Co., described responsibility accounting:

> In the modern business organization, control is exercised through individuals who compose the organization. If control of expenses is to be effected through members of the organization, it is necessary that they be classified so as to show responsibility for each class. If responsibility is taken as the controlling factor in an expense classification, each department will be charged with those expenses over which the executive head of the department exercises control. In addition it may be charged with some items of expense the amount of which is fixed or at least beyond the control of any officer.
>
> To illustrate, the production department will be charged for the supplies used in production, for these are under the control of the production manager, and in addition it will be charged with the depreciation on production equipment, the estimated amount of which is determined in most cases by others than the production manager.*

Notice that McKinsey advocates the use of responsibility accounting and he also argues in favor of charging not only expenses over which managers have direct control but also expenses they control indirectly, such as depreciation.

*J McKinsey, *Budgetary Control* (New York: Ronald Press, 1922), p. 281.

---

[1] This section draws heavily on M Jensen and W Meckling, "Divisional Performance Measurement," manuscript (Boston: Harvard Business School, 1986); and J Brickley, C Smith, and J Zimmerman, *Managerial Economics and Organizational Architecture,* 2nd ed. (New York: McGraw-Hill/Irwin, 2001).

TABLE 5–1   Summary of Cost, Profit, and Investment Centers

	Decision Rights	*Performance Measures*	*Typically Used When*
Cost center	Input mix (labor, materials, supplies	• Minimize total cost for a fixed output • Maximize output for a fixed budget	• Central manager can measure output, knows the cost functions, and can set the optimal quantity and appropriate rewards • Central manager can observe the quality of the cost center's output • Cost center manager has knowledge of the optimal input mix
Profit center	• Input mix • Product mix • Selling prices (or output quantities)	• Actual profits • Actual compared to budgeted profits	• Profit center manager has the knowledge to select the correct price/quantity • Profit center manager has the knowledge to select the optimal product mix
Investment center	• Input mix • Product mix • Selling prices (or output quantities) • Capital invested in center	• Actual ROI • Actual residual income • Actual compared with budgeted ROI or residual income	• Investment center manager has the knowledge to select the correct price/quantity • Investment center manager has the knowledge to select the optimal product mix • Investment center manager has knowledge about investment opportunities

subunit are the key determinants of how the unit's performance is evaluated and rewarded. Each of these categories implies a different assignment of decision rights and, accordingly, a different performance measurement system. In each case, decision rights are linked with the specialized knowledge necessary to exercise them. Responsibility accounting then dictates that the performance measurement system (the accounting system) measures the performance that results from the decision rights assigned to the responsibility center. For example, if an agent is assigned decision rights to sell products to customers in New York, the performance measurement of this agent should not include sales to customers in Maine.[2]

Matching the decision rights assigned to a subunit to its performance measure reduces the agency problems described in Chapter 4. A subunit is given a precise set of decision rights, a performance measure designed to evaluate the exercise of those rights, and rewards based on the measures. In this way the subunit focuses on those tasks the principal wants performed. Table 5–1 lists the differences among

---

[2] In certain circumstances, incorporating Maine sales into the New York salesperson's compensation is useful. If Maine and New York sales are correlated, then using Maine sales as a benchmark for general economic trends can reduce the total risk borne by the New York salesperson. See J Brickley, C Smith, and J Zimmerman, *Managerial Economics and Organizational Architecture* (Boston: McGraw-Hill/Irwin, 2004) pp. 426–28, for a discussion of relative performance evaluation.

the various responsibility centers. (In all cases, accounting numbers are used in the performance measurement system.)[3]

1. Cost Centers

Cost centers are established whenever a subunit is assigned the decision rights to produce some stipulated level of output and the unit's efficiency in achieving this objective is to be measured and rewarded. Cost center managers are assigned decision rights for determining the mix of inputs (labor, outside services, and materials) used to produce the output. Managers of cost centers are evaluated on their efficiency in applying inputs to produce outputs. Since they are not responsible for selling the final services or products, they are not judged on revenues or profits.

To evaluate the performance of a cost center, its output must be measurable. Moreover, some higher unit in the organization with the specialized knowledge and decision rights must specify the department's output or budget. Manufacturing departments like a parts manufacturing department in a factory are usually cost centers. The output of a parts department is measured by counting the number of parts produced. Cost centers are also used in service organizations for functions such as check processing in a bank (number of checks processed) or food services in a hospital (number of meals served). In addition to measuring the quantity of output, its quality must be monitored effectively. If not, cost center managers who are evaluated on costs can meet their targets by cutting quality.

Various objectives are used for evaluating cost center performance. One is to minimize costs for a given output; another is to maximize output for a given budget. Minimizing costs for a given output is consistent with profit maximization as long as central management has selected the profit-maximizing level of output. For example, the manager of a metal stamping department is told to produce 10,000 stampings per day of a fixed specification and quality. The manager is evaluated on meeting the production schedule and on reducing the cost of the 10,000 stampings while maintaining quality. The cost center manager does not have the decision rights to set the price or scale of operations.

The second potential evaluation criterion, maximizing output for a specified budget, provides incentives equivalent to the first criterion as long as the specified budget is the minimal budget necessary for producing the profit-maximizing quantity of output. For example, the manager has a fixed budget ($27,500 per week) and is evaluated based on the number of metal stampings produced that meet quality specifications within the fixed budget.

For both objectives, the manager is constrained either by total output or by budget. The two objectives are optimal if the central management chooses (1) the profit-maximizing output level or (2) the correct budget for efficient production of this output level. Nonetheless under both cost center arrangements, the cost center manager has incentives to reduce costs (or increase output) by lowering quality. Therefore, the quality of products manufactured in cost centers must be monitored.

Sometimes cost center managers are evaluated based on minimizing average cost. In this case the manager has the incentive to choose the output at which

---

[3] In this chapter, we focus on three centers (cost, profit, and investment centers). Other types, such as expense and revenue centers, are not as prevalent as the three discussed. For discussion of these additional types of centers, see R Kaplan and A Atkinson, *Advanced Management Accounting*, 3rd ed. (Upper Saddle River, NJ: Prentice Hall, 1998); Jensen and Meckling (1986); and Brickley et al. (2004).

TABLE 5–2   Example Demonstrating That Minimizing Average Cost May Not Yield the Profit-Maximizing Level of Sales

Quantity	Price	Revenue	Total Cost	Total Profits	Average Cost
1	$35	$ 35	$ 78	$−43	$78.0
2	33	66	83	−17	41.5
3	31	93	90	3	30.0
4	29	116	99	17	24.8
5	27	135	110	25	22.0
6	25	150	123	27	20.5
7	23	161	138	23	19.7
8	21	168	155	13	19.4
9	19	171	174	−3	19.3
10	17	170	195	−25	19.5

average costs are minimized and to produce this output efficiently. It is important to emphasize that profit maximization need not occur when average costs are minimized. In general, minimizing average unit cost is not the same as maximizing profit. For example, suppose a cost center has some fixed costs and constant variable costs per unit. In this case, average unit costs will continue to fall with increases in output. To illustrate, assume total costs are

$$TC = \$300{,}000 + \$6Q$$

Here fixed costs are $300,000 and variable costs are a constant $6 per unit. Given this equation, average costs are derived by dividing both sides of the equation by Q to get

$$AC = \frac{TC}{Q} = \frac{\$300{,}000}{Q} + \$6$$

With a constant variable cost, the average cost falls as the quantity produced increases. In this situation, a cost center manager who is evaluated based on minimizing average unit costs has incentives to increase output, even as inventories mount. Focusing on minimizing average unit cost can provide incentives for cost center managers to either overproduce or underproduce; it depends on how the profit-maximizing output level compares to the quantity where average costs are minimized.

Table 5–2 provides another simple example that minimizing average cost is not equivalent to profit maximization. This table shows that profits are maximized by selling six units. However, minimum average cost occurs by producing nine units.

Cost centers work most effectively if: (1) the central managers have a good understanding of the cost functions, can measure quantity, and can set the profit-maximizing output level and appropriate rewards; (2) the central managers can observe the quality of the cost center's output; and (3) the cost center manager has specific knowledge of the optimal input mix. Table 5–1 summarizes the decision rights and measures used to evaluate the performance of the various centers and when each particular center is used.

Frequency of Profit Center Use	A study of 400 large U.S. companies and hospitals reports the following frequencies of profit centers:*

Industry	Percentage with Profit Centers
Commercial banks	94%
Diversified financial	71
Diversified service	95
Hospitals	27
Life insurance	77
Large manufacturing	97
Medium manufacturing	95
Retailers or wholesalers	97
Transportation	76
Utilities	61
Miscellaneous	92

Profit centers are very prevalent in most large U.S. firms. The only exception is in hospitals, which use profit centers only 27 percent of the time.

*The wording of the question by the study does not distinguish between profit and investment centers. Thus, the percentages reported include both profit and investment centers.

SOURCE: S Umapathy, *Current Budgeting Practices in U.S. Industry* (New York: Quorum Books, 1987), p. 20.

2. Profit Centers

Profit centers are often composed of several cost centers. Profit center managers are given a fixed capital budget and have decision rights for input mix, product mix, and selling prices (or output quantities). Profit centers are most appropriate when the knowledge required to make the product mix, quantity, pricing, and quality decisions is specific to the division and costly to transfer.

Top-level managers rely on their internal accounting systems to measure the performance of profit centers. Profit centers are usually evaluated on the difference between actual and budgeted accounting profits for their division. Although measuring the profits of profit centers seems straightforward, two complications often consume managers' attention: how to price transfers of goods and services between business units (transfer pricing) and which corporate overhead costs to allocate to business units. In every firm managers constantly debate these two issues. We examine the transfer pricing problem in the next section. Chapters 7 and 8 discuss the allocation of corporate overhead costs to responsibility centers.

When there are interdependencies among business units, motivating individual profit centers to maximize their unit's profits will not generally maximize profits for the firm as a whole. For example, individual units focusing on their own profits frequently ignore how their actions affect the sales and costs of other units.[4] One division might free-ride on another division's quality reputation, thereby reaping short-run gains at the expense of the other division. For example, Chevrolet and Buick are two profit centers within General Motors. Suppose Chevrolet, in pursuit of higher profits, decides to raise the quality of its cars. This might affect

---

[4] Conceptually, other units could offer money to take these effects into account. However, in the presence of transactions costs these offers are likely to be limited.

Changing Performance Measures at Caterpillar	In 1990 Caterpillar reorganized. It changed from a functional organization to a product-line organization. Instead of being organized around departments such as engineering, manufacturing, and marketing with each department as a cost center, Caterpillar created 13 profit centers organized around groups of products: bulldozers, loaders, graders, and so forth. Each profit center contains engineering, manufacturing, and marketing. The goal of the reorganization was to increase responsiveness, flexibility, and customer focus.

In addition to changing the organization chart (and hence decision rights) Caterpillar also pushed decision making downward by empowering employees and holding them accountable. New performance measures replaced the old one—the ratio of direct labor hours to machine hours. Now the managers are measured on return on investment, return on sales, and several nonfinancial measures such as customer satisfaction and process improvement. The company also tied compensation to both corporate and division profits for all employees, not just for managers. Divisions have reported outstanding success and continuous improvement since these changes were implemented.

Caterpillar's example highlights a key point from the last chapter: Performance measurement systems are rarely changed in isolation. Successful organizational change usually requires modifying all three legs of the stool. Caterpillar changed all three: decision rights assignment (shifting from cost to profit centers and employee empowerment), performance measures (adopting ROI), and performance rewards (linking pay to corporate and division ROI).

SOURCE: J Hendricks, D Defretias, and D Walker, "Changing Performance Measures at Caterpillar," *Management Accounting* (December 1996), pp. 18–24.

---

consumers' perceptions of the average quality of all General Motors cars, including Buick's perceived quality. An enhanced reputation for all General Motors cars helps Buick. But if Chevrolet receives no credit for Buick's profits, Chevrolet managers will likely ignore the positive effects they generate for Buick and tend to underinvest in quality enhancements. To help managers internalize both the positive and negative effects that their actions impose on other profit center managers, firms often base incentive compensation not just on the manager's own profit center profits but also on a group of related profit centers' profits and/or firmwide profits. Unless the entire firm makes a certain profit target, no individual profit center manager earns a bonus.

3. Investment Centers

Investment centers are similar to profit centers. However, they have additional decision rights for capital expenditures and are evaluated on measures such as return on investment (ROI). Investment centers are most appropriate when the manager of the unit has specific knowledge about investment opportunities as well as information relevant for making operating decisions for the unit.

Investment centers are often composed of several profit centers. They have all the decision rights of cost and profit centers, as well as the decision rights over the amount of capital invested. For example, suppose the consumer electronics group of an electronics firm consists of three profit centers: the television division, the DVD division, and the stereo division. Consumer electronics has decision rights over the amount of capital invested in the group.

How Firms Organize into Cost, Profit, and Investment Centers	A survey of 121 large publicly traded firms inquired about the type of reporting relationship between the CEO and the line units reporting directly to the CEO's office. The study reported that in 21 percent of the firms, the line units reporting to the CEO are exclusively cost centers, in 54 percent they are exclusively profit or investment centers, and in the remaining 25 percent of the firms, a combination of profit, investment, and cost centers report to the CEO. The study did not distinguish between profit and investment centers. These findings suggest there is substantial variation in how firms are organized. SOURCE: A Christie, M Joye, and R Watts, "Decentralization of the Firm: Theory and Evidence," *Journal of Corporate Finance* (January 2003), pp. 3–36.

Investment center managers are usually constrained in terms of the quality of products they can sell and the market niches they can enter. These constraints prevent investment center managers from debasing the firm's reputation (also called its *brand name capital*). For example, Eastman Kodak entered the consumer battery market by creating an investment center, Kodak Ultra Technologies. Kodak has a reputation for high-quality products. One way the managers of Ultra Technologies could meet their profit and ROI targets would be to lower costs by offering lower-quality batteries than consumers expect. Over time, consumers would come to learn of the lower-than-expect quality of the batteries. Ultra Technologies's managers might exceed their budgeted profits, but the market would lower its expectations of quality for all Kodak products. To control this problem, senior Kodak managers continually monitored the quality of the batteries produced to ensure that they met Kodak's quality standards.[5]

Debasing the firm's reputation by lowering the quality of its products is one example of an adverse effect that one responsibility center can have on another. Responsibility centers can interact in many ways and can have adverse or favorable impacts on other centers. A plant's operating efficiency can be affected by the quantity and timing of the orders it receives from the marketing department. A purchasing department can affect the manufacturing department's operations by the timing and quality of the raw materials purchased. A responsibility center sharing a newly discovered cost-saving idea or R&D development with other centers is an example of a favorable (or positive) interaction. Managing these interactions (eliminating the negative ones and encouraging the positive ones) is critical to the successful linking of decision rights to individual(s) with the specialized knowledge. As discussed throughout the remaining chapters, the firm's internal accounting system can play a powerful role in either enhancing the positive interactions or exacerbating the negative ones.

In all of the responsibility centers in Table 5–1, the measure of performance is linked to the decision rights vested in the management. Investment center performance can be measured in at least three ways: net income, return on investment, and residual income. Each of these is described below.

Net income

The simplest of the three performance measures is accounting **net income** generated by the investment center (revenues minus expenses). However, net income

---

[5] In 1989, Kodak reorganized Ultra Technologies and merged it back into Consumer Products. In 1990, Kodak sold part of the battery business to a group of private investors.

The Du Pont Company ROI Method

In the early 1900s, the E.I. Du Pont de Nemours Powder Company was the leading firm manufacturing high explosives and was later to grow into one of the world's largest chemical companies. To control and evaluate its operations, Du Pont managers developed the concept of *return on investment*.

The financial staff traced the cost and revenues for each product produced. This gave management accurate information on profits, which provided a more precise way of evaluating financial performance. However, managers found product-line profits to be an incomplete measure of performance because these did not indicate the rate of return on capital invested. One manager said, "The true test of whether the profit is too great or too small is the rate of return on the money invested in the business and not the percent of profit on the cost."

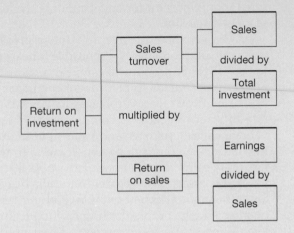

Developing a rate of return on each segment of business required accurate data on investment. Du Pont undertook a careful valuation of each of its plants, properties, and inventories by product line. These data, along with profits, allowed management to track ROI by product line. In addition, Du Pont managers decomposed ROI (Profits ÷ Investment) into its component parts to understand the underlying changes in ROI. The accompanying figure illustrates this decomposition.

ROI is the product of sales turnover (Sales ÷ Total investment) and return on sales (Earnings ÷ Sales). Given these data, managers could determine the causes of a product's change in ROI. Du Pont managers used these data to evaluate new capital appropriations by establishing the policy that there "be no expenditures for additions to the earnings equipment if the same amount of money could be applied to some better purpose in another branch of the company's business."

SOURCE: A Chandler, *The Visible Hand: The Managerial Revolution in American Business* (Cambridge, MA: Harvard University Press, 1977), pp. 445–49.

does not consider all the investment used in the investment center to generate that income. Net income incorporates interest on any debt used to finance the assets, but it does not include any equity financing charge. Measuring investment center performance using net income creates dysfunctional incentives in investment centers to overinvest. Managers have incentives to overinvest as long as the new investment yields positive net income, no matter how small it is relative to the investment. Two investment centers can have the same net income, but if one has substantially more investment than the other, the one with the smaller investment is yielding a substantially higher rate of return. If investment center managers have the decision rights over capital investments but are not held accountable for how efficiently that capital is employed, they likely will overinvest.

Return on investment

A commonly used investment center performance measure is **return on investment** (ROI). ROI is the ratio of accounting net income generated by the investment center divided by the total assets invested in the investment center. The other variants of ROI are ROA (return on total assets) and RONA (return on net assets — total assets less current liabilities). Exactly how the denominator is measured is unimportant for understanding the key conceptual issues. Hence, for subsequent discussion, ROI, ROA, and RONA are used interchangeably.

ROI overcomes the overinvestment problem of net income by holding the investment center manager responsible for earning a return on the capital employed in the center. It has intuitive appeal because ROI can be compared with external market-based yields to provide a benchmark for a division's performance. However, using ROI creates problems. ROI is not a measure of the division's economic rate of return because accounting net income (the numerator) excludes some value increases, such as land value appreciation, until the land is sold. Accounting net income tends to be conservative in that it recognizes most losses and defers most gains. The denominator of ROI, total assets invested, excludes many intangible assets such as patents and the firm's brand-name capital.

Whereas net income as an investment center performance measure creates an overinvestment problem, using ROI typically creates an underinvestment problem. Managers have incentives to reject profitable projects with ROIs below the mean ROI for the division because accepting these projects lowers the division's overall ROI. For example, suppose the division has an average ROI of 19 percent, 4 percent above its 15 percent cost of capital.[6] A new investment project that is 10 percent the size of the combined division is available. Its ROI is 16 percent, which is above the cost of capital of 15 percent, so that taking this project would increase the value of the firm. However, accepting this project lowers the division's average ROI to 18.7 percent (or $0.90 \times 19\% + 0.10 \times 16\%$). If the division is evaluated based on increasing ROI, the division management will reject the project, even though its return exceeds the opportunity cost of capital. Underinvesting results. In some cases overinvestment also can occur using ROI. For example, suppose a division has a 15 percent cost of capital, but only a 10 percent ROI. This division has incentive to seek out and accept a 12 percent ROI project. Doing so raises the division's ROI. But clearly this project is unprofitable because it is earning less than its cost of capital.

Riskier projects require a higher cost of capital to compensate investors for bearing this risk. If managers are rewarded solely for increasing their division's ROI without being charged for any additional risk imposed on the firm, they have an incentive to plunge the firm into risky projects. Also, a manager with a short time horizon who is evaluated based on ROI would prefer projects that boost ROI in immediate years (the horizon problem) even if they were expected to be unprofitable over the life of the project.

---

[6] Cost of capital is the rate of return the firm must pay the market to raise capital. If the firm can raise money at 15 percent and invest in projects earning 16 percent, the firm's value increases.

Quaker Oats's Use of Residual Income	Quaker Oats Company uses residual income to evaluate and reward internal performance. As described in its Proxy Statement,

The primary Company and business unit performance measure is Controllable Earnings, which is calculated as operating income (adjusted for certain financial costs) less a capital usage charge based on each business unit's invested capital. With incentives tied to maximizing Controllable Earnings, managers focus on generating greater profitable growth, investing in projects where returns exceed our cost of capital and efficiently utilizing assets. These are the drivers of long-term cash flow—ultimately the keys to building shareholder value.

On August 1, 2001, PepsiCo and Quaker Oats merged.

SOURCE: Quaker Oats Co. 1999 Proxy Statement (April 3, 2000). Also see http://www.sec.gov/Archives/edgar/data/81371/0000081371-00-000010-index.html.

TABLE 5–3   **Comparison of Residual Income to ROI ($000,000)**

	Division A	Division B
Invested capital	$100	$1,000
Net income	30	250
Capital charge (20%)	20	200
Residual income	10	50
ROI	30%	25%

Residual income

To overcome some of the incentive deficiencies of ROI, such as underinvesting, some firms use residual income to evaluate performance. **Residual income** measures divisional performance by subtracting the opportunity cost of capital employed from division profits (after excluding any interest expense included in division profits). Suppose a division has profits of $20 million and investment (total assets) of $100 million. This division also has a required cost of capital of 15 percent. Its ROI is 20 percent, which is in excess of its cost of capital (15 percent). Residual income is $5 million (or $20M − 15% × $100M). Under the residual income approach, divesting a project with an ROI of less than 20 percent, but above 15 percent, lowers residual income, although it raises average ROI.

Nonetheless, residual income is not without its own problems. Residual income is an absolute number, and thus larger divisions typically have larger residual incomes than smaller divisions, making relative performance-evaluation comparisons across investment centers of different sizes more difficult. To implement residual income measures, senior managers must estimate the cost of capital for each division. In principle each division will have a different cost of capital to allow more precise performance evaluations by controlling for risk differences.

Like ROI, residual income measures performance over one year. It does not measure the impact of actions taken today on future firm value. For example, cutting maintenance increases current period residual income (and ROI) but jeopardizes future cash flow and hence firm value.

Table 5–3 illustrates the differences between ROI and residual income. Division B has 10 times the invested capital and more than 8 times the net income of

Division A. Which division is the better performer? Division B has five times the residual income of Division A, but Division A has the higher ROI. Does this mean Division A is better? The larger division, B, is more important to the firm, since more of the firm's income is from Division B. Division A, if younger than B, will have a higher ROI partly because it has taken its most profitable projects first. As firms (or divisions) grow, their ROI tends to fall to the extent they invest in the most profitable projects first. Therefore, Division A's higher ROI does not imply that it is the better-managed division or has the best investment prospects.

Identifying the "better" division requires establishing a benchmark. Suppose Divisions A and B had budgeted residual incomes of $12 million and $45 million, respectively. We would likely conclude that Division B was the better performer because it exceeded its budget by $5 million, whereas Division A fell short of its budget by $2 million. Of course, these conclusions depend on whether, at the end of the year, we still believe the beginning-of-year budgets ($12 and $45 million) to be valid performance benchmarks.

4. Economic Value Added (EVA®)

A number of large companies, including AT&T, Briggs & Stratton, Coca-Cola Company, CSX Corp., Quaker Oats Company, and Whirlpool Corp., use **economic value added** or **EVA®** as a measure of performance.[7] EVA is widely heralded in the business press and several large consulting firms help companies implement EVA.[8] Other EVA-like terms have been created such as *economic profit, shareholder value added, total business return,* and *cash-flow return on investment.* And like EVA, these other metrics are variants of residual income. The formula for EVA is:

$$\text{EVA} = \frac{\text{Adjusted accounting}}{\text{earnings}} - \left(\begin{array}{c}\text{Weighted-average cost of}\\ \text{capital} \times \text{Total capital}\end{array}\right)$$

This formula is basically the same as residual income. EVA, like residual income, measures the total return after deducting the cost of all capital employed by the division or firm. Even though the formula is the same as the residual income formula, the two differ in three ways. First, different accounting procedures are often used to calculate "adjusted accounting earnings" than are used in reporting to shareholders.[9] For example, U.S. accounting rules require that the entire amount spent on research and development each year be deducted from earnings. This creates incentives for managers with a short horizon to cut R&D spending. One adjustment to accounting earnings that EVA advocates suggest is adding back R&D spending and treating it as an asset to be amortized, usually over three to seven years. Total capital in the EVA formula consists of all the division's or firm's assets, including the amount of capitalized R&D and other capitalized accounting adjustments. However, many firms using EVA choose not to make any accounting adjustments.

---

[7] EVA is a registered trademark of Stern Stewart & Co.

[8] S Tulle, "The Real Key to Creating Wealth," *Fortune,* September 20, 1993, pp. 38–50; R Myers, "Metric Wars," *CFO,* October 1996, pp. 41–50; S Stern, J Shiely, I Ross, *The EVA Challenge* (New York: John Wiley & Sons, Inc., 2001); A Ehrbar, *EVA: The Real Key to Creating Wealth* (New York: John Wiley & Sons, 1998).

[9] For a more complete description of EVA: see B Stewart, *The Quest for Value* (New York: Harper Business, 1991). Also see D Solomons, *Divisional Performance: Measurement and Control* (Homewood, IL: Richard D. Irwin, 1968) for a discussion of residual income.

Exercise 1:

A company has spent $1.2 million, $1.5 million, and $1.8 million over the last three years on R&D and spent $2.4 million this year. Calculate the amount of R&D assets and R&D expense in the current year under two alternative accounting procedures: (1) all current year R&D is expensed immediately, and (2) R&D is capitalized and then amortized over three years. (Assume that all R&D spending for the year occurs on the first day of the year.)

Answer:

If R&D is expensed immediately, the R&D asset on the balance sheet is $0 and current expense is $2.4 million. The following table amortizes R&D spending over three years. For example, three years ago $1.2 million was spent on R&D. If this amount is capitalized, its annual amortization would be $0.4 million per year. But this $1.2 million would have been completely amortized before the current year began; none of its amortization would be in the current year. The current year's amortization expense of $1.9 million consists of one-third of the R&D spending for the last two years and the current year ($1/3 \times \$5.7$ million).

	R&D Spending	Amortization of R&D Spending Incurred in				Total R&D Amortization Expense in Current Year
		Year 3	Year 2	Year 1	Current Year	
Year 3	$1.2	$0.4				
Year 2	1.5	0.4	$0.5			
Year 1	1.8	0.4	0.5	$0.6		
Current year	2.4		0.5	0.6	$0.8	$1.9

Using the amortization amounts in the previous table, the next table calculates the amount of the R&D asset at the end of the current year.

	Balance of the R&D Asset Acquired in				Total R&D Asset in Current Year
	Year 3	Year 2	Year 1	Current Year	
Beginning of Year 3	$1.2				
Beginning of Year 2	0.8	$1.5			
Beginning of Year 1	0.4	1.0	$1.8		
Beginning of current year	0.0	0.5	1.2	$2.4	
End of current year	0.0	0.0	0.6	1.6	$2.2

The $2.2 million of R&D asset remaining after the end of the current year consists of the remaining unamortized portion of last year's R&D spending ($0.6 million) plus the unamortized portion from this year's R&D spending ($1.6 million). The $1.2 million spent three years ago and $1.5 million spent two years ago are fully amortized, and hence no remaining portion of these amounts is in the R&D asset balance at the end of the current year.

Exercise 2:

The company in Exercise 1 has EVA before R&D of $15.2 million and a weighted-average cost of capital of 20 percent. Calculate its EVA under two alternative accounting procedures: (1) all current year R&D is expensed immediately, and (2) R&D is capitalized and then amortized over three years.

Answer:

1. If all R&D is expensed immediately, the company's EVA after R&D is $12.8 million ($15.2 − $2.4).

2. If R&D is capitalized and then amortized, the company's EVA after R&D is $12.86 million ($15.2 − $1.9 − 20% × $2.2).

Second, the EVA formula uses a weighted-average cost of capital, which reflects the cost of equity and debt. The cost of equity is the price appreciation and dividends the shareholders could have earned in a portfolio of companies of similar risk. This is the opportunity cost the shareholders bear by buying the company's stock. The cost of debt is the current market yield on debt of similar risk. The costs of debt and equity are weighted by the relative amounts of debt and equity. Suppose the cost of equity is 18 percent, the cost of debt is 10 percent, and the firm's capital structure is 40 percent debt and 60 percent equity. Then the weighted-average cost of capital is 14.8 percent (or 0.60 × 18% + 0.40 × 10%).[10]

Third, many companies implementing EVA not only adopt EVA as their performance measure but also link compensation to performance measured by EVA. For example, bonuses are paid only if managers achieve prestated EVA targets. Usually, firms adopting EVA put more of the total compensation paid to managers at risk. Instead of the bonus being 10 percent of the base salary, it becomes 30 percent. The pool of managers eligible to earn bonuses is expanded. Thus, firms adopting EVA increase the sensitivity of their managers' pay to performance. While adopting EVA-based compensation plans imposes more risk on managers, EVA also increases their incentives to maximize firm value.

Adopting EVA as a performance measure and then linking pay to EVA performance is a complicated process. Employees receiving EVA-based bonuses must be trained in how EVA is measured and how their actions affect EVA. For example, EVA creates incentives for managers to reduce unused assets, plant, equipment, and inventory. Eliminating underutilized assets lessens the capital charge applied to these assets and hence increases EVA.[11] Consulting firms that help companies adopt EVA train their employees in how to calculate EVA and how to manage the firm to increase EVA.

---

[10] EVA is calculated on an after-tax basis. In particular, adjusted accounting earnings are net of income taxes and the weighted-average cost of capital is computed as follows: The after-tax cost of debt is computed using 1 minus the marginal corporate tax rate times the market yield on debt of similar risk. For example, if the market yield on equivalent debt is 15 percent and the marginal corporate tax rate is 38 percent, the after-tax cost of debt is 9.3 percent (15% × [1 − 0.38]). If the cost of equity is 20 percent and the proportions of debt and equity are the same, the after-tax weighted-average cost of capital is 14.65 percent (0.50 × 9.3% + 0.50 × 20.0%).

[11] See J Wallace, "Adopting Residual Income-Based Compensation Plans: Do You Get What You Pay For?" *Journal of Accounting and Economics* 24 (1997), pp. 275–300.

| Georgia Pacific and EVA | Georgia Pacific, a large forest products company with more than $10 billion of sales, uses EVA to evaluate all projects, including environmental investments. Each environmental project is evaluated in terms of how it will reduce consulting fees, lower capital costs, increase revenues, reduce fines, and so forth. An internal environmental team for complex environmental permitting was formed and generated $2.1 million of EVA by speeding up the permitting process and by reducing outside consulting.

SOURCE: M Epstein and S Young, "Greening with EVA," *Management Accounting*, January 1999, pp. 45–49. |

TABLE 5–4   2002 EVA Rankings of U.S. Corporations

Rank	Company	2000 EVA ($billions)
1	General Electric Co.	$ 6.0
2	Federal Home Loan Mortgage Corp.	4.1
3	Merck & Co.	3.9
4	Citigroup Inc.	3.0
5	Wal-Mart Stores	2.9
2713	Intl Business Machines Corp.	−8.0
2714	SBC Communications Inc.	−8.4
2715	Lucent Technologies Inc.	−20.0
2716	AT&T Corp.	−27.1
2717	AOL Time Warner Inc.	−27.5

SOURCE: http://www.sternstewart.com/content/performance/200307mvaranking.pdf.

Table 5–4 lists the five companies with the best and worst EVA (in billions of dollars) in 2002. The most profitable company was General Electric with $6.0 billion of EVA. In other words, it earned $6.0 billion after a charge for all the capital employed (debt and equity). It ranked first out of 2,717 companies. AOL Time Warner ranked 2,717; it destroyed $27.5 billion of wealth in 2002.

EVA (and residual income) has several advantages over earnings as a performance measure. It creates incentives to use assets more efficiently. However, like ROI and residual income, EVA still focuses on short-run accounting earnings. Some of the accounting adjustments, such as capitalizing R&D, help reduce this problem. However, the future cash inflows from the R&D are not recognized in EVA (or ROI or residual income) until they are received. Thus, a company can be making very profitable investments, but the returns from these investments will not show up in EVA until the cash inflows from these investments are received.

5. Controllability Principle

Responsibility accounting seeks to identify the objectives of each part of the organization and then to develop performance measures that report the achievement of those objectives. For example, the department handling customer complaints might be evaluated based on how long customers wait for a representative or how many callers hang up. Holding managers responsible for only those decisions for which they have authority is called the **controllability principle. Controllable costs** are all costs affected by a manager's decisions. Uncontrollable costs are those that are not affected by the manager.

| Key Controllable Measures for a Manufacturing Firm | A multibillion-dollar global manufacturing company uses the following measures of performance to control and motivate managers: |

- Design products.
    1. Average time to market for new products.
    2. New product sales dollars as a percentage of total sales.
- Build products.
    3. Percent first-time quality.
    4. Actual-versus-planned production.
    5. Unit cost.
- Distribute products.
    6. Order/ship cycle time.
    7. Days supply of finished goods inventory.
- Market and sell products.
    8. Sales forecast accuracy.
    9. Sales dollars and percent growth.
    10. Market share percentage.
- Manage and develop people.
    11. Employee satisfaction.
- Satisfy customers.
    12. Customer satisfaction.
- Satisfy shareholders.
    13. Cash flow from operations.
    14. Profitability.
    15. Return on net assets.

SOURCE: B Birchard, "How Innovative Companies Use the New Metrics," CFO, October 1995, p. 50.

Some people argue that managers' performance should be judged solely on those items under their control but not on costs over which they have no influence. However, a strict application of the controllability principle has two major drawbacks. First, holding managers accountable for only those variables directly under their control does not give them an incentive to take actions that can affect the consequences of the uncontrollable event. For example, if the marina manager is not held accountable for damage done by hurricanes, the manager has less incentive to prepare the marina for severe storms. While managers cannot influence the likelihood of hurricanes, they can certainly influence the costs incurred when a hurricane strikes.[12]

Consider whether profit center managers should be evaluated based on their profits before or after taxes. One argument is that since profit center managers cannot control changes in state and federal tax policies, they should not be evaluated on after-tax profits. However, profit center managers' decisions affect corporate tax payments in a variety of ways. Export sales affect tax credits. Charitable contributions and inventory write-offs affect taxes. One company reports that before it started charging taxes to profit center managers, the corporation's income taxes

---

[12] G Baker, M Jensen, and K Murphy, "Compensation and Incentives: Practice vs. Theory," *Journal of Finance* 43 (July 1988), p. 611. Also see K Merchant, *Rewarding Results: Motivating Profit Center Managers* (Boston: Harvard Business School Press, 1989), pp. 87–141.

Gaming the System	A credit card company evaluated the performance of employees who answered telephone queries from cardholders about their accounts based on the number of calls answered per day. Cardholders with difficult questions or questions requiring time to retrieve the information had their calls forwarded to other departments. Customer satisfaction fell.

SOURCE: R Simons, *Levers of Control* (Boston: Harvard Business School Press, 1995), p. 84.

were between 46 and 48 percent of its profits. After it started charging taxes to the profit center managers, the average tax rate fell to 40.5 percent.[13] This example illustrates an important point. Evaluating managers on items that they can at least influence, if not control, such as corporate taxes, changes the managers' incentives regarding those items.

The second drawback of the controllability principle is that it ignores the often useful role of relative performance evaluation, in which performance is judged relative to how some comparison group performed instead of by absolute standards. The comparison group helps control for random events that affect both the person being evaluated and the comparison group. For example, many instructors curve grades. Instead of awarding As for scores of 94 to 100, they give As to the top 15 percent of the class. Curving the grades controls for unusually easy or hard exams and removes some of the risk from students.[14]

Whenever the controllability principle is applied and managers are held accountable for their actions, dysfunctional actions can occur. All of the performance measures in Table 5–1 are prone to managerial opportunism in the form of accounting manipulations. Managers can choose depreciation methods or estimates that reduce expenses and increase reported earnings (e.g., straight-line depreciation or longer estimated asset lives). These accounting choices artificially raise ROI. Investment center managers can increase ROI by rejecting (or divesting) profitable projects with ROIs below the division average. All of the accounting measures in Table 5–1 are short-term measures of performance that suffer from the horizon problem, whereby managers emphasize short-term performance at the expense of long-term returns. Each measure requires careful monitoring by senior managers to reduce suboptimal subordinate behavior from the viewpoint of the owners.

Two important points must be stressed regarding the controllability principle:

1. Performance measurement schemes (including accounting-based methods) used mechanically and in isolation from other measures are likely to produce misleading results and induce dysfunctional behavior. For example, in the former Soviet Union, Moscow cab drivers used to be evaluated on the number of miles driven. This scheme caused cab drivers to circle the city on the uncongested outer highways while most of the demand for cabs remained in the congested center of Moscow, where there were no cabs.

2. No performance measurement and reward system works perfectly. There will always remain some managerial action that can be used to enhance the manager's welfare at the expense of the shareholders. One should

---

[13] Merchant (1989), p. 99.
[14] Milgrom and Roberts (1992), p. 219.

avoid discarding a system because some managerial opportunism exists and it proves to be less than perfect. The key question is whether the current system outperforms the next best alternative after all costs and benefits are considered.

Concept Questions		
	Q5–1	What is *responsibility accounting*?
	Q5–2	What role does the firm's internal accounting system play in resolving organizational problems?
	Q5–3	Describe three different types of responsibility centers. Include any shortcomings the centers might have.
	Q5–4	How does EVA differ from residual income?
	Q5–5	What is the controllability principle and what are its limitations?
	Q5–6	What two points must be kept in mind when examining performance-based measurement systems?

B. Transfer Pricing

When goods are transferred from one profit (or investment) center to another, an internal price (the **transfer price**) is assigned to the units transferred. When Chevrolet manufactures an engine that is installed in a Buick, the transfer price is the internal charge paid by the Buick division of General Motors to the Chevrolet division of General Motors. Transfer prices are much more prevalent in organizations than most managers realize. Consider the charge that the advertising department receives from the maintenance department for janitorial service, or the monthly charge for telephones, security services, data processing, legal and personnel services, and so on. Most firms use cost allocations as a method of charging internal users for goods or services received from another part of the organization. These cost allocations are in reality transfer prices. Hence, transfer pricing and cost allocations are two closely related topics. (The specifics of cost allocations are discussed in Chapters 7 and 8.)

There are basically two main reasons for transfer pricing within firms: international taxation and performance measurement of profit and investment centers. Each of these is described below.

1. International Taxation

When products are transferred overseas, the firm's corporate tax liability in both the exporting and importing country is affected. For example, when a copier is manufactured in Rochester, New York, by Xerox Corp. and shipped to England and sold by Rank-Xerox (the Xerox joint venture), U.S. and British taxes paid by Xerox are affected. The transfer price of the copier is a revenue for U.S. tax purposes and a tax-deductible expense in England. To the extent allowed by the tax regulations, the firm will set a transfer price that minimizes the joint tax liability in the two countries. If the two tax jurisdictions have different income tax rates, then the firm will set the transfer price to shift as much of the profit into the lower-rate jurisdiction as possible, subject to the taxing authorities' guidelines.

For example, suppose Bausch & Lomb manufactures a box of contact lenses in the Netherlands and ships the lenses to an Australian subsidiary that sells them for 85 Australian dollars. The variable, out-of-pocket cost of manufacturing the

Frequency of Internal Transfer

A study of 400 large U.S. companies and hospitals reported the following frequencies of internal transfers:

Intracompany Sales as a Percent of Total Sales	Percent of Firms Reporting
0%	31%
1–5	43
6–10	11
11–20	6
21–40	6
41–60	2
Over 60	1

These data indicate that intracompany sales are a relatively small fraction (less than 5 percent) of total sales for over 70 percent of the firms sampled. However, 15 percent of the firms have in excess of 10 percent of their sales in internal transfers. Clearly, for these latter firms, transfer pricing can have a significant effect on divisional profits.

Even though internal transfers are not a large fraction of sales for the typical large U.S. firm, transfer pricing can still have a large effect on the profits of some divisions within these firms.

SOURCE: S Umapathy, *Current Budgeting Practices in U.S. Industry* (New York: Quorum Books, 1987), p. 136.

3. Co Trans Meth

contact lenses is 50 euros. The exchange rate is 0.70 Australian dollars to 1 euro. Suppose the Dutch corporate tax rate is 30 percent and the Australian corporate tax rate is 40 percent. Bausch & Lomb will want to set the transfer price on the lenses as high as permissible to recognize the most profits in the lower tax-rate jurisdiction, which is the Netherlands in this case. The transfer price of the contacts can vary, depending on what fixed costs are allocated to them and how. Suppose Australian and Dutch tax treaties allow Bausch & Lomb to set a transfer price at anywhere between 80 and 110 euros. Table 5–5 illustrates how the combined tax liability varies with the transfer price.

By choosing the highest allowed transfer price, 110 euros, Bausch & Lomb can recognize more profits in the country where the corporate income tax rate is the lowest. If Australia had the lower tax rate, then Bausch & Lomb would select the lowest transfer price, 80 euros, thereby reducing its Dutch tax liability and raising its Australian tax liability. But the higher taxes paid in Australia would be offset by the lower taxes paid in the Netherlands.

Each country has tax regulations that define how companies in its jurisdiction calculate the price of goods transferred in and out of the country. Section 482 of the U.S. Internal Revenue Code authorizes the Internal Revenue Service to regulate the allocation of revenues and costs to prevent tax evasion. International tax treaties regulate allowable transfer pricing methods.[15] Because tax codes vary across jurisdictions, we ignore the role of international taxation in setting transfer

---

[15] R Tang, "Transfer Pricing in the 1990s," *Management Accounting*, February 1992, pp. 22–26; and A King, "The IRS's New Neutron Bomb," *Management Accounting*, December 1992, pp. 35–38.

Negotiated transfer prices

Transfer prices can be set by negotiation between Manufacturing and Distribution. This method can result in transfer prices that approximate opportunity cost because Manufacturing will not agree to a price that is below its opportunity cost and Distribution will not pay a price that is above the product's price elsewhere.

With negotiated transfer prices, the two divisions have the incentive to set the number of units so as to maximize the combined profits of the two divisions. Once the value-maximizing number of units is agreed upon, the negotiated transfer price determines how the total profits are divided between the two divisions. If the two divisions negotiate both price and quantity, they have the joint incentive to maximize the total profit to be split. Yet, if the two divisions only negotiate the price, there is no guarantee that they will arrive at the transfer price that maximizes firm value.

While negotiation is a fairly common method, it too has drawbacks. It is time-consuming and can produce conflicts among divisions. Divisional performance measurement becomes sensitive to the relative negotiating skills of the two division managers. Moreover, if the two divisions negotiate a transfer price without at the same time agreeing on the quantity to be transferred at that price, there is no guarantee that they will arrive at the transfer price that maximizes the firm's value.

4. Reorganization: The Solution If All Else Fails

In some cases, transfer pricing conflicts among responsibility centers can become sufficiently divisive as to impose large costs on the firm. These costs take the form of both influence costs and the opportunity costs that arise when other than firm-value-maximizing transfer prices are chosen. Costly transfer pricing disputes usually occur when the relative volume of transactions among divisions is large. In such cases, a small change in the transfer price can have a large effect on the division's reported profits. Hence, the potential for (and destructive effects of) opportunistic transfer pricing actions by operating managers is substantial.

If transfer pricing becomes sufficiently dysfunctional, reorganize the firm. For example, senior management could combine two profit centers with a large volume of transfers into a single division. Alternatively, it might make more sense to convert Manufacturing into a cost center rather than a profit center and compensate the operating head based on efficiency in production. Or, both divisions might be reorganized as cost centers and keep the pricing and quantity decisions at the central office.

A final possibility is to change the decision rights allocation and give both Manufacturing and Distribution the rights to produce the transferred good. However, this alternative can be expensive due to duplication of resources and effort.

5. Recap

To review the discussion on transfer pricing, firms decentralize and create responsibility centers to take advantage of the divisional manager's specialized knowledge of local conditions. Incentives must then be provided for these managers to use their specialized knowledge to make profit-maximizing decisions for their firms. Forming responsibility centers and linking performance measures to their decision rights (as described in Table 5–1) provides these incentives. When one responsibility center buys or sells goods or services from another center, a transfer price must be established for this internal transaction in order that each center's performance measures, such as earnings, can be calculated. This provides each center the incentive to engage in internal transactions that benefit the firm. Hence, transfer

TABLE 5–6   Advantages and Disadvantages of Common Transfer Pricing Methods

Method	Advantages	Disadvantages
Market-based transfer prices	• Objective • Less subject to manipulation • Often leads to correct long-run make/buy decisions	• Might not exist for specialty items • Might not capture interdependencies among divisions
Variable-cost transfer prices	• Can approximate the opportunity cost of transferring one more unit • Gives the buying division incentive to purchase the correct number of units if selling division has excess capacity	• Does not allow the selling division to recover its fixed costs • Variable cost might vary with output • Selling division has incentive to classify fixed costs as variable costs
Full-cost transfer prices	• Avoids disputes over which costs are fixed and which are variable • Simplicity	• Selling division can export its inefficiencies to the buying division • Buying division purchases too few units
Negotiated transfer prices	• Both selling and buying divisions have incentives to transfer the number of units that maximize their combined profits	• Time-consuming • Depends on the relative negotiating skills of the two divisions
Reorganize the buying and selling divisions	• Eliminates costly disputes over transfer pricing	• Reduces the benefits from having two decentralized responsibility centers

pricing permits managers to exploit the specialized information they possess about local opportunities.[22] Various methods exist for calculating transfer prices. Table 5–6 summarizes the advantages and disadvantages of each method.

No single method is best in all circumstances. Since each method has its advantages and disadvantages, managers must choose the method that trades off decision making, control, and taxes given their unique circumstances. Market-based transfer pricing is objective, but might not capture interdependencies that exist within the firm. While variable-cost transfer pricing approximates the opportunity cost of producing one more unit when excess capacity exists, it is rarely used in practice. Market-based and full-cost transfer pricing methods are the most prevalent; each is used roughly 40 percent of the time.[23] While we do not know exactly why variable costing is used infrequently, we can speculate on some plausible

---

[22] For an expanded discussion of transfer pricing, see R Eccles, "Analyzing Your Company's Transfer Pricing Practices," *Journal of Cost Management,* Summer 1987, pp. 21–33; and R Eccles, *The Transfer Pricing Problem: A Theory for Practice* (Lexington, MA: Lexington Books, 1985). B Holmstrom and J Tirole, "Transfer Pricing and Organizational Form," *Journal of Law, Economics, & Organizations* 7 (1991), pp. 201–28, provide a more mathematical discussion.

[23] R Tang, "Transfer Pricing in the 1990s," *Management Accounting,* February 1992, pp. 22–26; R Benke, Jr. and J Edwards, *Transfer Pricing: Techniques and Uses* (New York: National Association of Accountants, 1980); D Keegan, *Transfer Pricing Practices of American Industry* (Price Waterhouse, March 31, 1984); R F Vancil, *Decentralization: Managerial Ambiguity by Design* (Homewood, IL: Dow Jones-Irwin, 1979), p. 114.

reasons. Full-cost transfer pricing approximates the costs of adding fixed capacity (in the absence of inflation and productivity changes). Also, with variable-cost transfer pricing it is difficult to separate fixed and variable costs. Finally, as discussed earlier, variable costing gives the selling division significant discretion in altering the transfer price by reclassifying fixed costs as variable costs.

The trade-off between decision making and control discussed in Chapter 1 also applies to transfer prices. The transfer price that most accurately measures the opportunity cost to the firm of transferring one more unit inside the firm may not be the transfer pricing method that gives internal managers the incentive to maximize firm value. For example, if the transfer pricing method that most accurately measures the opportunity cost of transferred units also requires managers producing these units to reveal privately held and hard-to-verify data of their costs, then these managers have considerable discretion over the transfer prices. If these transfer prices are important in rewarding managers, the producing managers can distort the transfer price to their benefit. Alternatively, a transfer pricing scheme that measures opportunity cost less accurately but more objectively might produce a higher firm value than a transfer pricing scheme that more closely approximates opportunity costs.

Managers often have authority for external sourcing. The ability to buy/sell outside is an important control device on the transfer pricing scheme. No matter how the internal transfer price is set, the ability to go outside limits the monopoly profits that can be earned by one responsibility center at the expense of another.

Changing transfer-pricing methods does more than shift income among responsibility centers. The level of the firm's output changes, as does firmwide profitability. The transfer price not only changes how the total profit pie is divided among responsibility centers, it also affects the size of the pie.

Finally, transfer pricing is more ubiquitous in organizations than many managers realize. Most organizations recharge inside users for information technology, telecommunications, janitorial service, maintenance, and so forth. In effect, these recharge schemes, based on cost allocations, are cost-based transfer prices. Since much of management accounting and cost accounting deals with cost allocations, many of the same issues that apply to transfer pricing also arise in later chapters.

Concept Questions		
	Q5–7	What are the two main reasons for transfer pricing within firms?
	Q5–8	Name four alternative methods for determining transfer prices.
	Q5–9	Is the choice of transfer pricing methods a zero-sum game?

C. Summary

Besides making operating decisions that involve pricing, marketing, and financing, managers must also ensure that employees perform tasks that add value to the firm. Chapter 4 described the general agency problem and how the firm's organizational architecture can provide incentives for self-interested employees to take value-adding actions. In particular, the organizational architecture, which consists of the three legs of the stool (the performance evaluation system, the performance reward system, and the partitioning of decision rights), helps align employees' and owners' interests. Accounting systems are an integral part of the firm's organizational architecture. This chapter described two central ways in which accounting systems are used: responsibility accounting and transfer pricing.

In responsibility accounting, decision rights within the firm are partitioned to cost, profit, and investment centers. Cost centers usually have decision rights over the mix of inputs used to produce the product or service. Cost centers are then evaluated based on the ability of the center to maximize output for a given cost or to minimize cost for a predetermined amount of output. Profit centers have decision rights over input mix and pricing and are evaluated based on profits. Investment centers have all the decision rights of profit centers plus the rights over how much capital is invested in the center. They are evaluated based on either return on investment or residual income.

Accounting is also often used in transfer pricing. Whenever goods or services are transferred across responsibility centers and the performance of these centers is measured, a transfer price for the transferred item must be calculated. Market prices, cost-based transfer prices, or negotiated transfer prices are used. Cost-based transfer prices include both variable costs and full costs (variable plus fixed costs). Each transfer pricing scheme has pros and cons that depend on the particular circumstances of the firm. Hence, each firm must determine the transfer pricing scheme that is best for its situation. In general, no transfer pricing scheme, just as no particular organizational architecture, is best for all firms or even best for a single firm over time. In transfer pricing schemes, as in other internal accounting methods, a trade-off exists between decision making and control. Transfer price schemes that are best for decision making are not always the best for control and vice versa.

Chapter 6 describes another example of how accounting systems are used to reduce agency problems: budgeting systems.

Self-Study Problems

Self-Study Problem 1:   Tam Burger

In the past five years, Tam Burger has expanded to more than 200 stores, 80 percent of which are franchised. Two of the company-operated units, Northside and Southside, are among the fastest-growing stores. Both are considering expanding their menus to include pizza. Purchase and installation of the necessary equipment costs $180,000 per store. The current investment in the Northside store totals $890,000. Store revenues are $1,100,500 and expenses are $924,420. Expansion of the Northside's menu should increase profits by $30,600. The current investment in the Southside store totals $1,740,000. The store's revenues are $1,760,800 and expenses are $1,496,680. Adding pizza to Southside's menu should increase its profits by $30,600.

Tam Burger evaluates its managers based on return on investment. Managers of individual stores have decision rights over the pizza expansion.

a. Calculate the return on investment for both stores before pizza is added, for the pizza project only, and for the stores after expansion.

b. Assuming a 14 percent cost of capital, calculate residual income for both stores before and after the potential expansion.

c. Will the Tam Burger stores choose to expand? How would the answer change if the stores were franchised units?

Solution:

a. Return on investment before and after the pizza expansion:

	Northside	Southside
ROI before Pizza		
Revenue	$1,100,500	$1,760,800
Expenses	924,420	1,496,680
Net income	$ 176,080	$ 264,120
÷ Assets	890,000	1,740,000
ROI	19.78%	15.18%
ROI of Pizza Only		
Increased profits from pizza	$ 30,600	$ 30,600
÷ Expansion cost	180,000	180,000
ROI of project	17.00%	17.00%
ROI after Pizza		
Total income	$ 206,680	$ 294,720
÷ Total assets	1,070,000	1,920,000
Total ROI	19.32%	15.35%

b. Residual income before and after the pizza expansion:

	Northside	Southside
Cost of capital	14.00%	14.00%
Residual Income before Pizza		
Net income	$176,080	$264,120
Less: Assets × 14%	(124,600)	(243,600)
Residual income	$ 51,480	$ 20,520
Residual Income of Pizza Only		
Increased profits from pizza	$ 30,600	$ 30,600
Less: 14% × Expansion cost	(25,200)	(25,200)
Residual income	$ 5,400	$ 5,400
Residual Income after Pizza		
Net income	$206,680	$294,720
Less: 14% × Assets	(149,800)	(268,800)
Residual income	$ 56,880	$ 25,920

c. The two units currently have different ROIs. The smaller Northside store is earning an ROI of just under 20 percent, while the larger Southside store is earning an ROI of just over 15 percent. Since the project's ROI is 17 percent, adding the project to the Northside store lowers its average ROI; adding the project to the Southside store raises its average ROI. The Northside manager will avoid adding pizza to the menu, since the store's ROI would drop as a result. The Southside manager, however, will want to add pizza since the store's ROI would subsequently rise.

If the stores were franchised units, both owners would definitely expand. The ROI of the project is higher than the cost of capital. This ensures a positive residual income for the project. As long as the residual income is positive, any franchise owner would jump at the opportunity. Franchise owners would not care if the store's ROI dropped as long as the residual income increased.

Self-Study Problem 2:   BioScience

Tomato beetles, a major pest to the tomato crop, are now being controlled by toxic pesticides. The firm BioScience invested $5 million in R&D over the last five years to produce a genetically engineered, patented microbe, MK-23, which controls tomato beetles in an environmentally safe way. BioScience built a plant with capacity to produce 10,000 pounds of MK-23 per month. The plant cost $12 million and has a 10-year life. MK-23 has a variable cost of $3 per pound. Fixed costs are $50,000 per month for such costs as plant management, insurance, taxes, and security. Plant depreciation is not included in the $50,000 fixed cost.

The following table summarizes the full cost of producing MK-23:

Depreciation per month ($12 million ÷ 120 months)	$100,000
Other fixed costs	50,000
Total fixed costs	$150,000
÷ Capacity per month (pounds)	10,000
Fixed costs per unit of capacity (pound)	$ 15.00
Variable costs per pound	3.00
Full cost per pound	$ 18.00

MK-23 is sold for $30 per pound. BioScience is currently selling 8,000 pounds per month to tomato farmers.

Another division of BioScience, Home Life, wants to secure 1,000 pounds per month of MK-23 that it will process further into a consumer product, Tomato Safe, for gardeners. Home Life is willing to pay an internal transfer price of $5 per pound. Home Life will incur an additional $4 of variable cost per pound of MK-23 in packaging and reducing the potency of MK-23 to make Tomato Safe more appropriate for home gardeners. Tomato Safe will sell for $20 per pound of MK-23.

a. Should the internal transfer be allowed?
b. What happens if the transfer price is set at full cost, $18? What happens if the transfer price is set at variable cost, $3?
c. After deciding to use variable cost as the transfer price, new farm orders for 2,000 pounds of MK-23 at $30 per pound per month are received. Suppose plants come only in fixed sizes of 10,000-pound capacities of $12 million each. Analyze the various options facing BioScience.

d. What is the opportunity cost of the excess capacity prior to producing MK-23 for Tomato Safe?

e. What happened to the $5 million R&D costs incurred to invent MK-23?

Solution:

a. The following table indicates that BioScience generates incremental cash flow of $13 for every pound of MK-23 it transfers to Home Life to be converted to Tomato Safe, assuming it does not forgo selling this pound of MK-23 directly to farmers for $30 per pound.

Contribution Margins for MK-23 and Tomato Safe

	MK-23	Tomato Safe
Selling price	$30.00	$20.00
Variable costs		
Manufacturing MK-23	3.00	3.00
Additional processing		4.00
Contribution margin	$27.00	$13.00

Clearly, if BioScience has excess capacity of 2,000 pounds of MK-23 production per month, then transferring 1,000 pounds of MK-23 enhances overall firm profits.

b. If a full-cost transfer price of $18 per pound is charged for MK-23, Home Life will not accept the transfer because its total cost of $22 ($18 transfer price plus $4 for further processing) is above the market price of $20. If the firm has unused capacity, then transferring at full cost causes it to forgo selling Tomato Safe and receiving $13 per pound for its unused capacity. Transferring at variable cost ($3) allows Tomato Safe to be produced. In the case where the firm has unused excess capacity, full-cost transfer pricing leads to the wrong decision.

If variable-cost transfer pricing is used, each month 1,000 pounds of MK-23 are transferred to Home Life.

c. After receiving new farm orders for 2,000 pounds of MK-23, management has three options. First, it can fill 1,000 pounds of the 2,000-pound order, because this is all the capacity available after transferring 1,000 pounds to Home Life. Second, management can cancel the 1,000 pounds transferred for Tomato Safe and fill all 2,000 pounds of the new farm order. Or third, management can build a new plant to increase capacity. Canceling the 1,000-pound transfer to Home Life and using this production capacity to fill the new farm orders increases BioScience's cash flows:

Contribution from new order	2,000 × $27	$54,000
Contribution forgone from Tomato Safe	1,000 × $13	13,000
Additional contribution		$41,000

Every additional pound of MK-23 sold to farmers instead of converted to Tomato Safe contributes $14 (or $27 − $13) to BioScience's cash flows, assuming the firm does not have enough capacity to meet demand in the farm market. The third option of adding capacity to meet both farm and home demand is not profitable. Each pound, including new capacity for MK-23, costs $18, and Tomato Safe cannot recover these costs. Therefore, full-cost transfer pricing includes the cost of adding additional capacity.

The managers of Home Life will object to canceling the internal transfer because their divisional profits will fall. They will most likely construct reasons that such a decision will adversely affect their other products. Undoing the decision to transfer MK-23 will require senior managers' time and patience. Thus, influence costs are likely to be generated. In general, internal transfers tend to be permanent and difficult to change.

d. Prior to accepting the internal transfer of MK-23 to produce Tomato Safe, BioScience has 2,000 pounds of unused capacity. If the demand for MK-23 is growing, then either consuming this capacity with an internal transfer causes the firm to forgo the contribution margin on lost sales of MK-23 or else the firm has to add capacity. The decision to permanently consume fixed capacity should not be based on the short-run incremental cost of the transfer unless it is highly likely that the internal transfer is the only long-run use of the unused capacity. Full-cost transfer pricing includes an estimate of the cost of adding capacity and reveals the past (historical) cost of a unit of capacity. A new unit of capacity will cost more than historical cost if there has been construction cost inflation. However, a unit of capacity can cost less than the historic cost if adding a second plant creates productivity enhancements or synergies.

e. These R & D costs were not included in the manufacturing costs of MK-23. The accounting system writes these costs off when incurred. The firm has an unrecorded but real economic asset, the patent on MK-23. The profit of $12 per pound of MK-23 ($30 − $18) represents the firm's return on this investment.

Problems

P 5–1:   Canadian Subsidiary

The following data summarize the operating performance of your company's wholly owned Canadian subsidiary for 2009 to 2011. The cost of capital for this subsidiary is 10 percent.

	($000,000)		
	2009	2010	2011
Subsidiary net income	$14.0	$14.3	$14.4
Total assets in subsidiary	125	130	135
Return on net investment* in subsidiary	20%	22%	24%

*Net investment is calculated as total assets less all liabilities.

Required:

Critically evaluate the performance of this subsidiary.

P 5–2:   Phipps Electronics

Phipps manufactures circuit boards in Division Low in a country with a 30 percent income tax rate and transfers them to Division High in a country with a 40 percent income tax. An import duty of 15 percent of the transfer price is paid on all imported products. The import duty is not deductible in computing taxable income. The circuit boards' full cost is $1,000 and variable cost is $700; they are sold by Division High for $1,200. The tax authorities in both countries allow firms to use either variable cost or full cost as the transfer price.

Required:

Analyze the effect of full-cost and variable-cost transfer pricing methods on Phipps's cash flows.

P 5–3:   EVA

At a Stern-Stewart conference, one of the topics discussed was "taking EVA to the shop floor." This session described "driving EVA analysis, decision making, and incentives down through every level of an organization." If you were attending this session, what questions would you ask the panelists?

P 5–4:   Economic Earnings

A large consulting firm is looking to expand the services currently offered its clients. The firm has developed a new performance metric called "Economic Earnings," or EE for short. The performance metric is argued to be a better measure of both divisional performance and firmwide performance, and hence "a more rational platform for compensating employees and managers." The consulting firm is seeking to convince clients they should replace their current metrics, such as accounting net income, ROA, EVA, and so forth, with EE.

EE starts with traditional accounting net income but then makes a series of adjustments. The primary adjustment is to add back depreciation and then subtract a required return on invested capital. The consultants argue for adding accounting depreciation back because it is a sunk cost. It does not represent a current cash flow. For example, suppose a client has accounting net income calculated as:

**Client's Traditional
Income Statement**

Revenues	$5,700
Cost of goods sold	(2,000)
Gross margin	$3,700
Depreciation	(900)
Selling, general, other	(700)
Interest	(500)
Earnings before taxes	$1,600
Income taxes (40%)	(640)
Net income	$ 960

Suppose the client has total assets of $6,000 and a risk-adjusted weighted-average cost of capital (WACC) of 25 percent. Then this client's EE is calculated as follows:

Client's Economic Earnings

Net income	$ 960
Depreciation	900
Capital charge*	(1,500)
Economic earnings	$ 360
*Total assets	$6,000
WACC	25%
Capital charge	$1,500

Required:

Critically evaluate EE as a performance measure. What are its strengths and weaknesses?

P 5–5: Eastern University

The Eastern University Business School teaches some undergraduate business courses for students in the Eastern University College of Arts and Science (CAS). The 6,000 undergraduates generate 2,000 undergraduate student course enrollments in business courses per year. The B-school and CAS are treated as profit centers in that their budgets contain student tuition revenues as well as costs. The deans have discretion to set tuition and salaries and determine hiring as long as they operate with no deficit (revenues = expenses). Undergraduate tuition is $12,000 per year and each student takes eight courses per year. Average undergraduate financial aid amounts to 20 percent of gross tuition. The current transfer price rule is gross tuition per course less average financial aid.

This transfer price rule gives net tuition to the B-school as a revenue and deducts an equal amount from the CAS budget. The CAS dean argues that the current system is grossly unfair. CAS must provide costly services for undergraduates in order to maintain a top-rated undergraduate program. For example, career counseling, academic advising, sports programs, and the admissions office are costs that must be incurred if undergraduates are to enroll at Eastern. Therefore, the CAS dean argues, the average cost of these services per undergraduate student course enrollment should be deducted from the tuition transfer price. These undergraduate student services total $9.6 million per year.

Required:

a. Calculate the current revenue the B-school is receiving from undergraduate business courses. What will it be if the CAS dean's proposal is adopted?

b. Discuss the pros and cons of the CAS dean's proposal.

c. As special assistant to the B-school dean, prepare a response to the CAS proposed tuition transfer pricing scheme.

P 5–6: Scoff Division

Scoff Division of Worldwide Paint is currently losing money and senior management is considering selling or closing Scoff. Scoff's only product, an intermediate chemical called Binder, is used principally by the latex division of the firm. If Scoff is sold, the latex division can purchase ample quantities of Binder in the market at sufficiently high quality levels to meet its requirements. Worldwide requires all of its divisions to supply product to other Worldwide divisions before servicing the external market.

Scoff's statement of operations for the latest quarter is:

SCOFF DIVISION
Profit/Loss
Last Quarter
($000s)

Revenues		
Inside	$200	
Outside	75	$275
Operating expenses		
Variable costs	$260	
Fixed costs	15	
Allocated corporate overhead	40	315
Net income (loss) before taxes		$(40)

Notes:

1. Worldwide Paint has the policy of transferring all products internally at variable cost. In Scoff's case, variable cost is 80 percent of the market price.
2. All of Scoff's fixed costs are avoidable cash flows if Scoff is closed or sold.
3. Of the $40,000 allocated corporate overhead, $4,000 will be avoided if Scoff is closed or sold.

Required:

Calculate the annual net cash flows to Worldwide Paint for closing or selling Scoff.

P 5–7:   Discretionary Cost Centers

Discretionary costs are defined as "costs that (1) arise from periodic (usually yearly) appropriation decisions regarding the maximum amounts to be incurred and (2) have no well-specified function relating inputs (as measured by the costs) and outputs (as measured by revenue or other objectives such as students' knowledge or patients' health). Examples include advertising, public relations, executive training, teaching, research, health care, and management consulting services. The most noteworthy aspect of discretionary costs is that one is seldom confident that the 'correct' amount is being spent."[24]

Discretionary cost centers are those parts of the organization that have large discretionary costs. Such subunits of the organization tend to have a high percentage of their costs in human resources performing nonrepetitive and nonroutine functions whose principal output is information-/service-oriented. The value of the output from discretionary cost centers is difficult to determine, as is the quality. Examples of discretionary cost centers include R&D, legal, public relations, and internal consulting organizations.

Max Jarvis, corporate controller for a midsize steel company, has just attended a seminar on discretionary cost centers. He decides to adopt this approach

---

[24] C Horngren and G Foster, *Cost Accounting: A Managerial Emphasis*, 6th ed. (Englewood Cliffs, NJ: Prentice Hall, 1987), p. 378.

in budgeting and controlling several corporate headquarters departments, including market research and environmental protection. These departments are currently cost centers.

Required:

    a. How do discretionary cost centers differ from cost centers and profit centers?

    b. What changes do you expect Max Jarvis's adoption of discretionary cost centers to produce?

P 5–8:   Metal Press

Your firm uses return on assets (ROA) to evaluate investment centers and is considering changing the valuation basis of assets from historical cost to current value. When the historical cost of the asset is updated, a price index is used to approximate replacement value. For example, a metal fabrication press, which bends and shapes metal, was bought seven years ago for $522,000. The company will add 19 percent to this cost, representing the change in the wholesale price index over the seven years. This new, higher cost figure is depreciated using the straight-line method over the same 12-year assumed life (no salvage value).

Required:

    a. Calculate depreciation expense and book value of the metal press under both historical cost and price-level-adjusted historical cost.

    b. In general, what is the effect on ROA of changing valuation bases from historical cost to current values?

    c. The manager of the investment center with the metal press is considering replacing it because it is becoming obsolete. Will the manager's incentives to replace the metal press change if the firm shifts from historical cost valuation to the proposed price-level-adjusted historical cost valuation?

P 5–9:   Lewis Corporation

Lewis is a large manufacturer of office equipment, including copiers. Its electronics division is a cost center. Currently, electronics sells circuit boards to other divisions exclusively. Lewis has a policy that internal transfers are to be priced at full cost (fixed + variable). Thirty percent of the cost of a board is considered fixed.

The electronics division is operating at 75 percent of capacity. Because there is excess capacity, electronics is seeking opportunities to sell boards to non-Lewis firms. The electronics division policy on non-Lewis sales states that each job must cover full cost and a minimum 10 percent profit. Electronics division management will be measured on its ability to make the minimum profit on any non-Lewis contracts that are accepted.

Copy products is another Lewis division. Copy products has recently reached an agreement with Siviy, a non-Lewis firm, for the assembly of subsystems for a copier. Copy products has selected Siviy because of Siviy's low labor cost. The subsystem Siviy will assemble requires circuit boards. Copy products has stipulated that Siviy must purchase the circuit boards from Lewis's electronics division because of their high quality and dependability.

Electronic products is anxious to accept this new work from copy products because it will increase electronic products' workload by 15 percent.

In negotiating a contract price with Siviy, copy products needs to take into account the cost of the circuit boards from electronics. The financial analyst from copy products assumes that electronics will sell the circuit boards to Siviy at full cost (the same as the internal transfer price). Electronics is considering adding the minimum 10 percent profit margin to its full cost and transferring at that price to Siviy.

Copy products is preparing to negotiate its contract with Siviy. Develop and discuss at least three options that may be used in establishing the transfer price between the electronics division and Siviy. Discuss the advantages and disadvantages of each.

SOURCE: L Harrington, R Lewis, P Siviy, and S Spector.

P 5–10:   ICB, Intl.

ICB has four manufacturing divisions, each producing a particular type of cosmetic or beauty aid. These products are then transferred to five marketing divisions, each covering a particular geographic region. Manufacturing and marketing divisions are free to negotiate among themselves the transfer prices for products transferred internally. The manufacturing division that produces all the hair care products wants a particular hair conditioner it developed and produces for Asian markets priced at full cost plus a 5 percent profit markup, which amounts to $105 per case.

The South American marketing division believes it can sell this conditioner in South America after redesigning the labels. However, most South American currencies have weakened against the dollar, putting further pressure on the prices of U.S.–produced products. The South American marketing division estimates it can make money on the hair conditioner only if it can buy it from manufacturing at $85 per case.

Manufacturing claims that it cannot make a profit at $85 per case. Moreover, the other ICB marketing divisions that are paying around $105 per case will likely want to renegotiate the $105 transfer price if South America marketing buys it for $85.

You work for the corporate controller of ICB, Intl. She has asked you to write a short, nontechnical memo to her that spells out the key points she should consider in her upcoming meeting with the two division heads regarding transfer pricing. You are not being asked to recommend a particular transfer price, but rather to list the important issues the controller should be aware of for the meeting.

P 5–11:   Microelectronics

Microelectronics is a large electronics firm with multiple divisions. The circuit board division manufactures circuit boards, which it sells externally and internally. The phone division assembles cellular phones and sells them to external customers. Both divisions are evaluated as profit centers. The firm has the policy of transferring all internal products at market prices.

The selling price of cellular phones is $400, and the external market price for the cellular phone circuit board is $200. The outlay cost for the phone division to complete a phone (not including the cost of the circuit board) is $250. The variable cost of the circuit board is $130.

Required:

a. Will the phone division purchase the circuit boards from the circuit board division? (Show calculations.)

b. Suppose the circuit board division is currently manufacturing and selling externally 10,000 circuit boards per month and has capacity to manufacture

15,000 boards. From the standpoint of Microelectronics, should 3,000 additional boards be manufactured and transferred internally?

c. Discuss what transfer price should be set for (*b*).

d. List the three most important assumptions underlying your analysis in (*b*) and (*c*).

P 5–12:   US Copiers

US Copiers manufactures a full line of copiers including desktop models. The Small Copier division (SCD) manufactures desktop copiers and sells them in the United States. A typical model has a retail price of less than $500. An integral part in the copier is the toner cartridge that contains the black powder used to create the image on the paper. The toner cartridge can be used for about 10,000 pages and must then be replaced. The typical owner of an SCD copier purchases four replacement cartridges over the life of the copier.

SCD buys the initial toner cartridges provided with the copier from the Toner Division (TD) of US Copiers. TD sells subsequent replacement cartridges to distributors that sell them to U.S. retail stores. Toner cartridges sell to the end consumer for $50. TD sells the cartridges to distributors for about 70 percent of the final retail price paid by the consumer. The Toner Division manager argues that the market price to TD of $35 (70% × $50) is the price SCD should pay to TD for each toner cartridge transferred.

Required:

a. Why does US Copiers manufacture both copiers and toner cartridges? Why don't separate firms specialize in either copiers or toner cartridges like Intel specializes in making computer chips and Gateway specializes in assembling and selling PCs?

b. You work for the president of SCD. Write a memo to your boss identifying the salient issues she should raise in discussing the price SCD should pay TD for toner cartridges included in SCD copiers.

P 5–13:   Cogen

Cogen's Turbine Division manufactures gas-powered turbines for generating electric power and hot water for heating systems. Turbine's variable cost per unit is $150,000 and its fixed cost is $1.8 million per month. It has excess capacity. Cogen's Generator Division buys gas turbines from Cogen's Turbine Division and incorporates them into electric steam generating units. Both divisional managers are evaluated and rewarded as profit centers.

The Generator Division has variable cost of $200,000 per completed unit, excluding the cost of the turbine, and fixed cost of $1.4 million per month. The Generator Division faces the following monthly demand schedule for its complete generating unit (turbine and generator):

Quantity	Price ($000)	Quantity	Price ($000)
1	$1,000	5	$800
2	950	6	750
3	900	7	700
4	850	8	650

Required:

  a. If the transfer price of turbines is set at Turbine's variable cost ($150,000), how many turbines will the Generator Division purchase to maximize its profits?

  b. The Turbine Division expects to sell a total of 20 turbines a month, which includes both external and internal sales. Calculate the (average) full cost of a turbine (fixed cost plus variable cost) at this level of sales.

  c. If the transfer price of turbines is set at Turbine's (average) full cost calculated in (b), how many turbines will the Generator Division purchase?

  d. Should Cogen use a variable-cost transfer price or a full-cost transfer price to transfer turbines between the Turbine and Generator divisions? Why?

P 5–14:   Assembly and Parts Departments

A large corporation has a manufacturing division with 40 parts departments and 20 assembly departments. The parts departments manufacture most of the parts for the products, and the assembly departments assemble the parts (some of which are purchased outside the firm) into final products. About 70 percent of the manufacturing operation occurs in one geographic location, and the remainder is in plants around the world. Several hundred different final products, some in very large unit volumes, are produced, involving thousands of different parts. The final products range from inexpensive consumer goods (selling price $50) to very expensive business products (selling price $500,000).

The marketing division forecasts sales six months in advance. These forecasts then become manufacturing's production quotas. As soon as manufacturing produces the product, it is turned over to marketing for either shipment or storage.

Manufacturing's production quotas are "exploded" into parts requirements and the parts departments begin producing parts for use by assembly. In order for assembly to meet its production quota on final products, every part in the product must be on hand for assembly. Not having a spring costing $0.0001 is just as costly to the assembly department as not having a motor costing $500; both shut down the assembly line.

If a part is not available, the assembly department tries to assemble another product, often by coercing a parts department to alter its schedule to produce parts for the alternative product assembly.

Assembly and parts departments are evaluated as cost centers. Parts departments are evaluated on being able to produce parts cheaper than last year while meeting quality standards. They must also meet their production quotas and schedules. Parts departments that continually force assembly lines to shut down because of parts shortages impose significant costs on assembly lines. Assembly departments are evaluated based on (1) their labor costs to assemble products versus budgeted labor costs and (2) their production quotas.

In order to minimize average costs, parts departments try to manufacture all the units of a particular part required for a six-month period at once. The major discretionary fixed cost per part is setup time. That is, when the machine is being converted from producing one part to another, no output is produced. Setup time is often half a day. Therefore, to reduce average unit costs, parts are produced in large lot sizes. As soon as parts are produced, they are sent to the assembly departments. Parts departments carry no inventories of final parts, only raw materials.

There is no transfer price for parts. There is no need for a transfer price because assembly and parts departments are evaluated as cost centers. One senior manager feels that considerable squabbling over transfer prices could be avoided by focusing on departmental costs that are under the control of the department managers. A modification is being proposed that would charge each department a holding cost for inventory on hand (12 percent cost of inventory). That is, each assembly department currently charged for its direct labor, overhead, and factory burden will also be charged 12 percent of all parts inventories. Assembly managers think this is unfair because they have no control over when and how many parts the parts departments produce. Assembly departments would like to get all the parts for one month's assembly instead of having to hold a six-month inventory of parts.

The parts department managers argue that the inventory holding cost charged to assembly departments is fair because assembly departments are always screaming for more inventory as safety stocks to their assembly lines, and this inventory holding charge will force assembly departments to bear the costs they are imposing on the firm by demanding large inventories. Parts department managers argue that it is inefficient to produce in one-month lot sizes.

Required:

Critically evaluate the existing management control system. Describe the strengths and weaknesses of the current and proposed systems. What dysfunctional behaviors exist in the current and proposed systems?

P 5–15: U.S. Pump Systems

U.S. Pump is a multidivisional firm that manufactures and installs chemical piping and pump systems. The valve division makes a single standardized valve. The valve division and the installation division are currently involved in a transfer pricing dispute. Last year, half of the valve division's output was sold to the installation division for $40 and the remaining half was sold to outsiders for $60.

The existing transfer price has been set at $40 per pump through a process of negotiation between the two divisions, with the involvement of senior management. The installation division has received a bid from an outside valve manufacturer to supply it with an equivalent valve for $35 each.

The manager of the valve division has argued that if it is forced to meet the external price of $35, it will lose money on selling internally.

The operating data for last year for the valve division are as follows:

VALVE DIVISION
Operating Statement
Last Year

	To Installation Division		To Outside	
Sales	20,000 @ $40	$800,000	20,000 @ $60	$1,200,000
Variable costs	20,000 @ $30	(600,000)		(600,000)
Allocated fixed costs		(135,000)		(135,000)
Gross margin		$ 65,000		$ 465,000

Analyze the situation and recommend a course of action. What should installation division managers do? What should valve division managers do? What should U.S. Pump's senior managers do?

P 5–16:   GM on ROA

General Motors's CFO, Michael Losh, converted GM's performance measure for compensation from net income to ROA. In explaining the move in *CFO* (August 1996), he said, "ROA was a logical next step because all those other measures generally have focused on the income statement. Moving to ROA means that we're going to focus not only on the income statement, but on the balance sheet and effective utilization of the assets and liabilities that are on the balance sheet as well.

"ROA is a better measure for us than EVA. . . . EVA is simpler conceptually, because it automatically builds on growth, whereas with this approach we know that we've got to have growth as an overlying objective. . . . EVA is more comprehensive. And that has a certain appeal to me. But, given our situation, particularly in our North American operations, it just would not have been the right measure.

"ROA works for us and EVA doesn't because our operations have to deal with those two different kinds of starting points. Within GM, in our North American operations, you've got a classic turnaround situation, and in our international operations, you've got a classic growth situation. You can apply ROA to both; you can't apply EVA to both."

Required:

   a. Explain how ROA focuses on both the income statement and the balance sheet.
   b. Explain why EVA is more "comprehensive" than ROA.
   c. Do you agree with Losh's statement that "you can apply ROA to both; you can't apply EVA to both"? Explain.

P 5–17:   PepsiCo, Inc.

Prior to 1997, PepsiCo, a major soft drink company, had a restaurant division consisting of Kentucky Fried Chicken, Taco Bell, and Pizza Hut.[25] The only cola beverage these restaurants served was Pepsi. Assume that the major reason PepsiCo owned fast-food restaurants was to increase its share of the cola market. Under this assumption, some Pizza Hut patrons who order a cola at the restaurant and are told they are drinking a Pepsi will switch and become Pepsi drinkers instead of Coke drinkers on other purchase occasions. However, studies have shown that some customers refuse to eat at restaurants unless they can get a Coke.

PepsiCo sells Pepsi-Cola to non-PepsiCo restaurants at $0.53 per gallon. This is the market price of Pepsi-Cola. Pepsi-Cola's variable cost is $0.09 per gallon, and its total (fixed and variable) cost is $0.22 per gallon. PepsiCo produces Pepsi-Cola in numerous plants located around the world. Plant capacity can be added in small increments (e.g., a half-million gallons per year). The cost of additional capacity is approximately equal to the fixed costs per gallon of $0.13.

Required:

What transfer price should be set for Pepsi transferred from the soft drink division of PepsiCo to a PepsiCo restaurant such as Taco Bell? Justify your answer.

---

[25] In October 1997, PepsiCo spun off its restaurant division to a new company, Tricon Global Restaurants Inc. The shares of Tricon were distributed to the shareholders of PepsiCo. Tricon and PepsiCo then began operating as separate, independent companies. However, Tricon entered into multiyear agreements with PepsiCo to sell Pepsi beverages in Tricon restaurants.

P 5–18: CJ Equity Partners

CJ Equity Partners is a privately held firm that buys small family-owned firms, installs professional managers to run the firms, and then sells them 3–5 years later, often for a substantial profit. CJ Equity is owned by four partners who raise capital from wealthy investors and invest this money in unrelated firms. Their aim is to provide a 15 percent rate of return on their investors' capital after paying the partners of CJ Equity a management fee. CJ Equity currently owns three operating companies: a tool and die company (Jasco Tools), a chemical bottling company (Miller Bottling), and a janitorial supply company (JanSan). The professional managers running these three companies are paid a fixed salary and bonus based on the performance of their company. Currently, CJ Equity is measuring and rewarding its three professional managers based on the net income after taxes of their individual companies. The following table summarizes the current year's operations of each of the three companies (all dollar amounts in millions):

	Jasco Tools	Miller Bottling	JanSan
Weighted average cost of capital	14%	12%	10%
CJ Equity management fee*	$0.200	$0.200	$0.200
Number of employees	84	120	85
Interest expense*	$1.600	$1.800	$0.800
Income tax rate	40%	40%	40%
Operating expenses	$33.600	$36.800	$18.200
Revenues	$38.600	$42.900	$21.200
Total assets	$20.1	$31.2	$16.3

* Not included in the operating expenses of the three companies.

CJ Equity charges each of the three operating companies an annual management fee of $200,000 for managing the companies, including filing the various tax returns. The weighted average cost of capital represents CJ Equity's estimate of the risk-adjusted, after-tax rate of return of similar companies in each operating company's industry.

You have been hired by CJ Equity as a consultant to recommend whether CJ Equity should change the way it measures the performance of the three companies (net income after taxes), which is then used to compute the professional managers' bonuses.

Required:

a. Design and prepare a performance report for the three operating companies that you believe best measures each operating company's performance and which will be used in computing the three professional managers' bonuses. In other words, using your performance measure, compute the performance of each of the three operating companies.

b. Write a short memo explaining why you believe the performance measure you chose in part (*a*) best measures the performance of the three professional managers.

P 5–19:   Sunstar Appliances

Sunstar sells a full line of small home kitchen appliances, including toasters, coffee makers, blenders, and bread machines. It is organized into a marketing division and a manufacturing division. The manufacturing division is composed of several plants, each a cost center, making one type of appliance. The toaster plant makes several different models of toasters and toaster ovens. Most of the parts, such as the heating elements and racks for each toaster, are purchased externally, but a few are manufactured in the plant, including the sheet metal forming the body of the toaster. The toaster plant has a number of departments including sheet metal fabrication, purchasing, assembly, quality assurance, packaging, and shipping.

Each toaster model has a product manager who is responsible for manufacturing the product. Each product manager manages several similar models. Product managers, with the help of purchasing, negotiate prices and delivery schedules with external part vendors. Sunstar's corporate headquarters sets all the toaster models' selling prices and quarterly production quotas to maximize profits. Product managers' compensation and promotions are based on lowering unit costs and meeting corporate headquarters' production quota.

The product manager sets production schedule quotas for the product and is responsible for ensuring that the distribution division of Sunstar has the appropriate number of toasters at each distribution center. Product managers have discretion over outsourcing, production methods, and labor scheduling to manufacture the particular models under their control. For example, they do not have to produce the exact number of toasters set by corporate headquarters quarterly, but rather product managers have some discretion to produce more or fewer toasters as long as the distribution centers have enough inventory to meet demand.

The following data were collected for one particular toaster oven, model CVP-6907. These data are corporate forecasts for model CVP-6907 in regard to how prices and total manufacturing costs are expected to vary with the number of toasters manufactured (and sold) per day.

MODEL CVP-6907
Total Cost and Price
by Quantity

Quantity	Manufacturing Cost	Price
100	$1,450	$120
105	1,496	116
110	1,545	112
115	1,596	108
120	1,650	104
125	1,706	100
130	1,765	96
135	1,826	92
140	1,890	88
145	1,956	84
150	2,025	80

In addition to the manufacturing costs reported in the table, there are $10 of variable selling and distribution costs per toaster.

Required:

    a. What daily production quantity would you expect the product manager for model CVP-6907 to set? Why?

    b. Evaluate Sunstar's performance evaluation system as it pertains to product managers. What behavior does it likely create among manufacturing product managers?

    c. Describe the changes you would recommend Sunstar consider making in its performance evaluation system for manufacturing product managers.

P 5–20:   Stale-Mart

Joan Chris is the Denver district manager of Stale-Mart, an old established chain of more than 100 department stores. Her district contains eight stores in the Denver metropolitan area. One of her stores, the Broadway store, is over 30 years old. Chris began working at the Broadway store as an assistant buyer when the store first opened, and she has fond memories of the store. The Broadway store remains profitable, in part because it is mostly fully depreciated, even though it is small, is in a location that is not seeing rising property values, and has had falling sales volume.

Stale-Mart owns neither the land nor the buildings that house its stores but rather leases them from developers. Lease payments are included in "operating income before depreciation." Each store requires substantial leasehold improvements for interior decoration, display cases, and equipment. These expenditures are capitalized and depreciated as fixed assets by Stale-Mart. Leasehold improvements are depreciated using accelerated methods with estimated lives substantially shorter than the economic life of the store.

All eight stores report to Chris, and, like all Stale-Mart district managers, 50 percent of her compensation is a bonus based on the average return on investment of the eight stores (total profits from the eight stores divided by the total eight-store investment). Investment in each store is the sum of inventories, receivables, and leasehold improvements, net of accumulated depreciation.

She is considering a proposal to open a store in the new upscale Horse Falls Mall three miles from the Broadway store. If the Horse Falls proposal is accepted, the Broadway store will be closed. Here are data for the two stores (in millions of dollars):

	Broadway *(Actual)*	*Horse Falls* *(Forecast)*
Average inventories and receivables during the year	$2.100	$2.900
Leasehold improvements, net of accumulated depreciation	0.900	4.600
Operating income before depreciation	1.050	3.300
Depreciation of leasehold improvements	0.210	1.425

Assume that the forecasts for Horse Falls are accurate. Also assume that the Broadway store data are likely to persist for the next four years with little variation.

The Lumber Division only purchases timber from the Forest Division. The purchase price is computed as Lumber's share of Forest's operating expenses where the share is based on Lumber's fraction of Forest's total board feet harvested. Lumber takes the timber from Forest, cuts it into lumber, and sells it to distributors. Lumber's total revenues, other operating expenses, and assets are $7.6 billion, $3.5 billion, and $2.7 billion, respectively. Lumber's operating expenses of $3.5 billion do not include its pro rata share of Forest's operating expenses.

Savannah Products uses economic value added (EVA) to evaluate and reward the performance of the senior managers in the two divisions. The risk-adjusted weighted-average cost of capital for the Forest and Lumber Divisions are 15 percent and 20 percent, respectively.

Required:

    a. Calculate the EVA of the Forest and Lumber Divisions.

    b. Based on your calculations in (*a*), identify the most profitable division.

    c. Do the calculations in (*a*) correctly identify the most profitable division? Explain why or why not.

    d. What changes would you recommend Savannah Products make in its performance measurement scheme?

P 5–24:   **Westinghouse Electric Supply Contract**

To induce utilities to award contracts to Westinghouse Electric to build nuclear reactors, Westinghouse contracted to supply uranium to these utilities at an average price of $9.50 per pound over a 20-year period. In 1966, Westinghouse disclosed in its annual report,

> Westinghouse Electric Corporation has entered into a number of long-term contractual agreements to sell up to 80 million tons of uranium to utility companies to encourage nuclear reactor construction and to secure sales of uranium. The contracts are optional to the purchasers at a fixed price. The average contract price is approximately $9.50 per pound, and the current market price is $8.00 per pound. We cannot reasonably estimate the amount of purchases that will be made under these agreements because of the optional nature of the contracts.[26]

By 1976, the market price of uranium was over $40 per pound. Westinghouse was unable to meet its commitments to deliver uranium and was faced with a potential loss of $2.275 billion, which was over six times the company's net income in 1976. In 1976, a new manager of the Westinghouse uranium supply division (USD) was hired. This division is responsible for the acquisition and sales of uranium to utilities, both those that have Westinghouse reactors and those with competitor reactors. USD purchases raw uranium in world markets and then processes it into nuclear reactor fuel cells. This division is evaluated as a profit center. The new manager argues that because a number of long-term supply agreements were signed before he joined Westinghouse, USD's revenues on these old contracts should be measured using the current market price rather than the original contract price.

---

[26] Cited in M Dugan and W Hughes, "Why Not Disclose Supply Commitments?" *Management Accounting*, July 1991, pp. 34–36.

Required:

a. How should the performance of the uranium supply division be measured?

b. Public utilities, including those with nuclear power generating plants, are regulated by state commissions. State regulatory commissions set the utilities' prices for electricity based on cost plus a "fair return on capital." Cost is based on transactions prices. Given the facts in the problem, how should managers of public utilities with Westinghouse Electric uranium contracts behave, in light of the difference between the contract price of $9.50 per pound of uranium and the current market price of $44.50?

P 5–25: XBT Keyboards

The keyboard division of XBT, a personal computer manufacturing firm, fabricates 50-key keyboards for both XBT and non-XBT computers. Keyboards for XBT machines are included as part of the XBT personal computer and are also sold separately. The keyboard division is a profit center. Keyboards included as part of the XBT PCs are transferred to the PC division at variable cost ($60) plus a 20 percent markup. The same keyboard, when sold separately (as a replacement part) or sold for non-XBT machines, is priced at $100. Projected sales are 50,000 keyboards transferred to the PC division (included as part of the XBT PC) and 150,000 keyboards sold externally.

The keys for the keyboard are fabricated by XBT on leased plastic injection-molding machines and then placed in purchased key sockets. These keys and sockets are assembled into a base, and connectors and cables are attached. Ten million keys are molded each year on four machines to meet the projected demand of 200,000 keyboards. Molding machines are leased for $500,000 per year per machine; maximum practical capacity is 2.5 million keys per machine per year. The variable overhead account includes all of the variable factory overhead costs for both key manufacturing and assembly. Studies have shown that variable overhead is more highly correlated with direct labor dollars than any other volume measure.

Cost Data per XBT Keyboard

Variable Costs		
Materials		
Plastic for keys	$ 3.00	
Base	11.00	
Key sockets	13.00	
Connectors and cables	9.00	
Direct labor, keys	4.00	
Direct labor, assembly	12.00	
Variable overhead*	8.00	$60.00
Fixed Costs†		
Key injection molding	$10.00	
Fixed overhead	18.00	28.00
Unit manufacturing cost		$88.00

*Based on direct labor dollars.

†At projected production of 200,000 keyboards.

Sara Litle, manager of the keyboard division, is considering a proposal to buy some keys from an outside vendor instead of fabricating them inside XBT. These keys (which do not include the sockets) will be used in the keyboards included with XBT PCs but not in keyboards sold separately or sold to non-XBT computer manufacturers. The lease on one of XBT's key injection-molding machines is about to expire and the capacity it provides can be easily shifted to the outside vendor.

The outside vendor will produce keys for $0.39 per key and will guarantee capacity of at least 2.5 million keys per year. Litle is compensated based on the profits of the keyboard division. She is considering returning one of the injection-molding machines when its lease expires and purchasing keys from the outside vendor.

Required:

a. How much will XBT save per key if it outsources the 2.5 million keys rather than producing them internally?
b. What decision do you expect Sara Litle to make? Explain why.
c. If you were a large shareholder of XBT and knew all the facts, would you make the same decision as Litle? Explain.
d. What changes in XBT's accounting system and/or organizational structure would you suggest, given the facts of the case? Explain why.

P 5–26: Infantino Saab

Infantino Saab is a car dealership that has been in business for 40 years at the same 20-acre location selling and servicing new and "pre-owned" (used) Saabs. Two years ago Infantino Saab replaced its aging showroom and service center with a new, state-of-the-art facility. When Ms. Infantino's father started the dealership, the business was on the outskirts of town. Now with city sprawl, the dealership is located on a busy commercial street surrounded by other dealerships, restaurants, and shopping centers.

The market for new cars is very competitive because many buyers shop on the Internet before visiting new car dealers. Once customers decide to purchase a new car from a dealer, they usually trade in their used car to avoid the hassle of selling the car themselves, and hence these new car buyers are willing to accept lower prices from car dealers for their trade-ins. Also, pre-owned cars have higher margins because there is less competition for used cars, as each used car differs in terms of mileage, condition, and options. Suppose a new car is sold for $45,000 ($500 over dealer cost) and the buyer receives a trade-in allowance on his old car of $8,000 and pays the difference in cash. That used car is then sold for $10,800. The dealer makes $500 on the new car and $2,800 on the used car. Infantino also offers parts and service for the new and pre-owned cars it sells.

Infantino Saab is organized into three departments: New Cars, Pre-owned Cars, and Service. All three share the same building and lot where the new and used cars are displayed. Ms. Infantino compensates her three department heads based on residual income. After careful analysis by her financial manager, they determine that all three departments should be charged for the capital invested in their departments at 16 percent.

The new building cost $12 million and the land cost $900,000. The following table summarizes the land and building utilization by each department, each department's net income, and other net assets invested in each department:

	New Cars	Pre-owned Cars	Parts & Service	Total
Percent of land	50%	40%	10%	100%
Percent of building	30%	10%	60%	100%
Department Income	$600,000	$1,725,000	$1,813,000	$4,138,000
Other net assets	$2,500,000	$6,700,000	$1,300,000	$10,500,000

For example, the new car department occupies 50 percent of the land and 30 percent of the building. It had net income of $600,000 and other net assets of $2,500,000. Other net assets consist of all inventories and receivables (net of external financing) invested in the department. For example, the new car department has a substantial inventory of new cars. But this new car inventory is mostly financed by short-term bank loans. The new car department pays interest on these loans, which is deducted (and hence included) in the new car department's net income of $600,000. Each department's income consists of all revenues and expenses directly traceable to that department, including interest on any debt used to finance the department's inventory. Income taxes are not included in each department's net income reported in the table. Infantino Saab uses the trade-in allowance of used cars taken in trade as the transfer price of used cars in calculating the net incomes of the new and pre-owned car departments.

Required:

    a. Calculate the residual income of each of the three divisions of Infantino Saab.

    b. Discuss the relative profitability of the three departments. Which is making the most money and which is making the least amount of money?

    c. Discuss whether the residual incomes of the three departments capture the true profitability of each department. What problems do you see in the way Ms. Infantino is evaluating the performance of the three department managers and of Infantino Saab as a whole?

P 5–27:   University Medical Lab

The University has a medical school that operates a large teaching hospital. Other smaller hospitals in the region are independent of University Hospital in the sense that they are owned and operated by unaffiliated not-for-profit corporations.

University Hospital has a Medical Laboratory Department (MLD) that provides a wide range of medical tests including hematology, biopsies, electron microscopy, immunology, toxicology, and virology. Few of the other independent hospitals in the region have the scale to provide the same comprehensive range of tests that MLD provides. Consequently, other hospitals rely on MLD for some of their lab tests.

For quality assurance and billing purposes, MLD tracks how much time laboratory technicians spend on each test performed. Based on these time sheets and the salaries of the technicians, 70 percent of MLD's lab technician salary expense (direct labor cost) is incurred performing lab tests for patients at University Hospital. The remaining 30 percent of MLD's lab technician direct labor cost is incurred performing tests for patients at the other, nonaffiliated hospitals. Direct labor cost consists of the salaries and benefits of the lab technicians while they are performing test procedures.[27]

MLD charges other departments at University Hospital the variable cost of performing the tests where variable cost is the actual direct labor cost of the lab technician (salary and benefits) plus direct materials. Direct materials (laboratory materials, supplies, chemicals, and other consumables) are 40 percent of direct labor. So, if the direct labor of a lab technician for a particular test is $120, the University Hospital department requesting the test is charged $168 ($120 + 40% × $120).

The reason for charging University Hospital departments requesting lab work only the variable (direct) cost of the tests is to keep the cost of lab work down. The vast majority of patients at University Hospital have HMO or other third-party insurance providers that pay University Hospital for providing care to their clients. Before University Hospital can get reimbursed from these third-party providers, the insurance provider must preapprove the treatment plan (including lab tests). If the Hospital does not get permission, the insurance provider might deny the charge. Since insurance providers base their approval decisions to some extent on the estimated cost of the treatment (including lab work), the Hospital wants to reduce the cost of lab tests to encourage the performance of adequate test procedures.

Outside, unaffiliated hospitals are charged 200 percent of the direct cost of performing a test. So, if an outside (unaffiliated) hospital sends a specimen to MLD and requests a test that has a direct labor cost of $120, it is charged $336 ([$120 + 40% × $120] × 2).

The following table lists the expenses incurred by MLD in the most recent fiscal year.

MEDICAL LABORATORY DEPARTMENT
University Hospital
Expenses
(Most Recent Fiscal Year)

Direct labor	$1,400,000
Direct materials & supplies	560,000
Fixed overhead cost	900,000

Fixed overhead cost of $900,000 consists of supervision and administrative costs, occupancy costs, depreciation and leases of equipment, training, and so forth.

Required:

a. Based on the existing pricing arrangements for inside and outside users, prepare an income statement for MLD for the most recent fiscal year.

---

[27] Suppose a technician who is paid $25 per hour and has benefits of 30 percent of her salary works 8 hours one particular day—6 hours performing tests and the other 2 hours in training. Then the direct labor cost of this lab technician is $195 (6 hours × $25 × 1.3) and the other $65 (2 hours × $25 × 1.3) is charged to Fixed Overhead.

b. Given the income statement you prepared in part (*a*), discuss the financial condition of MLD and the reasons for MLD's financial condition for the last fiscal year.

c. The manager of MLD believes that University Hospital departments sending specimens to his department for testing are not paying their fair share of the costs of his department under the current pricing arrangement. The MLD manager is proposing that inside users of MLD be charged the full cost that his department incurs to provide testing services (direct labor plus direct material plus fixed overhead). The manager proposes that since MLD's fixed costs are $900,000 and the direct labor costs are $1,400,000, then for every $1 of direct labor cost in each lab test, that lab test (for inside University Hospital departments) should be charged $0.6429 ($900,000/$1,400,000) of fixed overhead (in addition to the direct material charge of $0.40 and the direct labor charge of $1). The pricing of lab tests for outside users will not change. Prepare an income statement for MLD for the most recent fiscal year assuming the MLD manager's proposal is accepted.

d. Explain briefly why the net income figures computed in parts (*a*) and (*c*) differ.

e. Describe the likely consequences for MLD if its manager's suggestion described in part (*c*) is implemented.

P 5–28:   Swan Systems

Swan Systems developed and manufactures residential water filtration units that are installed under sinks. The filtration unit removes chlorine and other chemicals from drinking water. This Dutch company has successfully expanded sales of its units in the European market for the past 12 years. Swan started a U.S. manufacturing and marketing division six years ago and an Australian manufacturing and marketing division three years ago. Here are summary operating data for the last fiscal year:

SWAN SYSTEMS
Summary of Operations, Last Fiscal Year
(Millions of Euros)

	Australia	Netherlands	U.S.	Total
Sales	€50	€55	€75	€180
Divisional expenses	38	33	58	129
Net income	€12	€22	€17	€ 51

Senior management is in the process of evaluating the relative performance of each division. The Netherlands division generates the most profits and has the largest investment of assets, as indicated by the following table:

Year	Net Cash Flow (Millions)	Discount Factor	Present Value of Cash Flow
0	$(10.0)	1.000	$(10.00)
1	2.0	0.893	1.79
2	1.9	0.797	1.51
3	1.9	0.712	1.35
4	1.8	0.636	1.14
5	1.8	0.567	1.02
6	1.8	0.507	0.91
7	1.8	0.452	0.81
8	1.8	0.404	0.73
9	1.7	0.361	0.61
10	1.7	0.322	0.55
Net present value			$0.42

Judson realizes that Adams's projected cash flows are most likely optimistic, but she does not know how optimistic or even whether or not the project is a positive net present value project. She decides to change Adams's performance measure used in computing her bonus. Adams's compensation will be based on residual income (EVA). Judson also changes the accounting system to track asset expansion and depreciation on the expansion. Adams's profits from operations will now be charged for straight-line depreciation of the expansion using a 10-year life (assume a zero salvage value). Calculate Adams's expected residual income from the expansion for each of the next 10 years.

c. Based on your calculations in (b), will Adams propose the expansion project? Explain why.

d. Instead of using residual income as Adams's performance measure in (b), Judson uses net cash flows from operations less straight-line depreciation. Will Adams seek to undertake the expansion? Explain why.

e. Reconcile any differences in your answers for (c) and (d).

Cases

Case 5–1:   Troy Industrial Designs

Susan Willard, the CEO of Troy Industrial Designs (TID), has called a meeting to evaluate the present method of charging the two offices at Washington and Rochester for the shared services of the Creative Design Group (CDG). She wants to discuss the present transfer price system and suggest a better one.

TID is a reputable firm in the industrial design sector. It bids for design contracts from different firms. When a bid is accepted, TID either makes prototypes based on the client's blueprints, designs new products out of existing designs, or draws designs for a product the client has in mind. TID charges clients a fixed figure upon completion of the job and 1 percent of sales accruing to the client every year for the first seven years for the use of TID designs.

The two offices of TID are independently run by different managers and are both profit centers. Each manager assigns account executives to individual accounts. The account executives are paid a fixed salary, but a large part of their compensation is their bonus, which is based on the revenues accruing from the jobs they manage. Once receiving a job, each account executive informs George Scott, the head of CDG. They meet with the client and discuss the details of the job, including specifications, requirements, and expected completion time. The client is consulted when the account executive receives the preliminary design. As soon as the job for a client is finished, the account executive makes a detailed report explaining the work done, the number of designers employed for the job, the number of hours worked on it, the amount billed to the client, and any follow-up needed. Designing is a one-time job, and additional follow-up is rarely required. Account executives are responsible for any follow-up on the jobs done by them. If the client comes back with another project, it is treated as a separate job.

TID centralized the design departments of the two offices to take advantage of the specialized knowledge of the designers. Though CDG is only five years old, it employs the best talent and uses the latest technology. This has had a positive impact on customers, and because of this, TID has grown rapidly in the past few years. The two offices have a lot of confidence in the Creative Design Group and use it for all their design needs. The rapid growth has caused top management to rethink the transfer pricing procedures and other organizational aspects of the business.

CDG is totally responsible for the designing part of the job. It interacts with the client only at the design stage; all other aspects of the job are done by the appropriate account executive. CDG works in small teams, each led by a supervisor who reports to Scott daily. Scott is evaluated on the excess of revenues collected from the two offices over the costs of his department. The transfer price charged to each office is decided before the designing job is taken by CDG. Before the client is brought in for the discussion, the account executive and Scott decide what fees CDG will charge the office for the services. Revenues for CDG come from the predetermined fees charged to the two offices.

Willard suggests that CDG should provide its services free of charge. Under this proposal, Scott would receive a fixed salary and a bonus based on overall firm profits (i.e., a percentage of the combined profits of the two offices). She thinks that as the cost of the department is finally consolidated with the costs of the firm, there should be no transfer prices for the department. Removal of the transfer price will help reduce the work of the accounting department and streamline the department to cope with the firm's rapid growth. Willard says that the firm is committed to designing the best products and that transfer prices really do not matter.

Required:

Will the resources of the Creative Design Group be efficiently utilized under the new plan? Why? What are the merits and demerits of the existing plan? Is the proposed plan better than the existing one? Why or why not?

Case 5–2: IBM Data Center for Eastman Kodak

In 1989, IBM and Kodak entered into an agreement whereby IBM would build and operate a data processing center in Rochester, New York, that consolidates five Kodak data centers into one. Of the five original data centers, three were at separate sites in Rochester, one was in Colorado, and the fifth was in Canada. Over 300 Kodak data processing employees became IBM employees. Original Kodak-owned IBM computer equipment was purchased by IBM and moved into the IBM data center. IBM augmented this equipment with a significant amount of new equipment (both IBM and non-IBM products).

Kodak pays an annual fee to IBM based on the amount of computing services it receives (lines printed, amount of disk space, etc.). The IBM data center pays all labor costs, occupancy costs, and the costs of all software and hardware acquired. The IBM data center is evaluated based on profits and the satisfaction of Kodak customers.

Prior to the IBM–Kodak agreement, excess capacity in the mainframe business increased price competition. A third-party vendor made a bid to operate Kodak's five data centers at a substantial cost savings to Kodak. One source of the savings came from the vendor using less-expensive computers that are plug-compatible with IBM's machines. IBM made a successful counteroffer to keep the Kodak account and run the data center.

Kodak views this contract as very important because it allows it to get out of the business of operating computers and focus management's attention on more strategic issues, such as the design and maintenance of applications software directed at Kodak's core businesses. These application computer programs run at the data center and include billing, payroll, accounts payable and receivable, cost accounting, and manufacturing production control and scheduling.

IBM considers the data center an important test case for its other large corporate clients looking to move away from IBM hardware to cheaper plug-compatible mainframe clones. If IBM can successfully operate this data center for Kodak, it opens an important market of other Fortune 100 companies. IBM has the expertise in centralizing and standardizing different data centers into one using a common set of operating standards. There are economies of scale in corporate computing. Also, operating data centers allows IBM to learn about large corporate client computing, develop new software and hardware, and test new products before they are released.

One key issue that arises is the internal transfer price the IBM data center pays for the IBM hardware and software it "purchases" from other IBM divisions. This transfer price does not affect the price Kodak pays to IBM. Suppose a hypothetical IBM mainframe numbered A606 that sells for $3 million is installed in the Kodak data center. The variable cost of this machine is $1 million and its unit manufactured cost (UMC), including fixed and variable costs, is $1.6 million. Moreover, IBM's total selling, general, and administrative (SG&A) costs are 30 percent of revenue, of which half (15 percent) varies directly with revenue. The plug-compatible machine comparable to the A606 sells for $1.9 million. The other IBM divisions providing goods and services to the data center have profit responsibilities.

Required:

a. What factors should IBM consider when developing the transfer pricing rule used to charge the data center for IBM products installed in the data center?

b. Given the limited information in the case, what transfer price rule would you suggest IBM adopt for IBM products installed in the data center?

Using your transfer price rule, what price should be charged for the hypothetical A606 mainframe?

Case 5–3: Celtex

Celtex is a large and very successful decentralized specialty chemical producer organized into five independent investment centers. Each of the five investment centers is free to buy products either inside or outside the firm and is judged based on residual income. Most of each division's sales are to external customers. Celtex has the general reputation of being one of the top two or three companies in each of its markets.

Don Horigan, president of the synthetic chemicals (Synchem) division, and Paul Juris, president of the consumer products division, are embroiled in a dispute. It all began two years ago when Juris asked Horigan to modify a synthetic chemical for a new household cleaner. In return, Synchem would be reimbursed for out-of-pocket costs. After Synchem spent considerable time perfecting the chemical, Juris solicited competitive bids from Horigan and some outside firms and awarded the contract to an outside firm that was the low bidder. This angered Horigan, who expected his bid to receive special consideration because he developed the new chemical at cost and the outside vendors took advantage of his R&D.

The current conflict involves Synchem's production of chemical Q47, a standard product, for consumer products. Because of an economic slowdown, all synthetic chemical producers have excess capacity. Synchem was asked to bid on supplying Q47 for the consumer products division. Consumer products is moving into a new, experimental product line, and Q47 is one of the key ingredients. While the order is small relative to Synchem's total business, the price of Q47 is very important in determining the profitability of the experimental line. Horigan bid $3.20 per gallon. Meas Chemicals, an outside firm, bid $3.00. Juris is angry because he knows that Horigan's bid contains a substantial amount of fixed overhead and profit. Synchem buys the base raw material, Q4, from the organic chemicals division of Celtex for $1.00 per gallon. The organic chemical division's out-of-pocket costs (i.e., variable costs) are 80 percent of the selling price. Synchem then further processes Q4 into Q47 and incurs additional variable costs of $1.75 per gallon. Synchem's fixed manufacturing overhead adds another $0.30 per gallon.

Horigan argues that he has $3.05 of cost in each gallon of Q47. If he turned around and sold the product for anything less than $3.20, he would be undermining his recent attempts to get his salespeople to stop cutting their bids and start quoting full-cost prices. Horigan has been trying to enhance the quality of the business he is getting, and he fears that if he is forced to make Q47 for consumer products, all of his effort the last few months will be for naught. He argues that he already gave away the store once to consumer products and he won't do it again. He asks, "How can senior managers expect me to return a positive residual income if I am forced to put in bids that don't recover full cost?"

Juris, in a chance meeting at the airport with Debra Donak, senior vice president of Celtex, described the situation and asked Donak to intervene. Juris believed Horigan was trying to get even after their earlier clash. Juris argued that the success of his new product venture depended on being able to secure a stable, high-quality supply of Q47 at low cost.

Required:

    a. Calculate the incremental cash flows to Celtex if the consumer products division obtains Q47 from Synchem versus Meas Chemicals.

    b. What advice would you give Debra Donak?

Case 5–4: Royal Resort and Casino

Royal Resort and Casino (RRC), a publicly traded company, caters to affluent customers seeking plush surroundings, high-quality food and entertainment, and all the "glitz" associated with the best resorts and casinos. RRC consists of three divisions: hotel, gaming, and entertainment. The hotel division manages the reservation system and lodging operations. Gaming consists of operations, security, and junkets. Junkets offers complimentary air fare and lodging and entertainment at RRC for customers known to wager large sums. The entertainment division consists of restaurants, lounges, catering, and shows. It books lounge shows and top-name entertainment in the theater. Although many of those people attending the shows and eating in the restaurants stay at RRC, customers staying at other hotels and casinos in the area also frequent RRC's shows, restaurants, and gaming operations. The following table disaggregates RRC's total EVA of $12 million into an EVA for each division:

ROYAL RESORT AND CASINO
EVA by Division
(Millions $)

	Entertainment	Hotel	Gaming	Total
Adjusted accounting profits	$ 5	$ 10	$30	$ 45
Invested Capital	$40	$120	$60	$220
Weighted-average cost of capital	15%	15%	15%	15%
EVA	$(1)	$ (8)	$21	$ 12

Based on an analysis of similar companies, it is determined that each division has the same weighted-average cost of capital of 15 percent.

    Across town from RRC is a city block with three separate businesses: Big Horseshoe Slots & Casino, Nell's Lounge and Grill, and Sunnyside Motel. These businesses serve a less affluent clientele.

Required:

    a. Why does RRC operate as a single firm, whereas Big Horseshoe Slots, Nell's Lounge and Grill, and Sunnyside Motel operate as three separate firms?

    b. Describe some of the interdependencies that are likely to exist across RRC's three divisions.

    c. Describe some of the internal administrative devices, accounting-based measures, and/or organizational structures that senior managers at RRC can use to control the interdependencies that you described in part (*b*).

    d. Critically evaluate each of the "solutions" you proposed in part (*c*).

Chapter Six

Budgeting

Chapter Outline

Chapter 4 described the firm's organizational architecture as consisting of three integrated systems: assigning decision rights, measuring performance, and rewarding performance. The firm's organizational architecture reduces conflicts of interest among the various parties contracting with the firm. This chapter describes how budgeting is used for decision making and to control conflicts of interest. Budgeting systems are part of the firm's accounting system. A **budget** is management's formal quantification of the operations of an organization for a future period. It is an aggregate forecast of all transactions expected to occur.

Giving a manager an advertising budget of $8 million authorizes that manager to consume $8 million of firm resources on advertising. Put another way, the advertising budget authorizes the manager to spend $8 million on advertising by assigning these decision rights to the manager. At the end of the year, actual spending on advertising can be compared with the budget; any difference is a measure of the manager's performance and can be used in determining the manager's performance rewards. Budgets are thus part of the firm's organizational architecture; they partition decision rights and control behavior.

Budgets are an integral part of decision making by assembling knowledge and communicating it to the managers with the decision rights. Budgets are developed using key planning assumptions or basic estimating factors that are widely accepted forecasts of strategic elements faced by the firm. Typical planning assumptions are product prices, unit sales, foreign currency exchange rates, and external prices of key inputs. Budgets help assemble and then communicate these key planning assumptions. Various managers throughout the firm must accept these planning assumptions as reasonable and likely. Key planning assumptions represent those factors that are, to some extent, beyond management control and that set a limit on the overall activities of the firm.

Each key planning assumption must be forecast using past experience, field estimates, and/or statistical analysis. Making these forecasts usually involves accumulating the collective knowledge of numerous individuals in the firm. No single manager has detailed knowledge of total expected unit sales, but individual salespeople have knowledge of likely unit sales in their districts. Because salespersons have specific knowledge of their territories, the firm develops an accurate estimate of the planning assumption (firmwide sales) by adding sales forecasts from all the salespeople. From these key planning assumptions, a complete set of management

| Budgeting at the HON Company—I | The HON Company, a Fortune 500 manufacturer of office furniture with 14 plants in the United States, sells throughout the United States and Canada. The furniture business is very cyclical and competitive. Intense price pressure causes manufacturers to carefully plan expansions. All the departments at HON work closely to coordinate their operating plans. Budgeting allows the firm's strategy of productivity increases to be linked to action plans. "The budget has become the integral planning and control device for achieving two strategic objectives: ongoing new product and service development and rapid continuous improvement. The budget also serves as an important vehicle for ensuring that the corporate culture is unified in its understanding of—and commitment to—strategic objectives." |

SOURCE: R Drtina, S Hoeger, and J Schaub, "Continuous Budgeting at the HON Company," *Management Accounting*, January 1996, pp. 20–24.

Budgets Widely Used

A study of 400 large U.S. firms reports that budgets are used with the following frequencies:

Industry	Percent Using Budgets
Commercial banks	98%
Diversified financial	93
Diversified service	100
Hospitals	100
Life insurance	96
Large manufacturing	100
Medium manufacturing	98
Retailers or wholesalers	97
Transportation	94
Utilities	96
Miscellaneous	83

As indicated by these data, almost all large U.S. firms use budgets.

SOURCE: S Umapathy, *Current Budgeting Practices in U.S. Industry* (New York: Quorum Books, 1987), p. 20.

plans is developed regarding raw materials acquisition, labor requirements, financing plans, and distribution and marketing budgets.

Figure 6–1 summarizes the various functions performed by budgets. James McKinsey, founder of the consulting firm McKinsey & Co., describes budgetary control as involving the following:

1. The statement of the plans of all departments of the business for a certain period of time in the form of estimates.
2. The coordination of these estimates into a well-balanced program for the business as a whole.
3. The preparation of reports showing a comparison between the actual and the estimated performance, and the revision of the original plans when these reports show that such revision is necessary.[1]

FIGURE 6–1
Functions of budgets

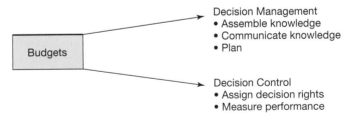

This chapter first describes some generic budgeting systems used by different organizations (section A). It then discusses how budgeting involves the trade-off between decision management and decision control (section B). Section C describes how budgets help reduce conflicts of interest between owners and managers. A comprehensive budget example is provided in the appendix.

---

[1] J McKinsey, *Budgetary Control* (New York: Ronald Press, 1922), p. 8.

A. Generic Budgeting Systems

The following discussion illustrates the essential aspects of budgeting using a simple organizational form (a hypothetical private country club), a more complicated organization (a university), and a large corporation. In all three examples, budgeting is part of the system whereby decision rights are partitioned and performance is measured and rewarded.

1. Country Club

This example illustrates the use of budgets to assign decision rights and create incentives for employees to act in the owners' interests.

Bay View Country Club is a private club with 350 members. Members pay a one-time initiation fee of $45,000 and dues of $385 per month. They have access to the golf course, pool, tennis courts, and restaurant.

Bay View Country Club has three departments (each managed by a full-time employee): the restaurant, the golf course, and the pro shop. The restaurant is managed by the club manager; the maintenance of the golf course is supervised by the golf course superintendent; and the pro shop is operated by the golf professional. The restaurant is treated as a profit center and the golf course and pro shop are treated as cost centers. The club manager is responsible for revenues and expenses in operating the restaurant, whereas the golf course superintendent and golf professional are responsible primarily for controlling expenses in their operations.

Table 6–1 is the operating statement for the club. Bay View Country Club is essentially a cash business. All of the members pay their dues on time and there are negligible inventories of food and liquor. Because it is a cash business, revenues are equivalent to cash receipts, while expenses are equivalent to cash disbursements. Table 6–1 lists the revenues and expenses for September 2008 and September 2007, and the budget for September 2008, including variances from budget. Parentheses denote negative numbers and unfavorable variances from budget. An unfavorable budget variance occurs when actual expenses exceed budgeted expenses or when actual revenues are less than budgeted revenues. The annual operating budget and monthly operating statement are the principal control devices used in most organizations, including Bay View Country Club.

At the beginning of the operating year, the board of directors submits an operating budget to the general membership for approval. This plan shows projected revenues (including dues) and projected expenses. To prepare the budget, management and the board examine each revenue and expense item for the previous year and adjust it for expected inflation and any change in operating plans. For example, the golf course superintendent reviews last year's spending on labor and supplies. The superintendent decides how to change the golf course maintenance schedule and forecasts how these changes, adjusted for price changes, translate into a total operating budget for the year. Knowing the maintenance program for each month, the superintendent estimates how the annual amount will be spent each month.

The annual budget, after approval by the members, authorizes the board and club management to operate the club for the next year under the limits it specifies. For example, the budgeted amount to be spent on the golf course in September 2008 is $80,000. The members (who are the owners of the club) control the operations by authorizing the board of directors and hence the management to spend club resources according to the plan. If there is a major unanticipated cost during

Table 6–1

BAY VIEW COUNTRY CLUB				
Operating Results September 2008				
	Actual September	*Budget September*	*Favorable (Unfavorable) Variance*	*Last Year*
Revenues				
Dues	$133,350	$134,750	$(1,400)	$129,600
Guest fees	2,900	2,500	400	2,200
Food and bar	46,000	44,500	1,500	45,000
Golf carts	2,200	1,900	300	2,100
Miscellaneous	1,600	1,800	(200)	1,700
Total revenue	$186,050	$185,450	$ 600	$180,600
Expenses				
Food & bar	$ 57,000	$ 51,300	$(5,700)	$ 49,700
Golf course	79,500	80,000	500	75,000
Administration & maintenance	47,050	45,350	(1,700)	45,600
Interest on debt	8,500	8,500	0	9,000
Total expenses	$192,050	$185,150	$(6,900)	$179,300
Net operating surplus (deficit)	$ (6,000)	$ 300	$(6,300)	$ 1,300

the year (e.g., the swimming pool heater breaks), the board of directors can either pay for this out of cash generated from prior years' accumulated surpluses or call a special meeting of the membership and propose an assessment from each member.

Table 6–1 reports the actual amounts received and spent in September 2008. The club had a net operating deficit of $6,000 in September. The budget projected a surplus of $300. Thus, September's operations were $6,300 below budget. Last year in September, actual revenue exceeded actual expenses by $1,300. Comparing budget with actual for individual line items indicates that most of this September's $6,300 unfavorable variance is from food and bar expenses, which were $5,700 over budget. At this point, additional information is needed to determine the reasons for the unfavorable variance in food and bar expenses. The operating statement merely identifies a budget variance. Additional analysis is required to identify its causes and any corrective action needed to solve the problem.

Table 6–2 provides additional information on the food and bar operations. It indicates that actual expenses exceeded actual revenues by $11,000. The budget called for only a $6,800 deficit. Thus, there was an unfavorable budget variance of $4,200 in the net operating deficit. September's unfavorable variances occurred because party revenue was $3,200 under budget and party expenses were $5,000 over budget. Further investigation reveals that the assistant manager in charge of parties quit in August. A large party was canceled in September, but no one at the club canceled the additional staff, food, and flower orders. The board criticized the club manager for not supervising these parties more closely during the absence of

TABLE 6–2

BAY VIEW COUNTRY CLUB
Food and Bar Operations
September 2008

	Actual September	Budget September	Favorable (Unfavorable) Variance	Last Year
Revenues				
Parties	$ 8,300	$11,500	$(3,200)	$11,000
Food	24,000	22,000	2,000	21,500
Bar	12,700	10,500	2,200	10,500
Miscellaneous	1,000	500	500	2,000
Total revenue	$ 46,000	$44,500	$ 1,500	$45,000
Expenses				
Parties	$ 9,000	$ 4,000	$(5,000)	$ 5,000
Food	44,000	43,000	(1,000)	40,000
Bar	4,000	4,300	300	4,700
Total expenses	$ 57,000	$51,300	$(5,700)	$49,700
Net operating surplus (deficit)	$(11,000)	$(6,800)	$(4,200)	$(4,700)

the assistant manager. A new assistant manager for parties was hired, and these problems were solved.[2]

Chapter 4 described organizational architecture as consisting of administrative systems that assign decision rights and evaluate and reward performance. Bay View Country Club's budgeting system illustrates how each of these three administrative systems is used to reduce agency problems at Bay View. *Decision rights*, which are initially held by the members, are assigned to the board of directors. The board hires professional managers who have the specialized knowledge to operate the various club functions: the club manager, the golf course superintendent, and the golf professional. These individuals submit their operating plans for the upcoming year via the budget.

Their budgets translate the plans for the next year into financial terms—the dollars of revenue and expenses that are expected to occur when their plans are implemented. The board reviews and modifies these plans to reflect member preferences and to ensure that monies are available to implement the plans. Once the membership approves the budget, the three managers have the decision rights to spend monies as specified in the budget. Decision rights are linked with knowl-

---

[2]A well-known agency problem with private clubs (and other nonprofit organizations) is that the board of directors has little financial incentive to oversee the club. Board members receive no cash compensation for serving on the board. Thus, firing the manager imposes costs on them because they have to spend their time replacing the manager. All the members gain from the improved operations with the new (better) manager. Each board member receives 1/350th of the benefit (if there are 350 members) but incurs 1/15th of the cost (if there are 15 board members). This free-rider problem is one of the reasons member-owned country clubs usually are run less efficiently than owner-managed, for-profit clubs. Members are willing to bear these higher agency costs because of the prestige and exclusivity of belonging to the club and because of social interactions from associating with a stable membership.

edge. For example, the golf course superintendent has the specialized knowledge of the golf course as well as the available chemicals and maintenance procedures to maintain the course. The budget assigns to the superintendent the decision rights to implement a specific set of actions.

Notice the bottom-up nature of the budgeting process. The operating managers submit their budgets to the board of directors, who adjust the budgeted figures and recommend the budget to the membership. The members then have final approval rights over the budget.

Budgets are also a *performance measurement system*. Monthly operating statements for each manager are prepared. Table 6–2 is the operating statement for the club manager's food and bar operation. This statement is only one component of the club manager's performance. It shows whether the club manager met revenue and expense targets. Another indication of the manager's performance is the level of member satisfaction with the food and bar operation. Member satisfaction will ultimately show up in revenues and expenses if quality falls and members stop using the restaurant. Similarly, it does little good for the golf course superintendent to meet financial targets if the golf course condition deteriorates. Also, the condition of the course relative to other courses in the area is an important consideration in evaluating the superintendent's performance.

Budget variances are indicators of whether managers are meeting expectations and they are used in the *performance reward system* to determine pay increases or, in the case of extremely unfavorable variances, the need to terminate the responsible manager. The large unfavorable variance in party operations caused the board of directors to search for reasons for the variance, which led to the discovery that the manager did not supervise the parties. The lack of supervision caused the board to criticize the club manager. If unfavorable variances continue and the board determines that they are the fault of the manager, they may be grounds for dismissal or for not granting a pay increase. On the other hand, favorable budget variances need not indicate superior performance. If less was spent than was budgeted, quality may have been sacrificed.

One danger inherent in annual budgets such as the Bay View Country Club example is their tendency to focus managers' attention on next year's operations only, ignoring the long-term well-being of the organization. For example, if budgeted expenses exceed budgeted revenues, there is pressure to reduce maintenance expenditures. Reducing maintenance and repairs brings the one-year budget into line, but the long-term goals of the organization are compromised. To reduce the tendency of short-term budgets to focus managers too narrowly on short-term performance, many organizations prepare long-term budgets of three- to five-year duration at the same time as the short-run budgets. A budget for five years is more likely to reveal the effects of reducing short-run maintenance than a one-year budget. Section C discusses short-run versus long-run budgets in greater detail.

Bay View Country Club's budget separates decision management (decision initiation and implementation) from decision control (decision ratification and monitoring):

1. *Decision initiation* (budget preparation) is done by the operating managers.
2. *Decision ratification* (budget approval) is done by the board and the members.
3. *Decision implementation* (operating decisions) is done by the managers.
4. *Decision monitoring* (reviewing monthly operating statements) is done directly by the board and indirectly by the members.

| Most Large Corporations Review Budgets Monthly | Most organizations compare actual operations with budget on a monthly basis. This comparison is usually made by the chief executive officer (CEO). A survey of 120 large publicly traded firms inquired how frequently budgeted and actual results are compared. The study reports that 90 percent of the line managers reporting to the CEO compare monthly, 4 percent compare weekly or biweekly, and 6 percent compare quarterly. CEOs compare actual and budgeted results monthly in 83 percent of the firms and quarterly in 15 percent of the firms. |

SOURCE: A Christie, M Joye, and R Watts, "Decentralization of the Firm: Theory and Evidence," *Journal of Corporate Finance* 118 (2001).

The managers prepare the budget and make day-to-day operating decisions in their area (decision management rights). The board of directors approves budget requests and monitors operations (decision control rights). The board not only examines financial operating variances (the favorable and unfavorable variances on the operating statements) but also monitors member satisfaction with the club's food and golf operations.

In the country club example, the budget and the monthly operating statements are an integral part of the various administrative mechanisms that reduce the club's organizational problems. We now turn to a larger, more complex organization—namely, a private university. Again, the budget is a key device in resolving organizational problems.

2. Private University

The private university example illustrates how budgets are used to assign decision rights to operating managers and then hold those managers responsible for their actions. Figure 6–2 is the organization chart for Eastern University, a nonprofit organization. The university has four separate colleges: liberal arts, engineering, medicine, and business. Liberal arts and engineering have both undergraduate and graduate programs. Engineering undergraduates take the first two years in liberal arts and the last two years in engineering. Medicine and business have only graduate programs. The auxiliary services department of the university provides dormitories, security, and food services.

The budgeting process begins with the chief financial officer (CFO) predicting general inflation and other key parameters for next year based on specialized knowledge of local markets. The managers of food service, dormitories, and security use this information and their specialized knowledge to prepare their budgets for the next year.

The deans of the colleges have specialized knowledge of faculty salaries in their areas and knowledge about the demand curve relating tuition to enrollments. Not all faculty markets have the same salary inflation. Each education program faces its own demand curve. Supply and demand for students vary across educational markets, thereby differentially affecting the cost of faculty and the tuition that can be charged in different disciplines.

At this university, liberal arts and engineering are treated as *cost centers*. That is, the deans have decision rights over expenditures, not revenues. This is because most of their revenues are from undergraduates who enter liberal arts and either stay in liberal arts or shift to engineering. The university administration believes neither the liberal arts nor the engineering deans are totally responsible for undergraduate enrollment and it is too complicated to account for the tuition revenue generated

FIGURE 6–2

Organization of Eastern University

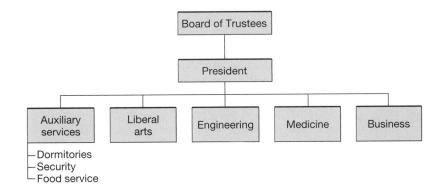

by undergraduates. Medicine and business are evaluated as *profit centers* in the sense that they are expected to generate revenues to cover their expenditures, where revenues include grants, annual alumni giving, fees, and tuition revenues.[3]

As profit centers, medicine and business must forecast revenues in addition to costs. Likewise, the CFO must forecast liberal arts and engineering revenues. Forecasting revenues requires estimates of the number of students enrolled, the tuition rate, and the financial aid budget. Net revenue received is the number of students enrolled times the stated tuition rate less financial aid awarded. Before the academic year begins, each school announces its tuition for next year. Half of the business school's total enrollment next year is reasonably easy to forecast based on the number of first-year students currently enrolled who are expected to return next year. The size of this group will not change much based on the tuition increase. However, the new entering class is more price sensitive than the class already enrolled. A large tuition increase may require an increase in the financial aid budget if the school is to maintain both the quantity and quality of entering students. Thus, estimating revenue requires trading off total revenue net of financial aid for student quality. Lowering student quality reduces the demand for the school's programs by high-quality students in the future.

Once the deans prepare their budgets for next year, they are sent to the CFO, who ensures that total projected revenues cover total projected expenditures. The CFO and the president also must ensure that the plans of each college are consistent with the overall strategy of the university. For example, if the president sees the university as primarily a graduate research institution, college budgets that put substantial additional resources into undergraduate education are inconsistent with that mission. The president would cut back these undergraduate resource requests. Through this back-and-forth negotiating process between the president, who has specialized knowledge of the university's mission, and the managers and deans of the various units, a consensus is reached and an overall budget for the university is prepared.

The budget is then sent to the board of trustees for approval. The board of trustees at this private institution consists of alumni, local leaders, and donors.

---

[3] Nonprofit institutions, such as private universities, do not like to admit that they maximize profits or that colleges are in fact profit centers. Thus, they invent terminology like *tubs on their own bottoms* to avoid using the term *profit centers*. In reality, all organizations must avoid generating negative cash flows or else they will not survive in a competitive environment. Their operating budgets can be subsidized through gifts and endowments, but these are just other services being provided by the nonprofit institution. Nonprofit institutions seek to make profits and hence to grow and survive, but legally they cannot distribute these profits to their "owners." There are no legal owners of the residual cash flow streams in nonprofit firms.

| "Budgeting for Curve Balls" | The Chicago White Sox baseball team has an annual budget of $50 to $100 million. Budget assumptions are set in August/September, and by October the new budget is prepared for the next year. The team owner first sets guidelines for the total player salary budget; this is the largest single expense category. Department heads assemble assumption sheets, books of 1,500–2,000 pages, one for every account in the general ledger. These sheets contain details such as the number of security people for each game based on expected attendance levels, their pay rates, union contracts, and so forth. These sheets explain any recommended changes from last year. Then the vice president of finance, the accounting manager, and the controller review the budgets with each department head. These meetings ensure consistent assumptions are being made across departments and that the budget requests are realistic. Department heads are asked to make any necessary revisions. The team owner then reviews the budget requests. Once the budget is set, department heads must submit revisions explaining cost overruns and underruns. |

SOURCE: A Dennis, "Budgeting for Curve Balls," *Journal of Accountancy*, September 1998, pp. 89–92.

Trustees do not receive any cash compensation from the university. They are appointed to the board for fixed terms and usually have a strong commitment to the preservation and improvement of the institution. The board of trustees examines the budget to ensure that it meets the university's mission and that it is fiscally prudent, meaning that the university will survive in the long run.

After the budget is approved, managers and deans have the decision rights to operate their units. Faculty are hired, food is purchased, and dormitory maintenance is provided consistent with the amounts in the budget. Monthly and annual reports, similar to Tables 6–1 and 6–2, are prepared to show each unit's compliance with the budget. These reports are part of the *decision-monitoring* process. This example again illustrates the linking of knowledge and decision rights and the separation of decision management and decision control via the use of the hierarchy. Like most budgeting systems, it is bottom up; lower levels in the organization prepare the initial budgets because they have much of the specialized knowledge. As the budget moves through the *decision ratification* process, higher levels review the budget and bring to bear their specialized knowledge.

Two points emerge from this example. First, managers and deans have an incentive to request "too large" a budget. The dean of liberal arts is under pressure from students and faculty in liberal arts to add more courses, more programs, and more student services, which can be done only by requesting more money. The dean of medicine is under pressure to provide more medical services in the hospital and more medical education. Even though medicine is treated as a profit center, the dean of medicine has an incentive to prepare a budget that shows a deficit (where expenditures exceed revenues) in hopes that the president will finance this deficit out of surpluses generated in other divisions. That is, the medical school dean hopes for *cross subsidization*.

The second point is that the deans of liberal arts and engineering have different incentives from the deans of medicine and business. Liberal arts and engineering are treated as cost centers, so they receive little benefit from additional revenues generated by adding more students. These deans have less incentive than the medicine and business deans to innovate cash-generating new programs because they do not directly capture the additional tuition. The liberal arts and engineering deans have incentives to lobby for more resources for new programs. But since these deans do not bear the full consequences of adding programs that cost more than they bring in, they are more likely to add unprofitable programs than are the business and medicine deans.

One problem the president faces with the medicine and business deans is their incentives to free ride on the university's reputation by offering lower-quality programs. For example, suppose the university has a reputation for high quality. The dean of medicine can generate additional revenues by starting low-quality programs, but this will debase the overall university reputation. The dean's incentive to reduce quality is controlled by presidential monitoring of faculty appointments and academic programs.

3. Large Corporation

The two previous examples described budgeting primarily as a process by which knowledge is assembled *vertically*, from both lower levels and higher levels in the organization's hierarchy. But budgeting is also an important device for assembling specialized knowledge *horizontally* within the firm. In a large, complex corporation, it is a major challenge to disseminate specific knowledge. Getting managers to share their knowledge among superiors and subordinates (vertically) as well as among peers in other parts of the organization (horizontally) and giving managers incentives to acquire valuable knowledge are important aspects of the budgeting system. Consider the case of Xerox Corporation.

Xerox produces, sells, leases, and services a wide range of copiers with different copy output rates, features, and sales and rental plans. The field organization consists of branch offices with sales, service, and administrative personnel. The manufacturing organization produces copiers at sites around the world and is treated as a cost center. Besides manufacturing copiers, Xerox also sells supplies, such as toner. The field offices that are part of marketing are cost centers; the supplies division is a profit center.

Each year Xerox must plan how many new copiers of each type will be placed in service and how many old copiers will be returned. These numbers drive the manufacturing plans for the year. The number of various types of copiers currently in the field, which is called the *installed base*, affects the number of service personnel in the field, the training programs they require, and the stock of spare parts needed to service the base. The installed base also affects the amount of supplies Xerox sells.

Each part of Xerox must communicate with the other parts of the firm. Manufacturing wants to know how many of each type of copier marketing expects to sell. Marketing wants to know what prices will be charged for each type of copier. Copier placements depend on the market's expectation of new product introductions. In setting their forecasts, manufacturing and marketing managers want to know about new products. Likewise, the toner division needs to know the size of the installed base and its composition so it can plan the production of supplies for the year.

Not only must the various parts of Xerox share their specialized knowledge but they must have incentives to acquire it. The sales force must acquire the knowledge about the forecasted quantities and prices of particular copiers to be sold (or leased). These sales estimates must be transmitted to manufacturing with enough lead time to build the projected quantities of new copiers.

An important part of the budgeting process is sharing and assembling knowledge about such key planning assumptions as unit placements, prices, and copier returns. Knowledge of these numbers is widely dispersed throughout the firm. In

Budgeting at the HON Company—II

The budget process at the HON Company consists of the following five steps:

1. Develop the sales budget by product line.
2. Convert the sales budget to a plant production and shipping schedule.
3. Prepare cost/expense budgets for production, distribution, and administration.
4. Consolidate department and plant budgets and compare budget results with the strategic plan.
5. Prepare a complete budget package for the parent company.

The budgeting process at HON illustrates the bottom-up process of assembling knowledge starting with salespeople, then manufacturing, and then distribution; finally the budget is reviewed by senior management. The salespeople in the field are asked for their forecasts. These are compared with marketing's forecasts; differences are reconciled. The scheduling department converts these sales forecasts into production plans and ensures that manufacturing can meet projected sales. In step 3, budgets are prepared for R&D, customer service, and distribution. Companywide productivity improvements are built into the budgets at this time. Step 4 forwards the budget to company headquarters for review. Here it is analyzed to ensure that strategic goals are being met. In step 5, the parent company, HON Industries, performs another review of the budget.

This example also illustrates the multiple review (decision control) at HON. "The HON Company's philosophy is that a change in the budget is not simply a change in numbers, but rather it means that the company's action plans also must be changed."

SOURCE: R Drtina, S Hoeger, and J Schaub, "Continuous Budgeting at the HON Company," *Management Accounting,* January 1996, pp. 20–24.

the process of assembling the knowledge, people will change their expectations of the key planning assumptions. In addition, all managers affected by a key planning assumption are usually required to approve it and then build their budgets using it. Each manager's approval helps ensure that expectations are consistent throughout the firm.

The corporate budgeting system is also a communication device through which some of the specialized knowledge and key planning assumptions are transmitted. It also involves a process by which various individuals arranged vertically and horizontally in the organization negotiate the terms of trade among the various parts of the organization. For example, for a given price schedule, the marketing organization estimates the quantity of each type of copier placed. Manufacturing agrees to produce this quantity of copiers and estimates the cost at which they will be produced. Usually, price schedules are adjusted to bring manufacturing (supply) in line with marketing (demand). In principle, when sales forecasts and production plans are produced, knowledge of cost (from manufacturing) and revenue (from marketing) is transferred to those agents with the decision rights to set prices, who ideally set the price for each product to maximize profits. Likewise, the supplies and service organizations accept their targets. Senior management ensures that all parts of the budget are consistent: Marketing and manufacturing are in agreement, the financing is in place, the parts inventory is

Budgeting Continuous Improvements

Many Japanese car companies, such as Toyota, use an elaborate system of continuous cost improvement called *Kaizen* costing. These systems have the following projections:

1. Unit sales and contribution margins.
2. Parts and material unit costs.
3. Variable cost reductions.
4. Direct labor and service department labor.
5. Capital projects.
6. Design costs, maintenance, advertising, sales and promotion, and general and administrative expenses.

The third item, variable cost reductions, sets a goal for each plant and each department within the plant. Monthly variance reports document differences between actual and budgeted cost reductions; managers in each department are held responsible for the variances.

SOURCE: Y Monden and J Lee, "How a Japanese Automaker Reduces Costs," *Management Accounting*, August 1993, pp. 22–26. Note that cost reduction goals are used by non-Japanese firms as well.

adequate to meet service requirements, and so on. Moreover, senior management likely has specialized knowledge to forecast some assumptions such as interest rates and salary levels and to arbitrate disputes that arise between departments during the budgeting process.

Many budgeting systems involve a bottom-up, top-down approach. Usually, some key planning assumptions are announced. Then, the lowest levels in the decision hierarchy submit first-round projections (budgets) for the next year. For example, product prices or the general inflation rate for next year is announced by a budget officer at the beginning of the budget process. These first-round, lowest-level projections are accumulated at the next level up in the organization, revised and submitted again to the next level, and so on up the hierarchy. At each level, managers ensure that the budget assumptions are consistent across their departments and that each department's forecast is reasonable. Each manager also modifies subordinates' plans with any specialized knowledge the manager has acquired. In a survey of 219 publicly traded firms, 79 percent indicated that lower-level managers have a significant role in both the initial and revision stages of the budget's preparation.[4]

As the budget is passed from one level of the organization up to a higher level, potential bottlenecks are uncovered before they occur. For example, if one department's budget calls for 10,000 units of a part and the parts fabrication department can produce only 7,500 units, this bottleneck is identified before production actually begins. At some point, the key assumptions may be challenged by managers with better specialized knowledge. On occasion, the assumptions are revised and the budgets updated.

The budget is revised at the top and passed back down through the organization. Either lower-level managers with specialized knowledge will agree with the

---

[4] W Cress, and J Pettijohn, "A Survey of Budget-Related Planning and Control Policies and Procedures," *Journal of Accounting Education* 3 (Fall 1985), p. 65.

changes and adapt to the new strategy or they will disagree. If there is enough disagreement and it is made known to senior management, another round of budget
revisions will occur.

Large corporations use budgets to

1. Assign decision rights.
2. Communicate information both vertically and horizontally.
3. Set goals through negotiation and internal contracting.
4. Measure performance.

Concept Questions		
	Q6–1	How are budgets developed?
	Q6–2	How are key planning assumptions derived?
	Q6–3	Define *budget variance*.
	Q6–4	Are budgets part of the performance measurement system or the performance reward system?
	Q6–5	What are some of the synergies that budgets provide within a large corporation?
	Q6–6	How do budgets partition decision rights within a firm?
	Q6–7	What purposes are served by the budgeting process in a large firm?

B. Trade-Off between Decision Management and Decision Control

The budgeting process is part of the system used to control behavior in organizations. In fact, a survey of senior managers in 219 publicly traded firms indicated
that 75 percent thought of the budgetary process as a managerial rather than an
accounting function.[5]

1. Communicating Specialized Knowledge versus Performance Evaluation

As the earlier examples describe, budgeting systems perform several functions
within firms, including decision management and decision control. In decision
management, budgets serve to communicate specialized knowledge about one part
of the organization to another part. In decision control, budgets are part of the
performance measurement system. Because budgets serve several purposes, trade-
offs must be made when a budgeting system is designed or changed. The budget
becomes the benchmark against which to judge actual performance. If too much
emphasis is placed on the budget as a performance benchmark, then managers
with the specialized knowledge will stop disclosing unbiased forecasts of future
events and will report conservative budget figures that enhance their performance
measure.

The trade-off between decision management and decision control is best illustrated in marketing. Salespeople usually have specialized knowledge of future
sales. This information is important in setting production plans. But if budgeted
sales are used to evaluate sales reps at the end of the year (i.e., actual sales are
compared with budget), then sales reps have an incentive to ex ante underforecast
future sales, thus improving their ex post performance evaluation. However,

---

[5] W Cress and J Pettijohn (1985), p. 64.

Budgets Used for Decision Management and Control

A study of 400 large U.S. firms reports the extent to which budgets are used for decision management (planning and coordination) versus evaluation:

	Percentage of Firms Responding
Two separate budgets are used.	7%
Only one budget is used and it is used for planning, coordination, and evaluation.	75
Only one budget is used and it is used for evaluation purposes.	5
Only one budget is used and it is used for planning and coordination purposes.	13

These data indicate that the vast majority of the responding firms (75 percent) use budgets for both decision management and decision control.

SOURCE: S Umapathy, *Current Budgeting Practices in U.S. Industry* (New York: Quorum Books, 1987), p. 29.

production plans will then be too low and the firm will not be able to plan the most efficient production schedules.[6] For example, suppose the salespeople underforecast sales by 20 percent. When actual sales are higher than the plant expects, overtime must be paid to produce the extra units. It would have been cheaper to expand the plant's permanent work force.

2. Budget Ratcheting

Using historical data on past performance is a common mechanism for setting next year's budget. Unfortunately, it often leads to a perverse incentive called the *ratchet effect*. The ratchet effect refers to basing next year's standard of performance on this year's actual performance. However, performance targets are usually adjusted in only one direction—upward. A bad year usually does not cause subsequent years' targets to fall. For example, if this year's sales budget is $1 million and the salesperson sells $1.3 million, next year's sales budget becomes $1.3 million. However, if actual sales are only $0.9 million, next year's budget is not cut back to $0.9 million.

H. J. Heinz, a producer of processed food (best known for its catsup) sets next year's profit center budgets at the greater of 115 percent of either last year's budget or last year's actual results. For example, if last year's budgeted earnings were $10 million and actual earnings were $11 million in a particular profit center, next year's profit for this center would be budgeted at $12.65 million ($11 million × 115%). However, if earnings last year were only $9 million, next year's budget would be $11.5 million ($10 million × 115%). Thus, at Heinz budgeted earnings only increase. One study of a large international conglomerate found that when the actual earnings of a subsidiary exceed budgeted earnings by, say, $100,000, the

---

[6] In some cases, it is possible to structure an incentive contract that induces managers to disclose their private information in an unbiased fashion. See J Gonik, "Tie Salesmen's Bonuses to Their Forecasts," *Harvard Business Review*, 1978, pp. 116–23; M Weitzman, "The New Soviet Incentive Model," *Bell Journal of Economics*, Spring 1976, pp. 251–57; and A Kirby, S Reichelstein, P Sen, and Y Paik, "Participation, Slack, and Budget-Based Performance Evaluation," *Journal of Accounting Research*, Spring 1991, pp. 109–28.

Budgeting at Sprint

In 1996, Sprint dropped its annual budget and went to quarterly reviews of a six-quarter rolling budget. The new process is quicker and offers increased flexibility and a stronger link between business drivers and forecasts. The old system required 137 days to prepare the annual budget. Now it takes half the time.

Once a year, corporate and division presidents set fixed high-level performance targets for the next six quarters. The targets are reviewed quarterly; however, there is no wholesale, bottoms-up reforecast. Targets are only revised under extraordinary circumstances, such as a price war.

SOURCE: S Arterian, "Sprint Retools the Budget Process," *CFO*, Summer 1997, pp. 88–91.

next year's budget is increased by $90,000. However, if actual earnings fall short of the budget by $100,000, next year's budget is only reduced by $40,000.[7] Hence, favorable budget variances are more likely to lead to larger increases than unfavorable variances are to lead to decreases.

This "ratcheting up" of budgets causes employees to temper this year's better-than-budgeted performance to avoid being held to a higher standard in future periods. Many illustrations of dysfunctional behavior induced by the ratchet effect exist:

- In the former Soviet Union, central planners would set a plant's production quota based on past experience. Plant managers meeting their targets received various rewards and those missing the target were punished. This created incentives for managers to just barely exceed their quota.
- Companies often base a salesperson's bonus on meeting a sales target that is based on last year's sales. If salespeople expect an unusually good year, they will try to defer some sales into the next fiscal year. They may take a customer's order but delay processing it until the next fiscal year.
- In one company, each department's target was based in part on last year's performance plus an increase. This created incentives for managers to defer making big productivity improvements in any one year, preferring instead to spread them over several years.[8]

Why do firms ratchet up their budgets given the perverse incentives induced? One possible reason is that even more perverse incentives might arise if they don't. For example, one simple solution to the dysfunctional incentives arising from the ratchet effect is to eliminate budget targets completely and simply base salespeople's salary on actual sales. Assume that budgeted sales next year are $1 million. Instead of paying a commission of 10 percent on all sales of more than $1 million, pay a commission of 2 percent on total sales. Suppose that both commission schemes have the same expected compensation. The 10 percent commission gives the employee five times the incentive (10 percent versus 2 percent) to make an additional sale. Thus, eliminating the $1 million target reduces the commission rate and hence the employee's marginal incentives.

Asking the salespeople to estimate next year's sales instead of ratcheting up next year's target based on this year's actual sales eliminates the perverse incentives of the ratchet effect. However, this alternative creates another problem. In

---

[7] A Leone and S Rock, "Empirical Tests of Budget Ratcheting and Its Effect on Managers' Discretionary Accrual Choices," *Journal of Accounting and Economics*, February 2002.

[8] R Kaplan and A Sweeney, "Peoria Engine Plant (A)," Harvard Business School Case 9-193-082 (revised June 29, 1993).

Improving Budgeting	Budgeting is the bane of many executives. "It's a wasteful effort, driven by a phenomenal amount of detail that generates precisely the wrong numbers." In 1998, only 12 percent of surveyed managers thought their budgeting process completely reliable and 90 percent labeled it cumbersome. One manager described the numerous budgeting iterations as, "We'd go through this exercise several times, up and down, and just keep cutting until someone felt good." At Nortel, budgets contained up to 100 line items for each unit and took four to five months to prepare. After streamlining the process by better tying the budget to strategic objectives, Nortel now reports only eight line items on a rolling quarterly basis.

Technology is improving budgeting. Web-based software is replacing numerous, nonstandard spreadsheets submitted by operating divisions that often have to be reentered and consolidated with other divisions' spreadsheets. For example, within one company each of 28 operating units would e-mail or send on diskette its own spreadsheet, which corporate would have to rekey or upload to create a consolidated budget. Just making simple changes delayed the process and maintaining all the spreadsheets cost $100,000 a year. Browser-based budgeting software now allows divisions to enter and revise data remotely using a standard format and allows corporate managers access to the consolidated numbers instantly. Conexant Systems Inc., a supplier of semiconductor products, uses a Web-based budgeting tool to manage 1,200 cost centers that each use up to 500 accounts. Cost center managers enter their own budget data with less help from financial analysts.

SOURCE: R Banham, "The Revolution in Planning," *CFO*, August 1999, pp. 46–56; and T Reason, "Building Better Budgets," *CFO*, December 2000, pp. 91–98.

particular, salespeople will forecast next year's sales far below what they expect to sell, thereby increasing their expected compensation and communicating too low an expected sales forecast to manufacturing.

Or, instead of ratcheting up to set next year's budget, a central planning group can prepare top-down budgets by using past sales and cost patterns, macroeconomic trends, and customer surveys. But this central forecasting group might be more expensive than a simple ratcheting-up budget algorithm. The direct costs of preparing budgets centrally (personnel and occupancy costs) could exceed the indirect costs from dysfunctional decision making induced by the ratchet effect.

Another way to reduce the problems caused by ratcheting up each year's performance targets is more frequent job rotation. If you know that next year someone else has to meet the sales figures you achieve this year, you will sell more now. However, job rotation destroys job-specific human capital such as customer-specific relationships.

In summary, while the ratchet effect creates dysfunctional behavior, the alternatives might prove more costly. In essence, one agency problem is replaced with another one. Depending on the particular situation, senior managers must choose the lesser of the two evils.

3. Participative Budgeting

The trade-off between decision management and decision control is often viewed as a trade-off between bottom-up and top-down budgeting. Bottom-up budgets are those submitted by lower levels of the organization to higher levels and usually imply greater decision management. An example of a bottom-up budget is

the three. A cost-benefit trade-off must be made somewhere in the firm. Exactly how and where this analysis and decision occurs is not specified by the proponents of the two-step approach to improving budgeting.

A second approach to improve budgeting involves breaking the so-called "annual performance trap." This approach does not use budgets as performance targets. Budgets are still constructed for financial planning (decision management), but they are not used for performance evaluation. Rather, firms use relative performance targets of other units or firms and compare these peer-units' performance to the actual performance achieved by the unit being judged. First a peer benchmark group is set for each budget unit. The benchmarks are either different units in the same firm or their leading competitors. Then the unit's actual achieved performance is compared to the actual performance achieved by the benchmark. Actual rewards are then determined subjectively, taking into account not just the benchmark's performance but other financial and nonfinancial performance measures. This approach to improving the budget process decouples financial planning, information communication, and coordination (decision management) from performance evaluation and performance rewards (decision control). Proponents of this approach claim that by decoupling decision management and decision control, decision management is improved because executives have less incentive to game the initial budget estimates. However, the use of relative performance evaluations and subjective evaluations are not without problems. Managers still have incentives to game how the benchmarks are chosen. There are no guarantees that the managers making the subjective evaluations will do so in an unbiased way, and therefore there is no guarantee that the person being evaluated based in part on the performance of some peer group will accept such an assessment without undue griping or without exerting undue influence costs.

No simple "one-size-fits-all" panacea exists for resolving the conflict between decision management versus decision control when it comes to budgeting. Nor is such a solution ever likely to be found. Budgets perform both decision management and decision control roles, and each firm must find the solution that is best tailored to its unique circumstances at that point in time. Budgeting processes (and associated compensation schemes) will evolve as the firm's circumstances change.

5. Managing the Trade-Off

To manage the trade-off between decision management and decision control, many organizations put the chief executive officer in charge of the budgeting process. While the actual collection of data and preparation of the budget are formal responsibilities of the chief financial officer or controller, the president or CEO has the final decision rights. There are several reasons for the chief executive to have ultimate control. First, it signals the importance of the budgeting process. Second, the CEO has the specialized knowledge and the overall view of the entire firm to make the trade-offs needed to resolve disagreements among departments regarding key planning assumptions or coordination of activities. McKinsey writes,

> [T]he sales department may desire to sell more than the production department thinks it can produce profitably, or the production department may desire to produce articles which the sales department does not think it can sell, or both the sales and production departments may desire to increase their activities beyond what the financial department

"Why Budgets Are Bad for Business" 	A June 4, 1990, *Fortune* magazine article entitled, "Why Budgets Are Bad for Business," concluded,

> Budgets, say experts, control the wrong things, like head count, and miss the right ones, such as quality, customer service—and even profits. Worse, they erect walls between the various parts of the company and between a company and its customers.
>
> When you're controlled by a budget, you're not controlling the business.
>
> Reliance on budgets is the fundamental flaw in American management. That's because they assume that everything important can be translated into this quarter's or this year's dollars, and that you can manage the business by managing the money. Wrong. Just because a budget was not overspent doesn't mean it was well spent.
>
> For tracking where the money goes, budgets are dandy. They become iniquitous when they are made to do more—when the budget becomes management's main tool to gauge performance. Managers do incredibly stupid things to make budget, especially if incentive pay is at stake. They woo marginal customers. They cut prices too deeply.
>
> The worst failure of budgets is what they don't measure. Budgets show what you spend on customer service, but not what value customers put on it.

The quote fails to recognize that budgeting systems are almost universally used and have survived. Thus, they must be yielding benefits at least as large as their costs. In some companies there very well may be incentives created by the budget system to be overly cautious or to "do incredibly stupid things to make budget." The question is whether even more dysfunctional behavior arises when budgets are not used. The fact that so many firms use budgets suggests that forgoing budgets is an unlikely formula for success.

While the quote offers insights into some of the problems with budgeting, it does not address the question of the benefits such systems provide that allow these systems to survive.

thinks can be financed. Obviously the only authority who can decide these questions is the chief executive who is superior to all executives interested in the controversy.[13]

In addition to placing the chief executive in charge of the budgeting process, many firms use a budget committee consisting of the major functional executives (vice presidents of sales, manufacturing, finance, and personnel), with the CEO as chair. This committee seeks to facilitate the exchange of specialized knowledge and reach consensus on the key planning assumptions. In essence, no budget or estimate is accepted until the budget committee approves. Then all the various parts of the organization agree to the inherent exchanges among the various parts of the organization. The budget is the informal set of contracts between the various units of the organization.

Concept Question		
	Q6–8	Why would managers bias their forecasts when preparing a budget?
	Q6–9	What is a bottom-up budgeting system?
	Q6–10	What is the *ratchet effect*?
	Q6–11	Describe participative budgeting.

[13] McKinsey (1922), pp. 44–45.

Individuals Involved in Approving Budgets

A study of 400 large U.S. firms reports that the following individuals are involved in formally approving the budget:

Individuals	% of Firms in Which the Individuals Are Involved in Budget Approval
Board of directors	58%
Executive committee	29
Chairman of the board	54
President	74
Executive vice president	39
Financial vice president	57
Controller	42
Management committee	22
Planning committee	8
Budget committee	14

Data add to more than 100 percent because formal approval can involve several groups or individuals. These data indicate two important results: (1) multiple levels of budget approval are necessary and (2) the most senior executives are involved in budget approval, including the board of directors in 58 percent of the surveyed firms.

SOURCE: S Umapathy, *Current Budgeting Practices in U.S. Industry* (New York: Quorum Books, 1987), p. 23.

C. Resolving Organizational Problems

As the three examples in section A illustrate, budgeting systems are an administrative device used to resolve organizational problems. In particular, these systems help (1) link knowledge with the decision rights and (2) measure and reward performance. The Bay View Country Club example illustrates how budgets provide performance measurements. The Eastern University example illustrates the concepts of cost centers and profit centers and how budgets assign decision rights. The Xerox Corporation example illustrates the linking of knowledge and decision rights. This section further describes various budgeting devices, such as short-run versus long-run budgets, line-item budgets, budget lapsing, flexible budgets, and incremental versus zero-based budgets.

1. Short-Run versus Long-Run Budgets

The budgeting examples in section A described annual budgeting processes. Starting in the prior year, firms develop detailed plans of how many units of each product they expect to sell at what prices, the cost of such sales, and the financing necessary for operations. These budgets then become the internal "contracts" for each responsibility center (cost, profit, and investment center) within the firm. These annual budgets are short-run in the sense that they project only one year at a time. But most firms also project 2, 5, and sometimes 10 years in advance. These long-run budgets are a key feature of the organization's strategic planning process.

Strategic planning refers to the process whereby managers select the firm's overall objectives and the tactics to achieve them. It involves deciding what markets to be in, what products to produce, and what price-quality combinations to offer. For example, Time Warner AOL faces the strategic question of whether to provide local

<table>
<tr>
<td>

Lenders Want Five-Year Budgets

</td>
<td>

Next to preparing annual budgets, what CFOs dread the most is creating five-year plans. Such documents take months to construct and generally are impossible to get right. Beyond year two, the numbers are guesses. So why do they do it?

One reason is that their bankers demand to see budgets that cover the period of the loans extended to the company. Many bank loans are for three to five years. A senior vice president at Bank of America says that the bank requires borrowers to produce forecasts that cover the duration of nearly any loan request: "We're looking for the cash-flow perspective and how we're getting paid. We build our loan agreements and covenants on that information. We're obviously asking so we understand the risk of a deal."

One company CFO who finds the process very useful says, "We do five-year plans to give ourselves a longer-term view to achieve long-term growth goals."

SOURCE: K Frieswick, "The Five-Year Itch," CFO, February 2003, pp. 68–70.

</td>
</tr>
</table>

telephone service in its cable markets. Making this decision requires specialized knowledge of the various technologies Time Warner and its competitors face, in addition to knowledge of the demand for various future products. Strategic planning also addresses questions of what the organization's future structure must be to support the strategy, including future R&D and capital spending and the financial structure.

Like short-run budgets, long-run budgets force managers with specialized knowledge to communicate their forecasts of future expected events under various scenarios. Long-run budgets contain future capital budgeting forecasts (and thus financing plans) required to implement the strategy. R&D budgets are long-run plans of the multiyear spending required to acquire and develop the technologies to implement the strategies.

In short-run budgets, the key planning assumptions involve quantities and prices. All parts of the organization must accept these annual key assumptions. In long-run budgets, the key planning assumptions involve what markets to be in and what technologies to acquire.

Chapter 3 described capital budgeting. Before a new investment is made, the future cash flows from that investment are projected. Capital budgets are long-run budgets for each project.

A typical firm integrates short-run and long-run budgeting into a single process. As next year's budget is being developed, a five-year budget is also produced. Year 1 of the five-year plan is next year's budget. Years 2 and 3 are fairly detailed and year 2 becomes the base to establish next year's one-year budget. Years 4 and 5 are less detailed but begin to look at new market opportunities. Each year, the five-year budget is rolled forward one year and the process begins anew.

The short-run (annual) budget involves both decision management and decision control functions, and as discussed earlier a trade-off arises between these two functions. Long-run budgets are hardly ever used as a decision control (performance evaluation) device. Rather, long-run budgets are used primarily for decision management. Five- and 10-year budgets force managers to think strategically and to communicate the specialized knowledge of their future markets and technologies. Thus, long-run budgets emphasize decision management more than decision control because less reliance is placed on using them as a performance measurement tool.

Long-run budgets also reduce managers' focus on short-term performance. Without long-term budgets, managers have an incentive to cut expenditures such as maintenance, advertising, and R&D to improve short-run performance or

Rolling Budgets

Many companies, such as Cisco, are replacing their static annual budgets with rolling 18-month budgets. Static annual budgets are often useless because they quickly become out of date. At the end of the fiscal year, when sales targets are missed, massive price discounts are offered to boost sales. Instead of preparing an annual budget that remains static for the year, companies such as Cisco produce an 18-month budget and then update the projections every month. So at the end of January, the monthly budgets for the next 17 months are revised and July of next year is added. In effect, the whole budget for the remainder of the year and the first five months of next year is recalculated and a new month 18 is added. Unlike static annual budgets, managers are encouraged to react more quickly to changing economic or business conditions. Rolling budgets force managers to better integrate planning and execution.

However, converting from a static to a rolling budget process often requires massive, expensive software upgrades. Firms are installing Internet-based systems that seamlessly integrate forecasts from numerous cost and profit (budget) centers. Previously, each budget center submitted its Excel spreadsheet to the budget office, which then had to transfer the data into a master budget. One company reported that 450 hours were required to consolidate the separate 130 budgets. Now each budget center enters its revised monthly budget into a single standardized Web page that automatically rolls up the revisions into a companywide budget.

Source: R Myers, "Budgets on a Roll," *Journal of Accountancy*, December 2001, pp. 41–46; and M Astley, "Intranet Budgeting," *Strategic Finance*, May 2003, pp. 30–33.

to balance short-term budgets at the expense of the long-term viability of the organization. Budgets that span five years help alert top management and/or the board of directors to the long-term trade-offs being taken to accomplish short-run goals.

Some firms use rolling budgets. A rolling budget covers a fixed time period, such as one or two years. A future period is added as the current period concludes. For example, suppose a two-year rolling budget is used with quarterly intervals. When the current quarter is concluded, a new quarter (two years ahead) is added. In this way, management is always looking at a two-year planning horizon.

2. Line-Item Budgets

Line-item budgets refer to budgets that authorize the manager to spend only up to the specified amount on each line item. For example, consider Table 6–3. In this budget, the manager is authorized to spend $12,000 on office supplies for the year. If the supplies can be purchased for $11,000, the manager with a line-item budget cannot spend the $1,000 savings on any other category such as additional office equipment. Because the manager cannot spend savings from one line item on another line item without prior approval, the manager has less incentive to look for savings. If next year's line item is reduced by the amount of the savings, managers have even less incentive to search for savings.

Line-item budgets reduce agency problems. Managers responsible for the line-item budgets cannot reduce spending on one item and divert the savings to items that enhance their own welfare. By maintaining tighter control over how much is spent on particular items, the organization reduces possible managerial opportunism.

Line-item budgets are quite prevalent in governments. They also are used in some corporations, but with fewer restrictions. Line-item budgets provide an extreme form of control. The manager does not have the decision rights to

TABLE 6–3   Line-Item Budget Example

Line Item	Amount
Salaries	$185,000
Office supplies	12,000
Office equipment	3,000
Postage	1,900
Maintenance	350
Utilities	1,200
Rent	900
Total	$204,350

substitute resources among line items as circumstances change. To make such changes during the year requires approval from a higher level in the organization.

Line-item budgets illustrate how the budgeting system partitions decision rights, thereby controlling behavior. In particular, a manager given the decision rights to spend up to $3,000 on office equipment does not have the decision rights to substitute office equipment for postage.

A survey of 120 large publicly traded firms found that among units reporting directly to the CEO, 23 percent cannot substitute among line items, 24 percent can substitute if they receive authorization, and 26 percent can make substitutions within specified limits.[14] The remaining 27 percent can substitute among line items to improve the unit's financial objective. These findings suggest that line-item budgets are prevalent even at fairly high levels in for-profit firms.

Governments use **encumbrance accounting** in addition to line-item budgets. When contracts for purchases are signed or purchase orders are issued, even though no legal liability for the goods or services exists until delivery occurs, encumbrance accounting requires the dollar amounts of such goods and services to be recorded in special encumbrance accounts. When the goods and services are delivered, the encumbrance entry is reversed and the purchase is charged to the appropriate line-item expenditure. By adding the actual purchases to the outstanding encumbrance, those responsible for monitoring the integrity of the budget can ensure that line-item spending authority is maintained.[15]

3. Budget Lapsing

Another common feature is **budget lapsing,** in which unspent funds do not carry over to the next year. Budget lapsing creates incentives for managers to spend all their budget. Otherwise, not only do managers lose the benefits from the unspent funds, but next year's budget may be reduced by the amount of the underspending.

Budgets that lapse provide tighter controls on managers than budgets that do not lapse. However, the opportunity cost of lapsing budgets can be less-efficient operations. Managers devote substantial time at the end of the year spending their remaining budget, even if it means buying items that have lower value (and a higher cost) than they would purchase if they could carry the remaining budget over to the next fiscal year.[16] Often the firm incurs substantial warehousing costs to

---

[14] A Christie, M Joye, and R Watts (2001).

[15] S Sunder, *Theory of Accounting and Control* (Cincinnati, OH: South-Western Publishing, 1997), pp. 196–97.

[16] J Zimmerman, "Budget Uncertainty and the Allocation Decision in a Nonprofit Organization," *Journal of Accounting Research* 14 (Autumn, 1976), pp. 301–19.

hold the extra end-of-year purchases. In one example, a Navy ship officer purchased an 18-month supply of paper to spend his remaining budget. The paper weighed so much that it had to be stored evenly around the ship to ensure the ship did not list to one side.

In addition, managers cannot adjust to changing operating conditions during the year if budgets lapse. For example, if managers have expended all of their budget authority and the opportunity to make a bargain purchase arises, they cannot borrow against next year's budget without getting special permission.

Without budget lapsing, managers could build up substantial balances in their budgets. Toward the end of their careers or before taking a new job in the same firm, these managers would then be tempted to make very large expenditures on perquisites. For example, they could take their staff to Hawaii for a "training retreat." Budget lapsing also prevents risk-averse managers from saving their budget for a rainy day. If it is optimum for a manager to spend a certain amount of money on a particular activity, then saving part of that amount as a contingency fund is not optimum. One way to prevent these agency problems is for budgets to lapse.

As in the case of budget ratcheting, the use of budget lapsing (or not) involves a choice between two evils. Agency costs can not be driven to zero; they can only be minimized.

4. Static versus Flexible Budgets

All of the examples in this chapter so far have presented **static budgets,** which do not vary with volume. Each line item is a fixed amount. In contrast, a **flexible budget** is stated as a function of some volume measure and is adjusted for changes in volume. Flexible budgets provide different incentives than do static budgets.

As an example of flexible budgeting, consider a concert where a band is hired for $20,000 plus 15 percent of the gate receipts. The auditorium is rented for $5,000 plus 5 percent of the gate receipts. Security guards costing $80 apiece are hired, one for every 200 people. Advertising, insurance, and other fixed costs are $28,000. Ticket prices are $18 each. A flexible budget for the concert is presented in Table 6–4.

Each line item in the budget is stated in terms of how it varies with volume (ticket sales in this case). Budgets are then prepared at different volume levels. At ticket sales of 3,000, an $11,000 loss is projected. At sales of 4,000 and 5,000 tickets, $3,000 and $17,000 of profits are forecasted, respectively.

Flexible budgets are better than static budgets for gauging the actual performance of a person or venture *after controlling for volume effects*—assuming, of course, that the individual being evaluated is not responsible for the volume changes. For example, 5,000 people attended the concert. Table 6–5 compares actual results with the flexible budget for 5,000 tickets. Total profits were $4,100 less than expected. Most of the difference of $3,000 resulted from not being able to sell all 5,000 tickets at $18 each. To sell 5,000 tickets, some were sold at a discount. The actual cost of the auditorium was $9,900 instead of the $9,500 estimated by the flexible budget. The additional $400 was for damage. The budget for the auditorium is automatically increased to $9,500 due to the 5,000 ticket sales, and the manager is not held responsible for volume changes. However, the manager is held responsible for the $400 difference that resulted from damage. Finally, "other costs" were higher by $700 because the promoters underestimated the cost of the rented sound system.

The key question is, should managers be held responsible for volume changes if the factors that cause the volume changes are outside their control? The initial reaction is no. Managers should be held responsible for volume effects only if they have some control over volume. However, this reasoning is incomplete. Recall the discussion of the controllability principle in Chapter 5. If the manager's actions

TABLE 6–4 Concert Operating Results

	Formula	Ticket Sales 3,000	4,000	5,000
Revenues	$18N*	$ 54,000	$ 72,000	$ 90,000
Band	$20,000 + 0.15(18N)	(28,100)	(30,800)	(33,500)
Auditorium	$5,000 + 0.05(18N)	(7,700)	(8,600)	(9,500)
Security	$80(N/200)	(1,200)	(1,600)	(2,000)
Other costs	$28,000	(28,000)	(28,000)	(28,000)
Profit/(loss)		$(11,000)	$ 3,000	$ 17,000

*N is the number of tickets sold.

TABLE 6–5 Concert Operating Results

	Flexible Budget at 5,000 Tickets	Actual Results	Favorable (Unfavorable) Variance
Revenues	$90,000	$87,000	$(3,000)
Band	(33,500)	(33,500)	0
Auditorium	(9,500)	(9,900)	(400)
Security	(2,000)	(2,000)	0
Other costs	(28,000)	(28,700)	(700)
Profit/(loss)	$17,000	$12,900	$(4,100)

influence the effects of volume changes, then the manager should not be insulated from the volume effects.[17] For example, if managers can reduce inventory holdings of perishable inventories during economic downturns, they should be held accountable for the entire inventory amount. This creates an incentive to take actions that mitigate or enhance the effect on the organization of the uncontrollable volume.

When should a firm or department use a static budget and when should it use a flexible budget? Since static budgets do not adjust for volume effects, volume fluctuations are passed through and show up in the variances. Thus, static budgets force managers to be responsible for volume fluctuations. If the manager has some control over volume or the consequences of volume, then static budgets should be used as the benchmark to gauge performance. Since flexible budgets do adjust for volume effects, volume fluctuations are not passed through and do not show up in the variances. Flexible budgets do not hold managers responsible for volume fluctuations. Therefore, if the manager does not have any control over either volume or the consequences of volume, then flexible budgets should be used as the benchmark to gauge performance. Flexible budgets reduce the risk of volume changes borne by managers.

Of 219 publicly traded U.S. firms, 48 percent said they use flexible budgets for manufacturing costs, but only 27 percent use flexible budgets for distribution, marketing, R&D, or general and administrative expenses.[18] These data suggest

---

[17] G Baker, M Jensen, and K Murphy, "Compensation and Incentives: Practice vs. Theory," *Journal of Finance* 43 (July 1988), pp. 593–616.

[18] W Cress and J Pettijohn (1985), pp. 65–66.

that flexible budgets are widely used in manufacturing where volume measures are readily available and costs vary with volume.

The preceding examples illustrate how budgets can be adjusted for different levels of volume, but flexible budgeting is more general. Budgets can be adjusted for variables other than volume levels, such as market share, foreign currency fluctuations, different rates of inflation, or any other variable outside of the manager's control that can cause the budget to vary.

5. Incremental versus Zero-Based Budgets

Most organizations construct next year's budget by starting with the current year's budget and adjusting each line item for expected price and volume changes. Since most budgeting processes are bottom up, where the detailed specialized knowledge resides, lower-level managers submit a budget for next year by making incremental changes in each line item. For example, the manager calculates the line item in next year's budget for "purchases" by increasing last year's purchases for inflation and including any incremental expenditures for volume changes and new programs. Only detailed explanations justifying the increments are submitted as part of the budget process. These incremental budgets are reviewed and changed at higher levels in the organization, but usually only the incremental changes are examined in detail. The core budget (i.e., last year's base budget) is taken as given.

Under **zero-based budgeting** (ZBB), each line item in total must be justified and reviewed annually. Each line item is reset to zero annually and must be justified in total. Departments must defend the entire expenditure (or program expenditure) each year, not just the changes. In a zero-based budget review, the following questions are usually asked: Should this activity be provided? What will happen if the activity is eliminated? At what quality and quantity level should the activity be provided? Can the activity be achieved in some other way, such as hiring an outside firm to provide the goods or service (outsourcing)? How much are similar companies spending on this activity?

In principle, zero-based budgeting causes managers to maximize firm value by identifying and eliminating those expenditures whose total cost exceeds total benefits. Under incremental budgeting, in which incremental changes are added to the base budget, incremental expenditures are deleted when their costs exceed their benefits. But inefficient base budgets can continue to exist.

In practice, ZBB is infrequently used. It is supposed to overcome traditional incremental budgeting, but it often deteriorates into incremental budgeting. Under ZBB, the same rationales and justifications as last year's are submitted and adjusted for incremental changes. Because the volume of detailed reports is substantially larger under ZBB than under incremental budgeting, higher-level managers tend to focus on the changes from last year. Moreover, firms usually promote people from within the firm rather than hiring from outside. Promotions tend to be vertical within the same department or division. Internally promoted managers bring with them specific knowledge of their previous job, including knowledge of previous budgets. Thus, managers reviewing detailed lower-level budgets have substantial knowledge of those operations, having earlier had decision management rights over at least some of the operations. These managers often already know the base budgets and now want to know the changes from the base level.

ZBB is most useful in organizations in which considerable turnover exists in middle- and senior-level ranks. Management turnover destroys specialized knowledge. Also, ZBB is useful in cases where there has been substantial strategic change or high uncertainty. For example, a defense contractor shifting into civilian markets

Budgeting Environmental Projects

Firms complying with environmental regulations install equipment to clean waste water and air emissions. Often firms must clean up existing plant sites to bring them into compliance with current law. Such environmental projects can be costly and thus require careful financial planning, including detailed budgets. A survey of 149 firms' environmental budgeting practices yielded some interesting results. The following costs are normally considered in their environmental budgets:

Budget Item (Partial List)	% of Firms
On-site air/water monitoring	79%
On-site hazardous waste treatment/disposal	71
Future regulatory compliance costs	59
Corporate image costs	55
Personal injury claims	54
Legal staff labor time	28
Additional sales of environmentally safe products	25

Of particular interest is the fact that 55 percent of the firms specifically consider the dollar cost of corporate reputation in their environmental planning.

SOURCE: A White and D Savage, "Budgeting for Environmental Projects: A Survey," *Management Accounting*, October 1995, pp. 48–54.

might want to use ZBB. In these cases, rejustifying each line item annually helps to inform managers with decision control rights of the total costs and benefits of each department or program. However, ZBB is significantly more costly to perform than incremental budgeting.

ZBB is often used in government budgets. President Carter used it both in Georgia when he was governor and in the federal government during the 1970s. In government, managers with decision management rights tend to be career civil servants in the departments and agencies. Decision control rights are vested in elected officials in the executive and legislative branches. Elected officials have short tenures in monitoring a specific agency and therefore lack detailed specialized knowledge of the department's functions. Zero-based budgets are useful in helping these elected officials make trade-offs between programs, as opposed to just making trade-offs among increments to programs.

Concept Question

Q6–12 What are short-run and long-run budgets?

Q6–13 What are the advantages and disadvantages of line-item budgets?

Q6–14 Why do some organizations practice budget lapsing? What are the disadvantages?

Q6–15 Define *static* and *flexible budgets*. Discuss their advantages and weaknesses.

Q6–16 Define *incremental* and *zero-based budgeting*. Discuss their advantages and weaknesses.

D. Summary

Budgets are an important mechanism for resolving firms' organizational problems. Budgets help partition decision rights and provide a benchmark against which performance can be measured. By preparing a budget, each unit in the organization implicitly recognizes the decision rights it has authority to exercise.

The advantages of budgeting consist of

1. Coordination of sales and production.
2. Formulation of a profitable sales and production program.
3. Coordination of sales and production with finances.
4. Proper control of expenditures.
5. Formulation of a financial program including investment and financing.
6. Coordination of all the activities of the business.

The process of building a budget via a bottom-up, top-down iterative procedure involves assembling specialized knowledge. Budgeting is a negotiation and consensus-building exercise. Thus, budgeting is part of the decision management process. Budgets are also used in decision control. In practice, budgeting involves a trade-off between decision making and control. Ideally, the budget system helps link specialized knowledge and decision rights, thus improving decision making. But if the budget is also used for control and incentives are provided for meeting it, then managers will bias their forecasts during budget preparation to enhance their reported performance relative to their forecast. Again, designers of the budgeting and performance evaluation systems must trade off more accurate forecasts (transfers of specialized knowledge) for incentive effects (control). We return to these incentive effects of budgeting and variance analysis again in Chapters 12 and 13.

One way to prevent managers from biasing their budgets is to set the budgets at the top, and one top-down method is referred to as the ratchet effect. Here, next year's budget is set based on last year's deviation of actual from budget. When last year's actual results are better than budget, next year's budget increases by more than it would fall were last year's actual results to fall short of last year's budget. This simple ratcheting up of budgets means that managers no longer need to set their own budgets, but it creates incentives for them to hold back effort when they are having a good year to prevent next year's budget from being too challenging.

Short-run budgets involve both decision management and decision control. Long-run budgets (3 to 10 years) place less emphasis on decision control. Managers are less likely to be held responsible for meeting long-term budget targets than short-term budget goals because long-term budgets are used for information sharing.

Line-item budgeting and budget lapsing are devices that constrain managers' decision rights. Line-item budgets prevent managers from shifting resources across different line items in the budget. Budgets that lapse prevent managers from shifting unspent funds from the current year into future years. Both line-item budgeting and budget lapsing reduce managers' incentives to search for cost savings because it is less likely that the manager can spend the savings.

Static budgets hold managers responsible for changes in volume, whereas flexible budgets do not. Even though they might not be able to control volume, managers evaluated under flexible budgets have less incentive to control the consequences of volume changes.

Finally, most budgeting processes are incremental in the sense that managers need only justify changes from last year's budgets. Under zero-based budgeting, managers must justify the entire budget. ZBB is most useful when those managers with decision ratification and monitoring rights over the budget do not have the specific knowledge of the operations. If managers with decision control rights have the knowledge because they have been promoted from within the organization, ZBB usually becomes incremental budgeting.

Appendix: Comprehensive Master Budget Illustration

Chapter 6 discussed the important conceptual issues of budgeting. This appendix illustrates how the various departments of a firm communicate their specialized knowledge via a firmwide master budget. This example demonstrates how various parts of the organization develop their budgets, the importance of coordinating the volume of activity across the different parts of the organization, and how budgets are then combined for the firm as a whole.

1. Description of the Firm: NaturApples

NaturApples is an upstate New York apple processor with two products, applesauce and apple pie filling. The applesauce is eaten as is, and the pie filling is used to make apple pies. Two types of apples are purchased from local growers, McCouns and Grannys. They are processed and packed in tin cans as either apple sauce or pie filling. Principal markets are institutional buyers, such as hospitals, public schools, military bases, and universities. NaturApples is a small processor. Its market is regional and is serviced by four sales reps who call on customers in a four-state area. A fifth salesperson markets the products to food distributors, who then sell them directly to restaurants.

The firm is organized into two departments: processing and marketing. Each is headed by a vice president who reports directly to the president. The vice president of finance is responsible for all financial aspects of the firm, including preparing budgets. The three vice presidents and the president make up NaturApples's executive committee, which oversees the budgeting process.

Apples are harvested in the fall of each year. The firm has long-term contracts with a number of local apple growers for their crops. If the local harvest is smaller than expected, additional apples can be purchased in the spot market. Likewise, if more apples are delivered than NaturApples wants to process, the extra apples can be sold in the spot market. Long-term contracts with local farmers and spot-market purchases and sales are the responsibility of the president and the vice president of finance.

Once harvested, the apples are stored either in coolers at NaturApples or in third-party warehouses until NaturApples processes them. Processing takes nine months. In October, the plant starts up after a three-month shutdown. Workers first thoroughly clean and inspect all equipment. The apples begin arriving in the middle of October. By the end of November, the apple harvest is in warehouses or started in production. By June, all of the apples have been processed and the plant shuts down for July, August, and September. NaturApples has a fiscal year starting October 1 and ending September 30.

Each of the two products (applesauce and pie filling) uses a combination of the two types of apples (McCouns and Grannys). The production process consists of inspection, washing, peeling, and coring. Then the apples are either mashed for applesauce or diced for pie filling. The apples are then combined with other ingredients such as spices and chemical stabilizers and cooked in vats. Both products are immediately canned on a single canning line in five-pound tins and packed in cases of 12 cans per case. The product has a two-year shelf life and is inventoried until ordered by the customer. Independent truckers deliver the apples to NaturApples and deliver the finished product to customers.

2. Overview of the Budgeting Process

The budgeting process begins in August for the next fiscal year's budget, which will begin in 14 months. That is, even though the current fiscal year beginning in October has not yet started, the preparation of next year's budget begins in August. In August, the coming fall harvest is reasonably well known. The president and the vice president of finance forecast the following year's crop harvest under long-term contract. The vice president of marketing begins forecasting sales that will be made from the harvest a year from this fall. Likewise, the processing vice president forecasts production costs and capacity. Every 2 months for the next 14 months, these budgets are revised with regard to marketing, processing, and apple procurement in light of any new information, and all three vice presidents and the president meet for a morning to discuss their revisions. In June of each year, the final master budget for the next fiscal year, which begins October 1, is adopted by the executive committee and approved by the board of directors. The executive committee also meets weekly to review current-year operations as compared with budget and to discuss other operational issues.

Figure 6–3 is a schematic diagram that illustrates the relations among component budgets and the NaturApples master budget. The master budget encompasses the budgeted income statement, budgeted balance sheet, and budgeted cash flows at the bottom of Figure 6–3. All the other budgets provide the supporting detail, including the various key planning assumptions underlying the master budget.

Three key pieces in NaturApples's budgeting process include apple procurement, sales, and production. These three components must be internally consistent with respect to the amount of each type of apple purchased and the volume of each product produced and sold. Once these three component budgets are determined, the budgeted ending inventory can be calculated. Given the production budget, the direct labor and factory overhead budgets can be generated. These last two budgets and the direct materials budget (from the apple procurement estimates) determine the cost-of-goods-sold budget. The budgeted income statement can then be prepared using these budgets and the budget for administration, which includes senior officer salaries and other administrative expenses not included elsewhere.

Toward the bottom of Figure 6–3 is the capital investment budget, which is based on an analysis of investment proposals. All profitable projects are in the capital investment budget, including those projects started in previous years but not yet completed. The capital investment budget and budgeted income statement are used to prepare NaturApples's budgeted balance sheet and then the cash flow budget. The remainder of this appendix illustrates the preparation of these various component budgets.

NaturApples uses the following accounting conventions:

1. FIFO is used for inventory accounting.
2. Factory overhead is estimated using a flexible budget.

FIGURE 6–3

Logical flow of components of the master budget

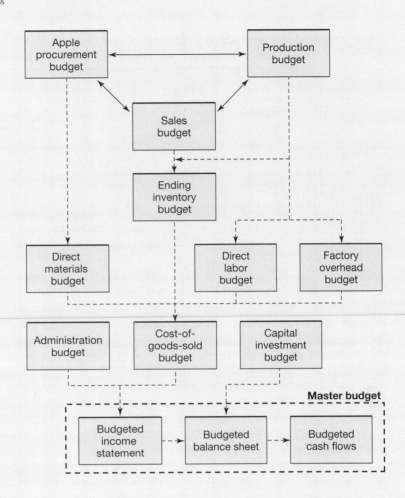

Variable overhead varies with the number of direct labor hours in the plant. Total overhead is then assigned to product costs using the number of hours of direct labor in the product. Chapter 9 further explains how overhead is assigned to products.

Table 6–6 provides the basic data for the budgeting illustration. This table contains some primary operating data, such as the beginning inventory figures. The bottom half of the table also shows the amount of each type of apple required to make a case of applesauce and a case of pie filling.

By June, the executive committee has agreed on next year's volumes. The sales budget for the next fiscal year is given in Table 6–7. These data are examples of the *key planning assumptions* described in the chapter. The executive committee agrees that the firm should be able to sell 140,000 cases of sauce at $68.95 per case and 60,000 cases of pie filling at $53.95 per case. These quantities and prices were derived after exploring alternative price-quantity combinations. In particular, these price-quantity points represent the managers' best judgment of where profits are maximized. Presumably, higher prices (and thus lower sales) or lower prices (and higher sales) would both result in lower profits than the combinations in Table 6–7.

3. Departmental Budgets

Table 6–8 presents the apple procurement budget. Given the harvest projections and the production plans, the executive committee is planning to purchase an

TABLE 6–6   **NaturApples**
Basic Data for Budgeting Example for Fiscal Year Beginning 10/1/08

	Cases	Cost/Case	Total
Beginning Inventory			
Sauce	13,500	$57.96	$782,460
Pie filling	2,300	$48.81	$112,263
	McCoun	Granny	
Pounds of Apples/Case			
Sauce	60	40	
Pie filling	50	30	

TABLE 6–7   **NaturApples**
Sales Budget for Fiscal Year Beginning 10/1/08

	Budgeted Cases	Budgeted Price/Case	Budgeted Revenue
Sauce	140,000	$68.95	$ 9,653,000
Pie filling	60,000	53.95	3,237,000
Total			$12,890,000

TABLE 6–8   **NaturApples**
Apple Procurement Budget for Fiscal Year Beginning 10/1/08

	Pounds (in 000s)		Price		Cost ($ in 000s)		
	McCoun	Granny	McCoun	Granny	McCoun	Granny	Total
Long-term contracts	10,900	8,000	$380	$310	$4,142.0	$2,480.0	$6,622.0
Market purchases (sales)	50	(910)	450	330	22.5	(300.3)	(277.8)
Total	10,950	7,090			$4,164.5	$2,179.7	$6,344.2
Pounds used					10,950	7,090	
Cost per thousand pounds					$380.32	$307.43	

additional 50,000 pounds of McCoun apples and sell 910,000 pounds of Granny apples. The total cost of apples is projected to be $6,344,200. The average cost per thousand pounds is $380.32 for McCoun apples and $307.43 for Granny apples. These average cost figures are used later in Table 6–12 to calculate the cost of applesauce and pie filling.

The third major budget component is the production budget presented in Table 6–9. The production budget, the apple procurement budget, and the sales budget must satisfy the following inventory-production-sales identity:

$$\text{Beginning inventory} + \text{Production} = \text{Sales} + \text{Ending inventory}$$

TABLE 6–9 **NaturApples**
Production Budget for Fiscal Year Beginning 10/1/08

	Budgeted Cases	Pounds of McCouns	Pounds of Grannys
Sauce	130,000	7,800,000	5,200,000
Pie filling	63,000	3,150,000	1,890,000
Total		10,950,000	7,090,000

TABLE 6–10 **NaturApples**
Ending Inventory Budget for Fiscal Year Beginning 10/1/08 (Cases)

	Sauce	Pie Filling
Beginning inventory	13,500	2,300
Plus: Production	130,000	63,000
Available for sale	143,500	65,300
Less: Cases sold	140,000	60,000
Ending inventory	3,500	5,300

The total units in beginning inventory and this period's production must be either sold or in ending inventory. The beginning inventory numbers are known in advance. Choosing two of the remaining three parameters uniquely determines the third. Given the number of apples purchased, the sales budget, and minimum inventory levels, the production budget is derived from the inventory-production-sales identity as long as the processing department has the capacity.

In the production budget in Table 6–9, notice first that the number of cases budgeted for production is different from the number of cases budgeted for sales in Table 6–7. Ten thousand fewer cases of sauce are planned to be produced than sold. Management has decided to reduce the applesauce inventory. On the other hand, the inventory of pie filling is being increased by 3,000 cases. The last two columns in Table 6–9 display the number of pounds of McCoun and Granny apples needed to produce the budgeted cases. The total pounds of each type of apple (10.95 million of McCouns and 7.09 million of Grannys) is the same as in the procurement budget in Table 6–8, reflecting the coordination process involved in budgeting. All the various parts of the organization end up agreeing on the volume of production.

Tables 6–7, 6–8, and 6–9 correspond to the top three boxes in Figure 6–3. Given these three key component budgets, the remainder of the master budget can be prepared. The next budget to compute is the ending inventory budget. This is presented in Table 6–10. The ending inventory of sauce is budgeted to be 3,500 cases and the ending inventory of pie filling is budgeted at 5,300 cases.

Next is the set of direct labor, direct materials, and factory overhead budgets. These budgets are presented in Tables 6–11, 6–12, and 6–13, respectively. Direct labor, as opposed to indirect labor, represents the time employees are actually

TABLE 6–11   **NaturApples**
Direct Labor Budget for Fiscal Year Beginning 10/1/08

	Direct Labor Hours/Case	
	Sauce	*Pie Filling*
Inspection, washing, peeling, coring	0.30	0.24
Saucing	0.10	0.00
Dicing	0.00	0.04
Cooking	0.10	0.16
Canning	0.10	0.10
Total hours per case	0.60	0.54
× Budgeted cases	130,000	63,000
Budgeted labor hours	78,000	34,020
× Budgeted labor rate	$8.75	$8.75
Budgeted labor cost	$682,500	$297,675

TABLE 6–12   **NaturApples**
Direct Materials Budget for Fiscal Year Beginning 10/1/08

	Sauce		*Pie Filling*	
Cost of Apples				
Thousands of pounds of McCouns	7,800		3,150	
× Average cost of McCouns	$ 380.32	$2,966,496	$380.32	$1,198,008
Thousands of pounds of Grannys	5,200		1,890	
× Average cost of Grannys	$ 307.43	$1,598,636	$307.43	$ 581,043
Total cost of apples		$4,565,132		$1,779,051
Cost of Other Ingredients				
Cost per case	$ 0.45		$ 0.33	
× Number of cases	130,000	$ 58,500	63,000	$ 20,790
Total direct materials cost		$4,623,632		$1,799,841

working to produce a particular product. Indirect labor represents the time workers are maintaining machines or are idle. (Chapter 9 explains these distinctions in greater detail.) Table 6–11 provides the number of direct labor hours needed to perform each of the processing functions to produce sauce and pie filling. Sauce requires 0.60 direct labor hours (36 minutes) per case and pie filling requires 0.54 labor hours (32.4 minutes). Multiplying these hours per case times budgeted cases determines the total number of direct labor hours for each product for next year (78,000 for sauce and 34,020 for pie filling).

The direct materials budget in Table 6–12 is a straightforward extension of the procurement budget for apples and includes the spices and other ingredients that are added to the sauce and pie filling. The average cost of 1,000 pounds of each type of apple from Table 6–8 is used to cost the quantity of each type of apple in

TABLE 6–13   NaturApples
Factory Overhead Budget for Fiscal Year Beginning 10/1/08

A. Factory Overhead Flexible Budget

Fixed factory overhead			$1,300,000
Variable overhead per direct labor hour		$13	
Direct labor hours			
Sauce	78,000		
Pie filling	34,020		
× Budgeted direct labor hours		112,020	
Budgeted variable overhead			$1,456,260
Budgeted factory overhead			$2,756,260
÷ Budgeted direct labor hours			112,020
Budgeted overhead rate per direct labor hour			$ 24.61

B. Factory Overhead

	Sauce	Pie Filling
Direct labor hours	78,000	34,020
Overhead rate per labor hour	× $24.61	× $24.61
Factory overhead cost	$1,919,580	$ 837,232

sauce and pie filling. To the cost of apples is added the cost of other ingredients: $0.45 per case for sauce and $0.33 per case for pie filling. Management estimates these costs by taking the known quantities of these other ingredients from the recipes and forecasting any price changes. The total cost of direct materials for sauce is budgeted at $4,623,632, and the total cost of direct materials for pie filling is budgeted at $1,799,841.

Table 6–13 presents the factory overhead budget for each product. The top part of Table 6–13 provides the flexible budget for factory overhead. Fixed factory overhead, which contains $650,000 of depreciation, is budgeted to be $1.3 million and variable overhead is budgeted at $13 per direct labor hour. Chapter 9 expands on how these parameters are forecasted. Given these forecasts and the number of direct labor hours from Table 6–11, management calculates the budgeted factory overhead as $2,756,260. This quantity is then divided by the budgeted direct labor hours (112,020 hours) to compute the budgeted overhead rate per hour of direct labor ($24.61). The $24.61 represents the average overhead cost assigned to sauce and pie filling for every direct labor hour worked on the two products.

Panel B of Table 6–13 calculates the factory overhead for sauce and pie filling. Since sauce is budgeted to use 78,000 direct labor hours, sauce is allocated $1,919,580 of factory overhead ($24.61 × 78,000 direct labor hours) and pie filling is assigned $837,232 (or $24.61 × 34,020).

Refer to Figure 6–3. Given the direct labor, direct materials, factory overhead, ending inventory budgets, and beginning inventory levels, management can now prepare the budget for cost of goods sold, as shown in Table 6–14. The beginning inventory cost is from Table 6–6. The direct labor and material and factory overhead costs are taken directly from Tables 6–11, 6–12, and 6–13. Added to these

TABLE 6–14   **NaturApples**
Cost-of-Goods-Sold Budget for Fiscal Year Beginning 10/1/08

		Sauce		Pie Filling
Beginning inventory		$ 782,460		$ 112,263
Cost of goods processed:				
Direct labor cost	$ 682,500		$ 297,675	
Direct materials cost	4,623,632		1,799,841	
Canning ($1.20/case)	156,000		75,600	
Factory overhead cost	1,919,580		837,232	
Total cost of processing		7,381,712		3,010,348
Available for sale		$8,164,172		$3,122,611
Less: Ending inventory*		(198,738)		(253,251)
Cost of goods sold		$7,965,434		$2,869,360

*Calculation of ending inventory (costs per case are not rounded for calculating ending inventories):

	Sauce	Pie Filling
Total cost of processing	$7,381,712	$3,010,348
÷ Cases produced	130,000	63,000
Cost per case	$ 56.78	$ 47.78
× Cases in ending inventory	3,500	5,300
Ending inventory	$ 198,730	$ 253,251

TABLE 6–15   **NaturApples**
Administration Budget for Fiscal Year Beginning 10/1/08

	Administrative Cost
Marketing	$ 470,000
Finance	160,000
Trucking	380,000
President's office	180,000
Total administration	$1,190,000

previous data is the cost of cans and packaging materials, $1.20 per case (see Table 6–14). The sum of the beginning inventory and the cost of goods processed is the amount available for sale. From this is deducted the ending inventory to arrive at the cost of goods sold. Since the firm uses FIFO, the ending inventory is valued at the cost of the current units processed. The current processing cost is the total cost of units processed divided by the units processed. The footnote to Table 6–14 indicates that the average cost to process a case of sauce is budgeted at $56.78 and the average cost to process a case of pie filling is budgeted at $47.78. These unit cost figures are used to value the ending inventory.

The administration budget in Table 6–15 contains the remaining operating expenses, including the marketing and finance departments' expenses, trucking costs, and the costs of the president's office. The total of all these administrative costs is $1.19 million.

TABLE 6–16 **NaturApples**
Budgeted Income Statement for Fiscal Year Beginning 10/1/08

	Sauce	Pie Filling	Total
Revenue	$9,653,000	$3,237,000	$12,890,000
Less			
Cost of goods sold	(7,965,434)	(2,869,359)	(10,834,793)
Gross margin	$1,687,566	$ 367,641	$ 2,055,207
Less			
Administration costs			(1,190,000)
Interest on debt			(380,000)
Net income before taxes			$ 485,207
Taxes (42%)			(203,787)
Net income			$ 281,420

4. Master Firmwide Budget

The budgeted income statement in Table 6–16 assembles the various pieces from all the earlier statements. The only additional data in Table 6–16 are interest on debt ($380,000) and the provision for corporate income taxes (a 42 percent combined state and federal rate is used). It projects net income after taxes to be $281,420. Clearly, an important question to ask is whether this budgeted profit is high or low, acceptable or unacceptable. To answer this question requires a benchmark for comparison. As we have seen, last year's budget and actuals can provide such a benchmark.

Some managers end their budgeting process with the budgeted income statement as in Table 6–16. But this statement does not address the firm's cash needs. Just because the firm forecasts positive profits does not mean there will be sufficient cash flow to finance operations. In NaturApples's case, the cost of apples represents about half of total revenues. The apples are harvested and paid for in the fall, but the revenue from selling the processed apples is received over the next 12 months. Therefore, NaturApples must find a source of operating cash to finance its apple procurement.

Table 6–17 presents the budgeted statement of cash flows by quarter. NaturApples must borrow $3,385,722 in the first quarter to finance operations, including the apple purchases. Its beginning cash balance of $1.5 million is insufficient to finance all the apple purchases and production costs. Of this $1.5 million, $400,000 must be kept as minimum cash reserves, leaving only $1.1 million to finance operations. In quarter 2, NaturApples repays $1,872,978 of the loan, leaving a balance of $1,512,744 to be repaid in quarter 3. Interest of 3 percent per quarter is paid in quarter 3 on the outstanding balances in quarters 1 and 2 ($101,572 + $45,382). In quarter 4, capital expenditures of $900,000 are budgeted. The budgeted ending cash balance is $2,424,834. The notes to Table 6–17 explain the quarterly timing of the various cash flows.

Having completed the budgeted statement of cash flows, NaturApples can prepare the budgeted statement of financial position (balance sheet) listing all the assets, liabilities, and equities (see Table 6–18). Cash is budgeted to increase from $1,500,000 to $2,424,834. There is no provision at this time to budget a dividend to shareholders, which would decrease the budgeted cash amount and the ending balance in shareholder equity. Budgeted fixed assets are increased by budgeted

TABLE 6–17

NATURAPPLES
Budgeted Statement of Cash Flows
For Fiscal Year Beginning 10/1/08

	Quarter 1	Quarter 2	Quarter 3	Quarter 4	Annual
Sales in the quarter	$ 3,222,500	$3,222,500	$3,222,500	$3,222,500	$12,890,000
80% collected in this quarter	2,578,000	2,578,000	2,578,000	2,578,000	10,312,000
20% collected from last quarter	630,000	644,500	644,500	644,500	2,563,500
Cash from sales	$ 3,208,000	$3,222,500	$3,222,500	$3,222,500	$12,875,500
Less:					
Apple purchases	$ 6,344,200	$ 0	$ 0	$ 0	$ 6,344,200
Direct labor	326,725	326,725	326,725	0	980,175
Other ingredients	26,430	26,430	26,430	0	79,290
Variable overhead	485,420	485,420	485,420	0	1,456,260
Fixed factory overhead	162,500	162,500	162,500	162,500	650,000
Administrative costs	297,500	297,500	297,500	297,500	1,190,000
Income taxes	50,947	50,947	50,947	50,947	203,787
Total cash expenses before interest	$ 7,693,722	$1,349,522	$1,349,522	$ 510,947	$10,903,712
Cash flows from operations	$(4,485,722)	$1,872,978	$1,872,978	$2,711,553	$ 1,971,788
Beginning cash balance	$ 1,500,000	$ 400,000	$ 400,000	$ 613,290	
Less: minimum cash reserves	400,000	400,000	400,000	400,000	
Cash available for operations	$ 1,100,000	$ 0	$ 0	$ 213,280	
New short-term borrowings	$ 3,385,722	$ 0	$ 0	$ 0	
Repayment of loan and interest	0	1,872,978	1,659,698	0	
Outstanding loan balance	$ 3,385,722	$1,512,744	$ 0	$ 0	
Interest at 3% per quarter	$ 101,572	$ 45,382	$ 0	$ 0	
Capital expenditures	$ 0	$ 0	$ 0	$ 900,000	
Ending cash balance	$ 400,000	$ 400,000	$ 613,280	$2,424,833	

Notes:

1. Sales, fixed factory overhead, administrative costs, and income taxes are incurred uniformly over four quarters.
2. Apple purchases are paid in quarter 1.
3. Direct labor, other ingredients, and variable overhead are incurred uniformly over the first three quarters.
4. One-half of the fixed factory overhead is depreciation.
5. 80% of sales are collected in the quarter; the other 20% are collected in the next quarter.
6. There are no uncollectible accounts.
7. $630,000 of accounts receivable from last year, quarter 4, are collected in quarter 1.
8. All interest in the first two quarters is paid in the third quarter.
9. Minimum cash reserves are $400,000.
10. Beginning cash balance is $1.5 million.
11. Interest on short-term borrowing is 3% per quarter.
12. Capital expenditures of $900,000 are paid in quarter 4.
13. Interest expense of $380,000 in Table 6–16 includes interest on short-term borrowing and long-term debt.

TABLE 6–18

NATURAPPLES
Statement of Financial Position
Years Ending 9/30/08 and 9/30/09

	Year Ending *9/30/08*	*Year Ending* *9/30/09*
Cash	$1,500,000	$2,424,834
Accounts receivable	630,000	644,500
Inventory:		
Sauce	782,460	198,738
Pie filling	112,263	253,251
Total inventory	894,723	451,989
Fixed assets	2,755,000	3,005,000
Total assets	$5,779,723	$6,526,323
Accounts payable	$1,300,000	$1,765,180
Long-term debt	1,950,000	1,950,000
Shareholder equity	2,529,723	2,811,143
Total liabilities	$5,779,723	$6,526,323

capital expenditures ($900,000) and decreased by depreciation ($650,000), for a net increase of $250,000. Accounts payable is budgeted to increase from $1,300,000 to $1,765,180. Shareholder equity is budgeted to increase by budgeted net income of $281,420.

Self-Study Problems

Self-Study Problem 1: GAMESS Inc.

GAMESS Inc. develops, markets, packages, and distributes multimedia computer games. GAMESS has outsourced production since it does not believe it can manufacture the games competitively. Its most recent development is an interactive adventure game. Since its multimedia games are different from other computer games in both physical size of the package and price, GAMESS established a new profit center for the adventure game and future CD computer games.

GAMESS is in the process of selecting the profit-maximizing price for the new adventure game. Management estimates demand for the new game at various wholesale prices. The retail stores then set the retail price of the game sold to the public. Estimated demand is shown in Table 1.

The manufacturer of the CDs charges GAMESS $9 per CD produced (assume CDs produced equal CDs sold). Packaging expense is $5 per unit sold. Distribution, which includes the amount paid to distributors for selling the game to retailers, is $3 per unit sold.

Note that although packaging and distribution are estimated to be $5 and $3, respectively, management is not sure how retailers will treat the different packaging size. Advertising contains fixed and variable elements. The fixed portion is

TABLE 1   Price and Quantity Demanded for Adventure Game

Wholesale sales price	$40	$44	$48	$52
Sales volume (units)	435,000	389,000	336,000	281,000

TABLE 2   First-Year Operating Results for Adventure Game

Sales price	$ 44
Sales volume (units)	389,000
Revenues	$17,116,000
Production costs	3,501,000
Packaging	1,798,700
Distribution	1,633,800
Advertising	1,148,232
Fixed overhead	2,506,200
Net income	$ 6,528,068

TABLE 3   Sales Price

	$40	$44	$48	$52
Sales volume (units)	435,000	389,000	336,000	281,000
Sales	$17,400,000	$17,116,000	$16,128,000	$14,612,000
Production	3,915,000	3,501,000	3,024,000	2,529,000
Packaging	2,175,000	1,945,000	1,680,000	1,405,000
Distribution	1,305,000	1,167,000	1,008,000	843,000
Advertising	1,034,800	1,034,232	1,032,256	1,029,224
Fixed overhead	2,500,000	2,500,000	2,500,000	2,500,000
Net income	$ 6,470,200	$ 6,968,768	$ 6,883,744	$ 6,305,776

$1 million. The variable portion is computed using the ratio of $1 advertising expense for each $500 of expected sales. Fixed overhead, which includes administration and management salaries, is projected at $2.5 million.

a. Compute the production, packaging, distribution, advertising, and fixed overhead expenses for the various sales prices and quantities in Table 1. Explain why GAMESS would not consider selling its adventure game for any price other than $44.

b. Actual data for the year are shown in Table 2. Calculate the budget variances.

c. Provide a possible interpretation for the variances.

Solution:

a. $44 is the profit-maximizing price, as seen in Table 3.

b. The variances from the flexible budget are computed as follows:

	Actual	Budgeted	Variance
Sales price	$44		
Sales volume (units)	389,000		
Sales	$17,116,000	$17,116,000	$ 0
Production	3,501,000	3,501,000	0
Packaging	1,798,700	1,945,000	146,300
Distribution	1,633,800	1,167,000	(466,800)
Advertising	1,148,232	1,034,232	(114,000)
Fixed overhead	2,506,200	2,500,000	(6,200)
Net income	$ 6,528,068	$ 6,968,768	$(440,700)

c. As displayed in the table above, packaging has a moderately large favorable variance, while distribution and advertising have large unfavorable variances and fixed overhead has a small unfavorable variance. One possible reason for this pattern of variances is that management cut corners on the packaging of the game. This change in package, combined with the difference in the packaging size between CD games and other computer games, resulted in higher shipping and distribution costs when stores insisted on smaller shipments since their shelf space was not designed for GAMESS CDs. The increase in advertising helped prevent lost sales because of the distribution problems. The fixed overhead variance is less than 1 percent of budgeted fixed overhead and is likely because of random fluctuations.

Self-Study Problem 2: Sandy Cove Bank

Sandy Cove is a new small commercial bank operating in Sandy Cove, Michigan. The bank limits interest rate risk by matching the maturity of its assets to the maturity of its liabilities. By maintaining a spread between interest rates charged and interest rates paid, the bank plans to earn a small income. Management establishes a flexible budget based on interest rates for each department.

The Boat and Car Loan Department offers five-year loans. It matches certificates of deposit (CDs) against car and boat loans. Given all the uncertainty about interest rates, management believes that five-year savings interest rates could vary between 2 percent and 16 percent for the coming year. The savings rate is the rate paid on CD savings accounts. The loan rate is the rate charged on auto and boat loans. Table 1 shows the expected new demand for fixed-rate, five-year loans and new supply of fixed-rate, five-year savings accounts at various interest rates. There are no loans from previous years. Note that the department maintains a 4 percent spread between loan and savings rates to cover processing, loan default, and overhead.

The amount of new loans granted is always the lesser of the loan demand and loan supply. For simplicity, this bank may lend 100 percent of deposits. Although rates are set nationally, the bank may pay or charge slightly different rates to limit demand or boost supply as needed in its local market.

The Boat and Car Loan Department incurs processing, loan default, and overhead expenses related to these accounts. The first two expenses vary, depending on the dollar amount of the accounts. The annual processing expense is budgeted to be 1.5 percent of the loan accounts. Default expense is budgeted at 1 percent of the amount loaned per year. Again, loans and savings would ideally be the same.

TABLE 1   **Demand and Supply of Five-Year Funds**

Loan Rate	Loan Demand	Savings Rate	Savings Supply
6%	$12,100,000	2%	$ 4,700,000
7	10,000,000	3	5,420,000
8	8,070,000	4	8,630,000
9	6,030,000	5	9,830,000
10	4,420,000	6	11,800,000

TABLE 2   **Actual Income Statement of the Boat and Car Loan Department**

Interest income	$ 645,766
Interest expense	314,360
Net interest income	$ 331,406
Fixed overhead	30,200
Processing expense	130,522
Default expense	77,800
Net income	$ 92,884
Loans	$8,062,000
Deposits	$8,123,000

Overhead expenses are estimated to be $30,000 for the year, regardless of the amount loaned.

a. Calculate the processing, loan default, and overhead expenses for each possible interest rate.

b. Create an annual budgeted income statement for five-year loans and deposits for the Boat and Car Loan Department given a savings interest rate of 4 percent. Remember to match supply and demand.

c. Table 2 shows the actual income statement for the Boat and Car Loan Department. Included are the actual loans and savings for the same period. Calculate the variances and provide a possible explanation.

Solution:

a. Flexible budget for the Boat and Car Loan Department:

			($ in Millions)			
Savings Rate	Loan Demand	Savings Supply	New Business	Loan Processing	Default Expense	Overhead Expense
2%	$12.10	$ 4.70	$4.70	$ 70,500	$47,000	$30,000
3	10.00	5.42	5.42	81,300	54,200	30,000
4	8.07	8.63	8.07	121,050	80,700	30,000
5	6.03	9.83	6.03	90,450	60,300	30,000
6	4.42	11.80	4.42	66,300	44,200	30,000

b. Budgeted income statement, 4 percent savings rate for the Boat and Car Loan Department:

Interest income	$645,600*
Interest expense	322,800†
Net interest income	$322,800
Fixed overhead	30,000
Processing expense	121,050
Default expense	80,700
Net income	$ 91,050

*$645,600 = $8,070,000 × 8%
†$322,800 = $8,070,000 × 4%

c. Variance report:

	Actual	Budgeted @ 4%	Fav. (Unfav.) Variance
Interest income	$ 645,766	$ 645,600	$ 166
Interest expense	314,360	322,800	8,440
Net interest income	$ 331,406	$ 322,800	$ 8,606
Fixed overhead	30,200	30,000	(200)
Processing expense	130,522	121,050	(9,472)
Default expense	77,800	80,700	2,900
Net income	$ 92,884	$ 91,050	$ 1,834
Loans	$8,062,000	$8,070,000	$ (8,000)
Deposits	$8,123,000	$8,070,000	$(53,000)

Even though loans were lower and deposits were higher than expected, interest income was higher and interest expense was lower than expected. The answer can be obtained by calculating the average interest rates earned and paid. On $8,062,000 worth of loans, Sandy Cove earned $645,766 interest, or 8.01 percent (0.01 percent more than expected). Similarly, it paid only 3.87 percent (0.13 percent less) on deposits. Therefore, the net interest income variance of $8,606 is a combination of two effects: the variance in the actual loans and deposits (quantity) and the variance in the interest rates (price). The combined effects are a favorable interest income variance, a favorable interest expense variance, and an overall favorable net interest income variance.

At a savings interest rate of 4 percent, there is an excess supply of deposits over demand for loans. The Boat and Car Loan Department lowered the interest rate on deposits to stem additional deposits. The increase in the interest rate on loans can be attributed only to an increase in the demand for loans, which resulted in the department charging a slightly higher average interest rate.

The higher processing expense could be related to the higher number of accounts processed and improvements in the default rate. That is, the favorable default expense could be attributed to an improved screening process—related to spending more on processing.

Problems

P 6–1:   Country Club

Using the data in Table 6–1 (on page 263), how much did it cost the members of Bay View Country Club to operate the club for September 2008?

P 6–2:   Shocker Company

Shocker Company's sales budget shows quarterly sales for next year as follows:

Quarter 1	10,000 units
Quarter 2	8,000 units
Quarter 3	12,000 units
Quarter 4	14,000 units

Company policy is to have a finished goods inventory at the end of each quarter equal to 20 percent of the next quarter's sales. Compute budgeted production for the second quarter of next year.

SOURCE: CMA adapted.

P 6–3:   The Jung Corporation

The Jung Corporation's budget calls for the following production:

Quarter 1	45,000 units
Quarter 2	38,000 units
Quarter 3	34,000 units
Quarter 4	48,000 units

Each unit of product requires three pounds of direct material. The company's policy is to begin each quarter with an inventory of direct materials equal to 30 percent of that quarter's direct material requirements. Compute budgeted direct materials purchases for the third quarter.

SOURCE: CMA adapted.

P 6–4:   G. Bennett Stewart on Management Incentives

I've given a good deal of thought to this issue of how companies . . . go about negotiating objectives with their different business units. The typical process in such cases is that once the parent negotiates a budget with a unit, the budget then becomes the basis for the bonus. And they are also typically structured such that the bonus kicks in when, say, 80 percent of the budgeted performance is achieved; and the maximum bonus is earned when management reaches, say, 120 percent of the budgeted level. There is thus virtually no downside and very limited upside.

Now, because the budget is negotiated between management and headquarters, there is a circularity about the whole process that makes the resulting standards almost meaningless. Because the budget is intended to reflect what management thinks it can accomplish—presumably without extraordinary effort and major changes in the status quo—the adoption of the budget as a standard is unlikely to motivate exceptional performance, especially since the upside is so limited. Instead it is likely to produce cautious budgets and mediocre performance.

So, because of the perverse incentives built into the budgeting process itself, I think it's important for a company to break the connection between the budget and planning process on the one hand and the bonus systems on the other hand. The bonuses should be based upon absolute performance standards that are not subject to negotiation.

Critically evaluate this quotation.

SOURCE: B Stewart, "CEO Roundtable on Corporate Structure and Management Incentives," *Journal of Applied Corporate Finance*, Fall 1990, p. 27.

P 6–5: Investment Banks

Rogers Petersen and Cabots are two of the five largest investment banks in the United States. Last year there was a major scandal at Cabots involving manipulation of some auctions for government bonds. A number of senior partners at Cabots were charged with price fixing in the government bond market. The ensuing investigation led four of the eight managing directors (the highest-ranking officials at Cabots) to resign. A new senior managing director was brought in from outside to run the firm. This individual recruited three outside managing directors to replace the ones who resigned. There was then a thorough housecleaning. In the following six months, 15 additional partners and over 40 senior managers left Cabots and were replaced, usually with people from outside the firm.

Rogers Petersen has had no such scandal, and almost all of its senior executives have been with the firm for all of their careers.

Required:

    a. Describe zero-based budgeting.

    b. Which firm, Rogers Petersen or Cabots, is most likely to be using ZBB? Why?

P 6–6: Ice Storm

In March, a devastating ice storm struck Monroe County, New York, causing millions of dollars of damage. Mathews & Peat (M&P), a large horticultural nursery, was hit hard. As a result of the storm, $653,000 of additional labor and maintenance costs were incurred to clean up the nursery, remove and replace damaged plants, repair fencing, and replace glass broken when nearby tree limbs fell on some of the greenhouses.

Mathews & Peat is a wholly owned subsidiary of Agro Inc., an international agricultural conglomerate. The manager of Mathews & Peat, R. Dye, is reviewing the operating performance of the subsidiary for the year. Here are the results for the year as compared with budget:

MATHEWS & PEAT
Summary of Operating Results for the Current Year ($000s)

	Actual Results	Budgeted Results	Actual as % of Budget
Revenues	$32,149	$31,682	101%
Less			
Labor	13,152	12,621	104
Materials	8,631	8,139	106
Occupancy costs[*]	4,234	4,236	100
Depreciation	2,687	2,675	100
Interest	1,875	1,895	99
Total expenses	$30,579	$29,566	103%
Operating profits	$ 1,570	$ 2,116	74%

[*]Includes property taxes, utilities, maintenance and repairs of buildings, and so on.

After thinking about how to present the performance of M&P for the year, Dye decides to break out the costs of the ice storm from the individual items affected by it and report the storm separately. The total cost of the ice storm, $653,000, consists of additional labor costs of $320,000, additional materials of $220,000, and additional occupancy costs of $113,000. These amounts are net of the insurance payments received due to the storm. The alternative performance statement follows:

MATHEWS & PEAT
Summary of Operating Results for the Current Year ($000s)

	Actual Results	Budgeted Results	Actual as % of Budget
Revenues	$32,149	$31,682	101%
Less			
Labor	12,832	12,621	102
Materials	8,411	8,139	103
Occupancy costs	4,121	4,236	97
Depreciation	2,687	2,675	100
Interest	1,875	1,895	99
Total expenses	29,926	29,566	101%
Operating profits before			
ice storm costs	2,223	2,116	105%
Ice storm costs	653	0	
Operating profits after			
ice storm costs	$ 1,570	$ 2,116	74%

Required:

a. Put yourself in Dye's position and write a short, concise cover memo for the second operating statement summarizing the essential points you want to communicate to your superiors.

b. Critically evaluate the differences between the two performance reports as presented.

P 6–7: Budget Lapsing versus Line-Item Budgets

a. What is the difference between budget lapsing and line-item budgets?

b. What types of organizations would you expect to use budget lapsing?

c. What types of organizations would you expect to use line-item budgets?

P 6–8: DMP Consultants

You work in the finance department of a telecommunications firm with a large direct sales force selling high-speed fiber optics access lines to companies wanting telephone and Internet access. Your firm uses a top-down budget that sets the sales quota for each of its 180 salespeople. The salespeople are compensated based on a commission as well as a bonus whenever actual sales exceed their individual budgeted sales quota. Each salesperson's quota is estimated by senior marketing managers in the corporate office based on the size of each customer in that salesperson's geographic territory and projected growth of business in that territory.

DMP Consultants specializes in redesigning antiquated budgeting systems. DMP has made a presentation to your finance department after conducting a thorough analysis of your firm's sales force budgeting system. DMP Consultants has emphasized that your current budgeting system does not take advantage of what your salespeople know about future sales to their customer regions. By ignoring this information, your firm does not effectively plan for this growth, and you are at a competitive disadvantage when deciding to add capacity to your fiber optic network in a timely and efficient way. Moreover, DMP points to extensive research documenting that when people participate in setting budgets that are used to evaluate their performance, these people more readily accept the budgets and there is an increase in employee morale. That is, "participative budgeting" (where employees who are judged against the budget participate in setting the budget) results in happier, more motivated employees. DMP Consultants has made a proposal to implement a bottom-up, participative budgeting scheme to replace your top-down system.

You have been asked to write a short memo to the head of the finance department that analyzes the pros and cons of DMP's proposal.

P 6–9: Budgeting

Describe (*a*) the *benefits* of top-down budgeting and (*b*) the *benefits* of bottom-up budgeting.

P 6–10: Essay

Describe how budgets and budgeting systems help solve the organization problem. Give examples.

P 6–11: Golf World

Golf World is a 1,000-room luxury resort with swimming pools, tennis courts, three golf courses, and many other resort amenities.

The head golf course superintendent, Sandy Green, is responsible for all golf course maintenance and conditioning. Green also has the final say as to whether a particular course is open or closed due to weather conditions and whether players can rent motorized riding golf carts for use on a particular course. If the course is very wet, the golf carts will damage the turf, which Green's maintenance crew will have to repair. Since she is out on the courses every morning supervising the maintenance crews, she knows the condition of the courses.

Wiley Grimes is in charge of the golf cart rentals. His crew maintains the golf cart fleet of over 200 cars, cleans them, puts oil and gas in them, and repairs minor damage. He also is responsible for leasing the carts from the manufacturer, including the terms of the lease, the number of carts to lease, and the choice of cart vendor. When guests arrive at the golf course to play, they pay greens fees to play and a cart fee if they wish to use a cart. If they do not wish to rent a cart, they pay only the greens fee and walk the course.

Grimes and Green manage separate profit centers. The golf cart profit center's revenue is composed of the fees collected from the carts. The golf course profit center's revenue is from the greens fees collected. When the results from April were reviewed, golf cart operating profits were only 49 percent of budget. Wiley argued that the poor results were due to the unusually heavy rains in April. He complained that there were several days when, though only a few areas of the course were wet, the entire course was closed to carts because the grounds crew was too busy to rope off these areas.

To better analyze the performance of the golf cart profit center, the controller's office recently implemented a flexible budget based on the number of cart rentals:

GOLF WORLD
Golf Cart Profit Center
Operating Results—April

	Static Budget	Actual Results	Variance from Static Budget	Flexible Budget	Variance from Flexible Budget
Number of cart rentals	6,000	4,000	2,000	4,000	0
Revenues (@ $25/cart)	$150,000	$100,000	$50,000U	$100,000	0
Labor (fixed cost)	7,000	7,200	200U	7,000	200U
Gas and oil (@ $1/rental)	6,000	4,900	1,100F	4,000	900U
Cart lease (fixed cost)	40,000	40,000	0	40,000	0
Operating profit	$ 97,000	$ 47,900	$49,100U	$ 49,000	$1,100U

Note: F = Favorable; U = Unfavorable.

Required:

a. Evaluate the performance of the golf cart profit center for the month of April.
b. What are the advantages and disadvantages of the controller's new budgeting system?
c. What additional recommendations would you make regarding the operations of Golf World?

P 6–12: Minimum Spending Plan at Bay View Country Club

Bay View Country Club is considering imposing a minimum spending plan on its members. Each member would prepay $50 of restaurant charges at the beginning of each month in addition to the normal dues. At the end of the month, a member who has restaurant charges in excess of $50 is billed the difference. A member who spends less than $50 in any month loses whatever he or she doesn't spend. (Note: Only members or their guests can eat at the club. The club's restaurant is not open to the general public.)

In explaining why the minimum is being proposed, the treasurer gave the following reasons:

The food operation is losing more money than budgeted. We have always budgeted to lose about $50,000 in the restaurant. But this year, the projected loss is $150,000. The problem is the revenue side of the budget. Revenues are down about 20 percent from budget, while costs are on target. If the members are unwilling to support the restaurant by eating here, then they have to pay for the unbudgeted deficit of $100,000 with either higher dues, a special assessment, or a minimum spending plan.

About one-third of the members spend in excess of $50 per month at the restaurant, but two-thirds spend less than $50 per month. It is not fair that one-third of the members are supporting the other two-thirds.

Knowing how much the members will be eating at the club each month will help tremendously in our budgeting and planning process. It will cut down on food waste because we will know how much revenue we will be generating and can plan accordingly.

Required:

Critically evaluate the costs and benefits of the proposed minimum spending plan. What consequences are likely to result?

P 6–13:   Coating Department

The coating department of a parts manufacturing department coats various parts with an antirust, zinc-based material. The parts to be processed are loaded into baskets; the baskets are passed through a coating machine that dips the parts into the zinc solution. The machine then heats the parts to ensure that the coating bonds properly. All parts being coated are assigned a cost for the coating department based on the number of hours the parts spend in the coating machine. Prior to the beginning of the year, cost categories are accumulated by department (including the coating department). These cost categories are classified as either fixed or variable and then a flexible budget for the department is constructed. Given an estimate of machine hours for the next year, the coating department's projected cost per machine hour is computed.

Here are data for the last three operating years. Expected coating machine hours for 2012 are 16,000 hours.

COATING DEPARTMENT
Operating Data

	2009	2010	2011
Machine hours	12,500	8,400	15,200
Coating materials	$ 51,375	$ 34,440	$ 62,624
Engineering support	27,962	34,295	31,300
Maintenance	35,850	35,930	36,200
Occupancy costs (square footage)	27,502	28,904	27,105
Operator labor	115,750	78,372	147,288
Supervision	46,500	47,430	49,327
Utilities	12,875	8,820	16,112
Total costs	$317,814	$268,191	$369,956

Required:

  a. Estimate the coating department's flexible budget for 2012. Explicitly state and justify the assumptions used in deriving your estimates.
  b. Calculate the coating department's cost per machine hour for 2012.

P 6–14:   Marketing Plan

Robin Jensen, manager of market planning for Viral Products of the IDP Pharmaceutical Co., is responsible for advertising a class of products. She has designed a three-year marketing plan to increase the market share of her product class. Her plan involves a major increase in magazine advertising. She has met with an advertising agency that has designed a three-year ad campaign involving 12 separate ads that build on a common theme. Each ad will run in three consecutive monthly medical magazines and then be followed by the next ad in the sequence. Up to five medical journals will carry the ad campaign. Direct mail campaigns and direct sales promotional material will be designed to follow the theme of the ad currently appearing. The accompanying table summarizes the cost of the campaign:

	Year 1	Year 2	Year 3	Year 4
Number of ads	4	4	4	12
Number of magazines	5	5	4	
Cost per ad	$ 6,000	$ 6,200	$ 6,500	
Advertising cost	$120,000	$124,000	$104,000	$348,000

The firm's normal policy is to budget each year as a separate entity without carrying forward unspent monies. Jensen is requesting that, instead of just approving the budget for next year (Year 1 above), the firm approve and budget the entire three-year project. This would allow her to move forward with her campaign and give her the freedom to apply any unspent funds in one year to the next year or to use them in another part of the campaign. She argues that the ad campaign is an integrated project stretching over three years and should be either approved or rejected in its entirety.

Required:

Critically evaluate Jensen's request and make a recommendation as to whether a three-year budget should be approved per her proposal. (Assume that the advertising campaign is expected to be a profitable project.)

P 6–15:   Potter-Bowen

Potter-Bowen (PB) manufactures and sells postage meters throughout the world. Postage meters print the necessary postage on envelopes, eliminating the need to affix stamps. The meter keeps track of the postage, the user takes the meter's counter to a post office and pays money, and the post office initializes the meter to print postage totaling that amount. The firm offers about 30 different postage systems, ranging from small manual systems (costing a few hundred dollars) to large automated ones (costing up to $75,000).

PB is organized into Research and Development, Manufacturing, and Marketing. Marketing is further subdivided into four sectors: North America, South America, Europe, and Asia. The North American marketing sector has a sales force organized into 32 regions with approximately 75 to 200 salespeople per region.

The budgeting process begins with the chief financial officer (CFO) and the vice president of marketing jointly projecting the total sales for the next year. Their staffs look at trends of the various PB models and project total unit sales by model within each marketing sector. Price increases are forecast and dollar sales per model are calculated. The North American sector is then given a target number of units and a target revenue by model for the year. The manager of the North American sector, Helen Neumann, and her staff then allocate the division's target units and target revenue by region.

The target unit sales for each model per region are derived by taking the region's historical percentage sales for that machine times North America's target for that model. For example, model 6103 has North American target unit sales of 18,500 for next year. The Utah region last year sold 4.1 percent of all model 6103s sold in North America. Therefore, Utah's target of 6103s for next year is 758 units (4.1% × 18,500). The average sales price of the 6103 is set at $11,000. Thus, Utah's revenue budget for 6103s is $8,338,000. Given the total forecasted unit sales, average selling prices, and historical sales of each model in all regions, each region is assigned a unit target and revenue budget by model. The region's total revenue budget is the sum of the individual models' revenue targets.

Each salesperson in the region is given a unit and revenue target by model using a similar procedure. If Gary Lindenmeyer (a salesperson in Utah) sold 6 percent of Utah's 6103s last year, his unit sales target of 6103s next year is 45 units (6% × 758). His total revenue target for 6103s is $495,000 (or 45 × $11,000). Totaling all the models gives each salesperson's total revenue budget. Salespeople are paid a fixed salary plus a bonus. The bonus is calculated based on the following table:

% of Total Revenue Target Achieved	Bonus
< 90%	No bonus
90–100%	5% of salary
101–110	10% of salary
111–120	20% of salary
121–130	30% of salary
131–140	40% of salary
141–150	50% of salary
>150%	60% of salary

Required:
Critically evaluate PB's sales budgeting system and sales force compensation system. Describe any potential dysfunctional behaviors that PB's systems are likely to generate.

P 6–16:   Feder Purchasing Department

The purchasing department at Feder buys all of its raw materials, supplies, and parts. This department is a cost center. It uses a flexible budget based on the number of different items purchased each month to forecast spending and as a control mechanism.

At the beginning of February, the purchasing department expected to purchase 8,200 different items. Given this expected number of purchased items, purchasing calculated its flexible budget for February to be $1,076,400. In reviewing actual spending in February, the purchasing department was over its flexible budget by $41,400 (unfavorable) when calculated using the actual number of items purchased. Actual spending in February was $1,175,000, and the department purchased 9,300 units.

Budgeted fixed cost and budgeted variable cost per item purchased remained the same in the flexible budgets calculated at the beginning and end of February.

Required:

Calculate the fixed cost and the variable cost per item purchased used in the purchasing department's flexible budget in February.

P 6–17: E-Commerce Companies

Two Internet-based, e-commerce companies were started about two years ago and both went public last month. They have about the same number of employees but offer different services (i.e., they are not competitors). Both firms use a one-year budgeting process, but only one firm also supplements its annual budget with a three-year budget.

Required:

Offer some plausible reasons why one firm uses only an annual budget and the other firm uses both an annual and a three-year budget.

P 6–18: Access.Com

Access.Com produces and sells software to libraries and schools to block access to Web sites deemed inappropriate by the customer. In addition, the software also tracks and reports on Web sites visited and advises the customer of other Web sites the customer might choose to block. Access.Com's software sells for between $15,000 and $20,000.

Three account managers (V. J. Singh, A. C. Chen, and P. J. Martinez) sell the software and are paid a fixed salary plus a percentage of all sales in excess of targeted (budgeted) sales. Vice President of Marketing S. B. Ro sets the budgeted sales amount for each account manager. The following table reports actual and budgeted sales for the three account managers for the past five years.

	A. C. Chen		V. J. Singh		P. J. Martinez	
	Actual	Budget	Actual	Budget	Actual	Budget
2003	$1.630	$1.470	$2.240	$2.400	$2.775	$2.695
2004	1.804	1.614	2.586	2.384	2.995	2.767
2005	1.685	1.785	2.406	2.566	2.876	2.972
2006	1.665	1.775	2.600	2.550	2.698	2.963
2007	1.924	1.764	2.385	2.595	3.107	2.936

Required:

a. Based on the data in the table, describe the process used by Ro to set sales quotas for each account manager.
b. Discuss the pros and cons of Access.Com's budgeting process for setting account managers' sales targets.

P 6–19: Videx

Videx is the premier firm in the security systems industry. Martha Rameriz is an account manager at Videx responsible for selling residential systems. She is compensated based on beating a predetermined sales budget. The last seven years' sales budgets and actual sales data follow. Videx sets its sales budgets centrally in a top-down fashion.

Year	Budget	Actual	Difference
1	$850,000	$865,000	$15,000
2	862,000	888,800	26,800
3	884,000	852,000	−32,000
4	884,000	895,000	11,000
5	893,000	878,000	−15,000
6	893,000	902,000	9,000
7	901,000		
Average	881,000	880,133	2,467
Standard deviation	18,385	18,970	21,715
Median	884,000	883,400	10,000

Required:

a. Martha Rameriz sells $908,000 in year 7. What budget will she be assigned for year 8?

b. Suppose Rameriz sells $900,000 of systems in year 7. What budget will she be assigned in year 8?

P 6–20:   New York Fashions

New York Fashions owns 87 women's clothing stores in shopping malls. Corporate headquarters of New York Fashions uses flexible budgets to control the operations of each of the stores. The following table presents the August flexible budget for the New York Fashions store located in the Crystal Lakes Mall:

NEW YORK FASHIONS—CRYSTAL LAKES MALL STORE
Flexible Budget
August

Expense	Fixed	Variable
Cost of goods sold		45%
Management	$ 7,000	1
Salespersons	2,000	8
Rent	12,000	5
Utilities	900	
Other	1,500	

Variable costs are based on a percentage of revenues.

Required:

a. Revenues for August were $80,000. Calculate budgeted profits for August.

b. Actual results for August are summarized in the following table:

NEW YORK FASHIONS—CRYSTAL LAKES MALL STORE
Actual Results from Operations
August

Revenues	$80,000
Cost of goods sold	38,000
Management	7,600
Salespersons	9,800
Rent	16,000
Utilities	875
Other	1,400

Prepare a report for the New York Fashions—Crystal Lakes Mall store for the month of August comparing actual results to the budget.

c. Analyze how the Crystal Lakes Mall store performed in August.

d. How does a flexible budget change the incentives of managers held responsible for meeting the flexible budget as compared to the incentives created by meeting a static (fixed) budget?

P 6–21:   August Company

August Company's budget for the month just ended called for producing and selling 5,000 units at $8 each. Actual units produced and sold were 5,200, yielding revenue of $42,120. Variable costs were budgeted at $3 per unit and fixed costs were budgeted at $2 per unit. Actual variable costs were $3.30 and fixed costs were $12,000.

Required:

a. Prepare a performance report for the current month's operation.

b. Write a short memo analyzing the current month's performance.

P 6–22:   International Telecon

You are working in the office of the vice president of administration at International Telecon (IT) as a senior financial planner. IT is a Fortune 500 firm with sales approaching $1 billion. IT provides long-distance satellite communications around the world. Deregulation of telecommunications in Europe has intensified worldwide competition and has increased pressures inside IT to reduce costs so it can lower prices without cutting profit margins.

IT is divided into several profit and cost centers. Each profit center is further organized as a series of cost centers. Each profit and cost center submits a budget to IT's vice president of administration and then is held responsible for meeting that budget. The VP of administration described IT's financial control, budgeting, and reporting system as "pretty much a standard, state-of-the-art approach where we hold our people accountable for producing what they forecast."

Your boss has assigned you the task of analyzing firmwide supplies expenditures, with the goal of reducing waste and lowering expenditures. Supplies include all consumables ranging from pencils and paper to electronic subcomponents and parts costing less than $1,000. Long-lived assets that cost under $1,000 (or the equivalent dollar amount in the domestic currency for foreign purchases) are not capitalized (and then depreciated) but are categorized as supplies and written off as expenses in the month purchased.

You first gather the last 36 months of operating data for both supplies and payroll for the entire firm. The payroll data help you benchmark the supplies data. You divide each month's payroll and supplies amount by revenues in that month to control for volume and seasonal fluctuations. The accompanying graph plots the two data series.

Payroll fluctuates from 35 to 48 percent of sales, and supplies fluctuate from 13 to 34 percent of sales. The graph contains the last three fiscal years of supplies and payroll, divided by the vertical lines. For financial and budgeting purposes, IT is on a calendar (January–December) fiscal year.

International Telecon monthly payroll and supply expenses, last 36 months

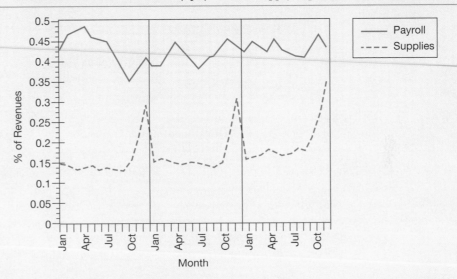

Besides focusing on consolidated firmwide spending, you prepare disaggregated graphs like the one shown, but at the cost and profit center levels. The general patterns observed in the consolidated graphs are repeated in general in the disaggregated graphs.

Required:

a. Analyze the time-series behavior of supplies expenditures for IT. What is the likely reason for the observed patterns in supplies?

b. Given your analysis in (a), what corrective action might you consider proposing? What are its costs and benefits?

P 6–23:   Adrian Power

Adrian Power manufactures small power supplies for car stereos. The company uses flexible budgeting techniques to deal with the seasonal and cyclical nature of the business. The accounting department provided the accompanying data on budgeted manufacturing costs for the month of January:

ADRIAN POWER
Planned Level of Production for January

Budgeted production (in units)	14,000

Variable costs (vary with production)	
Direct materials	$140,000
Direct labor	224,000
Indirect labor	21,000
Indirect materials	10,500
Maintenance	6,300
Fixed costs	
Supervision	24,700
Other (depreciation, taxes, etc.)	83,500
Total plant costs	$510,000

Actual operations for January are summarized as

ADRIAN POWER
Actual Operations for January

Actual production (in units)	15,400

Actual costs incurred	
Direct materials	$142,400
Direct labor	259,800
Indirect labor	27,900
Indirect materials	12,200
Maintenance	9,800
Supervision	28,000
Other costs (depreciation, taxes, etc.)	83,500
Total plant costs	$563,600

Required:

a. Prepare a report comparing the actual operating results with the flexible budget at actual production.

b. Write a short memo analyzing the report prepared in (*a*). What likely managerial implications do you draw from this report? What are the numbers telling you?

P 6–24:   Panarude Airfreight

Panarude Airfreight is an international air freight hauler with more than 45 jet aircraft operating in the United States and the Pacific Rim. The firm is head-quartered in Melbourne, Australia, and is organized into five geographic areas: Australia, Japan, Taiwan, Korea, and the United States. Supporting these areas are several centralized, corporate function services (cost centers): human resources, data processing, fleet acquisition and maintenance, and telecommunications. Each responsibility center has a budget, negotiated at the beginning of the year with the vice president of finance. Funds unspent at the end of the year do not carry over to the next fiscal year. The firm is on a January-to-December fiscal year.

After reviewing the month-to-month variances, Panarude senior management became concerned about the increased spending occurring in the last three months of each fiscal year. In particular, in the first nine months of the year, expenditure accounts typically show favorable variances (actual spending is less than budget), but in the last three months, unfavorable variances are the norm. In an attempt to smooth out these spending patterns, each responsibility center is reviewed at the end of each calendar quarter and any unspent funds can be deleted from the budget for the remainder of the year. The accompanying table shows the budget and actual spending in the telecommunications department for the first quarter of this year.

PANARUDE AIRFREIGHT
Telecommunications Department: First Quarter
Budget and Actual Spending (Australian Dollars)

	Monthly Budget	Cumulative Budget	Actual Spending	Cumulative Spending	Monthly Variance[*]	Cumulative Variance[*]
Jan.	$110,000	$110,000	$104,000	$104,000	$6,000 F	$6,000 F
Feb.	95,000	205,000	97,000	201,000	2,000 U	4,000 F
Mar.	115,000	320,000	112,000	313,000	3,000 F	7,000 F

[*]F = Favorable; U = Unfavorable.

At the end of the first quarter, telecommunications' total annual budget for this year can be reduced by $7,000, the total budget underrun in the first quarter. In addition, the remaining nine monthly budgets for telecommunications are reduced by $778 (or $7,000 ÷ 9). If, at the end of the second quarter, telecommunications' budget shows an unfavorable variance of, say, $8,000 (after the original budget is reduced for the first-quarter underrun), management of telecommunications is held responsible for the entire $8,000 unfavorable variance. The first-quarter underrun is not restored. If the second-quarter budget variance is also favorable, the remaining six monthly budgets are each reduced further by one-sixth of the second-quarter favorable budget variance.

Required:

a. What behavior would this budgeting scheme engender in the responsibility center managers?

b. Compare the advantages and disadvantages of the previous budget regime, where any end-of-year budget surpluses do not carry over to the next fiscal year, with the system of quarterly budget adjustments just described.

P 6–25:   Veriplex

Veriplex manufactures process control equipment. This 100-year-old German company has recently acquired another firm that has a design for a new proprietary process control system. A key component of the new system to be manufactured by Veriplex is called the VTrap, a new line of precision air-flow gauges.

Veriplex uses tight financial budgets linked to annual bonuses to control its manufacturing departments. Each manufacturing department is a cost center. The VTrap gauge is being manufactured in Veriplex's gauge department, which also manufactures an existing line of gauges. The gauge department's budget for the current year consists of two parts: €6.60 million for manufacturing the existing line of gauges and €0.92 million to develop and manufacture VTrap.

The gauge department is responsible for introducing VTrap, which has been in development in the gauge department since the beginning of the year. The new gauge will be manufactured using much of the same equipment and personnel as the existing gauges. VTrap is an integral part of the proprietary process control system that Veriplex hopes will give it a sustainable competitive advantage. Senior management is heavily committed to this strategy. Senior engineering staff members are always in the gauge department working with the manufacturing personnel to modify and refine both the gauges' design and the production processes to produce them. (Note: Engineering department costs are not assigned to the gauge department.)

By the end of the fiscal year, the gauge department had spent €1.30 million on the VTrap program and €6.39 million on existing gauge production. Both the new and existing gauge lines achieved their target production quotas and quality goals for the year.

Required:

a. Prepare a financial statement for the gauge department that details its financial performance for the fiscal year just completed.

b. Upon further investigation of previous new product introductions, you discover the same patterns in other departments between new and existing products and their budgets and actual costs. What are some possible reasons why the pattern in the gauge department is not an isolated occurrence but has occurred with other new product introductions and is likely to occur with future new product introductions?

P 6–26: Madigan Modems

Madigan produces a single high-speed modem. The following table summarizes the current month's budget for Madigan's modem production:

Projected production and sales	4,000 units
Variable costs	$ 640,000
Fixed costs	$ 480,000
Total production budget	$1,120,000

Actual production and sales for the month were 3,900 units. Total production costs were $1,114,800, of which $631,800 were variable costs.

Required:

a. Prepare an end-of-month variance report for the production department using the beginning-of-month static budget.

b. Prepare an end-of-month variance report for the production department using the beginning-of-month flexible budget.

c. Write a short memo evaluating the performance of the production manager based on the variance report in (*a*).

d. Write a short memo evaluating the performance of the production manager based on the variance report in (*b*).

e. Which variance report—the one in (*a*) or (*b*)—best reflects the performance of the production manager? Why?

P 6–27: Webb & Drye

Webb & Drye (WD) is a New York City law firm with over 200 attorneys. WD has a sophisticated set of information technologies—including intranets and extranets, e-mail servers, the firm's accounting, payroll, and client billing software, and document management systems—that allows WD attorneys and their expert witnesses access to millions of pages of scanned documents that often accompany large class action lawsuits. Bev Piccaretto was hired at the beginning of last year to manage WD's IT department. She and her staff maintain these various systems, but they also act as an internal consulting group to WD's professional staff. They help the staff connect to and use the various IT systems and troubleshoot problems the staff may encounter.

The IT department is a cost center. Piccaretto receives an annual operating budget and believes she is accountable for not exceeding the budget while simultaneously providing high-quality IT services to WD. Piccaretto reports to Marge Malone, WD's chief operating officer. Malone is responsible for IT, accounting, marketing, human resources, and finance functions for Webb & Drye. She reports directly to WD's managing partner, who is the firm's chief executive officer.

The fiscal year has just ended. The following table contains IT's annual budget, actual amounts spent, and variances from the budget.

WEBB & DRYE
IT Department
Budgeted and Actual Expenditures and Variances from Budget Last Year

	Budget	Actual	Variance	Fav./Unfav.
Salaries	$ 350,000	$ 336,000	$14,000	F
Benefits[*]	140,000	134,400	5,600	F
Software site licenses	143,000	168,000	(25,000)	U
Hardware leases	630,000	635,000	(5,000)	U
Travel	59,000	57,000	2,000	F
Supplies	112,000	110,000	2,000	F
Training	28,000	20,000	8,000	F
Occupancy costs	195,000	198,000	(3,000)	U
Total	$1,657,000	$1,658,400	$ (1,400)	U

[*] 40% of salaries

Malone expresses her concern that the IT department had substantial deviations from the original budgeted amounts for software licenses and salaries, and that Piccaretto should have informed Malone of these actions before they were implemented. Piccaretto argues that since total spending within the IT department was in line with the total budget of $1,657,000 she managed her budget well. Furthermore, Piccaretto points out that she had to buy more sophisticated antivirus software to protect the firm from hacker attacks and that, in paying for these software upgrades, she did not replace a staff person who left in the fourth quarter of the year. Malone counters that this open position adversely affected a large lawsuit because the attorneys working on the case had trouble downloading the scanned documents in the document management system that IT is responsible for maintaining.

Required:

Write a short memo analyzing the disagreement between Malone and Piccaretto. What issues underlie the disagreement? Who is right and who is wrong? What corrective actions (if any) do you recommend?

P 6–28:   City Hospital Nursing

City Hospital is a city government-owned and -operated hospital providing basic health care to low-income people. Most of the hospital's revenues are from federal, state, county, and city governments. Some patients covered by private insurance are also admitted, but most of the patients are covered by government assistance programs (Medicare and Medicaid).

Maxine Jones is the director of nursing for the 40-bed pediatrics unit at City Hospital. She is responsible for recruiting nurses, scheduling when they work (days, evenings, weekends), and preparing the nursing budget for the pediatrics unit. A variety of different nursing skills is needed to staff the unit: There are nursing aides, nurse practitioners, registered nurses, nursing supervisors, and clinical nurses. Each type of nurse provides different patient care services (care and feeding, drawing blood samples, giving injections, changing dressings, supervising, etc.). Not all types of nurses can provide all services, and each type of nurse has a different wage rate. Minimum nurse staffing levels per patient must be maintained. If the minimums are violated, new patients cannot be admitted.

Over 45 full-time nurses are required to staff the pediatrics unit. The number of each type of nurse is set in the budget (8 nurses aides, 12 nurse practitioners, 14 registered nurses, etc.). To change the mix of nurse types or their wage rates during the year requires time-consuming approval from the nursing administration, the hospital administration, and finally the city council. The director can change the staffing mix and pay scales in the next budget year by submitting a budget with the revised staffing levels and wage rates and having the budget approved through a lengthy review process that ultimately requires the city council's agreement.

In selecting where to work, nurses evaluate working conditions, pay, and amenities, as all employees do. A key working condition for nurses is flexibility in choosing their schedule. Because of the shortage of nurses in the community, all hospitals have become competitive in terms of work schedules and hours. Some private hospitals allow nurses to schedule when they want to work and how many hours a week they are willing to work. City Hospital often finds its nurses being hired away by private hospitals. If a nurse practitioner is hired away, Jones must replace her or him with another nurse practitioner. The private hospitals do not have such a constraint. If a nurse practitioner position is open, a private hospital will temporarily move a registered nurse with a higher level of skills into the position until a nurse practitioner can be found.

Required:

a. What type of specialized knowledge does Maxine Jones acquire in preparing the nursing schedule for the upcoming month?

b. What are some of the consequences of the constraints Jones must operate under?

c. Explain why City Hospital does not allow Jones as much freedom in her staffing decisions as her counterparts in private hospitals.

P 6–29: Madden International

Madden International is a large ($7 billion sales), successful international pharmaceuticals firm operating in 23 countries with 15 autonomous subsidiaries. The corporate office consists of five vice presidents who oversee the operations of the subsidiaries. These five vice presidents report to two executive vice presidents, who in turn report to the president of the firm.

The 15 subsidiaries specialize by pharmaceutical type and in some cases by country. The pace of innovation in this industry is very fast. In addition, each country has its own elaborate regulatory environment that controls new drug introduction, pricing, and distribution. Each market has its own peculiarities concerning hospital drug purchases. It is an understatement to say that Madden International operates in a very complex world that changes daily.

The corporate office requires each subsidiary to maintain an elaborate, detailed budget and control system. The following points summarize the budget and control system in each subsidiary:

- One-, three-, and five-year budgets are prepared each year.
- The vice president overseeing the subsidiary looks for three- and five-year budgets that stretch the subsidiary's capabilities. That is, subsidiaries are pushed to devise programs that increase value.
- These budgets are developed and approved first at the subsidiary level, then by corporate headquarters.
- Every three months the subsidiaries must reconcile actual performance to budget and write detailed reports to the corporate office explaining variances and corrective actions to be taken.
- The corporate vice president assigned to the subsidiary makes quarterly visits for three days of meetings that involve extensive reviews of the budgets and operating results. These meetings involve all the senior managers in the subsidiary.
- Subsidiary senior managers are not compensated or rewarded for meeting budget targets. Rather, they are evaluated on their ability to develop new markets, solve short-run problems, add value to their organization and to Madden International, and manage and motivate their subordinates. These performance evaluation criteria are quite subjective. But the corporate vice

presidents have a great deal of in-depth personal contact with each of the senior people in their subsidiaries and are able to arrive at suitable performance evaluations.

- Preparing for these meetings with the corporate vice president and developing the budgets requires the involvement of all the senior managers in the subsidiary. One manager remarked, "I'd hate to see how much more money we could be making if we didn't have to spend so much time in budget and financial review meetings."

It turns out that Madden International is not unique in the amount of senior management time spent on budgeting and financial reviews. A survey of large, publicly traded U.S. firms supports the Madden system. Researchers found that innovative firms in complex environments characterized by high uncertainty and change used much more elaborate formal financial control (budgeting) systems than did firms in more stable, mature industries. Innovative firms seem to employ more financial controls than less-innovative firms.

Required:

a. List the strengths and weaknesses of the budgeting and control system at Madden International.

b. Why might you expect firms like Madden International to rely so heavily on formal financial control systems?

P 6–30:   Calen Co.

Calen Co. manufactures and sells three products, which are manufactured in a factory consisting of four departments. Both labor and machine time are applied to the products as they pass through each applicable department. The nature of the machine processing and labor skills required is such that neither machines nor labor can be switched from one department to another.

Calen's management is attempting to plan its production schedule for the next several months. The planning is complicated by the fact that there are labor shortages in the community and some machines will be down several months for repairs. The following information regarding available machine and labor time by department and the machine hours and direct labor hours required per unit of product has been accumulated to aid in the decision. These data should be valid for at least the next six months.

Monthly Capacity Availability

	Department			
	1	*2*	*3*	*4*
Normal machine capacity in machine hours	3,500	3,500	3,000	3,500
Capacity of machine being repaired in machine hours	(500)	(400)	(300)	(200)
Available machine capacity in machine hours	3,000	3,100	2,700	3,300
Labor capacity in direct labor hours	4,000	4,500	3,500	3,000
Available labor in direct labor hours	3,700	4,500	2,750	2,600

Labor and Machine Specifications per Unit of Product

Product	Labor and Machine Time	Department 1	Department 2	Department 3	Department 4
401	Direct labor hours	2	3	3	1
	Machine hours	1	1	2	2
403	Direct labor hours	1	2	—	2
	Machine hours	1	1	—	2
405	Direct labor hours	2	2	2	1
	Machine hours	2	2	1	1

The sales department believes that the monthly demand for the next six months will be as follows:

Product	Monthly Sales Volume in Units
401	500
403	400
405	1,000

Inventory is satisfactory and need not be increased or decreased during the next six months. The unit price and cost data that will be valid for the next six months are presented in the table that follows.

	Product 401	Product 403	Product 405
Unit costs			
Direct material	$ 7	$ 13	$ 17
Direct labor			
Department 1	12	6	12
Department 2	21	14	14
Department 3	24	—	16
Department 4	9	18	9
Variable overhead	27	20	25
Fixed overhead	15	10	32
Variable selling	3	2	4
Unit selling price	$196	$123	$167

Required:

a. Calculate the monthly requirement for machine hours and direct labor hours for the production of products 401, 403, and 405 to determine whether the factory can meet the monthly sales demand for the three products.

b. What monthly production schedule should Calen Co. select in order to maximize its dollar profits? Explain how you selected this production schedule, and present a schedule of the contribution to profit that it would generate.

   c. Identify the alternative Calen Co. might consider so it can supply its customers with all the product they demand.

SOURCE: CMA adapted.

P 6–31:   Republic Insurance

Republic Insurance has a direct sales force that sells life insurance policies. All salespeople at the beginning of the year forecast the number of policies they expect to sell that year. At the end of the year, they are evaluated based on how many policies they actually sell. The compensation scheme is based on the following formula:

$$\text{Total compensation} = \$20,000 + \$100B + \$20(S - B) \quad \text{if } S \geq B$$
$$\$20,000 + \$100B - \$400(B - S) \text{ if } S < B$$

where

   B = Budgeted number of policies reported by the manager
   S = Actual number of policies sold

Required:

   a. Suppose a particular salesperson expects to sell 100 policies. This salesperson is considering reporting budgeted policies of 90, 99, 100, 101, 102, and 110. What level of budgeted policy sales should this person report at the beginning of the year?

   b. Critically analyze the Republic Insurance compensation scheme.

P 6–32:   Old Rosebud Farms

Old Rosebud is a Kentucky horse farm that specializes in boarding thoroughbred breeding mares and their foals. Customers bring their breeding mares to Old Rosebud for delivery of their foals and after-birth care of the mare and foal. Recent changes in the tax laws brought about a substantial decline in thoroughbred breeding. As a result, profits declined in the thoroughbred boarding industry.

Old Rosebud prepared a master budget for the current year by splitting costs into variable costs and fixed costs. The budget was prepared before the extent of the downturn was fully recognized. Table 1 on page 325 compares actual with budget for the current year.

Required:

Prepare an analysis of the operating performance of Old Rosebud Farms. Supporting tables or calculations should be clearly labeled.

P 6–33:   Troika Toys

Adrian and Pells (AP) is an advertising agency that uses flexible budgeting for both planning and control. One of its clients, Troika Toys, asked AP to prepare an ad campaign for a new toy. AP's contract with Troika calls for paying AP $120 per design hour for between 150 and 200 hours.

AP has a staff of ad campaign designers who prepare the ad campaigns. Customers are billed only for the time designers work on their project. Partner time is not billed directly to the customer. As part of the planning process, Sue Bent,

TABLE 1

OLD ROSEBUD FARMS
Income Statement for Year Ended 12/31

	Budget Formula (per Mare per Day)	Actual	Master Budget	Variance*
Number of mares		52	60	8
Number of boarding days		18,980	21,900	2,920
Revenues	$25.00	$379,600	$547,500	$167,900 U
Less variable expenses				
Feed & supplies	5.00	104,390	109,500	5,110 F
Veterinary fees	3.00	58,838	65,700	6,862 F
Blacksmith fees	.30	6,074	6,570	496 F
Total variable expenses	8.30	169,302	181,770	12,468 F
Contribution margin	$16.70	$210,298	$365,730	$155,432 U
Less fixed expenses				
Depreciation & insurance		$ 56,000	$ 56,000	$ 0
Utilities		12,000	14,000	2,000 F
Repairs & maintenance		10,000	11,000	1,000 F
Labor		88,000	96,000	8,000 F
Total fixed expenses		166,000	177,000	11,000 F
Net income		$ 44,298	$188,730	$144,432 U

*F = Favorable; U = Unfavorable.

partner-in-charge of the Troika account, prepared the following flexible budget. "Authorized Design Hours" is the estimated range of time AP expects the job to require and what the client agrees to authorize.

TROIKA TOYS
Flexible Budget

	Fixed Component	Variable Component	Authorized Design Hours		
			150	175	200
Revenues		$120	$18,000	$21,000	$24,000
Design labor	$ 0	45	6,750	7,875	9,000
Artwork	1,700	11	3,350	3,625	3,900
Office and occupancy costs*	0	6	900	1,050	1,200
Total costs	$1,700	$ 62	$11,000	$12,550	$14,100
Budgeted profits			$ 7,000	$ 8,450	$ 9,900

*Consists of rent, phone charges, fax costs, overnight delivery, and so on.

AP's executive committee reviewed Bent's budget and approved it and the Troika contract. After some preliminary work, Troika liked the ideas so much it expanded the authorized time range to be between 175 and 250 hours.

Bent and her design team finished the Troika project. Two hundred and twenty design hours were logged and billed to Troika at the contract price ($120 per hour). Upon completion of the Troika campaign, the following revenues and costs had been accumulated:

TROIKA TOYS
Actual Costs Incurred

Revenue ($120 × 220)	$26,400
Design labor	10,320
Artwork	4,350
Office and occupancy costs	1,690
Total costs	$16,360
Profits	$10,040

AP's accounting manager keeps track of actual costs incurred by AP on each account. AP employs a staff of designers. Their average salary is $45 per hour. New designers earn less than the average; those with more experience earn more. The actual design labor costs charged to each project are the actual hours times the designer's actual hourly cost. Artwork consists of both in-house and out-of-house artists who draw up the art for the ads designed by the designers. Office and occupancy costs consist of a charge per designer hour to cover rent, photocopying, and phones, plus actual long-distance calls, faxes, and overnight delivery services.

Required:

Prepare a table that reports on Sue Bent's performance on the Troika Toys account and write a short memo to the executive committee that summarizes her performance on this project.

P 6–34:   Cellular First

The sales department of a cellular phone company pays its salespeople $1,500 per month plus 25 percent of each new subscriber's first month's billings. A new subscriber's first-month bill averages $80. Salespeople work 160 hours a month (four weeks at 40 hours per week). If salespeople work more than 160 hours per month, they receive $12 per hour for hours in excess of 160.

Sales leads for the sales department are generated in a variety of ways—direct mailings to potential customers who then call to speak to a salesperson, lists of prospective customers purchased from outside marketing firms, and so forth. The manager of the sales department reviews potential leads and assigns them to particular salespeople who contact them. The manager of the sales department is expected to oversee the time spent by each salesperson per assigned lead and to approve overtime requests to work beyond the 40 hours per week. Each new customer added requires on average 2 hours of salesperson time to make the sale.

Last month, the sales department was budgeted for eight full-time salespeople. However, because of a new ad campaign, an additional salesperson was hired and overtime was approved, bringing actual hours worked up to 1,580. The department added 725 new customers.

Required:

a. Prepare a performance report comparing actual performance to budgeted performance using a static budget based on eight salespeople and no budgeted overtime.

b. Prepare a performance report comparing actual performance to budgeted performance using a flexible budget based on nine salespeople selling 725 new accounts.

c. Discuss when you would expect to see the report prepared in (*a*) used and when you would expect to see the report in (*b*) used.

P 6–35: Artisans Shirtcraft

Background

Artisans Shirtcraft manufactures and sells hand-painted shirts of original design. The company was founded in 1992 by three sisters: Cathy, Linda, and Valerie Montgomery. Shirtcraft started out as a means of financing a hobby; profits from shirt sales were used to pay the cost of supplies. However, word of the sisters' appealing products spread quickly, eventually creating strong and widespread demand for Shirtcraft shirts. By 1996, the year of Shirtcraft's incorporation, the company no longer relied on selling at the occasional crafts fair. It now earned almost all of its revenues through sales to upscale boutiques and department stores. Shirtcraft had grown into a legitimate business, but the hobby mentality remained. The company retained a simple approach that had served it well: Buy quality materials when available at a bargain price and produce them into shirts. At this time, the sisters had a ready market for whatever they could produce.

In 1997, the sisters loosely organized Shirtcraft into three functional areas, each based around a talent at which one of them excelled. Cathy would hunt high and low for the best prices, Linda would oversee the painting of the original designs, and Valerie would sell the shirts and deal with the general annoyances of business administration. No separate departmental financial records were kept.

Demand for Shirtcraft shirts continued to grow. To finance additional production, the company had become increasingly dependent upon debt. By the beginning of the 2000s, bankers had become an integral part of life at Shirtcraft. The sisters were devoting themselves primarily to executive administration, leaving most day-to-day operations to hired managers.

By the end of 2002, more than 75 employees were on the payroll. However, some of Shirtcraft's creditors began to get cold feet. Given the sluggish economy, some felt that continued investment in a company such as Shirtcraft would be foolish. In light of the scrutiny under which their industry presently operated, the bankers wondered about the prudence of increased and continued commitment to a company that was virtually devoid of financial controls. The bankers were particularly concerned by Shirtcraft's continuing reliance on the bargain purchase strategy. They thought the company would inevitably vacillate between periods of incurring excessive inventory holding costs for overpurchased materials and periods of lost sales due to underpurchasing. If Shirtcraft wanted the banks to commit long term to a rapidly growing credit line, the sisters would have to demonstrate their willingness to establish organizational structures and controls such as those found in larger companies.

Plan

In April 2003, a plan was established. Three functional areas were organized: purchasing, production, and sales and administration. Purchasing and production would be cost centers, each monitored by comparisons of actual costs to budgeted costs. Compensation for key personnel of the cost centers would be tied to the results of this comparison. The sisters would officially be employees of the sales and administrative department, which would hold final responsibility for all executive and corporate decisions. Key employees of sales and administration would be judged and compensated based on overall firm profitability.

For the 12 months beginning in September 2003, the sisters expected to sell 192,000 shirts at an average price of $23 per shirt. Expenses for the sales and administrative department are estimated at $750,000 for the year. Interest expenses for the period are estimated at $550,000. Incentive pay to the various departments is expected to amount to $75,000 per functional area. Under the plan, all expenses are charged to the individual department that incurs them, except for interest expenses, taxes, and incentive pay. These are treated as corporate profit and loss items. Taxes are expected to be 40 percent of corporate pretax income.

After considerable negotiations between the sisters and the purchasing manager, it was agreed that direct materials costs should average about $7 per shirt if purchases are made based on production department demand. Although this approach results in higher direct materials costs than a bargain purchase strategy, the demand-based purchase strategy is cheaper when opportunity costs such as inventory holding costs and contribution margin forgone due to lost sales are considered. Salaries and other overhead for the purchasing department are expected to amount to $150,000 for the year.

Discussions with the production manager led to estimates that production will use fixed overhead costing $240,000. Production's variable overhead consists wholly of direct labor. An average of 1/2 hour of direct labor, at a cost of $6 per hour, is needed for each shirt.

Previously, financial records were kept only on a corporate level. Under the new plan, cost records, both budgeted and actual, will be kept for each department. Of Shirtcraft's sales, 40 percent are expected to occur during September, October, November, and December. Sales are divided equally between months within each group of months. All costs that do not vary with shirt production are divided equally throughout the year. All monthly purchasing and production are based on that month's orders and are assumed to be completely sold during that month. Only negligible inventory is held.

Required:

a. Considering only costs, prepare budgeted annual and monthly financial statements for purchasing and production. (Assume that production is not responsible for any costs already assigned to purchasing.) Prepare an annual budgeted income statement for Artisans Shirtcraft for the period September 2003 through August 2004. Annual costs for income statement purposes consist of the following:

    Cost of goods sold
    Administrative expenses
    Interest
    Taxes

All salaries and overhead for purchasing and production are treated as product costs and assigned to individual units. Therefore, these costs should be included in Shirtcraft's annual income statement under cost of goods sold.

b. In general terms, consider the changes in Shirtcraft due to growth. How is the company different from an organizational standpoint? What role do budgeting and cost centers have in attempting to meet the challenges presented by this growth?

SOURCE: G Hurst.

P 6–36:   Wielson Company

Wielson Company employs flexible budgeting techniques to evaluate the performance of several of its activities. The selling expense flexible budgets for three representative monthly activity levels are shown here.

Representative Monthly Flexible Budgets for Selling Expenses

Activity Measures			
Unit sales volume	400,000	425,000	450,000
Dollar sales volume	$10,000,000	$10,625,000	$11,250,000
Number of orders	4,000	4,250	4,500
Number of salespersons	75	75	75
Monthly Expenses			
Advertising and promotion	$ 1,200,000	$ 1,200,000	$ 1,200,000
Administrative salaries	57,000	57,000	57,000
Sales salaries	75,000	75,000	75,000
Sales commissions	200,000	212,500	225,000
Salesperson travel	170,000	175,000	180,000
Total selling expenses	$ 1,702,000	$ 1,719,500	$ 1,737,000

The following assumptions were used to develop the selling expense flexible budgets:

- The average size of Wielson's sales force during the year was planned to be 75 people.
- Salespeople are paid a monthly salary plus commissions on gross dollar sales.
- Travel costs are best characterized as step-variable costs. The fixed portion is related to the number of salespeople, while the variable portion fluctuates with gross dollar sales.

A sales force of 80 people generated a total of 4,300 orders resulting in a sales volume of 420,000 units during November. Gross dollar sales amounted to $10.9 million. Selling expenses incurred for November were as follows:

Advertising and promotion	$1,350,000
Administrative salaries	57,000
Sales salaries	80,000
Sales commissions	218,000
Salesperson travel	185,000
Total	$1,890,000

Required:

Prepare a selling expense report for November that Wielson Company can use to evaluate its control over selling expenses. The report should have a line for each selling expense item showing the appropriate budgeted amount, the actual selling expense, and the monthly dollar variation.

Source: CMA adapted.

P 6–37:   Magee Inc.

Magee Inc. pays its sales manager a bonus of $10,000 if the manager meets the sales quota. The sales manager can exert either high effort or low effort. The additional disutility of the manager in exerting high effort relative to low effort to meet the sales quota is $1,500. Management can set a tight quota that is extremely difficult to achieve even with a great deal of effort, a loose quota that is achieved easily, or a medium-tight quota. The probability of achieving the sales figure under each quota is summarized in the accompanying table.

Probability of Achieving Quota

	Loose Quota	Medium-Tight Quota	Tight Quota
High effort	0.90	0.60	0.30
Low effort	0.60	0.40	0.25

The sales manager can either achieve the sales quota or not. Because each quota affects the total number of units sold and thus the gross margin earned by the firm, the following table outlines the gross margin earned by the firm when each quota is reached and is not reached.

Gross Margin of Achieving Quota

	Loose Quota	Medium-Tight Quota	Tight Quota
Quota achieved	$50,000	$70,000	$73,000
Quota not achieved	20,000	40,000	43,000

Should management set a loose, medium-tight, or tight quota?

Source: R Magee, *Advanced Managerial Accounting* (New York: Harper & Row, 1986), pp. 286–87.

P 6–38:   Kink Sales

The local sales manager of Kink Sales receives a fixed salary plus a bonus based on sales. Only the local sales manager knows the probability distribution over possible sales levels for the next year in her sales district, which is as follows:

Possible Sales	Probability	Expected Sales
100	0.10	10
200	0.20	40
300	0.50	150
400	0.20	80
		280

The manager's bonus is $100 for every unit above the budgeted sales figure she forecasts at the beginning of the year, with the bonus being nonnegative. That is,

$$\text{Bonus} = \$100 \times (\text{Actual sales} - \text{Budgeted sales}), \text{Bonus} \geq 0 \quad (1)$$

Senior management is considering changing the bonus scheme to the following:

$$\text{Bonus} = \$100 \times \text{Actual sales} - \$20 \times |\text{Budgeted sales} - \text{Actual sales}| \quad (2)$$

In this scheme, the local manager would receive $100 per unit sold but be penalized $20 for every unit sold that differs from budget. (Note: The symbol |...| denotes absolute value.)

If senior management changes the bonus, it will adjust the fixed component of salary to offset any gain or loss in the expected level of total compensation.

Required:

a. Graph the two bonus schemes.
b. Using the first bonus scheme, what budgeted sales figure will the local manager report?
c. Using the proposed bonus scheme, what budgeted sales figure will the local manager report?
d. Which method do you prefer? Why?

P 6–39:   James Marketing Campaign

James, Inc., a large mail-order catalog firm, is thinking of expanding into Canada. The Buffalo district office would manage the expansion and must decide how much to spend on the advertising campaign. The expansion project will be either successful (S) or unsuccessful (U). The probability of success depends on the amount spent on the advertising campaign. If the project is successful, the gross profit (before advertising) is $1.4 million. If the project is unsuccessful, the gross profit (before advertising) is $100,000. The accompanying table lists how the probability of success varies with the amount of spending on the Canadian venture.

Amount of Advertising (000s)	Probability of Success (S)	Gross Profit (000s)	
		If Successful	*If Unsuccessful*
$ 10	0.20	$1,400	$100
25	0.21	1,400	100
40	0.22	1,400	100
55	0.23	1,400	100
70	0.24	1,400	100
85	0.25	1,400	100
100	0.26	1,400	100
115	0.27	1,400	100
130	0.28	1,400	100
145	0.29	1,400	100

James, Inc., is a publicly traded firm and its senior managers and shareholders wish to maximize expected net cash flows from this venture. The Buffalo manager receives a bonus of 10 percent of the net profit (gross profit less advertising).

The bonus is paid only if the firm has gross profit net of advertising. If gross profit less advertising is negative, no bonus is paid. The manager wants to maximize her bonus and has private knowledge of how the probability of success varies with advertising.

Required:

a. What advertising level would senior managers choose if they had access to the Buffalo manager's specialized knowledge?
b. What advertising level will the Buffalo manager select, knowing that senior managers do not have the specialized knowledge of the payoffs?
c. If the advertising levels in (*a*) and (*b*) differ, explain why.

Cases

Case 6–1: Eastern University Catalog

Eastern University publishes and distributes over 100,000 copies of its *Official Bulletin on Undergraduate Studies* to prospective students, high school guidance counselors, faculty and staff of the university, and other interested parties. This 250-page catalog with four-color pictures is one of the primary marketing devices for the university's undergraduate programs. High school seniors expressing interest in attending the university receive the *Bulletin* along with other information about the university. It lists the various programs of studies, course offerings, and requirements. Each year it is revised and reprinted as courses and programs change, and the photographs are updated to improve it as a recruiting tool. The annual cost of preparing and printing the *Bulletin* is about $1 million, which includes the cost of photographers, nonuniversity graphic designers, typesetting, and printing but excludes the cost of university employees who rewrite the text, proofread the galleys, and manage the entire process.

The responsibility of preparing the catalog is shared by the admissions office and public relations. The admissions office coordinates collection of the basic data on course and program changes. Many of these are not known until May, after the various faculties have met and approved academic program and course changes. These changes are edited and the overall content of the publication is determined based on the admissions office's experience with high school applicants. Admissions then sends a draft copy of the brochure to public relations. Public relations is responsible for the overall image and publicity of the university and for ensuring that the university publications present a consistent image. Public relations, using outside graphic designers, marketing specialists, typesetters, and printers its staffers have come to know, takes the changes and produces an attractive, high-quality brochure. Admissions reports to the dean of the undergraduate college, who reports to the president. Public relations reports to the vice president of external affairs, who reports to the president. The admissions office affects the cost of the brochure in terms of the quantity of text to be included and how many *Bulletins* must be ordered to satisfy its distribution plan. Public relations affects the cost by using more color photographs, more expensive paper and cover materials, and elaborate layouts. Both admissions and public relations raise the cost by not meeting timely production schedules. If copy is returned late or the design is not completed on time, additional charges are incurred by typesetters and printers who work overtime to meet the publication schedule. It is critically important to the admissions process that the *Bulletin* be available for distribution in September to high school seniors beginning their college search process.

Admissions and public relations are both cost centers. They have been arguing over whether the cost of the *Bulletin* should be in the admissions office budget or the public relations department budget.

Required:

a. Discuss the advantages and disadvantages of placing the budget for the *Bulletin* in the public relations versus the admissions office budget.

b. What are some other ways of handling the *Bulletin*'s budget?

c. Based on your analysis, what recommendation would you make?

Case 6–2: Scion Corp.

Scion Corp. manufactures earth-moving equipment. Department A303 produces a number of small metal parts for the equipment, including specialized screw products, rods, frame fittings, and some engine parts. Scion uses flexible budgeting. The budget for each line item is based on an estimate of the fixed costs and variable costs per unit of volume for that item. The volume measure chosen for each line item is the one with the greatest cause-and-effect relation to the item. For example, the volume measure for utilities is machine hours, whereas the volume measure for supervision is direct labor hours of hourly employees.

At the beginning of the year, the plant is given an annual production quota consisting of the number of each piece of earth-moving equipment to produce. These equipment quotas are exploded into the total number of parts each department must produce, using data about what parts are required for each unit of equipment. Each department has a detailed set of standards, developed over a number of years, that translate each part produced into the number of machine hours, direct labor hours, raw materials, and so on. Table 1 summarizes the operating results of department A303—specifically, the budgeted cost per batch of 100 parts for part number UAV 672.

Given the production quotas and the detailed set of quantities of each input required to produce a particular part, Department A303's financial budget for the year can be developed. At the end of the year, the actual number of each type of part produced times the budgeting standards for each part can be used to calculate the flexible budget for that line item in the budget. That is, given the actual list of parts produced in Department A303, the flexible budget in Table 2 reports how much should have been spent on each line item. Price fluctuations in raw materials are not charged to the production managers. If low-quality materials are purchased and

---

TABLE 1   **Part Number UAV 672**
Budgeting Standards per 100 Parts per Batch

Raw materials	$26.72
Direct labor, salaried	2.5 hours
Direct labor, hourly	3.2 hours
Machine hours	6.3 hours

TABLE 2   Scion Corporation
Machining Department A303 Operating Results for Last Year

	Actual Last Year	Budget* Last Year	Favorable (Unfavorable) Variance
Volume Measures			
Machine hours	238,654	265,000	
Direct labor hours	146,400	152,000	
Parts machined	33,565,268	35,759,000	
Departmental Financial Performance			
Raw materials	$ 8,326,875	$ 8,150,000	$(176,875)
Direct labor, salaried	1,546,729	1,643,000	96,271
Direct labor, hourly	1,465,623	1,375,000	(90,623)
Supervision	451,597	460,000	8,403
Maintenance	315,864	325,000	9,136
Engineering	279,780	285,000	5,220
Utilities	69,539	82,000	12,461
Training	85,750	53,000	(32,750)
Factory overhead	188,500	210,000	21,500
Total operating expenses	$12,730,257	$12,583,000	$(147,257)

*Budget reflects expected fixed costs plus variable costs per unit volume times actual volume.

cause the production departments to incur higher costs, these variances are not charged to the production departments.

The manager of Department A303 does not have any say over which parts to produce. The manager's major responsibilities include delivering the required number of good parts at the specified time while meeting or bettering the cost targets. The two most important components of the manager's compensation and bonus depend on meeting delivery schedules and the favorable cost variances from the flexible budget.

Senior management of the plant is debating the process used each year to update the various budgeting standards. Productivity increases for labor would cause the amount of direct labor per part to fall over time. One updating scheme would be to take the budgeting standards from last year (e.g., Table 1) and reduce each part's direct labor standard by an average productivity improvement factor estimated by senior plant management to apply across all departments in the plant. The productivity improvement factor is a single plantwide number. For example, if the average productivity factor is forecast to be 5 percent, then for part UAV 672 the budgeting standard for "Direct labor, salaried" becomes 2.375 hours (95 percent of 2.5 hours). This is termed "adjusting the budget."

An alternative scheme, called "adjusting the actual," takes the actual number of direct labor hours used for each part and applies the productivity improvement factor. For example, suppose part UAV 672 used an average of 2.6 hours of salaried direct labor last year for all batches of the part manufactured. The budgeting standard for "Direct labor, salaried" for next year then becomes 2.47 hours (95 percent of 2.6 hours).

Under both schemes, last year's actual numbers and last year's budgeted numbers are known before this year's budget is set.

Required:

Discuss the advantages and disadvantages of the two alternative schemes (adjusting the budget versus adjusting the actual).

Case 6–3: LaserFlo

Marti Meyers, vice president of marketing for LaserFlo, was concerned as she reviewed the costs for the AP2000 laser printer she was planning to launch next month. The AP2000 is a new, commercial printer that LaserFlo designed for medium-sized direct mail businesses. The basic system price was set at $74,500; the unit manufacturing cost of the AP2000 is $46,295, and selling and administrative cost is budgeted at 33 percent of the selling price. The maintenance price she planned to announce was $85 per hour of LaserFlo technician time. While the $74,500 base price is competitive, $85 per hour is a bit higher than the industry average of $82 per hour. However, Meyers believed she could live with the $85 price. She is concerned because she has just received a memo from the Field Service organization stating that it was increasing its projected hourly charge for service from $35.05 to $38.25.

The $85 price Meyers was prepared to charge for service was based on last year's $35.05 service cost. She thought that using last year's cost was conservative since Field Service had been downsizing and she expected the cost to go down, not up. The $35.05 cost still did not yield the 60 percent margin on service that was the standard for other LaserFlo printers, but Meyers had difficulty justifying a higher maintenance price given the competition. With a service cost of $38.25, Meyers knows she cannot raise the price to the customer enough to cover the higher costs without significantly reducing sales. Given the higher cost of the LaserFlo field technicians and the prices charged for maintenance by the competition, she will not be able to make the profit target in her plan.

Background

LaserFlo manufactures, sells, and services its printers throughout the United States using direct sales and service forces. It has been in business for 22 years and is the largest of three manufacturers of high-speed laser printers for direct mailers in the United States. LaserFlo maintains its market leadership by innovating new technology. Direct mail marketing firms produce customized letters of solicitation for bank credit cards, real estate offers, life insurance, colleges and universities, and magazine giveaway contests. Personalized letters are printed on high-speed printers attached to computers that have the mailing information. The printers print either the entire letter or the address and salutation ("Dear Mrs. Jeremy McConnell") on preprinted forms. Direct mail firms have computer systems to manage their address lists and mailings, and LaserFlo printers are attached to the client's computer system.

Direct mail laser printers process very high volumes; a single printer commonly addresses 75,000 letters a day. Hence, LaserFlo printers for direct mail marketers differ from general-purpose high-speed printers. In particular, they have specialized paper transfer mechanisms to handle the often custom, heavy paper;

varying paper sizes; and high-speed paper flows. With such high paper flow rates, these printers require regular adjustments to prevent paper jams and misalignments. LaserFlo's nationwide field service organization of about 500 employees maintains these printers.

The standard LaserFlo sales contract contains two parts: the purchase price of the equipment and a maintenance contract for the equipment. All LaserFlo printers are maintained by LaserFlo field service personnel, and the maintenance contract specifies the price per hour charged for routine and unscheduled maintenance. Most of LaserFlo's profits come from printer maintenance. Printers have about a 5 to 10 percent markup over manufacturing and selling cost, but the markup on maintenance has historically averaged about 60 percent.

LaserFlo printers have a substantial amount of built-in intelligence to control the printing and for self-diagnostics. Each printer has its own microcomputer with memory to hold the data to be printed. These internal microcomputers also keep track of printing statistics and can alert the operator to impending problems (low toner, paper alignment problems, form breaks). When customers change their operating system or computer, this often necessitates a LaserFlo service call to ensure that the new system is compatible with the printer. The standard service contract calls for normal maintenance after a fixed number of impressions (pages); for example, the AP2000 requires service after every 500,000 pages are printed. Its microcomputer is programmed to call LaserFlo's central computer to schedule maintenance whenever the machine has produced 375,000 pages since the last servicing.

LaserFlo organization

LaserFlo is organized into engineering, manufacturing, marketing, field service, and administration divisions. Engineering designs the new printers and provides consulting services to marketing and field service regarding system installation and maintenance. Engineering is evaluated as a cost center.

Manufacturing produces the printers, which are assembled from purchased parts and subassemblies. LaserFlo's comparative advantage is quality control and design. Manufacturing also provides parts for field service maintenance. Manufacturing is treated as a cost center and evaluated based on meeting cost targets and delivery schedules. Manufacturing's unit cost is charged to marketing for each printer sold.

Marketing, a profit center, is responsible for designing the marketing campaigns, pricing the printers, and managing the field sales staff. LaserFlo sells six different printers; each has a separate marketing program manager. The six marketing program managers report to Marti Meyers, vice president of marketing, who also manages field sales.

Field sales is organized around four regional managers responsible for the sales offices in their region. Each of the 27 sales offices has a direct sales force that contacts potential customers and sells the six programs. Salespeople receive a salary and a commission depending on the printer and options sold. The salesperson continues to receive commissions from ongoing revenues paid by the account for service. Since ongoing maintenance forms a significant amount of a printer's total profit, the salesperson has an incentive to keep the customer with LaserFlo.

Field service contains the technical people who install and maintain the printers. Headed by Phil Hansen, vice president of field service, field service usually shares office space with field sales in the cities where they operate. Field service is a cost center, and its direct and indirect costs are charged to programs when the printers are serviced. The price charged is based on the budgeted rate set at the beginning of the year. Any difference between the actual amount charged to the programs and the total cost incurred by the field service group is charged to a corporate overhead account, not to the marketing programs.

Administration manages human resources, finance, accounting, and field office leases. It handles customer billing and collections, payroll, and negotiating office space for the field sales and field service people. Administration is evaluated as a cost center. While local office space is managed by administration, the cost of the office space is allocated to the field sales and service groups and included in their budgets and monthly operating statements.

Service contracts

Each LaserFlo printer sold requires a service contract. The AP2000's service contract calls for normal maintenance every 500,000 pages at a price of $0.51 per 1,000 pages. Normal maintenance requires three hours. The typical AP2000 prints 12 million pages per year. Besides normal maintenance (sometimes called *preventive maintenance*), unscheduled maintenance occurs due to improper operator setups, paper jams, system upgrades, and harsh usage of the equipment. Past statistical studies have shown that each normal maintenance hour generates 0.50 unscheduled maintenance hours. Unscheduled maintenance is billed to the customer at the service contract rate of $85 per hour.

When maintenance is performed on a particular machine, the service revenues less field service costs are credited to the marketing manager for that program. All the programs' actual service profits are compared with the plan; they form part of Meyers's performance evaluation. The field salesperson receives a commission based on the total service revenue generated by the account. In evaluating each new printer program, LaserFlo uses the following procedure. Profits from service are expected to create an annuity that will last for five years at 18 percent interest. To evaluate a proposed new printer, the one-year maintenance profits are multiplied by 3.127 to reflect the present value of the future service profits each printer is expected to generate over its life (about five years).

Parts

Any parts used during service are charged directly to the customer and do not flow through field service budgets or operating statements. LaserFlo purchases most of the printers' parts from outside suppliers, and the customer pays only a token markup. Marketing does not receive any revenue, nor is it charged any costs when customers use parts in the service process. The reason for not charging customers a larger markup on parts stems from an antitrust case filed against LaserFlo and other printer companies six years ago. A third-party service company, Servwell, sued the printer manufacturers for restraint of trade, claiming they prevented Servwell from maintaining the printers by only selling replacement parts at very high prices. To prevent other such claims, LaserFlo sells parts at a small markup over costs. Yet Servwell and other third-party service firms have never been able to penetrate LaserFlo's service markets because laser printing technology changes rapidly, and an outside company cannot keep a work force trained to fix the latest products. Besides, each printer usually has at least two engineering modifications each year to fix problems or upgrade the printer or its microcomputer hardware and/or software. An outside service company cannot learn of these changes and provide the same level of service as LaserFlo.

Recent changes in field service

LaserFlo field service had two types of technicians: Tech1 and Tech2. Both were trained to repair electromechanical problems, but Tech2s had more training in electronics and computers to work on the latest, most sophisticated printers.

Field service had been trying to reduce the size of the service force the last few years through voluntary retirements and attrition. As the printers became more sophisticated, they became more reliable. The newer systems had self-diagnosing software that allowed a service technician to call up a customer's printer and run a diagnostic program. Often the problem was solved over the phone line by having a LaserFlo technician make the repair in the software. If a mechanical problem was detected, the technician dispatched a repair person (often a Tech1) with the right part. Also, past customers replaced their older printers with newer ones that required less maintenance. The result was excess capacity in the field staff.

The voluntary retirements over the past few years did not produce the reductions necessary to eliminate the excess capacity. In 2010, field service went through a very large involuntary reduction of its workforce. Through attrition, early retirements, and terminations, LaserFlo reduced the number of technicians by 75, down to 500 budgeted for 2011. The company simultaneously improved the skill level of its remaining field force substantially.

AP2000 sales plan for 2011

Marti Meyers's 2011 sales plan for the AP2000 calls for 120 placements this year and a program profit projection of about $2.5 million based on capitalizing the service income using the 3.127 annuity factor. If she were to raise the service price much above $0.51 per 1,000 pages, LaserFlo would lose sales, which are already ambitious. She called Phil Hansen and raised her concerns with him.

"Phil," she began, "explain to me how you downsized your field personnel, cut some office locations, consolidated inventories, and reduced other fixed costs, yet the price I'm being charged for service increased from $35.05 per hour to $38.25. I thought the whole purpose of the field service reorganization was to streamline and make us more cost competitive. You know that our service costs were out of line with our competitors'. We were planning to charge $85 an hour for the AP2000 service contract. Even at $85 per hour, I would be violating the corporate policy of maintaining a 60 percent markup on service. If I were to follow the 60 percent rule, I would have to charge $87.63 per hour if you had kept your cost to me at $35.05. But with your cost of $38.25 and my price at $85, the margin falls to 55 percent. I already had to get special permission to lower the margin to 59 percent with $35.05."

Hansen replied, "Well, there are a number of issues that you've just raised. Let me respond to a few over the phone now and suggest we meet to discuss this more fully next week when I'm back in the office. In the meantime, I'll send you our projected budget for next year that derived the $38.25 rate. Regarding the key question as to how our hourly rate could go up after downsizing, it's really quite simple. We had a lot of idle time being built into the numbers. People just

TABLE 1   Field Service Projected Hourly Rate for 2011

Variable Costs		
Tech1[*]		
Salary & benefits	$ 42,800	
Number	× 175	
Total direct cost of Tech1		$ 7,490,000
Tech2[†]		
Salary & benefits	$ 54,800	
Number	× 325	
Total direct cost of Tech2		$17,810,000
Total variable cost		$25,300,000
Fixed Costs		
Supervision	$1,475,000	
Occupancy costs	1,864,000	
Utilities	772,000	
Insurance	368,000	
Other	56,000	
Total fixed cost		$ 4,535,000
Total cost		$29,835,000
Number of Tech1	175	
Number of Tech2	325	
Total technicians	500	
Number of technician months	6,000	
Average number of billable hours per month per technician[‡]	130	
Protected number of billable hours		780,000
Cost per hour projected for 2011		$38.25
Note: Cost per hour in 2010		$35.05

[*]300 Tech1s in 2010 with salary & benefits of $40,100.
[†]275 Tech2s in 2010 with salary & benefits of $52,900.
[‡]Same in 2010.

pretended to be busy. Had we not downsized, the hourly charge would have gone up even more than it did. For example, on the AP2000 that you mentioned, we would have used 3.25 hours per normal servicing had we kept our labor force mix of Tech1s and 2s the same as in 2010. Had we not downsized, our fixed costs in 2011 would have remained the same as they were in 2010, and our variable costs for Tech1s and 2s would have increased to the 2011 amounts because of wage increases and inflation. Let me get you our numbers so you can see for yourself how much progress we've been making."

That afternoon, Meyers received a fax from Hansen's office (see Table 1). In trying to decide how to proceed, Meyers would like you to address the following questions:

    a. Calculate the projected five-year profits of an AP2000 using first the $35.05 and then the $38.25 service cost.

b. Why did the field service hourly cost increase? What caused the hourly rate to go from $35.05 to $38.25?

c. Did the reorganization of field service reduce the cost of servicing the AP2000? Calculate what the total annual service cost of the AP2000 would have been had the reorganization not occurred.

d. Identify the various options Meyers has for dealing with the service cost increase and analyze them.

e. Why does LaserFlo make more money on servicing printers than selling them? Does such a policy make sense?

Chapter Seven

Cost Allocation: Theory

Chapter Outline

A central issue in all internal accounting systems is **cost allocation,** the assignment of indirect, common, or joint costs to different departments, processes, or products. The major problem in product costing is whether and how indirect costs (overheads) are allocated to products. The allocation of corporate headquarters costs and service department costs, such as data processing and security, is in fact a form of transfer pricing within the firm and is thus an integral part of the organization's architecture described in Chapter 4. This chapter presents a general framework for analyzing cost allocations in all organizations, using the earlier framework of costing for decision making (Chapter 2) and costing for control (Chapter 4).

Consider the following two examples. In the first example, a patient with abdominal pain is admitted to the hospital. After five days, a series of tests, and an operation to remove an ulcer, the patient is discharged. During the patient's stay, she used a variety of services: physicians, nurses, dietitians, laboratory technicians, social workers, and laundry services. Indirect services include the hospital's admitting and billing offices, building maintenance and security, data processing, and senior hospital administrators managing all the health providers. What was the cost of this patient's stay in the hospital? One could just examine the incremental (or marginal) cost of the patient's stay or the "average" or "full" cost, including all the indirect services. Calculating the average or full cost of the patients's stay requires allocating the costs of dieticians, social workers, laundry services, and so forth to patients.

In the second example, the drilling department in a manufacturing plant drills holes in the sheet-metal chassis that forms the base for a fax machine. Several types of fax machine chassis are drilled in the department, each with its own configuration and sizes of holes. The drilling department costs consist of labor, tools, supplies, space occupancy (utilities, maintenance, accounting, and plant administration), and accounting depreciation of the drilling machines. Last month, the department drilled 2,100 units of a particular chassis model. What was the "full" cost of drilling holes in this particular type of chassis? Answering this question requires allocating the drilling department costs to each chassis model produced.

Despite different organizational settings, both organizations face a similar problem: allocating a set of costs to a **cost object.** A cost object is a product, process, department, or program that managers wish to cost. In the two examples, a patient and a chassis are the cost objects. Corporate-level R&D expenses are allocated to the Chevrolet division of General Motors because senior executives at General Motors want to assess the total profitability of Chevrolet net of corporate R&D. The Chevrolet division is the cost object. Managers allocate common costs to cost objects for several reasons, including decision making and/or control. The framework developed in Chapters 2 and 4 will be used to illustrate the trade-off between decision management and decision control in designing cost allocations. Since cost allocations are used for multiple purposes, we will again see that no single way of allocating costs is always right or always wrong. Trade-offs must be made in choosing whether and how to allocate a given common cost. As we will see later, exactly how the cost allocation is performed depends on what purposes the allocation serves.

Section A in this chapter describes several different institutional settings and organizations in which cost allocation takes place. Costs are allocated for a variety of reasons, including taxes, financial reporting, cost-based reimbursement, decision making, and control. The various reasons for allocating costs, including organizational control reasons, are described in section B. The incentive effects of cost allocations are further examined in section C. Allocated costs are intended as proxies for certain hard-to-observe opportunity costs. While allocated costs measure the opportunity cost with error, they are much less expensive to compute than opportunity costs.

A. Pervasiveness of Cost Allocations

The vast majority of organizations allocate common costs. A **common cost** arises when a resource is shared by several users. For example, human resource department costs are a common cost because all employees in the firm utilize its services. Hospitals allocate the common costs of shared medical equipment to departments that use it. Telecommunications costs are allocated to users. Purchasing department costs are allocated to products.

Common costs are sometimes called **indirect costs** because they cannot be directly traced to units produced or cost objects precisely because such costs are incurred in providing benefits to several different product lines or users. Likewise, "overhead" refers to indirect, common costs. Following general practice, we will use the terms *common costs, indirect costs,* and *overhead* interchangeably.

The terms *cost allocation, cost assignment, cost apportionment,* and *cost distribution* are synonyms. All describe the process of taking a given common cost and dividing it between various cost objects (patients or fax machine chassis). Direct costs do not have to be allocated because they can be directly traced to the cost object. For example, if the firm's intranet is used only by the sales department, then the intranet costs are a direct cost of the sales department. However, if both the sales and the manufacturing departments share the same intranet, the intranet costs are not a direct cost of either department but rather a common cost that must be allocated to the cost objects—the two departments.

Cost allocation requires the following steps:

1. *Define the cost objects.* The organization must decide what departments, products, or processes to cost. For example, intranet users may be defined as cost objects. The cost object is often a subunit of the organization, such as a cost or profit center. Costs are often allocated to subunits to better evaluate the subunit's performance; or, costs are allocated to products or services being sold to assess product-line profitability.

2. *Accumulate the common costs to be assigned to the cost objects.* Suppose intranet costs are to be assigned to the intranet users. This step requires the identification and accumulation of the common costs such as the cost of the hardware, personnel expenditures, utilities, and software costs that will be distributed to the users.

3. *Choose a method for allocating common costs accumulated in step 2 to the cost objects defined in step 1.* An **allocation base,** a measure of activity associated with the pool of common costs being distributed to the cost objects, must be selected. The allocation base to distribute intranet center costs to users can be time used, computer memory, or some combination of these. As discussed later in this chapter, common costs usually are allocated to cost objects using an allocation base that approximates how the cost objects consume the common resources.

For example, to provide e-mail services for its employees a firm incurs expenses of $575,000 per year consisting of a computer lease ($273,000), labor ($195,000), software ($78,000), and other costs ($29,000). Four departments use

TABLE 7–1 E-Mail Users of Disk Space
(in Terabytes of Memory)

Users	Terabytes of Memory
Manufacturing	40
Sales	80
Research and development	20
Administration	60
Total	200

TABLE 7–2   Allocation of Annual E-Mail Cost to User Departments

Users	Cost per Terabyte	Terabytes of Memory	Allocated Cost
Manufacturing	$2,875	40	$115,000
Sales	2,875	80	230,000
Research and development	2,875	20	57,500
Administration	2,875	60	172,500
Total		200	$575,000

TABLE 7–3   Allocation of Corporate-Level Costs to Profit Centers

Type of Corporate-Level Expense	Percentage of Firms Allocating
Income taxes	44%
Interest expense and/or capital charges	62
Research and development	72
Finance and accounting	73
Selling costs	91
Distribution	100

SOURCE: R Vancil, *Decentralization: Managerial Ambiguity by Design* (Burr Ridge, IL: Irwin Professional Publishing, 1979), pp. 103, 112, 204.

various amounts of disk space for e-mail messages measured in terabytes (trillion characters). Table 7–1 shows disk space usage for the four departments.

Terabytes of storage are used as the allocation base to distribute the annual e-mail cost of $575,000 to the departments. The allocation rate is $2,875 per terabyte per year ($575,000 ÷ 200). Table 7–2 displays the resulting allocated costs to each user.

Table 7–3 illustrates the extensive use of cost allocations by U.S. firms. It lists some of the corporate-level common costs allocated to cost objects. Out of 1,010 large U.S. companies surveyed, 357 responded to a questionnaire regarding their cost allocation procedures. The expenses listed in Table 7–3 are most of the major cost categories incurred by firms at the corporate level. Two interesting facts emerge from Table 7–3. Most U.S. corporations allocate a significant amount of corporate overhead back to their profit centers and the extent of cost allocation varies by the type of cost category. More firms allocate corporate selling or distribution expense to their profit centers than income taxes.

At present, we have no theories that explain or predict which corporate expenses will be allocated to profit centers. However, the data in Table 7–3 suggest that these allocations are purposeful. If managers randomly chose the expenses to allocate the observed frequencies would not display the variability they do in Table 7–3; the frequencies would be nearly equal under random selection.

In a survey of 186 large Canadian firms, 70 percent indicated they allocate costs.[1] Of those allocating costs, the primary objective of cost allocation was:

Decision control	42%
Decision making	32
Other purposes:	
Cost determination	19
Overhead recovery	5
Equity or fairness	2

These findings reinforce the relative importance of cost allocations in decision management and control. In fact, in this survey, decision control is more important than decision making. The next three examples illustrate the prevalence of cost allocations in both profit and nonprofit organizations and another role of cost allocations: cost-based reimbursement.

1. Manufacturing Organizations

Cost allocations are quite prevalent in manufacturing. Manufacturers cannot deduct all their manufacturing costs for financial reporting and tax purposes. Rather, they must trace their direct manufacturing costs and allocate their indirect manufacturing costs between units sold and units remaining in inventory. Hence, for calculating cost of goods sold, net income, and inventories, financial reporting and taxes often mandate that indirect manufacturing costs be allocated. Cost allocations also arise whenever the firm has a cost-based reimbursable contract. In this case, the firm's revenues depend on reported costs, including allocated costs. For example, certain government defense contracts are cost based. The contractor's revenues are contractually tied to reported costs. In these circumstances, the contractor has an incentive to allocate as much cost to the government work as is permitted under the terms of the contract. Suppose an aircraft company manufactures both military and commercial aircraft. Military aircraft are produced under a cost-based contract. Subject to the contractual stipulations, the firm has an incentive to find the allocation basis that maximizes the fraction of the president's salary allocated to the military contract.[2]

---

[1] A Atkinson, *Intra-Firm Cost and Resource Allocations: Theory and Practice* (Toronto: Canadian Academic Accounting Association, 1987), p. 5.

[2] For a series of papers describing how cost-based contracts affect managers' incentives to allocate costs, see W Rogerson, "Overhead Allocation and Incentives for Cost Minimization in Defense Procurement," *Accounting Review* 67 (October 1992), pp. 671–90; J Thomas and S Tung, "Cost Manipulation Incentives under Cost Reimbursement: Pension Costs for Defense Contracts," *Accounting Review* 67 (October 1992), pp. 691–711; S Reichelstein, "Constructing Incentive Schemes for Government Contracts: An Application of Agency Theory," *Accounting Review* 67 (October 1992), pp. 712–31; J Demski and R Magee, "A Perspective on Accounting for Defense Contracts," *Accounting Review* 67 (October 1992), pp. 732–40; and F Lichtenberg, "A Perspective on Accounting for Defense Contracts," *Accounting Review* 67 (October 1992), pp. 741–52.

2. Hospitals

Hospitals rely on reimbursement by the government and by private medical insurance companies. At one time in the United States, these payments depended on the costs reported by the hospital. In some states, nursing home reimbursement under Medicaid is still based on reported costs. Under cost-based reimbursements, cost allocation becomes an important determinant of revenue. For example, suppose a hospital serves two patient populations: poor elderly cases and affluent maternity cases. Suppose the medical costs for the elderly are paid by the government at a fixed amount per case, whereas private insurance companies reimburse the hospital for maternity cases at "cost." Given these patient populations and reimbursement rules, the hospital administrator has an incentive to choose a cost allocation method that loads as much cost as possible onto the maternity cases in order to maximize revenues. For example, laundry costs can be assigned using various allocation bases: patient days, floor space, nursing hours, and so on. The hospital administrator wants to use the allocation base that allocates as much laundry cost as possible to maternity because this maximizes hospital revenue.

Today, hospital reimbursement in the United States is less tied to reported costs than previously. Hospitals basically are reimbursed at a flat amount for a given medical procedure (diagnostic-related groups, or DRGs). This change in hospital reimbursement rules has reduced the opportunity to maximize hospital revenues using cost allocations.[3]

3. Universities

Universities also allocate costs. A recurring debate at most campuses concerns *indirect cost pools*. Research-oriented universities derive significant revenues from government contracts and grants. Grants from organizations such as the National Science Foundation and the National Institutes of Health pay for basic research. University scientists submit research proposals to a government funding agency describing their experiments, anticipated contribution, and costs of the project. Besides the direct cost of the experiment, the research grant is expected to pay for the indirect costs of research such as building occupancy, library facilities, administration, and security. University research proposals include a reimbursable cost item for such indirect costs. The university estimates the total cost of all indirect expenses attributable to government-sponsored research as well as the total direct costs of government-sponsored research. The ratio of these estimates is the *indirect cost rate*, which varies from 40 to 75 percent across universities. If a cancer researcher seeks $250,000 of direct cost support for laboratory staff, supplies, and salaries, and the university has a 50 percent indirect cost rate, the grant proposal includes an additional $125,000 of indirect cost recovery.

Universities have an incentive to recover as much indirect cost as possible. Invariably, university administrators and researchers become embroiled in heated debates over who has the right to the indirect costs reimbursed by the federal grants. Researchers view the $125,000 as profits they are generating to help support the university. University administrators view the $125,000 as partial payment to help defray the costs of maintaining expensive libraries, computer centers, and university facilities.

---

[3] Many states now regulate hospitals by limiting the total revenues a hospital can receive in a given year. For example, the state of Washington places a cap on each hospital's total revenues based on its projected costs for the year and adjusted for actual volume. Such a scheme has been shown to provide hospital administrators with incentives to bias their forecasted costs in order to increase their budget. See G Blanchard, C Chow, and E Noreen, "Information Asymmetry, Incentive Schemes, and Information Biasing: The Case of Hospital Budgeting under Rate Regulations," *Accounting Review* 61 (January 1986), pp. 1–15.

The Legacy of the $7 Aspirin

Hospitals routinely justify the prices they charge for services and procedures based on costs. For example, a hospital explains the $7 price for two aspirin tablets as follows:

Two aspirin tablets	$0.012
Direct labor	
Physician	0.500
Pharmacist	0.603
Nurse	0.111
Indirect labor (recordkeeping and orderly)	0.400
Cup	0.020
Shared and shifted costs	
Unreimbursed Medicare	0.200
Indigent care	0.223
Malpractice insurance and uncollectible receivables	0.152
Excess bed capacity	0.169
Other administrative and operating costs	0.242
Product cost	$2.632
Hospital overhead costs @ 32.98%	0.868
Full cost (incl. overhead)	$3.500
Profit	3.500
Price (per dose)	$7.000

While the $7 price of the aspirin might at first appear ridiculous, this is the amount necessary to recover both the direct and indirect costs of prescribing the aspirin, costs that the hospital cannot recover from its other patients, and to provide a profit.

SOURCE: D McFadden, "The Legacy of the $7 Aspirin," *Management Accounting*, April 1990, pp. 38–41.

Stanford University received about $400 million to support research in 1988–89, which included about $91 million of overhead costs. A September 14, 1990, *Wall Street Journal* article reported that the federal government claims that Stanford "officials may have engaged in 'fraudulent acts' and made 'false claims' in its billing practices including 'excessive library cost reimbursement' amounting to $30 million to $40 million from 1983 to 1986." In 1991, the president, provost, and chief financial officer of Stanford resigned. The U.S. government reduced Stanford's indirect cost recovery rate from 78 percent to 55.5 percent, which reduced government payments to Stanford by $22 million per year. This Stanford example, while an isolated case, illustrates that cost allocations can at times have serious consequences for organizations and their leaders.

Cost allocations also affect the resources available to the various colleges and departments. Chapter 6 described a university budget system. If each college within the university is treated as a profit center, then cost allocations become relevant. If the business school must operate within a balanced budget, in which revenues equal expenditures plus allocated costs, then the amount of central administration, library, security, or human resource department costs allocated to the business school

The Allocation of Overhead Has Been Contentious for Decades	The allocation of overhead has received more attention than any other cost accounting topic and has been a hotly debated problem ever since accountants began recording indirect expenses. One commentator writing in 1916 described the situation as follows:

> Indirect expense is one of the most important of all the accounts appearing on the books of the manufacturer. Methods of handling its [allocation] have given rise to more arguments than the problem of the descent of man. It is the rock upon which many a ship of industry has been wrecked.
>
> SOURCE: C Thompson, *How to Find Factory Costs* (Chicago, IL: A. W. Shaw Co., 1916), p. 105. Quoted by P Garner, *Evolution of Cost Accounting to 1925* (Montgomery, AL: University of Alabama Press, 1954), pp. 170–71.

affects its other spending. A college within the university with positive net cash flows can be "taxed" and these cash flows used to subsidize colleges within the university with negative net cash flows. This is accomplished by allocating more university overhead to the positive cash-flow colleges and less overhead to the negative cash-flow colleges. These overhead allocations absorb some of the positive cash flows, allowing the president to use other funds that would otherwise have been used to pay the overheads to subsidize the negative cash-flow colleges. Cost allocations are no longer an idle academic speculation in such settings; they often consume a considerable amount of the deans' and central administration's time.

This discussion is not a thorough listing of all cost allocation situations, but it illustrates that cost allocations are important in many types of organizations. Cost allocations can affect real resource utilization and cash flows.

B. Reasons to Allocate Costs

Most organizations allocate costs. However, some responsibility accounting proponents argue that managers should only be allocated a cost if they have some control over that cost. For example, the maintenance department is a cost center. Its budget contains allocated costs such as a charge for office space over which the maintenance manager has no control. Why give the budget center manager a budget and then take some of it back via a cost allocation? Why not just give the manager a smaller budget?

This section describes three possible reasons that organizations allocate costs: external reporting (including taxes), cost-based reimbursements, and decision making and control.

1. External Reporting/Taxes

External financial reports and tax accounting rules require that inventory be stated at cost, including indirect manufacturing costs. For example, inventory includes not only direct labor and direct material but also a fraction of factory depreciation, property taxes, and the salaries of security guards at the factory. Overhead costs, including indirect costs, must be allocated to products. This does not require the firm to use cost allocations for internal reports. To avoid the extra bookkeeping costs of a second set of accounts that exclude the allocated costs, firms use the same accounts internally as externally. However, additional bookkeeping costs would likely be small and offset by the costs of dysfunctional decisions from using the external system for internal operating decisions. Thus,

Federal Reserve Banks: Reallocating Costs Due to Cost-Based Reimbursements

The Federal Reserve banks in the U.S. provide several services to their member banks: check-clearing, wire transfers, currency processing, and so forth. The Federal Reserve banks are an agency of the U.S. government, and they are required by law to charge private banks fees for their services. Moreover, the law mandates that these fees be based on all direct and allocated costs as if they were being charged by a private business. Some of the services provided by the Federal Reserve Banks (check-clearing) are also provided by private, for-profit competitors. Other Fed services (electronic transfer) face little outside competition.

A study found that the Fed shifted the allocation of costs from competitive services and markets to less competitive services. Because the prices charged by the Fed had to be documented based on costs (both direct and indirect), this reallocation of costs from more to less competitive services allowed the Fed to justify charging lower prices in its competitive services and higher prices in its less competitive services. This is an example of how cost-based reimbursement contracts create incentives for managers to design cost allocation schemes that maximize total revenues.

SOURCE: K Cavalluzo, C Ittner, D Larcker, "Competition, Efficiency and Cost Allocation in Government Agencies: Evidence on the Federal Reserve System," *Journal of Accounting Research* (Spring 1998), pp. 1–32.

external reporting requirements are not likely to explain the widespread use of cost allocations for internal reporting, such as divisional performance evaluation.

2. Cost-Based Reimbursement

Cost-based reimbursement is another reason for cost allocations. Government cost-based contracts and medical reimbursements for cost give rise to cost allocations. The U.S. Department of Defense purchases billions of dollars of goods a year under cost-plus contracts. Most weapons systems are procured under negotiated contracts in which the producer's revenues are in part a function of reported costs. To help regulate the cost allocations contractors use in government contracts, the federal government established the Cost Accounting Standards Board (CASB). The CASB has issued standards covering the cost accounting period, capitalization of tangible assets, accounting for insurance and pension costs, and the allocation of direct and indirect costs.

The revenues of public utilities such as electric and gas companies are also tied to reported costs. States often grant public utilities exclusive monopolies over service territories. In return, the state regulates the rates the utility can charge customers. In many cases, the regulated prices are based on reported costs, including allocated costs. In public utility regulation, the major issue is deciding how to allocate the common costs of capacity, such as the electricity-generating plant, among the different classes of users (residential versus business customers). In many public utility rate-setting cases, cost allocation is the preeminent issue.[4]

In firms whose revenues depend on reported costs, cost allocations can have a large impact on cash flows. But relatively few firms have revenues contractually based on costs, and cost allocations are prevalent in firms without cost-based revenues. Therefore, the widespread use of cost allocations cannot be explained by the existence of cost-based reimbursement contracts.

---

[4] See A Atkinson (1987), pp. 22–31.

or nonpecuniary rewards. If common costs are not allocated, the managers in the two divisions have less incentive to invest in the specialized knowledge necessary to determine the optimum level of the common costs. If the decision rights over the level of common costs do not reside with the managers of the two divisions and the common costs are not allocated back to the two divisions, the division managers will always be demanding more common resources. If these managers individually or collectively have the decision rights over the common resources but are not charged for the common costs, these costs will grow rapidly as the managers invent ways to substitute off-budget common costs for currently consumed factor inputs that are included in their budget. For example, security guards are a common cost. Suppose security costs are not charged to either division. The division managers have an incentive to substitute security guards for maintenance workers or even machine operators, thereby reducing the amount of direct labor charged to each division's budget.

As shown in Table 7–3, most firms allocate common costs, presumably to prevent individual divisions from overconsuming the common resource. The next task is choosing an allocation base. Choosing an allocation base causes it to be taxed and, as demonstrated earlier, managers will reduce their consumption of the taxed item. But this creates other incentives. Consider the following illustration.

Suppose our two manufacturing divisions have a significant amount of interaction: They hire from a common local work force, they use common shippers, and they deal with the same set of government officials for building permits, air quality standards, and safety standards. Ideally, the two division managers should cooperate with each other. However, within their firm, they are probably competitors, vying for the same promotion or assignment. If one division does poorly, it might enhance the other manager's chances when a promotion opportunity arises.

Cost allocations can promote or discourage cooperation between the two managers, depending on the type of allocation scheme. With an **insulating allocation** scheme, the costs allocated to one division do not depend on the operating performance of the other division. With a **noninsulating allocation** scheme, the allocated costs of one division do depend on the other division's operating performance. For example, our two divisions share the same factory building and both are profit centers. Assume that the common costs of the shared factory space are $1 million per month. In January and February, the computer modem division has profits of $8 million before allocations. The disk drive division has profits of $8 million in January and $2 million in February. If common costs are allocated using actual profits, then profits after cost allocations for one division depend on the performance of the other division, as illustrated in Table 7–6.

In part A of Table 7–6, common costs of $1 million per month are allocated based on actual profits. The modem division has the same level of division profits before allocation each month: $8 million. Yet its profits after cost allocation are smaller by $300,000 in February. This reduction occurs because the modem division is allocated more common costs when the disk drive division's profits fall; at the same time, the disk drive division receives lower allocated costs.

In Table 7–6, part A's allocation method is noninsulating because each division's allocation depends on the performance of the other. An insulating allocation scheme is presented in part B of Table 7–6 in which common costs are allocated using floor space. The modem division has 60 percent of the floor space and is therefore allocated $600,000 of common costs. To the extent that floor space does not vary with performance, at least in the short run, the performance of one division is not affected by the other division's performance. In the long run,

TABLE 7–6   Noninsulating and Insulating Cost Allocation Schemes ($000s)

	January		February	
	Modem Division	*Disk Drive Division*	*Modem Division*	*Disk Drive Division*
A. Noninsulating Scheme				
Division profits before allocation	$8,000	$8,000	$8,000	$2,000
Allocated common costs*	(500)	(500)	(800)	(200)
Net income	$7,500	$7,500	$7,200	$1,800
B. Insulating Scheme				
Division profits before allocation	$8,000	$8,000	$8,000	$2,000
Allocated common costs†	(600)	(400)	(600)	(400)
Net income	$7,400	$7,600	$7,400	$1,600

*Common costs are allocated based on actual division profits before allocated costs.
†Common costs are allocated based on square footage. The modem division has 60 percent of the square footage.

if one division expands floor space relative to the other, it will receive a larger fraction of the common costs.

Noninsulating systems can use sales or head count (employment) instead of profits. Either of these allocation bases will cause one division's profits to vary with the actual results of the other division. Insulating allocation systems use predetermined allocation rates that do not vary with actual results.

Both insulating and noninsulating methods give the division managers an incentive to economize on common costs. The noninsulating method (Table 7–6, part A) provides each division manager with incentives to increase the other division's profitability, thereby increasing the other division's share of the common costs. In this sense, noninsulating schemes create incentives for mutual monitoring and cooperation by managers. Noninsulating cost allocations are examples of cost allocations used for control purposes.

The disadvantage of a noninsulating method is that it distorts the performance measure of one division by tying it to another division's performance. Some argue that managers should be held responsible for only those cost items over which they have decision rights and hence control. (This controllability principle was discussed in Chapter 5.) In the above example, the common costs are jointly controllable by both managers. If there is a large interaction effect between the two managers in that one can significantly affect the other's performance, then each manager is held responsible for the other's performance through a noninsulating allocation method.

While noninsulating allocation schemes distort the performance measure by basing one division's share of overhead on another division's performance, they can reduce the risk managers bear. Suppose two divisions are affected by random events outside their control. Moreover, suppose these random events affecting the two divisions are not perfectly positively correlated. If one division has an unusually unfavorable random shock, the other division is unlikely to have such an adverse shock and will absorb more overhead in that period. The division with the adverse shock will absorb less overhead and will show a larger profit after common costs are allocated than it would if an insulating allocation method were used. Likewise, a highly favorable random event in one division is likely to occur when the other division does not have such a good period. The division with the good fortune will absorb more overhead, and its performance measure will not be as large as it would if overhead were allocated using an insulating method.

Noninsulating methods act like shock absorbers for random events and reduce the variability of all managers' performance measures. If managers were risk-neutral, such risk sharing would not matter. Variations in allocated costs due to noninsulating allocations wash out over time. And since a risk-neutral manager does not care about variability, the lower risk imposed by noninsulating cost allocation does not matter. But decreased variability does matter to risk-averse managers. Noninsulating methods reduce the variability of their performance measures.[10]

In the previous example, the two divisions shared common factory resources and controlled the level of common costs. Now consider corporate headquarters expenses, such as the president's staff expenditures. The divisions do not have decision rights over the level of corporate headquarters expenses, but noninsulating allocations still create incentives for mutual monitoring. Although they cannot directly control the level of the costs being allocated, subordinate managers can pressure senior management to control staff growth.

To summarize the discussion,

1. Common costs should be allocated for decision making and control whenever the marginal cost of a common resource, such as the human resource department, is equal to or greater than the resource's reported average cost.

2. Common costs should be allocated using an allocation base that does not insulate subunits whenever interactions among the subunits are high and cooperation is important. If interaction is unimportant, an allocation base should be chosen that does not fluctuate with other subunits' performance.

3. Noninsulating cost allocations can reduce the risk managers bear by diversifying that risk across other managers.

Concept Questions		
	Q7–3	How do cost allocations act as a tax system?
	Q7–4	Define *externality* and give an example of one.
	Q7–5	What is the difference between a positive and a negative externality?
	Q7–6	How are externalities reduced within a firm?
	Q7–7	Describe the three cases to consider when determining if a cost allocation is beneficial.
	Q7–8	Should common costs be allocated?
	Q7–9	Describe how a noninsulating allocation scheme promotes cooperation among managers and encourages mutual monitoring.
	Q7–10	Why would senior managers want to distort factor prices by using cost allocations?

[10]As long as the random events are not perfectly positively correlated, then noninsulating methods diversify some of the risk managers bear. The analysis is a straightforward application of portfolio theory as to why risk-averse investors want to hold a diversified portfolio of securities.

D. Summary

Cost allocations pervade all organizations. Managers allocate costs for a variety of reasons, including: financial reporting, taxes, cost-reimbursement contracts, and government regulation. But it appears that many organizations allocate costs for decision making and control. The important lessons from this chapter are

1. Cost allocations act as an internal tax on the factor input being used as the allocation base. And, like taxes in general, cost allocations change managers' incentives and hence the decisions they make.

2. Certain factor inputs, notably labor, impose externalities on the firm in the sense that when more of that input is used, other costs in the firm also rise. Managers and their accountants will want to tax that input if its reported cost does not fully reflect its cost plus the externality it generates. The way to tax the factor input is to use it as the allocation base for allocating some other cost to the manager with the decision rights over the taxed factor input. For example, labor can be taxed by allocating corporate overhead to departments based on the number of employees in each department.

3. Costs can be allocated in ways that increase or decrease managers' mutual monitoring and cooperation with each other. Noninsulating cost allocation schemes increase mutual monitoring and coordination; insulating schemes do the opposite.

4. Noninsulating cost allocations can reduce the risk managers face. For example, if a division's profits are unusually low, fewer costs are allocated to this division, thereby softening the full impact of the lower profits. Hence, noninsulating allocations induce risk-sharing among managers and can diversity the risk borne by managers.

Appendix: Cost Allocations as Taxes

This appendix presents a graphical representation of cost allocations serving as a tax system. The example of the computer company branch manager presented in Table 7–4 is used again. The manager must choose between salespeople and advertising. The standard economics solution is pictured in Figure 7–5. The axes represent the amount of advertising and the number of salespeople. The curve QQ is an isoquant. It reflects the various combinations of advertising (A) and salespeople (S) required to produce a given amount of sales. For example, at point X, fewer salespeople but more advertising are required to produce the same sales as at point Y. QQ takes the shape it does because each unit reduction in advertising (or salespeople) requires increasingly larger amounts of salespeople (or advertising) to produce the same level of sales. Isoquants farther from the origin represent higher levels of sales.

The branch manager's reported costs are

$$\text{Cost} = P_A A + P_S S$$

The price of an advertisement is P_A and the price of a salesperson is P_S. If the branch manager wants to produce sales equal to QQ, any combination of advertising and salespeople on curve QQ will suffice. But the optimum is point Y where the slope of the isoquant QQ is equated to the ratio of their prices. The straight-line

FIGURE 7–5

Profit-maximizing quantities of salespeople and advertising before cost allocation

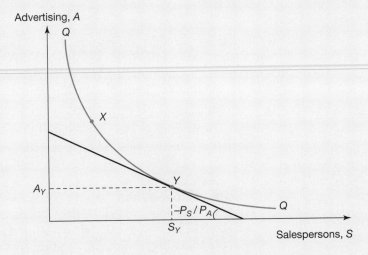

FIGURE 7–6

Profit-maximizing quantities of salespeople and advertising after cost allocation

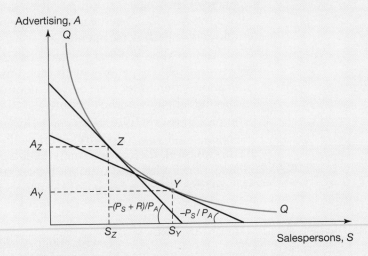

tangent to the isoquant in Figure 7–5 has a slope of -1 times the ratio of the prices, or $-P_S/P_A$.

To summarize, suppose the branch manager hires salespeople at P_S per person, purchases advertising at P_A per ad, and wants to produce the amount of sales equivalent to isoquant QQ. The manager chooses the amounts of salespeople and advertising to minimize cost (thereby maximizing profits), which is A_Y of advertising and S_Y of salespeople. This is the best the branch manager can do. Of course, there is no cost allocation yet.

Figure 7–6 introduces cost allocations. The no-allocation case of Figure 7–5 is reproduced in Figure 7–6 for comparative purposes. Suppose corporate expense is allocated based on the number of salespeople. The overhead rate, R, is in terms of the number of salespeople, S. The branch manager's reported costs are

$$\text{Cost} = P_A A + P_S S + R S$$

$$= P_A A + (P_S + R)S$$

The "price" the branch manager now "pays" for salespeople includes both the wage, P_S and the overhead rate, R. In Figure 7–6, the slope of the straight line

TABLE 1   Fitzhugh Investors Product Line Summary Data

	Money Market	Blue Chip	Fixed Income	Total Funds
Asset-based fees	0.75%	1.75%	1.25%	—
Per-account fee	$25	$8	$9	—
Net assets (millions)	$1,050	$1,150	$1,824	$4,024
Accounts (thousands)	275	110	185	570

TABLE 2   Fitzhugh Investors Direct Expenses by Fund

	Money Market	Blue Chip	Fixed Income
Sales and administration	$ 2,696,000	$2,332,000	$ 6,838,000
Fund management	1,400,000	2,750,000	1,800,000
Transfer agency	10,465,000	7,224,000	18,911,000

becomes steeper, and the reported cost-minimizing combination of advertising and sales becomes point Z, with combinations A_Z and S_Z. At this point, the branch manager uses more advertising and fewer salespeople than at point Y, where there was no overhead allocation. The branch manager uses less of the more expensive input, salespeople, and more of the relatively cheaper input, advertising.

Notice that allocating overhead based on the number of salespeople is a tax on salespeople, which causes the branch manager to use fewer salespeople ($S_Y - S_Z$). S_Z may or may not be the optimal number of salespeople. S_Z is the firm value-maximizing level of salespeople if each salesperson causes the firm to incur R of additional costs beyond the price, P_S (salary plus benefits), for each salesperson.

Self-Study Problem

Fitzhugh Investors

Fitzhugh Investors sells, manages, and operates three mutual funds: Money Market, Blue Chip, and Fixed Income. Each fund's prospectus specifies a schedule of fees payable to Fitzhugh Investors for its services. The company derives all of its revenue from two fees. The first fee Fitzhugh receives from each fund is based on the net assets in the fund. The second fee is based on the number of accounts. Table 1 itemizes the fee structure for each fund.

Each fund is operated as a separate line of business, incurring avoidable direct expenses for sales and administration, fund management, and transfer agency functions (brokerage fees, maintaining customer accounts, and safekeeping securities). Additionally, the funds employ several common corporate resources, such as a Web site, computer facilities, telephone representatives, security analysts, and corporate staff. Fitzhugh Investors allocates these corporate expenses to the respective funds based on the number of accounts. Corporate expenses total $2,595,000. Management estimates that closing any one fund could avoid $125,000 and any two funds $200,000 of the corporate expenses. Table 2 presents the direct expenses for each fund.

Required:

a. Prepare an income statement that shows the direct expenses and the allocated corporate expenses by mutual fund for Fitzhugh.

b. Fitzhugh's managers are reviewing the income statement prepared in part (*a*). Some of the funds are reporting a loss. What actions should management take?

Solution:

a. Revenues of each fund are composed of the asset-based fee times the net assets plus the per-account fee times the number of accounts. Corporate expenses are allocated based on the number of accounts.

FITZHUGH INVESTORS
Net Income by Fund Both before and after
Allocated Corporate Expenses

	Money Market	*Blue Chip*	*Fixed Income*	*Total Funds*
Revenues				
Asset-based fees	$ 7,875,000	$20,125,000	$22,800,000	$50,800,000
Per-account fees	6,875,000	880,000	1,665,000	9,420,000
Direct Expenses				
Sales and administration	2,696,000	2,332,000	6,838,000	11,866,000
Fund management	1,400,000	2,750,000	1,800,000	5,950,000
Transfer agency	10,465,000	7,224,000	18,911,000	36,600,000
Gross profit	$ 189,000	$ 8,699,000	$ (3,084,000)	$ 5,804,000
Corporate expense	1,252,000	501,000	842,000	2,595,000
Net income (loss)	$(1,063,000)	$8,198,000	$(3,926,000)	$ 3,209,000

b. Based on the current accounting system, the money market and fixed income funds are reporting losses after allocating corporate expenses. If the money fund is closed, Fitzhugh does not avoid losing $1,063,000 because this includes allocated corporate expense. Only $125,000 of corporate expense is avoided by closing one fund. The money fund is generating $189,000 of gross profit before corporate expenses. If this fund is eliminated, Fitzhugh forgoes $189,000 of cash flow but saves only $125,000. Thus it should not eliminate the money fund.

The fixed income fund is losing over $3 million before any corporate expense is allocated. Therefore it appears that if this fund is closed, Fitzhugh would save this loss plus corporate expenses of $125,000.

However, the preceding analysis fails to account for the positive externalities associated with having related funds. Exchange privileges between the funds—specifically, the ability to shift money across funds—are valued by investors. Before dropping the fixed income fund, Fitzhugh must consider how many blue chip and money market accounts such action would sacrifice now and in the future. An accounting system such as Fitzhugh's offers no real way of assessing the impact of such externalities.

Problems

P 7–1:   Peluso Company

Peluso Company, a manufacturer of snowmobiles, is operating at 70 percent of plant capacity. Peluso's plant manager is considering manufacturing headlights, which are now being purchased for $11 each (a price that is not expected to change in the near future). The Peluso plant has the equipment and labor force required to manufacture the headlights. The design engineer estimates that each headlight requires $4 of direct materials and $3 of direct labor. Peluso's plant overhead rate is 200 percent of direct labor dollars, and 40 percent of the overhead is fixed cost. If Peluso Co. manufactures the headlights, how much of a gain (loss) for each headlight will result?

SOURCE: CMA adapted.

P 7–2:   MRI

Magnetic resonance imaging (MRI) is a noninvasive medical diagnostic device that uses magnets and radio waves to produce a picture of an area under investigation inside the body. A patient is positioned in the MRI and a series of images of the area (say, the knee or abdomen) is generated. Radiologists then read the resulting image to diagnose cancers and internal injuries. The MRI at Memorial Hospital has the following projected operating data for next year.

	Fixed Cost	Variable Cost	Total Cost
Equipment lease	$350,000		$350,000
Supplies		$ 97,000	97,000
Labor	145,000	182,000	327,000
Hospital administration	63,000		63,000
Occupancy	48,000		48,000
Total projected costs	$606,000	$279,000	$885,000
Number of images			33,600
Number of hours			2,800

Memorial Hospital serves two types of patients: elderly, whose hospital bills are covered by governments (state and federal reimbursement), and other patients who are covered by private insurance (such as Blue Cross and Blue Shield). About one-third of Memorial's patients are elderly. Elderly patients using MRI services normally require more time per MRI image. The typical elderly patient requires one hour of MRI time to produce the 10 MRI images needed for the radiologist. Other patients only require about 45 minutes per patient to generate the 10 MRI images.

Governments reimburse MRI imaging based on the reported cost by the hospital. Reimbursable costs include both the fixed and variable costs of providing MRIs. Private insurers reimburse MRI imaging based on a standard fee schedule set by the insurance company. These fee schedules are independent of the hospitals' cost of providing MRI services.

Required:

   a. Calculate Memorial Hospital's projected cost per MRI image.
   b. Calculate Memorial Hospital's projected cost per hour of MRI time.

c. Suppose a typical elderly patient at Memorial Hospital requires 10 MRI images and takes one hour of MRI time. Calculate the cost of providing this service if Memorial Hospital calculates MRI costs based on cost per image.

d. Suppose a typical elderly patient at Memorial Hospital requires 10 MRI images and takes one hour of MRI time. Calculate the cost of providing this service if Memorial Hospital calculates MRI costs based on cost per hour of MRI time.

e. Should Memorial Hospital calculate the cost of MRI services based on the cost per image or the cost per MRI hour? Explain why.

P 7–3:   Network Systems

Network Systems (NS) offers telecommunications design and consulting services to organizations. The firm offers two types of contracts to its clients: a cost-plus 25 percent contract and a fixed-fee contract where NS offers a fixed price for the job. For cost-plus contracts, total cost includes both direct costs and indirect overheads. NS completes 10 cost-plus contracts at a total direct cost of $450,000 and 15 fixed-fee contracts. Revenues collected from the fixed-fee contracts total $2,400,000. The total direct cost of the fixed-fee contracts amounts to 75 percent of the collected revenues. NS has indirect overheads of $350,000.

Required:

a. Allocate the indirect overhead of $350,000 to the fixed-fee and cost-plus 25 percent contracts using direct cost as the overhead allocation base.

b. Allocate the indirect overhead of $350,000 to the fixed-fee and cost-plus 25 percent contracts using number of contracts as the overhead allocation base.

c. Should NS allocate overhead using direct cost or number of contracts? Explain why.

P 7–4:   Slawson

Slawson is a publicly traded Argentine company with three operating companies located in Argentina, the United States, and Germany. Slawson's corporate headquarters in Buenos Aires oversees the three operating companies. The annual cost of the corporate headquarters, including office expenses, salaries, and legal and accounting fees, is 2.4 million pesos. The following table summarizes operating details of each of the three operating companies.

	Argentina	*United States*	*Germany*
Number of employees	1,500	300	200
Net income (loss) in pesos (millions)	(100)	400	500

Required:

a. Allocate the 2.4 million pesos corporate headquarters cost to the three operating companies using number of employees in each operating company.

    b. Allocate the 2.4 million pesos corporate headquarters cost to the three operating companies using net income of each operating company as the allocation base.

    c. Discuss the advantages and disadvantages of allocating corporate headquarters costs using (i) employees and (ii) net income.

P 7–5:   The Corporate Jet

A large corporation maintains a fleet of three 30-passenger corporate jets that provide (weather permitting) daily scheduled service between Detroit and several cities that are home to its production facilities. The jets are used for business, not personal, travel. Corporate executives book reservations through a centralized transportation office. Because of the limited number of seats available, the planes almost always fly full, at least in the nonwinter months. Excess demand for seats is assigned by executive rank within the firm. The executive's budget is charged for the flight at the end of the month. The charge is based on the jet's total operating expenses during the month (including fuel, pilot's salary and fringes, maintenance, licensing fees, landing fees, and 1/12 of the annual accounting depreciation) divided by the actual passenger miles logged in the month. This rate per passenger mile is multiplied by each passenger's mileage flown in the month.

Required:

    a. Describe the formula being used to calculate the cost per passenger mile flown.

    b. As passenger miles flown increases, what happens to the cost per passenger mile?

    c. Describe what causes the monthly charge per passenger mile flown to fluctuate.

    d. What other problems are present in the current system and what improvements do you suggest making?

P 7–6:   Tuition Benefits

Eastern University prides itself on providing faculty and staff a competitive compensation package. One aspect of this package is a faculty and staff child tuition benefit of $4,000 per child per year for up to four years to offset the cost of a college education. The faculty or staff member's child can attend any college or university, including Eastern University, and receive the tuition benefit. If a staff member has three children in college one year, the staff member receives a $12,000 tuition benefit. This money is not taxed to the individual staff or faculty member.

Eastern University pays the benefit directly to the university where the staff/faculty member's child is enrolled or if the student is attending Eastern, it reduces the amount of tuition owed by the faculty/staff member. The university then charges this payment to a benefits account. This benefits account is then allocated back to the various colleges and departments based on total salaries in the college or department.

Evaluate the pros and cons of the present university accounting for tuition benefits. What changes would you recommend making?

technology and offers new markets. Transferring manufacturing and marketing ideas across products and customers provides important synergies.

The variable cost of Federal Systems and International is 50 percent of revenues. The only fixed cost in EI is its Engineering Design group.

Engineering Design is EI's R&D group. It designs new hardware and software that Federal Systems and International sell. Quarterly expenses for Engineering Design will be $0.60 million for the next two years. These expenses do not vary with revenues or production costs.

Engineering Design costs are to be included in calculating profits for the Federal Systems and International groups. Two ways of assigning the Engineering Design costs to Federal Systems and International are (1) group revenues, and (2) an even 50–50 split.

Required:

a. Prepare financial statements for Federal Systems and International illustrating the effects of the alternative ways of handling Engineering Design costs.

b. Which method of assigning Engineering Design costs do you favor? Why?

P 7–12:   Ball Brothers Purchasing Department

The purchasing department of Ball Brothers purchases raw materials and supplies for the various divisions in the firm. Most of the purchasing department's costs are labor costs. The costs of the purchasing department depend on the number of items purchased. The manager of the purchasing department estimates how her department's costs will vary with different levels of demand by the divisions. The following table provides her estimates of how the costs of purchasing vary with the aggregate number of items purchased by all divisions.

Number of Items Purchased per Week	Total Cost per Week
100–199	$1,000
200–299	1,100
300–399	1,200
400–499	1,400
500–599	1,700
600–699	2,100
700–799	2,600
800–999	3,200

In deriving this table, the manager of purchasing projects expanding the size of the department in order to keep roughly constant the time to purchase an item and the quality of the purchasing department's services at all levels of demand placed on the department. That is, if the department is processing 750 items per week, it will provide the same quality of services given a budget of $2,600 as it would processing 250 items per week given a budget of $1,100.

Required:

a. Suppose the purchasing department is currently purchasing 610 items per week. Should the department's costs of $2,100 per week be allocated back to the divisions, making the purchases at a charge of $3.44 per item purchased ($2,100 ÷ 610)? Explain why or why not.

b. Suppose the purchasing department is currently purchasing 210 items per week. Should the department's costs of $1,100 per week be allocated back to the divisions, making the purchases at a charge of $5.23 per item purchased ($1,100 ÷ 210)? Explain why or why not.

c. Reconcile (explain) why your answers to (a) and (b) are either the same or different.

P 7–13: Telstar Electronics

Telstar Electronics manufactures and imports a wide variety of consumer and industrial electronics, including stereos, televisions, camcorders, telephones, and VCRs. Each line of business (LOB) handles a single product group (e.g., televisions) and is organized as a profit center. The delivery of the product to the wholesaler or retailer is handled by Telstar's distribution division, a cost center. Previously, Telstar was organized functionally, with manufacturing, marketing, and distribution as separate cost centers. Two years ago, it reorganized to the present arrangement.

Distribution assembles products from the various LOBs into larger shipments to the same geographic area to capture economies of scale. The division is also responsible for inbound shipments and storage of imported products. It has its own fleet of trucks, which handles about two-thirds of the shipments, and uses common carriers for the remainder. Currently, the costs of the distribution division are not allocated to the LOBs, but LOBs do pay the cost for any special rush shipment using an overnight or fast delivery service, such as Federal Express or UPS. For example, if a customer must have overnight delivery, the LOB ships directly without using Telstar's distribution center and the LOB is charged for the special delivery.

The corporate controller is mulling over the issue of allocating the costs of distribution. Several allocation schemes are possible:

1. Allocate all distribution division costs based on gross sales of the LOBs.

2. Allocate all distribution division costs based on LOB profits.

3. Allocate the direct costs of each shipment (driver, fuel, truck depreciation, tolls) using the gross weight of each LOB's product in the shipment. Then allocate the other costs of the distribution division (schedulers, management, telephones, etc.) using the total direct shipping costs assigned to each LOB.

One argument against allocating is that it will distort relative profitability. The controller says, "Because allocations are arbitrary, the resulting LOB profitabilities become arbitrary." Another argument is that it is not fair to charge managers for costs they cannot control. LOBs cannot control shipping costs. For example, there are savings when two small separate shipments are combined into a single large shipment. LOBs will tend to avoid opening up new sales territories when other Telstar products are not being shipped to that area.

Required:
Write a memo addressing the controller's concerns. Should Telstar begin allocating distribution costs to the LOBs? If so, which allocation scheme should it use?

P 7–14: Diagnostic Imaging Software

Diagnostic Imaging Software (DIS) is the leading producer of imaging software for the health sciences. DIS develops, writes, produces, and sells its software through two direct selling organizations: North America and South America. Each of these direct selling forces is evaluated and rewarded as profit centers. The remaining world sales of DIS software are handled through independent distributors in Europe, Asia, and Africa. DIS has a software development group that designs, writes, and debugs the software before turning it over to the direct sales organizations (North and South America) and the independent distributors who then sell the software. The cost of designing, writing, and debugging the software is $12 million this year.

The following table presents the income statements of the two divisions (millions of $) for this year:

	North America	South America
Revenues	$17.800	$6.700
Operating expenses*	5.340	3.015
Profit before software development cost	$12.460	$3.685

*Does not include any costs of developing, writing, or debugging the software.

Senior management of DIS wants to allocate the software costs to the two direct selling forces in order to evaluate and reward their performance.

Required:

a. Calculate the profits of the two direct selling organizations (North and South America) after allocating the software costs of $12 million based on the relative revenues of the two organizations. (Round all decimals to 3 significant digits.)

b. Calculate the profits of the two direct selling organizations (North and South America) after allocating the software cost of $12 million based on the relative profits before software development cost of the two organizations. (Round all decimals to 3 significant digits.)

c. Calculate the profits of the two direct selling organizations (North and South America) after allocating the software cost of $12 million where 75 percent of the cost is assigned to North America and 25 percent to South America. (Round all decimals to 3 significant digits.)

d. Discuss the advantages and disadvantages of each of the three allocation methods used in parts (a), (b), and (c) above.

P 7–15: Fuentes Systems

Fuentes Systems provides security software to law enforcement agencies. It has a sales force of 70 and has plans to add another 10–15 salespeople. Fuentes allocates corporate administrative costs based on the number of salespeople. The current total administrative cost of $2,184,000 comprises the costs of the human resources, payroll, accounting, and information technology departments.

You manage the western region of Fuentes Systems with 18 salespeople and you plan to add one or two more salespersons. Each salesperson you hire costs

$120,000, which includes salary, benefits, and payroll taxes. If you hire one additional salesperson, you expect that person will generate $185,000 of net operating margin for your region. Net operating margin is revenues less cost of sales and less travel and entertainment expenses associated with that salesperson. Net operating margin does *not* include the salary, benefits, and payroll taxes of the salesperson. If you hire two salespeople, the combined additional net operating margin added to your region is expected to be $323,000. You are evaluated and rewarded as a profit center, where profits are calculated as net operating margin less the total salaries, benefits, and payroll taxes of all salespeople employed in the region, plus allocated corporate administrative costs.

Required:

   a. What is the current allocated administrative cost per salesperson?
   b. Assuming that your hiring of additional salespeople does not alter the allocated cost per salesperson, how many salespersons will you hire in the western region?
   c. Suppose that Fuentes hires an additional 10 salespeople, and the total corporate administrative cost rises from $2,184,000 to $2,640,000. Should Fuentes continue to allocate corporate administrative costs to the regions? Explain why or why not.
   d. Now suppose that Fuentes hires an additional 10 salespeople and the total corporate administrative cost rises from $2,184,000 to $2,200,000. Should Fuentes continue to allocate corporate administrative costs to the regions? Explain why or why not.

P 7–16:   Bio Labs

Bio Labs is a genetic engineering firm manufacturing a variety of gene-spliced, agricultural-based seed products. The firm has five separate laboratories producing different product lines. Each lab is treated as a profit center and all five labs are located in the same facility. The wheat seed lab and corn seed lab manufacture two of the five product lines. These two labs are located next to each other and are of roughly equal size in terms of sales. The two departments have close interaction, often sharing equipment and lab technicians. Both use very similar technology and science and usually attend the same scientific meetings.

Recent discoveries have shown how low-power lasers can be used to significantly improve product quality. The wheat seed and corn seed managers are proposing the creation of a laser testing department to employ this new technology. Leasing the equipment and hiring the personnel cost $350,000 per year. Supplies, power, and other variable costs are $25 per testing hour. The testing department is expected to provide 2,000 testing hours per year. The wheat seed manager expects to use 700 testing hours per year of the laser testing department and the corn seed manager expects to use 800 testing hours. The remaining 500 hours of testing capacity can be used by the other three labs if the technology applies or can be left idle for future expected growth of the two departments. Initially, only wheat and corn are expected to use laser testing.

The executive committee of Bio Labs has approved the proposal but is now grappling with how to treat the costs of the laser testing department. The committee wants to charge the costs to the wheat seed and corn seed labs but is unsure of how to proceed.

At the end of the first year of operating the laser, wheat seed used 650 testing hours, corn seed used 900 hours, and 450 hours were idle.

Required:

a. Design two alternative cost allocation systems.

b. Give numerical illustrations of the charges the corn and wheat seed labs will incur in the first year of operations under your two alternatives.

c. Discuss the advantages and disadvantages of each.

P 7–17:   World Imports

World Imports buys products from around the world for import into the United States. The firm is organized into a number of separate regional sales districts that sell the imported goods to retail stores. The eastern sales district is responsible for selling the imports in the northeastern region of the country. Sales districts are evaluated as profit centers and have authority over what products they wish to sell and the price they charge retailers. Each sales district employs a full-time direct sales force. Salespeople are paid a fixed salary plus a commission of 20 percent of revenues on what they sell to the retailers.

The eastern district sales manager, J. Krupsak, is considering selling an Australian T-shirt that the firm can import. Krupsak has prepared the following table of his estimated unit sales at various prices and costs. The cost data of the imported T-shirts were provided by World Imports's corporate offices.

WORLD IMPORTS
Eastern Sales District
Proposed Australian T-Shirt
Estimated Demand and Cost Schedules

Quantity (000s)	Wholesale Price	T-Shirt Imported Cost
10	$6.50	$2.00
20	5.50	2.20
30	5.00	2.50
40	4.75	3.00

The unit cost of the imported shirts rises because the Australian manufacturer has limited capacity and will have to add overtime shifts to produce higher volumes. Corporate headquarters of World Imports is considering allocating corporate expenses (advertising, legal, interest, taxes, and administrative salaries) back to the regional sales districts based on the sales commissions paid in the districts. It estimates that the corporate overhead allocation rate will be 30 percent of the commissions (for every $1 of commissions paid in the districts, $0.30 of corporate overhead will be allocated). District sales managers receive a bonus based on net profits in their district. Net profits are revenues less costs of imports sold, sales commissions, other costs of operating the districts, and corporate overhead allocations.

The corporate controller, who is proposing that headquarters costs be allocated to the sales regions and included in bonus calculations, argues that all of these costs must ultimately be covered by the profits of the sales districts. Therefore, the districts should be aware of these costs and must price their products to cover the corporate overhead.

Required:

a. Before the corporate expenses are allocated to the sales districts, what wholesale price will Krupsak pick for the Australian T-shirts and how many T-shirts will he sell? Show how you derived these numbers.

b. Does the imposition of a corporate overhead allocation affect Krupsak's pricing decision on the Australian T-shirts? If so, how? Show calculations.

c. What are the arguments for and against the controller's specific proposal for allocating corporate overhead to the sales districts?

P 7–18:   Painting Department

You are manager of a painting department of a large office complex. The painting department is responsible for painting the buildings' exteriors and interiors. Your performance is judged in part on minimizing your department's operating costs, which consist of paint and labor, while providing a high-quality and timely service.

The job of painting the halls of a particular building is being evaluated. Paint and labor are substitutes. To provide the quality job demanded, you can use less paint and more labor, or more paint and less labor. The accompanying table summarizes this trade-off. Paint costs $10 per gallon and labor costs $6.40 per hour.

Paint (Gallons)	Labor (Hours)
50	200
80	125
100	100
125	80
200	50

Required:

a. How much paint and how much labor do you choose in order to minimize the total cost of the hall painting job? (Show calculations in a neatly labeled exhibit.)

b. The accounting department institutes an overhead allocation on labor. For every dollar spent on labor, $0.5625 of overhead is allocated to the paint department to cover corporate overhead items, including payroll, human resource, security, legal costs, and so forth. Now how much labor and paint do you choose to minimize the total accounting cost of the hall painting job? (Show calculations in a neatly labeled exhibit.)

c. Explain why your decisions differ between parts (*a*) and (*b*).

d. Explain why the accounting department might want to allocate corporate overhead based on direct labor to your painting department.

P 7–19:   Scanners Plus

Scanners Plus manufactures and sells two types of scanners for personal computers, the Home Scanner and the Pro Scanner. The Home model is a low resolution model

The following are the costs incurred on the Lawson Company case:

Billable professional staff salaries	$150,000
Secretarial costs	25,000
Staff benefits	13,500
Telephone and mailing costs	8,000
Total costs	$196,500

Required:

a. Calculate the current year's overhead application rate under the old cost accounting system.

b. How would this application rate change if the secretarial costs, staff benefits, and telephone and mailing costs were reclassified as direct costs instead of overhead and overhead was assigned based on direct costs (instead of staff salaries)? Direct costs are defined as billable staff salaries plus secretarial costs, staff benefits, and telephone and mailing costs.

c. Use the overhead application rates from (*a*) and (*b*) to compute the cost of the Lawson Company case.

d. Nixon & Ross bills clients 150 percent of the total costs of the job. What will be the total billings to the Lawson Co. if the old overhead application scheme is replaced with the new overhead scheme?

e. Steve Nixon, managing partner, has commented that replacing the old allocation system with the direct charge method of the new accounting system will result in more accurate costing and pricing of cases. Evaluate the new system.

P 7–23:   Chicago Omni Hotel

The Chicago Omni Hotel is a 750-room luxury hotel offering guests the finest facilities in downtown Chicago. The hotel is organized into four departments: lodging, dining, catering, and retail stores. Each of these departments is treated as a profit center. Lodging is the largest profit center and is responsible for room rental, maids, reservations, main lobby, and bell captains. Dining operates the coffee shop, room service, and three restaurants out of a single kitchen. Catering services is separate from the dining operations. It offers banquet services to large parties, weddings, and business meetings through its own kitchen and staff separate from the dining department's kitchen. However, dining and catering coordinate purchasing and staff scheduling. Retail is responsible for leasing space off the lobby to independent store owners (gift shop, car rental agencies, airline ticket counters, jewelry, flowers, toys, liquor, etc.). There are currently 14 independent stores operating in the hotel. Profit center managers are paid a salary and a bonus. The annual bonus depends on a number of factors, including their unit's profits, customer satisfaction, and employee retention.

The following table presents budgeted operating data for the first year:

	Lodging	Dining	Catering	Retail Stores	Total
Revenues ($ millions)	$39.20	$9.80	$5.80	$1.90	$56.70
Separable operating expenses	$31.10	$6.20	$3.50	$0.30	$41.10
Square footage (1,000s)	625	50	125	80	880
Number of employees	1,000	140	35	4	1,179

Besides the separable expenses traced directly to each profit center, the hotel incurs the following additional expenses:

Occupancy costs (interest, taxes, insurance)	$5.6 million
Marketing costs	1.4 million
Administration (accounting, human resource, security, maintenance, and senior management)	1.1 million
Total	$8.1 million

Profit center performance is part of each profit center manager's annual bonus. Also, to evaluate how each department of the hotel is performing, senior management desires a statement calculating a performance measure.

Required:

a. Design a performance report for the Chicago Omni Hotel. Provide a statement calculating the performance of each unit using your performance report format. This statement should calculate for each unit a bottom-line profit/loss, which will be used as part of the performance evaluation and reward systems.

b. Discuss the rationale underlying the design of the performance report you chose.

c. Using your report, discuss the relative performance of each profit center. Which ones are the best and which are the worst?

P 7–24:   Reed Park, Inc.

Reed Park, Inc., is a bottler/supplier of bottled spring water to both commercial and residential customers. Reed Park's corporate headquarters is located in Clearwater Springs, Colorado. It operates distribution centers (DCs) in three territories throughout the metro Clearwater Springs area. The company began by selling to residential areas and small businesses in the region. In recent years, its sales have moved toward larger businesses. The Metro center was the first DC established. The newest center, Metro West, was established four years ago and continues to show great growth potential.

Bottling and distribution operations are treated as separate entities, and the costs associated with each are easily tracked and charged to the appropriate division. There have been no problems between the two divisions related to the accounting systems. However, the managers in the distribution division have recently begun raising some questions regarding the accounting systems in place within their division.

TABLE 1 Quarterly Income Statements for Reed Park's Three Distribution Centers
($000s)

	Metro		Metro East		Metro West	
Revenues		$865.0		$928.0		$766.4
Expenses:						
Delivery wages	$ 34.2		$ 40.0		$ 33.6	
Overtime wages	4.2		3.2		4.4	
Staff and administrative	150.0		120.0		125.0	
DC overhead	75.0		80.0		90.0	
Fuel	24.0		28.1		26.0	
Truck maintenance	105.0		65.0		75.0	
Corporate overhead	235.7	(628.1)	283.0	(619.3)	391.3	(745.3)
Net income		$236.9		$308.7		$ 21.1

Distribution center operations are relatively straightforward. Bottled water shipments are taken from the main bottling plant and stored at the DCs for delivery to customers at later dates. Most subscribing customers take delivery once every two weeks. Expenses associated with DC operations can be seen in the quarterly income statement (Table 1). DC overhead includes lease, building maintenance, security, and other costs related to running the warehouse facility. Staff and administrative expenses include salaries of sales and support staff as well as the cost of office supplies used in running the office.

Each distribution center has its own sales staff. The corporate office handles the subscription process and provides the drivers/delivery employees the information regarding delivery type and schedule. The majority of corporate overhead allocated to distribution centers results from the processing and maintenance of subscriptions and schedules. Reed Park allocates these overhead costs based upon the proportion of the book value of trucks at each DC facility to the total book value of the entire Reed Park delivery fleet. This allocation scheme was implemented at the time the company was founded to relate costs to the most significant cost item. Trucks are requested by distribution centers and purchased by the corporate offices under a corporate fleet contract with a major truck manufacturer. (See Table 2 for relevant data.) Each DC is treated as a profit center and DC management is evaluated based upon its territory's net income performance.

The bottled water industry is experiencing strong growth, as is Reed Park. While Reed Park's business seems to be profitable, all is not well within the ranks of the organization. Corporate has been pressuring DCs to expand their territories and increase delivery volume, but DCs have been reluctant to meet this request. Some DC managers are beginning to question the amount of overhead being charged to them. They complain that increased deliveries will only cause overhead costs to rise. DC drivers are also unhappy; they complain about being overburdened by their ever-expanding routes and the pressure to meet difficult delivery schedules. Steve Austin, assistant to the controller, has been assigned the task of examining the situation and developing alternatives if, indeed, a solution is needed.

TABLE 2   Data for Reed Park Analysis

	Metro	Metro East	Metro West
Delivery employees	80	70	50
Delivery employees wages (per hour)	$8	$8	$8
Total subscriptions	8,533	7,200	5,040
Deliveries per quarter	51,198	43,200	30,240
Bottles delivered per quarter	75,000	68,000	62,400
Average miles driven per delivery	4	4.5	5.2
New subscriptions this quarter	400	700	900
Trucks based at distribution center	70	65	60
Truck dollar value	$700,000	$690,000	$670,000
Accumulated depreciation (dollar value)	350,000	270,000	90,000
Allocation base	350,000	420,000	580,000
Overhead allocation percentage	26%	31%	43%

NOTES: Trucks average 15 mpg.   Fuel cost = $1.20 per gallon.   Delivery charge = $11 per bottle delivered.
Subscription fee = $100 per subscription.

Required:

   a. Describe the problems, if any, at Reed Park. Specifically, discuss items related to decision making, cost allocation, and incentives.

   b. Describe alternative overhead allocation systems.

   c. Which allocation system would you choose? What effects do you feel it would have upon Reed Park's distribution operations?

   d. Calculate net incomes for the three DCs under the system you have chosen and compare these results with those found under the present system.

SOURCE: D Lonczak, R Bingham, M Eisenstadt, and B Sayers.

P 7–25:   Plastic Chairs

Plastic Chairs manufactures plastic lawn chairs using a combination of new and recycled plastic. Varying amounts of each type of plastic can be used to produce a batch of 100 chairs. The table below lists the various combinations of recycled and new plastic required to produce one batch of 100 chairs.

Pounds of New and Recycled Plastic Required to Manufacture One Batch of 100 Chairs

Pounds of New Plastic	Pounds of Recycled Plastic
20	72
24	60
30	48
32	45
36	40
40	36
45	32
48	30
60	24
72	20

New plastic costs $16 per pound and recycled plastic costs $10 per pound. The manager of the chair manufacturing department receives a bonus based on minimizing the cost per batch of 100 chairs.

Required:

a. What combination of new and recycled plastic will the manager of the chair manufacturing department choose?

b. Overhead (including plant administration, utilities, property taxes, and insurance) is allocated to the chair manufacturing department based on the number of pounds of recycled plastic used in each batch. For each pound of recycled plastic used, the chair manufacturing department is charged $30 of plant overhead. What combination of new and recycled plastic will the manager of the chair manufacturing department select if the manager's bonus is based on minimizing the total cost per batch, which includes new and recycled plastic and plant overhead?

c. Why are your answers to (*a*) and (*b*) either the same or different?

d. Should the plastic chairs manufacturing manager's bonus be based on minimizing only the plastic costs or should it also be based on minimizing plastic costs plus allocated plant overhead?

P 7–26: Independent Underwriters Insurance Co.

The Independent Underwriters Insurance Co. (IUI) established a systems department two years ago to implement and operate its own information technology system. IUI believed that its own system would be more cost-effective than the service bureau it had been using.

IUI's three departments—claims, records, and finance—have different requirements with respect to hardware and other capacity-related resources and operating resources. The system was designed to recognize these differing demands. It was also designed to meet IUI's long-term capacity. The excess capacity designed into the system is being sold to outside users until IUI needs it. The estimated resource requirements used to design and implement the system are shown in the following schedule.

	Hardware and Other Capacity-Related Resources	Operating Resources
Records	30%	60%
Claims	50	20
Finance	15	15
Expansion (outside use)	5	5
Total	100%	100%

IUI currently sells the equivalent of its expansion capacity to a few outside clients.

When the system became operational, management decided to redistribute total expenses of the systems department to the user departments based upon actual computer time used. The actual costs for the first quarter of the current fiscal year were distributed to the user departments as follows:

Department	Percentage Utilization	Amount
Records	60%	$330,000
Claims	20	110,000
Finance	15	82,500
Outside	5	27,500
Total	100%	$550,000

The three user departments have complained about the cost distribution since the systems department was established. The records department's monthly costs have been as much as three times the costs experienced with the service bureau. The finance department is concerned about the costs distributed to the outside user category, because these allocated costs form the basis for the fees billed to outside clients.

James Dale, IUI's controller, decided to review the distribution method by which the systems department's costs have been allocated for the past two years. The additional information he gathered for his review is reported in Tables 1, 2, and 3. Dale has concluded that the method of cost distribution should be changed to reflect more directly the actual benefits received by the departments. He believes

TABLE 1   Systems Department Costs and Activity Levels

| | Annual Budget | | First Quarter | | | |
| | | | Budget | | Actual | |
	Hours	Dollars	Hours	Dollars	Hours	Dollars
Hardware and other capacity-related costs	—	$ 600,000	—	$150,000	—	$155,000
Software development	18,750	562,500	4,725	141,750	4,250	130,000
Operations						
Computer-related	3,750	750,000	945	189,000	920	187,000
Input-output-related	30,000	300,000	7,560	75,600	7,900	78,000
		$2,212,500		$556,350		$550,000

TABLE 2   Historical Utilization by Users

| | Hardware and Other Capacity Needs | Software Development | | Operations | | | |
| | | | | Computer | | Input/Output | |
		Range	Average	Range	Average	Range	Average
Records	30%	0–30%	12%	55–65%	60%	10–30%	20%
Claims	50	15–60	35	10–25	20	60–80	70
Finance	15	25–75	45	10–25	15	3–10	6
Outside	5	0–25	8	3–8	5	3–10	4
	100%		100%		100%		100%

TABLE 3 Utilization of Systems Department's Services for First Quarter (in Hours)

	Software Development	Operations Computer-Related	Operations Input/Output
Records	425	552	1,580
Claims	1,700	184	5,530
Finance	1,700	138	395
Outside	425	46	395
Total	4,250	920	7,900

that hardware and capacity-related costs should be allocated to the user departments in proportion to their planned, long-term needs. Any difference between actual and budgeted hardware costs should remain with the systems department.

The remaining costs for software development and operations would be charged to the user departments based upon actual hours used. A predetermined hourly rate based upon the annual budget data would be used. The hourly rates proposed for the current fiscal year are as follows:

Function	Hourly Rate
Software development	$ 30
Operations	
Computer-related	200
Input-output-related	10

Dale plans to use first-quarter activity and cost data to illustrate his recommendations. The recommendations will be presented to the systems department and the user departments for their comments and reactions. He then expects to present his recommendations to management for approval.

Required:

a. Prepare a schedule to show how the actual first-quarter costs of the systems department will be charged to the users if James Dale's recommended method is adopted.

b. Explain whether James Dale's recommended system for charging costs to the user departments will
   (i) Improve cost control in the systems department.
   (ii) Improve planning and cost control in the user departments.
   (iii) Be a more equitable basis for charging costs to user departments.

SOURCE: CMA adapted.

P 7–27: American Wood Products

American Wood Products is the world's largest integrated timber grower and wood processor. The forest group manages and harvests timber from company-owned and public forests. The lumber group buys cut trees from either the forest group or other timber companies and processes the trees into a full line of wood products, including plywood, lumber, and veneers. The building products group buys wood products (from the lumber group and other companies), as well as other building supplies such as drywall and roofing products, and distributes these products worldwide to retailers. The senior managers in each group receive a bonus based on their group's profit before taxes.

Central corporate overhead is allocated to each group based on actual sales revenues in each division. The current year's corporate overhead allocated to the three groups is

Corporate salaries and other	$ 50,000,000
Research and development	600,000,000
Interest	850,000,000
Corporate overhead	$1,500,000,000

Here are operating data for the last fiscal year (in millions of dollars):

	Forest Group	Lumber Group	Building Products Group	Total
Revenues	$5,000	$8,000	$12,000	$25,000
Operating expenses	3,500	7,000	11,500	22,000
Gross margin	$1,500	$1,000	$ 500	$ 3,000
Corporate overhead	300	480	720	1,500
Profit (loss) before taxes	$1,200	$ 520	$ (220)	$ 1,500
Group assets	$5,000	$2,000	$ 1,000	$ 8,000

Instead of allocating $1.5 billion of overhead to the groups on the basis of revenues, the controller is proposing a different allocation base for each of the overhead categories. In particular,

Overhead Category	*Allocation Base*
Corporate salaries and other	Sales revenue
Research and development	Gross margin
Interest	Group assets

Required:

a. Calculate each group's profits before taxes using the controller's proposed allocation scheme.

b. What are the pros and cons of allocating corporate overhead to operating divisions?

c. What are the advantages and disadvantages of the controller's proposed change relative to the existing method?

P 7–28:   BFR Ship Building

BFR is a ship-building firm that has just won a government contract to build 10 high-speed patrol boats for the Coast Guard for drug interdiction and surveillance. Besides building ships for the government, BFR has a commercial vessel division that designs and manufactures commercial fishing and commuting ships. The commercial division and the government division are the only two divisions of BFR, and the Coast Guard contract is the only work in the government division.

The Coast Guard contract is a cost-plus contract. BFR will be paid its costs plus 5 percent of total costs to cover profits. Total costs include all direct materials, direct labor, purchased subassemblies (engines, radars, radios, etc.), and overhead. Overhead is allocated to the Coast Guard contract based on the ratio of direct labor expense on the contract to firmwide direct labor.

BFR can either purchase the engines from an outside source or build them internally. The following table describes the costs of the commercial division and the Coast Guard contract if the engines are built by BFR versus purchased outside.

BFR
Cost Structure
($ in Millions)

	Commercial Division	Coast Guard Contract (Engines Manufactured Internally)	Coast Guard Contract (Engines Purchased Externally)
Direct labor	$14.600	$22.800	$18.200
Direct material		32.900	25.900
Purchased engines		0.000	17.000

Overhead for BFR is $83.5 million and does not vary if the engines are purchased outside or manufactured inside BFR. Overhead consists of corporate-level salaries, building depreciation, property taxes, insurance, and factory administration costs.

Required:

a. How much overhead is allocated to the Coast Guard contract if
   (i) The engines are manufactured internally?
   (ii) The engines are purchased outside?
b. Based on the total contract payment to BFR, will the Coast Guard prefer BFR to manufacture or purchase the engines?
c. What is the difference in net cash flows to BFR of manufacturing versus purchasing the engines?
d. Explain how cost-plus reimbursement contracts in the defense industry affect the make–buy decision for subassemblies.

P 7–29:   Kodak and NASCAR

Eastman Kodak sponsors a car in the NASCAR races. Like other major corporations that sponsor sports events, Kodak believes that the public's awareness of its products is enhanced by sponsoring a NASCAR car. For the right to have the car painted yellow with "Kodak" displayed prominently over the automobile, Eastman Kodak pays the racing team an annual fee in the millions of dollars.

Kodak is organized around some 25 business units that are profit centers. All Kodak products are sold by the business units. Senior management at Kodak believes that since the various business units at Kodak receive the benefits of NASCAR exposure through greater name recognition, and hence greater sales, the costs of the program should be allocated back to the business units and ultimately to all Kodak products. The cost of the NASCAR program is allocated back to the Kodak business units based on sales revenue. Suppose the allocation is 10 percent of revenues. That is, for every $1 of revenue, the business unit is allocated $0.10 of cost from the NASCAR car.

One of Kodak's business units sells X-ray film in 100-sheet packages. The following table summarizes possible pricing levels, packages sold at that price, and costs for the various number of packages.

Price	Number of Packages Sold	Total Cost
$564	218	$71,800
562	219	71,900
560	220	72,000
558	221	72,100
556	222	72,200
554	223	72,300
552	224	72,400
550	225	72,500
548	226	72,600

Required:

a. What price-quantity combination maximizes the profits of the X-ray film, ignoring the allocation of the NASCAR car?

b. If $0.10 of the NASCAR car is allocated for every dollar of X-ray revenue, what price-quantity combination of X-ray film maximizes profits after allocating NASCAR costs?

c. What price-quantity combination of X-ray film maximizes profits after allocating NASCAR costs using total costs (instead of revenues), where for every dollar of total costs, $0.20 of NASCAR costs are allocated?

d. Instead of allocating the NASCAR car based on revenues, it is allocated based on profits before allocated costs. For every $1.00 of profits before allocated costs, $0.30 of NASCAR costs are allocated. Now what price-quantity combination maximizes X-ray profits after allocating NASCAR costs?

e. Should NASCAR costs be allocated to the business units, and if so, what allocation scheme should be used (revenues, costs, or profits)?

P 7–30:   Durango Plastics

SCX is a $2 billion chemical company with a plastics plant located in Durango, Colorado. The Durango plastics plant of SCX was started 30 years ago to produce a particular plastic film for snack food packages. The Durango plant is a profit center that markets its product to film producers. It is the only SCX facility that produces this plastic.

A few years ago, worldwide excess capacity for this plastic developed as a number of new plants were opened and some food companies began shifting to a more environmentally safe plastic that cannot be produced with the Durango plant technology.

Last year, with Durango's plant utilization down to 60 percent, senior management of SCX began investigating alternative uses of the Durango plant. The Durango plant's current annual operating statement appears in the accompanying table.

DURANGO PLANT
Income Statement, 2008
(Millions)

Revenue		$36
Variable costs	$22	
Fixed costs		
Plant administration (salaries and other out-of-pocket expenses)	17	
Deprecation	5	44
Net loss before taxes		$ (8)

One alternative use of the Durango plant's excess capacity is a new high-strength plastic used by the auto industry to reduce the weight of cars. Additional equipment required to produce the automotive plastic at the Durango plant can be leased for $3 million per year. Automotive plastic revenues are projected to be $28 million and variable costs are $11 million. Additional fixed costs for marketing, distribution, and plant overhead attributable solely to auto plastics are expected to be $4 million.

All of SCX's divisions are evaluated on a before-tax basis.

Required:

a. Evaluate the auto industry plastic proposal. Compare the three alternatives: (i) close Durango, (ii) produce only film plastic at Durango, and (iii) produce both film and auto plastic at Durango. Which of the three do you suggest accepting? (If Durango is closed, additional one-time plant closing costs just offset the proceeds from selling the plant.)

b. Suppose the Durango plant begins manufacturing both film and auto plastic. Prepare a performance report for the two divisions for the first year, assuming that the initial projections are realized and the film division's 2009 revenue and expenses are the same as in 2008. Plant administration ($17 million) and depreciation ($5 million) are common costs to both the film and auto plastics divisions. For performance evaluation purposes, these costs are assigned to the two divisions based on sales revenue. All costs incurred for the Auto Plastics division should be charged to that division.

c. Does the performance report in (*b*) accurately reflect the relative performance of the two divisions? Why or why not?

d. In the year 2010, the Durango plant is able to negotiate a $1 million reduction in property taxes. Property taxes are included in the "plant administration account." In addition, the Film Division is able to add $3 million in additional revenues (with $2.1 of additional variable cost) by selling film to European food packagers. Assuming that these are the only changes at the Durango plant between 2009 and 2010, how does the Auto Plastics Division's performance change between these two years? Allocate the common costs using the method described in (*b*).

e. Write a short memo evaluating the performance of the Auto Plastics Division in light of the events in the year 2010 and describing how these events affect the reported performance of the Auto Plastics Division.

Case

Case 7–1: Phonetex

Phonetex is a medium-size manufacturer of telephone sets and switching equipment. Its primary business is government contracts, especially defense contracts, which are very profitable. The company has two plants: Southern and Westbury. The larger plant, Southern, is running at capacity producing a phone system for a new missile installation. Existing government contracts will require Southern to operate at capacity for the next nine months. The missile contract is a firm, fixed-price contract. Part of the contract specifies that 3,000 phones will be produced to meet government specifications. The price paid per phone is $300.

The second Phonetex plant, Westbury, is a small, old facility acquired two years ago to produce residential phone systems. Phonetex feared that defense work was cyclical, so to stabilize earnings, a line of residential systems was developed at the small plant. In the event that defense work deteriorated, the excess capacity at Southern could be used to produce residential systems. However, just the opposite has happened. The current recession has temporarily depressed the residential business. Although Westbury is losing money ($10,000 per month), top management considers this an investment. Westbury has developed a line of systems that are reasonably well received. Part of its work force has already been laid off. It has a very good work force remaining, with many specialized and competent supervisors, engineers, and skilled craftspeople. Another 20 percent of Westbury's work force could be cut without affecting output. Current operations are meeting the reduced demand. If demand does not increase in the next three months, this 20 percent will have to be cut.

The plant manager at Westbury has tried to convince top management to shift the missile contract phones over to his plant. Even though his total cost to manufacture the phones is higher than at Southern, he argues that this will free up some excess capacity at Southern to add more government work. The unit cost data for the 3,000 phones are as follows:

	Southern	Westbury
Direct labor cost	$ 70	$ 95
Direct materials cost	40	55
Variable factory overhead*	35	45
Fixed factory overhead*	40	80
General burden†	10	20
Total unit cost	$195	$295

*Based on direct labor costs.

†Allocated corporate headquarters expense based on direct labor cost.

Westbury cannot do other government work because it does not have the required security clearances. But Westbury can do the work involving the 3,000 phones. And it can complete this project in three months. "Besides," Westbury's manager argues, "my labor costs are not going to be $95 per phone. We are committed to maintaining employment at Westbury at least for the next three months. I can utilize most of my existing people who have slack. I will have to hire back about 20 production workers I laid off. For the three months, we are talking about $120,000 of additional direct labor."

Phonetex is considering another defense contract with an expected price of $1.1 million and an expected profit of $85,000. The work would have to be completed over the next three months, but Southern does not have the capacity to do the work and Westbury does not have the security clearances or capital equipment required by the contract.

Southern's manager says it isn't fair to make him carry Westbury. He points out that Westbury's variable cost, ignoring labor, is 33 percent greater than Southern's variable costs. Southern's manager also argues, "Adding another government contract will not replace the profit that we will be forgoing if Westbury does the telephone manufacturing. See my schedule."

Profits from Southern ($300 − 195)3,000		$ 315,000
Less: Profits from Westbury ($300 − 295)3,000		(15,000)
Forgone profits		$ 300,000
Profit in the next best government contract:		
Expected price		$1,100,000
Less:		
Direct labor	260,000	
Direct material	435,000	
Variable overhead	130,000	
Fixed factory overhead	150,000	
General burden	40,000	1,015,000
Expected profit		$ 85,000

Required:

Top management has reviewed the Southern manager's data and believes his cost estimates on the new contract to be accurate. Should Phonetex shift the 3,000 phones to Westbury and take the new contract or not? Prepare an analysis supporting your conclusions.

Chapter Eight

Cost Allocation: Practices

Chapter Outline

A. Death Spiral

B. Allocating Capacity Costs: Depreciation

C. Allocating Service Department Costs

1. Direct Allocation Method

2. Step-Down Allocation Method

3. Service Department Costs and Transfer Pricing of Direct and Step-Down Methods

4. Reciprocal Allocation Method

5. Recap

D. Joint Costs

1. Chickens

2. Net Realizable Value

3. Decision Making and Control

E. Segment Reporting and Joint Benefits

F. Summary

Appendix: Reciprocal Method for Allocating Service Department Costs

The previous chapter introduced the topic of cost allocations. Cost allocations are pervasive—most organizations, including profit, nonprofit, service, and manufacturing firms, allocate costs. Cost allocations serve numerous ends such as taxes, inventory valuation, cost-based reimbursements, and decision management and control.

In terms of creating incentives, cost allocations are like internal tax systems. The cost allocation base, such as direct labor or floor space, is taxed, causing decision makers to use less of the allocation base. Thus, the allocation bases chosen (what to tax) affects how resources are consumed inside the firm. Cost allocations create additional incentives, depending on the particular costs allocated and the allocation base chosen. For example, if two divisions are allocated a common cost such as the CEO's salary using a noninsulating method such as divisional profits, then these managers have greater incentives to cooperate. By helping the other division to perform better, that division's allocated costs increase and the other's decrease. Moreover, noninsulating methods help diversify the risk that managers bear.

This chapter continues the discussion begun in the last chapter by first discussing a problem arising in most cost allocations—the death spiral—and then describing some specific methods used to allocate costs. Alternative methods for allocating several interacting service departments' costs are described in section C. Section D describes joint cost allocation, or allocating costs to multiple products produced from a single input. Finally, section E discusses segment reporting and joint benefits. An appendix describes reciprocal cost allocations for service department costs.

A. Death Spiral

One problem arising when significant amounts of fixed costs are allocated and users have discretion over using the service being allocated involves the **death spiral**. For example, consider an internal telecommunications department that provides telephones for inside users. The department purchases, installs, and maintains a central switch, a phone-mail system, and individual phone sets. Users are charged for their phones, the options used, and long-distance charges. There are substantial fixed costs for the central switch, local access charges, installation costs, and maintenance of the phone-mail system.

Suppose the annual fixed costs are $600,000 and the annual cost of each of the 2,000 phone lines is $200. Most of the $600,000 represents depreciation of the existing equipment, which is largely a sunk cost. To recover all the costs from the users, each phone line is charged $500 (or $600,000 ÷ 2,000 + $200). Some users have multiple lines for voice, fax, and computer.

A local phone company will install private lines for $325 per year plus long-distance charges comparable to those available through the internal telecommunications department. Users with multiple lines start switching their fax and computer lines away from the telecommunications department to the outside phone company. At the end of the first year, 500 lines have been converted. To recover its costs, the telecommunications department raises its charge for each line to $600 (or $600,000 ÷ 1,500 + $200). This higher charge causes another 500 users to switch to the outside phone company and the cost rises to $800 per line ($600,000 ÷ 1,000 + $200). The final 1,000 users abandon the telecommunications department, citing exorbitant fees.

Cost Allocations at IBM	During the 1980s and early 1990s, IBM had the policy of allocating costs from one line of business to another. Managers in those lines of business constantly argued that some of their overhead should be carried by other IBM businesses. IBM also typically allocated all of the R&D of a new technology to the line of business first using the technology, and subsequent users were able to utilize it for free. The cost allocation system masked the true profitability of many IBM businesses for years. IBM claimed it was making money in its PC business. But in 1992, "as IBM began to move away from its funny allocation system, IBM disclosed that its PC business was unprofitable."

SOURCE: P Carroll, "The Failures of Central Planning—at IBM," *The Wall Street Journal*, January 28, 1993, p. A14.

The death spiral results when utilization of a common resource falls, creating excess capacity. Average (full) cost transfer pricing charges the users for the common resource. The fixed costs are borne by the remaining users who have incentive to reduce utilization, further raising the average cost and causing additional defections.

Notice that the death spiral can occur whenever full cost transfer pricing is used, there are significant fixed costs, and the user has some discretion over the quantity of the common resource to use. As discussed in Chapter 5, one of the problems with full cost transfer pricing is underutilization of the common resource. Too few units are transferred.

There are several solutions to the death spiral. When excess capacity exists, users should be charged for only the variable cost of the resource. Alternatively, some of the fixed costs could be excluded from the transfer price. For example, the $600,000 in fixed costs (accounting depreciation of existing equipment) should be excluded because with excess capacity the opportunity cost of this equipment is zero.

Example 8–1

Clay Sprays produces a line of aerosol sprays for hospitals and clinics, including air fresheners, spot removers, disinfectants, rug cleaners, and polishes. The plant has substantial excess capacity. The following table presents Clay's current financial situation:

CLAY SPRAYS
Net Income—Current Year

Revenue (1,000,000 units @ $6/unit)	$6,000,000
Variable costs (1,000,000 units @ $3)	(3,000,000)
Fixed costs (manufacturing overhead)	(2,800,000)
Net income before taxes	$ 200,000

Clay Sprays carries no beginning or ending inventories. All the products produced have the same variable cost of $3 per unit, and the fixed cost of $2.8 million represents manufacturing overhead.

continued

Wendy Clay, CEO and owner, worries that the low volume is causing the remaining products to absorb more overhead per unit, driving up their costs and thereby making Clay Sprays's remaining products less competitive than they would be otherwise.

Clay has asked her senior management team to find an acquisition that could add volume to the plant and thereby improve the overhead absorption problem. After analyzing several potential acquisition candidates, the team has found the Coronas Company. Also an aerosol manufacturer, Coronas's products are targeted at the household consumer. Coronas's products are produced by third-party custom-label manufacturers and Coronas has no manufacturing capacity—only a sales and marketing organization. Coronas, like Clay, is currently selling one million aerosol cans per year at an average wholesale price of $3 per can. Clay managers project that the variable cost of producing Coronas's aerosols will be $3 a can and that all of the Coronas volume can be handled by Clay's existing production facility without adding any additional fixed manufacturing overhead or affecting the current $3 variable cost of Clay's products.

Although purchasing Coronas and merging its volume into Clay does not add any incremental profits to Clay (since the wholesale price and the variable cost per can are both $3), Clay's management team still wants to proceed with the acquisition.

Mark Hendrickson, Clay's vice president of marketing, argues that Clay's products should appeal to its medical clients because of their high quality. But Clay's clients are switching to other manufacturers with lower quality and lower prices because hospital budgets are being squeezed. Clay cannot lower its prices because doing so would erode margins (price less manufacturing cost). Acquiring Coronas, Hendrickson argues, will lower the overhead absorption by the Clay products, thereby allowing Clay to lower its prices on the medical market's aerosols without adversely affecting margins.

Required:

  a. Does Clay's acquisition of Coronas improve overhead absorption?
  b. Does Clay's profitability improve with the Coronas acquisition?
  c. Reconcile any apparent inconsistencies between your answers in parts (*a*) and (*b*).
  d. Is Mr. Hendrickson's analysis correct?
  e. Should Clay acquire Coronas?
  f. Why do you think Clay's management team is recommending the Coronas acquisition?

Solution:

  a. The Coronas acquisition does improve Clay's overhead absorption. The average cost of producing Clay's existing products is:

$$\text{Average cost} = \$3 + \frac{\$2,800,000}{1,000,000} = \$5.80$$

Following the acquisition of Coronas, this falls to:

$$\$3 + \frac{\$2,800,000}{2,000,000} = \$4.40$$

continued

The average cost of Clay's existing products is now lower because the fixed cost of $2.8 million is spread over more aerosol cans.

b. Clay's profitability is not improved by the Coronas acquisition. Coronas is selling its aerosol products at $3 per can, which is variable cost. So Coronas is not adding any incremental profits to Clay.

Analysis of Clay's Profitability
from Coronas Merger

	Clay Alone	Coronas Alone	Clay and Coronas Combined
Revenue	$6,000,000	$3,000,000	$9,000,000
Variable cost	3,000,000	3,000,000	6,000,000
Fixed cost	2,800,000	—	2,800,000
Net income before taxes	$ 200,000	$ 0	$ 200,000

Clay's profits remain at $200,000 both before and after the acquisition.

c. The answers to parts (a) and (b) appear inconsistent. While overhead absorption appears to have improved under the acquisition, profits are not higher. The inconsistency is easily reconciled by noting the decline in average cost of Clay's existing products from $5.80 to $4.40. This decline in average cost does *not* represent a reduction in cash outlays. Rather, it represents a *shifting* of some of the fixed costs to the Coronas products. Suppose the $2.8 million fixed cost is allocated based on units. Then the following product line profitability analysis clearly shows the shifting of the fixed overhead.

Clay and Coronas
Product Line Profitability
Pro Forma

	Clay Products	Coronas Products	Firm Total
Revenues	$6,000,000	$ 3,000,000	$9,000,000
Variable cost	3,000,000	3,000,000	6,000,000
Allocated fixed cost (based on units)	1,400,000	1,400,000	2,800,000
Net income (loss) before taxes	$1,600,000	$(1,400,000)	$ 200,000

The Clay products now appear to be more profitable because half the overhead has been shifted to the Coronas products. But now these products appear to be losing $1.4 million. Overall, firm profitability has not changed.

d. Mr. Hendrickson is wrong. We know from economics that profit-maximizing prices are determined at the quantity where marginal cost equals marginal

continued

revenue. Fixed costs do not enter the pricing decision other than to determine whether or not to continue to produce at the optimum price. Mr. Hendrickson should not be setting Clay's aerosol prices based on average cost (or some cost-plus markup). To drive additional volume into the plant, instead of acquiring Coronas, Ms. Clay should carefully examine her pricing policies. By lowering her price, she will lose revenue from customers who would have bought at the higher price. But at a lower price, she will add more new customers. "Marginal revenue" is the difference between the revenue added from new customers purchasing at the lower price less the revenue lost from customers who would have paid the higher price. Clay should continue to drop its price until the marginal revenue from the last penny of price reduction equals $3, which is Clay's marginal cost.

e. If the desire to improve Clay's overhead absorption and hence its profitability is the only reason to acquire Coronas, then the acquisition makes no economic sense. Coronas should be acquired at a positive price if *real* synergies exist. Real synergies include additional sales of Clay or Coronas aerosols as a result of the expanded markets or product lines. Or, other synergies might arise if, by adding volume to the plant, operating efficiencies result and the variable cost of $3 per unit can be reduced.

f. Clay's management team might be interested in this acquisition because adding volume to the plant might mean additional job security.

B. Allocating Capacity Costs: Depreciation

As seen in the previous section, a death spiral can result when a common resource with significant fixed costs and excess capacity is allocated to users who have discretion over utilization of the resource. In the telecommunications example, depreciation of the existing phone system is the principal fixed cost. One way to solve the death spiral is to not allocate some (or all) of the fixed cost. For example, allocate only the fixed cost of the capacity actually being used. If there is 40 percent excess capacity, allocate only 60 percent of the depreciation. However, this solution to the death spiral creates other concerns.

Notice that the death spiral, or underutilization of the common resource, is really a problem of how to use an existing durable asset. How much of the *existing* common resource should each agent use? If there is excess capacity, any charge discourages its use. However, prior to deciding how to allocate the available capacity among existing agents, the firm had to decide how much capacity to acquire. In the previous example, the firm had to decide how large a phone system to buy (how much phone-mail capacity, how many lines, how fast a switch, and so forth). The current fixed costs of the phone system (including depreciation) were "variable" costs prior to acquiring the capacity. Accounting depreciation (such as straight line) represents the annual historical cost of acquired capacity. Depreciation is the allocation of the asset's historical cost over time.

How much capacity should the firm acquire? The future users of that capacity usually have specialized, private knowledge of how intensively they will use the common resource. If these users know they will not be charged for their future use because fixed costs are not allocated, they will overstate their future use. If they are not charged for the *excess* capacity, they will still overstate their use if the common resource exhibits economies of scale (average cost declines as acquired capacity increases). Therefore, charging accounting depreciation is a *commitment device*.[1] Future users, knowing they will be charged for the historical cost of a durable asset, have less incentive to overstate their utilization. Allocating accounting depreciation to users commits them to recovering at least the historical cost of the asset. (Note: Depreciation does not commit them to recovering the opportunity cost of capital tied up in the asset.)

In deciding whether to allocate depreciation on the common resource to its users, the firm makes a trade-off between the efficient investment in the common resource and its efficient utilization after acquisition. Charging depreciation helps control the overinvestment problem, but at the expense of underutilizing the asset after acquisition. Most firms charge users for depreciation. Thus, control of the overinvestment problem tends to dominate decision-making errors involving asset utilization (the death spiral). This is another example of how accounting systems tend to favor control when confronted with a choice between control and decision making.

C. Allocating Service Department Costs

Up to now, we have discussed allocating a single common cost to multiple users (either divisions or products). For example, Chapter 7 describes allocating personnel department costs and corporate-level costs to divisions. We now examine a more realistic situation in which a number of service departments exist whose costs are allocated to several operating divisions. Figure 8–1 illustrates the general case of N service departments and M operating divisions. In a manufacturing plant, the service departments consist of purchasing, janitorial, security, maintenance, information management, engineering, and so forth. The operating divisions might be separate product lines or manufacturing functions such as parts manufacturing and assembly lines. In order to compute the manufacturing cost of the final products for inventory valuation, the cost of the service departments must be allocated to the operating divisions. The service departments are like buckets of water that must be emptied into the operating divisions. The arrows

FIGURE 8–1

N service departments costs allocated to M operating divisions

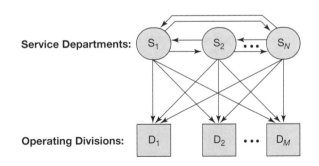

Service Departments: S_1 S_2 ... S_N

Operating Divisions: D_1 D_2 ... D_M

[1] See S Sunder, *Theory of Accounting and Control* (Cincinnati, OH: South-Western Publishing, 1997), pp. 55–56; and R Ball, S Keating, and J Zimmerman, "Historical Cost as a Commitment Device," *Maandblad voor Accountancy en Bedriifs-economie* (Netherlands), November 2000.

TABLE 8–1   **Capacity of Service Departments Used**

	Telecommunications	IT	Cars	Trucks	Total
Telecommunications	10%	20%	40%	30%	100%
IT	25	15	35	25	100

indicate the direction of the service flows. Complicating the allocation is the reciprocal use of services among the service departments. Service department S_1 not only provides service to operating divisions $D_1, D_2, \ldots D_M$, but it also provides service to the other service departments $S_2, S_3, \ldots, S_N$. For example, information technology provides data processing service to purchasing, while purchasing is involved in buying computer hardware and software for information technology.

To illustrate the allocation of service department costs, consider just two service departments (telecommunications and information technology, IT) and two operating divisions (Cars and Trucks). Table 8–1 contains the percentage of each service department's capacity consumed by the various users.

Telecommunications consumes 10 percent of its own capacity internally and IT consumes 15 percent of its capacity internally. Also, each service department uses the other service department. The goal is to assign the costs of the service departments (telecommunications and IT) to the operating divisions (Cars and Trucks). Cars and Trucks make the final products, and their cost should include the telecommunications and IT costs.

The following total costs of the two service departments are to be allocated to Cars and Trucks:

Telecommunications	$2 million
IT	6 million
Total costs	$8 million

The $2 million and $6 million costs are out-of-pocket costs incurred by the two departments and do not contain any costs allocated from the other service department.

There are several ways to allocate service department costs to the operating divisions: direct allocation, step-down allocation, and reciprocal allocation. These three methods and their advantages and disadvantages are discussed next.

1. Direct Allocation Method

Figure 8–2 illustrates the direct allocation of service department costs. Direct allocation ignores each service department's use of the other service departments. The allocation of S_1 is based only on the operating divisions' utilization of S_1. The fact that $S_2, S_3, \ldots, S_N$ also use S_1 is ignored. This greatly simplifies the allocation calculations, although we will see that inaccurate transfer prices for the services can result.

The divisional utilization rates in Table 8–1 are used to allocate service department costs. That is, the Cars division uses 40 percent of telecommunications and the Trucks division uses 30 percent. Together they use 70 percent. If 40 percent and 30 percent are used to allocate telecommunication's $2 million in costs, only

FIGURE 8–2
Direct allocation method

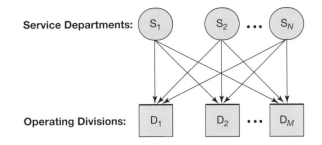

Service Departments: S_1 S_2 ... S_N

Operating Divisions: D_1 D_2 ... D_M

TABLE 8–2 **Service Department Percentages Used by Cars and Trucks**
($ in millions)

	Cars	Trucks	Total Allocated	Total Cost Incurred	Total Unallocated
Telecommunications	$0.8	$0.6	$1.4	$2.0	$0.6
	(40% × $2)	(30% × $2)			
IT	$2.1	$1.5	$3.6	$6.0	$2.4
	(35% × $6)	(25% × $6)			
Total			$5.0	$8.0	$3.0

$1.4 million of the total $2 million will be allocated to Cars and Trucks. The other $0.6 million remains unassigned. These results are shown in Table 8–2.

Allocating service department costs based on the divisions' actual use of each service department results in some of the service departments' costs remaining un-allocated: $5 million of service department costs are to be allocated and $3 million remain unassigned. If all service department costs are to be allocated to Cars and Trucks, then each division's percentage of the total used by the divisions is the allocation rate. That is, the percentages are recomputed so that the Cars and Trucks divisions' shares sum to one. This method is termed **direct allocation** because the service department costs are allocated directly to the operating divisions rather than to the other service departments first and then to the operating divisions. The direct allocations are in Table 8–3.

Since the revised shares in the first part of Table 8–3 sum to one, all the costs in telecommunications and IT are allocated to the two operating divisions and no costs remain unallocated. The allocated service department costs using these shares are in the bottom half of Table 8–3. Notice that the total cost of telecommunications and IT, $8 million, is now allocated to Cars and Trucks. However, this direct allocation method presents a problem in that the opportunity cost per unit of service is likely wrong. While we do not know the correct opportunity cost, we do know that the direct allocation method excludes the service departments' use of other service departments and therefore incorrectly states the opportunity cost of each service department.

Suppose that the Cars division increases its use of IT. This causes IT costs to rise. Since IT uses telecommunications, telecommunications' costs also rise when the Cars division uses more IT. But the direct allocation method does not charge IT for any telecommunications costs. Because each service department uses the

TABLE 8–3   Direct Allocation Method ($ in Millions)

	Cars	Trucks	Total
Revised Shares, Direct Allocation Method			
Telecommunications	$40/(40 + 30) = 4/7$	$30/(40 + 30) = 3/7$	100%
IT	$35/(35 + 25) = 7/12$	$25/(35 + 25) = 5/12$	100%
Allocated Costs, Direct Allocation Method			
Telecommunications	$4/7 \times \$2 = \$1.143$	$3/7 \times \$2 = \$0.857$	$2
IT	$7/12 \times \$6 = \$3.500$	$5/12 \times \$6 = \$2.500$	$6
Total	$4.643	$3.357	$8

other service department and the direct allocation method ignores these interactions, the cost allocated (i.e., the transfer price) is not the opportunity cost of the service department.

Another problem with the direct allocation method is that each service department will overuse the other service departments. Since each service department's costs are allocated only to the manufacturing departments, the other service departments view that service department as free. They are not charged for their use of other service departments and therefore have no monetary incentive to limit their use. Accordingly, nonfinancial methods must be employed to control the excessive use of each service department by the other service departments.

2. Step-Down Allocation Method

The **step-down method** partially overcomes the problems with direct allocations. The procedure begins by choosing a service department and allocating all of its costs to the remaining service departments and operating divisions. Then, a second service department is chosen and all of its costs (including its share of the allocated costs from the first service department) are allocated to the remaining service departments and operating divisions. This process continues until all service department costs are allocated. In this way, all service department costs cascade down through the service organizations and eventually are allocated to the operating divisions.

Figure 8–3 illustrates the step-down method. Service department S_1 is chosen first and all of its costs are allocated to $S_2, S_3, \ldots, S_N$ and $D_1, D_2, \ldots, D_M$. The solid arrows indicate the first step of the process. Then all of S_2's costs plus S_2's share of S_1's costs are allocated to $S_3, S_4, \ldots, S_N$ and $D_1, D_2, \ldots, D_M$. The dashed arrows indicate the allocation of S_2's costs. This continues until only service department S_N remains. All of its costs plus all of the costs allocated to S_N from the other service departments are allocated to the operating divisions as represented by the dotted arrows. Notice that half of the flows among service departments are captured by the step-down method. For example, S_2's use of S_1 is captured, although S_1's use of S_2 is not.

In our numerical example, the first service department to be allocated is telecommunications. The allocation shares are in the top half of Table 8–4, and the cost allocations are computed in the bottom half of the table. Telecommunications' costs are allocated to IT, Cars, and Trucks in the first step. Two-ninths of telecommunications are allocated to IT, 4/9 to Cars, and the remaining 1/3 to Trucks. In the first row of the bottom half of Table 8–4, these shares are used to

FIGURE 8–3

Step-down allocation method

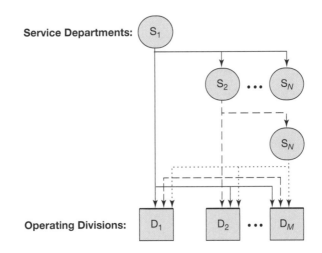

Service Departments: S_1

S_2 ... S_N

S_N

Operating Divisions: D_1 D_2 ... D_M

allocate telecommunications' costs. IT receives $444,000, the Cars division receives $889,000, and the Trucks division receives $667,000. All $2 million of the telecommunications costs are allocated.

In the second step, IT costs plus data processing's share of the telecommunications costs are allocated to Cars and Trucks. Total IT costs to be allocated include IT's direct costs of $6 million plus the $444,000 allocated in the first step. The total $6,444,000 is allocated to Cars ($7/12$) and Trucks ($5/12$).

Notice that all $8 million of the service department costs are allocated (far right column, last row of Table 8–4). The Cars division receives $4.648 million and the Trucks division receives $3.352 million. By chance, the costs allocated to each division, Cars and Trucks, are about the same using either the direct method or the step-down method.

The question arises as to the sequence of departments chosen in the step-down method. Had IT been chosen as the first service department in the sequence, the allocations in Table 8–5 would have been the result. Again, the step-down method starting with the IT department results in a cost allocation pattern to the operating divisions that is about the same as the one produced by the direct allocation method.

3. Service Department Costs and Transfer Pricing of Direct and Step-Down Methods

The costs allocated to Cars and Trucks differ by only $27,000 depending on whether telecommunications (Table 8–4) or IT (Table 8–5) is chosen first. In Table 8–4, the Cars division is allocated $4.648 million and in Table 8–5 the allocation is $4.621 million. The difference of $27,000 is less than 1 percent of the total costs allocated. Therefore, it would appear inconsequential as to whether telecommunications or IT is chosen over the direct allocation method. However, very different incentives result depending on which method is used. Allocated costs represent transfer prices. As we saw in Chapter 5, transfer pricing affects the quantity of the internal service demanded. If too high a transfer price is set, a death spiral can result when there are fixed costs included in the allocation.

To illustrate the effect of the cost allocation method on transfer prices, we expand the telecommunications and IT example. Suppose the allocation base in telecommunications is the number of telephones in each department and in IT the allocation base is the number of computer lines printed. Transfer prices are to be established for telephones and lines printed. Allocated costs will be used

TABLE 8-4 Step-Down Allocation Method—Telecommunications First ($ in Millions)

	Information Technology	Cars	Trucks	Total
Telecommunications	20/(20 + 40 + 30) = 2/9	40/90 = 4/9	30/90 = 1/3	100%
IT	—	35/60 = 7/12	25/60 = 5/12	100%

Using these shares, the allocated costs are as follows:

	Costs to Be Allocated	Information Technology	Cars	Trucks	Total Allocated to Cars and Trucks
Telecommunications	$2	2/9 × $2 = $0.444	4/9 × $2 = $0.889	1/3 × $2 = $0.667	$1.556
IT	$6 + $0.444	—	7/12 × $6.444 = $3.759	5/12 × $6.444 = $2.685	6.444
			$4.648	$3.352	$8.000

TABLE 8-5 Step-Down Allocation Method—Information Technology First ($ in Millions)

	Telecommunications	Cars	Trucks	Total
IT	25/(25 + 35 + 25) = 5/17	35/85 = 7/17	25/85 = 5/17	100%
Telecommunications	—	4/7	3/7	100%

Using these revised shares, the allocated costs are:

	Costs to Be Allocated	Telecommunications	Cars	Trucks	Total Allocated to Cars and Trucks
IT	$6	5/17 × $6 = $1.765	7/17 × $6 = $2.470	5/17 × $6 = $1.765	$4.235
Telecommunications	$2 + $1.765	—	4/7 × $3.765 = $2.151	3/7 × $3.765 = $1.614	3.765
			$4.621	$3.379	$8.000

Group Health

Group Health Cooperative of Puget Sound (GHC) is a Seattle-based HMO with 480,000 members. Its cost system consists of 70 percent of total delivery system costs being direct patient care department costs (such as radiology, dialysis, laboratory, inpatient departments) and 30 percent being overhead costs (administration departments). These overhead costs are allocated to the patient care departments using the step-down allocation method involving 26 layers, 180 actual step-down allocations, and 500 services delivery departments. The order of allocation was established so that departments receiving the most services absorb the most costs. These step-down costs are used in computing the cost of a unit of service in a patient care department (such as a dialysis treatment). The cost per unit of service for each department is the full cost (all allocated costs plus the direct costs in the patient care department) divided by the units of service for that department.

SOURCE: J Lee and P Nefcy, "The Anatomy of an Effective HMO Cost Management System," *Management Accounting* (January 1997), pp. 49–53.

to compute the transfer prices. The number of phones and lines printed are as follows:

	Allocation Base
Telecommunications	3,000 telephones
IT	12 million lines printed per year

The cost per phone will vary depending on the allocation method chosen. Part A of Table 8–6 computes the number of phones in each department, which is used in setting the allocated cost per phone. The Cars division has 40 percent of all telephones, or 1,200 phones. The Trucks division has 30 percent of all telephones, or 900 phones. Under direct allocation, only the phones in Cars and Trucks are used to allocate telecommunications costs. Hence, the allocation base is 2,100 phones. Under the step-down allocation with telecommunications chosen first, IT receives a charge for its phones. Thus, the number of phones used to allocate telecommunications costs rises to include the 600 phones in IT. On the other hand, if IT is chosen first in the step-down method, the number of phones in the allocation base is still 2,100 (those in Cars and Trucks), because the IT costs have already been allocated.

Part B of Table 8–6 reports the allocated cost per phone. The first line in part B is telecommunications costs divided by the total number of phones used to allocate costs (from part A). Notice that in the right column of part B, telecommunications costs are $3.765 million, the sum of the $2 million of telecommunications costs and the $1.765 million allocated to telecommunications when IT is allocated first (see Table 8–5). The last row reports the same cost allocations as in Tables 8–3, 8–4, and 8–5. For example, under the direct allocation method, the Cars division has 1,200 phones and will be charged $1.143 million. This is exactly the same charge as computed in Table 8–3. Likewise, the $0.889 million and $2.151 million in the last two columns correspond to the allocations computed in Tables 8–4 and 8–5, respectively.

TABLE 8–6 Allocated Cost per Phone

	Direct Allocation		Step-Down Allocation			
			Telecommunications Chosen First		Information Technology Chosen First	
A. Number of Phones						
Number of phones:						
Telecommunications	—		—		—	
IT	—		20% × 3,000 =	600	—	
Cars	40% × 3,000 =	1,200	40% × 3,000 =	1,200	40% × 3,000 =	1,200
Trucks	30% × 3,000 =	900	30% × 3,000 =	900	30% × 3,000 =	900
Phones used to allocate costs		2,100		2,700		2,100
B. Cost per Phone						
Cost per phone*	$2M/2,100 =	$ 952	$2M/2,700 =	$ 741	$3.765M/2,100 =	$1,793
Number of phones in Cars		1,200		1,200		1,200
Telecommunications charged to Cars		$1.143		$0.889		$2.151

*M denotes millions.

The first row in Part B of Table 8–6 also shows the computation of the transfer price, or cost allocated per telephone, under the three allocation methods. The cost per phone varies from $741 to $1,793 depending on which allocation scheme is used. The high cost per phone of $1,793 in the right column occurs because some of the $6 million of IT costs is allocated to telecommunications before the cost per phone is calculated. The IT costs allocated to telecommunications increase telecommunications' costs and, ultimately, the allocated cost per phone.

Because the cost per phone (which represents the transfer price) varies depending on which allocation method is used, the cost allocation scheme affects the decision of each department to add phones. The sequence of service departments in the step-down method can affect decision making because the last service department in the sequence will have a larger cost per unit of service. Remember that cost allocations are effectively internal tax schemes. How the taxes are applied will affect the "price" decision makers face in deciding to add or delete phones.

The same conclusions hold for the data processing department. The equivalent computations for the IT department, including the cost per line printed across the various allocation methods, are in Table 8–7. Again, note the wide variation in cost per line printed. The cost varies from $0.588 per line under the step-down method with IT chosen first to $0.895 under the step-down method with telecommunications chosen first. Also, note that the total charged to Cars (the last line) agrees with the previous calculations in Tables 8–3, 8–4, and 8–5.

We saw earlier that the various methods of allocating service department costs result in a difference of less than 1 percent of the total costs. However, these same methods can cause the cost-based transfer prices to vary by over 140 percent for telephones ([$1,793 ÷ $741] ÷ $741) and over 50 percent for lines printed

TABLE 8–7   Allocated Cost per Computer Line Printed

	Direct Allocation	Step-Down Allocation	
		Telecommunications Chosen First	*Information Technology Chosen First*
A. Number of Lines (in Millions)			
Number of lines printed:			
Telecommunications	—	—	25% × 12 = 3.0
IT	—	—	—
Cars	35% × 12 = 4.2	35% × 12 = 4.2	35% × 12 = 4.2
Trucks	25% × 12 = 3.0	25% × 12 = 3.0	25% × 12 = 3.0
Total lines printed	7.2	7.2	10.2
B. Cost per Line Printed (in Millions except Cost per Line Printed)			
Cost per line printed	$6/7.2 = $0.833	$6.44/7.2 = $0.895	$6/10.2 = $0.588
Number of lines printed in Cars	4.2	4.2	4.2
IT charged to Cars	$3.5	$3.759	$2.470

([$0.895 ÷ $0.588] ÷ $0.588). Why the discrepancy? Refer back to Table 8–1. In this example, the Cars division uses roughly equal fractions of the two service departments (57 percent and 58 percent), and the Trucks division uses roughly equal fractions of the service departments (43 percent and 42 percent). Because these fractions are roughly the same in both departments, the total costs allocated to the divisions vary little across the various methods. However, the transfer prices per phone and line printed vary dramatically. In general, the allocation methods can yield substantial differences in amounts allocated. The numbers chosen for this example illustrate that transfer prices can vary a great deal even when the cost allocation methods have little effect on the total amounts allocated.

The large variation in the cost-based transfer prices arises because the transfer prices in this setting are ratios. The numerator of the ratio is the sum of the department's direct costs and any costs allocated to the service department. The denominator of the ratio is the number of units in the remaining allocation base (number of phones or lines printed). The first service department in the step-down sequence has no allocated costs in its numerator and a large number of users (and hence a large denominator). If this service department gets shifted from the first to the last in the sequence, its cost-based transfer price rises for two reasons. First, the ratio's numerator goes up by all of the other service department costs now being allocated to it. Second, its denominator goes down because the only users of its services that are included in the allocation base are the operating units. The other service departments are excluded from the denominator. Thus, the ratio changes a lot because the numerator goes up while the denominator goes down. For example, refer to the cost per phone in Table 8–6. With telecommunications first in the step-down sequence, the transfer price is $2M/2,700 = $741. When it is last in the sequence, the cost per phone is $3.765M/2,100 = $1,793. Notice that both the numerator *and* the denominator change as telecommunications is shifted from first to last in the sequence.

One criticism of the step-down method is that the sequence used is arbitrary and large differences can result in the cost per unit of service using different sequences. Also, the step-down method ignores the fact that although departments earlier in the sequence use service departments later in the sequence, earlier departments are not allocated these costs.

The death spiral, described in section A, can be a significant problem with step-down allocations if the service departments contain significant amounts of fixed costs. If transfer prices are established for these service department costs, then users have incentives to use less of the high-cost service departments. (The high-cost departments are those last in the step-down chain.) As usage falls, total costs do not fall proportionately because of the fixed costs. This causes the costs allocated to the remaining users to rise further, and these users will seek to replace the inside service with outside vendors that offer lower costs.

4. Reciprocal Allocation Method

Under the step-down method, the transfer price of phones and printed lines can vary dramatically depending on the order selected for allocating the service departments' costs. The third allocation method, the **reciprocal allocation method**, is the most precise way to allocate service department costs when each service department uses other service departments. It captures all the service flows depicted in Figure 8–1. Under the reciprocal allocation method, a system of linear equations is constructed, one for each service department. Each equation contains the use of that department by all other service departments. If there are 20 service departments providing services to at least some of the other departments, there will be 20 equations with 20 unknowns. This system of equations is then solved to derive the cost shares for each operating department and the cost per unit of output in each service department. The appendix to this chapter illustrates the computations involved in the reciprocal method.

As demonstrated in the appendix, the reciprocal allocation method produces an allocated cost per phone of $1,492 and an allocated cost per line printed of $0.676. The following table compares these allocated costs with those of the direct and step-down allocation methods.

	Charge per Phone	Charge per Line Printed
Direct method	$ 952	$0.833
Step-down:		
Telecommunications first	$ 741	$0.895
IT first	$1,793	$0.588
Reciprocal method	$1,492	$0.676

The reciprocal allocation method produces neither the highest nor the lowest unit cost. By incorporating one service department's use of another service department, it avoids the distortions in unit allocated costs observed in the step-down method.

The cost per phone of $1,492 and the cost per line printed of $0.676 represent the opportunity cost of adding one more phone or printing one more line assuming all the costs being allocated are variable. The phone charge reflects the fact that the additional phone uses some additional telecommunications and IT resources. Likewise, the printed line charge reflects the fact that one more line uses some additional IT and telecommunications resources. Therefore, the reciprocal method is more accurate in assessing the opportunity cost of service departments than either the direct or step-down allocations, assuming all service department costs are variable.

The reciprocal method produces a transfer price that can be compared with an outside price for the service. If the outside bid is less than the internal price, it should be accepted. This assumes that the inside costs of service (the $2 million and $6 million cost of telecommunications and IT, respectively) represent all variable costs. If any of these costs contain fixed costs and there is excess capacity, then the reciprocal method does not produce opportunity cost transfer prices.

In many service departments, fixed and variable costs are not distinguished. Total costs are accumulated and allocated to the operating divisions. Combining fixed costs with variable costs in the service departments can compromise the reciprocal method's ability to produce opportunity cost transfer prices. To take full advantage of the reciprocal method's ability to estimate opportunity cost transfer prices, only the variable costs in each service department should be allocated using the system of equations. The fixed costs in each service department are either not allocated or allocated based on each operating division's planned use of the service department's capacity.

Another critical assumption underlying the reciprocal allocation method, and all other methods as well, is that the utilization rates do not change with increases or decreases in scale. That is, if the firm doubles in size, will IT continue to utilize 20 percent of telecommunications? (The assumption is that the system of linear equations is really linear.) If this assumption is violated, then no method based on past utilization rates can yield accurate forecasts of opportunity cost.

While the reciprocal allocation method has certain theoretical advantages, it is not widely used. Why? There is no good answer, but some conjectures are offered. First, calculating reciprocal allocations requires substantial computing power, especially when there are numerous service departments. Until recently, such large problems could only be solved with very large computers. Now, most spreadsheet programs can easily handle them. Second, few accountants were trained in solving systems of equations or how to formulate the problem. This conjecture seems implausible since many new innovations, such as derivative securities, suggest that financial managers have the ability to quickly adopt new analytic procedures when it is in their interest to do so. Third, it is difficult (and hence costly) to intuitively explain the reciprocal method to nonfinancial managers in the firm. The reciprocal method appears as a "black box," and the managers being asked to bear the allocated costs do not fully understand how the charges were computed. This conjecture also seems implausible, especially if the benefits of the reciprocal method outweigh the costs. It also relies on the questionable assumption that certain groups are stupid. One would think that financial managers would be able to devise suitable tutorials to explain the calculations. Fourth, the dysfunctional aspects of the step-down method can be minimized by ordering the departments in the step-down sequence. That is, by judiciously choosing the order, the step-down method produces allocated costs that are very similar to those produced by the reciprocal method in terms of the ultimate decisions managers make using the allocated costs. While simple textbook examples can be constructed showing large deviations in allocated costs produced by the step-down and reciprocal methods—and therefore, the potential for dysfunctional decision making—we have little evidence such differences exist in practice.

A final conjecture as to why reciprocal allocations are rarely used, and one consistent with other observed managerial accounting choices, is that the primary role of cost allocations is not decision making. If the primary function were decision making, then, since opportunity costs are the basis for decision making (and the reciprocal method approximates opportunity costs better than the other methods), we should observe fairly frequent use of the reciprocal method. The fact that we observe infrequent use of the reciprocal method suggests that internal accounting is not used for decision making, but rather for some other purpose such as decision control, financial reporting, or taxes. For example, using the step-down method affords managers considerable discretion in the resulting allocated costs because they can change the order of the departments and therefore manipulate the portion of the total cost allocated to each department. This discretion can be useful for strategic reasons, for financial reporting, or to minimize taxes.

5. Recap

There are three reasons to allocate service department costs (independent of which allocation method is chosen):

1. By charging a positive "price," users reduce their consumption from what it would be under a zero price (no cost allocations). Pricing the internal service helps allocate a scarce resource. At a zero price, demand usually exceeds supply. In the absence of a price mechanism to allocate department services, senior management will be confronted with requests to increase the amount of service via larger budgets and must devise nonprice priority schemes to manage the demand for service.

2. By allocating service department costs, senior management receives information about the total demand for the service at the allocated cost. This helps management to determine the optimum scale of the service department. For example, if the users are willing to pay a transfer price that recovers the cost of providing the service, then the service department is providing benefits to the users in excess of its costs.

3. By comparing the internal allocated cost with the outside external price of comparable services, senior management can assess the service department's operating efficiency. Gross inefficiencies are identified when the allocated cost per unit of service exceeds the external price.

Concept Questions		
	Q8–1	What is the death spiral and how is it prevented?
	Q8–2	What are some reasons to allocate service department costs, independent of which allocation method is chosen?
	Q8–3	What is step-down allocation? What are some criticisms of this allocation method?
	Q8–4	How do the direct allocation and step-down methods differ?
	Q8–5	How does the cost per unit of service vary over the sequence of service departments when the step-down method is used?

D. Joint Costs

A special case of cost allocations deals with allocating joint costs. A **joint cost** is incurred to produce two or more outputs from the same input. Joint products are produced from a single input. For example, hamburger and liver are joint products from a single joint input, the cow. In a mining operation, gold and silver are joint products from the joint input, ore. Usually, but not always, joint products are produced in fixed proportions, meaning that more gold cannot be produced if less silver is produced.

Firms convert one set of resources into another. Production is a process of assembling various factor inputs into a new combination. Many costs are thus common with other costs. Service department costs discussed in Section C are **common costs** of the various products manufactured. The fire insurance premium on the factory building used to manufacture various products in the plant is a common (and hence) inseparable cost of all the products manufactured in the building. Notice that joint costs and common costs are very similar in definition. The major distinction between the two is that common costs are incurred in both assembly and disassembly processes, but joint costs are incurred only in disassembly processes. In an assembly process, many inputs are assembled into a few final outputs. For example, tires, windows, a motor, seats, and more are assembled to produce an automobile. In a disassembly process, a few inputs are disassembled into many final products. For example, a barrel of crude oil is disassembled into gasoline, motor oil, jet fuel, and asphalt. Figure 8–4 illustrates the difference between an assembly and a disassembly process.

There are many ways to allocate joint costs to joint products. For example, in an oil refinery, the cost of each barrel of crude oil can be allocated to the joint products based on physical weight, physical volume, relative sales value, or net realizable value. Table 8–8 illustrates these various methods using a barrel of oil that is split into three products: gasoline, motor oil, and jet fuel. Part A provides the data used to allocate the $20 cost per barrel. Part B applies the percentages to allocate the barrel's $20 cost. Notice the wide variation in allocated costs across the various methods. The allocated cost of gasoline varies from $6 to $16. Jet fuel varies from $2 to $10.

FIGURE 8–4

Assembly and disassembly processes

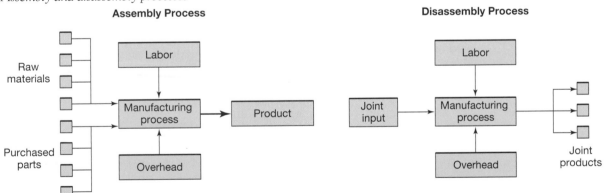

TABLE 8–8   Relative Weight, Physical Volume, Relative Sales Value, and Net Realizable Value

	Weight (%)	Volume (%)	Revenue of final product (%)	Net Realizable Value Costs	NRV*	(%)
A. Data						
Gasoline	60 lbs. (30%)	40 gals. (80%)	$20 (40%)	$15	$5	50%
Motor oil	40 lbs.(20%)	5 gals. (10%)	$20 (40%)	17	3	30
Jet fuel	100 lbs. (50%)	5 gals. (10%)	$10 (20%)	8	2	20
B. Allocated Joint Cost of $20 Barrel of Oil						
Gasoline	$ 6	$16	$ 8		$10	
Motor oil	4	2	8		6	
Jet fuel	10	2	4		4	
	$20	$20	$20		$20	

*NRV (net realizable value) = Revenue of final product − Costs. Costs are the additional costs required to produce the final product.

Physical measures such as weight and volume are convenient allocation bases because they are easily observed. If selling prices are used (relative sales value method), they must be recorded; frequent changes in sales prices introduce variability into the allocated costs. The **net realizable value** method of allocating joint costs uses as the allocation base the difference between sales revenue and the additional costs (beyond the joint costs) required to process the product from the point at which the joint products are split off until they are sold. Net realizable value is described more fully below. When analyzing situations involving joint costs, the fundamental point to remember is that *any joint cost allocated to final products is meaningless for assessing product line profitability.* More on this next.

1. Chickens

To illustrate the analysis of joint products, consider a chicken processor who buys live chickens and disassembles them into fillets, wings, and drumsticks. Suppose live chickens cost $1.60 each. The variable cost to process the live chicken into parts is $0.40 per chicken. The *joint cost* per chicken is then $2. Once the parts are obtained, separate processing is necessary to obtain marketable fillets, drumsticks, and wings. Each separate part must be cleaned, inspected, and packaged, at a cost of $0.80 for fillets, $0.16 for wings, and $0.04 for drumsticks. The **split-off point** is the point in processing at which all joint costs have been incurred. These data and selling prices are displayed in Table 8–9 along with the joint cost allocations based on weight.

Part A allocates the $2 joint cost to the chicken parts based on weight. Part B adds these allocated joint costs to the cost of further processing the chicken parts. The numbers in part B show that a loss of $0.11 per chicken is incurred from further processing of the wings. Based on this report, management's inclination is to stop processing the wings because they appear to be losing money.

Suppose that wings are no longer processed and sold. Assume that the unprocessed wings are hauled away for free and that eliminating wings has no effect on the revenue for fillets and drumsticks. Product line profitability after allocating the joint costs among the remaining parts—fillets and drumsticks—is recalculated in Table 8–10.

TABLE 8–9   Using Weight to Allocate Chicken Costs for Product Line Profitability of Fillets, Drumsticks, and Wings

	Total	Fillets	Drumsticks	Wings
A. Cost Allocation Based on Weight				
Weight	32 oz.	16 oz.	12 oz.	4 oz.
Percentage of weight	100%	50%	37.5%	12.5%
Allocated cost	$2.00	$1.00	$0.75	$0.25
B. Product Line Profitability, Including Joint Costs				
Sales	$3.50	$2.40	$0.80	$0.30
Costs beyond split-off point	(1.00)	(0.80)	(0.04)	(0.16)
Joint costs (from above)	(2.00)	(1.00)	(0.75)	(0.25)
Profit (loss) per chicken	$0.50	$0.60	$0.01	$(0.11)

TABLE 8–10   Using Weight to Allocate Chicken Costs for Product Line Profitability of Fillets and Drumsticks (Wings are Dropped)

	Total	Fillets	Drumsticks
A. Cost Allocation Based on Weight			
Weight	28 oz.	16 oz.	12 oz.
Percentage of weight	100%	57.14%	42.86%
Allocated cost	$2.00	$1.14	$0.86
B. Product Line Profitability, Including Joint Costs			
Sales	$3.20	$2.40	$ 0.80
Costs beyond split-off point	(0.84)	(0.80)	(0.04)
Joint costs (from above)	(2.00)	(1.14)	(0.86)
Profit (loss) per chicken	$0.36	$0.46	$(0.10)

Total profits have fallen from $0.50 per chicken to $0.36 per chicken, and we are now losing $0.10 on drumsticks. If we believed the analysis in Table 8–9 and eliminated the wings, we must also eliminate the drumsticks because of the analysis in Table 8–10. Table 8–11 presents the profit statement per chicken if we eliminate the drumsticks along with the wings.

Now we are losing $0.40 per chicken. (But at least we do not have to worry about allocating joint costs to joint products, as we have dropped all but one of the joint products.)

What is happening? Recall that any joint cost allocated to final products is meaningless for assessing product line profitability. The numbers in Tables 8–9 and 8–10 are meaningless for decision making. In fact, the allocated costs are causing a death spiral similar to that described in section A. The $2 joint cost of the chicken is fixed (sunk) with respect to further processing of the wings. If we no longer process and sell wings, we do not gain an additional $0.11 per chicken, as indicated by the reported loss in Table 8–9. It does not cost us $0.25 to get the wings in the first place because the wings are *free* with each chicken. It costs us

TABLE 8–11   Analysis of Processing Fillets Only

Sales	$ 2.40
Costs beyond split-off point	(0.80)
Joint costs	(2.00)
Profit (loss) per chicken	$(0.40)

FIGURE 8–5

Joint costs, costs beyond split-off, and selling prices

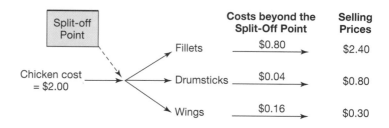

only the additional $0.16 per chicken incurred beyond the split-off point to get the wings.

2. Net Realizable Value

What is the correct analysis? Apply the concept of opportunity costs from Chapter 2. What is the benefit forgone if wings are not processed further? The answer is the revenues of $0.30 less the costs incurred of further processing wings of $0.16, or $0.14. The allocated joint costs of the wings have already been incurred when the chicken is purchased and processed to the split-off point. The *only* benefit of further processing is the revenues less costs incurred to process further. The joint cost of the chicken is sunk at the time of the decision to process the wings.

Figure 8–5 illustrates the relation among joint costs, joint products, costs beyond the split-off point, and selling prices. Using the data from Table 8–9, Figure 8–5 portrays the joint products (fillets, drumsticks, and wings) that result from the joint input (the chicken). Once the joint products emerge after the split-off point, further costs are incurred before they can be sold. The costs beyond the split-off point are separable from the other joint product costs and will be incurred only if the particular joint product is processed further.

Relying on the graphic intuition in Figure 8–5, Table 8–12 presents the analysis using the net realizable value (NRV) allocation method. The relative profitability of each joint product depends only on its selling price less its costs beyond the split-off point. The difference between selling price and costs beyond the split-off point is called *net realizable value* and is analogous to contribution margin. If a particular joint product has negative net realizable value, it should not be processed further. However, if the cost of disposing of it is greater than its negative NRV, further processing is the least costly alternative.

Table 8–12 shows that all three chicken parts are yielding incremental revenues in excess of their opportunity cost. For example, we can sell the wings for $0.30, yet the incremental cost (the cost of further processing) is only $0.16. Thus, the net realizable value of processing the wings is $0.14. Allocating joint costs using net realizable value as the allocation base does not distort product line profitability. In the footnote that accompanies Table 8–12, we see that fillets

TABLE 8–12   Profits from Further Processing (Allocating Joint Costs Using Net Realizable Value)

	Total	Fillets	Drumsticks	Wings
Sales	$3.50	$2.40	$0.80	$0.30
Costs beyond split-off point	(1.00)	(0.80)	(0.04)	(0.16)
Net realizable value from further processing	$2.50	$1.60	$0.76	$0.14
Less: Joint costs per chicken[*]	(2.00)	(1.28)	(0.61)	(0.11)
Profits	$0.50	$0.32	$0.15	$0.03

[*]Allocated based on net realizable value, as follows:

Net realizable value	$2.50	$1.60	$0.76	$0.14
Percentage of net realizable value	100%	64%	30.4%	5.6%
Joint cost	$2.00	$1.28	$0.61	$0.11

generate 64 percent of net realizable value and receive 64 percent of the joint costs. Wings generate only 5.6 percent of net realizable value and receive only 5.6 percent of the joint costs. Therefore, using net realizable value as the allocation base does not cause one product to bear a disproportionately larger percentage of joint costs than it generates in NRV.

After joint costs are allocated to the parts, wings show a "profit" of $0.03 per chicken. However, it is incorrect to say, "Wings generate $0.03 of profit per chicken." The correct statement is "Wings generate $0.14 of net cash flow per chicken if processed further."

Net realizable value does not distort product line profits because joint costs are allocated based on ability to pay. Products with the greatest contribution margins beyond the split-off point bear more of the joint cost. On the other hand, NRV allocation does not provide any additional information for decision making beyond whatever information is already contained in the net realizable value from further processing. That is, if a product is contributing positive cash flows beyond the split-off point, allocating joint costs to this product will not change the decision to process it further. Therefore, allocating joint costs using NRV is also irrelevant for product line profitability analysis. NRV allocations will not cause the wrong product line to be dropped, but they do not add anything for decision making beyond looking at the cash flows after the split-off point.

It is important to emphasize that when net realizable value is calculated, the costs beyond the split-off point must include only the direct costs associated with processing the joint product further. If no further processing is performed, then the firm should save all the costs beyond the split-off point. If costs beyond the split-off point contain any allocated fixed common costs, the decision to stop processing will not save the fixed common costs. For example, if costs beyond split-off contain allocated factory property taxes (because the further processing occupies shared factory space), the decision to stop further processing does not save these property taxes.

Often, a manufacturing process, besides producing joint products (fillets, drumsticks, and wings), also yields **by-products** (gizzards and feet). These are joint products that have small commercial value or are not the primary products of the

British Rail	After an analysis of profits by the various individual rail lines composing British Rail, management concluded that certain short trunk lines were unprofitable on a fully allocated cost basis. But after the unprofitable lines were closed, profits actually fell. Careful review of the facts revealed that labor was being charged to each rail line based on the amount of labor cost used on each line. But labor was a fixed, common cost. Labor union contracts prevented management from laying off employees when rail lines were closed. These employees were reassigned. Therefore, when lines were closed, revenues fell but the allocated common costs remained.

joint production process. Since management does not think of the by-products as being a managed part of the business, the sales revenue derived from them is subtracted from the joint costs. For example, suppose the by-products from each chicken (gizzard and feet) are sold for $0.07 and each chicken costs $1.67. Instead of treating the by-products as joint products and calculating a product line profit margin, management simply subtracts the $0.07 by-product revenue from the gross chicken cost of $1.67 to get the net chicken cost of $1.60. The net joint costs are then allocated to the joint products. This procedure allows management to focus on the major products being produced.

3. Decision Making and Control

Managers producing joint products must make two different, but interrelated, decisions: (1) which joint products to further process (and what prices to charge for them) and (2) given the answers in (1), whether to process any joint inputs (and how many). In step 1, managers decide whether to further process each joint product. A joint product should be further processed if its final sales price exceeds the additional processing cost plus its unprocessed sales value. Chicken wings should be processed further because their selling price of $0.30 exceeds the $0.16 additional processing cost (unprocessed wings have no value). Notice these decisions regarding further processing do not require any costs to be allocated.

In step 2, managers decide how many joint inputs (if any) to process. Here managers want to continue processing joint inputs (chickens) as long as the sum of the joint products' NRVs exceeds all the costs up to and including the split-off point. The analysis in step 1 determines the profit-maximizing mix of joint products. If the sum of the NRVs doesn't cover the cost of the joint input plus the cost of operating the split-off point, don't produce. If the price of chickens increases to $2.55, and the selling prices of the chicken parts remain the same, then the sum of the NRVs of $2.50 does not cover the cost of the chicken, and no chickens should be processed. Again, notice that cost allocations (even using NRV to allocate joint costs) play no role in making this decision.

Managers can make all the decisions regarding joint products without resorting to cost allocations. This suggests that joint cost allocations are not needed for decision making. Hence, given the pervasiveness of joint cost allocations, they must be serving other purposes such as inventory valuation for taxes and financial reporting or control.

Any joint cost allocation scheme other than net realizable value can lead to erroneous decisions regarding eliminating joint products. However, this does not mean that NRV is the best way of allocating joint costs. For the specific decision to eliminate a product, NRV is best because other allocation schemes distort the *incremental* profitability of the product or division. However, an allocation scheme other than NRV can be better for controlling agency problems. For example, NRV is a noninsulating allocation scheme in which each joint product's profitability depends on the other's profits (Chapter 7).

Consider the case of an oil refinery producing gasoline and jet fuel, sold by two separate profit centers. If refinery costs, including the cost of crude oil, are assigned to the two profit centers using NRV, the relative profitability of each profit center is not distorted. Suppose the airline industry is expanding and the price of jet fuel rises relative to gasoline. The jet fuel profit center's NRV increases, as does its share of the joint costs. Likewise, gasoline's share of the joint costs falls and the allocated joint cost per gallon of gasoline falls. With a lower cost per gallon of gasoline, the gasoline division might try to expand output by lowering price. But the opportunity cost of a gallon of gasoline is not lower; in fact, it is likely to be higher to the extent that the refining process allows some substitution between jet fuel and gasoline production. Allocating the joint refinery costs using a physical measure such as gallons or pounds insulates each division from price fluctuations in the other division. Net realizable value is better for product line profitability decisions but may not be best for other decisions such as pricing or control. Management usually must trade off decision making and control. A single cost allocation procedure is unlikely to be best for both.

The discussion of joint products highlights the problems of assessing product line profitability when the profits include allocated joint costs. Only NRV allocations do not distort product line profitability. The same cautions apply to assessing product line profits that contain allocated common costs. Companies can make major strategic decision errors if they focus on product line profits after joint or common costs are allocated using anything other than net realizable value.

Concept Questions		
	Q8–6	What are joint costs? How do they differ from common costs?
	Q8–7	Describe some methods for allocating joint costs.
	Q8–8	What are the advantages and disadvantages of the net realizable method of allocating joint costs?

E. Segment Reporting and Joint Benefits

Chapter 7 described insulating versus noninsulating allocations within the context of reporting the profitability of business segments—the modem and disk drive divisions that share a common factory. This section expands on some additional issues involved in segment reporting.

Again, consider the modem and disk drive divisions in the following financial statement. Some managers and accountants argue that each business segment report should be separated into those expenses that are controllable by the division and those expenses that are not controllable, but rather are allocated to the division. The following table illustrates the suggested format of a segment report.

	April	
	Modem Division	*Disk Drive Division*
Division revenues	$98,000	$103,000
Division controllable expenses	96,000	104,100
Controllable segment margin	$ 2,000	$ (1,100)
Allocated common costs	(700)	(300)
Net income	$ 1,300	$ (1,400)

In this statement the modem division is contributing $2,000 toward covering common costs whereas the disk drive division is losing $1,100 before any common costs are allocated to the segment. Proponents of separating controllable from noncontrollable segment expenses believe this format is more informative of segment performance. Since segments cannot control common costs, they should not be held responsible for them. If a segment is contributing a positive contribution toward the common costs, it should be retained. This is, again, another application of the controllability principle. It is similar in spirit to the argument that fixed costs should be ignored in setting transfer prices and that joint costs are irrelevant in assessing product profitability.

Unfortunately, simple rules of thumb like dropping segments with negative controllable segment margins can be wrong in some situations. Consider the following examples. Suppose a segment such as the modem division in the above table has a positive net income after all common cost allocations. Should it be retained? Not necessarily. The modem division could be producing very low-quality modems that are adversely affecting the demand for the disk drives. Or the modem division might be consuming so much of the attention of senior management that the other segments are suffering. In both of these cases, an apparently profitable segment based on its accounting statements should be dropped.

Now consider the example of a segment with a negative controllable segment margin such as the disk drive division. It appears this division should be dropped. Should it? Not necessarily. Suppose that the demand for disk drives and the demand for modems depend on each other because it is cheaper for customers to deal with one supplier of both disk drives and modems than two separate suppliers. Dropping either product adversely affects the demand for the other. The accounting segment report does not capture these interdependencies in demand.

In general, firms produce multiple products because there are synergies—in either production or demand. In Chapter 4 we argued that firms exist because they lower certain transactions costs below what it would cost to acquire equivalent goods or services in a series of market transactions. Firms have multiple segments because of synergies among segments. These synergies are "joint benefits" that are usually difficult to quantify, let alone allocate. Like joint costs, they cannot be allocated to segments in any meaningful way. Firms prepare segment reports as performance measures to help reduce agency costs. But to the extent there are large interdependencies among segments, these joint benefits make it very difficult to use the segment reports to decide which segments to drop without further analysis.

F. Summary

This chapter continues the cost allocation discussion begun in the previous chapter. Cost allocations can create a death spiral. The death spiral is a perverse problem that arises when (1) allocated costs contain fixed costs and (2) users reduce their demand for a service department in response to a high allocated cost. As usage falls, total costs do not fall proportionately because of the fixed costs. This causes the costs allocated to the remaining users to rise further, and the remaining users will seek to outsource the service to less expensive external vendors.

Two specific cost allocation situations are described: multiple service departments and joint costs. When the costs of several service departments are allocated to operating divisions, wide variations in transfer prices can result depending on how the service department costs are allocated and the order in which they are allocated if a step-down method is used. These variations in transfer price can then cause user departments to alter their consumption of service department resources.

Joint costs arise whenever a single joint input such as a barrel of oil is split into several joint products such as gasoline, motor oil, and jet fuel. Beware of all product line profitability studies that rely on allocated joint or common costs, unless these costs are allocated using net realizable value (revenues less the costs beyond the split-off point).

Chapters 7 and 8 introduce cost allocations and describe some general incentive issues arising from cost allocations. Cost allocations pervade almost all accounting topics, even financial accounting. For example, depreciation is a cost allocation. It involves allocating the asset's original cost over the time periods served by the asset. LIFO versus FIFO inventory valuation involves the allocation of the purchase prices for inventory over various time periods. Financial accounting typically involves the allocation of costs and revenues over various time periods, whereas managerial accounting typically involves allocating costs across products or divisions, usually within the same time period.

Chapters 9 through 13 expand the discussion begun in Chapters 7 and 8 by describing how costs are allocated to products. If a plant produces multiple products, the cost of each product must be computed for tax, inventory valuation, and decision management and control reasons. Chapters 9 through 13, based on the introductory material in Chapters 7 and 8, describe a number of complexities that arise in product costing within a manufacturing setting.

Appendix: Reciprocal Method for Allocating Service Department Costs

Section C of this chapter described various ways of allocating service department costs to operating divisions, including the direct allocation and step-down allocation methods. The reciprocal method was discussed, but its exact calculation was deferred to this appendix. To simplify the discussion, start by assuming that all costs in the service departments are variable.

When each service department uses the other service departments, the allocation of one service department's cost to another service department depends on the simultaneous utilization of each department. A simultaneous system of equations is needed to account for the reciprocal use among service departments. To illustrate the reciprocal method, the example of the telecommunications and information technology (IT) departments will be continued. Table 8–13 provides the computations of the reciprocal method.

TABLE 8–13   Reciprocal Method of Allocating Service Department Costs to Operating Divisions ($ in Millions)

	Service Departments		Operating Divisions		
	Telecommunications	Information Technology	Cars	Trucks	Total
Department providing service:					
Telecommunications	10%	20%	40%	30%	100%
IT	25%	15%	35%	25%	100%
Department costs before allocation of service costs	$ 2.000	$ 6.000			$ 8.000
Service department allocated costs:					
Telecommunications	$(4.475)*				$(4.475)
	$ 0.448	$ 0.895	$1.790	$1.343	$ 4.475
IT		$(8.112)*			$(8.112)
	$ 2.028	$ 1.217	$2.839	$2.028	$ 8.112
Total overhead allocated	$ 0.000	$ 0.000	$4.629	$3.371	$ 8.000
Overhead allocations bases:					
Allocated telecommunications costs	$ 0.448	$ 0.895	$1.790	$1.343	$ 4.475
÷ Number of phones	300	600	1,200	900	3,000
Cost per phone	$ 1,492	$ 1,492	$1,492	$1,492	$ 1,492
Allocated IT costs	$ 2.028	$ 1.217	$2.839	$2.028	$ 8.111
÷ Number of lines printed (millions)	3.0	1.8	4.2	3.0	12.0
Cost per line printed	$ 0.676	$ 0.676	$0.676	$0.676	$ 0.676

*Two simultaneous equations with two unknowns must be solved:

Let

T = Total cost to be assigned from telecommunications
I = Total cost to be assigned from information technology

T = Initial cost incurred + 0.10T + 0.25I

$T = \$2.0 + 0.10T + 0.25I$ (1)

I = Initial cost incurred + 0.20T + 0.15I

$I = \$6.0 + 0.20T + 0.15I$ (2)

Solve equations (1) and (2). Start with equation (1) and collect terms:

$0.9\,T = \$2.0 + 0.25\,I$

$T = \$2.0/.9 + (.25/.9)\,I$

$T = \$2.222 + 0.278I$ (3)

Now substitute the preceding equation into equation (2) and solve for I:

$I = \$6.0 + 0.20\,(\$2.222 + 0.278I) + 0.15I$

$I = \$6.0 + 0.444 + 0.056I + 0.15I$

$0.749\,I = \$6.444$

$I = \$8.112$

Substitute the value of $I = \$8.112$ into equation (3) and solve for T:

$T = \$2.222 + 0.278(\$8.112)$ (4)

$T = \$2.222 + \$2.253$

$T = \$4.475$

The reciprocal method operates in two steps. The first step focuses on the interactions among the service departments (ignoring the operating divisions) and develops a total charge for each service department. The second step takes the total charge and allocates it across the service departments and operating divisions. The first two lines in Table 8–13 repeat the utilization percentages by users reported in Table 8–1. These utilization percentages among the service departments are used to form a system of two equations with two unknowns (see the footnote to the table). The total cost, T, of operating the telecommunications department includes telecommunication's own cost ($2.0) plus a proportion of its own cost and IT's costs and is given by the following equation:

$$T = \text{Initial cost incurred} + 0.10T + 0.25I$$

The initial cost in the telecommunications department is $2 million, which allows this equation to be written as

$$T = \$2.0 + 0.10T + 0.25I$$

Likewise, the total IT cost assigned, I, is given by the following equation:

$$I = \$6.0 + 0.20T + 0.15I$$

We have two equations with two unknowns. Using some simple algebra outlined in Table 8–13, we can solve for the two unknowns:

$$T = \$4.475 \text{ million}$$

$$I = \$8.112 \text{ million}$$

The second step of the reciprocal method allocates these revised total costs to all the service departments and operating divisions using the utilization rates in Table 8–13. The resulting allocations are also shown in the table. Using these allocations, a charge per phone and cost per line printed are computed. Each department and each division pays the same per phone and line printed.

It is important to understand the relation between the initial cost of the service department and the total cost to be assigned using the reciprocal method. Telecommunications incurs costs of $2 million, yet $4.475 million is being allocated. The reason that more is being allocated than incurred is because some of the allocated costs are assigned to the service departments. In order for all $2 million of telecommunications costs to be allocated to the operating divisions, the total allocated has to be increased by the amount that is charged to the service departments.

So far the reciprocal method has been described as a system of two equations with two unknowns. Solving the two equations was straightforward: One equation was substituted into the other in order to solve for the remaining unknown. If there are more than three or four service divisions, this simple technique becomes very burdensome. At this point, some matrix algebra becomes quite useful. First, rewrite equations (1) and (2) in Table 8–13's footnote as

$$+0.90T - 0.25I = 2$$

$$-0.20T + 0.85I = 6$$

Next, express these equations in matrix form:

$$\begin{bmatrix} +0.90 & -0.25 \\ -0.20 & +0.85 \end{bmatrix} \begin{bmatrix} T \\ I \end{bmatrix} = \begin{bmatrix} 2 \\ 6 \end{bmatrix}$$

Solving for the unknown vector gives

$$\begin{bmatrix} T \\ I \end{bmatrix} = \begin{bmatrix} +0.90 & -0.25 \\ -0.20 & +0.85 \end{bmatrix}^{-1} \begin{bmatrix} 2 \\ 6 \end{bmatrix}$$

The -1 over the two-by-two matrix indicates the inverse matrix. Most spreadsheet programs have functions to compute the inverse of a matrix.

$$\begin{bmatrix} +0.90 & -0.25 \\ -0.20 & +0.85 \end{bmatrix}^{-1} = \begin{bmatrix} 1.19 & 0.35 \\ 0.28 & 1.26 \end{bmatrix}$$

Substituting the solution of the inverse into the preceding equation and solving yields the same solution as in Table 8–13,

$$\begin{bmatrix} T \\ I \end{bmatrix} = \begin{bmatrix} 4.475 \\ 8.112 \end{bmatrix}$$

The preceding analysis assumes that all the service department costs ($2 million and $6 million) are variable. If the service department costs contain any fixed costs, only the variable cost portion is allocated using the simultaneous solutions method. The fixed costs can be allocated based on planned usage.

Self-Study Problem

Medical Center

Eastern University has a medical center consisting of a medical school and a hospital. The primary function of the medical school is education. To accomplish this mission, the hospital provides teaching opportunities for medical students and residents. In addition, important research is conducted. Attracting top medical school faculty requires resources: good colleagues, good students, good research facilities, and competitive salaries. All faculty are expected to teach, conduct research, and provide medical care to patients. Good teaching requires knowledge of research and how to provide quality patient care. Patient care is enhanced by having faculty doing state-of-the-art research. Research is stimulated by inquisitive, bright students and actual patient cases. While the mix of activities varies substantially across faculty, a recent detailed study of their time utilization reported the following averages:

	% of Time Devoted to
Teaching	30%
Patient care	25
Research	45

Recent pressures to reduce hospital costs have caused the medical center to take a close look at its cost structure. In particular, hospital administrators have become concerned that they are at a competitive disadvantage with nonteaching hospitals that do not provide extensive teaching and research facilities. They have collected data on the medical center's operating revenues and expenses for the last fiscal year, 2008.

Medical Center Operating Revenues and (Expenses), 2008 Fiscal Year (Millions)

Direct patient care expenditures (nursing, pharmacy, laundry, etc.)[*]	$(297)
Direct research expenses (research supplies, lab technicians, etc.)[*]	(50)
Faculty salaries and benefits	(140)
Income from endowment	22
Medical school admissions and administration expenditures	(33)
Medical school tuition	82
Occupancy costs (utilities, maintenance, security, etc.)[†]	(80)
Patient revenues	370
Sponsored research funding	127

[*]Excludes faculty salaries.

[†]Square footage utilized:

Hospital	250,000
Medical school	50,000
Research labs	100,000

To help offset the high cost of medicine, the medical center solicits donations. The vast majority of the donations received are not specifically restricted to teaching, research, or hospital activities. Rather, most of the gifts are for the unrestricted use of the medical center. These contributions are invested in an endowment and the annual income from the endowment is a source of operating funds for the medical center.

Required:

    a. Prepare a financial statement that reports separately the operating performance of teaching, research, and patient care for the medical center. Explain and justify any assumptions you make in preparing the statement.

    b. Evaluate how accurately the report you have prepared reflects the financial performance of the three functions: teaching, research, and patient care. What inferences do you draw from your report in (*a*)?

Solution:

    a. This question illustrates the fundamental problems of trying to draw inferences about the profitability of joint products. The medical center produces three joint products: teaching, research, and patient care. All three are provided by the same organization rather than three separate organizations because synergies exist among the three. In addition to joint costs (faculty salaries), there are joint benefits (endowment income). Any attempt to try to allocate the joint costs (faculty salaries) and joint benefits (endowment income) is likely to lead to misleading inferences.

        One way of evaluating performance is to allocate the faculty salaries based on time utilization. The occupancy costs are probably not entirely joint or common costs and these can be assigned based on square footage. Allocating the endowment income is problematic and arbitrary. There is no completely rational basis for allocating these joint benefits. The accompanying table allocates endowment income based on the same percentages used to allocate the faculty salaries. This assumes that what ultimately drives gifts to the medical center is the same as what drives the joint costs.

Medical Center Operating Performance by Function, 2008 Fiscal Year (Millions)

	Teaching	Research	Hospital	Total
Revenue	$82	$127	$370	$579
Direct expenses	33	50	297	380
Faculty salaries	42	63	35	140
Occupancy costs	10	20	50	80
Surplus (deficit) before endowment	$(3)	$ (6)	$(12)	$(21)
Endowment income*	7	10	6	22
Surplus (deficit)	$ 4	$ 4	$ (7)	$ 1

*Allocated based on faculty salaries. Numbers do not add to total because of rounding.

It is important to note that, after including the endowment income of $22 million, the medical center actually had a surplus of $1 million.

We see from the above table that all three functions are operating at a deficit before endowment income. But it appears that the hospital is losing the most money, $12 million out of the total $21 million deficit. After considering the endowment income, teaching and research are both showing a surplus and the hospital is showing a loss.

If the endowment income is allocated based on total revenues, teaching breaks even, research reports a $1 million deficit, and the hospital reports a $2 million surplus. For public relations and fund-raising purposes, the medical center would probably not want the hospital to report a surplus. Thus, endowment income would most likely not be allocated based on revenues.

b. One problem with the previous table is that it produces misleading product line profitability information. Because faculty salaries are a joint cost, any attempt to allocate these costs using other than net realizable values can be misleading. The following table recasts the preceding table using NRV as the allocation base for both faculty salaries and endowment income.

Medical Center Operating Performance by Function
Net Realizable Value Method, 2008 Fiscal Year (Millions)

	Teaching	Research	Hospital	Total
Revenue	$82	$127	$370	$579
Direct expenses	33	50	297	380
Occupancy costs	10	20	50	80
Net realizable value	$39	$ 57	$ 23	$119
% NRV	33%	48%	19%	100%
Joint costs*	39	57	23	118
Surplus (deficit)†	$ 0	$ 0	$ 0	$ 1

*Faculty salaries less endowment income.
†Numbers do not add to total because of rounding.

The results in this table indicate that all three activities are contributing cash flows toward covering the joint costs. Research appears to be providing the most cash flows at $57 million. However, even this table is misleading in one important aspect.

None of the three functions (teaching, research, and patient care) is separable from the others. Unlike the chicken example in the text, where the firm can decide to further process a chicken part, the medical center does not have this option. Closing the hospital will have a large impact on the demand for teaching services. Few top students will attend a medical school that does not offer clinical experience. Since the demand for the three functions is interdependent, changing the scale of one function affects the revenues of the others. This would be equivalent to the case in which the demand for chicken fillets depends on the availability of wings. If supermarkets want to offer their customers both fillets and wings and will only buy from chicken processors who offer a full product line, then eliminating one chicken part reduces the demand for the other parts. This interdependency among demands is a primary reason that the medical center offers all three services. It also renders any attempt to disaggregate the firm into separate subunits for decision-making purposes a dangerous exercise.

While it is tempting to provide a disaggregated product line performance report, such an exercise provides very little insight. The medical center is generating a small surplus of $1 million. The source of this surplus cannot be attributable to any one of the three functions because demands for the service and the production functions of each service are so highly interdependent.

The financial performance of each function is probably best measured by comparing each unit's actual costs and revenues with budgeted costs and revenues estimated prior to the start of the fiscal year.

Problems

P 8–1: Step-Down

Critically evaluate the statement:

> The step-down method is better than the direct allocation method because at least the step-down method captures on average half of the service flows between service departments. By comparison, the direct allocation method ignores all the service flows.

P 8–2: Joint Costs versus Common Costs

What is the difference between joint costs and common costs?

P 8-3: Outback Opals

Outback Opals mines and processes opals from its Australian opal mines. The process consists of removing large chunks of stones, carefully splitting the stones and removing the opals, and then cutting and polishing the stones. Finally, the opals are sorted and graded (I, II, and III). The Grade I opals are sent to Outback's U.S. subsidiary for sale in the United States. The Graded II opals are sold through Outback's Hong Kong subsidiary in Hong Kong, and the Grade III opals are sold in Australia. It costs A$35,000 to mine, cut, polish, and sort a batch of opals. The following table summarizes the number of stones in each batch mined, the additional costs to package and sell each stone after it is polished and graded, the selling price of each grade of stone (in Australian dollars), and the income tax rates that apply to any income derived from stones sold in the country of final sale.

	Grade I	Grade II	Grade III
Number of stones per batch	70	105	175
Additional costs to package and sell each stone	A$250	A$120	A$5
Selling price per stone	A$800	A$300	A$110
Income tax rate	30%	15%	45%
Country of final sale	U.S.	Hong Kong	Australia

Required:

a. Calculate the joint cost per stone of each grade of opal (I, II, and III) using the number of stones in each batch to allocate the A$35,000 joint mining, cutting, polishing, and sorting costs. (Round all decimals to four significant digits.)

b. Calculate the joint cost per stone of each grade of opal (I, II, and III) using the net realizable value of each grade of stones (before taxes) to allocate the A$35,000 joint mining, cutting, polishing, and sorting costs. (Round all decimals to four significant digits.)

c. Which method of allocating the joint cost of A$35,000 (number of stones or net realizable value) should Outback Opals use? Explain why.

P 8–4: Walters Company

Walters Company produces 15,000 pounds of Product A and 30,000 pounds of Product B each week by incurring a common variable cost of $400,000. These two products can be sold as is or processed further. Further processing of either product does not delay the production of subsequent batches of the joint product. The accompanying table gives data regarding these two products.

	Product A	Product B
Selling price per pound without further processing	$12.00	$9.00
Selling price per pound with further processing	$15.00	$11.00
Total separate weekly variable costs of further processing	$50,000	$45,000

Required:

To maximize Walters Company's manufacturing contribution margin, how much total separate variable costs of further processing should be incurred each week?

SOURCE: CMA adapted.

P 8–5: Cosmo Inc.

Cosmo Inc. operates two retail novelty stores: the Mall Store and the Town Store. Condensed monthly operating income data for Cosmo Inc. for November appear in the accompanying table. Additional information regarding Cosmo's operations follows the statement.

	Total	Mall Store	Town Store
Sales	$200,000	$80,000	$120,000
Less variable costs	116,000	32,000	84,000
Contribution margin	$ 84,000	$48,000	$ 36,000
Less direct fixed expenses	60,000	20,000	40,000
Store segment margin	$ 24,000	$28,000	$ (4,000)
Less common fixed expenses	10,000	4,000	6,000
Operating income	$ 14,000	$24,000	$(10,000)

- One-fourth of each store's direct fixed expenses would continue through December of next year if either store were closed.
- Cosmo allocates common fixed expenses to each store on the basis of sales dollars.
- Management estimates that closing the Town Store would result in a 10 percent decrease in Mall Store sales, while closing the Mall Store would not affect the Town Store sales.
- The operating results for November are representative of all months.

Required:

a. A decision by Cosmo Inc. to close the Town Store would result in a monthly increase (decrease) in Cosmo's operating income during next year of how much?

b. Cosmo is considering a promotional campaign at the Town Store that would not affect the Mall Store. Increasing monthly promotional expenses at the Town Store by $5,000 in order to increase Town Store sales by 10 percent would result in a monthly increase (decrease) in Cosmo's operating income during the next year of how much?

c. Half of Town Store's dollar sales are from items sold at variable cost to attract customers to the store. Cosmo is considering deleting these items, a move that would reduce the Town Store's direct fixed expenses by 15 percent and result in the loss of 20 percent of Town Store's remaining sales volume. This change would not affect the Mall Store. A decision to eliminate the items sold at cost would result in a monthly increase (decrease) in Cosmo's operating income during next year of how much?

SOURCE: CMA adapted.

P 8–6:   Table 8–12:   Net Realizable Value

Table 8–12 allocates joint costs using net realizable value as the allocation base. What critical assumptions underlie the analysis in Table 8–12? That is, under what circumstances can the data in this table be used to assess product line profitability?

P 8–7:   Rose Hospital

Rose Hospital has two service departments (building services and food service), and three patient care units (intensive care, surgery, and general medicine). Building Services provides janitorial, maintenance, and engineering services as well as space (utilities, depreciation, insurance, and taxes) to all departments and patient care units. Food Service provides meals to both patients and staff members. It operates a cafeteria and serves meals to patients in their rooms. Building services costs of $6 million are allocated based on square footage, and food service costs of $3 million are allocated based on number of meals served. The following two tables summarize the annual costs of the two service departments and the utilization of each service department by the other departments.

	Annual Cost* (millions)
Building Services	$6.0
Food Service	3.0
Total overhead	$9.0

*Before allocated service department costs

Utilization Patterns

	Allocation Base	Building Services	Food Service	Intensive Care	Surgery	General Medicine	Total
Building Services	Square footage	2,500	15,500	10,000	20,000	40,000	88,000
Food Service	Meals	12,000	10,000	3,000	4,000	98,000	127,000

The following table summarizes the allocation of service department costs using the step-down method with Food Service as the first service department to be allocated:

Step-Down Method (Food Service First) (Millions)

	Intensive Care	Surgery	General Medicine
Food Service	$0.09	$0.09	$2.52
Building Services	0.88	1.83	3.59
Total	$0.97	$1.92	$6.11

Required:

(Round all allocation rates and all dollar amounts to two decimal places.)

a. Allocate the two service department costs to the three patient care units using the direct method of allocating service department costs.

b. Same as (*a*) except use the step-down allocation method with Building Services as the first service department allocated.

c. Write a short, nontechnical memo to management explaining why the sum of the two service department costs allocated to each patient care unit in (*b*) differs from the sum of the costs computed using the step-down method starting with Food Service.

P 8–8:   New View Products

New View is a chemical processor. Two chemicals, V7 and AC, are produced from a decomposition of M68JJ. Each batch of M68JJ costing $22,000 yields 300 pounds of V7 and 400 pounds of AC. Each unit of V7 can be sold for $35, and each unit of AC can be sold for $25. Either intermediate product can be processed further. It costs $2,000 to convert 300 pounds of V7 into 240 pounds of V7HX. Likewise, it costs $1,500 to convert 400 pounds of AC into 320 pounds of AC92. Each pound of V7HX can be sold for $50, and each pound of AC92 can be sold for $45. The $22,000 batch cost is allocated to the two intermediate products using pounds.

Required:

a. Prepare a financial statement assuming V7 and AC are sold and not processed further. Calculate the profit per batch of each intermediate product that includes the allocated batch cost.

b. If neither V7 nor AC is processed further, should New View produce V7 and AC?

c. Should New View further process V7 into V7HX and/or AC into AC92? Justify your answer with supporting calculations.

P 8–9:   Fidelity Bank

Fidelity Bank has five service departments (telecom, information management, building occupancy, training & development, and human resources). The bank uses a step-down method of allocating service department costs to its three lines of business (retail banking, commercial banking, and credit cards). The following table contains the utilization rates of the five service departments and three lines of business. Also included in this table are the direct operating expenses of the service departments (in millions of dollars). Direct operating expenses of each service department do not contain any allocated service costs from the other service departments. For example, telecom spent $3.5 million dollars and provided services to other units within Fidelity Bank. Information management consumed 15 percent of telecom's services. The order in which the service departments are allocated is also indicated in the table. The telecom department costs are allocated first, followed by information management, and the costs of the human resources department are allocated last.

FIDELITY BANK
Utilization Rates and Direct Operating Expenses of the Service Departments
(Dollars in millions)

	Direct Op. Exp.	Tele-com	Info. Mgmt.	Building Occ.	Training & Dev.	Human Res.	Retail Banking	Comm. Banking	Credit Cards
			Service Departments					Lines of Business	
1. Telecom	$3.5	—	0.15	0.05	0.05	0.05	0.20	0.15	0.35
2. Information Mgmt.	9.8	0.20	—	0.05	0.10	0.10	0.20	0.20	0.15
3. Building Occupancy	6.4	0.05	0.10	—	0.05	0.10	0.50	0.10	0.10
4. Training & Dev.	1.3	0.15	0.15	0.05	—	0.05	0.10	0.30	0.20
5. Human Resources	2.2	0.10	0.10	0.20	0.05	—	0.20	0.20	0.15

Required:

a. Using the step-down method and the order of departments specified in the table, what is the total allocated cost from information management to credit cards, including all the costs allocated to information management?

b. Information management costs are allocated based on gigabytes of hard disk storage used by the other service departments and lines of business. If, instead of being second in the step-down sequence, information management became fifth in the sequence, would the allocated cost per gigabyte increase or decrease? Explain precisely why it increases or decreases.

c. If instead of using the step-down method of allocating service department costs, Fidelity uses the direct allocation method, what is the total allocated cost from information management to credit cards, including all the costs allocated to information management? (Note: Information management remains second in the list.)

P 8–10:   Joint Products, Inc.

Joint Products, Inc., produces two joint products, X and V, using a common input. These are produced in batches. The common input costs $8,000 per batch. To produce the final products (X and V), additional processing costs beyond the split-off point must be incurred. There are no beginning inventories. The accompanying data summarize the operations.

	Products	
	X	V
Quantities produced per batch	200 lbs.	400 lbs.
Additional processing costs per batch beyond split-off	$1,800	$3,400
Unit selling prices of completely processed products	$40/lb.	$10/lb.
Ending inventory	2,000 lbs.	1,000 lbs.

Required:

    a. Compute the full cost of the ending inventory using net realizable value to allocate joint cost.

    b. If the selling prices at the split-off point (before further processing) are $35 and $1 per pound of X and V, respectively, what should the firm do regarding further processing? Show calculations.

P 8–11:   Talor Chemical Company

Talor Chemical Company is a highly diversified chemical processing company. The company manufactures swimming pool chemicals, chemicals for metal processing companies, specialized chemical compounds for other companies, and a full line of pesticides and insecticides.

Currently, the Noorwood plant is producing two derivatives, RNA–1 and RNA–2, from the chemical compound VDB, developed by Talor's research labs. Each week 1.2 million pounds of VDB are processed, at a cost of $246,000, into 800,000 pounds of RNA–1 and 400,000 pounds of RNA–2. The proportion of these two outputs is fixed. RNA–1 has no market value until it is converted into a product with the trade name Fastkil. The cost to process RNA–1 into Fastkil is $240,000 a week. Fastkil wholesales at $50 per 100 pounds.

RNA–2 is sold as is for $80 per 100 pounds. However, Talor has discovered that RNA–2 can be converted into two new products through further processing, which would require the addition of 400,000 pounds of compound LST to the 400,000 pounds of RNA–2. The joint process would yield 400,000 pounds each of DMZ–3 and Pestrol, the two new products. The additional raw material and related processing costs of this joint process would be $120,000 per week. DMZ–3 and Pestrol would each be sold for $57.50 per 100 pounds. Talor management has decided not to process RNA–2 further, based on the analysis presented in the following schedule. Talor uses the physical weight method to allocate the common costs arising from joint processing.

| | RNA–2 | Process Further | | |
		DMZ–3	Pestrol	Total
Production in pounds	400,000	400,000	400,000	
Revenue	$320,000	$230,000	$230,000	$460,000
Costs				
VDB costs	$ 82,000	$ 61,500	$ 61,500	$123,000
Additional raw materials (LST) and processing of RNA–2	—	60,000	60,000	120,000
Total costs	$ 82,000	$121,500	$121,500	$243,000
Weekly gross profit	$238,000	$108,500	$108,500	$217,000

A new staff accountant who was to review the analysis commented that it should be revised and stated, "Product costing of products such as these should be done on the basis of net relative sales value, not on a physical volume basis."

Required:

a. Discuss whether the use of the net relative sales value method would provide data more relevant for the decision to market DMZ–3 and Pestrol.

b. Critique Talor Company's analysis and make any revisions that are necessary. Your critique and analysis should indicate
  (i) Whether Talor has made the correct decision.
  (ii) The gross savings (loss) per week of Talor's decision not to process RNA–2 further, if different from the company-prepared analysis.

SOURCE: CMA adapted.

P 8–12: Donovan Steel

Donovan Steel has two profit centers: Ingots and Stainless Steel. These profit centers rely on services supplied by two service departments: electricity and water. The profit centers' consumption of the service departments' outputs (in millions) is given in the following table:

	Service Departments		**Profit Centers**		
Service Departments	*Electricity*	*Water*	*Ingots*	*Stainless Steel*	*Total*
Electricity	2,500 kwh	2,500 kwh	3,000 kwh	2,000 kwh	10,000 kwh
Water	1,000 gal.	800 gal.	1,000 gal.	2,000 gal.	4,800 gal.

The total operating costs of the two service departments are

Electricity	$ 80 million
Water	60 million
Total cost	$140 million

Required:

a. Service department costs are allocated to profit centers using the step-down method. Water is the first service department allocated. Compute the cost of electricity per kilowatt-hour using the step-down allocation method.

b. Critically evaluate this allocation method.

P 8–13: Sonimad Sawmill

Sonimad Sawmill manufactures two lumber products from a joint milling process. The two products developed are mine support braces (MSBs) and unseasoned commercial building lumber (CBL). A standard production run incurs joint costs of $300,000 and results in 60,000 units of MSB and 90,000 units of CBL. Each unprocessed unit of MSB sells for $2 per unit and each unprocessed unit of CBL sells for $4 per unit.

If the CBL is processed further at a cost of $200,000, it can be sold at $10 per unit but 10,000 units are unavoidably lost (with no discernible value). The MSB units can be coated with a preservative at a cost of $100,000 per production run and then sold for $3.50 each.

Required:

a. If no further work is done after the initial milling process, calculate the cost of CBL using physical quantities to allocate the joint cost.

b. If no further work is done after the initial milling process, calculate the cost of MSB using relative sales value to allocate the joint cost.

c. Should MSB and CBL be processed further or sold immediately after initial milling?

d. Given your decision in (c), prepare a schedule computing the completed cost assigned to each unit of MSB and CBL as charged to finished goods inventory. Use net realizable value for allocating joint costs.

SOURCE: CMA adapted.

P 8–14: Enzymes

Two genetically engineered enzymes are produced simultaneously from a series of chemical and biological processes: Q enzyme and Y enzyme. The cost per batch of Q and Y enzymes is $200,000, resulting in 300 grams of Q and 200 grams of Y. Before Q and Y can be sold, they must be processed further at costs of $100 and $150 per gram, respectively. Each batch requires one month of processing time and only one batch per month is produced.

The monthly demand for Q and Y depends on the price charged. The following table summarizes the various price-quantity combinations.

Quantity Sold	Price per Gram of Q	Price per Gram of Y
50	$1,200	$750
100	1,100	550
150	1,000	350
200	900	150
250	800	n.a.
300	700	n.a.

In the following analysis, the optimum price of Q is $900 per gram and the optimum price of Y is $750 per gram.

Quantity Sold	Price per Q	Revenue of Q	Total Cost of Q*	Total Profit	Price per Y	Revenue from Y	Total cost of Y†	Total Profit
50	$1,200	$ 60,000	$ 25,000	$35,000	$750	$37,500	$ 27,500	$10,000
100	1,100	110,000	50,000	60,000	550	55,000	55,000	0
150	1,000	150,000	75,000	75,000	350	52,500	82,500	(30,000)
200	900	180,000	100,000	80,000	150	30,000	110,000	(80,000)
250	800	200,000	125,000	75,000	n.a.			
300	700	210,000	150,000	60,000	n.a.			

*Cost per gram of Q = ($200,000/500) + $100 = $500/gram.
† Cost per gram of Y = ($200,000/500) + $150 = $550/gram.

Required:

    a. Critically evaluate the analysis underlying the pricing decisions of $900 for Q and $750 for Y.

    b. What should management do if the cost per batch rises to $225,000?

P 8–15:   Sunder Toys

Sunder manufactures hard rubber pet toys. The purple dog chewy has a variable cost of $3.00 per unit. It is produced on a machine that is leased. The three models of this machine have three different capacities.

Maximum Daily Capacity (units)	Daily Lease Cost
1,000	$10,000
1,200	10,800
1,400	11,200

The daily market demand for purple dog chewies at various prices is:

Price	Daily Quantity Demanded
$16.11	900
15.00	1,000
14.18	1,100
12.83	1,200
12.23	1,300
11.50	1,400

There is no uncertainty (daily variation) with respect to the daily demand for purple dog chewies. For example, if the price is set at $14.18, 1,100 chewies will be sold every day with certainty.

Required:

    a. Given all the data, how many purple dog chewies should Sunder produce and sell? (Show calculations, neatly labeled.)

    b. Suppose Sunder has the policy of not charging fixed costs to products whenever excess capacity exists. The manager of purple dog chewies receives a bonus based on the accounting profits from purple dog chewies. This manager has private knowledge of machine capacities, lease fees, and the demand for purple dog chewies, as well as the decision rights over how large a machine to lease. How big a machine will the manager lease and how many chewies will be produced and sold? (Show calculations, neatly labeled.)

    c. Comment on Sunder's policy of not charging fixed costs to products whenever excess capacity exists.

P 8–16: WWWeb Marketing

WWWeb Marketing is a decentralized firm specializing in designing and operating Internet marketing Web sites. The firm is four years old and has been growing rapidly, but it only shows a small profit. WWWeb has three profit centers: Design Division, Server Operations, and the Crawler Division. The Design Division devises Internet marketing strategies for external clients, including innovative Web sites and Web-based marketing strategies. Server Operations maintains the clients' Web sites on WWWeb's servers. The Crawler Division operates WWWeb's proprietary search engine that clients can use for Internet-based marketing research. In addition to these three profit centers, WWWeb has an IT group that maintains WWWeb's servers and telecommunication lines to the Internet.

The IT group is a cost center. The current annual IT budget is $548,000 for personnel, hardware and software leases for the servers, and telecommunication costs. The cost of the IT group is not allocated back to the three divisions. The CEO of WWWeb argues that the IT group is a common (shared) resource and is essentially a fixed cost. Adding another client Web site or performing a Web search does not generate any additional IT cost to the firm because WWWeb's IT group has excess capacity. WWWeb's CEO argues, "Any charge for IT back to the divisions will cause the divisions to avoid using our IT resources. As long as we have unused capacity on our systems we should be encouraging our people to use that capacity."

WWWeb currently uses about 80 percent of the capacity of its servers, routers, and fiber optic high speed lines to the Internet. The high speed lines are the "pipes" through which all client server Web traffic flows. These high speed lines are also used by WWWeb's e-mail traffic and the Crawler Divisions marketing research Web searches. Currently, the IT systems are performing well and WWWeb users experience few delays and minimal interference from other users. However, the three profit center managers are projecting growth in their businesses and expect to reach capacity on their servers and communication lines within the next 12 months. When this happens, the managers predict that they will experience significant service degradation.

Jose Coronas, head of WWWeb's IT group, has called a meeting of the three division managers to discuss the terrific deals being offered by telecom companies and hardware providers. Given the current slump in the economy, WWWeb can roughly double the capacity of its servers and high speed access lines and lock in these low rates for two years. The incremental cost of doubling the IT group's capacity is to raise its hardware lease costs and access line costs by 20 percent. IT currently spends $18,000 a month on hardware leases and access lines. If it were to double its existing capacity, the total monthly cost would rise to $21,600. Mr. Coronas believes his existing IT personnel can handle the additional server and line capacity. Coronas and the three division managers recommend that WWWeb acquire the additional capacity and lock in these attractive rates.

Required:

a. Analyze WWWeb's current policy of how the three divisions are charged for IT costs and whether WWWeb should acquire the additional capacity.

b. Should WWWeb change its policy of how it charges IT costs to the divisions? If so, what changes would you recommend?

P 8–17: ITI Technology

ITI Technology designs and manufactures solid-state computer chips. In one of the production departments, employees fabricate a six-inch circular wafer by laying down successive layers of silicon and then etching the circuits into the layers. Each wafer contains 100 separate solid-state computer chips. After a wafer is manufactured, the 100 chips are cut out of the wafer, tested, mounted into protective covers, and attached to electrical leads. Then a final quality control test is performed.

The initial testing process consists of successive stages of heating and cooling the chips and testing how they work. If 99 percent of a chip's circuits work properly after the testing, it is classified as a high-density (HD) chip. If between 75 percent and 99 percent of a chip's circuits work properly, it is classified as a low-density (LD) chip. If fewer than 75 percent of the circuits work, it is discarded. Twenty wafers are manufactured in a batch. On average, 50 percent of each batch are HD, 20 percent are LD, and 30 percent are discarded. HD chips are sold to defense contractors and LD chips to consumer electronics firms. Chips sold to defense contractors require different mountings, packaging, and distribution channels than chips sold to consumer electronics firms. HD chips sell for $30 each and LD chips sell for $16 each.

Each batch of 20 wafers costs $29,100: $8,000 to produce, test, and sort, and $21,100 for mounting, attaching leads, and final inspection and distribution costs ($14,500 for HD chips and $6,600 for LD chips). The $29,100 total cost per batch consists of direct labor, direct materials, and variable overhead.

The following report summarizes the operating data per batch:

ITI Technology Operating Summary of HD and LD Chips

	Total	HD Chips	LD Chips	Scrap
Percentage of chips	100%	50%	20%	30%
Revenue	$36,400	$30,000*	$6,400†	$ 0
Total costs	29,100	14,550	5,820	8,730
Profit per batch	$ 7,300	$15,450	$ 580	$(8,730)

*$30,000 = 50% × 20 wafers × 100 chips per wafer × $30/chip.
†$6,400 = 20% × 20 wafers × 100 chips per wafer × $16/chip.

The cost of scrap is charged to a plantwide overhead account, which is then allocated directly to the lines of business based on profits in each LOB.

Required:

a. Critically evaluate ITI's method of accounting for HD and LD chips.
b. What suggestions would you offer ITI's management?

P 8–18: Metro Blood Bank

Metro Blood Bank, a for-profit firm, collects whole blood from donors, tests it, and then separates it into two components: platelets and plasma. Three pints of whole blood yield two pints of platelets and one pint of plasma. The cost of collecting the three pints, testing them, and separating them is $300.

The platelets are sold for $165 per pint. But before they are sold they must be packaged and labeled. The variable cost of this additional processing is $15 per pint. Plasma is sold for $115 per pint after incurring additional variable processing costs of $45 per pint.

The selling prices of the platelets and plasma are set by competitive market forces. The prices of platelets and plasma quoted above are the current market prices, but they vary widely depending on supply and demand conditions. Metro Blood Bank ships its products nationwide to maximize profits. It has three operating divisions: blood collection and processing, platelets, and plasma. Collection and processing is a cost center, and platelets and plasma are profit centers.

Neither platelets nor plasma have any commercial value without further processing.

Required:

a. Prepare two statements showing the profits per pint of platelets and plasma with collection and processing costs assigned using

   (i) The number of pints of platelets and plasma produced from the whole blood.

   (ii) The net realizable value of platelets and plasma.

b. Discuss the advantages and disadvantages of each of the methods in (*a*) for assigning collection and processing costs to the blood products.

P 8–19:   Jason Rocks

Jason Rocks is small rock quarry that produces five different sizes of stones, from small crushed stones (#1 stones) to large (3-inch) rocks (#5 stones). The stones are first mined and sorted into the five grades. Once the stones are mined and sorted, they can be sold to a local distributor either washed or unwashed. Jason Rocks mines and sorts 500 tons of stone each day and is a price taker in the local stone market. The following table contains the percentage of each type of stone quarried each day and the market prices at which Jason Rocks can sell its five types of stones as either washed or unwashed:

		Selling Prices (per ton)	
Type of stone	% of daily production	Unwashed	Washed
#1	10%	$210	$219
#2	20	185	192
#3	20	150	170
#4	35	145	155
#5	15	160	165

The daily cost of mining and sorting the stones is $75,000, which includes the salaries and benefits of the employees who quarry and sort the stones, the depreciation on the equipment used in the process, the royalty payments to owners of the quarry for the stone removed, and an allocation of the utilities, insurance, property taxes, and administrative costs of the entire quarry operation. Washing any of the five types of stone costs $8 per ton and delivering the stone to the local distributor costs $7 per ton. Jason Rocks allocates the mining and sorting costs based on the tons of each type of stone produced.

manager argues, "More of my customers are located closer to the old plant than are residential sales' customers. Therefore, to economize on transportation costs, my products should be produced in the old plant." The residential sales department manager counters with the following argument: "Transportation costs are less than 1 percent of total revenues. The new plant should produce commercial products because we expect new commercial products to use more synthetic materials and the latest technology at the new mill is better able to adapt to the new synthetics." Senior management is worried about how to deal with the two sales department managers' reluctance to have their products produced at the new plant. One suggestion put forth is for each plant to produce about half of commercial sales products and about half of residential sales products. But this proposal would eliminate most of the economies of scale that would result from specializing production in each plant to one market segment.

Required:

   a. Calculate the overhead rates for the new plant and the old plant, where overhead is assigned to carpet based on normal yards per year.
   b. Calculate the expected total cost of carpet A6106 if run at the old mill and if run at the new mill.
   c. Put forth two new solutions that would overcome the resistance of the residential and commercial sales department managers to the new plant. Discuss the pros and cons of your two solutions.

P 8–25:   Four Service Centers

A firm has four service centers, S1, S2, S3, and S4, which provide services to each other, as well as to three operating divisions, A, B, and C. The distribution of each service center's output as well as its cost (in millions) is given in the following table.

| | | | Fraction of Service Center Output Used | | | | |
	S1	S2	S3	S4	Division A	Division B	Division C	Total Cost
S1	0.05	0.11	0.19	0.22	0.14	0.16	0.13	$ 4.80
S2	0.08	0.03	0.14	0.31	0.14	0.20	0.10	7.30
S3	0.09	0.16	0.04	0.16	0.24	0.08	0.23	6.50
S4	0.12	0.13	0.02	0.09	0.22	0.23	0.19	5.90
								$24.50

Required:

Using the reciprocal method, allocate the costs of the service centers to the three operating divisions.

P 8–26:   Beckett Manufacturing

Beckett Manufacturing is a contract manufacturer that assembles products for other companies. Beckett has two service departments, Maintenance and

Administration, and two operating divisions, Small Components and Large Components. The following data summarize the utilization of each service department:

	Maintenance	Administration	Small Components	Large Components	Allocation Base	Service Dept. Cost
Maintenance	50,000	300,000	400,000	250,000	Square feet of floor space	$950,000
Administration	17	34	68	221	Number of employees	$567,000

Square feet of floor space required by each user is the allocation base for allocating the Maintenance department cost of $950,000. Number of employees in each department and division is used to allocate the Administration department cost of $567,000. Beckett uses the step-down method of allocating service department costs to the two operating divisions. The $950,000 and $567,000 amounts represent the operating costs of the Maintenance and Administration departments, respectively, and they do not include any cost allocations from the other service departments.

Required:

a. Allocate the two service department costs to the two operating divisions using the step-down method where Maintenance is the first service department allocated and Administration is the second service department allocated.

b. Allocate the two service department costs to the two operating divisions using the step-down method where Administration is the first service department allocated and Maintenance is the second service department allocated.

c. Calculate the allocated cost per square foot and the allocated cost per employee resulting from using the step-down method where Maintenance is the first service department allocated and Administration is the second service department allocated (as in part [a]).

d. Calculate the allocated cost per square foot and the allocated cost per employee resulting from using the step-down method where Administration is the first service department allocated and Maintenance is the second service department allocated (as in part [b]).

e. Describe why the costs per square foot and the costs per employee vary in parts (c) and (d) above.

P 8–27:   Aurora Medical Center

Aurora Medical Center (AMC), located outside Phoenix, has an inpatient hospital and outpatient clinic. Because it is located in a retirement area, a substantial fraction of its patients are elderly, and hence their medical insurance is provided through the Medicare program of the federal government. Medicare outpatient clinic care is reimbursed by the federal government at cost. Each clinic with Medicare outpatients submits a reimbursement form to Medicare reporting the costs of treating these patients. Medicare inpatient reimbursement is based on pre-determined rates depending on the diagnosis. For example, all Medicare-paid hip replacements in Phoenix are reimbursed at $14,800 per patient, regardless of the hospital's cost.

AMC has two administrative departments that provide services to both the hospital and the clinic: accounting and information management (IM). The accompanying tables summarize the service levels provided by these two departments:

	Administrative Departments	
	Accounting	*IM*
Total cost	$3,800,000	$4,800,000
Allocation base	Number of transactions	Disk space (gigabytes)
	Service Levels	
	Transactions	*Gigabytes*
Accounting		8
IM	40,000	
Hospital	1,100,000	7
Clinic	600,000	9
Total	1,740,000	24

Accounting department costs are distributed to users based on the number of transactions posted to the general ledger generated by that user. IM costs are distributed to users based on the gigabytes of storage dedicated to the user. Medicare guidelines allow these allocation bases to be used. Medicare also provides some discretion to hospitals in the methods used to allocate costs, as long as they are reasonable and generally accepted.

Required:

a. Design a report for assigning the accounting and IM costs to the hospital and clinic. How much of the costs of accounting and IM should be allocated to inpatients and outpatients?

b. Justify your design in (a). Explain why AMC should follow your suggestions.

P 8–28:   Grove City Broadcasting

Grove City Broadcasting owns and operates a radio station and a television station in Grove City. Both stations are located in the same building and are operated as separate profit centers with separate managers, who are evaluated based on station profits. Revenues of both the radio and the TV station are from advertising spots. The price of a standard 30-second ad is based on audience size, which is measured by an independent outside agency. The radio station sells a 30-second ad for $100. (Assume that all 30-second ads sell for $100 regardless of the time of day they air.)

The $100 price is based on an expected audience size of 20,000 listeners. If the listener audience were to double, the 30-second ad would sell for $200. In other words, each radio listener is worth $0.005 ($100 ÷ 20,000) of advertising revenue per 30-second ad. Each TV viewer is worth $0.008 per 30-second ad. The radio station sells 3,550 ads per month, and the TV station sells 3,200 ads per month.

Sports Wire has approached both the radio and television managers about subscribing to its service, which brings all sports scores, sports news, and sports analyses to the station via an on-line computer system over the Internet. The radio and/or TV stations' sports announcers could download scores and news directly into sports scripts and read them over the air. Sports Wire is more comprehensive and contains more sports stories than the current general news wires that Grove City is receiving. If one of the two stations buys Sports Wire, the price is $30,000 per month. For an extra $5,000 per month, both the radio and the TV station can use Sports Wire. If both stations use Sports Wire, the $5,000 additional fee includes an extra computer terminal that allows two users to be on the system at the same time.

Sports Wire will not increase the number of ads each month, just the revenue per ad. The Grove City radio manager believes that purchasing Sports Wire would increase his audience by 1,500 listeners per ad. The television manager believes her audience size would increase by 500 viewers per ad.

Required:

a. If the two managers did not cooperate but rather each made a decision assuming he or she was the sole user of the system, would either buy Sports Wire? Support your answer with detailed calculations.

b. If the owner of Grove City Broadcasting had all the facts available to the two managers, would the owner buy Sports Wire?

c. The costs of the current wire services that Grove City purchases are allocated to the two stations based on the number of stories aired each month from the wire services. The owner of Grove City Broadcasting decides to purchase Sports Wire for both stations and to allocate its $35,000 cost based on the number of Sports Wire stories aired each month. During the first month, the radio station uses 826 Sports Wire stories and TV uses 574. Allocate the Sports Wire cost to the radio and TV stations.

d. What is the allocated cost per Sports Wire story in the first month?

e. Given the allocation of the Sports Wire cost, what behaviors can you predict from the radio and TV station managers?

f. Design an alternative allocation scheme that will avoid the problems identified in (e). Discuss the advantages and disadvantages of your allocation scheme.

P 8–29: Barry's Fashions

Barry's Fashions operates a Downtown Store and a Mall Store. Both department stores use three centralized, corporate service departments (human resources, maintenance, and information management). The following table summarizes the allocation bases used to allocate each service department, the operating expenses incurred by each service department, and the amount of each allocation base used by the three service departments and the two stores.

	Allocation Base	Operating Expenses (millions)	Human Resources	Maintenance	Info. Mgmt.	Downtown Store	Mall Store	Total
Human resources	Employees	$0.4	20	110	30	850	1,200	2,210
Maintenance	Square footage (thousands)	0.9	12	18	20	80	130	260
Information management	Lines printed (millions)	1.5	6	2	5	120	90	223

Required: (Round all fractions to three significant digits.)

a. Using the direct allocation method for allocating service department costs, calculate the amount of information management expense allocated to the Mall Store.

b. Using the direct allocation method for allocating service department costs, calculate the allocated cost per line printed for information management services.

c. Using the step-down allocation method for allocating service department costs, calculate the amount of information management expense allocated to the Mall Store. Note that the order of the service departments is as indicated in the table.

d. Using the step-down allocation method for allocating service department costs, calculate the allocated cost per line printed for information management services. Note that the order of the service departments is as indicated in the table.

e. Compare and contrast your answers in parts (b) and (d). First, describe why you get different answers. Second, which number would you recommend management use?

P 8–30: Janitorial Services

Janitorial services is one of five service departments in a firm that allocates service department costs using the step-down allocation method. Janitorial services is currently the third service department (S3) in the step-down process. The following table gives the allocation fractions of the five service departments to the other four service departments and the four operating departments.

		Service Departments					Operating Departments			
Service Departments		S1	S2	S3	S4	S5	D1	D2	D3	D4
S1		0.00	0.05	0.05	0.08	0.04	0.20	0.18	0.22	0.18
S2		0.03	0.00	0.04	0.02	0.08	0.23	0.20	0.16	0.24
S3	(Janitorial Services)	0.04	0.03	0.00	0.02	0.08	0.19	0.24	0.23	0.17
S4		0.08	0.07	0.01	0.00	0.11	0.08	0.04	0.18	0.43
S5		0.07	0.12	0.14	0.16	0.00	0.13	0.11	0.12	0.15

The costs ($100,000) for each of the service departments *before* making any cost allocations are:

	Total Service Department Cost
S1	$25.00
S2	32.00
S3	17.00
S4	29.00
S5	18.00

The next table details the step-down allocated costs to each service department *after* making cost allocations. (In other words, $1.25 is allocated from S1 to S2 and S3, $2.00 to S4, and $1.00 to S5.)

	S1	S2	S3	S4	S5	Total Service Dept. Cost
S1 allocated costs	$0.00	$1.25	$1.25	$2.00	$1.00	$25.00
S2 allocated costs	0.00	0.00	1.37	0.69	2.74	33.25
S3 allocated costs	0.00	0.00	0.00	0.42	1.69	19.62
S4 allocated costs	0.00	0.00	0.00	0.00	4.20	32.11
S5 allocated costs	0.00	0.00	0.00	0.00	0.00	27.63
Total	$0.00	$1.25	$2.62	$3.11	$9.63	

Service department S3 provides janitorial services (floor care, window cleaning, rest room sanitation) to the other service departments and the operating divisions. The allocation base used to allocate S3 costs is square footage of each department and operating divisions. Total square footage of S1, S2, S4, S5, D1, D2, D3, and D4 is 650,000 square feet. (Note: All costs are in terms of $100,000.)

Required:

a. Calculate the cost per square foot that janitorial services (S3) is currently charging its customers.

b. Suppose that janitorial services (S3) is moved from the third service department in the step-down method to the fifth (last) service department in the step-down process. Calculate the total cost of janitorial services including all service department costs allocated to janitorial services.

c. What is the cost per square foot that janitorial services will charge its customers if it becomes the last service department to be allocated in the step-down process?

d. Why might senior (corporate) management move janitorial services from the third service department to the last service department in the step-down process?

P 8–31: Jones Consortium

At the Hilton Applefest and Trade Expo, James Jones, owner of Jones Orchard, saw a sign displayed in front of a vendor's booth: I CAN GET YOU PESTICIDES AT $10.00 A GALLON—GUARANTEED IN WRITING! Over a one-year period, the vendor guarantees delivery of between 350,000 and 500,000 gallons of pesticide at a maximum price of $10 per gallon. Since Jones Orchard is currently paying $11.30 per gallon, the offer is appealing. However, Jones uses only 25,000 gallons and the annual management fee for this service is a whopping $275,000.

The only way Jones can see to make the offer work is to form a buying consortium with other farmers. As long as all of the farmers are located within 10 square miles, the vendor is willing to allow the formation of a consortium. Including Jones Orchard, five farms are within this area. Their pesticide needs and anticipated costs are as follows:

	Gallons	Price per Gallon
Jones	25,000	$11.30
Gilbert	35,000	11.20
Santos	50,000	11.12
Singh	100,000	10.90
Chen	150,000	10.70
Total	360,000	

All of the farmers are willing to participate in the buying consortium as long as there is an anticipated cost savings for each farmer. Everyone agrees that each farmer should pay the same amount for materials. But allocation of the management fee is left entirely up to Jones.

Required:

a. Based upon the numbers provided, demonstrate that this consortium could work.

b. Jones initially considers allocating the management fee either (i) equally between all members or (ii) based upon each farmer's percentage of total gallons needed. Would either method work? Show allocation by each method.

c. Jones believes it would make sense to allocate the management fee on an ability-to-pay basis. As the chapter allocates joint costs based upon net realizable value, allocate the management fee based upon the potential dollar savings opportunity of each farm. Is this method feasible?

d. Consider the issue of private versus public information as it relates to the cost allocation schemes presented in this problem. Address whether the information required to implement each scheme is essentially held in common by all of the farmers in the consortium or privately held by each individual farmer. In particular, given that the consortium will allocate the management fee by ability to pay, how might each farmer's privately held cost information serve to undermine the consortium's future existence?

Case

Case 8–1: Carlos Sanguine Winery

Carlos Sanguine, Inc., makes premium wines and table wines. Grapes are crushed and the free-flowing juice and the first-processing juice are made into premium

TABLE 1   **Summary of Operations for the Year**

Tons of grapes	10,000	
Average cost per ton	$190	

	Premium Wines	Table Wines
Number of cases produced and sold	400,000	70,000
Selling price per case	$11.00	$7.00
Revenues	$4,400,000	$490,000
Grape costs*	1,650,000	250,000
Packaging costs	1,000,000	140,000
Labor	200,000	35,000
Selling and distribution[†]	400,000	35,000
Manufacturing overhead	400,000	87,500
Operating profit (loss)	$ 750,000	$(57,500)

*Grape costs represent the cost of the juice placed into the two product categories and are calculated as

	Gallons of Juice Used in Each Product	% of Juice	×	Total Grape Costs	=	Grape Cost per Product
Premium wines	13,200,000	86.84%		$1,900,000		$1,650,000
Table wines	2,000,000	13.16		1,900,000		250,000
Total	15,200,000	100.00%				$1,900,000

NOTE: A greater quantity of juice is required per case of premium wine than per case of table wine because there is more shrinkage in the premium wines.

[†]Each product has its own selling and distribution organization. Two-thirds of S&D expenditures vary with cases produced; the remainder of the expenditures do not vary with output.

TABLE 2   **Manufacturing Overhead by Products**

	Premium Wines	Table Wines	Total
General winery costs*	$212,800	$37,200	$250,000
Production facilities costs[†] (depreciation and maintenance)	187,200	50,300	237,500
Manufacturing overhead	$400,000	$87,500	$487,500

*General winery costs do not vary with the number of cases or the number of product lines and are allocated based on cases produced.

[†]Premium and table wines have separate production facilities. One-fourth of each of their production facilities costs varies with cases produced. The remainder are fixed costs previously incurred to provide the production capacity.

wines (bottles with corks). The second- and third-processing juices are made into table wines (bottles with screw tops).

Table 1 summarizes operations for the year, and Table 2 breaks down manufacturing overhead expenses into general winery costs and production facilities costs.

Based on Tables 1 and 2, the accounting department prepared the report in Table 3.

Management is concerned that the table wines have such a low margin. Some of the managers urge that these lines be dropped. Competition keeps the price

TABLE 3   **Product Line Cost Structure per Case**

	Premium Wines		Table Wines	
Net sales		$11.00		$7.00
Variable costs				
Grapes	$4.13		$3.57	
Packaging	2.50		2.00	
Labor	0.50		0.50	
Selling and distribution	1.00	8.13	0.50	6.57
Margin		$ 2.87		$ 0.43
Less manufacturing overhead		1.00		1.25
Operating profit (loss)		$ 1.87		$(0.82)

TABLE 4   **Fixed and Variable Costs per Product and Product Break-Even Points**

	Premium Wines		Table Wines	
Sales		$11.00		$ 7.00
Less variable costs				
Grapes	$4.13		$3.57	
Packaging	2.50		2.00	
Labor	0.50		0.50	
Selling and distribution	0.66		0.33	
Manufacturing overhead	0.12*	7.91	0.18†	6.58
Contribution margin		$ 3.09		$ 0.42
Less unitized fixed costs per unit				
Selling and distribution	0.33		0.17	
Manufacturing overhead	0.88	1.21	1.07	1.24
Profit (loss)		$ 1.88		$(0.82)

Break Even

	Premium Wines		Table Wines	
Fixed costs	(400,000 × $1.21)	$484,000	(70,000 × $1.24)	$86,800
÷ Contribution margin		3.09		0.42
Number of cases to break even		156,634		206,667

*($187,200 × 25%) ÷ 400,000 cases.
†($50,300 × 25%) ÷ 70,000 cases.

down to $7 per case, which causes some managers to question how the competition could afford to sell the wine at this price.

Before making a final decision, top management asked for an analysis of the fixed and variable costs by product line and their break-even points. When management saw Table 4, the president remarked, "Well, this is the final nail in the coffin. We'd have to almost triple our sales of table wines just to break even. But we don't have that kind of capacity. We'd have to buy new tanks, thereby driving up our fixed costs and break-even points. This looks like a vicious circle. By next

TABLE 5   Effects of Discontinuing Table Wines

1. No effect on the sale of premium wines is expected.
2. The juice being used in the table wines can be sold to bulk purchasers to use in fruit juices for $150,000 per year.
3. The table wine production facilities (tanks, refrigeration units, etc.) have no use in premium wine production. These can be sold for $350,000, net of disposal costs.

month, I want a detailed set of plans on what it'll cost us to shut down our table wines." Table 5 summarizes the shutdown effects.

Based on the facts presented in the case, what should management do?

Case 8-2:   Wyatt Oil

Wyatt Oil owns a major oil refinery in Channelview, Texas. The refinery processes crude oil into valuable outputs in a two-stage process. First, it distills a barrel of crude oil at a variable cost of $2 per barrel into two types of outputs: light distillates (such as gasoline, jet fuel, diesel fuel, and kerosene) and heavy distillates. The light distillates are sold for $48 per barrel. The heavy distillates can either be sold for $30 per barrel or fed into a catalytic cracking unit ("cat cracker") at a variable cost of $3 per barrel to be converted into light distillates and sold, for $48 per barrel. The diagram in Figure 1 illustrates the refining process.

FIGURE 1

Crude oil distillation: the first step

SOURCE: http://www.eia.doe.gov/pub/oil_gas/petroleum/analysis_publications/oil_market_basics/Refining_text.htm#Crude%20Oil%20Quality.

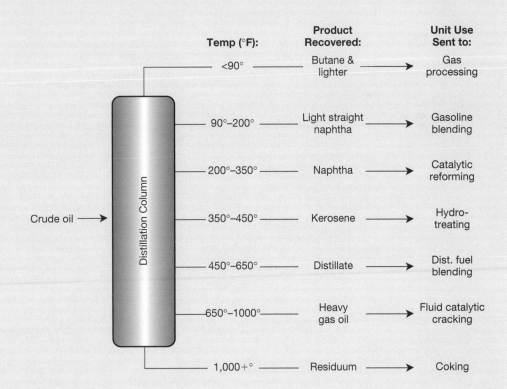

FIGURE 2

Product yield from simple distillation

SOURCE: http://www.eia.doe.gov/pub/oil_gas/petroleum/analysis_publications/oil_market_basics/Ref_image_Simple.htm.

NOTE: Arab Light is slightly lighter and sweeter than Kuwait Export. West Texas Intermediate is lighter than Kuwait Export (specific gravity of 40.8 for WTI versus 31.4 for Kuwait Export) and sweeter than Kuwait Export (sulfur percentage of 0.34% for WTI versus 2.52% for Kuwait Export).

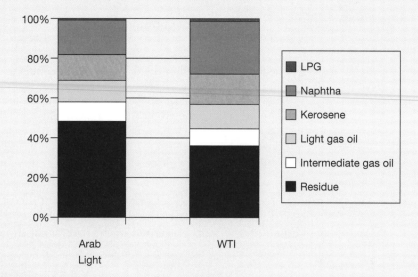

FIGURE 3

Price difference between light crude oil and heavy crude oil, 1988–2001

NOTE: Light crude oil is defined here as having an API gravity of 40.1 or greater and heavy crude oil is defined as having an API gravity of 20.1 or less.
SOURCE: http://www.eia.doe.gov/emeu/perfpro/ref_pi2/fig5.html.

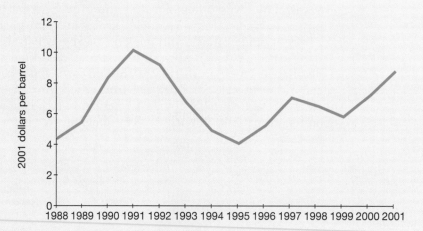

Wyatt's Channelview refinery can distill 60 million barrels of oil per year and feed 30 million barrels of heavy distillate a year into the cat cracker. It can process either light, sweet crude from Texas (such as West Texas Intermediate) or heavy, sour crude from the Middle East (such as Kuwait Export), depending on the market prices of the two types of crude. More valuable products are distilled from a barrel of light, sweet crude than from a barrel of heavy, sour crude (see Figure 2). Light, sweet crude currently costs $34 per barrel and heavy, sour crude costs $30; however, the price differential is volatile, as noted in Figure 3. The output from 60 million barrels of West Texas Intermediate and 60 million barrels of Kuwait Export is shown in Table 1.

The fixed and variable costs and capacities associated with distilling crude and cracking the heavy distillates are shown in Table 2.

Until recently, Wyatt's Channelview refinery processed West Texas Intermediate, but it switched to Kuwait Export when the price differential between the two reached $3.50 per barrel. Kim Quillen, manager of the refinery, is concerned because the switch to heavy, sour crude has resulted in the refinery selling only 50 million barrels of light distillates instead of 60 million—because the refinery has

TABLE 1

	West Texas Intermediate	Kuwait Export
Light distillates	30 million bbls./year	20 million bbls./year
Heavy distillates	30 million bbls./year	40 million bbls./year
Total	60 million bbls./year	60 million bbls./year

TABLE 2

	Distilling Crude Oil	Cracking Heavy Distillates
Variable cost	$2 per bbl.	$3 per bbl.
Annual fixed cost	$180 million	$90 million
Annual capacity	60 million bbls.	30 million bbls.

capacity to crack only 30 million barrels of heavy distillates. The refinery's projected accounting income for the year is shown below.

Revenue from light distillates	$ 960,000,000
Revenue from processed heavy distillates	1,440,000,000
Revenue from sold heavy distillates	300,000,000
Cost of crude oil	(1,800,000,000)
Variable distilling costs	(120,000,000)
Variable cracking costs	(90,000,000)
Fixed distilling costs	(180,000,000)
Fixed cracking costs	(90,000,000)
Net income	$ 420,000,000

Buying an additional cat cracker to increase cracking capacity by 10 million barrels would cost $900 million. It would last for 20 years, increasing the refinery's annual fixed costs by $45 million per year. Quillen has asked his accountant, John Hanks, to evaluate the investment, and Hanks has contemptuously dismissed the project. His analysis appears below.

Sales value of light distillates	$48.00 per bbl.
Cost of heavy distillates*	(35.00) per bbl.
Additional cat cracker accounting costs**	(7.50) per bbl.
Capital charge***	(13.50) per bbl.
Residual income (loss)	$ (8.00) per bbl.

* $\dfrac{\$180,000,000}{60,000,000 \text{ bbls.}}$ + $2 per barrel + $30 per barrel

** $\dfrac{\$45,000,000}{\$10,000,000 \text{ bbls.}}$ + $3 per barrel

*** $\dfrac{\$900 \text{ million} \times 15\%}{10,000,000 \text{ bbls.}}$

Hank concludes his evaluation by saying, "What an awful project! Our residual income decreases by $8 on every barrel. Not to mention the possibility that we might switch back to using West Texas Intermediate sometime. Then we would have excess cat cracker capacity, which would just rust away over time since expanding our distilling capacity is not feasible. There is no way we should pursue this project."

Quillen is puzzled, for he knows that many other refineries have been installing additional cat cracker capacity in response to the growing price differential between sweet, light crude and sour, heavy crude. Fortunately, he has just hired you to evaluate the capital investment.

Required:

a. Allocate the projected $420 million accounting income of the Channelview refinery among its three activities—light distillates, processed heavy distillates, and sold heavy distillates—by allocating joint costs on the basis of (*i*) physical volume and (*ii*) net realizable value. Compare the ratio of accounting profit to net realizable value of the three activities under both methods.

b. Did Quillen make the right decision to switch from West Texas Intermediate to Kuwait Export when the price differential reached $3.50 per barrel? Assuming there are no switching costs, find the optimal decision rule as a function of the price differential.

c. Would your decision rule be different if you were to expand the cracker capacity to 40 million barrels? Find the optimal switching rule if the refinery can crack 40 million barrels of heavy distillates each year.

d. Assume the price differential between West Texas Intermediate crude and Kuwait Export crude remains the same at $4 per barrel. Should Quillen expand the refinery's cat cracking capacity?

e. Now consider the possibility of changes in the price differential. Suppose that this year's price differential is $4, but next year's price differential could be anywhere between 75 percent and 125 percent of the current year differential (equally likely, so next year's price differential can be thought of as a random variable uniformly distributed on the interval [$3, $5]). Each succeeding year, the price differential follows the same pattern: between 75 percent and 125 percent of the prior year price differential. Should Quillen expand capacity? Why or why not?

SOURCE: R Sansing.

Chapter Nine

Absorption Cost Systems

Chapter Outline

A. Job Order Costing

B. Cost Flows through the T-Accounts

C. Allocating Overhead to Jobs

    1. Overhead Rates

    2. Over/Underabsorbed Overhead

    3. Flexible Budgets to Estimate Overhead

    4. Expected versus Normal Volume

D. Permanent versus Temporary Volume Changes

E. Plantwide versus Multiple Overhead Rates

F. Process Costing: The Extent of Averaging

G. Summary

Appendix A: Process Costing

Appendix B: Demand Shifts, Fixed Costs, and Pricing

461

Chapter 1 described the function of the internal accounting system as providing information for decision making and control. Chapters 2 and 4 provided the underlying economic framework for decision management and decision control. Chapters 7 and 8 introduced the topic of cost allocations and discussed various reasons why firms allocate costs. These reasons included: decision management, decision control, cost-plus pricing contracts, financial reporting, and taxes. This chapter continues the discussion of cost allocations by describing a particular costing system widely used in manufacturing called *absorption costing*.

Absorption cost systems ensure that all manufacturing costs are directly traced or allocated to the various products made. The cost objects are the products. If it costs $32 million to operate a factory that manufactures 620,000 pagers (16 different models), including units still in inventory, then an absorption cost system either directly traces or allocates the $32 million among the 620,000 pagers. Absorption cost systems display the same trade-off between decision making and control, but most of the discussion of this trade-off is deferred to the next two chapters; this chapter focuses on the mechanics of these cost systems.

Absorption cost systems are widely used in financial reporting for calculating the book value of inventory and cost of goods manufactured. These systems evolved in manufacturing firms. However, the same concepts have been applied to the service sector, including financial institutions and service firms such as law firms, hospitals, advertising agencies, and telecommunication firms. To keep the chapter focused, absorption cost systems in service industries are not described, although several problems at the end of this chapter and in other chapters illustrate absorption costing in nonmanufacturing settings. Actually, nonmanufacturing accounting systems are simpler in that they do not have work-in-process and finished goods inventories. On the other hand, defining the "product" to which costs are allocated is often more difficult. For example, in a bank that offers a wide range of services from loans to bank accounts, many of which involve numerous common costs, the list of products is not always clear cut. Nonetheless, since there are no substantive differences in absorption costing in manufacturing versus nonmanufacturing settings (except for inventories in manufacturing firms), the concepts described in this chapter should be mastered regardless of the actual organizational context.

There are different types of manufacturing processes:

- Job shops (customized production to a customer's specification).
- Batch manufacturing (standardized products manufactured in batches of given lot sizes either to meet customer orders or for inventory).
- Assembly processes (finished parts and subassemblies assembled into a finished product).
- Continuous flow processing lines (such as oil refineries and chemical processing plants).

Plants often consist of different production processes. For example, parts may be manufactured in batches in one department and assembled into finished products in another department. These different production processes usually require different accounting systems to accumulate the costs and assign them to products. There are basically two types of absorption systems: job order systems and process cost systems. **Job order costing** is used in departments that produce output in distinct jobs (job order production) or batches (batch manufacturing). Job order costing is also widely used in assembly processes. A job might consist of a single unit, such as the construction of an office building, or a batch of units, such as 200 windshield wiper motors for automobiles. In a service organization, a job might be handling a client's lawsuit or processing a loan application at a bank. The cost of each job is tracked separately, and job order cost systems accumulate costs by jobs. Alternatively, some assembly processes and continuous flow production processes use **process cost systems.** Production in these settings (e.g., soft-drink producers and oil refining) is continuous and distinct batches do not exist. Costs are assigned to the production processes and ultimately to the products flowing through the various processes. With either system, all manufacturing costs are assigned to the products produced.

In practice, there is great diversity in how firms' accounting systems assign costs to products, jobs, or activities. Even within batch processing departments, no two systems are exactly the same. Many plants use hybrids of job order and process costing. Each accounting system is tailored to the peculiarities of the department or plant. However, there are similarities across all these systems that are addressed in this chapter. Section A describes job order costing. Section B describes how job order costs flow through the manufacturing T-accounts. The central problem addressed in cost systems is how to treat costs that cannot be traced directly to the product, job, or service. The allocation of these overhead cost to products/production is often a key design issue in costing systems, and section C describes how overhead is allocated to manufacturing jobs. Section D discusses permanent versus temporary volume changes, and section E describes the use of single versus multiple overhead rates for allocating overhead to jobs. Process costing is addressed in section F. Section G summarizes the chapter. Appendix A provides a more in-depth discussion of the mechanics of process costing. Appendix B illustrates the relations among volume, average costs, and prices.

A. Job Order Costing

To illustrate job order costing in a manufacturing setting, consider a plant that produces multiple products. Each product is produced in a batch requiring several different raw material inputs and several different classes of direct labor. Moreover, the products utilize various combinations of common resources such as machines, supervisors, engineers, and factory space. Every job manufactured passes through a common machining process. The time spent in this machining center is recorded for each job and used to allocate overhead costs to the job. Each job has a job order cost sheet that records the costs attached to the products produced in the batch and the number of machine hours spent processing the job. A typical job order cost sheet appears in Table 9–1. The job sheet in Table 9–1 is the underlying source document in the job order cost system. Prior to computers, manufacturing firms maintained job order cost sheets manually. Today, job order cost sheets are electronic records in computer systems.

The job sheet records all direct materials issued for the job, including the type, quantity, and cost of materials. Each day, factory employees record the time they spent working on particular jobs and the hours they were idle or in a training program. All payroll costs not directly traced to particular jobs are charged to overhead. All direct labor worked on job #5167 is posted to the job order sheet. Notice

TABLE 9–1   Job Order Cost Sheet

Job Number 5167   **Date Started 3/10**

                                                      Date Completed 5/28

	Raw Materials					Direct Labor		
Date	Type	Quantity	Amount	Machine Hours	Date	Type	Hours	Amount
3/13	103a	205	$ 6,305	13	3/13	a65	15	$ 265
3/14	214	106	5,210	111	3/14	a68	20	596
4/1	217	52	786	45	4/18	b73	81	811
4/23	878	229	1,187	28	4/23	c89	368.5	7,370
5/23	331	113	659	16	5/28	c89	419	8,380
Totals			$14,147	213				$ 17,422

SUMMARY OF COSTS:

Total direct materials	$ 14,147
Total direct labor	17,422
Overhead (213 machine hours @ $25/hr)	5,325
Total job cost	**$36,894**
Divided by: Number of units in batch	1,560
Average cost per unit produced	$ 23.65

that different types of labor were used on the job. Job #5167 was started on March 10, completed on May 28, and yielded 1,560 completed units. It accumulated $14,147 of direct materials costs and $17,422 of direct labor costs.

Also recorded on the job sheet are the number of machine hours used by the job. In this plant, machine hours are used to allocate overhead costs at the rate of $25 per machine hour, a predetermined rate. (How overhead rates are determined is discussed later in this chapter.) Job #5167 used 213 machine hours. Multiplying 213 machine hours times $25 per hour yields $5,325 of overhead charged to this job. The total charges for this job amount to $36,894. Since there were 1,560 units in the job, the average cost was $23.65 per unit.

Machine hours are used as the allocation basis for indirect manufacturing costs accumulated in the overhead account. Remember from Chapter 7 that using machine hours as the allocation base taxes machine hours and creates incentives to substitute other inputs for machine hours. Job #5167 illustrates several important features of job order costing:

- The items being produced by the job are the objects being costed.
- All direct costs of manufacturing the job are traced directly to the job.
- Each job is charged for some indirect manufacturing overhead.
- An input measure, machine hours, is used to allocate overhead costs to jobs. An input measure is the allocation base.
- The overhead rate per input measure (here, the rate per machine hour) is set at the beginning of the year, before the first jobs are started. This overhead

Job Order Cost Sheets and United States Steel

In the 1870s, Andrew Carnegie built the Edgar Thompson Steel Works in Pittsburgh, which was later to become U.S. Steel. One of Carnegie's many management innovations and his obsession was a detailed cost accounting system. Each department in the steel works listed the amount and cost of labor and materials used by each job as it passed through the department. Carnegie received daily reports showing the direct costs of the products produced and would repeat, "Watch the costs and the profits will take care of themselves."

Carnegie's cost sheets were called a marvel of ingenuity and careful accounting. He required his people to explain the most minute change in unit costs. Carnegie and his managers used these data to evaluate the performance of his people, maintain the quality and mix of raw materials, evaluate improvements in process and product, and price products. New orders would not be accepted until costs had been carefully checked.

SOURCE: A Chandler, *The Visible Hand: The Managerial Revolution in American Business* (Cambridge, MA: Harvard University Press, 1977), pp. 267–68.

rate is the ratio of expected factory overhead for the year divided by the expected machine hours for the year.

- Reported product costs are average rather than variable or marginal costs. Each job is assigned a portion of the overhead. Since overhead contains both variable and fixed costs, overhead distributed to jobs contains some fixed costs.

B. Cost Flows through the T-Accounts

Job order cost sheets allow the assignment of all factory costs to the jobs flowing through the factory. As jobs enter the factory and remain in process, direct labor costs and direct materials costs are posted to job sheets via the computer system.

Table 9–1 illustrated the job order cost sheet for one job. Modern factories can have hundreds or even thousands of jobs in various stages of completion in the factory at any one time. The accounting system tracks the costs charged to each job by posting them to ledger accounts (T-accounts) via the usual mechanics of double-entry bookkeeping. As costs are charged to individual jobs, they are also entered in a work-in-process inventory account, which contains all the dollars of jobs in process, including the direct materials, direct labor, and overhead allocations. As raw materials move from the storeroom to the factory floor for individual jobs, their dollars are transferred out of the raw materials account and into the work-in-process account.

Figure 9–1 diagrams the flow of costs among the various T-accounts. When a job is finished and transferred to finished goods inventory, the total job cost from the job order cost sheet is transferred out of the work-in-process T-account and into the finished goods T-account. Similarly, when the goods are sold, the dollars flow out of the finished goods T-account and into the cost-of-goods-sold T-account.

The overhead T-account contains all indirect labor (supervisors as well as factory workers who are not working on jobs because they are either in training programs, setting up or maintaining machines, or idle), indirect materials (supplies not directly assignable to particular jobs), and other factory costs. Other factory

FIGURE 9–1

Schematic of a job order cost system

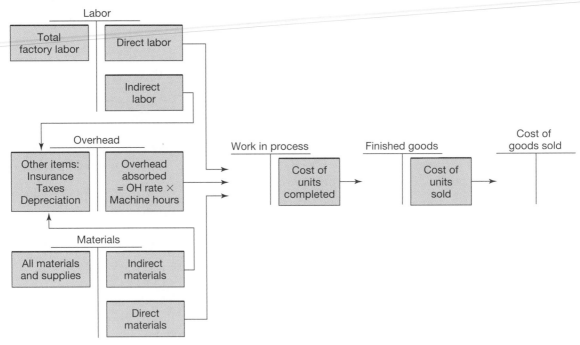

costs include insurance, property taxes, depreciation, accounting costs, purchasing, security, general factory management, and utilities. These costs represent the common resources used by all jobs. In a typical plant, direct labor is about 30 percent of total factory costs, direct materials is another 30 percent, and overhead is 40 percent.[1] These percentages can vary widely, however; direct labor can be as low as 1 percent of total manufacturing costs and overhead as high as 80 percent. The overhead T-account is a control account. It is used to temporarily accumulate and then distribute the indirect costs to the jobs. At the end of the accounting period, any remaining balance in this account must be charged to a balance sheet or income statement account.

Management must decide which inventory flow assumption to use in making the transfers between the various T-accounts. Should the costs follow a first-in, first-out (FIFO); last-in, first-out (LIFO); or specific identification flow? This decision is discussed in financial accounting, particularly with regard to the tax implications of the LIFO/FIFO choice. (In periods of rising costs, LIFO reduces reported income and hence taxes by taking the most recent and thus highest costs to the income statement.) However, the inventory accounting decision affects both decision making and control. For example, if LIFO is used, the most recent prices flow through the accounts and old prices remain in inventory. LIFO produces more timely (current) information regarding price changes than FIFO. In particular, LIFO-based product costs are computed using the most recent raw material prices and usually more closely reflect replacement costs.

---

[1] R Howell, J Brown, S Soucy, and A Seed, *Management Accounting in the New Manufacturing Environment* (Montvale, NJ: National Association of Accountants, 1987).

TABLE 9–2   Income Statement for a Manufacturing Firm

SAMPLE COMPANY
Income Statement
($000s)

Sales		$2,200
Cost of goods sold:		
Finished goods—Jan. 1	$ 217	
Cost of goods manufactured*	1,337	
Cost of goods available for sale	1,554	
Less finished goods—Dec. 31	(192)	
Cost of goods sold		(1,362)
Gross profit		$ 838
Less		
Selling and administrative expense		
Variable	$ 216	
Fixed	349	(565)
Net income		$ 273

*Cost of goods manufactured:

Direct materials		
Materials inventory—Jan. 1	$ 13	
Purchases	232	
Material available for use	245	
Less materials inventory—Dec. 31	(20)	
Material used		$225
Direct labor		480
Manufacturing overhead		665
Total manufacturing costs incurred		$1,370
Add work in process—Jan. 1		90
Total in process		$1,460
Less work in process—Dec. 31		(123)
Cost of goods manufactured		$1,337

To the extent replacement costs are good proxies for opportunity cost, LIFO is usually better for decision making. However, a LIFO system is usually more costly to implement and operate because more data must be maintained, particularly past prices and inventory layers. LIFO also creates control problems. Performance evaluation systems based on accounting profits create incentives for managers close to retirement or with a short horizon in the firm to liquidate old LIFO inventory levels, thereby generating large accounting profits (but also large tax liabilities). The choice of inventory flow assumptions is important because it affects taxes, financial statements (and the external contracts based on them), internal decision making, and control. To simplify the analysis, for the remainder of this text we assume that the firm uses the specific identification inventory valuation method, unless otherwise stated.

Table 9–2 illustrates how the various T-accounts in Figure 9–1 are used in constructing the firm's income statement. The cost of goods sold in the income statement consists of the change in finished goods inventory plus the cost of goods manufactured during the period, which in turn is composed of direct labor, direct materials, and overhead. Table 9–2 shows sales of $2.2 million. The cost of goods sold is $1.362 million, calculated by taking the sum of the beginning inventory and cost of goods manufactured and deducting the ending inventory. The cost of goods manufactured is calculated in the footnote to Table 9–2. It consists of direct materials, direct labor, and overhead plus the change in work-in-process inventories.

Concept Question		
	Q9–1	What are the two distinct absorption systems?
	Q9–2	Describe the flow of costs through the T-accounts in a job order cost system.
	Q9–3	Suppose that during the production of a particular job, a machine malfunctions, destroying $2,750 of raw materials. How should the cost of these materials be handled? Should they be charged to the job in process?

C. Allocating Overhead to Jobs

The previous two sections illustrated how a job order cost system accumulates product costs and how the accounting system tracks manufacturing costs through the ledger accounts. This section describes the mechanics of using overhead rates to distribute indirect costs to jobs. The use of prospective overhead rates (those estimated at the beginning of the year) results in over- or underabsorbed overhead at the end of the year, and this section discusses how this over/underabsorption is treated. The concept of flexible budgeting is reintroduced and applied to calculating overhead rates. This section concludes by describing alternative ways of estimating budgeted volume.

1. Overhead Rates

The most interesting aspect of job costing is its treatment of overheads because it involves management's judgment and offers managers discretion in product costing and income determination. If all resource utilization and factory costs could be traced directly to the products consuming those resources, then cost accounting would be nothing more than arithmetic. The innovation of job order costing is the accumulation of all indirect costs in an overhead account and the subsequent distribution of these costs to individual jobs through the use of an overhead rate. An overhead allocation base is chosen to allocate the indirect costs to jobs. Machine hours are used as the overhead allocation base in Table 9–1. As work is performed on the job, overhead is charged to the job based on total machine hours used. A *prospective* overhead rate, set at the beginning of the year, allows jobs to be costed as they are produced.

Most firms use prospective, not actual, overhead rates. Suppose overhead is charged to jobs based on the total actual machine hours used in the plant for the entire year. Then the total cost of each job (including overhead) is unavailable until the end of the year. The overhead costs for the first job cannot be determined until all the jobs are finished. For example, suppose the first job completed in the year uses 1,000 machine hours and overhead is assigned based on actual machine hours. Overhead on the first job could be 1 percent of actual overhead if actual total hours for the year end up being 100,000 hours or 2 percent if the final number of machine hours is 50,000 hours. Using a prospective overhead rate allows more timely reporting of total costs, including indirect costs.

Notice in Table 9–1 that factory volume is measured in machine hours, not units of production. That is, volume is being measured with an *input* measure, not an *output* measure. This practice is common in most plants. Inputs are used to measure volume because most plants produce heterogeneous products. If a factory manufactures small pumps and large pumps, the number of pumps manufactured can give a misleading measure of plant output. Plant volume can actually fall while the total number of pumps increases if there is a shift from large to small pumps. Therefore, volume in plants manufacturing heterogeneous products is based on an input measure rather than an output measure.

The input measure selected (machine hours, direct material dollars, direct labor hours, direct labor dollars) is usually the one that has the greatest association or cause-and-effect relationship with overhead. That is, the allocation base is the factor input most correlated with overhead. Overhead consists of both fixed and variable indirect costs. In the long run, fixed costs can be adjusted to changes in volume.

In a survey of 112 New York and American Stock Exchange firms, 92 percent said they chose their allocation base because there was a logical or statistical association with overhead.[2] For example, as plant output expands, additional supervisors must be hired. Therefore, the cost driver of supervision can be either the number of machine hours or the number of direct labor hours. If overhead costs are most closely related to direct labor hours, then direct labor hours should be the volume measure. In Chapter 7, overhead rates were shown in certain circumstances to serve as a proxy for hard-to-observe opportunity costs. If the overhead rate (which is the average cost) is less than or equal to the marginal cost imposed on the firm when output expands by one more unit, allocating overhead is better than not allocating it. The factor input used as the volume measure then becomes "taxed," and the choice of volume measure becomes, in essence, a decision regarding which factor input management wishes to tax. Usually, management wants to tax the input that imposes externalities on other parts of the organization. Ideally, the overhead rate provides an estimate of the opportunity cost of using one more unit of the allocation base.

Four points of this discussion and Figure 9–1 are worth noting:

1. The overhead rate equals annual budgeted overhead divided by budgeted volume. This measure averages out seasonal variability in monthly expenditures and volume. Each completed job can be costed, even though the total overhead and actual volume for the year are not known.
2. Budgeted volume is measured using an input, such as direct labor, instead of output. Typical volume measures are direct labor hours, direct labor dollars, direct material dollars, and machine hours.
3. The measure of volume chosen as the allocation base is usually the one that has the greatest association with overhead.
4. The choice of the overhead volume measure is critical; because it is the taxed input, managers will seek to reduce its use.

Point 2 suggests that direct labor and machine hours are common overhead allocation bases. In a survey of 198 Japanese companies in four industries (electronic

---

[2] H Schwarzbach, "The Impact of Automation on Accounting for Indirect Costs," *Management Accounting*, December 1985, p. 47.

<table>
<tr><td>

Over- and Underabsorbed Overhead Understood by 1910

</td><td>

By 1910, most large U.S. manufacturing companies had come to use overhead accounts to accumulate and distribute these costs to products. One writer described the typical accounting treatment as follows:

> The overhead account is charged each month . . . with the items composing the indirect expenses, and is credited through the fixed overhead percentage with the total amount applied to the various production orders and cost sheets. The balance, if a debit, shows the undistributed portion of the overhead, which means that the fixed percentage added to the labor cost was not sufficient to cover the indirect expenses. When there is a credit balance, however, it shows that the percentage allowed was more than sufficient.

Absorption cost systems, including the use of prospective overhead rates, have survived over 100 years and been used in a variety of firms, absent government regulations. The survival of those systems in firms that operate in competitive markets is evidence that absorption cost systems are providing benefits that exceed their costs.

SOURCE: J Nicholson, *Cost Accounting—Theory and Practice* (New York: The Ronald Press Co., 1913), p. 197. Quoted by P Garner, *Evolution of Cost Accounting to 1925* (Montgomery, AL: University of Alabama Press, 1954), p. 176.

</td></tr>
</table>

T-accounts based on the amount of overhead in these categories. For example, in the previous example there was $100,000 of overabsorbed overhead. Suppose that of the $3 million of overhead absorbed, $0.5 million is still in work in process, $1.0 million remains in finished goods inventory, and $1.5 million is in cost of goods sold. Then the following illustrates the proration of the $100,000 of overabsorbed overhead:

	Work in Process	Finished Goods	Cost of Goods Sold	Total
Overhead absorbed	$500,000	$1,000,000	$1,500,000	$3,000,000
Percentage of overhead absorbed	16.67%	33.33%	50%	100%
Overabsorbed overhead prorated	$(16,670)	$ (33,330)	$ (50,000)	$ (100,000)
Overhead before proration	500,000	1,000,000	1,500,000	3,000,000
Overhead after proration	$483,330	$ 966,670	$1,450,000	$2,900,000

The third method of disposing of over/underabsorbed overhead is to recalculate the cost of each job using actual overhead incurred and actual volume to compute a revised, end-of-year overhead rate. The second and third methods produce similar net income and inventory valuations. The third method is the most expensive in terms of bookkeeping and data processing costs, especially if a large number of jobs have been manufactured and each one is to be recosted. One reason to choose the third alternative of recosting all jobs is if the firm has cost-plus contracts whereby some of the firm's revenues are tied to reported costs. In this case, recosting each job can change the amount of overhead assigned to products manufactured under cost-plus contracts, thereby changing the firm's revenues, profits, and cash flows.

Usually the magnitude of the over/underabsorbed overhead is small, and thus disposing of the balance is inconsequential. Writing small balances off to cost of

Overhead Allocations and GAAP	One reason manufacturing overhead is allocated to work in process and therefore to product costs is for inventory valuation for external financial reports. Generally accepted accounting principles (GAAP) require:

> In keeping with the principle that accounting is primarily based on cost, there is a presumption that inventories should be stated at cost. . . . It should also be recognized that the exclusion of all overheads from inventory does not constitute an accepted accounting procedure. The exercise of judgment in an individual situation involves a consideration of the adequacy of the procedures of the cost accounting system in use, the soundness of the principles thereof, and their consistent application.

Thus, GAAP allows management significant discretion. It can either take over/underabsorbed overhead to the income statement by writing it off to cost of goods sold or allocate it among the inventory accounts.

SOURCE: Accounting Research Bulletin No. 43, "Restatement and Revision of Accounting Research Bulletins," in *Financial Accounting Standards Board, Original Pronouncements* (Burr Ridge, IL: Richard D. Irwin, 1992), Chapter 4, paragraph 5, pp. 15–16.

goods sold is expedient and senior managers do not concern themselves with such technical accounting issues. However, large balances remaining in the overhead account attract senior managers' and the external auditors' attention. External auditors have an incentive to be conservative since they are sued more frequently for overstatements of income than for understatements. The auditors are therefore more likely to allow a larger write-off to cost of goods sold of underabsorbed overhead than of overabsorbed overhead, assuming that these write-offs materially affect reported income. Underabsorbed overhead reduces income, whereas overabsorbed overhead increases income.

3. Flexible Budgets to Estimate Overhead

As described previously, most firms use prospective overhead rates, or those estimated before the fiscal year begins. This requires managers to forecast next year's overhead rate. One way to forecast the overhead rate is to use a flexible budget (Chapter 6). The first step requires estimating budgeted annual overhead.

$$\text{Budgeted annual overhead} = \text{Fixed overhead} + \text{Variable overhead}$$

$$= FOH + VOH \times BV$$

where

FOH = Fixed overhead
VOH = Variable overhead per unit of volume
BV = Budgeted volume

Suppose that fixed overhead is projected at \$500,000, variable overhead is projected at \$20 per machine hour, and 100,000 machine hours are budgeted. Then budgeted annual overhead is

$$\text{Budgeted annual overhead} = \$500,000 + \$20 \times 100,000 \text{ machine hours}$$

$$= \$500,000 + \$2,000,000$$

$$= \$2,500,000$$

Behavior of Overhead Costs	It has long been recognized that overhead costs contain both a fixed and a variable component:

> [Overhead costs] refer to costs that cannot be traced home and attributed to particular units of business in the same direct and obvious way in which, for example, leather can be traced to the shoes that are made of it. And most of the real problems involve one other fact; namely, that an increase or decrease in output does not involve a proportionate increase or decrease in cost.

SOURCE: J Clark, *Studies in the Economics of Overhead Costs* (Chicago: University of Chicago Press, 1923), p. 1.

The second step involves calculating the budgeted annual overhead rate:

$$\text{Budgeted overhead rate} = \frac{\$2,500,000}{100,000 \text{ machine hours}}$$

$$= \$25/\text{machine hour}$$

The advantage of using flexible budgets is the ability to derive an estimate of total overhead that varies with volume. Overhead is not treated as a purely fixed cost but rather as a mixture of fixed and variable costs. Analyzing how total overhead varies with volume should lead to a more accurate estimate of budgeted overhead.

Chapter 6 described the budgeting process. One important function of that process is estimating the budgeted overhead rate. This occurs prior to the beginning of the year. Hence, the budgeted overhead rate is a prospective rate. Most firms set their overhead rates prospectively. To simplify the terminology, throughout the remainder of this book, whenever the term *overhead rate* is used, it refers to the "budgeted overhead rate" unless otherwise specifically stated.

4. Expected versus Normal Volume

Previous sections have described prospective overhead rates as the ratio of budgeted overhead to budgeted volume. Budgeted volume can be determined in two ways. Budgeted volume can be estimated as either the volume expected for the coming year (**expected volume**) or the long-run average volume. Long-run average volume is called **normal volume,** or the average volume that is predicted over upturns and downturns in the economy.

The following example motivates the important difference between expected volume and normal volume. Fast Change offers automobile oil changes at $30 each. This is the only service provided. The variable cost ($20) of providing an oil change includes both direct labor and supplies (oil and oil filter). The fixed cost of $4,000 per month includes advertising, the manager's salary, rent, utilities, insurance, and so forth. Table 9–3 summarizes last month's operations.

Last month Fast Change had net income before taxes of $1,000 on 500 oil changes, and the full (average) cost of an oil change as shown in the table was $28.00 ($20 of variable cost plus $8.00 = $4,000 ÷ 500 of fixed cost).

This month, the price of an oil change ($30) remains constant, as does the variable cost and fixed cost. However, the number of oil changes falls from 500 to 350. Table 9–4 summarizes operations for this month.

Fast Change lost $500 this month. Notice that the average cost of an oil change has risen from $28.00 to $31.43 ($20 of variable cost plus $11.43 = $4,000 ÷ 350 of fixed cost). The accounting system reports that the cost of an oil change

TABLE 9–3   **Fast Change Summary of Operations Last Month**

	Oil Changes
Price per oil change	$30
Variable cost per service	$20
Number of oil changes	500
Revenue	$ 15,000
Variable cost	(10,000)
Fixed cost	(4,000)
Net income	$ 1,000
Total cost	$ 14,000
Number of oil changes	÷500
Cost per oil change	$ 28.00

TABLE 9–4   **Fast Change Summary of Operations This Month**

	Oil Changes
Price per oil change	$30
Variable cost per service	$20
Number of oil changes	350
Revenue	$ 10,500
Variable cost	(7,000)
Fixed cost	(4,000)
Net loss	$ (500)
Total cost	$ 11,000
Number of oil changes	÷350
Cost per oil change	$ 31.43

increased. A manager's natural tendency when confronted by a cost increase is to raise prices. But in Fast Change's case, average costs rose because volumes fell. The out-of-pocket costs (the variable cost) of the service did not change. The cost of doing one more oil change is still $20. The opportunity cost of an oil service has not changed. Therefore, the price of these services should not be raised. In fact, they probably should be lowered because the demand for oil changes has dropped. For example, if a new competitor has opened up down the street and is offering oil changes at lower prices, Fast Change will also have to lower its prices. Appendix B illustrates the relations among shifts in demand, changes in fixed costs, and price changes.

The preceding Fast Change example illustrates an important point. Basing overhead rates on short-run fluctuations in volume causes accounting costs, but not opportunity costs, to rise when volume falls and causes them to fall when

cost of facilities. In addition, they might want to treat 25 percent of the other fixed overhead costs (such as property taxes) as a period cost to avoid distorting unit costs. Similarly, if normal volume increases by 25 percent (a permanent increase), and the plant has the excess capacity to handle this larger volume, then the depreciable life of the plant and equipment can be shortened. This will increase the depreciation expense charged to overhead, offsetting the higher volume so that depreciation per unit of product does not fall.

While in theory managers can reduce the book value of plant and equipment for permanent reductions in volume, thereby reducing the overhead charges, managers are reluctant to make the write-off for other reasons. Such a write-off is a public admission by the managers that they overinvested in capacity, which can be damaging to their careers. Moreover, write-offs can provide competitors with useful strategic information to the extent that they are uninformed about the exact amount of the excess capacity.

In summary, temporary changes in volume are assumed to average out over the business cycle, and no asset write-offs or other accounting changes are necessary. However, to prevent dysfunctional pricing decisions, fixed asset write-offs can accompany permanent declines in volume, thereby preventing overhead rates and hence unit costs from rising.

| **Concept Questions** | Q9–9 | Why should normal volume be used to determine overhead rates? |
| | Q9–10 | Why should one-time write-offs of fixed capital be used in absorption cost systems? |

E. Plantwide versus Multiple Overhead Rates

This section describes alternative methods of aggregating overhead costs and allocating them to products. Figure 9–2 schematically represents a single, plantwide overhead rate, which is the method used in the examples so far. All of the overhead costs are first accumulated in a single overhead account or **cost pool,** a collection of accounts accumulated for the purpose of allocating the costs in the pool to activities, products, or processes, and then allocated to products using a single plantwide overhead rate.

A slightly more complicated way to allocate overhead costs is to use multiple overhead rates for different overhead cost items. In this case, each component of overhead is treated as a separate cost pool. Figure 9–3 illustrates this method.

For example, suppose the overhead account is composed of the following three categories:

Indirect labor	$ 750,000
Utilities	650,000
All other costs	1,100,000
Total overhead	$2,500,000

Each of these categories is then allocated to jobs through separate allocation bases. For example,

FIGURE 9–2

Single plantwide overhead rate

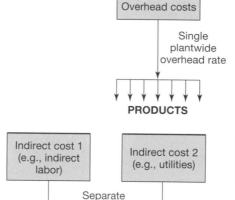

FIGURE 9–3

Multiple overhead rates based on overhead categories

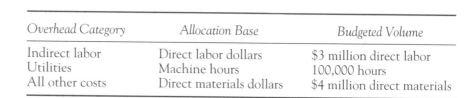

Overhead Category	Allocation Base	Budgeted Volume
Indirect labor	Direct labor dollars	$3 million direct labor
Utilities	Machine hours	100,000 hours
All other costs	Direct materials dollars	$4 million direct materials

A third method of accumulating overhead cost pools and allocating them to products involves developing different overhead rates by departments. Instead of being allocated by cost category, overhead costs are first grouped by departments. Each department is a separate cost pool. Separate allocation bases are developed for each department, and then overhead costs are allocated to products. Figure 9–4 illustrates this two step procedure.

Suppose the factory contains three departments: machining, painting, and assembly. The $2.5 million of total overhead costs is broken down into three different departments:

Department	Department Costs	Allocation Base
Machining	$ 900,000	Machine hours
Painting	750,000	Dollars of paint used
Assembly	850,000	Direct labor dollars
Total overhead	$2,500,000	

Under this method, all overhead costs are first accumulated by departments. Often, step-down allocations (discussed in Chapter 8) are used to assign service department costs (indirect cost pools) to manufacturing departments. These department costs are then allocated to jobs based on one of three allocation bases:

Borg-Warner

Borg-Warner's Muncie plant produces automobile and light truck transmissions and drive trains. Originally, the plant's products were manufactured in traditional production departments that were organized by function. Parts moved between departments depending on the operations required and when completed went to the components inventory waiting for assembly. Increased worldwide competition and new manufacturing technology changed the manufacturing process, how it was organized, and the accounting systems. A series of "focused factories" was created within the plant. The machines required for assembling each product were arranged to allow the product to flow from one stage to another. Component parts, produced in highly automated cells, were located around the assembly line to introduce the parts where they are required. The automated assembly line employed computer-controlled equipment and materials-movement robotic equipment. Each product (such as a transmission) had its own dedicated focused factory.

The accounting system also changed. Traditional line-item budgets based on direct labor hours were replaced by budgets for each dedicated focused factory. The new budgets were based on the number of units produced in the particular focused factory. Also, the accounting system was changed to provide more information to internal managers.

Section E in Chapter 1 describes the integral role played by the accounting system in the firm's organizational architecture and how the organizational architecture changes in response to environment shifts in competition and technology. Borg-Warner illustrates how one firm's organizational architecture (including its accounting system) adapted to changes in the firm's environment.

SOURCE: G Hanks, M Freid, and J Huber, "Shifting Gears at Borg-Warner Automotive," *Management Accounting*, February 1994, pp. 25–29.

FIGURE 9–4

Two-stage allocation of departmental overhead rates

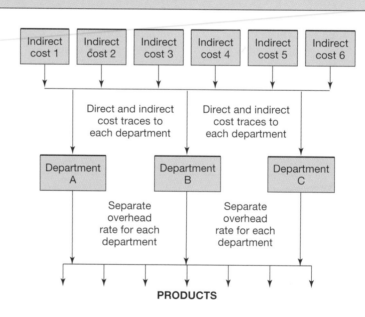

machine hours for machining department costs, dollars of paint used for painting department costs, and direct labor dollars for assembly department costs.

Whether managers use a single plantwide overhead rate, multiple rates, or departmental rates depends on the plant's organization, the incentive systems in place, management's demand for accurate cost data for decision making, and the incremental cost of using more complex cost systems. A plantwide overhead rate is acceptable if the plant has a single homogeneous production process. In this case, a single plantwide overhead rate is an accurate representation of the *average* cause-and-effect relation between volume and overhead.

It is commonly believed that a plantwide rate is a less accurate measure of the cause-and-effect relation in plants composed of several heterogeneous processes. Suppose a plant has three departments (parts fabrication, assembly, and testing) with overhead rates of $30, $50, and $100 per direct labor hour, respectively. To simplify the example, assume that each department has the same number of total direct labor hours per year. The simple average (the plantwide overhead rate) is $60, or ($30 + $50 + $100) ÷ 3. Suppose a particular job uses 500 direct labor hours in each of the first two departments and 2,000 hours in the third department. A plantwide overhead rate would charge this job $180,000 of overhead ($60 × 3,000 hours). Individual department overhead rates would charge the job $240,000 (or $30 × 500 + $50 × 500 + $100 × 2,000). However, if the overhead rates contain large amounts of fixed historical costs, such as depreciation, then neither plantwide overhead rates nor individual department rates accurately reflect the opportunity cost of capacity. If the plant is organized into production departments, separate departmental overhead rates usually are more useful for performance evaluation purposes.

A survey of U.S. manufacturing plants revealed the following frequencies of types of overhead schemes:[5]

Single plantwide overhead rate (Figure 9–2)	30% of respondents
Multiple overhead rates (Figure 9–3)	18% of respondents
Separate departmental overhead rates (Figure 9–4)	52% of respondents

In another study involving Korean, Japanese, and U.S. firms, the following data were reported:[6]

Allocation Scheme	Korea	Japan	United States
Single rate for entire plant	43%	18%	31%
Rate for groups of work centers	29	68	31
Rate for each work center	24	15	38
Rate for each machine	9	3	7

One must be careful about reading too much into the differences across countries because different survey techniques and different response rates exist. However, these findings suggest that substantial variation exists in the calculation of overhead rates. A large number of firms in each country use a single plantwide overhead rate, and a few firms calculate overhead rates by machine. These data

[5] U Karmarkar, P Lederer, and J Zimmerman, "Choosing Manufacturing Production Control and Cost Accounting Systems," *Measures for Manufacturing Excellence*, ed. R Kaplan (Boston: Harvard Business School, 1990).

[6] I Kim and J Song, "U.S., Korea, & Japan: Accounting Practices in Three Countries," *Management Accounting*, August 1990, pp. 26–30.

4. The overhead allocation base (volume measure) is usually the one with the greatest association with the common costs being allocated. That is, the volume measure selected is usually the most important cost driver of the overhead costs being allocated.

5. An overhead rate is estimated as the ratio of the budgeted overhead expenses to the budgeted (normal or expected) volume measure.

6. Adjusting overhead rates because of short-run changes in volume can cause dysfunctional decisions. If overhead rates are changed in response to short-run changes in volume, overhead rates rise as volume falls and vice versa. These are the wrong cost signals to send throughout the firm as the firm moves through expansionary and recessionary business cycles.

7. At the end of the year, any over/underabsorbed balance in the overhead account usually is written off to cost of goods sold.

8. Instead of using a single plantwide overhead rate, management can develop overhead rates for each overhead expenditure category or overhead department in the factory. However, these multiple overhead rates may or may not provide a more accurate estimate of opportunity cost than a single plantwide rate.

The ability of absorption costing systems to support decision making and control is discussed in the next two chapters.

Appendix A: Process Costing

A process cost system is based on equivalent units. An equivalent unit is the amount of output stated in terms of completed units. For example, if three units are one-third complete, this is equivalent to one complete unit. Or, if 200 units of product are in work in process at the end of the month and these units are 75 percent complete, then these 200 units represent 150 equivalent units (200 × 75%).

Process cost systems track direct materials and conversion costs (labor and overhead). A major function of all absorption cost systems, including process costing, is to divide total costs incurred into two pieces: those costs still in process and those that have completed manufacturing and thus are in either finished goods inventory or cost of goods sold. Computing the cost of ending work in process and the cost transferred to finished goods requires several distinct calculations. An average cost per equivalent unit of work is computed for materials and conversion costs. These average costs per equivalent unit are used to allocate the material and conversion costs among work-in-process inventory, finished goods inventory, and cost of sales.

Process cost systems view production as consisting of three batches of product: the beginning work-in-process inventory, units started and finished this period, and the ending work-in-process inventory. Consider the following example.

Cajun Peanut Butter Inc. uses process costing to compute product costs for inventory and cost of goods sold. This firm has discovered and patented a peanut butter machine that makes Cajun-flavored peanut butter through a continuous flow process whereby peanuts are dumped into the machine at the beginning of the process and Cajun flavoring is added at the very end. Conversion

TABLE 9–5   Cajun Peanut Butter Inc. Operating Data for March

There was no beginning inventory in process on March 1. The following summarizes the operating data for the month of March:

	Dollars	*Quantity*
Peanuts purchased and entered in process	$32,000	20,000 lbs.
Ending inventory in process (30% complete)	not available	1,200 lbs.
Cajun spices	$ 4,000	
All other factory costs (conversion costs)	$15,000	

costs are incurred continuously and evenly throughout the conversion process. The relevant information for March is presented in Table 9–5. All conversion costs (labor and overhead) are assumed to be incurred uniformly during the process. To simplify the discussion, we begin the analysis by assuming no beginning inventories (although later we will illustrate the case with beginning inventories).

Table 9–6 decomposes the mechanics of process costing into four steps. Step 1 summarizes the physical flow of the units and calculates the equivalent units of work in the physical flows. The summary of the physical flows is based on the accounting identity:

$$\text{Beginning inventory} + \text{Units started} = \text{Units transferred out} + \text{Ending inventory}$$

In step 1, this equation becomes

$$0 + 20,000 = 18,800 + 1,200$$

Since the ending inventory is 1,200 pounds and 20,000 pounds were started, 18,800 pounds must have been finished and transferred. These equations hold under the assumption of no spoilage. To simplify the calculations, we assume there is no spoilage or waste at Cajun Peanut Butter Inc.

Costs and the amount of work done are accumulated for each of the two batches: (1) *ending work-in-process (WIP) inventory* and (2) *transferred out* in March. Consider the batch of ending work-in-process inventory. In step 1 there are 1,200 pounds of ending WIP inventory, which are 30 percent complete with respect to conversion costs. This inventory was started in March. Conversion costs were incurred to produce this level of completion, requiring 360 equivalent units of work (1,200 lbs @ 30 percent). All the peanuts are added at the beginning, so there are 1,200 equivalent units of peanuts in the ending WIP inventory. On the other hand, since all the Cajun spices are added at the end of the process, the ending work-in-process inventory contains no equivalent units of spices. All the units transferred out (18,800) are complete with respect to conversion, peanuts, and spices, so there are 18,800 equivalent units of these items.

Step 2 in Table 9–6 computes the cost per equivalent unit for the conversion costs, peanuts, and spices. Total equivalent units is the sum of the equivalent units in the ending WIP inventory and units transferred out in March. The three cost categories (conversion, peanuts, and Cajun spices) have different equivalent units.

TABLE 9–6   Cajun Peanut Butter Inc.—Calculation of Ending Work in Process and Cost of Units Transferred Out for March

| | Units | Equivalent Units | | | |
		Conversion	Peanuts	Spices	Total
Step 1					
Physical flow:					
Units started	20,000				
Units to account for	20,000				
Ending work in process (30%)	1,200	360	1,200	0	
Transferred out	18,800	18,800	18,800	18,800	
Units accounted for	20,000				
Step 2					
Equivalent units		19,160	20,000	18,800	
Costs per unit:					
Total costs		$15,000	$32,000	$ 4,000	
Cost per equivalent unit		$0.7829	$1.6000	$0.2128	$2.5957
Step 3					
Total costs to account for:					
Conversion costs	$15,000				
Peanuts purchased	32,000				
Cajun spices	4,000				
Total costs	$51,000				
Step 4					
Ending work in process	$ 2,202	$282	$1,920	0	
		$0.7829 × 360	$1.60 × 1,200	$0.2128 × 0	
Transferred out (18,800 × $2.5957)	48,798				
Total costs	$51,000				

For conversion costs, 19,160 equivalent units were produced. For peanuts, 20,000 equivalent units were produced. For Cajun spices, 18,800 equivalent units were produced. The cost per equivalent unit is an average cost calculated as the ratio of the total costs incurred in the cost category and the number of equivalent units of work performed in that category. Costs per equivalent unit for conversion, peanuts, and spices are $0.7829, $1.6000, and $0.2128, respectively. The total cost of a complete pound of peanut butter is the sum of the conversion, peanuts, and spice costs ($2.5957).

Step 3 lists all the costs to be assigned to either the ending WIP inventory or the units transferred out, totaling $51,000. Step 4 uses the costs per equivalent unit to value work in process and units transferred out. Costs are assigned to the ending WIP inventory by taking the equivalent units in ending WIP inventory for each cost category and multiplying by the cost per equivalent unit in the same

TABLE 9–7   **Cajun Peanut Butter Inc.**
Revised Operating Data for March (Including Beginning Inventories)

	Dollars	*Quantity*
Beginning inventory in process (40% complete)	$ 3,600[*]	2,000 lbs.
Peanuts purchased and entered in process	$32,000	20,000 lbs.
Ending inventory in process (30% complete)	not available	1,200 lbs.
Cajun spices	$ 4,000	
All other factory costs (conversion costs)	$15,000	

[*]Composed of $600 conversion cost ($0.75 per equivalent unit × 2,000 lbs. × 40% complete) plus $3,000 peanut cost ($1.50 per equivalent unit × $2,000 × 100% complete).

cost category. These are then summed across categories to get the cost of the ending WIP inventory. For example, the ending WIP inventory of $2,202 is composed of $282 of conversion costs (360 equivalent units times $0.7829 per equivalent unit) and $1,920 of peanuts (1,200 equivalent units times $1.60 per equivalent unit). There is no Cajun spice cost in the ending WIP inventory because these spices are only added when the process is finished. The cost of the units transferred out is $48,798 (18,800 × 2.5957).

While highly simplified, the preceding example illustrates the key concepts in a process costing system. All costs incurred in March, $51,000, are either assigned to WIP or transferred out to finished goods. Like job order costing, process costing fully absorbs all manufacturing costs to units produced or in inventory.

We now make the example more realistic and complicated by introducing beginning inventories. With beginning inventories comes the decision of whether to use FIFO, weighted average, or LIFO. That is, do we assume the beginning inventory costs flow out first (FIFO), are averaged in with the costs incurred in March (weighted average), or are still in the ending inventory (LIFO)? The remainder of this appendix illustrates the FIFO and weighted average methods. LIFO is not illustrated, but it can be calculated by building LIFO layers from the beginning and ending inventories.

Table 9–7 provides the raw data, including the beginning inventory data. All the data are the same as before, except the beginning inventory of 2,000 pounds is 40 percent complete with respect to conversion costs and has a cost of $3,600.

Table 9–8 illustrates the computations assuming a FIFO cost flow. The first change to notice is that the units transferred out are different from those in Table 9–6. From the earlier accounting identity,

Beginning inventory + Units started = Units transferred out + Ending inventory

2,000 lbs. + 20,000 lbs.   = Units transferred out + 1,200 lbs.

Solving for units transferred out yields

Units transferred out = 2,000 lbs. + 20,000 lbs. − 1,200 lbs. = 20,800 lbs.

Given the revised transferred out amount, the equivalent units for conversion, peanuts, and spices are calculated in step 1 of Table 9–8. Under FIFO costing, the goal is to compute the cost per equivalent unit of only the work done in March. The equivalent units in the beginning WIP inventory (800 equivalent units of

TABLE 9–8   **Cajun Peanut Butter Inc. Revised Calculation of Ending Work in Process and Cost of Units Transferred Out for March**
(FIFO Cost Flow)

	Units	Equivalent Units			
		Conversion	Peanuts	Spices	Total
Step 1					
Physical flow:					
Beginning work in process (40%)	2,000				
Units started	20,000				
Units to account for	22,000				
Ending work in process (30%)	1,200	360	1,200	0	
Transferred out	20,800	20,800	20,800	20,800	
Units accounted for	22,000				
Step 2					
Less equivalent units in beginning WIP		(800)	(2,000)	0	
Equivalent units of work done in March		20,360	20,000	20,800	
Costs per unit:					
Total costs incurred in March		$15,000	$32,000	$ 4,000	
Cost per equivalent unit		$0.7367	$1.6000	$0.1923	$2.5290
Step 3					
Total costs to account for:					
Beginning work in process	$ 3,600				
Conversion costs	15,000				
Peanuts purchased	32,000				
Cajun spices	4,000				
Total costs	$54,600				
Step 4					
Ending work in process	$ 2,185	$265	$1,920	0	
		$0.7367 × 360	$1.60 × 1,200	$0.1923 × 0	
Transferred out:					
Beginning work in process	$ 3,600				
Cost to complete beginning WIP	884	60% × 2,000 × 0.7367			
	385			2,000 × 0.1923	
Started and completed: 20,800 − 2,000 = 18,800 × $2.5290	47,545				
Total costs	$54,600*				

*Rounding error.

conversion costs) are subtracted out under step 2 to make sure the equivalent units computed are for work done in March only. The beginning inventory contains equivalent units of work done in prior periods.

Step 2 also computes the cost per equivalent unit: $0.7367 for conversion costs, $1.60 for peanuts, and $0.1923 for spices. Total costs to account for now include the beginning WIP inventory ($3,600) plus the costs incurred in March (see step 3). The unit costs from step 2 are used to compute the ending amount of work in process ($2,185) in step 4. Ending WIP inventory ($2,185) is composed of the equivalent units of conversion, peanuts, and spices in the ending WIP inventory multiplied by the respective cost per equivalent unit of conversion ($0.7367) and peanuts ($1.60). (Remember, since spices are added at the end of the process, WIP contains no spice costs.)

In step 4, the cost of units transferred to finished goods consists of the beginning WIP inventory ($3,600), the costs to complete the beginning WIP inventory ($884 of conversion and $385 of spices), and the cost of units started and completed in March ($47,545).

Table 9–8 illustrates the FIFO method. Table 9–9 illustrates the weighted average method. FIFO calculates an average cost per equivalent unit using only the costs incurred this period and the equivalent units produced this period. The weighted average method calculates the average cost per equivalent unit using both the beginning inventory and current production. The weighted average cost includes not just the cost of work performed this period but also the costs incurred in previous periods that are still in the beginning inventory. Total equivalent units are the sum of both the beginning WIP inventory equivalent units and the equivalent units worked this period. For example, equivalent units of peanuts (22,000) consist of 1,200 units in the ending inventory plus 20,800 units transferred out. These 22,000 units include the peanuts in the beginning inventory. The total cost in step 3 is the sum of the costs in the beginning WIP inventory and costs incurred this period. Thus, the cost per equivalent unit is a weighted average of the costs in the beginning WIP inventory and those incurred this period.

Comparing Tables 9–8 and 9–9 reveals that the FIFO and weighted average methods give very similar numbers for the ending inventory and transferred-out costs. Whenever the beginning and ending inventories are a small fraction of the units started or finished, most of the cost incurred is transferred out.

Many continuous flow plants are composed of a series of production stages, each treated as a separate process costing unit. For example, an oil refinery consists of a crude splitter, various distillers, and refractors. Intermediate products flow from one stage to another. Each stage tracks beginning and ending work-in-process inventories and transferred-out costs for material and conversion costs. The costs of units transferred out of one stage become the transferred-in costs for the next stage downstream. Thus, stringing together a series of statements similar to Table 9–8 or 9–9 lets management compute each stage's separate costs as well as the entire plant's costs.

Finally, if the process has considerable scrap or waste, it is often accounted for and reported separately, which adds to the complexity of the calculations. But the conceptual issues remain: Process cost systems assign all costs to units. These systems report average unit costs, which are a mixture of fixed and variable costs—not measures of marginal or opportunity costs.

TABLE 9–9   Cajun Peanut Butter Inc. Revised Calculation of Ending Work in Process and Cost of Units Transferred Out for March
(Weighted Average Cost Flow)

	Units	Equivalent Units			
		Conversion	Peanuts	Spices	Total
Step 1					
Physical flow:					
Beginning work in process (40%)	2,000				
Units started	20,000				
Units to account for	22,000				
Ending work in process (30%)	1,200	360	1,200	0	
Transferred out	20,800	20,800	20,800	20,800	
Units accounted for	22,000				
Step 2					
Equivalent units of work done					
to date		21,160	22,000	20,800	
Costs per unit:					
Beginning work in process		$ 600	$ 3,000		
Current costs added		15,000	32,000	$ 4,000	
Total cost		$15,600	$35,000	$ 4,000	
Cost per equivalent unit		$0.7372	$1.5909	$0.1923	$2.5204
Step 3					
Total costs to account for:					
Beginning work in process	$ 3,600				
Conversion costs	15,000				
Peanuts purchased	32,000				
Cajun spices	4,000				
Total costs	$54,600				
Step 4					
Ending work in process	$ 2,174	$265	$1,909	0	
		$0.7372 × 360	$1.5909 × 1,200	$0.1923 × 0	
Transferred out:					
20,800 × $2.5204	52,424				
Total costs	$54,600*				

*Rounding error.

Appendix B: Demand Shifts, Fixed Costs, and Pricing

This appendix illustrates that when volumes drop causing average costs to rise, prices usually should be lowered, not raised. A photocopy store owner expects long-run average volume (normal volume) to be 175,000 copies per month. The store is leased for $1,000 per month, employees are paid $2,000 per month, and a copier is leased for $500 per month plus $0.005 per copy. Paper costs also are $0.005 per sheet. Each copy requires one page of paper (i.e., there is no two-sided copying). The store lease and employee costs do not vary with copy volume.

The store completes a customer order for 5,000 flyers at $0.04 per page, or $200. Assuming that taking this job did not require forgoing another job—that is, equipment and labor had excess capacity—the opportunity cost of this job was $50 (the paper at $0.005 per page and the additional copier fee at $0.005 per page). But the accounting cost of this order is $150, which incorporates some allocated overhead. The amount of overhead allocated to this job is the sum of the overhead items (store rental, labor, and copier rental) divided by normal volume for the year, multiplied by the volume for this job, or:

	Overhead Costs per Month
Office rental	$ 1,000
Labor	2,000
Copier rental	500
	$ 3,500
Divided by normal copy volume	175,000
Overhead costs per normal copy	$ 0.020
Plus: Paper costs	0.005
Additional copier charge per page	0.005
Total cost per page	$ 0.030
Times number of pages in job	5,000
Total job cost	$ 150

What does the $0.03 total cost per page represent? It is the long-run average cost. That is, at a normal volume of 175,000 copies per month, the store must charge at least $0.03 per page to break even over time. Suppose that copy volume this month falls from 175,000 copies to 100,000 copies. Overhead costs per copy increase to $0.035 (or $3,500 ÷ 100,000). Should prices be increased?

The profit-maximizing price occurs at the quantity that equates marginal cost and marginal revenue. Has marginal cost changed? No, it is still $0.01 per page. Has marginal revenue changed? Maybe—it depends on how the demand curve has shifted. Actually, it is possible that prices should be lowered. Figures 9–5 and 9–6 illustrate the typical case in which price should be lowered when demand falls.

In Figure 9–5, the demand curve labeled Normal demand corresponds to 175,000 copies being demanded at a price of $0.04 per copy. This demand curve has a marginal revenue curve, Normal marginal revenue. Equating the marginal cost of $0.01 to normal marginal revenue yields the profit-maximizing copy volume (175,000 copies) and price ($0.04).

Suppose that demand has shifted to the Low demand curve in Figure 9–6. At a price of $0.04, there is now demand for only 100,000 copies. (Take the price of $0.04 and move horizontally to the Low demand curve; then move down the vertical line and read off the quantity of 100,000.) In other words, if the demand curve shifts down and the price remains at $0.04 per copy, only 100,000 copies will be sold per month.

FIGURE 9–5

Photocopy store example

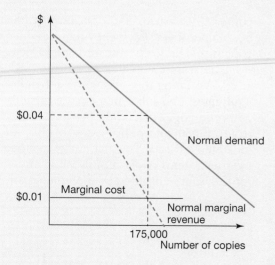

FIGURE 9–6

Photocopy store example: Reduce price when demand falls

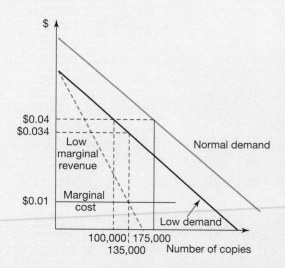

If demand is now represented by the Low demand curve in Figure 9–6, what is the profit-maximizing price to charge? Is it higher or lower than $0.04? Remember, profit maximization occurs at the quantity where marginal revenue equals marginal cost. Marginal cost has not changed; it is still $0.01 per copy. Marginal revenue for the Low demand curve is the dashed line in Figure 9–6 called Low marginal revenue. The Low marginal revenue and Marginal cost curves intersect at the output level of 135,000 copies per month. Following this quantity level up to the Low demand curve yields a price of about $0.034 per copy. Therefore, to maximize profits under the low demand situation, the copy store must *lower* the price from $0.04 to $0.034.

Table 9–10 compares total profits at the price of $0.04 and volume of 100,000 copies with the profits at a price of $0.034 and volume of 135,000 copies. Under both pricing scenarios, the store is losing money. However, the loss is smaller when the price is cut to $0.034 per copy. Notice that in both cases fixed costs remain constant at $3,500. Since fixed costs do not vary (by definition) between the two pricing scenarios, fixed costs are irrelevant for the *pricing decision*. But

TABLE 9–10 Photocopy Store Profits (Loss) at a Price of $0.04 per Copy versus $0.034 per Copy

	Price = $0.04 Copies = 100,000	Price = $0.034 Copies = 135,000
Revenue	$4,000	$4,590
Variable costs	(1,000)	(1,350)
Fixed costs	(3,500)	(3,500)
Loss	$ (500)	$ (260)

they are not irrelevant when it comes to the *shutdown decision*. Suppose the store lease and copier rental ($1,500 a month) are paid a year in advance but labor ($2,000 a month) is paid at the end of each month. Assuming that the store cannot be sublet, the firm should continue to operate until the current store and copier leases expire. It should then cease operations unless demand has increased sufficiently. Even though the store is not recovering all its fixed costs, fixed costs that have already been paid are sunk costs. Continuing to operate the store until the fixed costs (lease, copier rental, and labor) are payable again generates a positive cash flow.

Self-Study Problems

Self Study Problem 1: Cost Flows

The following is a job cost sheet for a special product:

Job Number 711					Date Started	5/26	
					Date Completed 6/15		

	Raw Materials				Direct Labor		
Date	Type	Cost	Qty.	Amount	Cost/Hr.	Hours	Amount
5/26	130	$30	6	$180	$18	5	$ 90
6/15	248	10	20	200	15	10	150
				$380		15	240

Total direct materials	$380
Total direct labor	240
Overhead (15 direct labor hours @ $10/hour)	150
Total job cost	$770

Overhead is allocated based on direct labor hours (DLH). The raw materials were in inventory before being used on job #711. The product is sold on 7/10. Identify the cost flows on each of these dates: 5/26, 6/15, and 7/10.

Solution:

Cost flows:

On 5/26: $180 from "Raw materials inventory" to "Work in process"

$90 from "Labor" to "Work in process"

$50 from "Overhead" to "Work in process" for overhead-related to direct labor hours (5 DLH × $10/DLH)

On 6/15: $200 from "Raw materials inventory" to "Work in process"

$150 from "Labor" to "Work in process"

$100 from "Overhead" to "Work in process" for overhead-related to direct labor hours (10 DLH × $10/DLH)

On 6/15: $770 from "Work in process" to "Finished goods"

On 7/10: $770 from "Finished goods" to "Cost of goods sold"

Self-Study Problem 2:   R&R Chairs, Inc.

R&R Chairs, Inc., manufactures two types of ergonomic chairs (the basic and the executive) in two departments (frame fabrication and cushion fabrication). In planning for the coming year, the managers would like to know the production cost of each chair. The main difference between the two chairs is additional padding in the executive chair. Budgeted direct costs for each department are as follows:

Budgeted Chair Production and Cost Data

	Frame Fabrication	Cushion Fabrication	Total
Basic			
Number of chairs			225,000
Direct labor/chair	$ 7.40	$6.40	
Direct materials/chair	6.70	2.40	
Total	$14.10	$8.80	$22.90
Executive			
Number of chairs			192,000
Direct labor/chair	$ 7.50	$ 8.70	
Direct materials/chair	6.80	6.20	
Total	$14.30	$14.90	$29.20

Currently the company uses a single plantwide overhead rate based on direct labor dollars to assign overhead costs to products. Budgeted overhead costs for the year are shown in the accompanying table.

Budgeted Overhead Costs

Rent	$1,680,000
Indirect labor	1,660,000
Indirect materials	1,125,000
Equipment lease payments	1,665,000
Total overhead	$6,130,000

Required:

    a. Given planned production rates of 225,000 basic chairs and 192,000 executive chairs, prepare a statement calculating the fully absorbed cost for each chair in each department.

    b. Management is considering switching to departmental overhead rates. Overhead costs in frame fabrication are assigned to chairs based on direct labor dollars, whereas cushion fabrication overhead costs are assigned based on direct material dollars. Calculate separate departmental overhead rates and prepare a new statement of the fully absorbed cost per chair given the following information:

Budgeted Overhead Costs

	Frame Fabrication	Cushion Fabrication
Rent	$ 500,000	$1,180,000
Indirect labor	650,000	1,010,000
Indirect materials	470,000	655,000
Equipment lease payments	280,000	1,385,000
Total overhead	$1,900,000	$4,230,000

    c. Explain the difference in costs between the two methods. Comment on which allocation scheme is likely to produce more accurate estimates of production costs.

Solution:

    a. Plantwide overhead rate:

Total overhead	$6,130,000
Divided by direct labor dollars*	÷ $6,215,400
Overhead rate/direct labor dollar	$ 0.986

*$6,215,400 = 225,000 × ($7.40 + $6.40) + 192,000 × ($7.50 + $8.70)

	Frame Fabrication	Cushion Fabrication	Total
Basic			
Direct labor/chair	$ 7.40	$ 6.40	$13.80
Direct materials/chair	6.70	2.40	9.10
Overhead ($0.986/DL$)	7.30	6.31	13.61
Total	$21.40	$15.11	$36.51
Executive			
Direct labor/chair	$ 7.50	$ 8.70	$16.20
Direct materials/chair	6.80	6.20	13.00
Overhead ($0.986/DL$)	7.40	8.58	15.97*
Total	$21.70	$23.48	$45.17*

*$.01 rounding difference.

b. Separate departmental overhead rates:

	Frame Fabrication	Cushion Fabrication
Total overhead	$1,900,000	$4,230,000
Total direct labor dollars	÷ $3,105,000*	
Total direct material dollars		÷ $1,730,400†
Overhead rate	$0.612	$2.445

	Frame Fabrication	Cushion Fabrication	Total
Basic			
Direct labor/chair	$ 7.40	$ 6.40	$13.80
Direct materials/chair	6.70	2.40	9.10
Overhead ($0.612/DL$)	4.53		4.53
Overhead ($2.445/DM$)		5.87	5.87
Total	$18.63	$14.67	$33.30
Executive			
Direct labor/chair	$ 7.50	$ 8.70	$16.20
Direct materials/chair	6.80	6.20	13.00
Overhead ($0.612/DL$)	4.59		4.59
Overhead ($2.445/DM$)		15.16	15.16
Total	$18.89	$30.06	$48.95

*$3,105,000 = $7.40 × 225,000 + $7.50 × 192,000.
†$1,730,400 = $2.40 × 225,000 + $6.20 × 192,000.

c. Going from a single plant overhead rate to separate department rates causes the basic chair's expected cost to fall $3.21 per chair and the executive chair's expected cost to rise $3.78 per chair. The basic chair's cost falls about 9 percent and the executive chair's cost rises about 8 percent. The reason for these changes is as follows. Cushion fabrication contains much of the overhead of the factory. Executive chairs contain a higher fraction of direct materials cost than direct labor cost. If all the overhead is allocated based on direct labor dollars, basic chairs bear a larger fraction of the overhead costs than if more of the overhead, in particular the cushion fabrication costs, is assigned to executive chairs. If cushion fabrication costs vary more with direct materials than direct labor, then the separate department overhead rates give a more accurate estimate of product costs than a single plantwide rate. However, if direct labor is the overhead cost driver in the cushion fabrication department, then a single overhead rate is likely to be more accurate.

Problems

P9–1: Accelerated Depreciation

What conditions are likely to exist when operating managers are compensated based on accounting earnings and accelerated depreciation methods are used to compute overhead charges to operating departments?

P9–2: Equivalent Units (See Appendix A)

Department 100 is the first step in the firm's manufacturing process. Data for the current quarter's operations are as follows:

	Number of Units
Beginning work in process (70% complete)	30,000
Units started this quarter	580,000
Units completed this quarter and transferred out	550,000
Ending work in process (60% complete)	60,000

Required:

Materials are added at the beginning of the process. Conversion costs (labor and capital costs) are incurred uniformly. The firm uses the FIFO method of inventory accounting. How many equivalent units of conversion cost were used in the current quarter in Department 100?

P9–3: IPX Packaging

IPX is a specialized packaging company that packages other manufacturers' products. Other manufacturers ship their products to IPX in bulk. IPX then packages the products using high-speed, state-of-the-art packaging machines and ships the packaged products to wholesalers. A typical order involves packaging small toys in see-through plastic and cardboard containers.

IPX uses a flexible budget to forecast annual plantwide overhead, which is then allocated to jobs based on machine hours. The annual flexible overhead budget is projected to be $6 million of fixed costs and $120 per machine hour. The budgeted number of machine hours for the year is 20,000.

At the end of the year, 21,000 machine hours were used and actual overhead incurred was $9.14 million.

Required:

a. Calculate the overhead rate set at the beginning of the year.
b. Calculate the amount of over/underabsorbed overhead for the year.
c. The company's policy is to write off any over/underabsorbed overhead to cost of goods sold. Will net income rise or fall this year when the over/underabsorbed overhead is written off to cost of goods sold?

P9–4: Rosen Company

The Rosen Company has two manufacturing departments: production and assembly. Each department has separate overhead rates. Rosen made the following estimates for its production and assembly departments for the calendar year 2003.

	Production	Assembly
Factory overhead	$ 300,000	$100,000
Direct labor cost	$1,000,000	$210,000
Machine hours	1,500	6,250
Direct labor hours	50,000	10,000

The company uses a budgeted overhead rate to apply overheads to orders. Machine hours are used to allocate overhead in the production department and direct labor hours are used to allocate overhead in the assembly department.

Required:

a. Calculate the overhead rate for each department.
b. A summary of job #77 follows:

	Production	Assembly
Direct materials used	$3,000	$2,000
Direct labor costs	$11,000	$15,500
Machine hours	100	250
Direct labor hours	500	750

What are overhead costs for job #77?

c. Actual operating results for 2003 are

	Production	Assembly
Factory overhead	$325,000	$65,000
Direct labor cost	$900,000	$230,000
Machine hours	1,550	6,250
Direct labor hours	47,000	10,500

Calculate the over/underapplied overhead for each department.

P9–5: MacGiver Brass

MacGiver Brass is a brass plating firm with sales of $8 million and profits before taxes of $625,000. MacGiver has a loan outstanding at its local bank for working capital purposes. As the loan officer reviewing MacGiver's loan application, you are charged with making a recommendation as to whether the $608,000 loan should be renewed for another year.

Upon reviewing MacGiver's most recent annual report, you find the following footnote:

Underabsorbed overhead of $462,000 was prorated to inventories (⅔) and cost of goods sold (⅓).

Required:

a. How should you evaluate MacGiver's annual report in light of this footnote? In particular, how does this footnote affect your recommendation regarding the loan?
b. In preparing for your meeting with MacGiver's president and chief financial officer, what questions do you want to ask regarding this footnote?

P9–6: Empco Inc.

Rose Bach has recently been hired as controller of Empco Inc., a sheet-metal manufacturer. Empco has been in the sheet-metal business for many years and is currently investigating ways to modernize its manufacturing process. At the first staff meeting Bach attended, Bob Kelley, chief engineer, presented a proposal for automating the drilling department. Kelley recommended that Empco purchase two robots that could replace the eight direct labor employees in the department. The cost savings outlined in Kelley's proposal include two elements. First, direct labor cost in the drilling department is eliminated. Second, manufacturing overhead cost in the department is reduced to zero because Empco charges manufacturing overhead on the basis of direct labor dollars using a plantwide rate.

The president of Empco thought that Kelley's explanation of the cost savings made no sense. Bach agreed and explained that as firms become more automated, they should rethink their manufacturing overhead systems. The president asked Bach to look into the matter and prepare a report for the next staff meeting.

To refresh her knowledge, Bach reviewed articles on manufacturing overhead allocation for an automated factory and discussed the matter with some of her peers. She also gathered the following historical data on the manufacturing overhead rates experienced by Empco over the years. Bach also wanted to have some departmental data to present at the meeting. Using Empco's accounting records, she was able to estimate these annual averages for each manufacturing department in the 1990s:

Historical Data

Date	Average Annual Direct Labor Cost	Average Annual Manufacturing Overhead Cost	Average Manufacturing Overhead Application Rate
1950s	$1,000,000	$ 1,000,000	100%
1960s	1,200,000	3,000,000	250
1970s	2,000,000	7,000,000	350
1980s	3,000,000	12,000,000	400
1990s	4,000,000	20,000,000	500

Annual Averages

	Cutting Department	Grinding Department	Drilling Department
Direct labor	$ 2,000,000	$1,750,000	$ 250,000
Manufacturing overhead	11,000,000	7,000,000	2,000,000

Required:

a. Disregarding the proposed use of robots in the drilling department, describe the shortcomings of Empco's current system for applying overhead.

b. Do you agree with Bob Kelley's statement that the manufacturing overhead cost in the drilling department will be reduced to zero if the automation proposal is implemented? Explain.

c. Recommend ways to improve Empco's method for applying overhead by describing how it should revise its overhead accounting system:
  (i) In the cutting and grinding departments.
  (ii) To accommodate the automation of the drilling department.

SOURCE: CMA adapted.

P9–7:   Ware Paper Box

Ware Paper Box manufactures corrugated paper boxes. It uses a job order costing system. Operating data for February and March are as follows:

Job	Date Started	Date Finished	Date Sold	Total Manufacturing Cost as of 2/28	Total Manufacturing Cost in March*
613	1/28	2/5	2/15	$12,500	
614	2/5	2/17	2/20	17,200	
615	2/20	2/27	3/5	18,500	
616	2/25	3/10	3/20	10,100	$13,400
734	2/21	3/15	4/1	4,300	8,200
735	2/27	4/1	4/9	9,100	2,400
736	3/2	3/22	4/19		16,300
617	3/15	3/20	3/26		19,200
618	3/22	4/5	4/15		14,400

*Manufacturing costs incurred only in March. Does not include any manufacturing costs incurred in prior months.

The factory was closed due to a labor strike prior to January 28, when job #613 was started. There were no other jobs in the plant at that time.

Required:
Calculate the following amounts:
   a. Work-in-process inventory as of 2/28.
   b. Work-in-process inventory as of 3/31.
   c. Finished goods inventory as of 2/28.
   d. Finished goods inventory as of 3/31.
   e. Cost of goods sold for February.
   f. Cost of goods sold for March.

P9–8:   DeJure Scents (See Appendix A)

DeJure Scents manufactures an aftershave and uses process costing. All materials are added at the beginning of the process and conversion costs are incurred uniformly over time. In May, DeJure started 15,000 gallons. There was no beginning inventory. May's ending inventory of work in process was 2,000 gallons, which were 50 percent complete with respect to conversion costs.

In May, conversion costs were $28,000 and materials costs were $45,000.

Required:

   a. Calculate the equivalent units of conversion and materials.
   b. Calculate the cost per equivalent unit of conversion and materials.
   c. Calculate the cost of the ending inventory and the cost transferred to finished goods inventory.

P9–9:   Chemtrex (See Appendix A)

Chemtrex is an agricultural chemical producer. Process costing is used in its mixing department. At the beginning of July, Chemtrex had 700,000 gallons 70 percent complete in work in process. During July, it started another 4,000,000 gallons and produced 3,700,000 gallons. One million gallons of ending work in process were 60 percent complete at the end of July. Conversion costs are incurred uniformly over the mixing process.

Required:
Calculate the number of equivalent units of conversion work performed during July.

P9–10:   Northridge Plant

The Northridge plant manufactures two different ski boots: the Runner and the Racer. These are the only two products planned for production in the plant this year. The following data provide planned production for this year and the associated projected cost data.

	Models	
	Runner	*Racer*
Projected production (units)	2,500	6,200
Unit costs		
Direct materials	$ 16.00	$11.75
Direct labor ($18/hour)	36.00	27.00
Manufacturing overhead	54.00	40.50
Selling and administrative	8.60	19.40
Unit cost	$114.60	$98.65

Overhead is assigned to products based on direct labor dollars. The overhead rate is established at the beginning of the year using a flexible budget. The variable manufacturing overhead rate in the flexible budget is projected to be 70 percent of direct labor dollars.

Required:
What estimate of fixed manufacturing overhead was used in setting the overhead rate at the beginning of the year?

P9–11:   Media Designs

Media Designs is a marketing firm that designs and prints customized marketing brochures. The design department designs the brochure and the printing department prints and binds it. Each department has separate overhead rates. The following estimates for the two departments were made for the calendar year 2010.

	Design	*Printing*
Overhead	$800,000	$500,000
Direct labor cost	$3,250,000	$410,000
Direct materials cost	$8,500	$250,000
Direct labor hours	50,000	10,000

Media Designs uses a budgeted overhead rate to apply overhead to jobs. Direct labor hours are used to allocate overhead in the design department, and direct materials cost is used to allocate overhead in the printing department.

Required:

a. What are the overhead rates for the design and printing departments?

b. A summary of the Matsui job follows:

	Design	Printing
Direct materials used	$3,000	$12,000
Direct labor costs	$46,200	$28,500
Direct labor hours	700	750

What are overhead costs for the Matsui job?

c. Actual operating results for 2010 are

	Design	Printing
Overhead	$802,000	$490,000
Direct labor cost	$3,193,000	$451,500
Direct materials cost	$11,550	$230,000
Direct labor hours	51,500	10,500

Calculate the over/underapplied overhead for each department.

P9–12:   Simple Plant

Simple Plant manufactures DNA test strips. Manufacturing overhead is applied to units produced using direct labor dollars as the allocation base. The overhead rate is calculated prior to the beginning of the fiscal year that runs January 1 to December 31. Simple Plant has one manufacturing employee, J. Kusic, and one overhead expense besides indirect labor, property taxes. J. Kusic's salary and fringe benefits for next year are forecast to be $50,000. Kusic is expected to work 2,000 hours at a cost of $25 per hour ($50,000/2,000). Eighty percent of Kusic's time is budgeted to be direct labor, and the remainder is budgeted to be indirect labor. Property taxes are projected to be $110,000. There was no beginning balance of work in process on January 1.

Required:

a. Calculate Simple Plant's overhead rate for next year.

b. On January 2, the first working day of the new fiscal year, Kusic works eight hours (five hours on manufacturing test strips and three hours waiting for raw materials to arrive). Each day Simple Plant posts all entries (transactions) to the accounts. What are the balances in the Overhead account and the Work-in-Process account at the close of business on January 2?

    c. At the end of the year, Kusic's salary and benefits are $50,000, with $44,000 of the total charged to test strips manufactured. Kusic worked 2,000 hours during the year. Property taxes paid during the year amounted to $103,000. What, if any, is the balance in the overhead account before an adjusting entry is made to transfer the balance to other accounts?

P9–13: First Eastern Bank

First Eastern Bank is a large, multibranch bank offering a wide variety of commercial and retail banking services. Eastern uses an absorption costing system to monitor the costs of various services and provide information for a variety of decisions.

One set of services is a retail loan operation providing residential mortgages, car loans, and student college loans. All loan applications are filed by the applicant at a branch bank, where the branch manager fills out the loan application. From there, the loan application is sent to the loan processing department, where the applicant's credit history is checked and a recommendation is made regarding loan approval based on the applicant's credit history and current financial situation. This recommendation is forwarded to the loan committee of senior lending officers, who review the file and make a final decision.

Thus, there are three stages to making a loan: application in a branch, the loan processing department, and the loan committee. Mr. and Mrs. Jones visit the West Street branch and file an application for a residential mortgage. Their loan application is processed through the three stages.

- *West Street branch bank.* The branch manager spends one hour taking the application. The branch manager spends 1,000 hours per year of her total time taking loan applications and the remainder of her time providing other direct services to customers. Total overhead in the West Street branch is budgeted to be $259,000, excluding the manager's salary, and is allocated to direct customer services using the branch manager's time spent providing direct customer services. The branch manager's annual salary is $42,600.

- *Processing department.* The processing department budgets its total overhead for the year to be $800,000, which is allocated to loans processed using direct labor hours. Budgeted direct labor hours for the year are 40,000 hours. Direct labor hours in the processing department cost $18 per hour. The Joneses' loan requires five direct labor hours in the loan processing department.

- *Loan committee.* Ten senior bank executives are on the loan committee. The loan committee meets 52 times per year, every Wednesday, all day, to approve all loans. The average salary and benefits of each member of the loan committee are $104,000. The loan committee spends 15 minutes reviewing the Joneses' loan application before approving it.

For costing purposes, all employees are assumed to work eight-hour days, five days per week, 52 weeks per year.

Required:
Calculate the total cost of taking the application, processing, and approving the Joneses' mortgage.

P 9–14:   Rick's Bags

Rick's Bags manufactures both golf bags and tennis totes. Fixed manufacturing overhead is budgeted to be $187,200, variable manufacturing overhead is budgeted to be $1.10 per direct labor hour, and fixed selling and administration costs are budgeted to be $346,000. Each golf bag is expected to use 2.5 direct labor hours and each tennis tote is expected to use 1.8 direct labor hours. Planned production consists of 12,000 golf bags and 18,000 tennis totes.

During the year, 34,060 direct labor hours are used to make golf bags and 16,250 direct labor hours are used to make tennis totes. Manufacturing overhead incurred during the year was $207,500. Overhead is absorbed into products using actual direct labor hours.

Required:

a. Calculate the manufacturing overhead rate used to absorb overhead to golf bags and tennis totes.
b. A batch of tennis totes is produced in May. The batch uses 1,900 direct labor hours. How much overhead is charged to this batch of tennis totes?
c. Calculate the amount of over/underabsorbed overhead at the end of the year.
d. Describe in nontechnical terms what the over/underabsorbed overhead calculated in part (c) means.

P9–15:   Unknown Company

Compute the unknowns:

Sales	$100,000
Direct materials used	29,000
Direct labor	10,000
Variable selling and administration expenses	16,000
Fixed manufacturing overhead	30,000
Fixed selling and administration expenses	9,000
Gross profit	?
Opening material inventory	3,000
Closing material inventory	10,000
Variable manufacturing overhead	?
Purchase of direct material	?
Cost of goods manufactured	?
Net income	1,000

There is no opening or closing finished goods or work-in-process inventory.

P9–16:   Wellington Co.

The following figures were taken from the records of Wellington Co. for the year 2008. At the end of the year, two jobs were still in process. Details about the two jobs include:

	Job A	Job B
Direct labor	$10,000	$28,000
Direct materials	$32,000	$22,000
Machine hours	2,000	3,500
Direct labor hours	1,000	2,000

Wellington Co. applies overhead at a budgeted rate, calculated at the beginning of the year. The budgeted rate is the ratio of budgeted overhead to budgeted direct labor costs. Budgeted figures for 2008 were

Budgeted direct labor costs	$250,000
Budgeted overhead	$187,500

Actual figures for 2008 were

Direct labor	$350,000
Overhead	$192,500
Finished goods inventory	$ 75,000
Cost of goods sold	$550,000

There were no opening inventories. It is the practice of the company to prorate any over/underabsorption of overhead to finished goods inventory, work in process, and cost of goods sold based on the total dollars in these categories.

Required:

a. Compute the cost of work in process before over/underapplied overheads are prorated.

b. Prepare a schedule of finished goods inventory, work in process, and cost of goods sold after over/underapplied overheads are prorated.

c. What is the difference in operating income if the over/underapplied overhead is charged to cost of goods sold instead of being prorated to finished goods inventory, work in process, and cost of goods sold?

P9–17: Building Services Department

Increased global competition has spurred most firms to take a hard look at their costs and become "lean and mean." Rochco, a large industrial complex, has seen offshore competition erode its market share. This industrial site of over 100 functional departments (some cost centers and others profit centers) has over the past few years undergone several restructuring and labor reduction programs in order to make the firm more cost competitive.

Five years ago, the many service groups supporting Rochco's manufacturing operations were broken up into well-defined business centers. Top management

b. Calculate the projected overhead rates for 2010 to 2012 using *normal* volume.

c. Even though actual overheads for 2010 to 2012 are not known yet, using your estimated overhead rate based on *expected* volume from (*a*), forecast Pacemakers's over/underabsorbed overhead for 2010 to 2012.

d. Even though actual overheads for 2010 to 2012 are not known yet, using your estimated overhead rate based on normal volume from (*b*), forecast Pacemakers's over/underabsorbed overhead for 2010 to 2012.

e. Comment briefly on the relative advantages and disadvantages of using expected versus normal volumes in setting overhead rates.

P9–21:   Jacklin Stampings

Jacklin Stampings allocates overhead to products based on machine hours. It uses a flexible overhead budget to calculate a predetermined overhead rate at the beginning of the year. This rate is used during the year to allocate overhead to the various stampings produced. The following table summarizes operations for the last year:

Budgeted fixed overhead	$3,800,000
Overabsorbed overhead variance	$220,000
Actual machine hours	46,000
Variable overhead per machine hour	$100
Actual overhead incurred	$8,750,000

Required:

In setting the overhead rate at the beginning of the year, what budgeted volume of machine hours was used?

P9–22:   Bartolotta Company

The Bartolotta Company had an overabsorbed overhead balance at year-end. The firm wrote off one-third of it to Cost of Goods Sold, thereby raising net income by $100,000, and the remainder was charged to inventory accounts. Overhead is allocated to products using direct labor dollars. The firm uses a flexible budget to calculate its overhead rate. Before the year began, the variable overhead rate and budgeted volume were estimated to be $7.00 per direct labor dollar and $1 million, respectively. Actual overhead incurred for the year was $9.7 million, and actual direct labor cost was $1,250,000. What budgeted fixed overhead amount did the Bartolotta Company use in calculating the overhead rate?

P9–23:   Kitchen Rite

Kitchen Rite is considering outsourcing the production of a steel chassis that is used in a kitchen appliance. Two thousand chassis are produced per month. An outside vendor will supply an identical chassis for $9.90. The chassis is manufactured in two steps. A stamping press punches out the part from sheet metal, bends the sides, and cuts holes in it, all in one operation. Then a welding machine welds the corners. Both the welding and stamping machines are used to produce only this one chassis model. The following job order cost sheet summarizes the costs of producing a single chassis.

	Cost per Unit
Steel plate	$ 4.75
Direct labor:	
Stamping ($20/hour)	1.60
Welding ($30/hour)	2.50
Overhead:	
Stamping (depreciation)	3.60
Welding (lease payment)	2.15
General plant	5.90
	$20.50

The stamping machine is old and has little economic value. A used equipment dealer is willing to remove the machine and haul it away at no cost. The stamping machine was purchased 13 years ago for $1,728,000. For both tax and reporting purposes, it is being depreciated using a 20-year life, straight-line method, and it has zero salvage value. The welding machine is leased for $4,300 per month, and the lease can be canceled at any time and the machine returned. However, an early termination penalty of $1,800 per month for the next 42 months must be paid.

General plant overhead consists primarily of the allocated cost of depreciation on the plant, property taxes, and fire insurance on the plant. Kitchen Rite currently has excess plant space. The manufacturing space freed up if the chassis is outsourced has no other use.

Employees are unionized and have a clause in their contract that prevents the firm from firing them if their jobs are eliminated due to outsourcing. The employees working on the stamping machine will be placed on indefinite furlough at 75 percent of their current pay. The employees operating the welding machine can be reassigned to other positions in the firm as job openings occur. Given the high demand for welders, these reassignments will occur within a few weeks of outsourcing the chassis.

Kitchen Rite has a tax loss for the current and the previous two years.

Required:
Should Kitchen Rite outsource the chassis? Support your recommendation with a clear financial analysis of the facts.

P9–24: Frames, Inc.

Frames, Inc., manufactures two types of metal frames: large and small. Steel angle iron is first cut to the appropriate sizes; the pieces are then welded together to form the frames. The process involves a high degree of automation. There is considerable indirect labor by skilled technicians and engineers who maintain the automated equipment. There are two manufacturing departments: cutting and welding. The following report details the actual costs of production for the year:

FRAMES, INC
Year Ending 12/31

Direct Costs

Frame Type	Units Produced	Direct Labor	Direct Materials
Large	10,000	$ 480,000	$950,000
Small	30,000	1,140,000	800,000

Overhead Costs by Department

Overhead Costs	Cutting	Welding	Total
Utilities	$ 58,000	$174,000	$ 232,000
Indirect labor	430,000	480,000	910,000
General factory costs			150,000
Total overhead costs			$1,292,000

Kilowatt-Hours (000s)

Frame Type	Cutting	Welding	Total
Large	530	1,040	1,570
Small	910	1,200	2,110
Total kilowatt-hours	1,440	2,240	3,680

Required:

a. Compute the unit costs of large frames and small frames for the year using a single, factorywide overhead rate. The factorywide overhead allocation base is direct labor cost.

b. Compute the unit costs of large frames and small frames for the year using different overhead rates for utilities, indirect labor, and general factory costs. Utility costs and indirect labor costs are allocated to frames using kilowatt-hours. General factory costs are allocated to frames using direct costs (the sum of direct labor and direct materials).

c. Compute the unit costs of large frames and small frames for the year using departmental overhead rates for the cutting and welding departments. General factory overhead costs are evenly divided between the two departments before departmental overhead is allocated to the frames. Cutting department overhead costs are allocated based on direct materials costs; welding department overhead costs are allocated based on kilowatt-hours in the welding department.

d. Analyze why different unit costs result from the different methods of allocating overhead costs to the products. Which method is best?

P9–25: Hurst Mats

Hurst Mats manufactures custom replacement floor mats for automobiles. The floor mats are made of spun nylon on highly automated, expensive machinery.

Hurst manufactures two mat styles: Plush and Deluxe. Hurst's unionized work force makes it difficult for Hurst to compete on price. So far it has been able to successfully compete on quality, innovative design, and delivery schedule. However, the leaders of Hurst's union are aggressive and are seeking additional work-related job guarantees. Hurst management would like to reduce its dependence on unionized labor.

Hurst's manufacturing process is overhead-driven; most of the overhead arises from the common machinery that produces the Plush and Deluxe floor mats. Nonunionized engineers and technicians maintain the equipment. Expensive lubricants and filters are required to operate the machines, which require large amounts of electricity and natural gas. Each mat style is produced in batches that consist of 10 mats per batch. Plush and Deluxe do not put differential demands on the equipment other than through the amount of machine time required to produce each batch of mats. The following table summarizes the operating data for each mat style:

	Plush	Deluxe
Machine minutes per batch of 10 mats	12	9
Direct labor per batch of 10 mats	$4	$6
Direct material per batch of 10 mats	$7	$5
Number of batches per year	14,000	9,000

Overhead is allocated to the two mat styles using a predetermined overhead rate estimated from a flexible budget at the beginning of the year. Fixed overhead is estimated to be $680,000, and variable overhead is estimated to be $1.50 per machine minute. Management is debating whether to use machine minutes or direct labor cost as the overhead allocation base to allocate overhead to the two mat styles.

Required:

a. Calculate two overhead rates. The first uses machine minutes as the allocation base, and the second overhead rate uses direct labor cost as the allocation base. Round both overhead rates to two decimals.

b. Calculate the *total* product cost per batch of Plush and Deluxe mats using the two overhead rates calculated in (*a*).

c. Discuss the advantages and disadvantages of using machine minutes or direct labor cost as the allocation base for assigning overhead to the two mat styles.

P9–26: Mutual Fund Company

Mutual Fund Company (MFC) is considering centralizing its overnight mail function. Five departments within MFC use overnight mail service: trades processing, trades verifications, securities processing, accounts control, and customer service. Although these departments send different types of packages (weight and content), they often send packages to the same destinations. Currently, each of these

Magic Floor allocates the fill line costs to the various bottled products using a predetermined overhead absorption rate calculated based on budgeted costs divided by budgeted volume. Budgeted volume is measured in seconds on the fill line. Pints are filled in 3 seconds, quarts in 5 seconds, half-gallons in 9 seconds, and gallons in 17 seconds.

During 2012, the following times (in seconds) were recorded for filling bottles on the fill line:

	Pints	Quarts	Half-Gallons	Gallons
Wax stripper	118,000	246,000	542,000	800,000
Soap	145,000	305,000	703,000	1,180,000
Wax	130,000	270,000	608,000	840,000

Actual overhead costs incurred in 2012 on the fill line are:

Maintenance	$ 76,000
Indirect labor	179,000
Depreciation	127,000
Utilities	28,000
Indirect supplies	25,000

Required:

a. Calculate the expected volume of the bottling fill line for 2012.

b. Calculate the normal volume of the bottling fill line for 2012.

c. Calculate the overhead absorption rate for the bottling fill line for 2012 based on expected volume (round overhead rate to four decimals).

d. Calculate the overhead absorption rate for the bottling fill line for 2012 based on normal volume (round overhead rate to four decimals).

e. Calculate the over/underabsorbed overhead amount for the bottling fill line for 2012 based on expected volume.

f. Calculate the over/underabsorbed overhead amount for the bottling fill line for 2012 based on normal volume.

g. Explain in intuitive terms why your answers in parts (e) and (f) differ.

P9–31:   Sportway Inc.

Sportway Inc. is a wholesale distributor supplying a wide range of moderately priced sporting equipment to large chain stores. About 60 percent of Sportway's products are purchased from other companies and the remainder are manufactured by Sportway. The company has a plastics department that is currently manufacturing molded fishing tackle boxes. Sportway is able to manufacture and sell 8,000 tackle boxes annually, making full use of its direct labor capacity at available workstations. Presented below are the selling price and costs associated with Sportway's tackle boxes.

Selling price per box		$86.00
Costs per box		
Molded plastic	$8.00	
Hinges, latches, handle	9.00	
Direct labor ($15.00/hr.)	18.75	
Manufacturing overhead	12.50	
Selling and administrative cost	17.00	65.25
Profit per box		$20.75

Because Sportway believes it could sell 12,000 tackle boxes if it had sufficient manufacturing capacity, the company has looked into the possibility of purchasing the tackle boxes for distribution. Maple Products, a steady supplier of quality products, would be able to provide up to 9,000 tackle boxes per year at a price of $68 per box delivered to Sportway's facility.

Bart Johnson, Sportway's product manager, has suggested that the company could make better use of its plastics department by manufacturing skateboards. To support his position, Johnson has a market study that indicates an expanding market for skateboards and a need for additional suppliers. Johnson believes that Sportway could expect to sell 17,500 skateboards annually at $45 per skateboard. Johnson's estimate of the costs to manufacture the skateboards follows:

Selling price per skateboard		$45.00
Costs per skateboard		
Molded plastic	$5.50	
Wheels, hardware	7.00	
Direct labor ($15.00/hr.)	7.50	
Manufacturing overhead	5.00	
Selling and administrative cost	9.00	34.00
Profit per skateboard		$11.00

In the plastics department, Sportway uses direct labor hours as the application base for manufacturing overhead. Included in manufacturing overhead for the current year is $50,000 of factorywide, fixed manufacturing overhead that has been allocated to the plastics department. For each product that Sportway sells, regardless of whether the product has been purchased or is manufactured by Sportway, a portion of the selling and administrative cost is fixed at $6 per unit. Total selling and administrative costs for the purchased tackle boxes would be $10 per unit.

Required:

Prepare an analysis based on the data presented that will show which product or products Sportway Inc. should manufacture and/or purchase to maximize the company's profitability. Show the associated financial impact. Support your answer with appropriate calculations.

SOURCE: CMA adapted.

P9–32: MumsDay Corporation

MumsDay Corporation manufactures a complete line of fiberglass attaché cases and suitcases. MumsDay has three manufacturing departments (molding, component, and assembly) and two service departments (power and maintenance).

The sides of the cases are manufactured in the molding department. The frames, hinges, locks, and so on are manufactured in the component department. The cases are completed in the assembly department. Varying amounts of materials, time, and effort are required for each type of case. The power department and maintenance department provide services to the three manufacturing departments. MumsDay has always used a plantwide overhead rate. Direct labor hours are used to assign overhead to products. Management calculates the predetermined rate by dividing the company's total estimated overhead by the total estimated direct labor hours to be worked in the three manufacturing departments.

Whit Portlock, manager of cost accounting, has recommended that MumsDay use departmental overhead rates. He developed the planned operating costs and expected levels of activity for the coming year, presented by department in the following schedules:

Manufacturing Departments (000s)

	Molding	Component	Assembly
Departmental activity measures			
Direct labor hours	500	2,000	1,500
Machine hours	875	125	0
Departmental costs			
Raw materials	$12,400	$30,000	$ 1,250
Direct labor	3,500	20,000	12,000
Variable overhead	3,500	10,000	16,500
Fixed overhead	17,500	6,200	6,100
Total departmental costs	$36,900	$66,200	$35,850
Use of service departments			
Maintenance			
Estimated usage in labor hours for coming year	90	25	10
Power (in kilowatt-hours)			
Estimated usage for coming year	360	320	120
Maximum allotted long-term capacity (in kilowatt-hours)	500	350	150

Service Departments

	Power	Maintenance
Departmental activity measures		
Maximum capacity	1,000 kwh	Adjustable
Estimated usage in coming year	800 kwh	125 hours
Departmental costs		
Materials and supplies	$ 5,000	$1,500
Variable labor	1,400	2,250
Fixed overhead	12,000	250
Total service department costs	$18,400	$4,000

Required:

a. Calculate the plantwide overhead rate for MumsDay Corp. for the coming year using the same method as used in the past.
b. Whit Portlock has been asked to develop departmental overhead rates for comparison with the plantwide rate.
  (i) Allocate maintenance department costs to the three manufacturing departments using labor hours.
  (ii) Allocate the fixed costs in the power department to the three manufacturing departments according to long-term capacity and the variable costs according to planned usage.
  (iii) Calculate departmental overhead rates for the three manufacturing departments using a machine-hour base for the molding department and a direct-labor-hour base for the component and assembly departments.
c. Should MumsDay use a plantwide rate or departmental rates to assign overhead to its products? Explain your answer.

SOURCE: CMA adapted.

P9–33: Neweway Plastics (See Appendix A)

Neweway Plastics manufactures an acrylic compound used in automobile bumpers in a continuous flow process. Raw material is added at the beginning of the process and conversion costs are incurred uniformly over the process. The accompanying table summarizes the results of operations for May:

Beginning work in process (units)		6,000
Raw materials	$2,680	
Conversion costs (50%)*	892	$3,572
Units completed and transferred out		40,000
Units started in May		38,000
Ending work in process (units)		4,000 (70%)*
Conversion costs incurred in May		$17,512
Material costs incurred in May		$19,760

*Percentages denote percentage complete.

Required:

Compute the cost of goods transferred out and the ending work in process for the month of May using both the weighted average and FIFO methods.

P9–34: Targon Inc.

Targon Inc. manufactures lawn equipment. A job order system is used because the products are manufactured on a batch rather than a continuous basis. Targon employs a full absorption accounting method for cost accumulation. The balances in selected accounts for the 11-month period ended August 31, 2010, are presented below:

Stores inventory	$ 32,000
Work-in-process inventory	1,200,000
Finished goods inventory	2,785,000
Factory overhead	2,260,000
Cost of goods sold	14,200,000

The work-in-process inventory consists of two jobs:

Job. No.	Units	Items	Accumulated Cost
3005-5	50,000	Estate sprinklers	$ 700,000
3006-4	40,000	Economy sprinklers	500,000
			$1,200,000

The finished goods inventory consists of five items:

Items	Quantity and Unit Cost	Accumulated Cost
Estate sprinklers	5,000 units @ $22 each	$ 110,000
Deluxe sprinklers	115,000 units @ $17 each	1,955,000
Brass nozzles	10,000 gross @ $14 per gross	140,000
Rainmaker nozzles	5,000 gross @ $16 per gross	80,000
Connectors	100,000 gross @ $5 per gross	500,000
		$2,785,000

The factory cost budget prepared for the 2009–10 fiscal year is presented below. The company applies factory overhead on the basis of direct labor hours.

Activities during the first 11 months of the year were quite close to budget. A total of 367,000 direct labor hours have been worked through August 31, 2010.

Factory Cost Annual Budget for the Year
Ending September 30, 2010

Direct materials	$ 3,800,000
Purchased parts	6,000,000
Direct labor (400,000 hours)	4,000,000
Overhead	
Supplies	190,000
Indirect labor	700,000
Supervision	250,000
Depreciation	950,000
Utilities	200,000
Insurance	10,000
Property taxes	40,000
Miscellaneous	60,000
Total factory costs	$16,200,000

All direct materials, purchased parts, and supplies are charged to stores inventory. The September purchases were as follows:

Materials	$410,000
Purchased parts	285,000
Supplies	13,000

The direct materials, purchased parts, and supplies were requisitioned from stores inventory as shown in the table that follows:

	Purchased Parts	Materials	Supplies	Total Requisitions
3005-5	$110,000	$100,000	$ —	$210,000
3006-4	—	6,000	—	6,000
4001-3 (30,000 gross rainmaker nozzles)	—	181,000	—	181,000
4002-1 (10,000 deluxe sprinklers)	—	92,000	—	92,000
4003-5 (50,000 ring sprinklers)	163,000	—	—	163,000
Supplies	—	—	20,000	20,000
	$273,000	$379,000	$20,000	$672,000

The payroll summary for September is as follows:

	Hours	Cost
3005-5	6,000	$ 62,000
3006-4	2,500	26,000
4001-3	18,000	182,000
4002-1	500	5,000
4003-5	5,000	52,000
Indirect	8,000	60,000
Supervision	—	24,000
Sales and administration	—	120,000
		$531,000

Other factory costs incurred during September were

Depreciation	$62,500
Utilities	15,000
Insurance	1,000
Property taxes	3,500
Miscellaneous	5,000
	$87,000

Jobs completed during September and actual output were

Job. No.	Quantity	Items
3005-5	48,000 units	Estate sprinklers
3006-4	39,000 units	Economy sprinklers
4001-3	29,500 gross	Rainmaker nozzles
4003-5	49,000 units	Ring sprinklers

The following finished products were shipped to customers during September:

Items	Quantity
Estate sprinklers	16,000 units
Deluxe sprinklers	32,000 units
Economy sprinklers	20,000 units
Ring sprinklers	22,000 units
Brass nozzles	5,000 gross
Rainmaker nozzles	10,000 gross
Connectors	26,000 gross

Required:

a. Calculate the over- or underapplied overhead for the year ended September 30, 2010. Be sure to indicate whether the overhead is over- or underapplied.

b. Calculate the dollar balance in the work-in-process inventory account as of September 30, 2010.

c. Calculate the dollar balance in the finished goods inventory as of September 30, 2010, for the estate sprinklers using a FIFO basis.

SOURCE: CMA adapted.

Cases

Case 9–1: Heath Metal Products

Chris Maynard, one of Heath Metal Products's three customer engineers, is reviewing the costs of the radar housings for Lingle Aerospace (LA). LA is one of Maynard's largest accounts and the radar housing is a fabricated piece of sheet metal LA uses to assemble an aircraft's radar system installed in the nose of the plane. In reviewing the detailed cost record for this job, Maynard is concerned that the direct labor posted to the job appears too high. He estimated the direct labor in the welding department to be six hours per batch of 130 units. But the job sheet reports that 9.5 hours were used.

Background

Heath Metal Products is a custom machine shop that bids on orders and produces sheet metal parts in batches. It was founded 30 years ago by two tool and die makers in their mid-30s: Jack Spence and Don Carter. Spence and Carter were previously employed by a national automobile company. They started Heath to make parts for local, large manufacturing firms that did not have sufficient capacity to meet short-run production schedules. Now Heath competes by supplying certain types of parts more cheaply than large companies can produce them internally. It does this by (1) bidding on jobs with run lengths that match Heath's machine configurations, (2) employing nonunion labor, and (3) avoiding much of the overhead existing in big factories. Heath Metal Products now manufactures sheet metal parts used in a variety of office products, computers, and printers. The firm has grown in recent years and has benefited from the outsourcing movement whereby large firms seeking to reduce their manufacturing costs outsource non-critical metal fabricated parts.

Heath's single plant has a number of sheet metal presses (the largest being a 500-ton press), numerically controlled cutting and drilling machines, lathes, drill presses, and electric arc welders. Engineers contact customers to see if they have parts they are willing to outsource. Usually, the customer is introducing a new model and has not produced the tools necessary to fabricate the part internally. Heath's customer engineer works with the client on the manufacturing and design specifications for the part and submits a bid to produce and deliver a set number of parts over a given time period at a fixed price. In the process of preparing the bid, the customer engineer forecasts the cost of the job by estimating direct labor, direct material, and machine time required in each factory department.

Due to intense competition from other firms (as large office equipment companies constantly shift production worldwide to find the lowest-cost, highest-quality producers), shops such as Heath have high variability in volumes. In response to these volume changes, Heath is always laying off and rehiring employees. If Heath loses a large contract, it often requires six to nine months to replace the work. In the meantime, employees are laid off until new work can be found.

Two hundred employees now work at Heath, including sales, administrative, and factory employees. Besides production workers, Heath has a maintenance and janitorial staff. To improve cost competitiveness, Spence and Carter have been trying to get production employees to take over more of the maintenance and clean-up tasks when they have idle time. They would also like to see the workers cross-trained in more production and maintenance tasks to help better balance work flow in the factory. These actions will raise productivity and reduce costs. However, the attempts at cross-training have achieved very limited success.

Compensation system

Heath does not have a formal pay-for-performance or bonus system. All employees are paid straight salary with annual raises. Customer engineers do not receive commissions for sales. In good years, raises are higher. Management has explored incentive pay and piece-rate systems. They have concluded that the constantly changing product mix would cause such systems to be very expensive to implement and maintain.

At a sales staff meeting in February, Phil Matson, Heath's vice president of operation, mentioned they were going to award bonuses to the customer engineers if they could achieve their target sales forecasts. In July, Chris Maynard, whose sales were up 22 percent over the previous year, asked Matson whether total sales were ahead of the target needed for the bonus. Matson said that while sales were up for the year, the plant still had excess capacity and it appeared they would not achieve the forecast.

Accounting system

A job order cost system is used to accumulate direct labor and direct materials to individual jobs. At the end of the day, employees fill out a time sheet indicating the jobs they worked on and the time spent on each job. All the indirect costs are accumulated into a separate overhead cost pool for each factory department (pressing, drilling, and welding). The indirect costs for each department include equipment depreciation and lease charges, the department supervisor's salary, employees' idle time, and allocated utilities and occupancy charges (property taxes, plant building depreciation). Then, separate overhead rates are set for each department using direct labor hours as the allocation base. When an employee posts time to a particular job, the overhead rate for the employee's department multiplied by the employee's time charged to the job is the amount of overhead for that department charged to the job.

Problem with the Lingle Aerospace job

Chris Maynard contacts Phil Sanchez, supervisor of the welding department, and asks about the discrepancy between Maynard's estimate of 6.0 hours in the welding department and the 9.5 hours actually charged to the LA contract. Sanchez admits that there were two other jobs in the welding department at that time and that it is possible the employee had mistakenly charged some time to the LA contract instead of the other jobs.

Maynard then asks Linda Rawlings, supervisor of the drilling department, about the 67 labor hours charged to LA. Maynard had estimated the drilling time to be 53 hours for the batch. Rawlings said she was too busy now to look into the matter but she would contact him later. That was two weeks ago. Maynard is concerned that if the costs charged to the LA contract are too high, Phil Matson will ask LA for a higher price. If this happens, LA might shift the radar housing from Heath to another supplier.

When Jack Spence learned of the accounting errors on the LA account, he replied, "I don't see any problem. As long as the time cards are charged to jobs, our tax returns are right."

Required:

    a. Identify various problems at Heath.

    b. What improvements would you suggest Heath implement?

Case 9–2:   WoodCo

WoodCo is a wholesale distributor supplying a wide range of equipment and tools to the logging industry. About half of WoodCo's products are purchased from other companies, and the remainder are manufactured by WoodCo for distribution. One item WoodCo makes is a fiberglass-reinforced case used to carry long-bladed chainsaws. In a normal year, WoodCo manufactures and sells 5,000 of these cases. This production makes full use of WoodCo's capacity in the fiberglass processing department, which is limited by the amount of direct labor that can be expended at a fixed number of workstations. WoodCo believes it could sell 7,000 cases if it had the manufacturing capacity. Here are the actual revenue and cost data for manufacturing chainsaw cases:

Selling price per case		$80.00
Costs per case		
Fiberglass and resin	$24.00	
Handle, hinges, latch	7.00	
Direct labor ($12.00/hour)	12.00	
Manufacturing overhead	6.00	
Selling and administrative cost	16.00	65.00
Profit per case		$15.00

WoodCo has looked into the possibility of purchasing chainsaw cases for distribution. The company learned that Murphy Supply could provide the cases in volume quantities at a price of $60 each delivered to WoodCo's facility. The maximum number of cases that Murphy could supply to WoodCo in any given year would be 6,000, and the cases must be bought in increments of 1,000. Other goods supplied from Murphy in the past have been of very good quality, and WoodCo regards Murphy as a reliable vendor.

The only other product that WoodCo's fiberglass processing department could make is a brightly colored hard hat. At present, WoodCo does not sell hard hats; however, a market analysis indicates there is room for another producer. The market analysis revealed that a sales price of $35 per hat would be best; at this price, WoodCo could expect to sell 9,500 hard hats annually. The data indicate that the profit per hard hat would be considerably less than the profit per chainsaw case. Estimated manufacturing costs for the hard hats are as follows:

Selling price per hat		$35.00
Costs per hat		
Fiberglass and resin	$12.00	
Liner, strap, rivets	5.00	
Direct labor ($12.00/hour)	4.80	
Manufacturing overhead	2.40	
Selling and administrative cost	3.50	27.70
Profit per hat		$ 7.30

WoodCo employs departmental rates for applying manufacturing overhead to its products. Direct labor hours are used as the application base for the fiberglass processing department. Included in the manufacturing overhead for the current year is $20,000 of factorywide fixed manufacturing overhead that has been allocated to the fiberglass processing department.

In addition, $80,000 per year of companywide fixed selling and administrative costs are allocated to the fiberglass processing department using a 20-percent-of-sales application base. To encourage new products, however, WoodCo's policy is to allocate companywide fixed selling and administrative costs at only 10 percent of sales rather than the usual 20 percent.

WoodCo's management is, of course, interested in increasing the profitability of the firm. The company controller has been asked to review the available data and recommend what combination of products WoodCo should manufacture and/or purchase in the future.

Required:

   a. In formulating this recommendation on the nature of WoodCo's future business,

     (i) Explain the decision rule the controller should apply.

     (ii) Discuss the important factors the controller needs to identify when preparing the analysis.

b. Prepare an analysis based on the data presented that will show which product or products WoodCo should manufacture and/or purchase in order to maximize the company's profitability. Support your answer with appropriate calculations.

SOURCE: CMA adapted.

Case 9–3:   PortCo Products

PortCo Products is a divisionalized furniture manufacturer. The divisions are autonomous segments, each responsible for its own sales, costs of operations, working capital management, and equipment acquisition. Each division serves a different market in the furniture industry. Because the markets and products of the divisions are so different, there have never been any transfers between divisions.

The commercial division manufactures equipment and furniture that is purchased by the restaurant industry. The division plans to introduce a new line of counter and chair units that feature a cushioned seat for the counter chairs. John Kline, the division manager, has discussed the manufacturing of the cushioned seat with Russ Fiegel of the office division. They both believe a cushioned seat currently made by the office division for use on its deluxe office stool could be modified for use on the new counter chair. Consequently, Kline has asked Russ Fiegel for a price for 100-unit lots of the cushioned seat. The following conversation took place about the price to be charged for the cushioned seats.

FIEGEL: John, we can make the necessary modifications to the cushioned seat easily. The raw materials used in your seat are slightly different and should cost about 10 percent more than those used in our deluxe office stool. However, the labor time should be the same because the seat fabrication operation basically is the same. I would price the seat at our regular rate—full cost plus 30 percent markup.

KLINE: That's higher than I expected, Russ. I was thinking that a good price would be your variable manufacturing costs. After all, your capacity costs will be incurred regardless of this job.

FIEGEL: John, I'm at capacity. By making the cushioned seats for you, I'll have to cut my production of deluxe office stools. Of course, I can increase my production of economy office stools. The labor time freed by not having to fabricate the frame or assemble the deluxe stool can be shifted to the frame fabrication and assembly of the economy office stool. And you will save the cost of the framing raw materials. However, I am constrained in terms of the number of hours I have for cushion fabrication. Fortunately, I can switch my labor force between these two models of stools without any loss of efficiency. As you know, overtime is not a feasible alternative in our community. I'd like to sell it to you at variable cost, but I have excess demand for both products. I don't mind changing my product mix to the economy model if I get a good return on the seats I make for you. Here are my budgeted costs for the two stools and a schedule of my manufacturing overhead (see the tables that follow).

KLINE: I guess I see your point, Russ, but I don't want to price myself out of the market. Maybe we should talk to corporate to see if they can give us any guidance.

Office Division Budgeted Costs and Prices

	Deluxe Office Stool		Economy Office Stool
Raw materials			
Framing	$ 8.15		$9.76
Cushioned seat			
Padding	2.40		—
Vinyl	4.00		—
Molded seat (purchased)	—		6.00
Direct labor			
Frame fabrication			
(0.5 × $7.50/DLH*)	3.75	(0.5 × $7.50/DLH)	3.75
Cushion fabrication			
(0.5 × $7.50/DLH)	3.75		—
Assembly†			
(0.5 × $7.50/DLH)	3.75	(0.3 × $7.50/DLH)	2.25
Manufacturing			
Overhead (1.5 DLH × $12.80/DLH)	19.20	(0.8 DLH × $12.80/DLH)	10.24
Total standard cost	$45.00		$32.00
Selling price (30% markup)	$58.50		$41.60

*Direct labor hours.
†Attaching seats to frames and attaching rubber feet.

Office Division Manufacturing Overhead Budget

Overhead Item	Nature	Amount
Supplies	Variable—at current market prices	$ 420,000
Indirect labor	Variable	375,000
Supervision	Nonvariable	250,000
Power	Use varies with activity; rates are fixed	180,000
Heat and light	Nonvariable—light is fixed regardless of production, while heat/air conditioning varies with fuel charges	140,000
Property taxes and insurance	Nonvariable—any change in amounts/rates is independent of production	200,000
Depreciation	Fixed dollar total	1,700,000
Employee benefits	20% of supervision, direct and indirect labor	575,000
	Total overhead	$3,840,000
	Capacity in DLH	÷ 300,000
	Overhead rate/DLH	$12.80

Required:

a. John Kline and Russ Fiegel ask PortCo corporate management for guidance on an appropriate transfer price. Corporate management suggests they consider using a transfer price based upon opportunity cost. Calculate a transfer price for the cushioned seat based upon variable manufacturing cost plus forgone profits.

b. Which alternative transfer price system—full cost, variable manufacturing cost, or opportunity cost—would be better as the underlying concept for an intracompany transfer price policy? Explain your answer.

SOURCE: CMA adapted.

Chapter Ten

Criticisms of Absorption Cost Systems: Incentive to Overproduce

Chapter Outline

Traditional cost data tend to be irrelevant and mischievous. These systems of simple proportional divisions followed by allocations and reallocations do not provide data appropriate for managerial use in planning or controlling operations. Moreover, they tend to put such data as do exist in an inaccessible form. Unless other purposes for such data exist, the systems should be discontinued to save the clerical costs of operating them.[1]

The last chapter described traditional absorption cost systems. These systems have been widely used for 90 years, and some elements of them have been traced back to the beginning of the Industrial Revolution. For as long as these systems have been used, they have been criticized for producing misleading information and creating incentives that are inconsistent with maximizing the value of the firm. The quotation above is just one example of the charges leveled at traditional cost accounting systems. Despite such criticism, absorption cost systems are the predominant systems in use in manufacturing firms today. Moreover, nonmanufacturing systems are based on elements of absorption cost systems. This chapter and the next chapter examine some common complaints and present some alternatives to solve the problems.

As described in Chapter 1, cost systems serve numerous functions, including decision making, control, and external reporting. No single system can satisfy all the requirements of each function, so trade-offs must be made. Costing systems are constantly being revised and updated as technology and firms' organizational architecture change. Examining the well-known problems in costing systems provides a greater appreciation of how to implement them and how to become a more intelligent user of their data. Also, one must be careful not to reject a particular type of cost system (e.g., absorption costing) merely because a particular firm or industry implements it badly.

Section A of this chapter describes how absorption cost systems can create incentives for managers to produce more than they sell (the incentive to overproduce). Section B presents an alternative to absorption costing called *variable costing* that purportedly eliminates the incentive to overproduce. However, there are still incentives to overproduce under variable costing in some situations. Furthermore, variable costing creates other dysfunctional incentives, which are described in section C. The lesson of this and the following chapter is described in section D, "Beware of unit costs." All cost systems generate product costs (average unit costs) that are inaccurate to some extent and inappropriate for some decisions because all cost systems rely on historical costs, not opportunity costs. The degree of inaccuracy varies across products and decisions. The concept of unit cost implies a relation between the unit cost figure and volume. When a unit cost figure is reported—say, $5.12—the first reaction is that it will cost $5.12 to produce one more unit. But in many (if not most) cases, unit costs are mixtures of variable and fixed costs and thus do not represent the incremental cost of producing one more unit.

Chapters 10 and 11 illustrate that all cost systems produce misleading information for some decisions and that average unit costs are misleading because costs per unit implies that these are the variable (or marginal) costs of production. A unit cost figure unlikely measures both the opportunity cost of producing one more unit (marginal cost) and the opportunity cost of doubling output. Producing one more unit unlikely requires additional capacity, while doubling output most likely

---

[1] B Goetz, *Management Planning and Control: A Managerial Approach to Industrial Accounting* (New York: McGraw-Hill, 1949), p. 143.

requires adding more (costly) capacity. Reported unit costs can be long-run average costs, short-run marginal costs, or neither. Without detailed knowledge of the production process and accounting system, it is easy to misinterpret unit cost data.

A. Incentive to Overproduce

Absorption cost systems include both job order and process cost systems. These systems are designed to *absorb* all manufacturing costs into product costs. All costs incurred by the factory are absorbed by products. All of the costs unloaded onto the delivery docks are shipped out by the shipping department or are still in raw material and work-in-process inventories. Some complaints about these systems arise from their full absorption character. In particular, it is claimed that absorption cost systems create incentives to overproduce.

1. Example

To illustrate the incentive to overproduce, consider a department with $10,000 of fixed costs and constant variable costs of $5 per unit. Assume that (1) the department produces a single homogeneous product and (2) actual overhead incurred equals overhead absorbed and actual production is the same as budgeted production. The first assumption allows volume to be measured in units produced. The second assumption ensures that there is no over/underabsorbed overhead. These assumptions greatly simplify the arithmetic of the example without altering any of the basic conclusions.

The firm sells 2,000 units at $12 per unit but can produce 2,000, 2,200, or 2,400 units. There is no beginning inventory. Table 10–1 shows how reported profits vary with different production levels.

Sales revenue is constant at $24,000, but production varies from 2,000 units to 2,400 units. Variable costs for the 2,000 units sold remain constant at $10,000. Fixed costs are allocated to units sold using overhead absorption:

$$\text{Fixed costs absorbed to units sold} = \frac{\text{Fixed costs}}{\text{Units produced}} \times \text{Units sold}$$

Notice that the overhead rate is lower when more units are produced. Also, while sales, variable costs per unit, and fixed costs remain constant, profits increase as production (not sales) increases.[2] Why? The fixed costs charged off to

TABLE 10–1 Reported Profits Increase with Production

	Production (Units)		
	2,000	*2,200*	*2,400*
Sales revenue (2,000 @ $12)	$24,000	$24,000	$24,000
Variable costs (2,000 @ $5)	(10,000)	(10,000)	(10,000)
Fixed costs ($10,000/2,000) × 2,000	(10,000)		
($10,000/2,200) × 2,000		(9,091)	
($10,000/2,400) × 2,000			(8,333)
Profit	$ 4,000	$ 4,909	$ 5,667

---

[2] This example allocates fixed costs to products using actual production instead of expected or normal production. Since we are assuming actual and budgeted fixed costs are equal (as are units produced and budgeted units), using actual data gives the same allocations as using budgeted data.

TABLE 10–2   Fixed and Variable Costs in Inventory

	Production (Units)		
	2,000	2,200	2,400
Units in inventory	0	200	400
Fixed costs in inventory: ($10,000/2,000) × 0	$ 0		
($10,000/2,200) × 200		$ 909	
($10,000/2,400) × 400			$ 1,667
Fixed costs charged to profits (from Table 10–1)	10,000	9,091	8,333
Total fixed costs	$10,000	$10,000	$10,000
Total inventory:			
Variable costs (@ $5/unit)	$0	$1,000	$2,000
Fixed costs (from above)	0	909	1,667
Inventory	$0	$1,909	$3,667

income for the 2,000 units sold declines from $10,000 to $8,333 at 2,400 units. When more units are produced than sold, some of the fixed costs are inventoried. When the number of units in inventory is increased, the fraction of fixed costs in inventory increases. With more fixed costs in inventory, fewer fixed costs are transferred to the income statement. Absorption costing systems spread all the costs (including fixed costs) against all the units worked on. When production is increased (holding sales constant), average unit costs fall and reported accounting profit per unit sold increases.

Table 10–2 illustrates that as more units are produced with sales held constant, a greater fraction of the fixed costs flow into inventory. The total dollars of fixed costs remain constant; they are just shifted from the income statement to the balance sheet. The amount added to inventory increases from zero to $3,667 at a production level of 2,400 units. However, building inventories to shift fixed costs to the balance sheet is not costless. Additional cash is needed to pay the variable costs. When 2,400 units are produced, the firm must find financing for the $2,000 variable costs in inventory.

Managers rewarded on total profits calculated using absorption costing can increase reported profits by increasing production (if sales are held constant). A major criticism of absorption costing is that it creates incentives for managers to overproduce, thereby building inventories.

This analysis makes the critical assumption that variable cost *per unit* remains constant as production is increased. If marginal cost (and hence variable cost) per unit rises as production increases, then average unit costs can actually increase. An increasing marginal cost reduces the incentives of managers to overproduce with absorption costing. The remainder of this chapter assumes that marginal (and variable) cost per unit is constant as volume changes.

2. Reducing the Overproduction Incentive

There are several ways to mitigate the incentive to overproduce. The first is to charge inventory holding costs against profits. That is, inventory values are increased by the cost of capital plus warehousing costs. Managers oppose this policy because inventory holding costs then have to be backed out of profits for

TABLE 10–3   Residual Income and Overproduction

	Production (Units)		
	2,000	*2,200*	*2,400*
Profits (from Table 10–1)	$4,000	$4,909	$5,667
Inventory (from Table 10–2)	0	1,909	3,667
Cost of inventories (@ 20%)	0	382	733
Residual income	4,000	4,527	4,934

external reporting, which increases accounting and data processing complexity and causes division profits (with the inventory holding costs) to be lower than firm profits (without the holding costs). If a manager is evaluated based on residual income instead of net income, the effect is to charge managers an inventory holding cost. Remember from Chapter 5 that residual income is net income less the firm's cost of capital times the amount of investment during the year, including inventories. If the manager overproduces, inventories increase and residual income falls.

For example, consider the example in Tables 10–1 and 10–2. Suppose the manager is evaluated and rewarded based on residual income. Furthermore, assume that the only asset is inventory and the firm's cost of capital is 20 percent. Table 10–3 illustrates how residual income varies with production.

We see from Table 10–3 that at a cost of capital of 20 percent, residual income does not eliminate the incentive to overproduce. It does, however, make it less profitable to the manager. For example, by producing 2,400 units, the manager raises profits from $4,000 to $5,667. Residual income cuts the gain from overproducing from $1,667 (or $5,667 − $4,000) to $934 (or $4,934 − $4,000).

A second method of reducing the overproduction incentive is a strict senior management policy against building inventories. Compensation plans can contain a clause that bonuses tied to net income will not be paid if inventories exceed a certain amount. However, such strict constraints are cumbersome and generate influence costs. Circumstances can arise under which firm value is maximized by increasing inventories (e.g., new product introductions, unexpected market shocks to supply or demand, or growing sales). Therefore, it is difficult to know at the beginning of the year what upper bound to place on inventory levels.

Third, in a single-plant, publicly traded firm, compensation can be based on stock prices instead of on accounting earnings, which removes the incentive for managers to overproduce. For example, awarding the plant manager stock or stock options forces the manager to bear the consequences of decisions that do not maximize firm value. However, this method imposes additional risk on managers for general marketwide events. In publicly traded firms with many plants, any plant manager's overproduction has a small effect on the value of the firm. Hence, free-rider problems in multiplant firms decrease the ability of stock-based compensation to eliminate the overproduction incentive.

A fourth possibility is to use just-in-time (JIT) production systems to reduce inventory levels. (Chapter 14 describes JIT in greater detail.) In a JIT system, manufacturing does not typically begin until the part or final product is ordered by a customer. Intermediate products flow immediately from one stage of production to another with little work-in-process inventories. If the production schedule is determined by demand, then the plant manager or product-line manager does not have the discretion to set production levels in excess of demand. In essence, a JIT system removes from managers the decision rights to set production levels. These decision rights are replaced by demand-driven market orders. JIT systems can reduce inventories and thus the incentive to overproduce in order to increase reported profits. A final option is to change the costing system. Variable costing systems, discussed next, reduce the incentive to overproduce.

Concept Questions	Q10–1	What is the danger in viewing unit costs as variable costs?
	Q10–2	How can managers increase profit artificially when an absorption cost system is used?
	Q10–3	Name four ways to mitigate the incentives for managers to overproduce.

B. Variable (Direct) Costing

Absorption cost systems can distort reported profits as production volumes change, creating incentives for managers to overproduce and thereby create larger inventories. Variable costing (sometimes called *direct costing*) is claimed to eliminate the incentive to build inventories, although it is not entirely successful.

1. Background

Under **variable costing,** all fixed costs are written off against income in the year they are incurred. Fixed manufacturing costs are not absorbed into product costs and do not flow through the inventory accounts. Product costs contain only the variable components. Fixed manufacturing costs are treated as period costs and are written off. Thus, the only difference between absorption costing and variable costing is in the treatment of fixed manufacturing costs: Fixed manufacturing costs are included as part of product costs under absorption costing and written off as period expenses (and not included in product costs) under variable costing. The purported advantages of variable costing are that it eliminates distortions to income and product costs when volume changes, and it reduces the dysfunctional incentives to overproduce.

Variable costing attracted much attention in the 1950s and 1960s. A few companies still use it. We discuss it here because it helps us to better understand absorption costing systems. Also, variable cost transfer pricing is the same as variable costing. The transfer price consists of only the variable costs. The same weaknesses of variable costing also apply to variable cost transfer pricing (see Chapter 5). Moreover, many firms use variable costing to some degree for some fixed expenditures. For example, Allegheny Ludlum Steel Co. wrote off depreciation, plant insurance, property taxes, and factory management salaries to income. These fixed costs were not part of Allegheny Ludlum's product costs and were treated as period costs.

2. Illustration of Variable Costing

As an example of variable costing versus absorption costing, consider the data in Table 10–4. The same assumptions made earlier continue to apply: A single homogeneous product is produced, budgeted volume equals actual volume, and variable cost per unit does not increase as production is expanded. In Table 10–4, the company sells 10,000 units each year and produces 10,000 units in year 1 and

A Nineteenth-Century Example of Variable Costing

Two very influential nineteenth-century English accountants, Garcke and Fells, recognized the problems of letting fixed costs enter unit costs. Garcke was a managing director of British Electric Traction Co., and Fells was the general manager of Salt Union Limited. They argued that fixed overhead charges should be written off to net income:

> [Fixed overheads] do not vary proportionately with the volume of business. . . . [They] are, in the aggregate, more or less constant, while the manufacturing costs fluctuate with the costs of labor and the price of materials. To distribute the charges over the articles manufactured would, therefore, have the effect of disproportionately reducing the cost of production with every increase, and the reverse with every diminution of business. Such a result is to be deprecated.

SOURCE: E Garcke and J Fells, *Factory Accounts*, 4th ed. (London: Crosby, Lockwood, and Son, 1893), p. 73. Quoted by P Garner, *Evolution of Cost Accounting to 1925* (Montgomery: University of Alabama Press, 1954), p. 124.

TABLE 10–4   **Data for Direct Costing and Absorption Costing Example**[*]

Price		$11/unit sold
Direct materials and labor (all variable)		$2/unit produced
Flexible overhead budget		$40,000 + $3/unit produced

	Sales	*Production*	*Overhead*
Year 1:	10,000 units	10,000 units	$70,000
Year 2:	10,000 units	11,000 units	$73,000

[*]To simplify all examples, assume there are no beginning inventories.

11,000 units in year 2. Actual overhead costs in both years are the same as predicted by the flexible budget ($70,000 in year 1 and $73,000 in year 2).

Table 10–5 provides the absorption costing and variable costing income statements for the two years. In part A, net income under absorption costing rises in year 2 even though sales are flat, because some of the fixed costs are inventoried.

In part B, all of the fixed overhead of $40,000 is written off each year and net income is the same across the two years. All overhead costs are written off to the income statement under variable costing. Inventoried units are charged for variable overhead costs under both absorption and variable costing. Only the fixed overhead is treated differently. Under variable costing, in year 2 only variable overhead of $30,000 is written off to income. The remaining $3,000 of variable overhead (1,000 units × $3 of variable overhead) remains in inventory along with the other $2 of direct cost per unit. Two points should be noted from this example:

1. When production and sales are equal, absorption costing and variable costing give identical profit amounts (assuming no beginning inventories). When production and sales are equal, both costing methods write off all fixed costs to income.

2. Absorption cost net income is higher in year 2 than in year 1 because some of the fixed costs in year 2 end up in inventory. In contrast, variable cost net income is constant over the two years.

TABLE 10–5   Absorption Costing and Variable Costing Income Statements for Years 1 and 2

	Year 1		Year 2	
A. Absorption Costing Net Income				
Sales		$110,000		$110,000
Direct materials and labor	(20,000)		(20,000)	
Overhead absorbed:				
$\frac{\$70,000}{10,000} \times 10,000$	(70,000)	(90,000)		
$\frac{\$73,000}{11,000} \times 10,000$			(66,364)	(86,364)
Net income		$ 20,000		$ 23,636
B. Variable Costing Net Income				
Sales		$110,000		$110,000
Direct materials and labor	(20,000)		(20,000)	
Variable overhead	(30,000)		(30,000)	
Fixed overhead	(40,000)	(90,000)	(40,000)	(90,000)
Net income		$ 20,000		$ 20,000

3. Overproduction Incentive under Variable Costing

In Table 10–5 note that under variable costing, profits do not vary with production volume changes. Proponents claim that variable costing eliminates the incentives of managers to show higher profits by overproducing. However, this claim is not entirely accurate. To illustrate, the example is modified slightly in Table 10–6. Actual overhead incurred is no longer the same as that predicted by the flexible budget ($70,000 in year 1 and $73,000 in year 2), but rather is $17,000 higher in both years ($87,000 in year 1 and $90,000 in year 2).

The issue becomes whether this $17,000 of additional overhead is a variable cost or a fixed cost. At the beginning of the year, the flexible budget is a useful tool to forecast total overhead as a function of volume. But at the end of the year, any deviation between actual spending and the flexible budget can be due to changes in fixed costs, changes in the variable cost per unit of volume, or both. In the absence of specific knowledge regarding whether the $17,000 budget variance is a fixed cost or a variable cost, managers can use their discretion to manage earnings. If the $17,000 is treated as a variable cost, then even under variable costing, managers have an incentive to overproduce. Table 10–6 presents the revised net income numbers with the additional $17,000 of overhead.

As displayed in parts A, B, and C of Table 10–6, net income is always $3,000 when production volume and sales are the same. (See year 1.) When production exceeds sales (as in year 2), absorption costing shows higher income in year 2 than in year 1 (part A). Under absorption costing, managers can show larger profits by overproducing. In part B, the extra $17,000 is treated as an additional fixed cost under variable costing. These additional dollars are written off in both years and net income is the same in both years.

Under variable costing, with the $17,000 of additional overhead treated as a variable cost (part C), the variable overhead per unit is composed of two pieces.

TABLE 10–6   Net Income under Absorption Costing and Variable Costing with an Additional $17,000 of Overhead

	Year 1		Year 2	
A. Absorption Costing				
Sales		$110,000		$110,000
Direct labor and materials	(20,000)		(20,000)	
Overhead absorbed:				
$\dfrac{\$87,000}{10,000} \times 10,000$	(87,000)	(107,000)		
$\dfrac{\$90,000}{11,000} \times 10,000$			(81,818)	(101,818)
Net income		$ 3,000		$ 8,182
B. Variable Costing, with $17,000 Treated as Additional Fixed Cost				
Sales		$110,000		$110,000
Direct labor and materials	(20,000)		(20,000)	
Variable overhead	(30,000)		(30,000)	
Fixed overhead				
($40,000 + $17,000)	(57,000)	(107,000)	(57,000)	(107,000)
Net income		$ 3,000		$ 3,000
C. Variable Costing, with $17,000 Treated as Additional Variable Cost				
Sales		$110,000		$110,000
Direct labor and materials	(20,000)		(20,000)	
Variable overhead:				
$\left(\$3 + \dfrac{\$17,000}{10,000}\right) \times 10,000$	(47,000)			
$\left(\$3 + \dfrac{\$17,000}{11,000}\right) \times 10,000$			(45,455)	
Fixed overhead	(40,000)		(40,000)	
		(107,000)		(105,455)
Net income		$ 3,000		$ 4,545

There is the original $3 of variable overhead per unit plus the $17,000 of extra overhead (assumed to be variable), which is converted to a per-unit amount by dividing by the number of units produced. When unit production exceeds units sold, some of the extra variable overhead is inventoried.

In the preceding example, management has discretion over classifying the additional $17,000 as either a fixed or variable cost. If each component of overhead, such as depreciation, utilities, property taxes, or indirect labor, is separately classified as fixed or variable, then at the end of the year management has no discretion to classify the over- or underabsorbed overhead as either fixed or variable. For example, suppose indirect labor is classified as variable overhead and at the end of the year indirect labor is underabsorbed. Then management has no discretion in classifying this underabsorbed indirect labor. It is a variable cost. However, some overhead components are mixed costs—they contain both fixed and variable elements. For example, utilities contain a fixed amount for turning on the lights and heat in the plant and a variable component for operating the machinery. At the end of the year, the total bill for utilities is a mixture of both fixed and variable costs. In this case, management can exercise discretion by classifying any budget variance in the total utility bill as either a fixed or variable cost.

C. Problems with Variable Costing

1. Classifying Fixed Costs as Variable Costs

The principal benefit of variable costing is it eliminates (or reduces) the incentive to overproduce as a way to boost reported earnings. However, the preceding example illustrates a potential problem with variable costing. How does one determine which costs are fixed and which costs are variable *at the end of the year?* At the beginning of the year, the fixed and variable components can be estimated. At the end of the year, however, when total overhead is known and is probably different from that forecast by the flexible budget, it is difficult and time-consuming to sort out whether the difference is due to a change in fixed costs, variable costs, or both. By classifying all of the excess overhead costs as variable, managers using variable costing can *inventory* some of these extra costs by overproducing.

Therefore, even under variable costing, building inventories can result in higher reported profits whenever actual overhead exceeds the flexible budget amount. The use of variable costing introduces another element of discretion into the accounting system. Someone must have the decision rights to determine at the end of the year how much of the actual overhead was fixed and how much was variable. This additional discretion, if exercised by the individuals being monitored by the accounting system, reduces the system's value as a control device. The managers responsible for the day-to-day operations that generate the overhead usually have more information regarding what causes actual overhead to exceed budget than their superiors. These managers can often argue more persuasively than their superiors about the causes of the excess overhead and whether it should be classified as a fixed or variable cost. Determining the fixed and variable portions of overhead is often arbitrary and creates incentives for the people being monitored to manipulate the classification. While the incentive to overproduce is lessened under variable costing as compared with absorption costing, the tendency to build inventories must still be monitored.

2. Ignores Opportunity Cost of Capacity

Another problem with variable costing is that it produces misleading unit cost figures. The opportunity cost of manufacturing a given product includes the direct costs and the forgone opportunities of using the plant and equipment in other ways. Inside the firm, market prices do not exist to guide the allocation of scarce resources. Management must devise alternative accounting and administrative systems to allocate scarce resources. (See Chapter 4.) Unit cost data are a substitute inside the firm for the lack of market prices. If variable costing is used, unit cost figures do not contain any amount for the opportunity cost of the production capacity. Full absorption costs, while not an exact measure of opportunity costs, can be a better measure than variable costs especially when the firm is capacity-constrained. If fixed costs are ignored, managers have incentives to overconsume the fixed resources.

On the other hand, if the firm has excess capacity, including fixed charges in unit costs overstates opportunity cost and discourages use of the excess capacity. On average, to the extent that the economy is growing and surviving firms in general are growing, firms face capacity constraints. Then, average firms will want to include fixed costs in product costs to proxy for the opportunity cost of capacity. Is variable costing better than absorption costing? Economic Darwinism (the marmot-and-bear parable) suggests that commonly used procedures such as absorption costing probably yield benefits in excess of their costs. Since variable costing is not widely used, its benefits are probably less than its costs. Also, variable costing is rarely used for external reporting. Generally accepted accounting principles, financial accounting standards, and the U.S. Internal Revenue Service require the allocation of fixed costs to products. If variable costing is used for internal reports and absorption costing is used for external reports, internal and external reporting systems will produce different numbers. As discussed in Chapter 1, reconciling the different numbers is time-consuming and diverts senior managers' attention from more important issues.[3]

Concept Questions		
	Q10–4	What is the major difference between absorption costing and variable costing?
	Q10–5	Give two claimed advantages of variable costing. Give two potential problems with variable costing.

D. Beware of Unit Costs

All cost systems, whether absorption or variable systems, produce unit cost figures. Such product costs are used for both decision making (pricing, outsourcing, product mix) and decision control (transfer pricing, performance evaluation). This section presents an example of how unit-based costs can be wrong for some decisions.

A glass bottle producer makes only two types of bottles: gallon wine jugs and quart juice bottles. Only one input, natural gas, is used to make both bottles. Labor, capital, and silica are all free. Natural gas is purchased for an annual fixed fee of $100,000 plus $0.20 per cubic yard up to 500,000 yards and then $0.30 per cubic yard thereafter. The following summarizes how much natural gas is needed to produce the two bottles:

	Natural Gas
100 gallon jugs	9 cubic yards
100 quart bottles	3 cubic yards

Current production consists of 3 million gallon jugs and 7 million quart bottles.

Table 10–7 summarizes production, gas used, and the variable and fixed costs. To arrive at a full absorption cost per bottle, the fixed gas cost is allocated based on gas used. Gallon jugs use 270,000 ÷ 480,000 or 56.25 percent of the gas, and quart bottles use the remaining 43.75 percent. Allocating the fixed cost of gas in these

---

[3] A prevalent argument holds that managers who prefer variable costing use absorption costing for external reporting only because generally accepted accounting principles (GAAP) require full costing of inventories. An alternative, more controversial position argues that GAAP does not require full costing. Managers have significant discretion in valuing inventories for financial reporting. (See Accounting Research Bulletin No. 43, "Restatement and Revision of Accounting Research Bulletins," in Financial Accounting Standards Board, *Original Pronouncements* [Burr Ridge, IL: Irwin, 1992], Chapter 4, paragraph 5.) Moreover, if an overwhelming majority of firms wanted to use variable costing for GAAP, they could influence the standard-setting process to allow such a change. In many ways, GAAP reflects what most managers consider preferred accounting practices.

TABLE 10–7   **Bottle Production and Gas Utilization**

	Gallon Jugs	Quart Bottles	Total
Current production (in bottles)	3,000,000	7,000,000	
Current production (in 100 units)	30,000	70,000	
Gas per 100 units	9	3	
Gas used (cubic yards)	270,000	210,000	480,000
Gas cost:			
Fixed cost			$100,000
Variable cost (@ $0.20/cubic yard)	$54,000	$42,000	$ 96,000

TABLE 10–8   **Full Cost and Variable Cost per Bottle**

	Gallon Jugs	Quart Bottles
Variable cost	$ 54,000	$ 42,000
Allocated fixed cost	56,250	43,750
Total cost	$ 110,250	$ 85,750
÷ Bottles produced	3,000,000	7,000,000
Full cost/bottle	$ 0.03675	$ 0.01225
Variable cost/bottle	$ 0.01800	$ 0.00600

proportions yields $56,250 assigned to gallon jugs and $43,750 assigned to quart bottles. Table 10–8 summarizes the full cost and variable cost of the two bottles.

The full cost per bottle is about twice the variable cost. Both the full and variable cost figures lead to inappropriate conclusions for some decisions. For example, suppose a customer asks to purchase 1 million additional gallon jugs at $0.022. The variable cost of $0.018 is less than the price. It appears we should accept the offer. However, since we are currently using 480,000 cubic yards of gas, the additional production pushes gas purchases above the 500,000-cubic-yard limit and we have to purchase additional gas at $0.30 per cubic yard instead of $0.20 per cubic yard.

The additional gallon jugs require 90,000 cubic yards of gas (1,000,000 jugs ÷ 100 bottle lots × 9 cubic yards per 100-bottle lot). The cost of this gas is

Cost of first 20,000 cubic yards @ $0.20	$ 4,000
Cost of last 70,000 cubic yards @ $0.30	21,000
Incremental cost	$25,000
Number of gallon jugs	÷ 1,000,000
Incremental cost per jug	$0.0250

Notice that neither the variable cost nor the full cost figures accurately estimate the opportunity cost of the additional 1 million gallon jugs. The reason is that neither the full cost nor the variable cost estimates include the higher gas cost per cubic yard when more than 500,000 cubic yards are required. Both full and variable costing rely on historical costs. If the firm expands or contracts into areas of its cost curve where it has not been before, there is no historical information regarding the level of costs in these unexplored regions.

By now, you should have acquired a healthy skepticism of accounting costs, particularly *unit* costs. One writer summarized absorption costing 50 years ago as follows:

> (Accounting) product costs are never actual costs, but leveled, smoothed, or "normal" costs. It should be clear, then, that product costs are the result of specific tracing of some cost items (direct costs) plus the assignment of indirect (variable and fixed) costs by the use of average-expected or "normal" indirect cost rates. The unit costs thus computed are technically compiled average costs; they are "normal" costs—never actual costs.[4]

Not only are unit costs not actual costs, they are not marginal costs. Although stated in terms of dollars per unit, unit costs do not tell us the cost of producing one more unit.

E. Summary

This chapter discusses one of the criticisms of traditional absorption costing systems: Absorption cost systems create incentives to overproduce. By producing more units than the firm can sell, some of the fixed costs are absorbed to units in inventory. These fixed costs in inventory are not in the cost of products sold. As long as variable costs per unit do not rise faster than average fixed costs fall as more units are produced, then the average full unit cost falls and the profits on these units rise. This creates the incentive to overproduce.

A firm can reduce (but not eliminate) the incentive to overproduce by adopting variable (direct) costing systems. Variable costing writes off all fixed manufacturing costs as a period cost. As a result, profits cannot be increased by overproducing and thereby spreading these fixed costs over more units.

While variable costing systems reduce the incentives to overproduce, these systems are not generally observed in practice, which suggests that their total costs exceed their total benefits. There are alternative mechanisms for controlling managers' incentives to overproduce, such as flat prohibitions on increasing inventory levels, charging managers for inventory holding costs, and just-in-time production scheduling. Moreover, writing off all fixed costs gives managers an additional degree of discretion over their performance evaluation system. They often have discretion over classifying expenditures as fixed or variable. Also, if fixed costs are written off, product costs are distorted to the extent that they do not reflect the opportunity cost of the plant's capacity.

Self-Study Problems

Self-Study Problem 1:   Dial Cards

A plant with $1 million of fixed overhead costs makes decks of playing cards with a variable cost per deck of $1.00. The plant only makes playing cards and allocates all the fixed costs to the product by the number of decks produced. The firm can

---

[4] W Vatter, *Managerial Accounting* (New York: Prentice Hall, 1950), p. 402.

sell 200,000 decks a year for $10.00 each. There is no beginning inventory. The plant manager has the opportunity to make 200,000 decks, 220,000 decks, or 240,000 decks. Handling excess inventory costs $0.10/deck. Handling costs are expensed in the year they are incurred. Which production level causes the highest reported income for the year?

Solution:

	Production Levels		
	200,000	*220,000*	*240,000*
Fixed costs	$1,000,000	$1,000,000	$1,000,000
Variable costs ($1/unit)	200,000	220,000	240,000
Total costs	$1,200,000	$1,220,000	$1,240,000
Average cost per deck	$6/deck	$5.55/deck	$5.17/deck
Revenues (200,000 decks)($10/deck)	$2,000,000	$2,000,000	$2,000,000
Cost of goods sold			
(200,000 decks)($6/deck)	(1,200,000)		
(220,000 decks)($5.55/deck)		(1,109,091)	
(240,000 decks)($5.17/deck)			(1,033,333)
Excess inventory handling costs	0		
(220,000 − 200,000)($.10/deck)		(2,000)	
(240,000 − 200,000)($.10/deck)			(4,000)
Net income	$ 800,000	$ 888,909	$ 962,667

Self-Study Problem 2: Kiddo Inc. (A)

Kiddo Incorporated manufactures running shoes. Recently, it added a new line of pump sneakers. Over the past two years, sales of both the Runner and the Pump have been flat at 5,000,000 and 2,400,000 pairs, respectively. However, in anticipation of increased sales, production was increased from 5,140,000 to 5,200,000 for the Runner and from 3,000,000 to 3,564,000 for the Pump from year 1 to year 2.

The production costs for the two sneakers are very different. Materials cost $14.00 per Runner and $17.75 per Pump. Labor costs are $4.60 and $5.00 and variable overhead costs are $6.60 and $7.30 for the Runner and the Pump, respectively. Fixed overhead costs are $50 million and are allocated based on direct labor cost. Kiddo uses LIFO to value inventory. Round ratios to two decimal digits.

Required:

   a. Based on revenues of $32 per Runner and $46 per Pump, prepare an income statement for each year.

   b. Explain the change in net profit from year 1 to year 2. Be sure to explain any differences between the Runner and the Pump.

Solution:

   a. Income statements for years 1 and 2:

	Runner	Pump	Total
Year 1			
Revenue	$160,000,000	$110,400,000	$270,400,000
Expenses:			
Material	70,000,000	42,600,000	112,600,000
Labor	23,000,000	12,000,000	35,000,000
Variable overhead	33,000,000	17,520,000	50,520,000
Fixed overhead*	29,650,000	15,480,000	45,130,000
Net income	$ 4,350,000	$ 22,800,000	$ 27,150,000
Year 2			
Revenue	$160,000,000	$110,400,000	$270,400,000
Expenses:			
Material	70,000,000	42,600,000	112,600,000
Labor	23,000,000	12,000,000	35,000,000
Variable overhead	33,000,000	17,520,000	50,520,000
Fixed overhead†	27,550,000	14,376,000	41,926,000
Net income	$ 6,450,000	$ 23,904,000	$ 30,354,000

*Year 1

	Runner	Pump	Total
Direct labor per pair	$ 4.60	$ 5.00	
× Units produced	5,140,000	3,000,000	
Direct labor cost	$23,644,000	$15,000,000	$38,644,000
Fixed overhead rate per direct labor dollar			
($50,000,000/$38,644,000)			$1.29
Direct labor per pair	$ 4.60	$ 5.00	
× Fixed overhead rate	1.29	1.29	
Fixed overhead per pair	$ 5.93	$ 6.45	
× Number of pairs sold	5,000,000	2,400,000	
Allocated fixed overhead	$29,650,000	$15,480,000	$45,130,000

†Year 2

	Runner	Pump	Total
Direct labor per pair	$ 4.60	$ 5.00	
× Units produced	5,200,000	3,564,000	
Direct labor cost	$23,920,000	$17,820,000	$41,740,000
Fixed overhead rate per direct labor dollar			
($50,000,000/$41,740,000)			$1.20
Direct labor per pair	$ 4.60	$ 5.00	
× Fixed overhead rate	1.20	1.20	
Fixed overhead per pair	$ 5.51	$ 5.99	
× Number of pairs sold	5,000,000	2,400,000	
Allocated fixed overhead	$27,550,000	$14,376,000	$41,926,000

b. Net income increased from year 1 to year 2 even though sales were constant. This change results from increased production. The fixed costs are allocated based on direct labor cost. Increasing production decreases the fixed cost per pair of sneakers, thereby increasing profits per pair sold. In year 1, 90.26 percent of the $50 million of fixed overhead was included in profits. This fell to 83.85 percent, causing year 2 profits to increase.

Problems

P 10–1:   Federal Mixing

Federal Mixing (FM) is a division of Federal Chemicals, a large diversified chemical company. FM provides mixing services for both outside customers and other Federal divisions. FM buys or receives liquid chemicals and combines and packages them according to the customer's specifications. FM computes its divisional net income on both a fully absorbed and variable costing basis. For the year just ending, it reported

	Net Income
Absorption costing	$13,800,000
Variable costing	12,600,000
Difference	$ 1,200,000

Overhead is assigned to products using machine hours.

There is no finished goods inventory at FM, only work-in-process (WIP) inventory. As soon as a product is completed, it is shipped to the customer. The beginning inventory was valued at $6.3 million and contained 70,000 machine hours. The ending WIP inventory was valued at $9.9 million and contained 90,000 machine hours.

Required:

Write a short, nontechnical note to senior management explaining why variable costing and absorption costing net income amounts differ.

P 10–2:   Xerox

An October 25, 1999, article in *Business Week* by D. Brady, "Why Xerox Is Struggling," reported:

> President and Chief Executive G. Richard Thoman is a big-picture guy. For the past two years, he has preached a digital revolution at the copier giant. Get down to the detail, though, and it's clear that the revolution isn't going as planned: In both copiers and printers, Xerox is losing ground. On October 18, the company announced lower than expected earnings and the stock price tumbled more than 13% on that day. Xerox stock is down 60% from its recent high of $60 in July. Xerox blamed the bad news on short-term surprises: sagging productivity in the sales force after a big reorganization as well as weakness in Brazil. But the sheer scope of bad news shocked even Thoman, who told investors in a conference call that he was "disappointed and sad about this quarter."
>
> Thoman took the top job in April and vowed annual earnings growth in the "mid-to-high teens."

Beginning November 1, 1999, Xerox factories increased their hours from five eight-hour days a week to six ten-hour days a week through the end of the year.

The factory managers were told to build inventories in expectation of higher sales in the fourth quarter of 1999. Fourth-quarter sales were expected to be higher because of anticipation that the new sales force reorganization would increase sales.

Required:

Offer an alternative reason(s) for Xerox's decision to increase output in its factories.

P 10–3: Matson Metal Works

Matson manufactures a metal dog cage that has variable cost of $50 per cage. Budgeted and actual fixed manufacturing overhead are $900,000. Cages sell for $60 per cage.

Required:

Calculate variable cost net income and absorption cost net income under each of the following independent cases:

- *a.* Sales and production are 100,000 cages.
- *b.* Sales are 90,000 cages and production is 100,000 cages.
- *c.* Sales are 100,000 cages and production is 90,000 cages. The beginning inventory consists of 20,000 units manufactured last year. Last year 100,000 units were manufactured, 80,000 were sold, variable costs were $50 per cage, and fixed manufacturing overhead costs were $900,000. For inventory valuation purposes, all of this year's production is sold and 10,000 units in the beginning inventory are sold. LIFO is used to value inventories.

P 10–4: Goldratt

Eli Goldratt advocates that all manufacturing costs other than materials be treated as operating expenses for the period. Periodic profits would be calculated as

Sales	xxx
Less cost of material	xxx
Less all nonmaterial operating expenses	xxx
Net income	xxx

Operating data for last year are

Units produced	12,000
Unit sales	10,000
Material cost/unit produced	$0.45 per unit
Labor cost/unit produced	0.35
Overhead/unit produced	0.38

There is no beginning inventory.

Required:

    a. Compare profits under absorption costing and Goldratt's method.

    b. Evaluate Goldratt's proposal.

P 10–5:   Varilux

Varilux manufactures a single product and sells it for $10 per unit. At the beginning of the year, there were 1,000 units in inventory. Upon further investigation, you discover that units produced last year had $3 of fixed manufacturing costs and $2 of variable manufacturing costs. During the year, Varilux produced 10,000 units of product. Each unit produced generated $3 of variable manufacturing cost. Total fixed manufacturing cost for the current year was $40,000. Selling and administrative costs consisted of $12,000 of variable costs and $18,000 of fixed costs. There were no inventories at the end of the year.

Required:

Prepare two income statements for the current year: one on a variable cost basis and the other on an absorption cost basis. Explain any difference between the two net income numbers and provide calculations supporting your explanation of the difference.

P 10–6:   Truini Paints

Using the data from Table 10–6, recast the analysis with one change of assumption: Instead of assuming that an additional $17,000 of overhead was incurred in both years, assume that overhead was lower each year by $10,000. How do incentives change regarding the treatment of the $10,000 savings?

P 10–7:   Zipp Cards

Zipp Cards buys baseball cards in bulk from the companies that produce them. Zipp buys sheets of 48 cards, then cuts the sheets into individual cards, and sorts and packages them, usually by team. Zipp then sells the packages to large discount stores. The accompanying table provides information regarding operations for 2010 and 2011.

Zipp Cards—Summary of Operations

	2010	2011
Unit sales (of 48 cards)*	50,000	48,000
Price	$5.00	$4.90
Production in units		
(budgeted = actual)	50,000	75,000
Variable cost	$1.00	$1.00
Fixed manufacturing overhead	$160,000	$160,000

*One unit equals 48 cards.

Volume is measured in terms of 48-card sheets processed. Budgeted and actual production in 2010 were both 50,000 units. There were no beginning inventories on January 1, 2010. In 2011, budgeted and actual production rose to 75,000 units.

At the beginning of 2012, the president of Zipp was pleasantly surprised when the accountant showed her the income statement for the year 2011. The president remarked, "I'm surprised we made more money in 2011 than 2010. We had to cut prices and we didn't sell as many units, yet we still made more money. Well, you're the accountant and these numbers don't lie."

Required:

    a. Prepare income statements for 2010 and 2011 using absorption costing.

    b. Prepare a statement reconciling the change in net income from 2010 to 2011. Explain to the president why the firm made more money in 2011 than in 2010.

P 10–8: TransPacific Bank

You are working as a loan officer at TransPacific Bank and are analyzing a loan request for a client when you come across the following footnote in the client's annual report:

> Inventories are priced at the lower of cost or market of materials plus other direct (variable) costs. Fixed overheads of $4.2 million this year and $3.0 million last year are excluded from inventories. Omitting such overhead resulted in a reduction in net income (after taxes) of $720,000 for this year. Our tax rate is 40 percent.

In preparing to present the loan application to the bank's loan committee, write a brief paragraph in nontechnical terms describing what this footnote means and how it affects the bank's evaluation of the financial condition of the borrower.

P 10–9: Valezquez Designs

Valezquez Designs, a wholly owned subsidiary of Tura Products, manufactures wallpaper. Managers are paid quarterly bonuses based on net income. Management at Valezquez expects sales next quarter to be 10,000 rolls of wallpaper at $8 per roll. Valezquez has limited inventory of wallpaper and wants to increase its inventory. Valezquez uses a traditional absorption costing system where product costs are based on both fixed and variable manufacturing costs. The table below shows how costs are expected to behave at various production levels.

	Alternative Production Levels				
Production (rolls of wallpaper)	10,000	11,000	12,000	13,000	14,000
Fixed manufacturing cost	$40,000	$40,000	$40,000	$40,000	$40,000
Variable manufacturing cost	$30,000	$35,900	$41,600	$48,270	$55,900

Required:

Based on the above data, what level of production do you expect management to choose?

P 10–10: Filters Plus

Filters Plus manufactures paper filters for swimming pools. It uses an absorption costing system and writes off over/underabsorbed overhead to cost of goods sold.

Overhead is applied to products based on direct labor hours. For 2010, overhead was applied at the rate of $6.30 per direct labor hour (DLH). Total variable overhead is budgeted at $72,600 and 22,000 hours were expected. The accompanying table presents the income statement for 2010.

FILTERS PLUS
Income Statement (Absorption Costing)
Year Ending 12/31/10

Sales		$824,500
Cost of goods sold		571,400
Contribution margin		$253,100
Selling and administrative costs		
Variable	$172,900	
Fixed	67,600	240,500
Net income		$ 12,600

Filters Plus had no beginning inventories of filters in 2010. The ending inventory as of 12/31/10 consists of 1,400 filters, each of which required 2 DLHs to manufacture.

Required:
What would Filter Plus's net income be under variable costing? (Show calculations and explain the logic of your methodology.)

P 10–11:   Alliance Tooling

Alliance Tooling produces a single product in its plant. At the beginning of the year, there were no units in inventory. During the year, Alliance produced 120,000 units and sold 100,000 units at $26.75 per unit. Variable manufacturing costs are $13.50 per unit. Alliance pays $2.70 per unit for sales commissions and shipping. It has fixed costs of $720,000 for selling and administration. Its tax rate is 40 percent.

Required:
a. Prepare an income statement for Alliance Tooling using absorption costing.
b. Prepare an income statement for Alliance Tooling using variable costing.
c. Explain why the net income figures computed in (a) and (b) differ.

P 10–12:   Aspen View

Aspen View produces a full line of sunglasses. This year it began producing a new model of sunglasses, the Peak 32. It produced 5,300 pairs and sold 4,900 pairs. The following table summarizes the fixed and variable costs of producing Peak 32 sunglasses. Aspen View uses variable costing to value its ending inventory.

	Fixed Cost	Variable Cost	Total Cost
Direct labor		$ 3.50	$ 3.50
Direct material		7.50	7.50
Manufacturing overhead	$3.20	4.50	7.70
Advertising	1.20	1.70	2.90
Distribution	.70	.25	.95
Selling	1.20	.90	2.10
Total cost	$6.30	$18.35	$24.65

Required:

a. What is Aspen View's ending inventory value of Peak 32 sunglasses?

b. Aspen View is considering switching from variable costing to absorption costing. Would this year's net income from Peak 32 sunglasses be higher or lower using absorption costing? Explain why.

c. Suppose Aspen View uses absorption costing. If, instead of producing 5,300 pairs of Peak 32s it produced only 5,000, would net income from Peak 32 sunglasses be higher or lower from the smaller production compared to the larger production? Explain why.

d. Aspen View has an opportunity cost of capital of 20 percent. What is the cost of producing 5,300 pairs of Peak 32s instead of 4,900 pairs?

P 10–13:   CLIC Lighters

CLIC manufactures two types of cigarette lighters: Basic and Super. A new plant began producing both lighter models this year. The following variable costing statement summarizes the first year of operations:

CLIC LIGHTERS
Income Statement—Manufacturing
For the Year Ended December 31

	Basic	Super	Total
	Products		
Number of units produced	200,000	160,000	
Number of units sold	180,000	110,000	
Selling price	$ 0.50	$ 0.70	
Sales revenue	$90,000	$77,000	$167,000
Cost of goods sold	18,000	22,000	40,000
Manufacturing margin	$72,000	$55,000	$127,000
Fixed overhead			103,000
Income from manufacturing			$ 24,000

For internal control purposes, variable costing is used. Management also wants income from manufacturing calculated using absorption costing. Fixed overhead is allocated to the two lighters using actual machine minutes. Each Basic lighter requires 1.1 machine minutes and each Super lighter requires 1.2 machine minutes.

Required:

a. Calculate the fixed overhead rate per machine minute.

b. Calculate the plant's income from manufacturing for both Basic and Super lighters and for the entire plant using absorption costing.

c. Prepare a table that reconciles the difference in income from manufacturing reported using variable costing and absorption costing.

d. Explain in one or two sentences why income from manufacturing differs depending on whether variable costing or absorption costing is used.

P 10–14: Medford Mug Company

The Medford Mug Company is an old-line maker of ceramic coffee mugs. It imprints company logos and other sayings on mugs for both commercial and wholesale markets. The firm has the capacity to produce 50 million mugs per year, but the recession has cut production and sales in the current year to 15 million mugs. The accompanying table shows the operating statement for 2010.

MEDFORD MUG COMPANY
Income Statement
Year Ending 2010 ($ in Millions)

Sales (15 million @ $2)		$ 30.0
Less costs of goods sold		
Variable cost (15 million @ $0.50)	(7.5)	
Fixed cost	(20.0)	(27.5)
Gross margin		$ 2.5
Less selling and administration		(4.0)
Operating profit		$ (1.5)

At the end of 2010, there was no ending inventory of finished goods.

The board of directors is very concerned about the $1.5 million operating loss. It hires an outside consultant who reports back that the firm suffers from two problems. First, the president of the company receives a fixed salary, and since she owns no stock, she has very little incentive to worry about company profits. The second problem is that the company has not aggressively marketed its product and has not kept up with changing markets. The current president is 64 and the board of directors makes her an offer to retire one year early so that they can hire a new president to turn the firm around. The current president accepts the offer to retire and the board immediately hires a new president with a proven track record as a turnaround specialist.

The new president is hired with an employment contract that pays a fixed wage of $50,000 a year plus 15 percent of the firm's operating profits (if any). Operating profits are calculated using absorption costing. In 2011, the new president doubles the selling and administration budget to $8 million (which includes the president's salary of $50,000). He designs a new line of "politically correct" sayings to imprint on the mugs and expands inventory and the number of distributors handling the mugs. Production is increased to 45 million mugs and sales climb to 18 million mugs at $2 each. Variable costs per mug remain at $.50 and fixed costs at $20 million in 2011.

At the end of 2011, the president meets with the board of directors and announces he has accepted another job. He believes he has successfully gotten Medford Mug back on track and thanks the board for giving him the opportunity. His new job is helping to turn around another struggling company.

Required:

a. Calculate the president's bonus for 2011.

b. Evaluate the performance of the new president in 2011. Did he do as good a job as the numbers in (a) suggest?

P 10–15:   Kothari Inc.

The telecom division of Kothari Inc. produces and sells 100,000 line modulators. Half of the modulators are sold externally at $150 per unit, and the other half are sold internally at variable manufacturing costs plus 10 percent. Kothari uses variable costing to evaluate the telecom division. The following summarizes the cost structure of the telecom division.

	Variable Manufacturing Costs
Materials	$27.00
Labor	12.00
Overhead	4.00
Total manufacturing cost	$43.00
Fixed manufacturing overhead	$1,700,000
Variable period costs (per units)	$18.00
Fixed period costs	$1,900,000

Required:

a. Calculate the net income of the telecom division (before taxes) using variable costing.

b. Telecom can outsource the final assembly of all 100,000 modulators for $9.00 per modulator. If it does this, it can reduce variable manufacturing cost by $1.00 per unit and fixed manufacturing overhead by $700,000. If the managers of the telecom unit are compensated based on telecom's net income before taxes, do you expect them to outsource the final assembly of the modulators? Show calculations.

c. What happens to the net cash flows of Kothari Inc. if the final assembly of the modulators is outsourced?

P 10–16:   Mystic Mugs

Sanjog and Rajiv Gupta have started a business that manufactures and sells thermal mugs. Users personalize the mugs by plugging them into a laptop and downloading their favorite images from a digital camera. The company makes two mug sizes: 16 and 24 ounce mugs. This is its first year of business. The following data summarize operations for the first year.

	16 oz. mug	24 oz. mug	Total
Selling price	$9.75	$11.20	
Direct materials/unit	$1.10	$1.45	
Direct labor/unit	$0.60	$0.80	
Variable overhead/unit	$0.30	$0.40	
Variable selling and distribution/unit	$1.65	$1.75	
Units sold	22,500	16,400	
Units produced	24,000	16,400	
Fixed manufacturing overhead			$85,000
Fixed selling and distribution			$148,000

There were no beginning inventories. Overhead is assigned to products using direct labor dollars.

Required:

a. Calculate Mystic Mugs's net income before taxes using absorption costing.

b. Calculate Mystic Mugs's net income before taxes using variable costing.

c. Prepare a table that reconciles any difference between the two net income figures calculated in parts (*a*) and (*b*).

d. Write a short memo explaining in lay terms any difference between the two net income figures calculated in parts (*a*) and (*b*).

P 10–17:   Avant Designs

Avant Designs designs and manufactures polished-nickel fashion bracelets. It offers two bracelets: Aztec and Mayan. The following data summarize budgeted operations for the current year:

AVANT DESIGNS
Summary of Budgeted Operations
Current Year

	Aztec	Mayan
Sales price/unit	$12	$15
Variable cost/unit	$4	$5
Units sold	30,000	20,000
Machine minutes/unit	2	3
Beginning inventory	0	0
Ending inventory	3,000	1,000

Budgeted fixed manufacturing overhead for the year was $258,000.

Required:

  a. Prepare the budgeted income statement for the year using variable costing.
  b. Prepare the budgeted income statement for the year using absorption costing. Budgeted fixed manufacturing overhead is allocated to the two bracelets using machine minutes.
  c. Explain the difference in the two net income figures computed in parts (*a*) and (*b*). That is, reconcile any difference in earnings and explain why it occurs.

P 10–18:   MAPICS Co.

MAPICS Co. uses full absorption costing and has the following cost structure:

Variable costs per unit	$0.30
Fixed manufacturing costs	$2.0 million
Normal production	1.0 million units
Selling price	$2.50/unit

In the first year of production, MAPICS produced 1.4 million units and sold 1.0 million units. In the second year, MAPICS sold 1.0 million units but produced 0.8 million units. Fixed manufacturing costs are allocated to products using normal volume. There was no beginning inventory in year 1, and FIFO is used to value inventories. Any unabsorbed or overabsorbed overhead is written off to cost of goods sold.

Required:

  a. Analyze the change in profitability between years 1 and 2.
  b. What would profits have been if 0.6 million units were produced in the second year?

P 10–19:   Smidt & Sons

Smidt & Sons produces a single product and has the following operating data:

	2010	2011	2012
Units produced	22,000	16,000	15,000
Units sold	20,000	15,000	18,000
Fixed manufacturing overhead	$800,000	$880,000	$950,000
Variable manufacturing cost	$3.00	$3.10	$3.20
Variable selling costs	$0.25	$0.30	$0.35
Selling price	$45.00	$50.00	$53.00

The firm uses FIFO inventory costing and there was no beginning inventory in 2010.

Required:

a. Calculate net income using absorption costing.

b. Calculate net income using variable costing.

c. Reconcile the annual differences between the two costing methods.

P 10–20: Easton Plant

The Easton plant produces sheet metal chassis for television sets. Its customer is General Electric Appliances. The chassis are manufactured on a computerized, numerically controlled (NC) machine that cuts, drills, and bends the metal to form the chassis for the television set. Two different chassis are produced: HX–3 and DX–55.

Easton has a single plantwide overhead account. Actual machine minutes on the NC machine are used to distribute overhead to the two products. There were no beginning inventories of work in process or finished goods. The following table summarizes the planned and actual production data for the year:

	HX–3	DX–55
Planned unit production	6,500	3,400
Budgeted machine minutes per unit	× 6.2	× 9.8
Expected machine minutes	40,300	33,320
Actual units produced	7,200	3,900
Actual volume (machine minutes)	44,640	38,220

The following data summarize the flexible overhead budget:

	Fixed	Variable (per Minute)
Depreciation	$695,000	
Indirect labor		$0.80
Indirect materials		1.00
Property taxes	28,000	
Utilities	55,000	0.90
Other	42,000	0.30
Total	$820,000	$3.00

At the end of the year, the following overhead amounts had been incurred:

	Actual
Depreciation	$ 695,000
Indirect labor	71,288
Indirect materials	84,860
Property taxes	31,000
Utilities	133,074
Other	68,858
Total	$1,084,080

Any over- or underabsorbed overhead is written off to cost of goods sold. The ending finished goods inventory consists of 2,000 units of HX–3 and 1,000 units of DX–55, representing 13,400 minutes and 10,300 minutes of actual machine time, respectively.

Required: (Round all dollars, including overhead rates, to two decimal places.)

    a. Calculate the overhead absorption rate set at the start of the year.

    b. Calculate the over- or underabsorbed overhead for the year.

    c. The firm is considering switching to variable costing. What effect would this decision have on Easton's reported profit for this year? To implement variable costing at the end of the year, variable overhead is calculated as $3.00 per machine minute times the actual number of machine minutes. Fixed overhead is the difference between total actual overhead and variable overhead.

    d. Instead of defining fixed overhead as all overhead in excess of variable overhead as in part (*c*), assume the following: Fixed overhead is budgeted fixed overhead ($820,000), and variable overhead is the difference between total actual overhead and budgeted fixed overhead. What is the difference between absorption net income and variable costing income given these new assumptions?

P 10–21:   Weststar Appliances

Weststar manufactures and distributes a complete line of home appliances worldwide. Lynn Tweedie is the U.S. Space Saver Dishwasher product manager for Weststar Appliances. Her responsibilities include pricing, planning, and sales of Weststar's Space Saver dishwasher in the United States. It is the end of the third quarter and Tweedie is deciding how many Space Saver washers to produce in the fourth quarter. Given sales from the first three quarters and orders for the last quarter, she expects total sales for the year to be 73,000 washers at $200 per unit. There are 12,000 washers in inventory at a (LIFO) cost of $90 per washer. The factory produced 58,000 washers in the first three quarters of this year and Tweedie is considering ordering an additional 10,000, 15,000, or 20,000 washers in the fourth quarter. The plant's capacity can easily accommodate any of these volume levels without affecting fixed costs or variable cost per unit. The variable manufacturing cost of the washer is $75 and the plant has fixed annual costs of

$1.3 million. Manufacturing overhead is allocated to dishwashers based on units. Tweedie's selling and administrative expenses consist of $15 of variable cost per washer and fixed cost of $2.92 million. The dishwasher division has a 17 percent weighted-average cost of capital and invested capital (not including inventories) of $18 million. Weststar uses full absorption costing.

Required:

    a. Prepare a table showing annual accounting earnings prepared under absorption costing for the Space Saver dishwasher for annual production levels of 68,000, 73,000, and 78,000 washers.

    b. If Lynn Tweedie's bonus depends on reported accounting earnings from Space Saver dishwashers, what production quantity is she likely to select for the fourth quarter?

    c. Prepare a table computing the valuation of the ending inventory (under LIFO) for annual production levels of 68,000, 73,000, and 78,000 washers.

    d. If Lynn Tweedie's bonus depends on residual income from Space Saver dishwashers, what production quantity is she likely to select for the fourth quarter?

    e. How would your answer change in part (*d*) if Tweedie's bonus was based on return on assets?

P 10–22: Blauvelt Products

Blauvelt Products uses a flexible budget to set the overhead rate at the beginning of the year based on units produced. In year 1 budgeted fixed overhead is $1 million and budgeted variable overhead is $2 per unit. Direct material and direct labor together are $5 per unit. Blauvelt sells the completed product for $30. There is no beginning inventory. Budgeted volume is 80,000 units. Production and sales are 80,000 units. Actual overhead incurred in year 1 is $1,160,000. Any under- or overabsorbed overhead is written off to cost of goods sold.

    In year 2, budgeted volume and production are again both 80,000 units. However, only 60,000 units are sold. Budgeted fixed overhead is $1 million and budgeted variable overhead is $2 per unit. Direct material and direct labor are $5 per unit. Final selling price remains at $30 per unit. Actual overhead incurred in year 2 is $1.35 million.

Required:

    a. Calculate net income in year 1 first using absorption costing and then using variable costing. Explain any difference between the two net income numbers.

    b. Calculate net income in year 2 using absorption costing, where the overhead rate used to assign overhead to products is based on actual overhead incurred.

    c. Calculate net income in year 2 using variable costing, where any difference between budgeted overhead and actual overhead is treated as a fixed cost.

    d. Calculate net income in year 2 using variable costing, where any difference between budgeted overhead and actual overhead is treated as a variable cost.

    e. Explain why your answers in parts (*b*), (*c*), and (*d*) differ.

P 10–23:   Sants Brakes Co.

The current year's income statement for Sants Brakes Co. on a variable costing basis appears in the accompanying table.

SANTS BRAKES COMPANY
Income Statement—Manufacturing
For the Year Ended December 31 ($000s)

| | Product Lines | | | |
	G-226	G-348	G-714	Total
Number of units sold (in thousands)	650	280	120	—
Sales revenue	$7,800	$2,240	$1,920	$11,960
Cost of goods sold	5,200	840	480	6,520
Manufacturing margin	$2,600	$1,400	$1,440	$ 5,440
Fixed overhead				3,600
Income from manufacturing				$ 1,840

Inventories of finished stock were increased during the year in anticipation of increases in sales volume in the current year. Inventories in units of product for the beginning and end of the year follow.

	Beginning Inventory	Ending Inventory
G-226	20,000	90,000
G-348	50,000	90,000
G-714	20,000	50,000

The budgeted operating level for assigning fixed overhead to production is 1.8 million machine hours. One-half hour is required to produce a unit of G-226, two hours are required for a unit of G-348, and four hours are required for a unit of G-714.

Required:

a. Recast the income statement on an absorption costing basis.
b. Explain why the income from manufacturing on the absorption costing statement differs from the income on the variable costing statement. Show your computations.

P 10–24:   BBG Corporation

BBG Corporation is a manufacturer of a synthetic chemical. Gary Voss, president of the company, has been eager to get the operating results for the just-completed fiscal year. He was surprised when the income statement revealed that income before taxes had dropped to $885,000 from $900,000, even though sales volume had increased by 100,000 kilograms. The drop in net income occurred even though Voss had implemented two changes during the past 12 months to improve the company's profitability:

1. In response to a 10 percent increase in production costs, the sales price of the company's product was increased by 12 percent. This action took place on December 1, the first day of the current fiscal year.
2. The managers of the selling and administrative departments were given strict instructions to spend no more in the current fiscal year than last year.

BBG's accounting department prepared and distributed to top management these comparative income statements.

BBG CORPORATION
Statements of Operating Income
For the Years Ended November 30

	Last Year	Current Year
Sales revenue	$9,000	$11,200
Cost of goods sold	$7,200	$ 8,320
Under/overabsorbed overhead	(600)	495
Adjusted cost of goods sold	$6,600	$ 8,815
Gross margin	$2,400	$ 2,385
Selling and administrative expenses	1,500	1,500
Income before taxes	$ 900	$ 885

The accounting staff also prepared related financial information to assist management in evaluating the company's performance. BBG uses the FIFO inventory method for finished goods. Budgeted and fixed overhead are equal and the beginning inventory last year has $3.00/kg. of fixed overhead.

BBG CORPORATION
Selected Operating and Financial Data

	Last Year	Current Year
Sales price	$10.00/kg.	$11.20/kg.
Material cost	1.50/kg.	1.65/kg.
Direct labor cost	2.50/kg.	2.75/kg.
Variable overhead cost	1.00/kg.	1.10/kg.
Fixed overhead cost	3.00/kg.	3.30/kg.
Total fixed overhead costs	$3,000,000	$3,300,000
Normal production volume	1,000,000 kg.	1,000,000 kg.
Selling and administrative (all fixed)	$1,500,000	$1,500,000
Sales volume	900,000 kg.	1,000,000 kg.
Beginning inventory	300,000 kg.	600,000 kg.
Production	1,200,000 kg.	850,000 kg.

Required:

a. Explain to Gary Voss why BBG Corporation's net income decreased in the current fiscal year despite the sales price and sales volume increases.

b. A member of BBG's accounting department has suggested that the company adopt variable costing for internal reporting purposes.

 (i) Prepare an operating income statement through income before taxes for the current year ended November 30, using the variable costing method.

 (ii) Present a numerical reconciliation of the difference in income before taxes using the absorption costing method as currently employed by BBG and the proposed variable costing method.

c. Identify and discuss the advantages and disadvantages of using variable costing for internal reporting purposes.

SOURCE: CMA adapted.

P 10–25:   Joon

Joon manufactures and sells to retailers a variety of home care and personal care products. Joon has a single plant that produces all four of its product lines: Stick Goods (brooms and mops), Floor Care (strippers, soaps, and waxes), Brushes (hair brushes and shoe brushes), and Aerosols (room deodorizers, bug spray, furniture wax). The following statement summarizes Joon's financial performance for the most recent fiscal year.

	Stick Goods	Floor Care	Brushes	Aerosols	Total
Quantity (000 cases)	20	35	15	30	
Direct labor hours/case	1.5	1	2	1.6	
Total direct labor hours (000)	30	35	30	48	143
Manufacturing cost per case:					
Direct material	$ 51.00	$ 21.00	$ 31.00	$ 11.00	
Variable overhead	5.25	3.50	7.00	5.60	
Direct labor cost	31.50	21.00	42.00	33.60	
Fixed overhead	46.50	31.00	62.00	49.60	
Total cost per case	$ 134.25	$ 76.50	$ 142.00	$ 99.80	
Selling price per case	$ 165.00	$122.00	$ 189.00	$ 145.00	
Total revenue (000)	3,300	4,270	2,835	4,350	$14,755.00
Operating margin per case	30.75	45.50	47.00	45.20	
Total operating margin (000)	615	1,592.5	705	1,356	$ 4,268.50
Selling, general & administrative (000):					
Fixed					(1,350.00)
Variable (20% of revenues)					(2,951.00)
Net income (loss) (000)					$ (32.50)

Direct labor costs $21 per hour. Fixed manufacturing overhead of $4.433 million is allocated to products based on direct labor hours. Last year, the fixed manufacturing overhead rate was $31 per direct labor hour ($4.433 million/143,000 direct labor hours). Variable manufacturing overhead is $3.50 per direct labor hour. Selling, general, and administrative (SG&A) expenses consist of fixed costs ($1.35 million) and variable costs ($2,951 million). The variable SG&A is 20 percent of revenues.

The Joon plant has considerable excess capacity. Senior management has identified a potential acquisition target, Snuffy, that sells a line of automotive products (car waxes, soaps, brushes, and so forth) that are complimentary to Joon's existing products and that can be manufactured in Joon's plant. Snuffy does not have any manufacturing facilities, but rather outsources the production of its products to contract manufacturers. Snuffy can be purchased for $38 million. The following table summarizes Snuffy's current operating data:

Snuffy Operating Data Most Recent Fiscal Year	
	Car Care
Quantity (000 cases)	60
Direct labor hours per case	1.9
Direct material per case	$18
Selling price per case	$138
Additional fixed manufacturing overhead	$450,000
Additional fixed SG&A	$400,000

Senior management argues that the reason Joon is currently losing money is because volumes have fallen in the plant and that the remaining products are having to carry an increasingly larger share of the overhead. This has caused some Joon product managers to raise prices. Senior managers realize that they must drive more volume into the plant if Joon is to return to profitability. Since organic growth (i.e., growth from existing products) is difficult due to a very competitive marketplace, management proposes to the board of directors the purchase of Snuffy as a way to drive additional volume into the plant. With volume of 60,000 cases and 1.9 direct labor hours per case, Snuffy's car care product line will add 114,000 direct labor hours to the plant and increase volume about 80 percent (114,000/143,000). This additional volume will significantly reduce the overhead the existing products must absorb and allow the product managers to lower prices. To incorporate Snuffy's manufacturing and distribution into Joon's current operations, Joon will have to incur additional fixed manufacturing overhead of $450,000 per year for new equipment, and $400,000 per year for additional SG&A expenses.

Required:

    a. Prepare a pro forma financial statement that shows Joon's financial performance (net income) for the most recent fiscal year assuming that Joon has already acquired Snuffy's car care products and has incorporated them into Joon's manufacturing and SG&A processes. In preparing your analysis, make the following assumptions:

        (i) Snuffy's products have the same fixed and variable cost structure as Joon's exisiting lines (i.e., variable overhead is $3.50 per direct labor hour and variable SG&A is 20 percent of revenues).

    (ii) The addition of Snuffy products does not change the demand for Joon's existing products.

    (iii) There are no positive or negative externalities in manufacturing from having the additional Snuffy volume in the plant.

    (iv) There is sufficient excess capacity in the plant and the local labor markets to absorb the additional Snuffy volume without causing labor rates or raw material prices to rise.

    b. Based on your financial analysis in part (a), should Joon acquire Snuffy?

    c. Evaluate management's arguments in favor of acquiring Snuffy.

    d. What other advice would you offer Joon's management?

Case

Case 10–1: Olat Corporation

Olat Corporation produces three gauges. These gauges measure density, permeability, and thickness and are known as D-gauges, P-gauges, and T-gauges, respectively. For many years the company was profitable and operated at capacity. However, in the last two years prices on all gauges were reduced and selling expenses increased to meet competition and keep the plant operating at full capacity. Third-quarter results in this table are representative of recent experience:

OLAT CORPORATION
Income Statement, Third Quarter 2010 ($000s)

	D-Gauge	P-Gauge	T-Gauge	Total
Sales	$900	$1,600	$ 900	$3,400
Costs of goods sold	770	1,048	950	2,768
Gross profit	$130	$ 552	$ (50)	$ 632
Selling and administrative expenses	185	370	135	690
Income before income taxes	$ (55)	$ 182	$(185)	$ (58)

Mel Carlo, president of Olat, is very concerned about the results of the pricing, selling, and production policies. After reviewing the third-quarter results he asked his management staff to consider a course of action that includes the following three suggestions:

1. Discontinue the T-gauge line immediately unless the problems with the gauge can be identified and resolved.

2. Increase quarterly sales promotion by $100,000 on the P-gauge product line to increase sales volume 15 percent.

3. Cut production on the D-gauge line by 50 percent, a quantity sufficient to meet the demand of customers who purchase P-gauges. In addition, cut the traceable advertising and promotion for this line to $20,000 each quarter.

George Sperry, controller, suggested a more careful study of the financial relations to determine the possible effect on the company's operating results of the president's proposed course of action. The president agreed, and JoAnn Brower, assistant controller, was assigned to prepare an analysis. To do so, she gathered the following information:

- All three gauges are manufactured with common equipment and facilities.
- The quarterly general, selling, and administrative expenses of $170,000 are allocated to the three gauge lines in proportion to their dollar sales volumes.
- Special selling expenses (primarily advertising, promotion, and shipping) are incurred for each gauge as follows:

	Quarterly Advertising and Promotion	Shipping Expense (per Unit)
D-gauge	$100,000	$ 4
P-gauge	210,000	10
T-gauge	40,000	10

The unit manufacturing costs for the three products are as follows:

	D-Gauge	P-Gauge	T-Gauge
Raw material	$17	$ 31	$ 50
Direct labor	20	40	60
Variable manufacturing overhead	30	45	60
Fixed manufacturing overhead	10	15	20
	$77	$131	$190

The unit sales prices for the three products are as follows:

D-gauge	$90
P-gauge	$200
T-gauge	$180

The company is manufacturing at capacity and is selling all the gauges it produces.

Required:

a. JoAnn Brower has suggested that Olat Corporation's product line income statement as presented for the third quarter of 2010 is not suitable for analyzing Mel Carlo's proposals.

(i) Explain why the product line income statement as presented is not suitable for analysis and decision making.

(ii) Describe an alternative income statement format more suitable for analysis and decision making. Explain why it is better.

b. Use the operating data presented for Olat Corp. and assume that Mel Carlo's proposed course of action was implemented at the beginning of the third quarter of 2010. Evaluate the president's proposed course of action by specifically responding to the following points:

   (i) Are each of the three suggestions cost effective? Your discussion should be supported by a differential analysis that shows the net impact on income before taxes for each of the three suggestions.

  (ii) Was the president correct in eliminating the T-gauge line? Explain your answer.

 (iii) Was the president correct in promoting the P-gauge line rather than the D-gauge line? Explain your answer.

 (iv) Does the proposed course of action make effective use of Olat's capacity? Explain your answer.

c. Are there any nonquantitative factors that Olat should consider before dropping the T-gauge line?

SOURCE: CMA adapted.

Chapter Eleven

Criticisms of Absorption Cost Systems: Inaccurate Product Costs

Chapter Outline

Rockwell International Axle Plant

Rockwell International allocated overhead costs to products in its truck axle plant using direct labor costs. After reviewing its cost allocation scheme, Rockwell concluded that high-volume product costs were approximately 20 percent too high and some of the low-volume product costs were 40 percent too low. Since Rockwell based its prices on fully absorbed product costs, competitors were entering the high-volume market and taking business away by underpricing Rockwell.

SOURCE: F Worthy, "Accounting Bores You? Wake Up," *Fortune*, October 12, 1987, pp. 43–53.

and will appear more profitable. Plant M will deemphasize Tide and further differentiate its product line by adding more specialty soaps. But doing so will drive up overhead costs as production becomes more complex with the additional resources required for scheduling, purchasing, and managing several different soap inventories.

The problem in plant M is the way the absorption costing system traditionally allocates costs. Even though producing Tide in both factories uses the same resources, plant M has higher overhead costs than plant S. Many costs in a plant are driven not so much by the number of units produced as by the number of transactions, such as machine setups, purchase orders, or shipments. Allocating these transaction-based costs using unit volume causes products with large production volumes to be assigned too large a share of these costs.

When managers and accountants speak of inaccurate product costs they mean that overhead costs are not being tracked to the activities causing the costs (such as setups). Rather, these costs are being combined with other cost pools (such as maintenance) and these overly aggregated cost pools are then being allocated to products using allocation bases (like direct labor) that do not capture the cause-and-effect relation driving the particular costs in the overly aggregated cost pool. In the above example, Tide does not really cost more to produce in plant M than in plant S. However, the accounting system inaccurately reports this. Overhead costs are higher in plant M because of the additional products produced. If Tide were the only soap produced in plant M its cost would be the same as in plant S. Thus, the accounting system in plant M is inaccurately charging Tide for some overhead costs that should be charged to the other products in plant M that are causing the higher costs.

Traditional absorption systems can be modified to provide more accurate product costs in plant M. An activity-based cost system is one such modification. Whether activity-based systems are truly alternatives to absorption systems or simply modifications is a legitimate question, although such questioning ultimately deteriorates into a semantic debate. The important point, however, is that managers seeking to control costs must manage the cost drivers. Controlling costs requires identifying and managing the key factors that generate costs, not massaging the cost numbers or cost allocation procedures. Activity-based cost systems (described next) are intended to provide more accurate product costs and to give managers the data to manage the cost drivers. Activity-based costing recognizes that overhead costs vary not only with volume but also with the range of items manufactured—that is, their diversity and complexity. Finally, examining activity-based systems furthers our understanding of costing systems in general.

Concept Questions	Q11–1	Why does traditional absorption costing often yield inaccurate product costs?
	Q11–2	In a plant producing multiple products, would absorption costing overcost or undercost the more complex products? Why?

B. Activity-Based Costing

This section describes a type of absorption costing called *activity-based costing* (ABC). While a manufacturing setting is chosen to describe activity-based costing, this technique has also been applied in insurance and banking institutions, nonprofit organizations, and the marketing and distribution departments of firms.

Activities are repetitive tasks performed by each specialized group or activity center within the factory. Activity centers are cost centers (see Chapter 5). Costs are assigned to activities (i.e., cost centers) in the initial step of the process, and then these activity center costs are either directly traced or allocated to products. In this sense, activity-based cost systems are very similar to the two-stage allocation procedure depicted in Figure 9–4. However, activity-based cost systems differ from more traditional absorption cost systems in how department/activity center costs are allocated to products.

An entire vocabulary has developed surrounding activity-based costing, including activity-based management, activity drivers, resource drivers, cost driver analysis, and value-chain costing. Since the purpose of this section is to introduce the concepts of activity-based costing, not to treat the subject comprehensively, the terminology used in this chapter is simplified from that found in practice.[4]

1. Choosing Cost Drivers

Installing an activity-based cost system begins with an analysis of the types of transactions that generate costs in each factory support department (e.g., purchasing, engineering, maintenance, and quality control). Cost analysts examine each factory department to understand what drives the costs in that support department. Examples of typical cost drivers are the number of inspections or testings, receipts of raw materials and parts, the number of part numbers in inventory, machine setups, and engineering change orders. For each factory support department studied, the principal cost driver is identified.

Once the cost driver is determined, it can be classified into one of four mutually exclusive categories: unit level, batch level, product level, or production sustaining. Figure 11–1 illustrates these four categories in an activity-based costing system. **Unit-level costs** arise from activities that are performed at least once for each unit of product. For example, machining a surface, drilling a hole, or attaching a subassembly must be done for each and every unit produced. These costs include direct labor and material, machine costs, and direct energy costs.

Batch-level costs arise from activities performed once for each batch or lot of products. For example, machine setups, cleanup, and moving the batch to the

---

[4] The interested reader is referred to R Cooper and R Kaplan, *The Design of Cost Management Systems* (Englewood Cliffs, NJ: Prentice Hall, 1991); and N Raffish and P Turney, "Glossary of Activity-Based Management," *Journal of Cost Management,* Fall 1991, pp. 53–63.

FIGURE 11–1

Activity-based cost system categorization and allocation of indirect costs

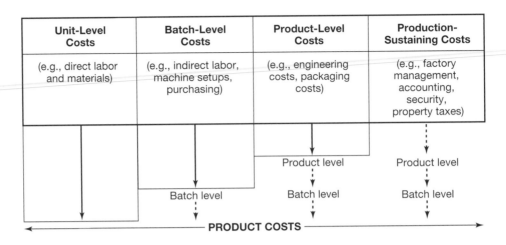

Unit-Level Costs	Batch-Level Costs	Product-Level Costs	Production-Sustaining Costs
(e.g., direct labor and materials)	(e.g., indirect labor, machine setups, purchasing)	(e.g., engineering costs, packaging costs)	(e.g., factory management, accounting, security, property taxes)

next step in the production process depend on the number of batches rather than the number of units in each batch. Purchase orders and inspections are also examples of batch-level activities. They occur once for each batch, independent of how many units are in the batch.

Product-level costs arise from activities to support the production of the product type or model. For example, engineering support costs for process modifications and product design depend on the existence of the product line and do not vary with the number of units or number of batches produced. Other examples of product-level costs include the costs of engineering change orders and product enhancement and packaging costs unique to the product.

Finally, **production-sustaining costs** arise from all remaining activities required for the overall productive capacity of the factory. For example, plant security, maintenance, administration, insurance, and property taxes are incurred to maintain the production capability of the plant and do not depend on the number of units, batches, or product lines produced. These are common costs, shared by all the products produced. The company pays property taxes for the right to use the land and facilities for manufacturing. These taxes are not caused by and hence cannot be tracked to any particular product, batch, or product line.

Some writers suggest splitting out additional levels such as process-level costs, which arise from the engineering activities necessary to maintain a particular production process, or customer-sustaining costs, which arise from sales or engineering activities required to support a particular customer. Conceptually, these are similar to product-level activities. To simplify the exposition, only four cost levels are discussed here. (In practice, however, ABC system designers tailor the number of levels used by a particular system to the firm's specific circumstances.)

In Figure 11–1, direct costs that are unit-level costs are traced directly to the units produced. Other costs, such as indirect labor to set up machines or to purchase materials for each batch, cannot be traced directly to units; they depend not on the number of units in the batch, but only on the number of batches. For example, the work load in the purchasing department usually depends on the number of purchase orders issued, receipt of the order, and inspection of the order. The amount of work is about the same whether 100 units or 10,000 units are in the order. Once these batch-level costs are traced to a batch, they can be allocated to the product by dividing by the number of units in the batch.

AT&T and ABC	The business billing center of AT&T, with $30 million annual expenses, prints, sorts, and mails invoices to business customers. Its activities include monitoring the billing process, editing and checking the data, and correcting errors. It installed ABC to control costs. First, a thorough analysis of the process revealed the underlying cost drivers for each activity (number of customers tested, change requests, service orders, and pages printed). Second, costs were assigned to cost objects based on the cost drivers. Armed with the new cost data, management benchmarked their operations with billing centers in other companies. In two years, AT&T's billing center reduced operating expenses 26 percent even though billable minutes increased 46 percent. SOURCE: T Hobdy, J Thompson, and P Sharman, "Activity-Based Management at AT&T," *Management Accounting*, April 1994, pp. 35–39.

Product-level costs, such as engineering costs and some maintenance costs, are incurred only if the particular product line exists. These costs vary with the number of distinct products in the plant, not with the number of batches or units. For example, the number of engineers needed to maintain the product line often depends on the complexity of the product, which in turn is a function of the number of different parts in the product. Some firms allocate product-level costs based on the number of different parts in the product. These costs are then averaged over the number of units produced.

All remaining factory costs that cannot be traced directly to units, batches, or product lines, such as general factory management, accounting department costs, and property taxes, are production-sustaining costs. They can be allocated to units by first allocating them to product lines, then to batches, and finally to the units in the batches. Alternatively, they can be allocated directly to units using direct labor or machine hours.

When each cost is segregated into one of these four categories, the factory is broken up into distinct sets of activities, or identifiable operations that consume resources. Costs are accumulated by activity centers. Cost drivers should accurately reflect the underlying factors that cause a particular overhead activity's costs to vary. Cost drivers are both financial and nonfinancial measures of activity that mimic how products consume resources in activity centers. ABC attempts to refine the set of internal "tax rates" (Chapter 7) used to tax externalities inside the firm. Instead of taxing direct materials for purchasing department costs, purchase orders or part numbers are the cost drivers and become the taxed activity.

Exercise 1:

Southridge is a 200-bed hospital. Southridge has the following cost structure: $250 per bed per day for nursing care, food, linen, and janitorial services; $50 per bed per day for occupancy costs such as depreciation, administration, and utilities; and $120 per patient for admission in the admitting department and social work discharge planning. The bed cost of $250 varies with the number of bed days. Occupancy cost represents the cost of

continued

providing capacity and does not vary with bed days. The $120 admission cost varies with the number of patients admitted. Each patient, regardless of the number of days in the hospital, must be admitted and then discharged. Two years ago the average patient stayed seven days. Now the average patient stays four days. To simplify the illustration, assume all hospital beds are always occupied. Note that prescription drugs and medical procedures such as X-rays and lab tests are billed directly to patients and are not included in Southridge's operating costs.

Required:

    a. What was the total annual cost of operating Southridge two years ago?

    b. What is the total annual cost of operating Southridge today?

    c. Describe why total costs increased from two years ago to today.

    d. How has the average cost of a patient stay changed?

    e. Categorize the three cost categories above using the ABC labels: unit-level, batch-level, product-level, and production-sustaining costs.

Solution:

    a. Calculating the total annual cost two years ago first requires determining the number of admissions per year:

Bed days per year	365
Bed days per admission	÷7
Admissions per bed per year	52.14
Number of beds	× 200
Admissions per year	10,428

Total cost (millions):

Variable bed cost (200 beds × $250 × 365 days)	$18.25
Occupancy cost (200 beds × $50 × 365 days)	3.65
Costs of admission (10,428 admissions × $120)	1.25
Total annual cost	$23.15

    b. Total annual cost today:

Bed days per year	365
Bed days per admission	÷4
Admissions per bed per year	91.25
Number of beds	× 200
Admissions per year	18,250

Total cost (millions):

Variable bed cost (200 beds × $250 × 365 days)	$18.25
Occupancy cost (200 beds × $50 × 365 days)	3.65
Costs of admission (18,250 admissions × $120)	2.19
Total annual cost	$24.09

    c. Total operating cost increased about $940,000 (7,822 additional admissions × $120 per admission) because average length of stay has fallen from seven to four

continued

days, and the number of patients admitted has increased. To service the increased number of admissions requires more admission and discharge resources.

d. The average cost of a patient stay two years ago was $2,220 ($23.15 million ÷ 10,428 patients). The average cost of a patient stay today is $1,320 ($24.09 million ÷ 18,250 patients). The average cost per patient has decreased because length of stay (and hence the cost that varies with days) is lower. However, total hospital costs are higher because Southridge is incurring more costs admitting and discharging the greater volume of patients.

e. Unit-level costs: The $250 per bed per day cost for nursing and so forth. These costs vary with the number of patient bed days.

Batch-level costs: The $120 per admission cost. Each patient admitted consumes some admissions and social work costs, regardless of the patient's length of stay.

Product-level costs: Lab tests, X-rays, and surgical departments are like production-sustaining costs. These costs are accumulated in the various service areas, and then patients are charged for the medical services they use.

Production-sustaining costs: The $50 per bed per day occupancy cost. Even though these costs are being allocated based on bed days, they do not vary with either bed days or the number of admissions. Occupancy costs provide the basic capacity to serve the 200 patients per day.

Activity-based systems can be related back to the discussion of cost curves in Chapter 2. Chapter 2 presented a linear cost curve of the form

$$TC = VC \times Q + FC$$

where

TC = Total cost
VC = Variable cost per unit
Q = Number of units produced
FC = Fixed cost

That is, total cost, TC, can be disaggregated into variable costs, $VC \times Q$, and fixed cost, FC. Fixed costs, by definition, do not vary with Q, units produced.

Under activity-based costing, a more complex cost function is assumed to exist in the factory—namely,

$$TC = VC \times Q + BC \times B + PC \times L + OC$$

where

TC = Total cost
VC = Variable cost per unit
Q = Number of units produced
BC = Cost per batch
B = Number of batches
PC = Cost per product line
L = Number of product lines
OC = All other costs that do not vary with some activity measure

Activity-Based Costing in the Railroads	In the 1870s, the railroads developed a sophisticated unit-cost measure: the cost of hauling a ton of freight one mile. The accounts were segregated into four groups:

1. Maintenance of the roadway and general management.
2. Station expenses.
3. Movement expenses.
4. Interest on the capital investment.

The first group involves costs that do not vary with volume of traffic. Group 2 contains costs that vary with volume of freight. Group 3 contains costs that vary with the number of trains run. The last group represents interest on the capital investment. Three cost drivers were used to allocate the four cost pools:

- Average number of tons transported over one mile of road per year (groups 1 and 4).
- Length of haul (2).
- Average number of tons of freight in each train (3).

This complex calculation of cost per ton-mile resembles current activity-based costing systems that separate costs into unit-level, batch-level, product-level, and production-sustaining-level costs. Unit-level costs are roughly the movement expenses (3). Batch-level costs are like station expenses (2). Product-line costs resemble maintenance of roadway expenses. (1). And interest on capital investment is required to sustain the entire system.

A Chandler, *The Visible Hand: The Managerial Revolution in American Business* (Cambridge: Harvard University Press, 1977), pp. 116–19.

In addition,

$$FC = BC \times B + PC \times L + OC$$

That is, a large fraction of the fixed costs, FC, that do not vary with units produced do vary with the number of batches and product lines.

The more complex ABC cost function recognizes that costs vary due to more than just changes in units produced, Q. Costs also vary with the number of batches and the number of product lines. If the two cost functions are viewed as multiple regressions, the second equation has more explanatory (right-side) variables. Therefore, assuming that the additional variables correctly capture how costs vary in the particular factory under study, this equation will have more explanatory power (i.e., a higher R^2).[5]

While the ABC cost function captures more of the complexity in the factory, it still makes a number of simplifying assumptions that potentially reduce its

[5] Multiple regression is not being advocated as a way to estimate cost functions. Regressions estimated using monthly accounting cost data are usually misleading and inaccurate. Well-known problems include autocorrelated residuals, nonstationary processes, seasonality, and errors in variables. Appendix B in Chapter 2 describes these problems in more detail.

accuracy. For example, every batch is assumed to cost $BC regardless of the number of units in the batch, the types of products in the batch, and what was produced before the current batch. Also each product line is assumed to cost $PC regardless of the complexity of the product lines.

Activity-based costing tries to identify the factors that drive cost and then use these factors to allocate overhead costs. The following exercise illustrates an activity-based cost system.

Exercise 2:

A tree nursery is considering a change in product mix in its inventory. The manager wants to estimate the effect of each type of tree on indirect costs. Indirect costs are identified and estimated for the following activities: watering, repotting (transferring trees to larger pots), and administration. Total estimated annual costs for each activity, the cost driver for each activity, and the expected annual usage of each cost driver are as follows:

Activity	Estimated Costs	Cost Driver	Estimated Usage of Cost Driver
Watering	$100,000	Number of trees	500,000
Repotting	200,000	Number of repots	200,000
Administration	45,000	Number of different types of trees	50

Required:

a. What are the application rates for each of the activities?

b. Given the choice of cost driver, determine the activity level (unit-level, batch-level, product-level, production-sustaining level) of each of the activities.

c. What are the indirect costs of 100 weeping birches, each of which requires repotting once a year?

Solution:

a. The application rate for each activity is calculated by dividing the estimated costs of the activity by the estimated usage of its respective cost driver:

Activity		Application Rate
Watering	$100,000/500,000	$0.20/tree
Repotting	$200,000/200,000	$1.00/repot
Administration	$45,000/50	$900/type of tree

b. Both watering and repotting are unit-level activities because their cost drivers vary with the number of units. Administration is treated as a product-level activity because each product receives the same indirect costs.

continued

c. The indirect costs traced to the 100 weeping birches are as follows:

Activity	Application Rate	Usage	Costs
Watering	$0.20/tree	100	$ 20
Repotting	$1.00/repot	100	100
Administration	$900/type of tree	1	900
Total annual indirect costs			$1,020

2. Unit-Based versus Activity-Based Costing: An Example

An example is used to compare a single unit-based allocation system and activity-based costing. The term a *single, unit-based allocation system* refers to an absorption cost system whereby all manufacturing overhead is allocated using a single allocation base that varies with units produced, such as direct labor, direct material, or machine hours. VBL Co. manufactures a complete line of DVD players in its plant: three four-head models and two six-head models. The four- and six-head models make up two separate product lines, each with its own engineering department. The five models are manufactured in separate jobs consisting of 100 DVDs per batch.

The following table contains the production and direct costs for each model:

DVD Players

	Four-Head Models			Six-Head Models	
	105	*205*	*305*	*801*	*901*
Number of batches/year	800	1,000	600	400	200
Cost/Batch of 100 DVD Players					
Direct labor	$3,400	$3,500	$3,600	$4,200	$4,400
Direct material	$6,000	$6,400	$6,500	$8,000	$8,500

The plant's overhead consists of the following items and amounts:

Factory Overhead Costs
($ in Millions)

Testing, setups, and supplies		$ 9.30
Product-line costs:		
Four-head models	$5.40	
Six-head models	4.20	9.60
Other factory costs		2.98
Total overhead costs		$21.88

The following tables calculate the total manufacturing cost per unit by model using a single, unit-based allocation scheme. Overhead is assigned to models by a plantwide overhead rate using direct labor dollars as the allocation base.

FIGURE 11–2
DVD player unit-based cost system

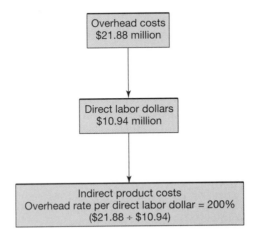

The first step is to calculate the plantwide overhead rate based on direct labor costs.

| | DVD Player Models | | | | | |
	105	205	305	801	901	*Total*
Number of batches	800	1,000	600	400	200	
Direct labor/batch	$3,400	$3,500	$3,600	$4,200	$4,400	
Total direct labor cost (millions)	$2.72	$3.50	$2.16	$1.68	$0.88	$10.94
Total factory overhead (millions)						$21.88
Overhead rate (percentage of direct labor)						200%

Using the estimated plantwide overhead rate of 200 percent of direct labor cost, the cost of each product line is calculated next.

Model Costs per Batch of 100 DVD Players
(Unit-Based Costing)

| | Models | | | | |
	105	205	305	801	901
Direct labor	$ 3,400	$ 3,500	$ 3,600	$ 4,200	$ 4,400
Direct material	6,000	6,400	6,500	8,000	8,500
Overhead (200% of direct labor)	6,800	7,000	7,200	8,400	8,800
Total cost	$16,200	$16,900	$17,300	$20,600	$21,700
Cost per DVD player	$162	$169	$173	$206	$217

Under this costing scheme, the unit cost of the DVD players ranges from $162 to $217. Figure 11–2 illustrates the unit-based costing computation.

VBL Co. was concerned that using a single plantwide overhead allocation base might distort product costs. An activity-based costing study reveals that the cost of manufacturing a batch consists of indirect labor for machine setups and testing and supply costs. There are 3,000 batches per year. Product-line costs consist of engineering and equipment specialized in each particular product line. Other factory costs consist of plant administration and general maintenance.

Using the data in the preceding paragraph, overhead is assigned to the models using an activity-based costing system with three cost pools: batch-related costs, product-line costs, and production-sustaining costs. Batch-related costs and product-line-related costs are assigned to models based on the number of batches. Production-sustaining activities consist of other factory costs of $2,980,000. These costs are allocated to models based on direct labor cost.

The following tables illustrate the activity-based costing overhead cost assignment. The first step in the activity-based costing method is to calculate the unit cost for each of the three activity cost drivers.

(1) Batch-related costs: $9.3 million ÷ 3,000 batches = $3,100 per batch
(2) Product-line–related costs:

	Four-Head	Six-Head
Product-line costs	$5,400,000	$4,200,000
Number of batches	2,400	600
Product-line cost/batch	$ 2,250	$ 7,000

(3) Production-sustaining costs:

Other factory costs (millions)	$ 2.98
Total direct labor cost (millions)	÷ $10.94
Overhead rate per direct labor dollar	27.24%

Given the three cost drivers, the activity-based cost of each DVD player is calculated in the following table.

Model Costs per Batch of 100 DVD Players
(Activity-Based Costing)

	Models				
	105	205	305	801	901
Direct labor	$ 3,400	$ 3,500	$ 3,600	$ 4,200	$ 4,400
Direct material	6,000	6,400	6,500	8,000	8,500
Overhead:					
Batch-related costs	3,100	3,100	3,100	3,100	3,100
Product-line-related costs	2,250	2,250	2,250	7,000	7,000
Production-sustaining costs (27.24% of direct labor)	926	953	981	1,144	1,199
Total cost	$15,676	$16,203	$16,431	$23,444	$24,199
Cost per DVD player	$ 157	$ 162	$ 164	$ 234	$ 242
Ratio of activity-based cost to absorption cost	−3%	−4%	−5%	+14%	+12%

Under activity-based costing, the unit cost of the DVD players ranges from $157 to $242. Figure 11–3 illustrates the activity-based costing computation.

FIGURE 11–3
*DVD player plant's
activity-based costing
system*

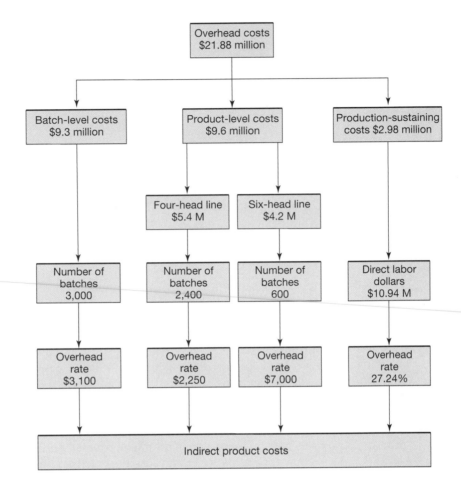

Notice that all costs are allocated under both unit-based and activity-based costing. There is no distinction between fixed and variable costs. All costs are viewed as being variable in the long run and assigned to the products.

Under activity-based costing, the four-head models' costs are 3 to 5 percent lower than under a plantwide overhead rate, and the six-head models' costs are 12 to 14 percent higher. The product-line costs under unit-based costing are assigned to models using direct labor costs. Since the four-head models require about 77 percent of the direct labor dollars [($2.72 + $3.50 + $2.16) ÷ $10.94], they are assigned 77 percent of the $9.6 million of product-line costs. However, the four-head models account for only 56 percent of the product-line costs ($5.4 ÷ 9.6). Thus, unit-based costing assigns more product-line costs to the four-head models than does activity-based costing.

The key point of this example is that traditional unit-based costing overcosts the high-volume models and undercosts the low-volume models. Since the six-head models are more complex, they require more product-line costs per unit than the four-head models. Unit-level allocation bases (e.g., direct labor) overcost the less complex products and undercost the more complex, more resource-consuming products.

In this example, batch-level costs do not cause any miscosting because all of the DVD models are produced in equal lot sizes of 100.

Concept Questions	Q11–3	What are the four mutually exclusive categories used in activity-based cost accounting?
	Q11–4	Does activity-based costing allocate more or less total costs to products than unit-based costing?

C. Analyzing Activity-Based Costing

Having described activity-based costing (ABC) and how cost drivers are selected, this section discusses some of the reasons firms adopt it, why most firms do not, and the costs and benefits of ABC.

1. Reasons for Implementing Activity-Based Costing

An interesting study compares product costs computed using a traditional unit-based absorption costing system with product costs computed using an activity-based system.[6] The site is an electronics factory producing over 800 different analog and digital multimeters and computer-controlled instrument systems. The factory manufactures the circuit boards and assembles them into a completed instrument, which is then tested. Under the traditional absorption costing system, all overhead costs were assigned to one of the two overhead cost pools. One pool was allocated to individual products based on direct materials and the other pool was allocated based on direct labor. Both of these pools were treated as unit-level costs. Direct materials averaged 65 percent of total product costs, direct labor averaged 2 percent of total product costs, and overhead averaged 33 percent of product costs. Six-month product volumes range from 1 to 4,826 units; half of the products have volumes of fewer than 50 units every six months. Thus, the plant produces both high- and low-volume products.

The factory converted to an activity-based costing system, which identified 14 different activity centers and accumulated the costs in each center separately. The new system identified cost drivers for each activity center. For example, one activity center maintains part numbers and its cost driver is number of parts per instrument. Another activity center is robotic insertions and its cost driver is number of insertions. Instead of just two allocation bases (direct labor and direct materials), 14 allocation bases are used to allocate overhead costs.

The authors of the study compare the traditional absorption cost of each product with its activity-based cost by computing the ratio of activity-based cost to absorption cost for each product. Seventy percent of the activity-based product costs are within about 20 percent of the traditional absorption costs. Fewer than 20 percent of the product costs vary by more than 50 percent. These data indicate that for most of the products, activity-based costing and traditional absorption costing generate comparable product costs. But for a few products, there are dramatic changes in product costs when computed under activity-based costing. One percent of the products has activity-based costs equal to five times their traditional absorption-based costs.

The authors of the study find that (1) high-volume products have lower activity-based unit costs relative to absorption-based unit costs and (2) low-volume products tend to have higher activity-based costs than absorption costs. Traditional

---

[6] G Foster and M Gupta, "Implementation of an Activity Accounting System in the Electronics Industry," in *Measuring Manufacturing Performance*, ed. R Kaplan (Boston: Harvard Business School, 1989).

Insteel Industries

Insteel manufactures and markets concrete-reinforcing products such as industrial wire, fasteners, nails, and mesh. Its South Carolina plant produced 477 individual products. About 20 percent of its products accounted for 85 percent of its revenues, and 20 percent of its customers accounted for 95 percent of its revenues. Senior managers at this plant formed an ABC team that identified 80 cost pools and appropriate cost drivers for these pools. For example, materials-handling costs were assigned to products based on the number of moves required by each product. Based on the new ABC cost data, management at this plant undertook a series of profit-enhancing actions: they discontinued unprofitable products, increased prices on other unprofitable items, and dropped unprofitable customers. After the success of ABC at its South Carolina plant, Insteel rolled out ABC at its other plants.

SOURCE: V Narayanan and R Sarkar, "The Impact of Activity-Based Costing on Managerial Decisions at Insteel Industries—A Field Study," *Journal of Economics and Management Strategy*, Summer, 2002, pp. 257–88.

Acxiom Corporation

Acxiom is a publicly traded firm that provides data and computer processing services to Fortune 500 companies. Its services include market databases, mailing list processing, data warehousing, and facilities management. Acxiom owns InfoBase, the largest consumer database in the United States, covering 95 percent of all households.

Acxiom uses activity-based costing to trace costs to activities and processes. A software project involves the following activities: planning the project, designing software, writing code, and testing code. Acxiom's ABC system accumulates the costs of these activities and assigns them to products, projects, and customers. This allows Acxiom to assess customer and product profitability and to hold its people accountable. It also allows it to further decentralize decision making because lower-level employees, knowledgeable of the firm's cost structure, can make decisions about changing a project's specification without approval by higher-level managers.

absorption costing systems tend to assign more costs to large-volume jobs relative to small-volume jobs, particularly when overhead contains a high fraction of indirect costs that do not vary with units produced but do vary with batches and product lines. When these batch and product-line costs are allocated to jobs based on a volume measure such as units or direct materials, large-volume jobs bear a high fraction of these costs.

This study of an actual manufacturing plant that converted to an activity-based costing system shows that activity-based costing does make a difference in reported product costs, although for most products the cost changes are not terribly large.

Activity-based costing systems claim to offer several advantages. ABC increases the percentage of product costs directly traced to individual products. Also, ABC provides an understanding of how costs are consumed by individual products, the activities required to produce them, the direct and indirect costs in the various activity centers, and how indirect costs are generated by cost drivers. Activity-based cost systems focus cost control at the activity level and the product design level. Allocating overhead costs using direct labor encourages managers to reduce the direct labor content in products. Activity-based systems focus managers' attention on controlling costs in the activity center and reducing the content of the cost drivers in the products.

Activity-based costing systems are promoted as a way to develop more accurate product or product-line costs. *Accuracy* means that changes in product volume, batch size, or product design characteristics (number of parts, manufacturing complexity, etc.) cause reported cost changes to be more highly correlated with changes in opportunity cost. Besides being more accurate, ABC changes the incentives of operating managers. Identifying the underlying cost drivers allows managers to focus their attention on them. For example, product designers will change the way products are designed and manufactured to reduce the reported ABC costs. To the extent that the chosen cost drivers are in fact associated with the factors that cause costs to change, an activity-based cost system will cause managers to change their behavior and thus reduce costs.

But these managers must have the *decision rights* to alter the levels of the cost drivers and there must be a *performance evaluation system* that gives them incentives to minimize cost. Adopting an activity-based costing system is a change in the *performance measurement system*. For behavior to be changed in the desired way, the other two parts of the organizational architecture (performance reward and decision-right partitioning) must encourage the appropriate changes. (Recall from Chapter 4 that all legs of the organization's three-legged stool must be coordinated with one another.)

Activity-based cost systems are directed primarily at decision management, not decision control. In fact, to emphasize their importance as a decision-making tool, ABC proponents have coined the term *activity-based management* (ABM) to describe decisions that use ABC information to satisfy customers and improve profitability. ABM includes using activity-based costs to make better pricing and product-mix decisions, reduce costs, improve manufacturing and administrative processes, and design better products. ABM is about planning and managing activities. ABC presumably provides more accurate information that leads to better decisions (decision management). ABC and ABM proponents *do not* argue that activity-based costs are better as performance measures and that incentive compensation schemes be redesigned around activity-based costs (decision control).

2. Benefits and Costs of Activity-Based Costing

Most proponents argue that activity-based costing produces more accurate product cost data for decision making (decision management). A central tenet of activity-based costing is that more accurate product costs are always preferable to less accurate product costs and that accuracy generally increases with the number of cost drivers.

Adding more cost drivers allows more of the factors that cause overhead to vary (such as the number of batches, the number of part numbers, or the number of product lines) to be included in the ABC system. This increases the accuracy of the product cost numbers generated by the accounting system and, presumably, better operating, pricing, and resource utilization decisions result. However, adding additional cost pools and cost drivers for these pools is not free. Separate cost pools for each cost driver must be developed and data on each cost driver must be collected. At some point, the cost of adding more cost pools and cost drivers exceeds the benefit, in terms of better decisions resulting from the additional accuracy. Hence, it is unlikely that the ABC system ever achieves 100 percent

FIGURE 11–4

Net benefits versus number of cost drivers (decision making only and decision making and control)

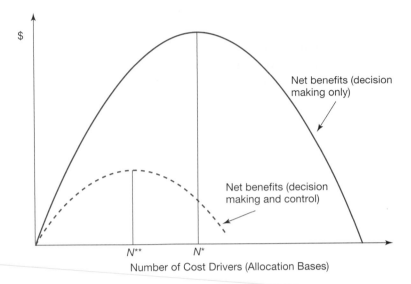

accuracy. The solid curve in Figure 11–4 depicts the net benefits (benefits less costs) as a function of the number of cost drivers. Up to N^* cost drivers, the net benefits are increasing. But beyond N^*, the net benefits decline.

So far, the analysis has focused exclusively on how the costs and benefits of decision making vary with the number of cost drivers. Now let us introduce decision control. As more cost drivers are introduced, lower-level managers have more control over the allocation bases chosen as the "cost drivers" because they usually have specialized knowledge of the factors driving costs in their departments. Increasing the number of cost drivers means giving more discretion over the cost system to the managers whose performance is being measured by these systems. Increasing the discretion of managers being evaluated by the cost system usually reduces the ability of the system to monitor their behavior.

The costs of ABC systems include both the direct costs of collecting and reporting data on the activity levels and the costs incurred from the loss of control arising from less effective monitoring of managers because these managers have more discretion in choosing the cost drivers. Some of this discretion will be exercised opportunistically by these managers to manipulate their performance measures. When this second set of costs is included, the net benefits curve is lower and the optimum number of cost drivers, becomes N^{**} in Figure 11–4.

The dashed line in Figure 11–4 suggests that fewer cost drivers, or even inaccurate product costs, can be desirable. More accurate product cost knowledge is undesirable if it leads to poorer decision control. For example, some firms prefer to bias their costs upward to prevent the sales force from shaving margins by setting prices so low that they cover only variable costs.[7] This is partly a problem with the performance reward system and partly a problem with how product costs are measured. Nonetheless, some managers are reluctant to report lower product costs for decision control reasons.

Other companies systematically understate product costs, as in targeting costing, which is described more fully in Chapter 12. Many Japanese firms, in particular,

---

[7] K Merchant and M Shields, "When and Why to Measure Costs Less Accurately to Improve Decision Making," *Accounting Horizons*, June 1993, pp. 76–81.

The Costs of ABC Exceed the Benefits at a Hewlett-Packard Plant	Many Hewlett-Packard (HP) plants have successfully implemented ABC, but not the Colorado Springs Division. This division produces test and measurement equipment. Two finance and four information technology personnel spent one and one-half years helping the division design and implement the ABC system. Wages, benefits, occupancy costs, and depreciation were largely fixed and composed 85 percent of total costs. By treating these costs as though they were largely variable, the ABC system was not useful in managing short-term cost fluctuations. The ABC system had numerous cost drivers, one for just about every activity in a process. In pursuit of accurate costs for extremely heterogeneous products, the system became unwieldy trying to explain the monthly variance reports. Employees constantly tweaking the driver rates created an administrative "nightmare" for the accounting system. Finally, the division simplified the accounting system by allocating overhead using material dollars, thereby eliminating two people in the cost accounting function.

SOURCE: S Landry, L Wood, and T Linquist, "Can ABC Bring Mixed Results?" *Management Accounting,* March 1997, pp. 28–33.

set cost targets based on what the item should cost in order for the firm to compete. Such target costs are well below the costs that the firm can currently achieve. However, low target costs encourage innovation and cost improvement. Other incentive-control reasons can cause firms to choose less accurate cost systems. Zytec simplified its cost system to just one cost driver: time to manufacture the product (cycle time). While such a system produces less accurate product costs than multiple-cost-driver ABC systems, senior management wanted to focus employee attention on what it believed was the single most important cost reduction factor in the firm.

3. ABC Measures Costs, Not Benefits

Suppose a firm produces a single product in its only plant. Such a firm is not likely to use ABC because the average cost of its only product is easily computed. As we have seen, product costing becomes more challenging in multiproduct plants that produce a variety of low- and high-volume products that place differential demands on the plant's common resources (purchasing, setup, engineering, etc.). Presumably, ABC provides a more accurate representation of how each product consumes common factory resources. However, ABC does not capture the benefits of producing and selling multiple products.

As discussed in Chapter 4, firms sell multiple products if they can do so more economically than separate, single-product firms. Multiproduct plants can be low-cost producers due to demand- or supply-side synergies. For example, because product quality information is expensive for consumers to acquire, firms develop brand-name capital that allows them to offer broad product lines. Ford Motor can introduce and sell a new small, sports utility vehicle (SUV) at lower cost than can a new start-up company because the marketplace already knows the Ford name and its overall quality reputation. A start-up company would need to invest millions of dollars to assure the consumer of its SUV's quality.

Another example of a demand-side benefit of being a multiproduct firm is offering consumers one-stop shopping. Catalog companies such as L.L. Bean include many clothing items, often arranged in outfits that allow the consumer to order matching pants, shirt, and sweater. This reduces consumers' transaction costs of assembling a coordinated outfit.

ABC Can Be Costly	A large aerospace company has a centralized procurement department that purchases parts and material for three product lines. Direct labor dollars and material dollars were used to allocate procurement costs to the three product lines. However, procurement processing time was the same whether purchase orders were for higher quantities and more expensive parts or for single parts and low dollar parts. After an extensive survey, purchase order line items was selected as the best cost driver of procurement time. Procurement costs were reassigned using purchase order line items.

Overall reaction to the ABC system was quite negative. The finance group felt that the new system was too complicated and would require additional work to forecast the cost drivers. Procurement had misgivings because the cost per purchase order line item seemed expensive. The product line managers objected. The government contract agency, which audited the contracts for product lines sold to the government, was overwhelmed by the complexity of the system—as were other users of the cost data.

The original ABC system was modified and simplified. Instead of using purchase order line items, head count in the procurement department assigned to each product line was used to allocate procurement costs.

Source: D Pattison and C Arendt, "Activity-Based Costing: It Doesn't Work All the Time," *Management Accounting*, April 1994, pp. 55–61.

On the supply side, producing multiple products in the same plant allows the firm to capture economies of scope, learning curve effects, or smoothing production over time. For example, some tire companies produce both snow tires and all-weather tires in the same plant, since separate plants would be too small to provide low-cost production. Or, if one plant produced only snow tires, they would have to be inventoried during spring and summer until they could be sold in fall and winter.

Although ABC systems capture how different products consume resources, they are unable to capture the joint benefits of having multiple products. For example, an ABC analysis might demonstrate that producing a particular sunglasses model has an ABC cost greater than its price. However, if this sunglasses model is worn by movie stars (which increases the sales of the firm's other sunglasses models), then this "loss leader" provides significant brand-name marketing benefits.

Likewise, suppose a new product allows the firm to smooth production and utilize excess capacity. An ABC analysis might still show this product is unprofitable. Suppose an engineering department requires five engineers to support peak production, which occurs over nine months. In the three months that are off peak, two engineers could be let go, but because it is too expensive to recruit and train new engineers, they are retained. A new product is added to utilize the two engineers and other excess capacity in the off-peak period. Three or four years after this product is added, it is unlikely that anyone will remember why the product was added to the plant. Hence, an ABC analysis probably charges this new product the full cost of the two engineers, which could cause the firm to drop the product. Adding the new product did not increase the number of engineers. The plant had two "extra" engineers in the off-peak period to staff the peak period.

Finally, recall the discussion of joint costs in Chapter 8, which described the futility of allocating joint costs to joint products. All joint cost allocation schemes, other than net realizable value, distort product costs for decision making. If the cost of the chicken is allocated to the wings based on weight, the cost of wings is distorted. Wings might be dropped even though they provide incremental net cash flow. Analogously, multiple products can yield joint benefits from the demand or supply side. ABC, like all cost allocation schemes, ignores these benefits by focusing on allocating costs. And even if these joint benefits are identified, they cannot be allocated meaningfully. Suppose L.L. Bean offers a matching shirt and sweater in its catalog. If each is offered without the other, L.L. Bean sells either 1,000 shirts or 1,000 sweaters. By offering both as an outfit, they sell 1,200 of each, or 400 outfits more in total. How should the additional joint benefits of these 400 be allocated? They shouldn't be allocated because any attempt to do so will likely distort the relative profitability of both the shirt and the sweater.

D. Acceptance of Activity-Based Costing

Many people have the impression that activity-based costing is a recent invention. However, over 30 years ago Peter F. Drucker, a well-known management consultant, wrote that absorption costing systems can produce misleading product cost data.[8] Professor Goetz advocated activity-based costing principles in 1949 when he wrote

> Each primary (overhead) class should be homogeneous with respect to every significant dimension of managerial problems of planning and control. Some of the major dimensions along which (overhead) may vary are number of units of output, number of orders, number of operations, capacity of plant, number of catalogue items offered.[9]

A few firms in the United States and Europe installed *activity-based systems* in the 1970s before the term *activity-based costing* was coined.

Many manufacturing plants have experimented with activity-based costing systems but have not integrated the activity-based cost data into their accounting systems. The activity-based cost systems are primarily stand-alone, supplemental analyses conducted as special studies. They are off-line and are updated once or twice a year to produce revised product cost data for strategic analysis, not for product costing and periodic internal reporting. In a field study of eight firms, researchers found

> No site considered or intended the activity-based model to be a replacement for the organization's financial transaction system. At all eight cases, this system continued to function as before and was expected to remain in the future. *The activity-based model was treated as a management information system, not as part of the accounting system.* (Emphasis in original.)[10]

Most firms adopting ABC use it for decision making outside the accounting function. In one article, the authors conjecture: "Thousands of companies have adopted or explored the feasibility of adopting ABC. However, we estimate that no more than 10 percent of them now use activity-based management in a significant number of operations. The other 90 percent have given up, or their programs are

---

[8] P Drucker, "Managing for Business Effectiveness," *Harvard Business Review* (May–June 1963), pp. 53–60. Also, see C Horngren, "Management Accounting: This Century and Beyond," *Management Accounting Research*, September 1995, pp. 281–86.

[9] B Goetz, *Management Planning and Control: A Managerial Approach to Industrial Accounting* (New York: McGraw-Hill, 1949), p. 142.

[10] R Cooper, R Kaplan, L Maisel, E Morrissey, and R Oehm, "From ABC to ABM," *Management Accounting*, November 1992, pp. 54–57.

A Nineteenth-Century Example of ABC	Founded around 1813, the Boston Manufacturing Co. produced equipment for cotton and silk mills. This firm's cost accounting system is described in the following passage:

> There was a painstaking tabulation of all direct costs, together with a careful allocation of such costs to the department in which they were incurred. . . . A definite attempt was made to charge many overhead costs to the production accounts. An outstanding example of this attempt to assign such costs to the department in which they were incurred is provided by the company's treatment of executive salaries. The salaries of Paul Moody and Patrick Tracy Jackson were spread over several different accounts, and the allocations were varied from period to period as the supervisory attention of these men shifted. Presumably the basis employed in making these charges was the number of hours . . . devoted by the agent and the treasurer to the various phases of the business.

SOURCE: G Gibb, *The Saco-Lowell Shops* (Cambridge: Harvard University Press, 1950), pp. 50–51, quoted in P Garner, *Evolution of Cost Accounting to 1925* (Montgomery: University of Alabama Press, 1954), p. 84.

stagnating or floundering."[11] The evidence suggests that firms implementing ABC use it for decision making, not control, because firms rarely incorporate the ABC cost allocation bases into their financial reporting of inventories and cost of goods sold.

Two studies conducted by consulting firms report that as many as 60 percent of all U.S. organizations have attempted to implement ABC, but only 20 percent have sustained it. Eight percent continue to use traditional absorption costing methods.[12] A U.K. survey reports that 17.5 percent of the U. K.'s largest firms use ABC and 15.3 percent rejected ABC after assessing it. Of those firms using ABC, half of them use it in only a few applicable parts of their organization.[13]

Several problems exist in implementing ABC.[14] First, to implement ABC, cost analysts use interviews, time logs, and direct observation of the time people spend on various activities to estimate the resource expenses assigned to an activity. Interviewing and surveying employees to get their time allocations is time-consuming and costly. One money center bank required 70,000 employees at over 100 facilities to submit monthly surveys of their time. The bank had 14 full-time people managing the ABC data collection and processing. The high cost to maintain the ABC model has caused many firms to update the information infrequently, leading to out-of-date activity cost driver rates and inaccurate estimates of product and customer costs. Consequently, most ABC models are often not maintained, their cost estimates soon become obsolete, and the firm abandons ABC.

A second problem involves the complexity of many ABC systems. To generate accurate ABC cost estimates, more cost drivers are added to capture the underlying complexity of the various processes performed by the firm. This dramatically increases the demands on the computer model used to store and calculate the cost estimates. One company uses 150 activities in its ABC model to cost 600,000 cost objects (products and customers); running the model monthly requires data estimates, calculations, and storage for more than 2 billion items. The company's computer systems often take days to process one month's data.

---

[11] J Ness and T Cucuzza, "Tapping the Full Potential of ABC," *Harvard Business Review* (July–August 1995).

[12] P Sharman, "The Case for Management Accounting," *Strategic Finance* (October 2003), pp. 43–47.

[13] J Innes, F Mitchell, and D Sinclair, "Activity-Based Costing in the U.K.'s Largest Companies," *Management Accounting Research* (2000), pp. 349–62.

[14] The first two problems are described in R Kaplan and S Anderson, "Time-Driven Activity-Based Costing," *Harvard Business School* (November 2003).

The third problem encountered in ABC is the increased ability of employees and managers to game the numbers. To the extent that ABC numbers are used to evaluate performance or decide which processes or products to outsource, employee welfare is affected. ABC requires people to estimate how they spend their time and identify specific cost drivers. These are inherently subjective estimates that are difficult to verify objectively and can lead to inaccurate estimates of activity-based costs. ABC's inherent subjectivity makes it susceptible to gaming and hence lowers its value in decision control.

Few calls for activity-based costing are based on decision control reasons. The trade-off between decision management and decision control described in Chapter 1 helps to predict some of the observed tendencies:

1. Proponents of activity-based costing are operating managers who want better information for decision making.
2. Most ABC systems are stand-alone, off-line systems. Firms are reluctant to change accounting systems, which are primarily for decision control.
3. Most of the resistance to ABC comes from corporate management and the accounting staff. ABC systems tend to sacrifice decision control for decision management, thereby reducing the usefulness of accounting numbers for decision control.

Activity-based costing systems are most often adopted in plants producing multiple products, where product diversity is large, fixed factory overheads are a large fraction of product costs, and there is increased pressure from competitors. Single-product plants have little trouble computing product costs because all of the costs are assigned to the single product. Product diversity can arise because of different production volumes (some products run in large numbers and others in small volumes) or the products' complexity (some products are simple and others complicated to manufacture). Simple unit-based cost drivers cannot capture the diversity of plants with different product volumes or manufacturing complexities. If fixed factory overhead is a small fraction of total product cost, reallocating a small cost pool using more accurate cost drivers does not cause individual product costs to vary. Finally, firms facing little competition are able to price their products above cost, so that inaccurate average unit costs are not as critical as when competition is driving prices down to or even below average cost. Activity-based costing systems will not be adopted everywhere, and the value of ABC is not the same across all plants.

While much has been written about the benefits of activity-based costing for decision management, few proponents have gone back to companies that experimented with it to follow up on the outcomes and understand why the ABC systems were not fully implemented. In one firm, activity-based costing was implemented and abandoned after a year. The controller explained that under the old system, with just a few cost drivers, everyone understood the weaknesses of the system and accepted its faults. With the new system, managers were constantly arguing over the appropriate cost drivers, because switching cost drivers changed product costs and the managers' performance measures. Real resources were being consumed debating the merits of particular cost drivers. To stop the bickering, the controller abandoned ABC.

Many firms have redesigned their products and production processes with the effect of converting what were once indirect costs into direct costs. These companies set up machines more rapidly. Faster setups mean more setups. These plants

Simplify Operations versus ABC	A small family-owned manufacturing company formed a team of 15 employees to implement ABC. Two years of study and $200,000 later, the committee discovered that low-volume products cause more overhead than high-volume products. However, before fully implementing ABC, this company was bought by Illinois Tool Works, which had a different strategy in mind. Instead of trying to come up with better cost allocations, ITW decided to simplify and eliminate nonvalue-added activities. Instead of implementing ABC, ITW converted the plant to just-in-time (JIT) production, redesigned its production processes, eliminated certain overhead costs, converted indirect costs into direct costs, and dropped low-volume products. The switch to JIT eliminated most setups. The plant adopted a flatter organizational structure by decentralizing more decision-making authority to lower levels and eliminating some levels. The plant now uses direct costing and has eliminated most arbitrary cost allocations. The profitability of the plant has improved. SOURCE: L Tatikonda, D O'Brien, and R Tatikonda, "Succeeding with 80/20," *Management Accounting*, February 1999, pp. 40–44.

Overhead Allocations in the Hitachi VCR Plant	Hitachi, a large Japanese electronics producer, manufactures VCRs in one of its plants. This plant is very heavily automated but continues to allocate overhead based on direct labor, even though the managers know that direct labor does not reflect the cause-and-effect relation between overhead and the overhead cost drivers. The Hitachi managers continue to use direct labor as the allocation base because they are committed to long-term aggressive automation. Taxing direct labor is a way to reduce direct labor and thereby lower production costs. Hitachi's decision to use direct labor as the allocation base is an example of sacrificing decision management for decision control. The Hitachi managers are willing to accept less precise estimates of product costs for decision making because they achieve desirable incentives that further their automation goals. SOURCE: T Hiromoto, "Another Hidden Edge—Japanese Management Accounting," *Harvard Business Review* (July–August 1988).

have fewer workers associated with overhead costs such as moving, storing, inspecting, and expediting. Production is more of a continuous flow process, eliminating the need for work to stop, start, and wait. With a lower fraction of total cost in overhead, activity-based systems are far less valuable. More of the cost is directly traceable to the products. When a high fraction of the total cost of the production process is directly traceable to the products, product costs are more accurate. In addition, when multiple products are produced, firms design cost centers around product lines rather than by functions. Costs are then reported by product line, which avoids allocating costs to individual products within the product line. Activity-based costing systems in these settings add little value over simpler traditional absorption costing systems.[15]

---

[15] See M Sakurai, "The Influence of Factory Automation on Management Accounting Practices: A Study of Japanese Companies," in *Measuring Manufacturing Performance*, ed. R Kaplan (Boston: Harvard Business School, 1989). "Japanese managers and academics actually prefer simple methods for allocating overhead to the more complex activity accounting allocation methods advocated by several U.S. academics" (p. 43).

Concept Questions	Q11–5	What are two purposes for implementing activity-based costing?
	Q11–6	What are some advantages of activity-based costing systems?
	Q11–7	What problems are associated with tracking historical costs?
	Q11–8	How does the trade-off between decision management and decision control affect the form that an absorption cost system takes within a particular firm?
	Q11–9	Under unit-based absorption costing systems, are high- or low-volume products overcosted? Why?

E. Summary

This chapter discusses the second of two major criticisms of traditional absorption costing systems: They can in some circumstances produce misleading or inaccurate estimates of product costs, especially in multiproduct plants producing high- and low-volume products or products of varying complexity. Absorption cost systems typically allocate overhead using unit-level allocation bases, such as direct labor or direct materials. However, overhead costs can vary at the batch and product levels. Products that use relatively greater proportions of batch and product-line costs will be undercosted if unit-level allocation bases are chosen.

The accuracy of product costs can be increased if overhead cost drivers can be identified so as to assign costs in activity centers to products. Greater accuracy in product costs is beneficial in decision making. However, activity-based systems are costly to design and implement. Moreover, these systems exacerbate decision control by giving more discretion over the control system (the accounting system) to lower-level managers, the people these systems are designed to control. Numerous firms have experimented with activity-based costing systems, yet only a minority have adopted ABC and changed their performance evaluation systems to incorporate the new cost system.

Self-Study Problem

Kiddo Inc. (B)

(For the basic data, refer to Chapter 10 self-study problem Kiddo Inc. [A].) Further analysis of Kiddo's production process has allowed it to allocate costs using activity-based costing. Engineering costs, rework expenses, and equipment maintenance and depreciation were estimated for each production line. Product-line costs for the Runner and Pump sneakers are $5 million and $12 million, respectively. Setup costs for each batch are $2,500. The batch size for the Runner is

1,000 pairs of sneakers. The batch size for the Pump in year 1 is 500 pairs and 600 pairs for year 2. Remaining fixed overhead costs total $5,150,000 and were allocated based on direct labor cost.

Required:

a. Prepare a revised income statement for each year using activity-based costing.

b. Explain changes in the net profit between the original cost allocation system and activity-based costing.

Solution:

a. Here are income statements for years 1 and 2 under activity-based costing:

	Year 1		
	Runner	*Pump*	*Total*
Revenue	$160,000,000	$110,400,000	$270,400,000
Expenses:			
Material	70,000,000	42,600,000	112,600,000
Labor	23,000,000	12,000,000	35,000,000
Variable overhead	33,000,000	17,520,000	50,520,000
Gross margin	$ 34,000,000	$ 38,280,000	$ 72,280,000
Batch costs*	12,500,000	12,000,000	24,500,000
Product-line costs†	4,863,813	9,600,000	14,463,813
Fixed overhead‡	3,065,159	1,599,213	4,664,372
Net profit	$ 13,571,028	$ 15,080,787	$ 28,651,815

	Runner	Pump	Total
*Batch Costs			
Cost per batch	$ 2,500	$ 2,500	
× Units sold	5,000,000	2,400,000	
÷ Units per batch	1,000	500	
Allocated batch costs	$12,500,000	$12,000,000	
†Product-Line Costs			
Total product-line costs	$ 5,000,000	$12,000,000	
÷ Units produced	5,140,000	3,000,000	
× Units sold	5,000,000	2,400,000	
Allocated line costs	$ 4,863,813	$ 9,600,000	
‡Fixed Overhead Costs			
Remaining fixed overhead			$ 5,150,000
Units produced	5,140,000	3,000,000	
× Direct labor per pair	$4.60	$5.00	
Total labor cost	$23,644,000	$15,000,000	$38,644,000
Fixed overhead per direct labor $			$ 0.1333
Direct labor of units sold	$23,000,000	$12,000,000	
Fixed overhead allocated (× $0.1333)	$ 3,065,159	$ 1,599,213	

Year 2

	Runner	Pump	Total
Revenue	$160,000,000	$110,400,000	$270,400,000
Expenses:			
Material	70,000,000	42,600,000	112,600,000
Labor	23,000,000	12,000,000	35,000,000
Variable overhead	33,000,000	17,520,000	50,520,000
Gross margin	$ 34,000,000	$ 38,280,000	$ 72,280,000
Batch costs*	12,500,000	10,000,000	22,500,000
Product-line costs†	4,807,692	8,080,808	12,888,500
Fixed overhead‡	2,837,805	1,480,594	4,318,400
Net profit	$ 13,854,502	$ 18,718,598	$ 32,573,100

	Runner	Pump	Total
*Batch Costs			
Cost per batch	$ 2,500	$ 2,500	
× Units sold	5,000,000	2,400,000	
÷ Units per batch	1,000	600	
Allocated batch costs	$12,500,000	$10,000,000	
†Product-Line Costs			
Total product-line costs	$ 5,000,000	$12,000,000	
÷ Units produced	5,200,000	3,564,000	
× Units sold	5,000,000	2,400,000	
Allocated line costs	$ 4,807,692	$ 8,080,808	
‡Fixed Overhead Costs			
Remaining fixed overhead			$ 5,150,000
Units produced	5,200,000	3,564,000	
× Direct labor per pair	$ 4.60	$ 5.00	
Total labor cost	$23,920,000	$ 17,820,000	$41,740,000
Fixed overhead per direct labor $			$ 0.1234
Direct labor of units sold	$23,000,000	$ 12,000,000	
Fixed overhead allocated			
(× $0.1234)	$ 2,837,905	$ 1,480,594	

b. Profits are higher in both years 1 and 2 under activity-based costing than under traditional absorption costing. Under the original allocation system, profits increase in year 2 since more of the fixed overhead was inventoried. Now, the $50 million fixed overhead is split so that a greater portion goes to the Pump line. Since more of the Pump shoes are inventoried than the Runner shoes, more of the overhead is also inventoried. Consider the costs per unit for the two years under both allocation systems:

Per-Unit Summary	Runner	Pump
Price	$32.00	$46.00
Material	14.00	17.75
Labor	4.60	5.00
Variable overhead	6.60	7.30
Gross margin	$ 6.80	$15.95

Per-Unit Summary	Runner	Pump
Year 1		
Absorption costing:		
Fixed overhead*	$ 5.93	$ 6.45
Net profit	$ 0.87	$ 9.50
ABC costing:		
Gross margin	$ 6.80	$15.95
Batch costs	2.50	5.00
Product-line costs	0.97	4.00
Fixed costs	0.61	0.67
Total costs	$ 4.08	$ 9.67
Net profit	$ 2.72	$ 6.28
Year 2		
Gross margin	$6.80	$15.95
Absorption costing:		
Fixed overhead	5.51	5.99
Net profit	$1.29	$ 9.96
ABC costing:		
Gross margin	$6.80	$15.95
Batch costs	2.50	4.17
Product-line costs	0.96	3.37
Fixed costs	0.57	0.62
Total costs	$4.03	$ 8.16
Net profit	$2.77	$ 7.79

*From Chapter 10, Kiddo Inc. (A)

For both years under both systems, the direct costs and selling price remain constant, providing margins of $6.80 and $15.95 for the Runner and the Pump, respectively. The fixed overhead in cost of goods sold is divided by number of units sold to calculate fixed overhead per unit for both years under the original system. Under that system, net profits increase from $0.87 to $1.29 per Runner and $9.50 to $9.96 per Pump. When the overhead is divided into product-line and batch costs, the cost structure changes significantly. The Runner's net profits jump to $2.72 and $2.77 for the two years. Profits on the Pump in turn drop to $6.28 and $7.79.

Problems

P 11–1:   Activity-Based Costing

Required:

    a. What is activity-based costing and how does it differ from traditional absorption costing?

    b. Describe the advantages and disadvantages of activity-based costing systems.

P 11–2:   The Maui Seminar

Your boss, the vice president of corporate accounting, has just returned from a two-week seminar in Maui on activity-based cost accounting. He says he wants to completely overhaul the company's existing absorption-based accounting system. "Activity-based costing is the wave of the future and will allow us to make better product-line decisions and therefore be more competitive in the marketplace," he asserts.

He wants you to start implementation immediately, but he would like your comments before you begin. How do you respond?

SOURCE: L McGinn.

P 11–3:   GAMMA

GAMMA produces over a hundred different types of residential water faucets at its Delta, Florida, plant. This plant uses activity-based costing to calculate product costs. The following table summarizes the plant's overhead for the year and the cost drivers used for each activity center:

Summary of Plant Overhead and Activity Centers

Activity Center	Total Cost (Millions of Dollars)	Cost Driver	Amount of Cost Driver	Activity Cost per Unit of Cost Driver
Materials handling	$20.8	Direct materials	$130 million	$0.16
Purchasing	13.8	Part numbers	800	$17,250
Set-up labor	6.8	Batches	500	$13,600
Engineering	10.9	Number of products	125	$87,200
Occupancy	16.2	Direct labor	$90 million	$0.18
Total plant overhead	$68.5			

One faucet model GAMMA manufactures is Explorer. Its total product cost is as follows:

Direct labor			$121,700
Direct materials			90,500
Materials handling	$90,500	$0.16	14,480
Purchasing	9	17,250	155,250
Setup	8	13,600	108,800
Engineering	1	87,200	87,200
Occupancy	$121,700	$0.18	21,906
Total cost			$599,836
Number of units manufactured			12,500
Product cost per unit			$ 47.99

Required:

Calculate the product cost per unit of the Explorer faucet using absorption costing where plant overhead is assigned to products using direct labor dollars.

P 11–4: ABC and Volume Changes

Required:

a. What differentiates unit-level costs, batch-level costs, product-line costs, and production-sustaining costs? Give examples.

b. "One advantage of an activity-based cost system is that it prevents unit costs from rising when volumes fall and unit costs from falling as volumes rise." True or false? Discuss why.

P 11–5: Milan Pasta

At its Lyle Avenue plant, Milan Pasta produces two types of pasta: spaghetti and fettuccine. The two pastas are produced on the same machines, with different settings and slightly different raw materials. The fettuccine, being a wider noodle and more susceptible to curling edges, requires more inspection time. The total daily cost of inspection is $500. Here are daily production data for the two products:

	Spaghetti	Fettuccine
Pounds produced	6,000	2,000
Machine minutes per pound	0.20	0.40
Inspection hours per product line	8	24

Required:

a. Calculate the inspection cost per pound of pasta using traditional absorption costing with number of machine hours as the allocation base.

b. Calculate the inspection cost per pound of pasta using activity-based costing. Assume inspection time is the cost driver.

c. Analyze why inspection costs differ between the methods used in (*a*) and (*b*).

P 11–6: Implementing ABC

Critically discuss the following quotation:

ABC (activity-based cost) information, by itself, does not invoke actions and decisions leading to improved profits and operating performance. . . . For ABC systems to be effective, everyone in the company—from top management to operating personnel—must view them as cost management tools rather than as accounting tools. To achieve this objective, the accounting or finance department must relinquish ownership of these systems to the users. If accounting or finance fails to understand this key point, then ABC is unlikely to succeed. . . . While traditional systems are the property of accounting and are used to support the financial accounting process, successful ABC systems are owned by the functions and are designed to support the needs of cost management, not financial accounting. The result is a reduction in the role of accounting in the management of costs. [M]ost companies that implement ABC systems run them in parallel to their financial accounting systems. Parallel systems remove the risk of compromising the cost management capabilities of ABC to accommodate financial accounting rules and regulations.[16]

---

[16] R Cooper, "Look Out, Management Accountants," *Management Accounting*, May 1996, pp. 20–21.

P 11–7: Astin Car Stereos

Astin Car Stereos manufactures and distributes four different car stereos. The accompanying table summarizes the unit sales, selling prices, and manufacturing costs of each stereo.

ASTIN CAR STEREOS
Summary of Operations
Current Fiscal Year

	A 90	B200	B300	Z7
Sales price	$100	$120	$140	$180
Manufacturing cost (all variable)	$80	$90	$100	$120
Units sold	15,000	13,000	12,000	9,000

Selling and distribution (S&D) expenses are $1,270,000. They are treated as a period cost and written off to the income statement. To assess the relative profitability of each product, S&D expenses are allocated to each product based on sales revenue.

Upon further investigation of the S&D expenses, half are shown to be for marketing and advertising. Each product has its own advertising and marketing budget, administered by one of four marketing managers. Z7, the premier product, is advertised heavily. Forty percent of the marketing and advertising budget goes toward Z7, 30 percent to B300, 20 percent to B200, and 10 percent to A90.

The remaining S&D expenses consist of distribution and administration costs (25 percent) and selling costs (25 percent). The distribution and administration department is responsible for arranging shipping and for billing the customers. (Customers pay transportation charges directly to the common carrier.) It also handles federal licensing of the car radios. Upon analysis, each product line places equal demands on the distribution and administration department and each consumes about the same resources as the others. Selling costs consist primarily of commissions paid to independent salespeople. The commissions are based on gross margin on the product (sales revenue less manufacturing cost).

Required:

a. Allocate all S&D expenses based only on sales revenue. Identify the most and least profitable products.

b. Allocate all S&D expenses based only on the advertising and marketing budget. Identify the most and least profitable products.

c. Allocate all S&D expenses. Use the advertising and marketing budget for advertising and marketing costs, the demand for these resources by product for distribution and administration costs, and commissions for selling costs. Identify the most and least profitable products.

d. Discuss the managerial implications of the various schemes. Why do the different schemes result in different product-line profits? Which product is really the most profitable? The least profitable?

P 11-8: Haking Cameras

Haking Cameras, a Hong Kong firm, assembles digital cameras in its plant located in the south of China. It assembles cameras for Kodak, Fuji, and Canon. These companies purchase the parts for their cameras and send them to Haking, which builds the complete digital cameras.

Haking uses an ABC system to cost the three digital cameras that it assembles. There are two activity cost pools comprising total factory overhead: parts management costs, and engineering and general factory costs. Parts management arranges for the delivery, unpacking, and inspection of each part and then inventories the parts and delivers them as needed by the assembly department to build the cameras. The number of parts in each camera is the assumed cost driver of the parts management activity cost pool. The engineering and general factory activity cost pool consists of all other indirect costs incurred in the plant. The cost driver of this activity cost pool is assumed to be the number of different digital cameras assembled during the year. There are only three different cameras being assembled this year.

The following table computes the ABC cost of each camera in Hong Kong dollars (HK$).

	Kodak 86	Fuji 910	Canon 135	Total
Parts per product	30	45	75	150
Percent parts	20%	30%	50%	100%
Parts inventory management cost				$536,000
Allocated parts management cost	$107,200	$160,800	$268,000	$536,000
Engineering and general factory cost				$630,000
Allocated by camera line	$210,000	$210,000	$210,000	$630,000
Total cost allocated to each camera line	$317,200	$370,800	$478,000	$1,166,000
÷ Number of cameras assembled	8,000	5,000	4,000	
Total factory overhead per camera	$39.65	$74.16	$119.50	
Direct labor assembly cost per camera	$11.75	$15.05	$ 22.80	
Total cost per camera	$51.40	$89.21	$142.30	

Required:

a. Haking is considering adopting a traditional absorption costing system where all the factory costs (parts inventory management and engineering and factory overhead) are allocated to cameras based on the direct labor cost of assembling each camera. Calculate the absorption-based full cost per camera of assembling each of the three camera types using total direct labor cost to allocate all the factory overhead costs.

b. Discuss some possible reasons why Haking might want to shift from its ABC system to absorption costing.

P 11-9: Tilist Golf

Tilist Golf is a premier producer of golf clubs and golf balls. The Ball Division makes two types of balls: a professional ball (the "Masters") played by professional and top amateur players, and a mass-market ball (the "Distance") which targets weekend players. Although most golf balls are very similar in construction and performance, slight differences exist between them. The Master ball is a little softer and allows skilled players to put more spin on the ball for control. The Distance ball is a little harder with a more durable cover. While the two balls perform similarly, many golfers perceive the differences are larger than they really are, especially across ball manufacturers. Most golfers have a favorite brand of ball. Golf ball manufacturers compete over ball design (dimples, cover, core composition), price, and marketing. The principal way balls are marketed is through the endorsements of major professional golfers. Tilist pays professional golfers up to $500,000 per year to wear Tilist hats or shirts during tournaments, to allow Tilist to use their image in commercials, and to play Tilist balls (which are provided free to the professional) in all tournaments.

Tilist's Ball Division has separate profit centers managing each type of ball. The following table summarizes the operations of the Ball Division for last year.

	Masters	Distance
Price per dozen	$26	$7
Variable cost per dozen	$12	$3
Quantity sold	300,000	25,000,000

In addition, the Ball Division has $61.429 million of overhead, consisting of sponsorships, promotions, R&D, and so forth.

Required:

a. Prepare income statements for the two ball types after allocating the $61.429 million of overhead based on revenue.

b. Senior management of the Ball Division has undertaken a review of the cost allocation methodology used in part (*a*). They hired an ABC consultant and formed an ABC task force to design a new allocation scheme that better allocates the $61.429 million overhead to the two ball types. The overhead consists of the following items:

Promotional samples	$ 1,075,000
Sponsorships	18,500,000
Advertising	34,837,000
R&D	3,450,000
Ball Division headquarters expenses	3,567,000
Overhead	$61,429,000

Promotional samples consist of Tilist balls given away to touring pros under Tilist sponsorships, marketing opportunities, and charity events. $950,000 of Masters and $125,000 of Distance balls comprise the $1,075,000 of promotional samples.

The $18.5 million of sponsorships consists of payments to touring professional golfers expected to do well in televised tournaments. Sponsored pros are paid to play Tilist balls and wear the Tilist name on their hats or shirts. Sponsorships are aimed at increasing Tilist's name recognition across all types of golfers. Senior managers and the ABC task force believe the sponsorships expenditure is best assigned to the two divisions based on the number of balls sold.

The advertising expenditure of $34,837,000 covers television and print ads ($1.35 million for Masters and $33.487 million for Distance).

Tilist has a research lab where it designs new balls by experimenting with different dimple patterns, covers, and cores. About one-third of the R&D effort is devoted to improving the Masters, and two-thirds of the R&D effort is directed toward improving the Distance.

After an extensive study of the various functions of the Ball Division's headquarters expenses, including the time spent by the various personnel in the two ball divisions, the ABC task force has agreed that 40 percent of the $3.567 million headquarters expenses should be allocated to Masters and the remainder to Distance.

Prepare income statements based on the findings of the ABC task force.

c. Based on the income statements prepared in part (a) (overhead allocated using revenues) and part (b) (ABC overhead allocations), what conclusions can you draw about the relative profitability of the two ball types?

P 11–10:   DVDS

DVDS manufactures and sells DVD players in two countries. It manufactures two models—Basic and Custom—out of the same plant. The Basic DVD has fewer options and provides lower-quality output than the Custom DVD. The basic model is sold only in a developing country and the custom model is sold only in a developed country. DVDS pays income taxes to the country where the final sale of the DVD player takes place. The following table summarizes DVDS operations.

DVDS
Summary of Operations
Current Year

	Basic	Custom
Quantity produced and sold	60,000	70,000
Price	$75	$140
Direct labor/unit	$15	$30
Direct materials/unit	$40	$80
Income tax rate	15%	35%

Besides direct materials and direct labor, manufacturing overhead amounts to $2 million and is currently assigned to products based on direct labor dollars. Manufacturing overhead is a fixed cost (does not vary with the number of units produced).

Required:

a. Calculate the unit manufacturing costs of the Basic and Custom DVD models using traditional absorption costing. Manufacturing overhead is allocated based on direct labor dollars.

b. DVDS hires a consulting firm to analyze its costing methods. After performing an extensive review, the consultants determine that the vast majority of the $2 million of overhead varies with the number of different parts in the two DVD models. The number of parts drives purchasing department activities. More engineering time is spent on the more complex Custom DVD models. More accounting depreciation of assembly and testing equipment is incurred producing the Custom DVD model than the Basic DVD model. The Basic DVD has 140 different parts and the Custom DVD model has 160 different parts. Calculate the unit manufacturing costs of the Basic and Custom DVD models using activity-based costing.

c. Should DVDS change its costing methodology from its traditional absorption costing to ABC? Explain why it should or should not.

P 11–11:   Roderiques

Roderiques manufactures five products (P1, P2, P3, M1, and M2) in two product lines (P product line and M product line). The firm uses activity-based costing to allocate the four activity centers comprising manufacturing overhead to the five products. It assigns batch-level costs using number of batches, product-level costs using number of product lines, part-level costs using number of parts in each product, and facility-level costs using direct labor dollars.

The following table summarizes the total costs in each of the four activity centers:

Batch-level costs	$ 895,000
Product-level costs	1,120,000
Facility-level costs	1,392,000
Part-level costs	943,000

The following table summarizes the operating data for each product:

Activity Centers	P1	P2	P3	M1	M2	Total
Number of batches	550	500	425	350	210	2,035
Batch size	100	90	90	80	60	420
Number of units produced	55,000	45,000	38,250	28,000	12,600	178,850
Part numbers per product	28	28	30	35	40	161
Total direct labor	$187,000	$171,000	$160,650	$156,800	$122,220	$797,670

Based on the data in the preceding table, the firm calculates the following percentages used by the ABC system to allocate costs to the five products. Note that product-line costs are first allocated to the two product lines evenly and then assigned to each product within the product line based on units.

ABC Allocation Percentages Used to Allocate Activity Center Costs to Products

	P1	P2	P3	M1	M2	Total
Number of batches	27.03%	24.57%	20.88%	17.20%	10.32%	100.00%
Product-level	16.67	16.67	16.67	25.00	25.00	100.00
Part numbers	17.39	17.39	18.63	21.74	24.84	100.00
Facility level costs	23.44	21.44	20.14	19.66	15.32	100.00

The final table presents the ABC product costs based on the preceding data.

ABC Product Costs

	P1	P2	P3	M1	M2
Direct material	$13.50	$17.25	$22.10	$24.60	$ 42.00
Direct labor	3.40	3.80	4.20	5.60	9.70
Batch-level costs	4.40	4.89	4.89	5.50	7.33
Product-level costs	3.39	4.15	4.88	10.00	22.22
Part-level costs	2.98	3.64	4.59	7.32	18.59
Facility-level costs	5.93	6.63	7.33	9.77	16.93
Total cost	$33.60	$40.36	$47.99	$62.79	$116.77

Senior management at Roderiques is considering converting back to a more traditional absorption costing system. In particular, they want to allocate batch-level costs and part-level costs using direct material dollars and product-level costs and facility-level costs using direct labor dollars.

Required:

a. Calculate product costs per unit for each of the five products, where batch-level and part-level costs are allocated based on total direct material dollars, and product-level and facility-level costs are allocated based on total direct labor dollars.

b. Describe how the product costs per unit change relative to those computed using activity-based costing. What is causing product costs to change in the particular ways that they do?

c. Offer some plausible reasons why management might want to abandon ABC and revert to a more traditional product-costing methodology.

P 11–12: True Cost Manufacturing, Inc.

True Cost Manufacturing, Inc., manufactures and sells large business equipment for the office and business markets. The primary function of Manufacturing is to provide components and subassemblies for the profit centers within the company. To maintain competitiveness, each profit center can purchase parts either from Manufacturing or from outside firms. Manufacturing operates as a cost center and charges the profit centers for the full cost of the parts. Costs are computed once a

TABLE 1   Finishing Annual Cost Structure

	Annual Cost	
Fixed asset depreciation	$400,000	$4,000,000 machine purchased 2 years ago
Tank operations costs	250,000	Cost to operate tanks—fixed cost, not volume dependent
Tank material cost	50,000	Cost to operate tanks—$0.007575/inch
Variable labor cost	210,000	$10/hour × 21,000 hours of operation
Total	$910,000	

year using full absorption costing. The volume of parts used to calculate costs is provided by the profit centers to Manufacturing in August; the fiscal year begins in January. With these numbers, Manufacturing projects costs per part for the year. These cost estimates are then used throughout the year to charge the profit centers. Any over/underabsorbed overhead goes directly to the bottom line of the company, not to any of the profit centers.

Within Manufacturing there is a department called finishing. The finishing department provides a service to other Manufacturing departments and profit centers as well as generating some external sales. Types of finishing include painting and plating. The facility has large investments in fixed assets in both automation and environmental compliance for finishing. The finishing operation believes it provides value to customers through its high quality and its close location to the manufacturing departments.

During the past year, the profit centers have begun taking work away from Manufacturing and giving it to outside vendors with lower quoted costs. Manufacturing then has lower volumes and has to raise the prices on the products it is producing, causing the profit centers to send even more work out. Manufacturing feels it is caught in a death spiral.

The death spiral situation has affected finishing the most. The finishing department is currently operating at 30 percent of capacity and has facilities that are too large for the low volume of work. Table 1 summarizes the data pertaining to finishing. Fixed costs make up 71 percent of the current cost structure. Other manufacturing departments are beginning to tell finishing that they will be sending their work out to get plating and painting so as not to lose any work because of the high internal cost of finishing.

Finishing is trying to attract business from outside True Cost Manufacturing. The external sales guidelines require a 35 percent profit margin applied to the full cost for all external work. With the current low level of work and high fixed costs, finishing cannot attract external sales due to cost.

In an effort to gain control of the true cost drivers of the business, the manager of the finishing operation has implemented activity-based costing. Tables 2 and 3 project the cost for products and volumes for one plating operation. The problem that the finishing manager now faces is that the manufacturing departments are about to send the 12-inch and 18-inch work to an outside shop due to lower costs.

In implementing activity-based costing, the manager thinks he has truly identified the proper system. The larger parts tend to run in smaller lot sizes and

TABLE 2   Finishing Costs before and after Activity-Based Costing

	Volume of Pieces per Year*	Old Cost per Piece	Activity-Based Cost per Piece	Outside Cost per Piece
3" parts	1,000,000	$0.50	$0.31	$0.30
6" parts	200,000	1.00	1.00	1.10
12" parts	50,000	1.20	2.00	0.90
18" parts	100,000	1.50	3.00	1.20

*This volume of work uses only 30 percent of capacity.

TABLE 3   Forecasted Costs

	Old Cost	Activity-Based Cost	Outside Cost
3" parts	$500,000	$310,000	$300,000
6" parts	200,000	200,000	220,000
12" parts	60,000	100,000	45,000
18" parts	150,000	300,000	120,000
Total per year	$910,000	$910,000	$685,000

generate more paperwork. Smaller parts tend to be run in larger lot sizes and generate less paperwork.

In a recent meeting with the management of the manufacturing department and profit centers, it was stated that the installation of activity-based costing is in direct conflict with the change in the mix of work from small parts to large parts and the need to run smaller lot sizes. The manufacturing department and profit centers would like to pursue just-in-time manufacturing and further reduce the lot sizes for both small and large parts. During this meeting, the profit centers and manufacturing departments said the implementation of activity-based costing would force them to move their work out of the finishing department to outside shops.

Required:

   a. Analyze the current situation in this company. What should be done?
   b. Compare and comment on the costs before and after ABC is implemented.
   c. Has finishing management made a mistake by installing activity-based costing?

SOURCE: R Bradley, J Buescher, L Campbell, and B Florance.

P 11–13:   O'Reilly Manufacturing

O'Reilly Manufacturing produces three models of a product: Super, Supreme, and Ultra. These models are basically the same design, but different quality standards are applied in the production process. Frequent production line stops, adjustments, and startups cause a certain amount of scrap costs. Also, scrap occurs when inspectors reject a product for not meeting specifications. Once rejected, the product has no commercial value and is hauled away. All costs incurred to produce a scrapped product are charged to a scrap account, which is part of overhead. The budgeted operating statement for the firm, by product, follows.

O'REILLY MANUFACTURING
Budgeted Operating Statement

	Super	Supreme	Ultra	Total
Unit volume	85,000	42,000	13,000	
Selling price	$205	$225	$235	
Revenue	$17,425,000	$9,450,000	$3,055,000	$29,930,000
Less:				
Raw materials	$ 8,500,000	$4,200,000	$1,300,000	$14,000,000
Direct labor*	5,312,500	3,150,000	975,000	9,437,500
Overhead†	3,478,245	2,062,395	638,360	6,179,000
Total cost	$17,290,745	$9,412,395	$2,913,360	$29,616,500
Profits	$　134,255	$　37,605	$　141,640	$　313,500

*Direct labor cost is $25 per hour.
†Overhead costs are allocated to products based on direct labor dollars.

Overheads consist of

Depreciation	$3,500,000
Indirect labor	450,000
Scrap	1,679,000
Other	550,000
Total	$6,179,000

	Super	Supreme	Ultra
Direct labor hours per unit	2.5 hours	3 hours	3 hours
Total scrap	$850,000	$504,000	$325,000
Profits per unit	$1.58	$0.90	$10.90

Management is concerned about the relatively low profit per unit on the Supreme line as compared with the Ultra line and is considering a variety of marketing strategies to increase sales of Ultra since its profit margin is substantially higher.

Required:

Critically analyze management's conclusion that profits are substantially higher on Ultra. Present supporting figures to back up your analysis and conclusions.

P 11–14:　Friendly Grocer

Friendly Grocer has three departments in its store: beverages, dairy and meats, and canned and packaged foods. Each department is headed by a departmental manager. Operating results for the last month (in thousands) are given in the table.

	Beverages	Dairy and Meats	Canned and Packaged Foods	Total
Sales	$250.00	$470.00	$620.00	$1,340.00
Direct costs:				
Cost of goods sold (COGS)	200.00	329.00	527.00	1,056.00
Indirect costs:				
SG&A (20% of COGS)	40.00	65.80	105.40	211.20
Operating income	$ 10.00	$ 75.20	$(12.40)	$ 72.80

The direct costs consist of the cost of goods sold. Indirect costs consist of selling, general, and administrative (SG&A) costs and are allocated to each department at the rate of 20 percent of costs of goods sold. Based on the preceding report, beverages had operating income of $10,000, dairy and meats had operating income of $75,200, and canned and packaged foods lost $12,400.

Senior management is concerned that the allocation of costs might be distorting the relative profitability of the three departments. Further analysis of the SG&A account yields the following breakdown:

Shelf space costs	$ 90.00
Handling costs	20.00
Coupon costs	15.00
Shrinkage	28.00
Other indirect costs	58.20
Total	$211.20

Shelf space costs consist of store occupancy costs such as depreciation on the building and fixtures, utilities, store maintenance, property taxes, and insurance. Beverages make up 25 percent of the shelf space, dairy and meats make up 35 percent of the space, and canned and packaged goods make up 40 percent of the shelf space.

Handling costs consist of the labor required to stock the shelves and remove outdated products. The beverage suppliers (Coca-Cola, Pepsi, etc.) provide the labor to shelve their products (i.e., the beverage delivery people stock their products on the shelf). Dairy and meats' labor costs for stocking are three-quarters of the handling costs; canned and package foods' labor and handling costs are one-quarter of the total.

Coupon costs consist of the labor costs to process the redeemed coupons. Dairy and meats do not have any coupons. Twenty percent of the coupons redeemed are for beverages and 80 percent are for packaged and canned foods.

Shrinkage consists of the cost of products spoiled, broken, and stolen. Shrinkage by product category comes to

Beverages	$ 1
Dairy and meats	21
Canned and packaged foods	6

The remaining indirect costs are allocated based on cost of goods sold.

Required:

   a. Apply an activity-based costing system and recalculate the operating income of the three departments.

   b. Based on the statement you prepared in part (*a*), write a short memo to management discussing the revised operating income of the three departments and which statement (yours or the one in the question) management should use.

P 11–15:   Houston Milling

Houston Milling is a subcontractor to Pratt & Whitney, which makes jet engines. Houston Milling makes two different fuel pump housings for two Pratt & Whitney jet engines: the A11 housing and the D43. These pump housings are received from Pratt & Whitney, which buys them from an outside (independent) foundry and ships them to Houston for precision machining. Houston performs two machining operations on the housings. These are performed in two separate machining departments (Department 1 and Department 2). Both housings, A11 and D43, require machining in both Departments 1 and 2. Before the parts are machined, the machines must first be set up, which includes cleaning the machine, checking the tools in the machine, adjusting the tolerances, and then finally machining some trial parts. Houston's current accounting system tracks the number of setups and direct labor hours used by each part. Table 1 summarizes the indirect costs of producing A11 and D43. (The direct costs such as direct labor and materials are ignored to simplify the computations.)

Setup and machine hours in the two departments are pooled into two cost pools: setup and machining. Table 1 allocates the costs in these two pools to the two products. Under this accounting system, A11 has indirect costs of $8,600 and D43 has indirect costs of $6,400. Management believes that the current accounting system is not producing accurate costs for the two products because the two cost pools are too aggregate. They decide to disaggregate the data and use four cost pools. They collect some additional data, which are summarized in Table 2.

TABLE 1   **Houston Milling Allocated Indirect Costs
of Producing Parts A11 and D43**

	Functions		
	Setup	*Machining*	*Total*
Indirect cost	$5,000	$10,000	$15,000
Allocation base	Number of setups	Direct labor hours	
Usage: A11	10	66	
D43	15	34	
Total	25	100	
Allocation rate	$200/setup	$100/DL hr.	
Allocations: A11	$2,000	$ 6,600	$ 8,600
D43	3,000	3,400	6,400
Total	$5,000	$10,000	$15,000

Required:

a. Calculate revised cost allocations based on the disaggregated data in Table 2. Number of setups is used to allocate the indirect cost of setups in both Departments 1 and 2 and direct labor hours are used to allocate the machining costs in Departments 1 and 2.

b. Prepare a short memo describing the pros and cons of the revised allocated indirect costs in (*a*) compared to those in Table 1.

c. After completing the analysis in (*a*) and (*b*), some additional data are collected from a special study of setup hours and machine hours in the two departments. These data are presented in Table 3. In particular, setup hours and machine hours are collected in the two departments. Management now believes that setup hours and machine hours more accurately reflect the true cause-and-effect relations of setup costs and machining costs in Departments 1 and 2 than number of setups and direct labor hours, respectively.

   Based on the data presented in Table 3, calculate revised cost allocations for A11 and D43. Setup costs in Departments 1 and 2 are to be allocated based on setup hours, and machining costs in Departments 1 and 2 are to be allocated based on machine hours.

d. Compare the total product costs for A11 and D43 in Table 1 and parts (*a*) and (*c*). What conclusions can you draw?

TABLE 2   **Houston Milling Disaggregated Cost Pool Data**

	Setup		Machining		
	Department 1	*Department 2*	*Department 1*	*Department 2*	*Total*
Total cost	$3,000	$2,000	$8,000	$2,000	$15,000
Allocation base	Number of setups	Number of setups	Direct labor hours	Direct labor hours	
Usage: A11	7	3	32	34	
D43	13	2	18	16	
Total	20	5	50	50	

TABLE 3   **Houston Milling Setup Hours and Machine Hours in Departments 1 and 2**

	Department 1		Department 2	
	Setup	*Machining*	*Setup*	*Machining*
Total cost	$3,000	$8,000	$2,000	$2,000
Allocation base	Setup hours	Machine hours	Setup hours	Machine hours
Usage: A11	15	115	6	120
D43	15	85	4	80
Total	30	200	10	200

P 11–16: Sanchez Gadgets

Sanchez Gadgets purchases innovative home kitchen gadgets from around the world (such as a kitchen torch, a pasta maker, and an automatic salad spinner) and sells them to specialty cooking retail stores. Sanchez has a marketing department that locates and purchases the innovative gadgets and prepares price lists and catalogs for Sanchez's direct selling force. Sanchez's salespeople are assigned geographic sales territories and are responsible for all the specialty kitchen stores in their geographic territories.

Management at Sanchez is concerned that with over 450 different items it is currently carrying too many different SKUs (SKUs are "stock keeping units"). Management is currently looking for a methodology to eliminate unprofitable SKUs. To focus on developing that methodology, assume that Sanchez has just four SKUs: SKU1, SKU2, SKU3, and SKU4. The following data summarize the current sales, selling prices, and cost (purchase price plus freight) for each SKU:

	SKU 1	SKU 2	SKU 3	SKU 4
Wholesale price (to retailer)	$51.00	$13.00	$85.00	$7.00
Cost (including all freight)	$29.00	$8.00	$49.00	$5.00
Sales volume	12,000	25,000	8,000	30,000

Sanchez purchases items for sale and inventories them. The cost of inventorying each item (including the opportunity cost of financing the item) is 20 percent of the annual cost of the item. So if 100 units of a gadget are sold each year, and the cost of the item is $4, Sanchez's inventory holding cost is $80 (20% × 100 × $4).

The annual cost of the marketing department is $135,000. This amount consists of the salaries and fringe benefits of the employees who purchase the products and prepare the catalogs and price lists. Management determines that marketing department costs vary with the number of SKUs.

The annual cost of the direct sales force is $350,000. This amount consists of the salaries, fringe benefits, and travel expenses of the salespeople who call on the retail specialty kitchen stores to sell Sanchez gadgets. After extensive conversations with the salespeople, management believes that the salespeople spend their time in proportion to the sales volume of the gadgets. In other words, if a particular gadget accounts for 10 percent of Sanchez's total revenue, then the sales force spends about 10 percent of its time selling that item.

Required:

a. Design a reporting methodology that identifies possible SKUs that Sanchez should consider dropping from its product mix. Using your methodology, compute the profitability of each of the four SKUs.

b. Based on your analysis in part (*a*), which SKUs should Sanchez drop? Which ones should Sanchez retain?

c. Discuss the critical assumptions underlying your analysis in part (*a*).

P 11–17: Wedig Diagnostics

Wedig Diagnostics manufactures two laser photometers that are used in preparing DNA tests. The U.S. model is designed for use in the U.S. and the EU model is designed to meet the specifications in most of the European Union. Both models are manufactured in the U.S. The EU models are shipped to Wedig's wholly owned European subsidiary, which sells them. All units manufactured are sold. The following table summarizes the selling prices, direct materials and labor, and number of units sold.

	U.S. Model	EU Model
Selling price/unit	$2,500	$2,200
Direct materials/unit	$235	$260
Direct labor/unit	$560	$500
Number of units sold annually	15,000	16,800

The EU units are sold in U.S. dollars. Wedig has total manufacturing overhead of $39 million annually. This overhead is allocated to both U.S. and EU models using total direct labor dollars. Wedig transfers its EU model to its European subsidiary at full cost (direct materials and labor plus allocated overhead). Assume that Wedig pays U.S. taxes only on the profits it makes on sales in the U.S. and the Wedig EU subsidiary pays taxes only on the profits it makes on sales in the EU. The U.S. income tax rate is 30 percent and the Wedig European subsidiary has a tax rate of 15 percent.

Wedig hires a consulting firm to perform an ABC analysis of its overhead costing methodology. This analysis reveals that the $39 million of overhead consists of three cost pools: batch-related costs ($12 million), parts-related costs ($9 million), and direct labor-related costs ($18 million). Each model is produced in batches, and batch-related costs consist of engineering, quality control, and machining costs that vary with the number of batches produced. The U.S. model is produced in 45 batches each year and the EU model is produced in 55 batches a year.

The U.S. and EU models differ in terms of the number of different parts in each unit. The U.S. model has 40 different part numbers and the EU model has 80 different part numbers. Parts-related costs consist of the costs of operating the purchasing department (excluding the costs of the parts purchased), inspecting the parts upon arrival, inventorying the parts, and managing the parts inventory. Parts-related costs vary with the number of part numbers in each product. Finally, the direct labor-related costs consist of human resources, accounting, and other overhead costs that vary with the amount of direct labor in each model.

Required:

a. Calculate the unit manufacturing cost of the U.S. and EU models using total direct labor dollars to allocate the $39 million of manufacturing overhead.

b. Calculate the unit manufacturing cost of the U.S. and EU models using the ABC analysis to allocate the $39 million of manufacturing overhead.

c. Prepare income statements (including income tax expense) for Wedig and its European subsidiary using the unit manufacturing costs calculated in part (a) (overhead is allocated using total direct labor dollars).

d. Prepare income statements (including income tax expense) for Wedig and its European subsidiary using the unit manufacturing costs calculated in part (b) (overhead is allocated using the ABC analysis).

e. Discuss the advantages and disadvantages of using direct labor versus ABC to allocate the $39 million of overhead.

P 11–18:   Toby Manufacturing

Toby Manufacturing produces three different products in the same plant and uses a job order costing system to estimate product costs. A flexible budget is used to forecast overhead costs. Total budgeted fixed factory overhead is $450,000 and variable overhead is 120 percent of direct labor dollars.

Projected volumes, selling prices, and direct costs for the three products for the next calendar year are as follows:

	Product AAA	Product BBB	Product CCC
Projected number of units	6,000	3,000	1,000
Direct materials per unit	$22	$25	$30
Direct labor per unit	$11	$12	$16
Selling price	$98	$115	$140

Upon closer analysis of the overhead account, warehousing costs are determined to be a major fraction of overhead. The manufacturing process requires six operations. Between operations, intermediate products are moved and warehoused until the next production stage. Each product requires 10 days of processing time to complete all six operations. But the products have different total cycle times because of different waiting times between operations. Cycle time is the total time from when raw materials are ordered until the product is completed and shipped. Product AAA has the shortest cycle time (20 days) because the large volume allows more accurate forecasts and more continuous scheduling of production. Product BBB has a total cycle time of 40 days; product CCC has a total cycle time of 50 days. Product BBB and CCC have longer warehousing times of work in process because of more frequent scheduling changes and supplier delays.

Half of what is currently treated as fixed overhead cost is involved in the warehousing function.

Required:

a. Prepare a pro forma income statement by product line for the year based on full absorption costing. Product costs should include overhead assigned on direct labor cost.

b. Prepare a revised pro forma income statement by product line using activity-based costing.

c. Comment on the differences.

P 11–19:   Kay Enterprises

Kay Enterprises is a small, family-owned and managed business. It has a patented production process for manufacturing a digital switch used in large telephone switches. It manufactures two models in its plant in Atlanta, Georgia. The U.S. model is sold to U.S.-based telephone companies and the European switch is transferred to Kay's wholly owned subsidiary in Ireland, where it is sold to European telephone companies. U.S. switches are sold only in the United States and

European switches can be sold only in Europe. One brother, Lloyd Kay, manages the U.S. company and his brother, Colin Kay, manages the Irish firm. The two switches share the same proprietary production process but have different design specifications to match the different telephone systems.

All switches manufactured are sold; Kay does not have any work-in-process or finished goods inventories. Because of the patented nature of the production process, Kay faces very little competition for its switches either in the United States or Europe. This allows the firm to set a relatively high price above its costs.

The following table summarizes the annual number of U.S. and European switches produced and the costs of manufacturing each switch. All manufacturing overhead of $24 million is a fixed cost that does not vary with the number of switches produced. Overhead is allocated to units produced based on direct labor dollars.

	Switches	
	European	*United States*
Units produced (000s)	1,000	900
Units transferred (000s)	1,000	N/A
Final selling price*	$30	$32
Direct labor per unit	$2.00	$3.00
Direct material per unit	$8.00	$9.00

N/A not applicable.

*Final selling price to the external market, not to the Irish company.

Because Kay operates in two countries, it must calculate and report income by country. Assume that the United States has a 35 percent income tax rate on U.S. derived income. Profits of firms in Ireland are taxed at 10 percent to encourage foreign investment. In recent years, the U.S. and Irish tax authorities have scrutinized Kay's full-cost transfer pricing policy. The tax authorities become suspicious if a different transfer price is used for taxes than for other purposes. Kay transfers the European switches at full accounting cost (direct labor, direct material, and allocated overhead).

Required:

a. Prepare separate income statements for each country for Kay Enterprises for the current operating year using direct labor dollars to allocate manufacturing overhead to the switches.

b. Kay is considering switching to activity-based costing for allocating overhead to the two models of switches. Upon analysis of the production process it is determined that most of the $24 million of manufacturing overhead varies with the number of batches produced. The equipment is set up between batches; raw materials are ordered and inspected on a batch basis. The quality control department checks five units per batch. Packing and shipping costs vary to a large degree based on batches, and so forth. After conducting this analysis, Kay decides to switch to ABC for allocating manufacturing costs. European switches are produced in batch sizes of 20,000 and U.S. switches are produced in batch sizes of 30,000. Prepare separate income statements for each country for Kay Enterprises for the current operating year using ABC to allocate manufacturing overhead to the switches.

c. Which set of income statements (those in part [a] or [b]) should Kay Enterprises use?

P 11–20:   Vangard Inc.

Vangard Inc. manufactures shafts for golf clubs. The shafts are sold to golf club manufacturing companies that attach the heads and grips to complete the club. Vangard makes two types of shafts: steel and beryllium. The beryllium shaft is a steel shaft with small amounts of beryllium alloy added to give the shaft a distinctive (and prestigious) copper color. The steel shaft accounts for 90 percent of unit sales and the beryllium shaft accounts for 10 percent. Vangard faces a very competitive market for steel shafts. There are four other domestic producers, and the Japanese have entered the market and are capturing an ever-increasing market share of steel shafts. The market for shafts is growing at 15 percent per year due to the growing popularity of golf, but Vangard's market share is dropping a percentage point per year and is now down to 23 percent.

Raw tube stock, either steel or beryllium, is purchased from a supplier. Vangard has two production processes: forming and tempering. The forming process takes the raw tube stock, cuts it to the desired lengths, and then crimps the shafts in various places to reduce the tube's diameter from the thicker end where the grip is attached down to the narrower diameter at the club head. Forming is a highly automated, continuous machining process. Once the machinery is adjusted, raw tube stock is fed in, cut, and sized, and crimped shafts emerge from the other end of the machinery.

The second and final stage of the process is tempering. Here the cut and crimped shafts are first heated in special ovens and then cooled. This process hardens the steel and gives it the desired whip and flex necessary for the golf swing. Steel tubes are processed in batch sizes of 500 shafts per batch. Because of the higher temperatures needed for beryllium, only 100 beryllium shafts can be processed per batch. Currently, 180 batches of steel shafts and 100 batches of beryllium shafts are tempered per year. Annual capacity of the tempering process is 300 batches per year.

Vangard Inc. produces 100,000 shafts per year. Its cost structure is as follows:

	Tubing	*Forming*	*Tempering*	*Total*
Steel	$180,000			$ 180,000
Beryllium	30,000			30,000
Direct labor		$120,000	$ 50,000	170,000
Variable overhead		35,000	180,000	215,000
Fixed overhead		440,000	780,000	1,220,000
Total manufacturing costs				$1,815,000

Overhead costs are applied to products based on the number of shafts produced. The costs of each type of shaft are as follows:

	Steel	Beryllium	Total
Tubing	$ 180,000	$ 30,000	$ 210,000
Direct labor			
Forming	108,000	12,000	120,000
Tempering	45,000	5,000	50,000
Overhead			
Variable	193,500	21,500	215,000
Fixed	1,098,000	122,000	1,220,000
Total cost	$1,624,500	$190,500	$1,815,000
Units produced	90,000	10,000	100,000
Cost per shaft	$18.05	$19.05	$18.15

The profit margin on each type of shaft is as follows:

	Steel	Beryllium
Selling price per shaft	$23.00	$43.00
Cost per shaft	(18.05)	(19.05)
Profit per shaft	$ 4.95	$23.95

Vangard is one of only two companies currently manufacturing beryllium shafts. While the market for these shafts is small, it is growing. Management feels that it would be wise to become the dominant manufacturer of beryllium shafts and begin shifting more output into the beryllium market. The Japanese, who make only steel shafts, are starting to put increasing pressure on steel shaft prices, often bidding large orders at less than $20 per shaft. Vangard management sees its niche as being the premier beryllium shaft maker.

Required:

    a. Evaluate management's strategy to expand beryllium shaft output and become the dominant firm in beryllium shafts.

    b. Evaluate Vangard's current cost accounting system.

P 11–21: Hospital Admissions Office

The admissions office of a large hospital has an annual operating budget of $700,000. These costs are distributed to inpatient departments (surgery, medicine, pediatrics, psychiatry) and to outpatient departments (drug treatment, prenatal care, dialysis). In the past, the admissions office's costs have been allocated to inpatients and outpatients based on the number of patients processed. But now hospital management is seeking some alternative ways to distribute these costs.

The following data for the last 12 months summarize the number of patients, average days per stay, average patient bill, and average number of minutes to register inpatients and outpatients.

	Number of Patients	Average Days per Patient Stay	Average Patient Bill	Average Minutes to Register a Patient
Inpatient	25,000	6.50	$8,200	12
Outpatient	120,000	1.00	700	8

Required:

a. Allocate the admissions office's annual operating budget to inpatient and outpatient categories based on
   (i) Total number of patients.
   (ii) Total number of patient days.
   (iii) Total patient billings.
   (iv) Total minutes used registering.
b. Discuss the managerial implications of these various alternative ways to distribute the admissions office's costs. Which method should the hospital adopt?

P 11–22:   ABC and Taxes[17]

A plant manufactures two products, Hi-V and Lo-V. High-V is the high-volume product that represents most of the plant's revenue. It is produced 10 times per year, inventoried, and shipped to customers twice a month. Lo-V is a specialty product. It is made to order in small but frequent batches (usually once a week) and shipped immediately to customers. The plant uses an absorption costing system that assigns manufacturing overhead to products based on direct labor hours.

   This table summarizes the annual cost structure and operating data for the plant.

		Hi-V	Lo-V
Direct materials	4 @ $13	$ 52	
	10 @ $2		$ 20
Direct labor	.75 hrs. @ $12	9	
	.25 hrs. @ $12		3
Overhead	.75 hrs. @ $40	30	
	.25 hrs. @ $40		10
Total cost per unit		$ 91	$ 33
Selling price		$ 95	$ 100
Ending inventory		700	0
Production (units)		12,000	4,000
Setups per year		10	40

continued

---

[17] This problem is based on S Dilley, F Jacobs, and R Marshall, "The Tax Benefits of ABC," *Journal of Accountancy*, March 1997, pp. 34–37.

Manufacturing overhead:

Fixed overhead	$390,000
Variable overhead per direct labor hour	$ 1
Budgeted volume:	
Hi-V (12,000 × .75)	9,000
Lo-V (4,000 × .25)	1,000
Budgeted direct labor hours	10,000
× Variable overhead per hour	$ 1
Variable overhead	$ 10,000
Fixed overhead	390,000
Budgeted overhead	$400,000
÷ Budgeted volume	10,000
Overhead rate	$ 40

A careful analysis of the plant's fixed overhead reveals that $350,000 of the $390,000 varies with the number of setups. The remaining $40,000 of fixed overhead will still be allocated to products based on direct labor hours.

There were no beginning inventories.

Required:

a. Compute product costs per unit of Hi-V and Lo-V using activity-based costing.

b. Prepare a table that compares the *profits of the two product lines* using the current absorption costing allocation method and activity-based costing.

c. Income taxes are 50 percent. Calculate the plant's total tax liability under absorption costing and under activity-based costing.

d. In general, will switching to activity-based costing lower a firm's taxes? Describe the general conditions necessary for activity-based costing to lower taxes.

P 11–23: Familia Insurance Company

Familia Insurance Company (FMC) specializes in offering insurance products to the Hispanic community. It has its own direct sales organization of agents that sells three lines of insurance: life insurance, auto insurance, and home insurance. FMC is organized around three profit centers (Life, Auto, and Home) and several cost centers (Sales, Accounting and IT, Human Resources, and Underwriting and Claims). Each agent sells all three insurance lines. Accounting and IT processes all transactions, including customer billing, claims, payroll, and so forth. Human Resources hires employees and manages the employee benefits plans. Underwriting and Claims sets the rates for the three types of policies, calculates the insurance premiums for each policy written, and processes insurance claims.

The three profit center managers are responsible for designing their marketing materials, training the common sales force to sell their policies, and designing their policies to appeal to their market demographics. Each profit center manager is compensated based on net income before taxes in their profit center.

The sales strategy of FMC is to heavily market the auto insurance and then sell the customer life and home insurance products. The following statement (in millions of dollars) summarizes operations for the last fiscal year:

	Life Insurance	Home Insurance	Auto Insurance	Total
Premium revenue	$ 500.00	$ 900.00	$ 600.00	$ 2,000.00
Investment income	87.50	157.50	105.00	350.00
Total revenue	$ 587.50	$1,057.50	$ 705.00	$ 2,350.00
Expenses:				
Insurance losses and loss adjustments	$(300.00)	$ (540.00)	$(560.00)	$(1,400.00)
Policy acquisition expenses	(112.50)	(202.50)	(135.00)	(450.00)
Operating and administrative expenses	(100.00)	(180.00)	(120.00)	(400.00)
Net income before taxes	$ 75.00	$ 135.00	$(110.00)	$ 100.00

Policy premiums are invested in securities and income from these investments is reported as "Investment income." "Insurance losses and loss adjustments" represent the actual insurance claims paid plus anticipated losses not yet paid for policies written that year. "Policy acquisition expenses" are the costs of the direct sales force. Operating and administrative expenses (in millions) consist of the following:

Operating and Administrative Expenses:	
Underwriting and claims	$ 90.00
Accounting and IT	70.00
Human resources	40.00
Advertising	120.00
Profit center expenses	30.00
Corporate office	50.00
Total O&A expenses	$400.00

In the statement of operations for last year, "Investment income," "Policy acquisition expenses," and "Operating and administrative expenses" are allocated to the three profit centers based on premium revenues. "Insurance losses and loss adjustments" are based on the actual and estimated losses on each policy written as calculated by the actuaries in the Underwriting and Claims department.

Profit center expenses consist of the salaries and benefits of the management and staff operating the profit centers and other direct costs incurred by the profit center. The $30 million consists of $6 million in the Life Insurance profit center, $15 million in the Home Insurance profit center, and $9 million in the Auto Insurance profit center. Corporate office expense consists of FMC's senior managers and their staff. They oversee all the profit and cost centers and design FMC's advertising campaigns.

FMC management and the board of directors worry about the large losses being reported in the Auto Insurance profit center and question the methodology being used to allocate both the investment income and the expense items. A consultant hired by senior (corporate) management to analyze these items finds the following relations:

- Investment income generated by each insurance line depends on the difference between premium revenues and insurance losses and loss adjustments.
- Policy acquisition expenses are driven by the time each agent spends on selling a particular line of insurance. Based on a questionnaire sent to FMC's agents, the consultant reports that on average agents spend 30 percent of their time selling auto policies, 30 percent selling home policies, and 40 percent selling life policies.
- Underwriting and Claims expenses are driven by the number of policies in each area. There are 150,000 life policies, 375,000 home policies, and 225,000 auto policies.
- The number of policies in each insurance line is a reasonable approximation of what causes resource consumption in Accounting and IT.
- Human resource costs are driven by the number of employees at FMC. Most of the employees at FMC are in either "Policy Acquisition expenses" or "Profit Center expenses." A reasonably accurate proxy for human resources consumed by employees is salary and benefit expenses of the direct sales force (policy acquisition expenses) plus the profit center expenses.
- Advertising and Corporate office expenses represent firmwide common resources. All FMC ads promote the FMC brand and not individual lines of insurance. After much discussion, management agrees the most commonly accepted allocation scheme for these two expense items is premium revenue.

Required:

a. Based on the consultant's recommendations, prepare a revised statement of operations for the current year that reports revised net income before taxes for each of the three profit centers.

b. Should FMC replace its current methodology for computing net income before taxes with the statement of operations you prepared in part (a)? Present the advantages and disadvantages of the two methodologies and make a recommendation.

P 11–24:   Brickley Chains

Brickley Chains produces five different styles of silver chains, A, B, C, D, and E, in a highly automated batch machining process. The following table summarizes the production and cost data for the five products.

Product	Annual Volume	Direct Labor per Unit	Direct Material per Unit
A	5,000	$2.00	$4.00
B	3,000	2.50	4.50
C	1,000	3.00	5.00
D	800	4.00	6.00
E	500	5.00	7.00

Annual overhead is $80,000.

Required:

a. Compute the unit cost of each chain, A–E, using absorption costing. Overhead is assigned to individual products using direct labor cost.

b. Upon further analysis, you discover that the annual overhead of $80,000 consists entirely of the highly automated machining process. Each chain type is produced in batches with chains of the same type. Each batch requires the same amount of machine time. That is, producing a batch of 100 style A chains requires the same amount of machine time as a batch of 25 style E chains. The following table summarizes the batch size for each type of chain:

Product	Batch Size
A	100
B	100
C	50
D	40
E	25

Compute the unit cost of each chain, A–E, using activity-based costing.

c. Prepare a table comparing the activity-based cost and absorption cost of each product. Discuss why the product costs differ between the two costing methods.

Cases

Case 11–1:   NSB Accounting Firm

The NSB accounting firm generates revenues from the following services:

- Basic bookkeeping services for small- to medium-size firms.
- Financial audits as required for publicly held firms or for private and public companies as required by bank loan covenants and state regulations. NSB provides this service for a wide variety of clients.
- Tax return preparation and consulting. NSB has historically used the SPEEDTAX service (a computerized tax-return service located in Chicago) to complete returns after specified information is obtained. This service is particularly useful when several state returns must be completed for an individual client.

NSB is a very labor-intensive firm. Its professional staff is grouped into the following categories:

Category	Description	Number of Staff	Average Salary
Staff accountant	Primarily responsible for bookkeeping services, simple tax returns, and basic sections of financial audits	30	$ 20,000
Senior accountant	Primarily responsible for the day-to-day supervision of financial audits and the completion of more complicated tax returns	10	40,000
Manager	Responsible for overall administration and supervision of financial audits and tax returns	5	100,000
Partner	Reviews financial audits and tax returns for completeness, accuracy, and compliance with applicable regulations, and responsible for obtaining new clients	2	250,000

NSB operates on a job cost basis by requiring all professionals to submit detailed time sheets. NSB estimates that professionals will work approximately 2,000 hours annually. Jobs are charged the number of hours by professional type (staff, senior, etc.) multiplied by the hourly rate for that professional type (annual salary for that staff category divided by 2,000 hours). When the staff is idle (not generating billable hours), the idle time is included with the other overhead items. Overhead is allocated to jobs based upon billable hours times the overhead rate. The overhead areas with projected spending are as follows:

Overhead Category	Budget
SPEEDTAX service	$ 200,000
Outside accounting technical services (for advice on complex issues)	200,000
Training	150,000
Idle time	380,000
Benefits (25% of salary)	500,000
Supplies	70,000
Rent/other	100,000
Total	$1,600,000

The amount for outside accounting technical services represents payments to outside experts for help on complex tax and audit questions that arise on certain NSB jobs.

The total budget for billable hours based on 2,000 potential hours per employee is summarized as follows:

	Potential Hours	Billable Hours	Percentage Billable	Billing Rate	Revenue
Staff accountant	60,000	51,000	85%	$ 25	$1,275,000
Senior accountant	20,000	18,000	90	60	1,080,000
Manager	10,000	9,000	90	100	900,000
Partner	4,000	2,400	60	200	480,000
					$3,735,000

NSB's budget by service category is summarized next. NSB is concerned about the lackluster performance of its bookkeeping operation and is thinking of discontinuing it.

Profit and Loss Budget and Billable Hours

	Bookkeeping	Audit	Tax	Total
Revenue	$955,000	$1,525,000	$1,255,000	$3,735,000
Expenses:				
Professional staff	380,000	690,000	550,000	1,620,000
Overhead	591,045	555,223	453,732	1,600,000
Total expenses	$971,045	$1,245,223	$1,003,732	$3,220,000
Net income (loss)	$(16,045)	$ 279,777	$ 251,268	$ 515,000
Billable Hours				
Staff accountant	25,000	15,000	11,000	51,000
Senior accountant	4,000	7,000	7,000	18,000
Manager	500	4,500	4,000	9,000
Partner	200	1,400	800	2,400
Total	29,700	27,900	22,800	80,400

Required:

a. Comment on NSB's budget with a focus on the overhead allocation.

b. If you disagree with the NSB methodology, prepare an alternative analysis documenting all assumptions. Prepare a supporting income statement.

SOURCE: T Murray, D Quinn, R Rabideau, H Reitz, and D Wierzbicki.

Case 11–2: SnapOn Fasteners

SnapOn makes snap-together button fasteners (a male top and female bottom) for designer clothes. Each top and bottom consists of several metal parts that, when attached to the garment, allow the shirt, jacket, or pants to be closed without the use of a zipper. The top of each button consists of a shiny or painted metal surface, usually embossed with the designer's logo or design. Fashion design houses contract with manufacturers to produce their fashion lines. The fashion house specifies the particular SnapOn fasteners the manufacturer will use. The manufacturer then purchases the top and bottom sections of the fasteners and leases SnapOn attaching machines to attach the fasteners to the garments. Because each fastener is designed specifically for a particular designer, SnapOn attaching machines must be tailored to each fastener so that the fastener can be attached to the garment without scratching or marring the snap and the machine can operate reliably without jamming. Each machine is specialized to a particular fastener by the tooling in the machines, which have tight tolerances for the particular fastener shape, size, and finish. This tooling is the materials handling device that moves the various components of the tops and bottoms through the machine and positions them in the correct location so that the machine can then compress the metal parts and fabric together.

SnapOn has achieved a good reputation among top design houses for producing high quality, unique fasteners and a line of attaching machines that do not jam and do not mar the fastener. SnapOn has a staff of service technicians who maintain the attaching equipment 24–7. If a machine malfunctions, SnapOn guarantees that it will repair it within 24 hours, anywhere in North America. This service is very important to SnapOn's customers because fashion designers operate on short cycle times. Once they design their spring, summer, fall, or winter lines and show them to the buyers, the designers have eight weeks to produce and deliver the lines. Keeping their designs secret until they are released keeps other fashion houses and knock-off producers from copying their designs. The top fashion designers are willing to pay premium prices for high-quality fasteners that can be attached using highly reliable equipment.

SnapOn has two product lines (fasteners and attaching machines) and produces both lines in the same plant. Separate managers are responsible for the two product lines, and each manager receives 50 percent of his/her bonus based on reported net income of his/her product line and 50 percent of his/her bonus based on SnapOn's total net income. All manufacturing overhead of $59.615 million is applied to all products (attaching machines and fasteners) using direct labor dollars. All selling and service costs of $47.210 million are allocated to fasteners and attaching machines based on revenue dollars generated by each product line. The following table summarizes the operations of SnapOn (in millions) for the most recent fiscal year.

SNAPON FASTENERS
Summary of Operations
Last Fiscal Year

	Machines	*Fasteners*
Revenue	$95.750	$132.895
Direct labor	22.650	43.680
Direct materials	24.640	21.840

Required:

a. Prepare income statements for SnapOn's two lines of business (fasteners and attaching machines) that include manufacturing overhead and selling and service expenses allocated to each business line using the methodology described previously. Assume there are no beginning or ending inventories of either attaching machines or fasteners.

b. Senior management is concerned that its current costing methodology of allocating manufacturing overhead based on direct labor dollars is too simplistic and is not producing unit manufacturing costs that accurately reflect the true consumption of indirect manufacturing overheads. Since manufacturing overhead is about 50 percent of total manufacturing cost (direct labor, direct materials, and manufacturing overhead), small errors in cost allocations could materially affect the calculated unit manufacturing costs. Some foreign competitors are entering SnapOn's traditional fashion markets and are offering fasteners at prices below SnapOn's unit manufacturing costs. Garment manufacturers who use these foreign fasteners have to lease attaching machines from other U.S. manufacturers as the foreign fastener-makers do not provide their own attaching machines. SnapOn will not allow non-SnapOn fasteners to be used in SnapOn attaching equipment.

Senior management organizes a task force to study SnapOn's manufacturing overhead and selling and service costs and asks the task force to devise a better methodology for tracing these costs to individual products and the two lines of business. After three months of analysis, the task force presents the following breakdown of last year's manufacturing overhead amount:

	Manufacturing Overhead Amount	Cost Driver
Purchasing	$ 9.812	Direct materials
Depreciation of machinery	17.611	Traced directly
Supervision	3.665	Direct labor
Occupancy	19.873	Square footage
Engineering	8.654	Traced directly
Total	$59.615	

The task force determines that costs in the purchasing department are driven by the dollars spent on direct materials. The depreciation of machinery should be charged to the two product lines based on the machinery used by the two product lines. Since attaching machine production and fastener production use different equipment, the depreciation of the manufacturing equipment can be directly traced to the two product lines. Of the $17.611 million of total depreciation, 70 percent is for equipment used to manufacture the attaching machines and 30 percent is for equipment used to manufacture fasteners. Employees are supervised either manufacturing attaching machines or manufacturing fasteners. So, direct labor dollars is the cost driver of supervision expenses. The production of attaching machines occupies 75 percent of the total manufacturing space (square footage) and fastener production occupies the remaining 25 percent. Hence, occupancy costs (depreciation of the building, property taxes, property insurance, and utilities) should be assigned to products using square footage as the cost driver. Finally, engineers are assigned exclusively to either attaching machine production (60 percent of the engineering costs) or fastener production (40 percent).

The task force also examined the selling and service costs and determined that $11.850 million of the total $47.210 million consisted of service costs for the attaching machines (salaries, travel, and parts to maintain the attaching machines in the field). The task force also determined that selling costs of $35.36 million vary with revenues.

Using the task force's findings, prepare revised income statements for SnapOn's two lines of business (attaching machines and fasteners) for the last fiscal year. Assume there are no beginning or ending inventories of either attaching machines or fasteners.

c. Briefly describe any changes in the relative profitability of the two lines of business after implementing the task force's analysis.

d. Should SnapOn stay with its current costing system as portrayed in part (a), or should SnapOn convert to the new costing methodology based on the task force's analysis as portrayed in part (b)? Be sure to justify your recommendation based on the advantages and disadvantages of each alternative.

Case 11–3:   Pilot Plant

The Bion Co. has an R&D building that is shared by three R&D groups: High-Voltage, Medium-Voltage, and Low-Voltage. Adjacent to the R&D building is Pilot Plant, a small-scale production facility designed for limited runs of experimental and commercial products. The groups rely on Pilot Plant to produce samples of their formulations.

At Pilot Plant, sample sizes vary from about 1,000 pounds to 10,000 pounds. The R&D groups, including Pilot Plant, are run as cost centers. Pilot Plant also accepts special production runs for external customers that are too small for a regular plant. Pilot Plant consists of three combination blending/extruding machines, which produce pellets of compounded material. Unlike large commercial compounding machines (which can operate 24 hours a day), each of these machines is run for approximately 2,700 hours a year. In the past, Pilot Plant has costed its jobs based on direct materials, variable machine time, and allocated overhead. Overhead is allocated by machine time. A single plantwide machine rate pools all three machines. The overhead pool includes plant fixed costs plus the labor cost of Pilot Plant.

Approximately 20 percent of the machine technicians' time is spent performing general cleanup and maintenance. Machine time is calculated before each job by a computer program that outputs feed rate and setup parameters. Each product is scheduled to a specific machine based on its formulation. The cost schedule of each machine is shown here. Capacity represents the historical annual average capacity.

	Cleanup (Hours per Batch)	Capacity (Pounds per Year)	Variable Cost (Dollars per Hour)	Technicians
Machine 1	4	250,000	25	2
Machine 2	6	250,000	25	2
Machine 3	8	500,000	50	1

Fixed costs		$200,000/yr.
Labor costs:	1 manager	@ $45,000/yr.
	6 technicians	@ $30,000/yr.

While formulations vary considerably, 90 percent of the blends are either resin or flame-retardant magnesium hydroxide. These bulky materials are normally ordered one or two weeks ahead of time and take up much of the floor space. The additives are quite standard and are kept in stock. Weigh-ups and general setup are time consuming and vary from job to job; a formulation that requires seven additives takes considerably more time to prepare than a similar run with two additives. Time spent on setup was not tracked, but it is a simple matter for the technician to include these numbers with the run report. One of the technicians is not assigned to a particular machine but rather is responsible for arranging stock on the floor. Technicians work 2,000 hours per year. The manager spends most of his time scheduling runs and attending to administrative work.

In a typical job, total weigh-up time is the amount of labor time required to locate, prepare, and mix the direct materials prior to inserting them in the machine.

Job #71302
Composition and Direct Cost

Sample run 5,000 lbs:	90% NCPE–0600, resin	$0.10/lb.
	8% Kisuma, flame retardant	$0.12/lb.
	2% Compound Z, antioxidant	$0.14/lb.
Run on machine 1	250 pounds per hour for 20 hours	
Total weigh-up time	16 technician hours	

Required:

a. Calculate the cost of the sample run as charged to Low-Voltage.

b. What is wrong with this system? Construct an alternative costing system and describe its benefits.

c. Recalculate the cost of this run using the new system.

SOURCE: B Graham, R Mardsen, J Quinn, P Leparulo, N Ahmed, and J Vallandingham.

Case 11–4:   Dyna Golf [18]

Joe Bell, president and chief executive officer of Dyna Golf, has called a meeting of the executive committee of his board of directors. He is concerned about the price competition and declining sales of his golf wedge line of business. Bell summarizes the current situation by saying,

As you know, we set target prices to maintain a gross margin on sales of 35 percent. On some products, such as our drivers, we have been able to achieve the target price. We have been able to achieve higher prices than a target 35 percent gross margin would dictate on our putters. But our wedges are a totally different story.

Our factory is among the most efficient in the world. I think that some foreign companies are dumping wedges in the U.S. market, driving down prices and unit sales. We've been reluctant to further cut our prices for fear of what this will do to our gross margins. Fortunately, we've been able to offset the decline in sales of wedges by significantly raising the price of our putters. We were pleasantly surprised when our customers readily accepted the price increases of our putters, and we haven't experienced much reaction from our competitors on the putter price increases.

---

[18] This case is based on J Shank and V Govindarajan, "The Perils of Allocation Based on Production Volumes," *Accounting Horizons*, December 1988, pp. 71–79.

Steve Barber, an outside director on the board asks:

> Joe, I don't pretend to know a lot about the golf club business, but how confident are you in your cost data? If your costs are off, won't your prices be off as well?

Joe Bell responds:

> That's a good point, Steve, and one I've been worried about. We've been modernizing our production facilities and I've asked our controller, Phil Meyers, to look into it and report back after he has undertaken a thorough analysis. My purpose for calling this meeting was to update you on our current situation and let you know what we are doing.

Background

Dyna Golf has been in business for 15 years. Its one plant manufactures three different types of golf clubs: drivers, wedges, and putters. Dyna does not produce a complete club with a shaft and grip. It makes the metal head that is sold to other companies that assemble and market the complete club. Dyna holds four patents on a unique golf club head design that forges together into one club head three different metals: steel, titanium, and brass. It also has a very distinctive appearance. These three metals weigh different amounts, and by designing a club head with the three metals, Dyna produces a club with unique swing and feel properties. While the Dyna club is unique and covered by patents, other manufacturers have recently introduced similar technology using comparable manufacturing methods.

The Dyna driver is sold to a single distributor that adds the shaft and grip and sells the driver to retail golf shops. Dyna first made its reputation with its driver. It became an "instant hit" with amateurs after a professional golfer won a major tournament using the Dyna driver. Based on the name recognition from its driver, Dyna introduced a line of putters and then wedges. The wedges are sold to three different distributors and the putters to six different distributors. Specialty, high-end putters like Dyna's have a retail price of $120 to $180 and drivers a retail price of $350 to $500. Golfers like to experiment with new equipment, especially when they are playing badly. Therefore, it is not uncommon for golfers to own several putters and switch among them during the year. Putter manufacturers seek to capitalize on this psychology with aggressive advertising campaigns. It is less common for players to switch among wedges as they do with putters. Since it takes several rounds of golf playing with a new wedge to get its feel and distance control, most players don't experiment as much with wedges as with putters, or even drivers.

Production process

All three clubs (drivers, wedges, and putters) use the same manufacturing process. Each of the three clubs consists of between 5 and 10 components. A component is a precisely machined piece of steel, brass, or titanium that Dyna buys from outside suppliers. The components are positioned in a jig, which is placed in a specially designed computer-controlled machine. This machine first heats the components to a very high temperature that fuses them together, then cools them, and polishes the finished club.

The factory is organized into five departments: Receiving, Engineering, Setup, Machining, and Packing. Before a production run begins, Receiving issues a separate order for each component comprising the club head and inspects each order when it arrives. Engineering ensures that the completed club heads meet the product's specifications and maintains the operating efficiency of the machines. Because of the preciseness of the production process, Engineering is constantly

TABLE 1   **Dyna Golf Basic Product Information**

	Drivers	Wedges	Putters
Production	10,000 units in 1 run	15,000 units in 3 runs	5,000 units in 10 runs
Shipments	10,000 units in 1 shipment	15,000 units in 5 shipments	5,000 units in 20 shipments
Selling prices:			
Target	$162.61	$134.09	$ 81.31
Actual	162.61	125.96	105.70

having to issue Engineering change orders in response to small differences in purchased components. Setup first cleans out the machine and jigs, adjusts the machine to the correct settings to produce the desired club head, and then makes a few pieces to ensure the settings are correct. Machining contains several machines, any of which can be used to manufacture drivers, wedges, or putters once it is equipped with the proper jigs and tools. Packing is responsible for packaging and shipping completed units.

Table 1 summarizes the basic product information for the three products: production, shipments, target prices, and actual prices. For example, Dyna manufactured all 10,000 drivers in a single production run and shipped them all out in a single shipment. The 5,000 putters were manufactured in 10 separate runs and shipped in 20 shipments. Dyna set a target price for drivers to be $162.61 (wholesale price) and achieved it. However, it was not able to achieve its target price for wedges ($134.09 versus $125.96), but it exceeded its target price for putters ($105.70 versus $81.31).

Accounting system

Table 2 summarizes raw material, setup and run labor, and machine time for each of the three products. Each product is produced in the machining department by assembling the metal components. Drivers require 5 components, whereas wedges and putters require 6 and 10 components, respectively. Before the production begins, the machine must be set up, requiring setup labor. Then to produce clubs, operating the machines requires both machine time and run labor time. Both setup and run labor cost $20 per hour. Machining has a total budget of $700,000 consisting of the depreciation on the machine, electricity, and maintenance. Drivers take more run labor time than machine time because several operators are required to operate the machinery when drivers are produced. During putter machining, the operator can be operating two machines at once.

Table 3 summarizes the overhead accounts.

Phil Meyers, Dyna's controller, and Joe Bell meet a week after the executive committee meeting of the board of directors. Joe Bell asks Phil to report on what he has found. Phil begins,

> Joe, as you know, our current accounting system assigns the direct material costs of the components and the direct labor for run time to the three products. Then it allocates all overhead costs, including setup time and machine costs, to the three products based on

TABLE 2   Dyna Golf Production Information

	Drivers	*Wedges*	*Putters*
Raw material	5 components @ $4 each = $20	6 components @ $5 each = $30	10 components @ $1 each = $10
Labor ($20/hr.)			
Setup labor	10 hrs per production run	10 hrs per production run	11 hrs per production run
Run labor	1/2 hr per driver	1/3 hr per wedge	1/4 hr per putter
Machine time	1/4 hr per driver	1/3 hr per wedge	1/2 hr per putter

TABLE 3   Dyna Golf Overhead

Receiving department	$ 300,000
Engineering department	500,000
Machining department	700,000
Packing department	200,000
Setup department	3,000
	$1,703,000

direct run labor dollars. Setup labor is considered an indirect cost and is included in overhead. Based on these procedures we calculate our product costs for drivers, wedges, and putters to be $105.70, $87.16, and $52.85, respectively.

I've been looking at our system and have become worried that our overhead rate is getting out of line. It's now over 750 percent of direct labor cost. Since we've introduced more automated machines, we're substituting capital or overhead dollars for labor dollars. The Engineering department schedules its people based on change orders it receives. Drivers are pretty standard and only generate 25 percent of the change orders and wedges about 35 percent. Putters are our most complex production process and require the remainder of the change orders.

I'm thinking we should refine our accounting system along the following lines. First, we should break out setup labor from the general overhead account and assign that directly to each product. We know how much time we are spending setting up each machine for each club-head run. Second, we should stop allocating receiving costs based on direct labor dollars but rather on raw material dollars. And third, the remaining overhead (excluding setup and receiving) should be allocated based on machine hours. If we make these three changes, I think we'll get a more accurate estimate of our products' costs.

Joe Bell responded,

These seem to be some pretty major changes in our accounting system. I'll need some time to mull these over. Let me think about it and I'll let you know in a few days how to proceed.

Required:
What advice would you offer Joe Bell?

Chapter Twelve

Standard Costs: Direct Labor and Materials

Chapter Outline

A. Standard Costs

    1. Reasons for Standard Costing

    2. Setting and Revising Standards

    3. Target Costing

B. Direct Labor and Materials Variances

    1. Direct Labor Variances

    2. Direct Materials Variances

    3. Risk Reduction and Standard Costs

C. Incentive Effects of Direct Labor and Materials Variances

    1. Build Inventories

    2. Externalities

    3. Discouraging Cooperation

    4. Mutual Monitoring

    5. Satisficing

D. Disposition of Standard Cost Variances

E. The Costs of Standard Costs

F. Summary

The cost systems described so far report actual (historical) labor and material costs. Historical costs satisfy financial reporting requirements for valuing inventories (balance sheet) and determining cost of goods sold (income statement). Historical costs can also be a useful starting point for estimating opportunity costs. But historical costs do not tell us what costs should be; they only state what the costs actually were. An over- or underabsorbed overhead number is reported, which conveys information about whether the plant has met expectations with respect to overhead. But there are no benchmarks for whether direct labor or direct materials are too high or too low, except by comparing the actual numbers to the same numbers from prior periods. Historical costs are useful as benchmarks only if future costs are expected to be similar to past costs.

Standard costs are benchmarks. They represent the expected or desired future cost of a product, process, or subcomponent. Once standards are set, managers can gauge performance by comparing actual operating results against the standards. The amount by which actual and standard costs differ is the standard cost **variance.** Variances provide useful information for senior management in gauging whether the production system is in control. Variances are an important part of the decision control process described in Chapter 4. Variances are attention-getters. They alert senior managers that something is amiss. Variances also provide information for performance evaluation. In addition to their role in control, standard costs are useful in making decisions on product pricing, outsourcing, and resource allocation.

This chapter describes the use of standard costs for decision making and control. The trade-off between decision management and decision control described in previous chapters also exists with standard costs. Direct labor and direct materials variances are described in this chapter. Overhead variances and marketing variances are described in the next chapter. This chapter focuses on the costs and benefits of standard cost systems.

A. Standard Costs

Standard costs arise from the budgeting process described in Chapter 6. In setting the budget for the firm for the next year, managers determine the per-unit costs of the goods manufactured, the expected volume of production, and the prices to charge for the output. For example, suppose a firm manufactures two products (200GB hard disk drives and 500GB drives) and has an assembly department where the units are assembled. The following table summarizes the key data:

	200 GB Drive	500 GB Drive	Total
Planned production	25,000	14,000	
Standard cost per drive	$ 40	$ 50	
Total standard cost	$1,000,000	$700,000	$1,700,000

Standard cost is the expected cost that is reasonably required to achieve a given objective under specified conditions. In the assembly department, the objective is to assemble 200GB and 500GB drives, and the specified conditions are that 25,000 200GB and 14,000 500GB drives are assembled in the existing department.

TABLE 12–1   **Standard Cost Sheet**
Smith Art Book, 1,000 Copies

Direct Materials				Direct Labor			
Type	*Quantity*	*Price*	*Amount*	*Type*	*Hours*	*Wage*	*Amount*
Paper	800 lbs.	$2	$1,600	Typesetters	80	$15	$ 1,200
Covers	2,000	3	6,000	Printers	55	40	2,200
Binding	500 lbs.	4	2,000	Binders	70	20	1,400
Total			$9,600				$ 4,800

Total direct materials	$ 9,600
Total direct labor	4,800
Total overhead ($100/printer hour)	5,500
Total cost	$19,900
Number of copies	÷ 1,000
Cost per book	$ 19.90

A standard cost represents the relation between inputs and outputs. The $40 standard cost of the 200GB drive in the assembly department states that $40 of both direct and indirect inputs is required to assemble each 200GB drive (the output).

In a standard cost system, each product has a set of standards associated with each input. Consider the following example of a book printer. Table 12–1 presents the standard cost sheet for a particular print run. Each type of direct labor and each type of direct material has a standard quantity and a standard price per unit of that quantity. In addition, the overhead rate (in this example, $100 per printer hour) is set at the beginning of the year and is used to estimate the total overhead each printed book will absorb. Producing a particular book requires a set of cost estimates (standards) such as in Table 12–1.

Before publishing the Smith art book, senior managers will assess the book's expected profitability, which requires projected costs and revenues. The "projected costs" are the standard costs. So, for decision management (whether to publish the book) the company estimates production costs. These estimates form the standards or benchmarks against which the actual costs of producing the book are compared. Comparing actual costs against standards creates a control system. After the book is produced, senior management can use the variance from standard as a performance measure. This approach is the same as that in Chapter 6 for developing annual budgets. (For example, recall the country club discussion.)

1. Reasons for Standard Costing

Standard costs are useful for both decision management and decision control. Historical costs can often prove misleading if operating conditions have changed, if materials prices or wages have changed, or if these factors are expected to change. Operating conditions in the past may have been atypical because new products were introduced or a new manufacturing process was implemented. Lot sizes may have changed, causing both raw materials prices and setup labor costs to be different in the future.

Standard costs are used in a wide variety of decision-making contexts: product pricing, contract bidding, outsourcing decisions, and assessing alternative production technologies. As discussed in Chapter 4, market prices do not exist to guide resource allocations within firms. Instead, administrative devices are used to convey information about alternative uses of scarce resources. Standard costs are part of the internal repetitive contracting process within the firm.

Chapter 6 described how various parts of the organization must coordinate their operating plans for the coming year. Manufacturing and marketing must agree on how many units of each product to manufacture and sell. A key parameter in this coordination is the cost per unit. At the beginning of the year, manufacturing and marketing must agree not only on the number of units but also on their cost. The estimated cost at the beginning of the year is the standard cost. Throughout the year, manufacturing and marketing then have an implicit contract to manufacture and sell the agreed-upon number of units at the agreed-upon standard cost. Standard costs often serve as transfer prices for intrafirm transfers of goods and services.

The standard cost of an hour of mainframe computer time is a proxy for the opportunity cost of using one hour of computer time. This standard cost per hour of mainframe time conveys to other managers throughout the firm the opportunity cost of using the firm's mainframe computer. Likewise, the $40 standard cost of assembling a 200GB drive conveys to other managers an estimate of the opportunity cost of assembling 200GB drives.

Standard costs also provide benchmark information for decision control. Large differences between standard and actual costs signal that a particular process or raw material input differs significantly from what was expected when the standard was set. In labor standards, variances can be traced to specific processes and individual machine operators. Chapter 6 described how variances can be used as a measure of performance—not the sole measure of performance, but one measure. Standard cost variances do not necessarily incorporate information about whether a manager met the production schedule or whether the quality of the units produced met or exceeded specifications.

Actual costs and standard costs for individual processes or materials usage are expected to differ. Random variation causes such deviations. But when summed over a day, a week, or a month, are these deviations in the aggregate positive or negative? Random fluctuations will wash out over time. Positive variances will offset negative variances so that the aggregate variance should be about zero if the process is in control. Therefore, the aggregate variance, like a large sample, gives supervisors confidence that the variance is not due to random chance.

Standard costs are pervasive in manufacturing. In a random sample of 112 New York and American Stock Exchange firms, 85 percent responded that they use standard costs.[1] In another survey involving 219 publicly traded firms, 85 percent again said that they used standard costs.[2] While standard cost systems are common in manufacturing firms, some managers are questioning their costs and benefits. Some firms are scaling back on their reliance on standard costs, changing how they estimate standard costs, or even abandoning their standard cost systems. Section E discusses these trends and the factors that may be causing managers to change or eliminate standard cost systems.

---

[1] H Schwarzbach, "The Impact of Automation on Accounting for Indirect Costs," *Management Accounting*, December 1985, p. 46.

[2] W Cress and J Pettijohn, "A Survey of Budget-Related Planning and Control Policies and Procedures," *Journal of Accounting Education* 3 (Fall 1985), p. 66.

2. Setting and Revising Standards

A standard cost is the product of a standard quantity or usage and a standard price. Standard quantities are usually defined by the technical characteristics of the production process and are often estimated by industrial engineering studies that examine how long a particular manufacturing process takes or how much raw material is required to produce the product. Standard prices are usually forecast at the beginning of the year and are part of the key planning assumptions in the firm's budgeting process (described in Chapter 6).

Standard costs are estimated in manufacturing by taking the *bill of materials* (the list of all the materials required for the product) and forecasting how much of each material is required for the product and the expected price for each material. Standard quantity times standard price is the *standard material cost* of the product. *Routing sheets* contain information about how much labor time is required in each department to produce each product. The expected labor time from industrial engineering estimates and the expected wages for each labor process are used to calculate the *standard labor cost* for the product. Often, managers determine the standards for next year by taking the current year's actuals and making adjustments for inflation, productivity changes, and product mix changes.

No universal method exists for deriving standard costs, and considerable variation and debate exist in practice. Some experts argue that standard costs (standard quantity multiplied by standard price) should be those that are currently attainable, meaning the cost that is achievable if normal effort and luck prevail. Others argue that standard costs should be those that will occur with abnormal effort and/or luck. How tight the standards should be and how much weight to place on meeting them in performance evaluation are important issues in designing the firm's organizational structure, issues that involve trading off the costs and benefits of tight versus loose standards.[3] In the aforementioned survey of 219 publicly traded U.S. firms, 50 percent of the firms say they set standards based on expected, yet difficult-to-attain, actual costs; 42 percent set standards based on average past performance; and 8 percent set standards as the maximum theoretical efficient level.[4]

As described in Chapter 6 regarding the budgeting process in general, setting and revising standards requires gathering specific knowledge about the standards from the individuals who have the requisite knowledge. Usually managers with the specialized knowledge for updating the standard will be evaluated, at least in part, on the difference between their actual performance and the standard. If the standard is to reflect the opportunity cost of the resource, it should contain all of the specific knowledge pertaining to the standard. Standards that accurately capture opportunity costs are the most useful in conveying information within the firm about alternative resource utilization. But the accuracy of the standard as a measure of opportunity cost is often compromised for decision control reasons (i.e., to provide managers with incentives to reduce agency problems). For example, some firms specifically set standard costs below expected actual costs. One reason for biasing the standard cost downward is to exert more pressure on managers to eliminate waste and other operating inefficiencies. Other firms set standard costs above expected actual costs in order to prevent setting selling prices too low.

---

[3] For a general discussion of the issues and related literature, see C Chow, "The Effects of Job Standard Tightness and Compensation Scheme on Performance: An Exploration of Linkages," *Accounting Review* 58 (October 1983), pp. 667–85.

[4] W Cress and J Pettijohn (1985), p. 66. A related study finds "a large majority of profit center budget targets are set so they can and will be achieved," K Merchant, *Rewarding Results: Motivating Profit Center Managers* (Boston: Harvard Business School Press, 1989), p. 30.

<table>
<tr><td>

Standard Costing at Parker Brass

</td><td>

Parker Brass, a subsidiary of Parker Hannifin Corporation, manufactures tube and brass fittings, valves, hose, and hose fittings. Parker Brass uses its standard costing system as an important business tool to target problems so it can develop solutions for continuous improvement. If a standard cost variance exceeds 5 percent of sales for that business unit, the manager must explain the cause of the variance and construct a corrective action plan to solve the problem. Variance reports are prepared the day after each job is closed. Variances greater than $1,000 are listed on exception reports. Weekly summary reports show each variance in dollars as well as by product line and each batch within product line. Managers use the reports to explain to the production employees each variance and the earnings statements for each business unit. These meetings educate the production people about how their production decisions affect business unit profits.

SOURCE: D Johnsen and P Sopariwala, "Standard Costing Is Alive and Well at Parker Brass," *Management Accounting Quarterly*, Winter 2000, pp. 10–20.

</td></tr>
</table>

The choice of tight versus loose standards often involves trading off decision control (tight standards) for decision management (loose standards). Decision management requires assembling the specialized knowledge that often resides only with the person or unit of the firm that later will be judged by the standard (decision control). For example, the purchasing department has the specialized knowledge required to set the standard price of raw materials used in the manufacturing process. But if the purchasing department also has the decision rights to set the standard price, then the standard becomes less useful in evaluating the performance of the purchasing department manager. One solution is to separate decision management (setting the standard) from decision control (ratifying and monitoring the standard).

Usually, the accounting or industrial engineering departments have the decision management rights to set or change the standards. The individuals responsible for the standard cost variance have some decision ratification rights over the standards. Standards are then reviewed and revised each year as part of the annual budgeting cycle. In the study of 219 publicly traded firms referred to earlier, 79 percent of the respondents said that three or more of the following groups participated in setting the standards: industrial engineering, purchasing, human resources, accounting, top management, and line managers with specific cost responsibility. Standard costs are reviewed annually for possible revision by 62 percent of the firms and quarterly by 15 percent.[5]

Most firms are very reluctant to change standards during the year. Once a standard is set at the beginning of the year, it is rarely revised during the year. Managers are held accountable for the standard cost variance. The only exception to this practice occurs when there is a large, unexpected change in a standard. For example, oil is an important input in plastics. If oil prices suddenly jump, the standard cost of plastic is too low. If managers inside the firm continue to use the old standard cost of plastic for internal operating decisions, they will not respond to relative price changes and decision management will be compromised. However, if standards are revised frequently during the year, operating managers have less incentive to control costs. Unfavorable variances will be avoided by changing the standards. Therefore the decision to revise standards

---

[5] W Cress and J Pettijohn (1985), p. 74.

Target Costing at Nissan	Nissan first determines the target price to attract potential buyers to the new car model being designed. After deducting the desired profit margin from this target price, a target cost is derived. This total target cost is divided between design and engineering, manufacturing, sales, and marketing. Within the manufacturing target cost, each part of the car such as the windshield and the engine block is assigned a target cost. "'This is where the battle begins.' The battle is an intense negotiating process between the company and its outside suppliers, and among departments that are responsible for different aspects of the product. The sum of the initial estimates may exceed the overall target cost by 20 percent or more. By the time the battle is over, compromises and trade-offs by product designers, process engineers, and marketing specialists generally produce a projected cost that is within close range of the original target."

SOURCE: F Worthy, "Japan's Smart Secret Weapon," *Fortune*, August 12, 1991, pp. 72–75.

during the year again involves the trade-off between decision management and decision control. Frequent revisions of standards improve decision management but harm decision control.

3. Target Costing

The traditional approach for deriving standard costs is a bottom-up technique. Usually, the manager who will be held responsible for meeting the standard submits an initial estimate, which is reviewed and ratified by industrial engineers, controllers, and high-level managers. Sometimes industrial engineering submits the initial estimate of the standard. In all cases, setting and revising standards involves assembling specialized knowledge from various individuals in the firm. The standard cost of each factor input is estimated and the standard cost of the complete product is built up from the sum of these individual standard costs.

Target costing is a top-down approach conducted during new product planning. It starts with the long-run price (often estimated by the marketing department) required to achieve a desired market share. From this price, the required return on investment (profit) is subtracted to derive a total target product cost. Or,

$$\text{Target cost} = \text{Target price} - \text{Target profit}.$$

This total target cost is then broken down into subcomponent costs, including selling and distribution costs. These subcomponent costs become the targets or standards to be achieved if the firm is to meet its goals for market penetration and return on capital. The target costs become part of the performance evaluation system.[6]

For many products, once the product is designed, most of the opportunities to reduce the cost of the product are gone. The only way to reduce the costs is to redesign the product. Unlike traditional cost control systems, which do not control costs until production begins, target costing requires aggressive cost management during planning, product design, and production. Target costing focuses management's attention on cost control during the critical design stage when most costs are controllable.

---

[6] T Tani et al., "Target Cost Management in Japanese Companies: Current State of the Art," *Management Accounting Research*, 1994, pp. 67–81; and M Sakurai, "Target Costing and How to Use It," *Journal of Cost Management for Manufacturing Industry*, Summer 1989, pp. 39–50.

Changing Organizational Architecture at ITT	This book has emphasized that successful firms rarely change just one leg of their three-legged stool. When one leg is changed (adopting target costing), other legs (decision rights assignment and performance rewards) must also be changed. ITT Automotive Division, one of the world's largest suppliers of auto parts—such as anti-lock brake systems—adopted target costing. ITT formed cross-functional teams (a change in the decision rights assignment) to do value engineering to reduce costs during design and preproduction stages. The cross-functional team consists of members from purchasing, production, engineering, cost targeting, and finance. The team has decision rights to set the target cost (subject to review and ratification by senior management) and is empowered to find the optimal processes, outsourcing, materials used, tooling, and capital investment. Target costing at ITT takes a bottom-up, team-oriented approach in which the team is held responsible for the targets set and the development of further cost reducing methods. Responsibility for solving particular problems is assigned to individual team members.

SOURCE: G Schmelze, R Geier, and T Buttross, "Target Costing at ITT Automotive," *Management Accounting*, December 1996, pp. 26–30.

Setting standards is similar to the budgeting process (Chapter 6) in that both processes force the communication of specialized knowledge. Setting and revising the standards are in fact part of budgeting. Consider the example of Nissan's use of target costing. Setting the target cost of all parts comprising the car forces the product designers, manufacturing engineers, and marketing people to make trade-offs. In the process of making these compromises, specialized knowledge from throughout the firm is shared.

Once standards are set, the variance, or difference between standard and actual cost, is used to judge performance. In general, most firms produce three sets of standard cost variances: direct labor variances, direct materials variances, and overhead variances. Because direct labor and materials are quite similar, they are discussed together in this chapter (section B). The incentive effects of these variances are discussed in section C. Overhead variances are described in the next chapter. It is important to keep in mind that the variances described here are generic to a wide range of applications. Any given department, plant, and company will not use all of the variances described and will invent others. The variances used will be tailored to the organization's specific requirements and become an important component of the firm's organizational architecture.

Concept Questions		
	Q12–1	Define standard cost.
	Q12–2	Name three areas in which standard costs can be used in the decision-making process.
	Q12–3	Can standard costs be viewed as a proxy for opportunity costs?
	Q12–4	How do standard costs illustrate the trade-off between decision making and control?
	Q12–5	What is target costing? How does it differ from traditional standard costing?

Kaizen Costing	A number of Japanese car companies have adopted an elaborate system of continuous cost improvement called Kaizen costing. Such systems used by Toyota and Daihatsu start with a companywide cost reduction goal, say 5 percent. This goal applies to the variable costs (fixed cost reduction goals are set separately). For example, suppose a particular car model has a variable cost base of $9,000 and the company sets the goal to reduce this by 5 percent next year, to $8,550. Each plant is then assigned a target reduction rate. Some plants may be asked to reduce their variable costs by 6 percent and others by 4 percent depending on the plant's particular circumstances. Each plant then disaggregates its plantwide target rate reduction into individual targets by department, such that if each department meets its target, the plant will meet its goal. Each department's annual cost reduction target is translated into a monthly goal of usually one-twelfth the annual goal. If a particular department is to reduce its unit variable cost by $18 for the year, January's goal is $1.50 (or $18 ÷ 12). Monthly variance reports are prepared for each department comparing actual costs to the cost reduction targets. Kaizen costing is a very aggressive scheme to reduce costs. It usually follows target costing, which is performed while the product is still in development. Once the product is being manufactured, Kaizen costing seeks to continually find further cost reduction opportunities. Source: Y Monden and J Lee, "How a Japanese Auto Maker Reduces Costs," *Management Accounting*, August 1993, pp. 22–26. Note that cost reduction goals are also used by non-Japanese firms as well. See R Kaplan and A Sweeney, "Peoria Engine Plant (A)," Harvard Business School Case 9–193–082 (revised June 29, 1993).

B. Direct Labor and Materials Variances

Once standard costs are estimated, they can be used for decision management and control. This section describes how direct labor and materials cost variances are calculated and how they are used for decision control. Direct labor and materials variances are very similar.

1. Direct Labor Variances

The difference between what the direct labor actually costs and what it should have cost (the direct labor variance) can be disaggregated into wage and efficiency variances in the following fashion:

$$\text{Direct labor variance} = \text{Actual cost of labor} - \text{Standard cost of labor}$$

$$= (\text{Actual wage} \times \text{Actual hours})$$
$$- (\text{Standard wage} \times \text{Standard hours})$$

$$= (\text{Actual wage} - \text{Standard wage}) \times \text{Actual hours}$$
$$+ (\text{Actual hours} - \text{Standard hours}) \times \text{Standard wage}$$

$$= \text{Wage variance} + \text{Efficiency variance}$$

Suppose that in producing the Smith art book (Table 12–1), 85 typesetter hours were used at a wage of $15.40 per hour. Actual typesetter cost was thus $1,309, instead of the $1,200 standard cost. The typesetting labor had a $109 unfavorable variance from standard. This variance can be further disaggregated:

FIGURE 12–1

Direct labor variances

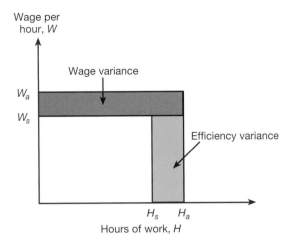

W_a is the actual wage. H_a is the actual hours.
W_s is the standard wage. H_s is the standard hours.

$$\text{Total labor variance} = W_aH_a - W_sH_s$$
$$\text{Wage variance} = (W_a - W_s) \times H_a$$
$$\text{Efficiency variance} = (H_a - H_s) \times W_s$$

Wage variance	($15.40 − $15.00) × 85	$ 34 (unfavorable)
Efficiency variance	(85 − 80) × $15.00	75 (unfavorable)
Typesetter labor variance		$109 (unfavorable)

This analysis indicates two reasons why typesetter labor costs exceeded standard: (1) $0.40 more per hour was paid than expected, and (2) five more typesetter hours were used than expected. If management believes that the standards are correct, then the typesetter labor variances indicate that the person responsible for assigning typesetters to the Smith art book assigned typesetters with a higher actual wage rate per hour than expected and that the person responsible for supervising the typesetters allowed more typesetting hours than expected. The costs of these two "errors" are $34 for paying too much per hour and $75 for using too many hours. Clearly, the ability to draw these inferences depends on whether the standards represent what the typesetting wage rates should have been and how many hours of typesetting should have been used.

Notice that the wage and efficiency variances are calculated after the Smith art book job is completed. The variances pertain to the entire batch of 1,000 books.

The foregoing analysis is illustrated graphically in Figure 12–1, where W denotes the wage rate, H denotes hours, subscript a denotes actual amounts, and subscript s denotes standard amounts. The rectangle $W_s \times H_s$ represents what the labor should have cost, and the rectangle $W_a \times H_a$ represents what the labor actually cost. The total typesetting labor variance is the difference between what the typesetting actually cost and what it should have cost, $W_aH_a - W_sH_s$. This difference is the shaded area in Figure 12–1, which is disaggregated into a wage variance (the top shaded rectangle) and an efficiency variance (the shaded rectangle on the right).

The total labor variance can be disaggregated algebraically as follows:

Total labor variance	$W_a H_a - W_s H_s$
Wage variance	$(W_a - W_s) \times H_a$
Efficiency variance	$(H_a - H_s) \times W_s$

Notice that the sum of the wage variance and the efficiency variance is the total typesetting labor variance:

$$\text{Wage variance} + \text{Efficiency variance} = \text{Total labor variance}[7]$$

Referring back to the standard cost sheet for the Smith art book (Table 12–1), suppose that 50 hours of printers are used at a cost of $41 per hour. To calculate the printers' labor variances, we apply the preceding formulas:

Total printer labor variance:

$$W_a H_a - W_s H_s = (\$41 \times 50) - (\$40 \times 55) = \$2,050 - 2,200$$
$$= -\$150 \text{ (favorable)}$$

Wage variance: $(W_a - W_s) \times H_a = (\$41 - 40) \times 50 = \$50 \text{ (unfavorable)}$

Efficiency variance: $(H_a - H_s) \times W_s = (50 - 55) \times \$40 = -\$200 \text{ (favorable)}$

Notice that the wage variance is unfavorable since the actual wage rate exceeds the standard wage rate. However, the efficiency variance is favorable, as denoted by the minus sign. Actual printer hours were less than standard. The minus sign occurs because we defined the variance as the difference between actual and standard. (Had we defined the variance as the difference between standard and actual, then a minus sign would denote an unfavorable variance. It is arbitrary whether the variance is calculated as the algebraic difference between actual and standard or as the algebraic difference between standard and actual as long as there is consistency.)

Exercise 1:

A CPA firm estimates that an audit will require the following work:

Type of Auditor	Expected Hours	Cost per Hour	Standard Costs
Manager	10	$50	$ 500
Senior	20	40	800
Staff	40	30	1,200
Totals	70		$2,500

continued

---

[7] Algebraically $(W_a - W_s) H_a + (H_a - H_s)W_s = W_a H_a - W_s H_a + W_s H_a - W_s H_s = W_a H_a - W_s H_s$.

The actual hours and costs were as follows:

Type of Auditor	Actual Hours	Actual Cost per Hour	Actual Costs
Manager	9	$52	$ 468
Senior	22	38	836
Staff	44	30	1,320
Totals	75		$2,624

Calculate the direct labor, wage rate, and labor efficiency variances for each type of auditor.

Answer:

The direct labor variance for each type of auditor is

Type of Auditor	Actual Costs	Standard Costs	Direct Labor Variance
Manager	$ 468	$ 500	$(32) Favorable
Senior	836	800	36 Unfavorable
Staff	1,320	1,200	120 Unfavorable
Totals	$2,624	$2,500	$124 Unfavorable

The wage rate variance for each type of auditor is

Manager ($52/hour − $50/hour)(9 hours)	$ 18 Unfavorable
Senior ($38/hour − $40/hour)(22 hours)	(44) Favorable
Staff ($30/hour − $30/hour)(44 hours)	0
Total wage rate variance	$(26) Favorable

The labor efficiency variance for each type of auditor is

Manager (9 − 10 hours)($50/hour)	$ (50) Favorable
Senior (22 − 20 hours)($40/hour)	80 Unfavorable
Staff (44 − 40 hours)($30/hour)	120 Unfavorable
Total labor efficiency variance	$150 Unfavorable

As a check of the calculations of the wage rate and labor efficiency variances, notice that the total variance on this audit is $124 unfavorable ($2,624 − $2,500). The total wage rate variance ($26 favorable) plus the total labor efficiency variance ($150 unfavorable) sum to the total variance ($124 unfavorable).

Large variances, either favorable or unfavorable, can mean that the system is out of control. An accounting variance can indicate that either the operating unit deviated from the prescribed standard or that faulty assumptions were used to develop the standard. In the first case, supervisors of the direct labor did not operate at the levels assumed in the standards. In the second case, the standards were set at a level that could not be attained. If the standards are set as biased forecasts of future expected wages and labor hours, then future accounting variances will reflect the extent of the bias built into the standards when they were established.

Just because a large unfavorable variance is reported does not mean that the person responsible is performing below expectations. The standard could be set at an unrealistic, unattainable level. Also, actuals and standards will deviate due to random causes. Small variances (favorable/unfavorable) are probably not worth senior management's time to investigate. If a variance is small, the costs of investigating the variance will probably exceed the benefits of learning its cause. Clearly, the decision to investigate a variance depends on the inherent variability (uncertainty) of the item. Variances from standards subject to greater variability require a greater threshold before they are investigated.

Large favorable variances are not necessarily good news because they could mean that quality is being reduced. For example, one way to generate favorable labor efficiency variances is to use too few labor hours and produce lower-quality products. Likewise, favorable wage variances might mean that less-skilled, lower-paid employees were used more than expected; this too can compromise product quality. The human resource department is held responsible for the wage variance if that department has the decision rights for hiring employees with given job skills at a given standard wage rate. In other cases, the shop floor supervisor is held responsible for wage variances if the supervisor can schedule different employees with varying skills and wage rates to produce the product. If the supervisor can change the mix of employees and thus the cost of the job by substituting more- or less-skilled employees at different wage rates, then he or she is usually assigned the total direct labor variance and there is no reason to separately compute a wage variance and an efficiency variance except to provide information about what caused the labor variance. The extent to which wage and efficiency variances are used to measure performance and the weight they receive in a manager's performance evaluation depend on three things: the reliability of the underlying standards, the inherent variability of the wages and hours due to random fluctuations, and how much of the variance is potentially controllable by the manager. Some firms place large weight on variances in performance evaluation; other place little or no weight on them.

2. Direct Materials Variances

Direct materials variances are identical to those computed for direct labor, with one exception that will be introduced later. Figure 12–2 portrays the material variances. P denotes the unit price of the material, Q denotes the quantity of the material, and the subscripts a and s again denote actual and standard amounts, respectively. As with direct labor, the total materials variance can be disaggregated into a price variance and a quantity variance.

The analysis in Figure 12–2 assumes that *all purchases are used immediately for production;* there is no raw materials inventory. (This assumption is relaxed later.) However, in the usual case, raw materials are purchased for inventory and then released to production as called for by the production schedule. Only in a just-in-time production system or in custom manufacturing are raw materials received and used simultaneously. In Figure 12–2, the total variance is the difference be-

FIGURE 12–2

Direct materials variances (materials used as purchased)

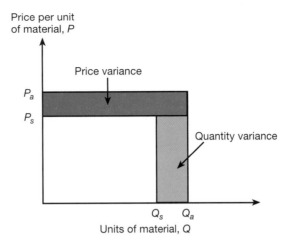

Price per unit of material, P

Price variance

P_a

P_s

Quantity variance

Q_s Q_a

Units of material, Q

P_s is the standard price. Q_s is the standard quantity.
P_a is the actual price. Q_a is the actual quantity.

Total materials variance $= P_a Q_a - P_s Q_s$
Price variance $= (P_a - P_s) \times Q_a$
Quantity variance $= (Q_a - Q_s) \times P_s$

tween what the material actually cost and what it should have cost, $P_a Q_a - P_s Q_s$. As in Figure 12–1, this difference is disaggregated into two variances: a price variance and a quantity (usage) variance. The price variance, $(P_a - P_s)Q_a$, is typically reported to the purchasing manager and is one measure of the purchasing manager's performance. Other performance measures for purchasing might include the percentage of on-time delivery of materials and the quality of materials. The materials quantity variance, $(Q_a - Q_s)P_s$, is the difference between actual and standard quantity times standard price. It measures the inefficient or efficient use of materials. The quantity variance is reported to the manager responsible for the efficient use of materials (usually the shop supervisor) and is one performance measure of this manager.

The price variance and quantity variance are often interrelated. For example, if substandard materials are purchased at a price below the standard price, usually an unfavorable materials quantity variance is generated because more materials than standard are used. If a less-expensive exterior house paint is purchased, more of it will probably be required to provide the same coverage as a higher-quality, higher-priced paint. A variance in one area is likely to be related to other variances. A favorable price variance might cause an unfavorable quantity variance, or a favorable labor quantity variance might be the result of another unfavorable labor quantity variance if one type of labor is substituted for another. A favorable materials price variance and a resulting unfavorable materials quantity variance can cause unfavorable labor efficiency variances if extra material and labor are used due to the substandard materials. A less-expensive exterior house paint requires more labor to apply the extra coats. Therefore, to assess performance in the manufacturing process, all the variances must be analyzed as an integrated whole.

In a standard cost system, materials are recorded in the raw materials inventory account at standard cost. That is, inventory is stated at standard price, not actual price. The price variance is recorded in a separate ledger account, which is usually written off to cost of goods sold at the end of the year instead of flowing

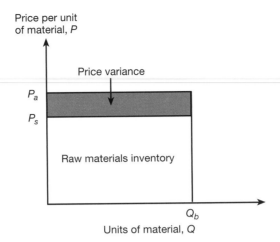

P_a is the actual price. Q_b is the actual quantity bought.
P_s is the standard price.

Price variance $= (P_a - P_s) \times Q_b$

through inventory and product costs. For example, suppose 100 pounds of copper are purchased for $12 per pound when the standard price is $10 per pound. The purchase is recorded in the raw materials inventory account at $1,000 and the $200 difference is recorded in a separate materials price variance account. Future products using this copper are charged $10, not $12, per pound. When the $200 is recorded in a separate materials price variance account and written off to cost of sales directly, the unit costs of the products using the copper are not distorted by the $2-per-pound price variation.

Figure 12–3 depicts the case in which raw material is bought, placed in raw materials inventory, and then used at a later date. In Figure 12–3, the price variance is removed as soon as the raw material is purchased. The raw materials inventory is then stated at standard cost, P_s. The price variance is reported as soon as the material is bought, not when it is used at some later date. Once the price variance is removed at purchase, all the remaining withdrawals from the raw materials account are stated at the same standard cost per unit.

Timely reporting of price variances is important so managers can act quickly to mitigate or capitalize on the price change. For example, if a raw material's price rises, managers might want to use less of the more expensive material and more of a relatively less expensive material, if such substitution is possible. Or, management might want to raise the selling price of the final product.

Figure 12–4 represents how the raw material purchased is divided up after some of the raw material is used in production. If Q_b units are purchased and Q_a units are actually used in production, then $Q_b - Q_a$ units are left in raw materials inventory. These are valued at P_s, standard cost. Thus, the vertical rectangle on the right-hand side of Figure 12–4, $(Q_b - Q_a)P_s$, is the dollar value of the raw material remaining in the raw materials inventory account. Likewise, the dollar amount of raw materials transferred to work in process is P_sQ_s, the standard price at the standard quantity (i.e., the unshaded rectangle).

Notice that Figure 12–4 has three quantity measures on the horizontal axis: standard quantity, actual quantity used in production, and quantity bought. The standard quantity, Q_s, is the number of units of output produced times the standard quantity of raw materials that should have been used per unit of output. The

FIGURE 12–4

Direct materials variances (materials purchased and used later)

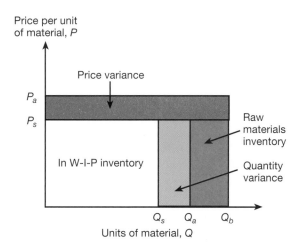

Price per unit of material, P

Price variance

P_a

P_s

Raw materials inventory

In W-I-P inventory

Quantity variance

Q_s Q_a Q_b

Units of material, Q

P_a is the actual price. Q_a is the actual quantity used in production.
P_s is the standard price. Q_s is the standard quantity used in production.
   Q_b is the actual quantity bought.

$$\text{Price variance} = (P_a - P_s) \times Q_b$$
$$\text{Quantity variance} = (Q_a - Q_s) \times P_s$$

actual quantity (Q_a) is the number of units of the raw material actually used to produce the product. The quantity bought (Q_b) is the number of units of the raw material actually purchased. Suppose three pounds of fiberglass cord is the standard quantity per automobile tire. In May the plant purchased 98,000 pounds of fiberglass cord and manufactured 30,000 tires using 95,000 pounds of fiberglass cord. The three quantity measures are as follows:

Standard quantity (30,000 tires × 3 pounds per tire)	90,000 pounds
Actual quantity	95,000 pounds
Quantity bought	98,000 pounds

It is important to understand that the standard quantity of raw materials, 90,000 pounds, is the number of actual tires produced (30,000 tires) times the standard amount of fiberglass cord per tire (three pounds per tire). Standard quantity is the amount of cord that should have been used to produce the 30,000 tires.

Recall that when raw materials are purchased for inventory and then issued into production as needed, the price variance is computed based on the total units bought. In Figures 12–3 and 12–4, the price variance is based on Q_b. The price variance is stripped out of the total amount paid for the raw material, and the raw materials inventory account is stated at the standard price of the raw material.

The total amount paid for the raw materials, P_aQ_b, is disaggregated into four pieces, as illustrated in Figure 12–4: the price variance, the amount transferred to work in process, the quantity variance, and the amount remaining in raw materials inventory. The only difference between Figures 12–4 and 12–2 is that the price variance is calculated based on total units bought (Figure 12–4) versus units used (Figures 12–2).

3. Risk Reduction and Standard Costs

Insurance and capital markets reduce risk through diversification. Stock options, interest rate swaps, and commodity futures allow investors to hedge risk. Thus, risk reduction is an important service individuals are willing to buy from financial markets. Standard cost systems also provide a mechanism inside the firm to reduce certain risks managers bear because their compensation is linked to accounting-based performance measures.

Recording labor and materials at standard cost strips out price and quantity (efficiency) deviations and places them into variance accounts. Then downstream users in the plant see only standard costs. Stripping out price and efficiency fluctuations reduces the risk borne by downstream "purchasers" of the product, such as the marketing department. Downstream users know at the beginning of the year what they will be charged for final products throughout the year. If raw materials prices or wage rates change, or if material or labor is used more (or less) efficiently than originally planned, downstream managers do not bear the risk of these deviations. Thus, standard costs remove some uncontrollable factors from the performance measures of downstream users. Because they bear less risk, these managers do not have to be paid higher salaries to compensate them for bearing this additional risk. Hence, total compensation can be lower.

Concept Questions		
	Q12–6	What are the three sets of standard cost variances produced by most firms?
	Q12–7	What are the two components of direct labor variances?
	Q12–8	When might large favorable variances be viewed as bad?
	Q12–9	What are the components of the direct materials variance?

C. Incentive Effects of Direct Labor and Materials Variances

Standard costs and variances, when used as part of the performance evaluation system, create incentives for managers to control costs; this is one of their intended purposes. Standards are part of the performance evaluation system, as described in Chapter 4. However, if the standard cost system is not designed properly and integrated consistently with the other parts of the performance evaluation and reward systems and the decision-partitioning system, then dysfunctional behavior can result. The fault does not lie with the standard cost system per se but rather in how it is implemented within the particular firm. (Similarly, modern pharmaceuticals are extremely important in treating disease, but they can be misused as well.)

Standard cost variances create subtle incentive effects. This section describes five: the incentive to build inventories, externalities, discouraging cooperation, mutual monitoring, and satisficing.

1. Build Inventories

When purchasing managers are evaluated based on direct materials price variances, they have an incentive to build inventories. Price discounts are often granted for volume purchases. Therefore, one way to generate favorable price variances is to purchase raw materials in lots larger than necessary for immediate production and hold these inventories until they are needed.

It is costly to hold inventory because of warehousing, materials handling, obsolescence, and financing costs. When purchasing managers are rewarded based on favorable price variances, quantity discounts will often lead to buying raw materials in larger-than-optimum lot sizes. Purchasing large quantities lowers materials costs, which are included in accounting earnings. However, the opportunity cost of capital tied up in inventory is not included in accounting earnings. Moreover, the costs of warehousing the inventories and insuring them are often in general factory overhead and are neither traced nor allocated to specific inventories.

One way to reduce the incentive to hold large inventories is to charge the purchasing department for inventory holding costs. For example, if the firm's opportunity cost of capital is 13 percent and warehousing and handling costs are 15 percent, then charging the purchasing department 28 percent of the average dollar balance in raw materials inventory reduces the incentive to purchase in large lots. In other words, the performance report for the purchasing department should include the sum of all favorable and unfavorable price variances generated during the period as well as the inventory holding costs.

Most firms do not charge purchasing managers for inventory holding costs because such costs then have to be backed out of the various accounts for external reporting purposes. An alternative mechanism for controlling dysfunctional inventory building is to adopt just-in-time (JIT) purchasing rules. That is, the purchasing department can order materials only as they are needed for production.

2. Externalities

Purchasing managers can impose externalities on production by purchasing substandard materials. Recall from Chapter 7 that externalities are costs (or benefits) that one department imposes on another (without being charged). Lower-quality materials often require more labor hours and more skilled workers (paid higher wages) to process them. The substandard materials impose costs on the downstream production managers because additional production resources are consumed for rework or machine downtime. To offset the purchasing manager's incentive to acquire low-quality raw materials, purchases are inspected when received, engineering specifications are set for each product, and purchasing is not allowed to buy materials that deviate from these standards. Alternatively, part of the purchasing manager's performance evaluation can be tied to the amount of rework generated in production and/or the raw materials quantity variance. In this last case, when performance is judged in part on the outcomes in manufacturing, purchasing managers are forced to bear some of the costs they impose on manufacturing when they purchase substandard materials. However, the purchasing manager is responsible for only part of any manufacturing variances. So we would expect to see purchasing managers evaluated based on manufacturing variances only when purchasing substandard materials can impose a large cost on manufacturing.

Production managers impose externalities on purchasing by requesting that materials be purchased on short lead times and in small lot sizes to reduce the quantity of materials in storage. By making frequent design changes, engineering can increase the actual price of the purchases. These are just a few examples of the types of externalities that purchasing and production can impose on each other.

3. Discouraging Cooperation

Evaluating individuals within an organization based on variances can discourage cooperative effort. In some firms, employees are evaluated and rewarded based on a labor efficiency variance. Such systems often cause the employees to be reluctant to support others if their evaluation reflects only what they produce as an individual.

An alternative is to measure variances for a team or department within the organization. Team performance measures encourage cooperative effort but can lead to shirking (the free-rider problem) on the part of some individuals. For example, a group project for a class is given a single grade that is shared by all the students in the group. Some individuals will take advantage of the group grading system by shirking their duties, because they know other responsible students in the group will complete the group task.

To encourage cooperative effort and reduce shirking, many organizations measure performance and calculate variances at multiple levels. For example, an individual worker would be evaluated based on an individual labor efficiency variance and a departmental labor efficiency variance. Bonuses would be paid for both individual and group accomplishments.

4. Mutual Monitoring

The usual method of monitoring behavior within firms is for superiors to monitor subordinates. But another important form of monitoring occurs between managers who are not in a direct reporting relationship with each other. Monitoring can occur between managers at the same level in the same subunit or between managers in different subunits. Sometimes managers or employees at the same level monitor each other; this is called **mutual monitoring.** (Examples of mutual monitoring via noninsulating cost allocations were described in Chapter 7.)

If the purchasing department manager is held responsible for materials variances (including the quantity variance), then the purchasing manager has the incentive to monitor the production supervisor's usage of materials. Likewise, the production supervisor monitors the quality of the materials bought by the purchasing manager. Basing the purchasing manager's performance evaluation on both the price and quantity variances encourages the purchasing manager to help devise ways in which the production manager can economize on materials. The performance evaluation and reward systems can be designed to contain mutual monitoring incentives that encourage managers to acquire and use their specialized knowledge to improve the performance of other managers.

5. Satisficing

If standards are used as a benchmark for evaluating managers, the reward system is often tied to achieving the standard. If the manager works sufficiently hard to achieve the standard, a bonus is often paid to the manager. The problem with this type of reward system is that managers have incentives to achieve the standard, but they have no incentive to go further. This is often referred to as *satisficing behavior.*[8] The ratchet effect described in Chapter 6 provides a further disincentive to perform beyond the standard. Next year's standards are usually based on past performance and therefore will be harder to achieve if they are raised due to exceptional performance this year. The organization, of course, would like managers to continually improve and not stop when the standard is met.

Firms must respond to their competitors. If managers focus only on achieving the standard and ignore competition, the organization will not change to meet new demands. Rewarding managers for simply achieving the standards tends to make the managers think that the status quo is appropriate; it stifles innovation. Therefore, rewarding managers for meeting the standard is less appropriate in industries that are rapidly changing with new, innovative products. The problem is

---

[8] Technically, *satisficing* refers to selecting actions that are satisfactory, not optimal, because finding the optimum is too difficult. Instead of searching for the sharpest needle in the haystack, the haystack is searched for a needle sharp enough for sewing. See J March and H Simon, *Organizations* (New York: John Wiley & Sons, 1958).

not so much with using standards as performance measures but rather in how the compensation schemes reward performance. Compensation schemes should motivate managers to continuously improve beyond the standard, with higher payments for greater improvement.

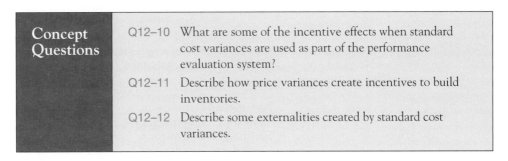

Concept Questions	Q12–10 What are some of the incentive effects when standard cost variances are used as part of the performance evaluation system?
	Q12–11 Describe how price variances create incentives to build inventories.
	Q12–12 Describe some externalities created by standard cost variances.

D. Disposition of Standard Cost Variances

Up to this point, the discussion has focused on the calculation, interpretation, and incentive effects of standard cost variances for direct materials and direct labor. We have not discussed what happens to the standard cost variances once they are calculated and recorded in the ledger accounts. Chapter 9 discussed three ways of disposing of over/underabsorbed overhead: (1) writing it off to cost of goods sold, (2) allocating it among work in process, finished goods, and cost of sales, or (3) recalculating the cost of each job. The same options are also available for disposing of the labor and materials variances.

Writing off all of the variances to cost of sales prevents the inventory accounts of work in process and finished goods from being affected. Product costs are not changed from standard cost. In many firms, variances are written off to cost of goods sold and hence income. The alternative is to prorate the total amount of the

Dysfunctional Incentives and Standard Costing	Charles Machine Works, Inc., manufactures a line of underground trenching equipment. Under the old standard cost system, the standard cost variance report promoted a "pounds-in-the-barrel" mentality. Employees tried to beat their standard cost quotas without sufficient regard for quality. One worker said, "If I waste time testing for burrs, and if I find one (which requires redeburring and retesting), I'll be held responsible for not meeting my quota and for the unfavorable labor variance. If there is a burr, it won't be discovered for a long time, and there's plenty of parts inventory on hand so assembly won't be hurt. By not testing for burrs, I can beat my quota and the standard time allowed."

To change employees' incentives, management developed detailed variance control tables that relate quality problems detected later in the production process back to earlier processes causing the problem. For example, in step 23 where parts are assembled and tested, if hydraulic fluid leaks, this means that interior surface burrs were not deburred in step 7. The employee producing the bad parts in step 7 is held responsible for these defects.

SOURCE: M Thomas and J Mackey, "Activity-Based Cost Variances for Just-in-Time," *Management Accounting*, April 1994, pp. 49–54. |

standard cost variances to inventories (work in process and finished goods) and cost of goods sold. The reason for writing off the variances to the income statement is expediency. Writing off variances to cost of goods sold is easy and does not require detailed computations if there are numerous inventory accounts.

Exercise 2:

Total materials variances for the year were $150,000 unfavorable. Total material purchased during the year at standard cost was $1 million, which is now in the following accounts:

Raw materials inventory	$ 100,000
Work-in-process inventory	200,000
Finished goods inventory	150,000
Cost of goods sold	550,000
Total purchases	$1,000,000

Prorate the materials variances to the various accounts.

Answer:

	Purchases in Account	%	Prorated Variance	Adjusted Balance
Raw materials inventory	$ 100,000	10%	$ 15,000	$ 115,000
Work-in-process inventory	200,000	20	30,000	230,000
Finished goods inventory	150,000	15	22,500	172,500
Cost of goods sold	550,000	55	82,500	632,500
Total	$1,000,000	100%	$150,000	$1,150,000

Since the total materials variance is unfavorable, too little materials cost was charged to products. Thus, prorating this variance increases the balances in the inventory and cost-of-goods-sold accounts. Had the variance been favorable, the account balances would be reduced by prorating.

There are also organizational reasons for writing off all of the variances to cost of goods sold and not restating product costs. As discussed in Chapter 9, when volumes fall, average unit costs rise if fixed overheads are allocated based on actual volume. Unfavorable purchase price variances may occur if smaller lot sizes are purchased. Unfavorable labor efficiency variances usually result as employees are idle. If all of these unfavorable variances are then prorated back to inventories, the managers responsible for selling these inventories are now confronted with higher reported product costs. Their first reaction is to try to raise the selling price. But as illustrated in Chapter 9, this is usually the wrong thing to do.

When volumes are higher than normal, dysfunctional decisions can again result. Standard cost variances tend to be favorable, and prorating them to inventories lowers inventory costs. Therefore, one reason not to prorate cost variances is to avoid sending incorrect signals to managers in the firm that marginal costs have changed when, in fact, they have not.[9]

E. The Costs of Standard Costs

Standard cost systems are costly to implement and operate. Not only must detailed standards be maintained for each labor and material input, but these standards must be revised in a timely fashion. Rapid technological change and continuous improvement efforts (total quality management programs) cause standards to become obsolete. Workers tend to anchor on old standards rather than seeking continuous cost reductions. It is also expensive, in terms of the opportunity cost of the manager's time, to investigate cost variances. Managers should investigate only those variances that indicate that the process is out of control and management intervention is required. Investigating variances caused by random or temporary fluctuations is usually not a productive use of a manager's time. Managers usually examine only large variances.

However, there can be some value to investigating variances caused by random or temporary fluctuations. To the extent that such an investigation creates a better understanding of the firm's environment, the manager creates specialized knowledge. This specialized knowledge, when combined with decision rights, results in higher firm value if the manager is able to exploit some heretofore unrealized profit opportunity.

A large Japanese automobile parts supplier, Atsugi Motor Parts (an affiliate of Nissan), used detailed standard costing systems for over 25 years for cost control but dropped the system in the mid-1980s.[10] Likewise, Toyota has abandoned standard costing. Several reasons may explain these changes. As factories become more automated, the fraction of direct labor in product costs falls. Since many standard cost systems were aimed at controlling direct labor costs, the benefits of a standard cost system are smaller in more highly automated factories. Second, highly automated factories are no longer stable production processes. New machines, technologies, and processes can be introduced more quickly because of flexible manufacturing systems. Frequent changes in products or processes require frequent revisions of the cost standards. For example, suppose a plant manufactures 15,000 different parts, and a typical part has 10 separate machining operations. Introducing new computer-controlled machines that perform work on 5 percent of the operations requires that 7,500 standards be changed (15,000 × 10 × 5 percent), often necessitating detailed studies by industrial engineers. As the frequency of product changes or process changes increases, the costs of maintaining a standard cost system increase. Therefore, flexible manufacturing systems appear to be causing some companies to abandon standard cost systems because they increase the costs of standard cost systems and hence lower their value.

While Atsugi and Toyota have moved away from their standard cost systems, a survey of 198 Japanese companies in four automated industries concludes that

---

[9] Product costs will still vary inversely with volume if overhead rates are based on next year's expected volume and not long-run average (normal) volume.

[10] M Sakurai, "The Influence of Factory Automation on Management Accounting Practices: A Study of Japanese Companies," in *Measures for Manufacturing Excellence*, ed. R Kaplan (Boston: Harvard Business School, 1990), pp. 46–48.

<table>
<tr><td>

NEC Revises Its Standard Cost System

</td><td>

NEC, a large diversified Japanese electronics firm, installed its standard cost system in the 1950s, when it was in a stable market supplying a small number of products, mainly telephones and switching equipment, to Nippon Telegraph & Telephone. But by the 1980s, NEC was supplying a vast number of different electronic products that were subject to rapid technological obsolescence.

It is very expensive to keep standard costs up to date as products and the production technology change. The life expectancy of any one cost standard is now much shorter. NEC still uses its standard cost system as a factory management tool, but it no longer uses standard costs on a product-by-product basis.

Source: T Hiromoto, "Another Hidden Edge—Japanese Management Accounting," *Harvard Business Review*, July–August 1988.

</td></tr>
</table>

most Japanese firms are maintaining their standard costs.[11] The authors report that 70 percent of the firms in electronic and transportation equipment industries and 58 percent of the firms in chemical products and iron and steel manufacturing use standard costs. Japanese managers were evenly split in their opinion as to whether factory automation increased or decreased the use of standard costs.

One U.S. textile manufacturer, Milliken, substantially revised its standard cost system but did not eliminate it. The firm upgraded its computer and communication systems to improve manufacturing productivity by monitoring the production process. Computer-aided manufacturing (CAM) provided detailed data on output per machine, downtime, and the reason for the downtime. The CAM technology provides managers daily detailed, nonfinancial information such as set-up time. The availability of extensive nonfinancial data generated by CAM allowed Milliken to simplify the existing variance reports and reduce the number of detailed cost standards estimated by industrial engineers, accountants, and production managers. However, Milliken still relies on standard costs for pricing decisions and performance evaluation. The experience at Milliken illustrates how accounting systems are one part of the firm's decision management and control systems. When technological change allows improvements in other parts of the decision management and control system, these changes are likely to affect the accounting system.[12]

While some companies may abandon their detailed standard cost systems, they are not likely to abandon their annual budgeting process. Recall from Chapter 6 that budgeting is an important coordination mechanism for communicating specialized knowledge of prices, quantities, costs, and revenues within the firm. Annual budgets require managers to forecast next year's cost structure. These costs, while not built on detailed standards, are still aggregate standard costs. That is, instead of deriving the standard cost of a manufactured personal computer as the sum of the detailed standard costs of each part and assembly process, management derives next year's standard cost by adjusting this year's actual costs for price

---

[11] P Scarbough, A Nanni, Jr., and M Sakurai, "Japanese Management Accounting Practices and the Effects of Assembly and Process Automation," *Management Accounting Research* 2 (March 1991), pp. 27–46.

[12] J Edwards, C Heagy, and H Rakes, "How Milliken Stays on Top," *Journal of Accountancy*, April 1989, pp. 63–74.

changes and process changes. When firms say that they are abandoning their standard cost system, they usually mean they are no longer maintaining detailed standard quantities and standard prices for each part and production process. Rather, they are using standard costs at a more aggregate subassembly or product level for budgeting and performance evaluation purposes.

A standard cost system must be designed carefully to maximize firm value. Carelessly designed standard cost systems that serve as performance evaluation schemes can lead to dysfunctional behavior. For example, if too much emphasis is placed on labor efficiency variances, then incentives are created that can lead to large work-in-process inventories and plant scheduling rules that keep employees busy instead of producing products that maximize firm profits. In some plants, a few machines or manufacturing cells are the scarce resource or bottleneck. To maximize firm profits, these bottlenecks should be scheduled to maximize the contribution margin per unit of scarce resource. Keeping nonbottlenecks operating at capacity does not increase throughput of the bottleneck and can actually decrease it if the excess inventory waiting to be processed clogs up the smooth flow of the high-contribution-margin units at the bottleneck.[13]

For example, the steps to make plywood include debarking the logs, heating the logs, cutting the log into veneer (thin layers of wood), cutting the veneer into sheets, sorting the veneer, drying the veneer, layering and gluing the veneer, trimming the plywood, and sanding and patching the plywood. Each of these steps has a different capacity in terms of tons of wood product processed per day:

Process	Tons of Wood Product per Day
Debarking log	300,000
Heating log	200,000
Cutting log into veneer	100,000
Cutting veneer into sheets	150,000
Sorting veneer	120,000
Drying veneer	130,000
Layering and gluing veneer	150,000
Trimming plywood	250,000
Sanding and patching plywood	300,000

The cutting of the log into veneer is the bottleneck because only 100,000 tons per day can be cut into veneer. All the other steps can produce more tons per day. Bottlenecks can usually be identified even if the capacity of the different processes are unknown because work in process (unfinished inventory) accumulates prior to the bottleneck process. The bottleneck process should be operated as many hours as possible. Maintenance of the bottleneck is extremely important, and methods of increasing the capacity of the bottleneck should be considered. Managers should focus on the bottlenecks (in this example, cutting the log into veneer and sorting the veneer). Standard cost systems that focus management attention on nonbottleneck processes (in this case, sanding and patching) can often be counterproductive.

---

[13] See E Goldratt and J Cox, *The Goal*, rev. ed. (Croton-on-the-Hudson, NJ: North River Press, 1986).

Concept Questions	Q12–13	Why are variances usually written off to cost of goods sold?
	Q12–14	What are some of the costs and benefits of standard cost systems?
	Q12–15	Why are some firms dropping standard cost systems?

F. Summary

Standard costs of parts, processes, and subassemblies are set during the budgeting process before the fiscal year begins. The standard costs of products are then the agreed-upon costs accepted by various units of the organization for the repetitive exchanges among parties internal to the firm. Standard costs and variance analyses are used for several reasons: (1) to provide information to senior managers regarding whether the system is in control or not, (2) to provide a basis for the performance evaluation system, (3) to provide information to other managers in the firm regarding the normal or expected (opportunity) cost of producing a repetitive activity, part, or product, and (4) for product pricing. Accounting systems using standard costs are an administrative device firms use because market prices do not exist to guide internal production.

When actual costs differ from standard costs, standard cost variances filter out the differences, allowing only standard costs to flow downstream to other internal contracting parties. Thus, a properly designed standard cost system acts as a huge filtration mechanism that separates actual costs into the agreed-upon standard costs and variances. However, detailed standard cost systems are costly to maintain, and industrial engineers are often required to update the numerous standards.

The variances described in this chapter are generic to a wide range of applications. However, no department, plant, or company will use all of the variances described. They will use some of the variances, modify some, and invent others, because firms differ in the trade-offs they face between decision management and control. Variances will be tailored to an organization's specific requirements.

Standard cost systems can produce dysfunctional decision making if they are improperly designed and then used in conjunction with other performance evaluation and reward systems. Standard costs used in a performance reward system create incentives for managers to (1) change behavior and maximize the performance measure and/or (2) manipulate the standards. The first option is one purpose of the standard cost system. All too often, however, the second alternative occurs. When a manager has input into setting a standard, basing the manager's performance on beating that standard creates incentives for that manager to bias the standard. This is not a failure of the standard cost system but rather of the performance reward system.

Standard cost systems can produce functional or dysfunctional behavior. Moreover, the incentive effects can be very subtle. Building excess inventories, creating quality externalities, discouraging cooperation, mutual monitoring, and satisficing behavior are just some of the subtle behavioral changes induced by standard costs used in conjunction with performance reward systems.

Standard cost systems are costly to maintain. Without offsetting increases in the systems' benefits, short product life cycles and rapid technological innovation increase the cost of standard cost systems and lower their value.

Self-Study Problem

Injection Molding Department

Injection molding has the following materials and direct labor standards:

		Per Finished Lot
Materials	10 pounds @ $3.00/pound	$30.00
Direct labor	0.5 hour @ $20.00/hour	10.00
Total cost per lot		$40.00

The number of finished lots produced for the period totaled 9,810. The following quantities were used:

Actual materials	97,200 pounds used	
Actual direct labor	3,950 hours	at a total cost of $81,765

During the month, purchases amounted to 100,000 pounds at a total cost of $310,000. Price variances are isolated upon purchase.

There were no beginning inventories.

Required:

a. Show computations of all variances.

b. Comment on the likely interpretation of each variance and describe what each means.

Solution:

a. Variances:

	Materials Variances	Labor Variances
Price variance = $(P_a - P_s)Q_a$	$0.10† × 100,000‡ = $10,000U	$0.70* × 3,950 = $2,765U
Quantity variance = $(Q_a - Q_s)P_s$	900# × $3 = 2,700F	955§ × $20 = 19,100F
Total	$ 7,300U	$16,335F

---

†$310,000 ÷ 100,000 − $3.00.

‡100,000 pounds is used to calculate the price variance because this is the amount purchased. If 98,150 pounds is used for the actual quantity, the price variance is not as timely a performance measure if raw material sits in inventory until it is used.

#97,200 − 9,810 × 10.

*$81,765 ÷ 3,950 − $20.

§3,950 − 9,810 × 0.5.

b. The price variances represent the difference in what was paid and what should have been paid for labor and materials. The quantity variances represent the difference between what was used and what should have been used.

The materials variances in total were $7,300 unfavorable. This was due primarily to a $10,000 unfavorable price variance that was partially offset by a favorable quantity variance of $2,700. Thus, it appears that high-quality materials were purchased because fewer-than-expected units of material were needed to produce the final product. This seems to be reinforced by the labor variances. The wage rate was slightly higher than expected ($0.70), causing an unfavorable wage variance of $2,765. However, the more highly paid employees, coupled with the better-than-standard materials, caused a $19,100 favorable labor efficiency variance. That is, the work force was much more efficient (in the sense of requiring fewer direct labor hours) in producing the final output. The overall result was that the final product was produced for $9,035 (or $16,335 − $7,300) less than standard. The higher-quality direct materials and higher-paid employees more than made up for their higher unit cost.

Problems

P 12–1: Todco

Todco planned to produce 3,000 units of its single product, Teragram, during November. The standard specifications for one unit of Teragram include six pounds of material at $0.30 per pound. Actual production in November was 3,100 units of Teragram. The accountant computed a favorable materials purchase price variance of $380 and an unfavorable materials quantity variance of $120.

Required:
Based on these data, calculate how many pounds of material were used in the production of Teragram during November.
Source: CMA adapted.

P 12–2: Medical Instruments

Medical Instruments produces a variety of electronic medical devices. Medical Instruments uses a standard cost system and computes price variances at the time of purchase. One product, a thermometer, measures patient temperatures orally. It requires a silver lead with a standard length of five inches per thermometer. To make the leads, hollow silver tubing is purchased at a standard price of $4 per inch, cut into the required length, and then assembled into the thermometer.

There was no silver tubing in inventory when a batch of 200 thermometers was scheduled for production. Twelve hundred inches of silver tubing were purchased for $4,680 by the purchasing department for this 200-unit batch of thermometers, and 1,100 inches were used in production.

Required:
Compute the materials variances for silver tubing and comment on their meaning.

P 12–3:   Mickles Ltd.

Mickles Ltd. uses a standard cost system. In June, Mickles's direct labor efficiency variance was $1,470 unfavorable and its direct labor rate variance was $825 favorable. Mickles manufactured 460 batches of product in June. Actual direct labor hours in June were 980 hours. Each batch calls for two standard direct labor hours per batch.

Required:

Calculate the standard direct labor wage rate used by Mickles in computing its direct labor variances in June.

P 12–4:   Arrow Industries

Arrow Industries employs a standard cost system in which direct materials inventory is carried at standard cost. Arrow has established the following standards for the direct costs of one unit of product:

	Standard Quantity	Standard Price	Standard Cost
Direct materials	8 pounds	$1.80 per pound	$14.40
Direct labor	0.25 hour	$8.00 per hour	2.00
			$16.40

During May, Arrow purchased 160,000 pounds of direct materials at a total cost of $304,000. The total factory wages for May were $42,000, 90 percent of which were for direct labor. Arrow manufactured 19,000 units of product during May using 142,500 pounds of direct materials and 5,000 direct labor hours.

Required:

a. Calculate the direct materials price variance for May.
b. Calculate the direct materials quantity variance for May.
c. Calculate the direct labor wage rate variance for May.
d. Calculate the direct labor efficiency variance for May.

SOURCE: CMA adapted.

P 12–5:   Raw Materials Variances

Thirty-six thousand pounds of plastic pellets were purchased for $8,640. These pellets are used in injection-molding machines to produce plastic parts. The pellets have a standard cost of $0.25 per pound. Thirty thousand pounds of these pellets were used in two jobs. The first job called for 14,000 pounds of pellets but actually used 15,000 pounds. The second job also used 15,000 pounds but it called for 15,500 pounds. The company uses a standard cost system, calculates price variances at purchase, and had no beginning inventory of this plastic pellet.

Required:

At the end of the two jobs and before any more of the plastic pellets are used (and before proration or write-off of variances), prepare a table that indicates the financial disposition of the historical cost of the pellets. (That is, account for the $8,640.)

P 12–6: Oaks Auto Supply

Oaks Auto Supply just acquired a patent on an antifreeze recycler that flushes used antifreeze from a car, filters it, removes dissolved chemicals, and then returns it to the automobile without having to dispose of the old antifreeze or use new antifreeze. It is a cheaper and environmentally safer process than replacing the old antifreeze. The recycler will be sold to garages and auto service shops. The patent cost Oaks $2.2 million. The firm will have to invest another $12.6 million in plant, equipment, and working capital. Oaks has a pretax cost of capital of 20 percent. In order to achieve a dominant position in the recycler market, it must sell 2,960 units the first year. To achieve this level of sales, the firm forecasts that the sales price cannot exceed $2,500 per recycler. Variable selling commissions will be $500 per unit. Purchased parts are projected to cost $750 per unit.

Required:
Calculate the target conversion cost (labor and overhead) per recycler if Oaks is to achieve its sales projections and return on investment objectives.

P 12–7: AN7-X1

A new pharmaceutical drug calls for 4.5 ounces of compound AN7-X1 per batch of 250 tablets. AN7-X1 has a standard price of $2 per ounce. An initial inventory of 8,000 ounces of AN7-X1 is purchased for $17,200. The firm produces 1,000 batches of the new drug and uses 4,600 ounces of AN7-X1. All variances are calculated as soon as possible.

Required:
Calculate the price and quantity variances for AN7-X1.

P 12–8: Changing Standards

The empirical evidence reveals that very few firms change their standard prices and standard quantities during the fiscal year. Most firms have the following policy, "We set our standards before the fiscal year begins and we NEVER, NEVER change them during the year (except when we have to)."

Required:

a. Evaluate the "never change" policy. Does it make any sense? Why would firms adopt such a policy?
b. When would you expect firms to change their standards during the fiscal year?

P 12-9: Standard Cost Systems

Consider the following two separate firms. One firm manufactures flexible packaging films for the snack, bakery, confectionery, and tobacco industries. Its manufacturing process has been quite stable for many years, with few technological innovations. Moreover, its products have a long life cycle. The other firm manufactures complex printed circuit boards, primarily for laptop computers and cell phones. It does contract assembly for original equipment manufacturers. Its products have short life cycles and the firm itself faces rapid technological change in its manufacturing processes. Both firms have about the same cost structure; the percentage of unit manufacturing cost that is direct labor is roughly the same for both firms, as is the percentage of unit manufacturing cost that is direct materials.

Required:

a. Which firm is more likely to use a standard cost system to control labor costs? Explain why.

b. How would you expect the two firms' compensation plans for their first-line supervisors to vary? (First-line supervisors manage production employees and are responsible for controlling direct labor and direct materials costs.)

P 12–10: Healing Touch

Healing Touch manufactures massage chairs with the following standard cost structure:

Standard Cost Sheet: Massage Chair

Metal tubing	6 meters @ $3	$ 18.00
Leather	2 square meters @ $7	14.00
Padding	3 kilograms @ $4	12.00
Direct labor	4 hours @ $15	60.00
Total standard cost		$104.00

During the month 500 chairs are manufactured and the following costs incurred:

Actual Costs Incurred for the Month: Massage Chair

Metal tubing	3,100 meters	$ 9,455
Leather	1,100 square meters	7,722
Padding	1,600 kilograms	6,560
Direct labor	1,800 hours	27,270
Total cost		$51,007

Required:

a. Calculate all materials and labor variances (including price, quantity, wage rate, and labor efficiency variances).

b. Write a short report summarizing and analyzing the manufacturing operations for the month.

P 12–11: Marian Health Care System

Marian Health Care is a large hospital system outside Chicago that offers both hospital (inpatient) and clinic (outpatient) services. It has a centralized admissions office that admits and registers clients, some of whom are seeking inpatient hospital services and others outpatient services. Marian uses a standard cost system to control its labor costs. The standard labor time to admit an inpatient is 15 minutes. Outpatient admissions have a standard labor time of 9 minutes. The standard wage rate for admissions agents is $14.50 per hour. During the last week, the admissions office admitted 820 in-patients and 2,210 out-patients. Actual hours worked by the admissions agents last week were 540 hours, and their total wages paid were $8,235.

Required:

    a. Prepare a financial report that summarizes the operating performance (including the efficiency) of the admissions office for last week.

    b. Based on the financial report you prepared in (a), write a short memo summarizing your findings and conclusions from this report.

P 12–12:   Zinc Faucets

The standard cost sheet calls for 80 pounds of zinc per batch of 70 faucets. Zinc has a standard price of $5.10 per pound. One thousand pounds of zinc are purchased for $5,530. Ten batches of the faucets are produced, and 840 pounds of zinc are used. There was no beginning zinc inventory. All variances are calculated as soon as possible.

Required:

Prepare a table that decomposes the total purchase price of the zinc ($5,530) into its various components as calculated by the standard cost system.

P 12–13:   Hospital Software, Inc.

Hospital Software sells and installs computer software used by hospitals for patient admissions and billing. Every sale requires that Hospital Software modify its proprietary software for the specific demands of the client. Prior to each installation, Hospital Software estimates the number of hours of programming time each job will require and the cost of the programmers. Programmers record the amount of time they spend on each modification, and variance reports are prepared at the end of each installation.

    For the Denver General Hospital account, Hospital Software estimated the following labor standards:

	Standard Hours	Standard Rate per Hour
Junior programmer	85	$23
Senior programmer	33	31

After the job was completed, the following costs were reported:

Junior programmer (98 hours)	$2,352
Senior programmer (36 hours)	1,044

Required:

Calculate the labor efficiency and labor wage rate variances for the junior and senior programmers on the Denver General Hospital account.

P 12–14: Johnson Quote

More research is needed to explain the tenacity with which businesses cling to accounting performance information. More empirical research into the consequences of managing with accounting information is also in order. But there already is much evidence that businesses impair their competitiveness and profitability by managing with the information found in standard cost variances, flexible budgets, product cost, return on investment, and other financial measures. Less well understood is why "world-class" manufacturing companies persist in using accounting-based financial performance measures.

Required:

Critically evaluate this quotation.

SOURCE: H T Johnson, "Performance Measurement for Competitive Excellence," *Measures for Manufacturing Excellence*, ed. R Kaplan (Boston: Harvard Business School Press, 1990), p. 84.

P 12–15: Labor Efficiency Ratio

A number of companies use the following ratio to measure operating efficiency:

$$\frac{\text{Earned direct labor dollars}}{\text{Actual direct labor dollars}}$$

Earned direct labor dollars is the number of units produced times the standard direct labor dollars per hour. For example, the machine department produced four jobs today:

Job Number	Number of Units Produced	Standard Labor Dollars per Unit	Earned Direct Labor Dollars
101	100	$3	$ 300
102	200	2	400
103	150	1	150
104	100	2	200
	Total earned direct labor dollars		$1,050

Actual direct labor dollars for today total $1,350.

$$\frac{\text{Earned direct labor dollars}}{\text{Actual direct labor dollars}} = \frac{\$1,050}{\$1,350} = 0.777$$

The higher the ratio, the more output per actual direct labor dollar. Operating managers are rewarded for high ratios.

Required:

Discuss the advantages and disadvantages of using this ratio to measure and reward the performance of factory managers.

P 12–16: Ogwood Company

Ogwood Company is a small manufacturer of wooden household items. The corporate controller plans to implement a standard cost system for Ogwood. The controller has information from several co-workers that will assist him in developing standards for Ogwood's products.

One of Ogwood's products is a wooden cutting board. Each good cutting board requires 1.25 board feet of lumber and 12 minutes direct labor time to prepare and cut each board. The cutting boards are inspected after they are cut. Because the cutting boards are made of a natural material that has imperfections, one board is normally rejected after cutting for each five that are accepted. Four rubber foot pads are attached to each good cutting board. A total of 15 minutes of direct labor time is required to attach all four foot pads and finish each cutting board. The lumber for the cutting boards costs $3.00 per board foot, and each foot pad costs $0.05. Direct labor is paid at the rate of $8.00 per hour.

Required:

a. Develop the standard cost for the direct cost components of the cutting board. For each direct cost component of the cutting board, the standard cost should identify the

   (i)   Standard quantity.

   (ii) Standard rate.

   (iii) Standard cost per unit.

b. What are the advantages of standard cost systems?

c. Explain the role of each of the following persons in developing standards:

   (i)   Purchasing manager.

   (ii) Industrial engineer.

   (iii) Cost accountant.

SOURCE: CMA adapted.

P 12–17:   Associated Media Graphics

Associated Media Graphics (AMG) is a rapidly expanding company involved in the mass reproduction of instructional materials. AMG is organized into a number of production departments, each of which is responsible for a particular stage of the production process, such as copyediting, typesetting, printing, and binding. An engineering department provides technical assistance to the various production units. Ralph Davis, owner and manager of AMG, has made a concentrated effort to provide a quality product at a competitive price with delivery on the promised due date. Expanding sales have been attributed to this philosophy. Davis is finding it increasingly difficult to personally supervise the operations of AMG and is beginning to institute an organizational structure that would facilitate management control.

One change recently made was the designation of operating departments as cost centers, with control over departmental operations transferred from Davis to each departmental manager. However, quality control still reports directly to Davis, as do the finance and accounting functions. A materials manager was hired to purchase all raw materials and to oversee the inventory handling (receiving, storage, etc.) and recordkeeping functions. The materials manager is also responsible for maintaining an adequate inventory based upon planned production levels.

The loss of personal control over the operations of AMG caused Davis to look for a method of efficiently evaluating performance. Dave Cress, a new cost accountant, proposed the use of a standard cost system. Variances for materials and labor could then be calculated and reported directly to Davis.

Required:

a. Assume that AMG is going to implement a standard cost system and establish standards for materials, labor, and manufacturing overhead. For each of these cost components, identify and discuss.

  (i) Who should be involved in setting the standards.

  (ii) The factors that should be considered in establishing the standards.

b. Describe the basis for assignment of responsibility under a standard cost system.

SOURCE: CMA adapted.

P 12–18: Howard Binding

Howard Binding manufactures two types of notebooks: large and small. The large and small notebooks are made of the same cloth cover (direct materials) but in different quantities. The standard cost sheet for each follows.

	Large	*Small*
Cloth covering	3 feet @ $0.30/foot	2 feet @ $0.30/foot
Ring holder	1 @ $0.12 each	1 @ $0.12 each
Direct labor	0.15 hour @ $6.00/hour	0.10 hour @ $6.00/hour

At the beginning of the month, the purchasing department bought 35,000 feet of cloth for $10,850. There were no beginning inventories. During the month, 5,000 large and 8,000 small notebooks were produced. The production records for the month indicate the following actual production quantities:

	Large	*Small*
Cloth covering	16,000 feet	15,500 feet
Ring holders	5,000 @ $0.12 each	8,000 @ $0.12 each
Direct labor	800 hours @ $5.80/hour	780 hours @ $6.10/hour

Required:

a. Calculate the cloth covering price variance (i) at purchase and (ii) when the materials are actually used.

b. Discuss why the two price variances calculated in (a) differ. Which is superior (and why)?

P 12–19: Fast Fax

Sue Young sells fax machines for Fast Fax. There are two fax machines: model 700 and model 800. At the beginning of the month, Sue's sales budget is as follows:

	Model 700	*Model 800*
Budgeted contribution margin per unit	$ 200	$ 300
Forecasted sales in units	100	100
Budgeted margins	$20,000	$30,000

At the end of the month, the number of units sold and the actual contribution margins are as follows:

	Model 700	Model 800
Actual contribution margin	$ 150	$ 350
Number of units sold	150	80
Actual contribution	$22,500	$28,000

Contribution margins have changed during the month because the fax machines are imported and foreign exchange rates have changed.

Required:

Design a performance evaluation report that analyzes Sue Young's performance for the month.

P 12–20: ABC versus Standard Costs

Activity-based costs and standard costs are not necessarily substitutes. However, very few firms use both activity-based costs and standard costs. In fact, some management consultants who advocate ABC argue that before adopting ABC, firms should abandon their standard cost systems.

Required:

a. Concisely describe activity-based costing.
b. Concisely describe standard costing.
c. Why do so few firms use both ABC and standard costing together?

P 12–21: Flower City Cartridges

Flower City Cartridges (FCC) manufactures replacement cartridges for desktop printers. FCC uses standard costs within a job order cost system. In June, FCC purchased 18 gallons of blue ink for $385.20 and produced the following four different cartridge jobs using the blue ink (and other inks, materials, and direct labor):

Jobs	Blue Ink Gallons Used
CJ120	4.2
HP9X2	3.9
CN417	3.8
XRX776	4.4

All four jobs have a blue ink materials standard that calls for four gallons of blue ink per job. Blue ink has a standard cost of $20 per gallon. These were the only jobs calling for blue ink in June. There was no beginning blue ink inventory on June 1.

Required:

Prepare a table that indicates the financial disposition of the historical cost of the blue ink purchased in June. (That is, account for the $385.20 blue ink purchase.)

P 12–22: Great Southern Furniture

Ed Koehler started Great Southern Furniture five years ago to assemble prefabricated bedroom furniture for large hotel chains. Hotels purchase furniture (beds, night stands, and chests of drawers) from manufacturers who ship the furniture to the hotels unassembled. Koehler sends a site supervisor and a small crew of employees to the hotel. The site supervisor first hires additional local employees to help assemble the furniture and then trains them. The locally hired employees along with the small crew of Great Southern employees assemble the furniture at the hotel. This significantly reduces the shipping charges and damage to the furniture. Before sending a crew to the site, Koehler has a crew in his office assemble several sets to make sure there are no problems and also to estimate the expected time required to assemble the particular furniture.

The 500-room Hyatt opens in Tampa and Koehler sends a crew to assemble the 500 bedroom sets. He establishes that 4.5 hours are required to assemble one complete room and the estimated cost per hour is $22. Upon completing the job, the crew reports they had total wages of $49,693 for 2,170 hours worked.

Required:

Write a report evaluating the performance of the crew at the Hyatt in Tampa.

P 12–23: Software Associates

Software Associates (SA) is a computer software consulting firm that specializes in designing and implementing integrated marketing database warehousing programs. Humphrey Catalog is a client. In preparing its bid for Humphrey, SA estimates its total labor cost for this project to be $222,500, broken down as follows:

	Budgeted Hours	Budgeted Wage	Budgeted Cost
Partner	100	$175	$ 17,500
Associate	300	120	36,000
Senior analyst	600	90	54,000
Analyst	1,000	40	40,000
Programmer	3,000	25	75,000
Total			$222,500

After the completion of the Humphrey contract, the following data are reported:

	Actual Hours	Actual Cost
Partner	90	$ 15,750
Associate	280	35,000
Senior analyst	750	63,750
Analyst	1,400	49,000
Programmer	3,600	82,800
Total		$246,300

Required:

a. Prepare a performance report for the Humphrey Catalog project.
b. Offer a plausible explanation for SA's performance on the Humphrey project.

P 12–24:   ColdKing Company

ColdKing Company is a small producer of fruit-flavored frozen desserts. For many years, ColdKing's products had strong regional sales on the basis of brand recognition; however, other companies have begun marketing similar products in the area, and price competition has become increasingly important. John Wakefield, the company's controller, is planning to implement a standard cost system for ColdKing and has gathered considerable information from his co-workers on production and materials requirements for ColdKing's products. Wakefield believes that the use of standard costing will allow ColdKing to improve cost control and make better pricing decisions.

ColdKing's most popular product is raspberry sherbet. The sherbet is produced in 10-gallon batches, and each batch requires six quarts of good raspberries. The fresh raspberries are sorted by hand before entering the production process. Because of imperfections in the raspberries and normal spoilage, one quart of berries is discarded for every four quarts of acceptable berries. Three minutes is the standard direct labor time for sorting to obtain one quart of acceptable raspberries. The acceptable raspberries are then blended with the other ingredients; blending requires 12 minutes of direct labor time per batch. After blending, the sherbet is packaged in quart containers. Wakefield has gathered the following pricing information:

- ColdKing purchases raspberries at a cost of $0.80 per quart. All other ingredients cost a total of $4.50 per 10-gallon batch.
- Direct labor is paid at the rate of $9.00 per hour.
- The total cost of materials and labor required to package the sherbet is $0.38 per quart.

Required:

a. Develop the standard cost for the direct cost components of a 10-gallon batch of raspberry sherbet. For each direct cost component of a batch of raspberry sherbet, the standard cost should identify the
   (i)   Standard quantity.
   (ii) Standard rate.
   (iii) Standard cost per batch.
b. As part of the implementation of a standard cost system at ColdKing, John Wakefield plans to train those responsible for maintaining the standards in the use of variance analysis. Wakefield is particularly concerned with the causes of unfavorable variances.
   (i) Discuss the possible causes of unfavorable materials price variances and identify the individual(s) who should be held responsible for them.
   (ii) Discuss the possible causes of unfavorable labor efficiency variances and identify the individual(s) who should be held responsible for them.

SOURCE: CMA adapted.

P 12–25: Starling Coatings

Starling Coatings produces weather-proofing coatings that protect metal from oxidation. One of Starling's patented coatings, zurtan, is composed of two inputs, magna45 and zelon. While both inputs are required, they can be substituted for each other. The following table describes how many gallons of magna45 and zelon are required to produce a single batch of zurtan.

Gallons of Magna45 and Zelon Needed to Make One Batch of Zurtan	
Magna45	*Zelon*
1	30.00
2	15.00
3	10.00
4	7.50
5	6.00
6	5.00
7	4.30
8	3.75
9	3.33
10	3.00

In other words, one batch of zurtan can be produced using one gallon of magna45 and 30 gallons of zelon, or 2 gallons of magna45 and 15 gallons of zelon, or 3 gallons of magna45 and 10 gallons of zelon, and so forth. Starling has a long-term contract with a defense contractor to supply a fixed quantity of zurtan at a fixed price, neither of which can be altered. The price of zurtan is far above its manufacturing cost. Starling uses a standard cost system and at the beginning of the year establishes the standard quantities of the various raw materials used to manufacture its coatings. Before Starling's fiscal year begins, management estimates that magna45 will have a standard price of $4 per gallon and zelon will have a standard cost of $5 per gallon.

The manager in charge of producing zurtan has decision-making authority to alter the mix of magna45 and zelon used to produce zurtan and is evaluated and rewarded based on two criteria: meeting delivery schedules of zurtan (including quantities and quality specifications) and materials quantity variances of magna45 and zelon.

Required:

a. Before Starling's fiscal year begins, determine the cost-minimizing (standard) quantities of magna45 and zelon per batch of zurtan.

b. Soon after the fiscal year begins, the price of magna45 falls to $3 per gallon and the price of zelon rises to $7 per gallon. What are the efficient (cost-minimizing) quantities of magna45 and zelon that Starling should use to produce a batch of zurtan?

c. Starling has a policy of never changing standards during the year. Standard prices and standard quantities are changed only before the next fiscal year begins. What quantities of magna45 and zelon will the zurtan production manager choose after the price of magna45 falls to $3 per gallon and zelon rises to $7 per gallon?

d. Why doesn't Starling alter its policy of never changing standards after the fiscal year begins?

P 12–26: Seville Techtronics

Seville Techtronics, a manufacturer of subcomponents for a large power supplier, uses a standard cost system. One particular product, M-303, called for a silver-iridium compound that Seville did not have in inventory. Seville purchased the compound and used a portion of it in producing M-303. Upon purchase, the compound was recorded in the raw materials inventory at standard price. The following data summarize the disposition of the silver-iridium compound:

Silver-iridium price variance	$110,000 U
Silver-iridium quantity variance	$60,000 F
Silver-iridium charged to work-in-process	$2,850,000
Actual pounds of silver-iridium used in producing M-303	9,300 pounds
Actual cost of silver-iridium purchased	$3,410,000

Required:

a. Calculate the standard quantity (in pounds) of the silver-iridium compound that Seville should have used in producing M-303.

b. Calculate the number of pounds of the silver-iridium compound initially purchased.

c. Calculate the standard price per pound of the silver-iridium compound.

d. Calculate the actual price paid per pound of the silver-iridium compound.

P 12–27: Trevino Golf Balls

Golf ball manufacturer Trevino is generally regarded as the industry leader. It commands a 40 percent market share in its targeted channels of distribution and reported net profits of $31.5 million on sales of $171 million in the last fiscal year.

A recent trend in the golf ball industry is the movement toward a 15-ball dozen (a so-called value pack). This value-oriented offering provides the consumer with 15 golf balls for the price of a standard (12-ball) dozen. Using one of its less popular, lower-quality golf ball brands, Trevino entered this market in a temporary, special promotion context. The entry was primarily in response to competitive pressures from smaller, lower-quality ball manufacturers who were flooding the market with value packs.

Initially, Trevino encountered several start-up problems relating to the unorthodox 15-ball packaging. Since the packaging machinery had been tooled to accommodate 12-ball dozens, it could not be converted to run packaging for 15-ball dozens. These 15-ball value packs had to be packed by hand. Nonetheless, as the market developed, the value pack became a permanent product offering. Trevino continued to offer its higher-quality, more popular brands exclusively in a 12-ball dozen configuration.

Trevino uses a standard cost system based on cost per 12-ball unit. When the value pack was introduced, it was costed at the 12-ball standard. As a result, the standard cost for the value pack includes only the costs associated with the manufacturing of 12 balls. The cost of the remaining three balls is written off to a value-pack sales promotion account when the balls are manufactured and is treated as a marketing expense for that period. Trevino calculates this written-off amount by taking the standard cost per golf ball (12-ball standard divided by 12) and multiplying it by three.

The table below, drawn from Trevino's most recent business plan, displays how the standard cost of the value pack did not increase to account for the additional three balls.

Product	Units*	Trade List Price	Standard Manufacturing Cost	Gross Margin $	Gross Margin %
Standard dozen (12 balls)	2 million	$17.00	$6.75	$10.25	60.3%
Value pack (15 balls)	1 million	17.00	6.75	10.25	60.3

*A unit is considered a "dozen" package regardless of the actual number of balls in the package.

The senior product manager, defending the use of sales incentives to increase market share in the value-pack market, commented that increasing value-pack sales was appropriate for a number of reasons, including the fact that "we're still making a 60 percent margin on that line, as reflected in the business plan." When asked about the value-pack standard cost, a senior financial officer commented, "Look, we're still accounting for the cost, but just doing it somewhere else, so the bottom line isn't affected. Since we've given marketing a bigger budget to account for the balls, everyone is happy."

Trevino uses standard units as a means for allocating certain categories of overhead in a FIFO inventory system and uses standard gross margin as a component of the manufacturing group's compensation package. Marketing is treated as a cost center and marketing costs are not traced to the product.

Required:

a. What effect is the accounting treatment of the value pack having on Trevino?

b. Why do you think the company implemented such an accounting treatment?

c. Should the accounting treatment of the value pack be changed?

SOURCE: D Arvan, A Thomas, D Titus, and C Webber.

P 12–28: Domingo Cigars

To generate needed foreign exchange, the Cuban government entered into a joint venture with Domingo Cigars of Spain. The joint venture manufactures Domingo Cigars in Cuba using Cuban tobacco and employees. Domingo and the Cuban government split all profits evenly. The contract calls for all financial transactions, including employee salaries, to be in U.S. dollars.

Spanish managers came to Cuba and opened a cigar factory. All cigars are handmade. Domingo hires the best Cuban cigar makers who formerly worked for the Cuban government making cigars. The average cigar roller makes $2.50 per hour in a government factory. Domingo decides to set the effective wage rate at $3.00 per hour to attract the best employees, but will pay them piece rates.

Domingo makes three types of cigars: panatellas, coronas, and churchills. All three use the same type of tobacco, but in varying amounts. Among the many management practices installed by Domingo are an employee incentive system and a standard cost system. Because the time to roll each type of cigar varies, employees are paid different amounts for each cigar type. The following standards are established for production:

	Panatella	Corona	Churchill
Labor time (minutes)	3	4	6
Grams of tobacco per cigar	6	10	20
Effective labor rate (hour)	$3.00	$3.00	$3.00
Tobacco price (per gram)	$0.20	$0.20	$0.20

Each cigar roller selects an outer wrapper and inner leaves. These are cut and hand-rolled to the desired tightness, size, and weight. Then, an outer leaf is rolled on. The cigar is trimmed and placed in a wooden press to provide a symmetric shape. Employees are paid purely on a piece rate for good cigars produced. Inspectors discard defective cigars and employees are not paid for these cigars.

Employees are assigned each day to one of three rolling rooms: panatella, corona, or churchill. Each room is stocked with tobacco leaves. Each roller selects a batch of outer leaves and inner leaves to use from the common tobacco stocks in the room. Sometimes rollers in the same room will share a tobacco pile and will often hand each other leftover pieces if they need some additional filler. At the start of the day, each room is stocked with a preweighed amount of tobacco. At the end of the day, any unused tobacco is weighed and returned to storage. Thus, management tracks the amount of tobacco used in each room each day. Cigars not meeting quality standards are sold to a bulk buyer. However, the roller is not paid for these cigars. Scrap tobacco pieces are sold to jobbers for cigarettes.

Domingo buys only the highest-quality tobacco from state communes who grow the tobacco for government-run factories or Domingo. Since Domingo pays more than the government, the communes willingly sell their best tobacco to Domingo.

The following table summarizes production for the month of March.

	Panatella	Corona	Churchill
Cigars produced	115,000	125,000	60,000
Actual labor hours	4,900	7,000	5,600
Actual tobacco used (grams)	740,000	1,360,000	1,400,000

Domingo purchased 3.5 million grams of tobacco for $805,000.

Required:

a. The piece rate for each cigar type is based on the standard labor minutes for each cigar and a $3.00 per hour wage rate. Calculate the piece rate per cigar paid for panatellas, coronas, and churchills.

b. Calculate the tobacco price variance.

c. Calculate the tobacco quantity variances for each type of cigar.

d. Calculate the labor efficiency variances for each type of cigar.

e. Analyze the quantity and labor efficiency variances calculated in parts (c) and (d) above. What managerial implications do you draw from these variances?

f. What suggested changes would you recommend to Domingo Cigars's management? Be specific.

Case

Case 12–1:   Rust Belt Mufflers

Dr. Madison, inventor and owner of Madison Corrosion Treatment, has discovered that ordinary mufflers and pipes, when treated with his patented process, will become permanently impervious to corrosion. To reap the rewards from his ingenuity, he has opened Rust Belt Mufflers, a chain of 30 corporate-owned muffler shops. Rust Belt unconditionally warrants all of its muffler and pipe installations for the life of the vehicle. From minor adjustments to complete replacement, a Rust Belt customer must be a satisfied customer!

Although Rust Belt's service has become the rage of the Great Lakes, profits have been unimpressive. Simon, one of Madison's employees, scolds his boss: "Here you are, with the greatest competitive advantage in the history of muffler service, doing no better than any of your rivals." Madison retorts, "I'm devoted to science, not business. As long as the enterprise is profitable, I will not interfere with my shop managers." Simon says that the profitability problem is due to squandering of resources by shop managers. The product's superior price, strong demand, and Madison's policy of benign neglect have given managers a virtual blank check when it comes to expenditures. Simon says that Madison's solution is to reduce costs by monitoring shop performance via a standard cost system. Due in large part to early childhood conditioning, Madison does as Simon says.

Each Rust Belt shop provides two services:

1. Replacement of non-Madison mufflers and pipes with modern Madison mufflers and pipes.
2. Warranty replacement of defective Madison mufflers and pipes with new Madison mufflers and pipes.

These services require materials (including corrosion treatment) and direct labor. Materials purchases, installation procedures, and labor allocation are strictly the responsibility of each individual shop manager. Since Madison mufflers and pipes are merely ordinary mufflers and pipes that are treated with Madison's corrosion process, shop managers purchase mufflers and pipes from any supplier of their choosing. Corrosion treatment is done at each shop.

After careful study, Madison adopts the following cost standards per installation. Actual installations include both original and warranty installations.

Materials	$60 per installation
Direct labor	1 hour per installation
Standard labor rate	$11.80

Cost data for the three shops in Buffalo, New York, for the first year of the standard cost system follow.

	State St.	Dewey Ave.	Mt. Hope Ave.
Expected installations	15,000	22,500	10,000
Actual installations	14,500	22,250	11,500
Materials costs	$710,500	$1,346,125	$759,000
Direct labor hours	11,600	21,138	12,650
Actual labor rate	$11.00	$12.00	$13.00

Required:

a. Calculate materials and labor variances for each of the three Buffalo shops. Evaluate the relative performance of each shop based on the calculated variances.

b. Madison's cousin Milty, Rust Belt's MBA intern, presents the following in his analysis of the Buffalo shops under standard costing:

   During the standard costing period, 500 of the installations performed by State Street involved the originally installed Madison mufflers and pipes being fully replaced under warranty with new Madison mufflers and pipes. Work at the Dewey Avenue shop has produced 100 original installations requiring full warranty replacement. At the Mt. Hope Avenue shop, only eight installations have required full warranty replacement. This accounts for all known warranty work in Buffalo for installations performed under standard costing. (Warranty replacement services performed before standard costing were not considered.)

   Has your interpretation changed? In broad terms, is the standard costing system effectively meeting its objectives? What general improvements should be made?

Chapter Thirteen

Overhead and Marketing Variances

Chapter Outline

Chapter 12 described standard cost systems. These systems are used for both decision management and decision control. Standard costs provide information regarding the opportunity cost of providing a repetitive activity, part, or product. These data are useful for allocating scarce resources within the firm and for external pricing. As part of the budgeting process (Chapter 6), standard costs also provide benchmarks for judging performance. Hence, standard cost variances can provide performance measures. Two types of standard cost variances (direct labor and direct materials variances) were introduced in Chapter 12. This chapter completes that discussion by describing some additional variances: manufacturing overhead variances, which help to identify the causes of the over/underabsorbed overhead calculated in Chapter 9, and marketing variances, which pinpoint why total revenues differ from budgeted revenues. Marketing variances illustrate how variance analysis can be applied to nonmanufacturing settings.

A. Budgeted, Standard, and Actual Volume

Before describing overhead variances, it is useful to review some concepts and terminology involving the notion of volume. As described in Chapter 9, most plants or departments within plants produce a diverse set of outputs, not a single homogeneous product. Volume is measured not in terms of output but rather in terms of a common input such as direct labor, machine time, or raw material dollars.

Once an input measure such as machine time is selected as the definition of volume in the plant or department, there are three different ways to quantify volume: budgeted volume, standard volume, and actual volume. **Budgeted volume** is sometimes called denominator volume. As described in Chapter 9, it is set at the beginning of the year and is used as the denominator to calculate the overhead rate. There are two ways to estimate budgeted volume: *expected volume* (which is based on the projected units to be produced next year) or *normal volume* (which is the long-run average production). If budgeted volume is based on forecasted units for next year (expected volume), then budgeted volume falls during business recessions and rises during business expansions, causing overhead rates to vary inversely with actual output. If budgeted volume is based on normal volume, overhead rates do not vary as the business moves through recessionary and expansionary periods. Budgeted volume is denoted by the variable BV.

Standard volume is the amount the plant would have generated if each unit of product manufactured used precisely the standard units of volume allowed. Given the output actually produced, standard volume measures how much input should have been used. For example, suppose direct labor hours are used as the measure of volume. After completing each job, the number of units produced times the standard number of direct labor hours per unit is the standard volume. Standard volume, sometimes called earned or allowed volume, is denoted by the variable SV.

The third volume concept is **actual volume,** the amount of the volume measure actually incurred (e.g., actual machine hours, actual direct labor hours, or actual direct labor dollars). Standard volume focuses on the relation between inputs and outputs. Actual volume just focuses on inputs. Actual volume is denoted by the variable AV.

The three volume measures (budgeted, standard, and actual) differ in terms of when they are computed. Budgeted volume is estimated before the fiscal year begins and before production starts. Both standard and actual volume are computed after production is completed.

An example illustrates the different volume concepts and how they interrelate. The Toronto Engine Plant of Eastern Corp. manufactures engine blocks for automobiles. Three types of engine blocks are produced: four-, six-, and eight-cylinder blocks. An engine block, a one-piece iron casting, is the basic component of an automobile engine and contains the cylinders into which the pistons are fitted. After assembling the block with the heads, pan, pistons, spark plugs, rods, camshafts, and valves, the motor is ready to be fitted with the fuel and exhaust systems and installed in the automobile. The cylinders are bored by high-precision, computer-controlled machine tools, and then other machine tools tap and thread the block to attach the other engine components. Cylinder boring is the key process after the engine block is cast.

Overhead is tracked to departments. Volume is measured in the cylinder boring department as machine hours, or the number of hours each block spends in the computer-controlled machine tool having its cylinders bored. The three motor blocks require the following standard machine hours per block:

four-cylinder block	0.50 machine hours
six-cylinder block	0.70 machine hours
eight-cylinder block	0.90 machine hours

Each block requires some set-up time to mount and correctly position the block in the computer-controlled machine tool. Hence, an eight-cylinder block does not require twice the machining time of a four-cylinder block. Also, a cylinder in a four-cylinder block is larger and requires more boring time than does a cylinder in a six- or eight-cylinder block.

Budgeted volume in the engine plant is based on projected production next year. In other words, expected volume is used in setting budgeted volume. At the beginning of the year, management forecasts the number of blocks to be manufactured based on the projected unit sales of car models requiring four-, six-, and eight-cylinder engines. Using the projected number of blocks per product and the number of standard machine hours per block, management converts the projected number of blocks of each engine into an overall measure of projected volume in terms of machine hours. The calculation of budgeted volume is illustrated in Table 13–1. The plant plans to produce 95,000 engine blocks using 67,500 machine hours. Notice that the expected volume of 67,500 machine hours is not normal volume. The budgeted volume measure used in the boring department is based on the expected number of blocks to be produced next year. If fewer blocks are expected, fewer expected machine hours are calculated. Overhead rates vary inversely with expected engine production in the cylinder boring department.

During the year, production plans change as customer preferences become known. An unexpected increase in oil prices causes consumers to shift toward smaller, more fuel-efficient automobiles with smaller engines. Fewer eight-cylinder engines are made and more four- and six-cylinder engines are manufactured. Table 13–2 presents the actual operating results for the year and calculates actual and standard volumes.

Although more blocks were bored (96,000) than were expected at the beginning of the year (95,000), the standard volume of 67,400 machine hours (which is based on actual blocks produced) was less than the budgeted volume of 67,500 machine hours because more four-cylinder blocks were produced. The budgeted

TABLE 13–1   Calculation of Budgeted Volume (Using Expected Volume)—
Toronto Engine Plant's Cylinder Boring Department

Product	Expected Production	×	Standard Machine Hours per Block	=	Budgeted Volume (Machine Hours)
4-cylinder blocks	25,000 blocks		0.50		12,500
6-cylinder blocks	40,000 blocks		0.70		28,000
8-cylinder blocks	30,000 blocks		0.90		27,000
	95,000 blocks				
Budgeted volume					67,500

TABLE 13–2   Calculation of Actual and Standard Volumes—
Toronto Engine Plant's Cylinder Boring Department

Product	Actual Blocks Produced	×	Standard Machine Hours per Block	=	Standard Volume	Actual Machine Hours
4-cylinder blocks	27,000		0.50		13,500	14,200
6-cylinder blocks	41,000		0.70		28,700	29,000
8-cylinder blocks	28,000		0.90		25,200	25,000
	96,000					
Standard (earned) volume (SV)					67,400	
Actual volume (AV)						68,200

volume of 67,500 is based on expected production, which was set at the beginning of the year using the production quotas of the three engines. During the year, the mix of the three products differed from the forecasts, causing the plant's volume to differ from the budgeted amount set at the beginning of the year. Given the actual mix of blocks bored, total machine hours should have been 67,400 hours (standard volume). In fact, actual boring time was 68,200 machine hours, or 800 more than standard. The right-hand column in Table 13–2 provides the actual machine hours used for each type of block. The four- and six-cylinder blocks used more machine hours than standard, whereas the eight-cylinder blocks used slightly fewer machine hours. Upon investigation, it was learned that to meet the increased demand for small engines, some of the four- and six-cylinder block casting molds were not prepared properly. These blocks were slightly warped and required more boring time to bring the cylinder bore back to specification.

Table 13–3 summarizes the three volume measures for Toronto's Boring Department. Total budgeted and standard volumes are about the same. However, there has been a shift in the mix from large to smaller engines. Actual volumes exceeded standard primarily due to the increased production of four-cylinder blocks.

In the next section, these volume concepts form the basis of the overhead variances.

TABLE 13–3   Budgeted, Actual, and Standard Volumes—
Toronto Engine Plant's Cylinder Boring Department

	Budgeted Volume	*Standard Volume*	*Actual Volume*
4-cylinder blocks	12,500	13,500	14,200
6-cylinder blocks	28,000	28,700	29,000
8-cylinder blocks	27,000	25,200	25,000
Total	67,500	67,400	68,200

Concept Questions	Q13–1	What are three definitions of volume? Describe each.
	Q13–2	Describe the two different ways of estimating budgeted volume. How do they differ?

B. Overhead Variances

Chapter 12 described direct labor and direct materials variances. This section describes overhead variances. Overhead variances are more complicated than direct labor and materials variances, but the following sections based on Chapter 9 clarify the accounting process.

1. Flexible Overhead Budget

At the beginning of the year, the firm estimates its **flexible overhead budget** for the year, as illustrated in Figure 13–1. The flexible budget consists of fixed overhead, FOH, and variable overhead, $VOH \times V$. Or

$$\text{Flexible overhead budget} = FOH + VOH \times V$$

where V is the volume measure (e.g., machine hours). Recall that FOH, fixed overhead, is a total dollar amount per year (e.g., \$1,350,000). VOH, the variable overhead rate, is in terms of dollars per unit of the volume measure (e.g., \$14 per machine hour). In Figure 13–1, the flexible overhead budget is plotted as a straight line with intercept FOH and slope VOH. This straight line shows how total overhead is expected to vary with the volume measure.

At the beginning of the year, management also estimates total budgeted volume, BV (e.g., machine hours), for the year. As described in section A, budgeted volume, BV, can be estimated using expected volume (based on next year's planned production) or normal volume (based on long-run average volume). Given BV, fixed overhead (FOH), and the variable overhead rate (VOH), the flexible budget is used to estimate budgeted overhead (BOH):

$$BOH = FOH + VOH \times BV$$

Continuing with the cylinder boring department example from the last section, assume that the flexible overhead budget is

Fixed overhead	\$1,350,000
Variable overhead	\$14 per machine hour

Fixed overhead is composed mainly of the depreciation charges on the computer-controlled machines. Variable overhead is composed mainly of power, lubricants to cool the cutting tools in the machines, maintenance, and replacement

FIGURE 13–1

Flexible overhead budget

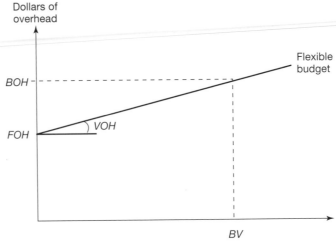

BOH: Budgeted overhead
FOH: Fixed overhead (expected for the year)
BV: Budgeted volume
VOH: Variable overhead per unit of volume

of the cutting tools. From Table 13–1, budgeted volume is 67,500 machine hours. Using these data, budgeted overhead is projected:

$$BOH = \$1,350,000 + (\$14 \times 67,500) \text{ machine hours} = \$2,295,000$$

2. Overhead Rate

As described in Chapter 9, budgeted overhead is converted into an overhead absorption rate, which is used to apply overhead to jobs. Figure 13–2 illustrates the relation between the flexible budget and the overhead rate. Again, *BOH* is the budgeted overhead for the year and *BV* is the budgeted volume (e.g., in machine hours).

As in Chapter 9, the overhead rate, *OHR*, is calculated as

$$OHR = \frac{BOH}{BV} = \frac{FOH + VOH \times BV}{BV} = \frac{FOH}{BV} + VOH$$

OHR is the slope of the line through the origin and the point (*BV*, *BOH*). This overhead rate consists of the fixed overhead per budgeted unit of volume, *FOH ÷ BV*, plus the variable overhead per unit of volume, *VOH*.

The overhead rate in the cylinder boring department is calculated as

$$OHR = \frac{BOH}{BV}$$

$$= \frac{\$2,295,000}{67,500}$$

$$= \$34$$

3. Overhead Absorbed

As work is done in the factory, overhead is absorbed to product (and entered into the work-in-process account) along the line labeled "Overhead absorbed" in Figure 13–2. In other words, the line shows the quantity of overhead absorbed to

FIGURE 13–2

Flexible budget and overhead absorbed

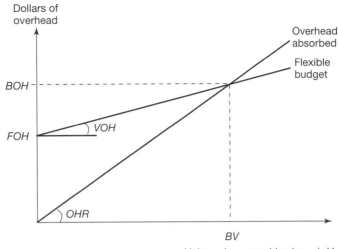

BOH: Budgeted overhead
BV: Budgeted volume
FOH: Fixed overhead (expected for the year)
OHR: Overhead rate = $(FOH + VOH \times BV)/BV = BOH/BV$
VOH: Variable overhead rate per unit of volume

product as production occurs. By chance, if the plant ends the year having produced the budgeted volume *BV* and actual overhead incurred equals budgeted overhead, then overhead absorbed will coincide with budgeted overhead (*BOH*), and overhead absorbed to product will just equal total overhead incurred, leaving no over- or underabsorbed amount in the overhead account.

Overhead is absorbed using *SV* (standard machine hours, not actual machine hours). Most firms use standard volume to apply overhead to products. This produces job costs and product costs based on standard costs. If actual machine hours are used to apply overhead and actual hours differ from standard hours, the overhead charged to each job differs from what the standard cost sheet shows. If work in process and finished goods were charged overhead using actual hours, downstream users would receive cost reports with product costs that differed from standard costs. When all the cost variances are stripped out as they are incurred, deviations from standard are not transferred to downstream users. Using standard volume to absorb overhead prevents cost variations from being passed downstream because of the inefficient use of the input used to measure volume (machine hours).

Table 13–4 illustrates how overhead is absorbed to the engine blocks in the cylinder boring department. Overhead is charged to engine blocks at the rate of $34 per standard machine hour. It is important that standard machine hours, not actual machine hours, be used to assign overhead in the boring department. In Table 13–2, the four-cylinder blocks used 14,200 actual machine hours, which was 700 hours more than the standard machine hours of 13,500. If actual machine hours were used to apply overhead, then the four-cylinder blocks would be charged an additional $23,800 (or 700 hours × $34) of overhead, and the machining inefficiency caused by the warped blocks would be added to the cost of the engines. Instead, standard hours are used and none of the blocks bored is charged for the extra boring time; the additional overhead caused by the extra boring hours is placed into a variance account (described next).

TABLE 13–4   Applying Overhead Based on Standard Volume—Toronto Engine Plant's Cylinder Boring Department

Product	Standard Volume (Machine Hours)	×	Overhead Rate per Machine Hour	=	Overhead Absorbed
4-cylinder blocks	13,500		$34		$ 459,000
6-cylinder blocks	28,700		34		975,800
8-cylinder blocks	25,200		34		856,800
	67,400				
Total overhead absorbed					$2,291,600

4. Overhead Efficiency, Volume, and Spending Variances

At the end of the accounting period (month, quarter, or year), overhead variances are computed. The total overhead variance is

Total overhead variance = Actual overhead costs incurred − Overhead absorbed

This total overhead variance is the same as the over/underabsorbed overhead in the overhead account in Chapter 9. (Often the terms *absorbed overhead* and *applied overhead* are used interchangeably.) Alternatively,

$$\text{Over/underabsorbed overhead} = \frac{\text{Actual overhead}}{\text{cost incurred}} - \frac{\text{Overhead}}{\text{absorbed}}$$

$$= \underset{(AOH)}{\frac{\text{Actual overhead}}{\text{cost incurred}}} - \underset{(OHR)}{\frac{\text{Overhead}}{\text{rate}}} \times \underset{(SV)}{\frac{\text{Standard}}{\text{volume}}}$$

$$\text{Over/underabsorbed overhead} = AOH - OHR \times SV$$

The total overhead variance is disaggregated into three variances that sum to the total overhead variance (over/underabsorbed):

$$\text{Overhead spending variance} = \frac{\text{Actual overhead}}{\text{cost incurred}} - \frac{\text{Flexible budget at}}{\text{actual volume}}$$

$$\text{Overhead efficiency variance} = \frac{\text{Flexible budget}}{\text{at actual volume}} - \frac{\text{Flexible budget}}{\text{standard volume}}$$

$$\text{Overhead volume variance} = \frac{\text{Flexible budget at}}{\text{standard volume}} - \frac{\text{Overhead}}{\text{absorbed}}$$

These three variances sum to the over/underabsorbed overhead amount. In terms of the variables,

Overhead spending variance = $AOH - (FOH + VOH \times AV)$

Overhead efficiency variance = $(FOH + VOH \times AV) - (FOH + VOH \times SV)$

Overhead volume variance = $(FOH + VOH \times SV) - OHR \times SV$

As in Chapter 12, positive variances are unfavorable and negative variances are favorable. Each of these variances has the following specific interpretation:
Overhead spending variance.   This variance measures the difference between how much overhead was actually incurred versus how much overhead should have been incurred for the actual volume worked. That is, given the flexible budget

(FOH and VOH) and actual volume (AV), the factory should have incurred *FOH* + *VOH* × *AV* of overhead. Instead, the factory incurred *AOH* of overhead. The difference indicates to management the accuracy of the flexible budget and/or the extent to which more or less overhead was incurred given actual volume. The overhead spending variance is a catchall variance that captures everything not explained by the efficiency and volume variances. A spending variance can result for a variety of reasons:

- Unexpected changes in the prices of variable overhead items, such as lubricating oil used to cool cutting tools.
- Changes in fixed costs, such as lower-than-expected property tax assessments.
- Changes in the plant's production technology. For example, automating a previously labor-intensive process causes overhead to vary more closely with machine hours than the currently used direct labor hours; the result is that the flexible budget based on labor hours is less accurate as a predictor of overhead costs than if it were based on machine hours.

Overhead efficiency variance.   This variance is the difference in flexible budgets using actual volume and standard volume:

$$FOH + VOH \times AV - (FOH + VOH \times SV) = VOH(AV - SV)$$

That is, because standard volume is different from actual volume, the amount of variable overhead will differ. In the cylinder boring example, actual volume is 68,200 machine hours instead of 67,400 standard machine hours, indicating that for the actual cylinder blocks bored, 800 too many machine hours were used. These 800 additional machine hours cause additional variable overhead. Since overhead costs are presumed to vary at the rate of $14 per machine hour and machine hours were used inefficiently, additional overhead of $11,200 (or $14 × 800 hours) is incurred primarily because the blocks were warped.

Overhead volume variance.   This variance is the difference between the flexible budget at standard volume and overhead absorbed. The volume variance is an estimate of unused or overused capacity of the facility. From the earlier equation,

$$\text{Overhead volume variance} = (FOH + VOH \times SV) - OHR \times SV$$

Since

$$OHR = \frac{FOH + VOH \times BV}{BV} = \frac{FOH}{BV} + VOH$$

we can substitute this equation into the preceding one:

$$\text{Volume variance} = FOH + VOH \times SV - \left[\frac{FOH}{BV} + VOH\right] \times SV$$

$$= FOH - FOH \times \frac{SV}{BV}$$

$$= FOH \left[1 - \frac{SV}{BV}\right]$$

$$= FOH \left[\frac{BV - SV}{BV}\right]$$

If budgeted volume (*BV*) equals standard volume (*SV*), the volume variance is zero. Remember, budgeted volume is set at the beginning of the year. Standard volume is the number of units produced times the standard volume per unit. If *BV* = *SV*, the plant produced work equal to expectations. If *SV* < *BV*, the plant produced less work than budgeted and an unfavorable volume variance results. If *SV* > *BV*, the plant overproduced and the volume variance is favorable (a negative number).

Suppose *BV* = 100,000 machine hours, *SV* = 80,000 machine hours, and *FOH* = $2,000,000. The volume variance is

$$\$2,000,000 \times \frac{100,000 - 80,000}{100,000} = \$400,000 \text{ unfavorable}$$

Actual work performed, stated at standard, is 20 percent less than budgeted. The plant's fixed overhead of $2 million presumably is incurred to provide the firm with capacity of 100,000 machine hours. Since the firm used only 80 percent of its capacity, $200,000 of the fixed overhead was wasted. In this sense, the volume variance reflects the cost of deviating from budgeted volume. Likewise, if *SV* = 115,000 machine hours or 15 percent over budget, then a $300,000 *favorable* overhead volume variance results.

The volume variance does not measure the opportunity cost of the unused capacity. The opportunity cost is the contribution margin from units that could have been produced and sold but were not. Measuring and rewarding performance using the volume variance induces managers to build inventories.

Table 13–5 illustrates the calculation of the three overhead variances for the cylinder boring department of the Toronto Engine Plant. Actual overhead incurred by the department was $2.3 million. With an overhead rate of $34 per machine hour and 67,400 standard machine hours, total overhead absorbed to engine blocks was $2,291,600. (See Table 13–4.) The difference between overhead incurred and overhead absorbed is $8,400, representing the amount of underabsorbed overhead in the cylinder department. Table 13–5 disaggregates this total underabsorbed overhead into the three overhead variances.

In Table 13–5, most of the underabsorbed overhead of $8,400 was caused by the unfavorable efficiency variance of $11,200. This $11,200 represents the additional variable overhead incurred (cooling oil and tools) that resulted from the additional machine time required to correct the warped engine blocks. Because the castings did not conform to specification when they arrived to be bored, additional machine hours were used, which increased the consumption of lubricating oil and cutting tools in the cylinder boring department. Upon further investigation, the favorable $4,800 spending variance was caused by a drop in the price of lubricant. The unfavorable $2,000 volume variance reflects the fact that the department operated at slightly below budgeted volume. (Budgeted volume was 67,500 hours but standard volume was 67,400.)

5. Graphical Analysis

To this point, overhead variances have been described both verbally and algebraically. The same overhead variances can be described graphically as in Figure 13–3. Figure 13–3 is based on Figure 13–2. In the particular case diagrammed, all three variances are unfavorable. The spending variance (computed using actual volume, *AV*) is the vertical distance between points *C* and *D* on the graph. The vertical height of point *C* is the amount of actual overhead incurred (*AOH*), and the vertical height of point *D* is the flexible budget at actual volume.

TABLE 13–5 Calculating Overhead Variances—
Toronto Engine Plant's Cylinder Boring Department

$$\text{Overhead efficiency variance} = \frac{\text{Flexible budget}}{\text{at actual volume}} - \frac{\text{Flexible budget at}}{\text{standard volume}}$$

$$= [\$1,350,000 + (\$14 \times 68,200)] - [\$1,350,000 + (\$14 \times 67,400)]$$

$$= \$2,304,800 - \$2,293,600$$

$$= \underline{\$11,200} \text{ unfavorable}$$

$$\text{Overhead volume variance} = \frac{\text{Flexible budget}}{\text{at standard volume}} - \text{Overhead absorbed}$$

$$= (\$1,350,000 + \$14 \times 67,400) - (\$34 \times 67,400)$$

$$= \$2,293,600 - \$2,291,600$$

$$= \underline{\$2,000} \text{ unfavorable}$$

$$\text{Overhead spending variance} = \frac{\text{Actual overhead}}{\text{cost incurred}} - \frac{\text{Flexible budget at}}{\text{actual volume}}$$

$$= \$2,300,000 - [\$1,350,000 + (\$14 \times 68,200)]$$

$$= \$2,300,000 - \$2,304,800$$

$$= \underline{\$4,800} \text{ favorable}$$

Summary of overhead variances:

Efficiency variance	$11,200 unfavorable
Volume variance	2,000 unfavorable
Spending variance	4,800 favorable
Underabsorbed overhead	$ 8,400 unfavorable

The overhead efficiency variance (computed using the difference between actual and standard volume, $AV - SV$, multiplied by the variable overhead rate) is the vertical distance between points D and E. In other words, the overhead efficiency variance, DE, is the horizontal distance between AV and SV (meaning $AV - SV$) multiplied by the slope of the flexible budget, VOH.

The volume variance (computed using standard volume, SV) is the vertical distance between points F and B. The height of point F is the flexible budget at standard volume; the height of point B is the amount of overhead absorbed. The sum of the three vertical distances, $CD + DE + FB$, equals the underabsorbed overhead amount, AB.

6. Inaccurate Flexible Overhead Budget

The engine boring example illustrates how a standard cost system is able to assign responsibility and estimate the financial costs that one department can impose on another or on the firm. However, the ability of the standard cost system to accomplish these goals depends on the accuracy of the flexible budget. For example, one factor affecting the accuracy of the flexible budget is whether variable overhead per unit, VOH, is invariant to volume changes. Is the flexible budget really a straight line? Chapters 1 and 2 described how congestion costs in a plant tend to

FIGURE 13–3
Overhead variances

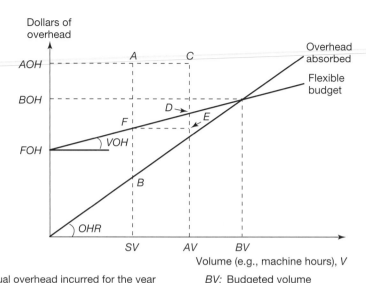

AOH: Actual overhead incurred for the year
BOH: Budgeted overhead
FOH: Fixed overhead
VOH: Variable overhead per unit of volume
OHR: Overhead rate = (FOH + VOH × BV) ÷ BV
Spending variance = Vertical distance between points *C* and *D*
Efficiency variance = Vertical distance between points *D* and *E*
Volume variance = Vertical distance between points *F* and *B*
Total overhead variance = Vertical distance between points *A* and *B*

BV: Budgeted volume
AV: Actual volume based on inputs used
SV: Volume based on actual output × standard
  units of volume per unit of output

rise as plant utilization increases. Congestion costs include such overhead expenses as the additional materials handlers, expenditures, and rush delivery costs. These congestion costs can cause variable overhead per unit of volume to rise as plant utilization increases. (That is, the flexible budget is nonlinear.)

If total overhead costs do not vary as captured by the linear flexible budget, then using the flexible budget to disaggregate the under- or overabsorbed overhead into three variances produces misleading numbers. As performance measures, overhead variances are only as good as the flexible overhead budget.

Concept Questions	Q13–3	Describe the various steps used to determine overhead variances.
	Q13–4	What are the three components of the overhead variance? Describe each.
	Q13–5	Give three reasons why a spending variance could occur.

C. Marketing Variances

Chapter 12 and the first half of this chapter described standard costs and variances for a manufacturing firm. Standards and variances are useful for both decision making and control. Nonmanufacturing organizations also use standards and variances for decision making and control. This section illustrates how standards and variances can be used in a marketing organization.

Trane Company's Standard Cost System	Trane Co., a part of American Standard, is a leading producer of air conditioning systems. Trane Co. built a new plant in 1990 to produce water chillers. This plant operates on a continuous shift, seven days a week, 24 hours a day. Materials constitute 70 percent of product cost; direct labor is only 5 percent of product cost. Standard costs are used to monitor and control cost changes. But the standard cost system was designed to match the plant's unique operating characteristics, namely the high raw materials cost component and low direct labor cost component. The following describes Trane's standard cost system at this plant: • The standard cost system exposes materials cost changes that result from engineering change orders and part substitutions. • There are no direct labor standards or tracking. Labor efficiency and rate variances are not calculated. • In developing overhead standards, the philosophy is to get it close enough, as opposed to using a lot of engineering time. • The system is kept simple and inexpensive. Costs are allocated to the finished unit, not each individual part of the unit. <small>SOURCE: R Clements and C Spoede, "Trane's SOUP Accounting," *Management Accounting,* June 1992, pp. 46–52.</small>

1. Price and Quantity Variances

Table 13–6 provides the basic data used to illustrate the marketing application. The context involves a Pepsi-Cola bottler who supplies the Friendly Supermarket with Pepsi in quart bottles and 12-ounce cans. Quarts and cans are sold by the case, and a case of quarts contains about the same number of fluid ounces of Pepsi as a case of cans. The bottler projects 6,000 cases of quarts and 4,000 cases of cans will be sold to the Friendly Supermarket in May at prices of $3.80 and $5.40, respectively. However, 6,100 cases of quarts and 4,500 cases of cans at $3.81 and $5.38, respectively, were sold. A total favorable variance of $3,051 (or $47,451 − $44,400) occurred. This can be broken down into the usual price and quantity variances illustrated in Chapter 12 for direct materials.

Disaggregating the total variance of $3,051 into various subcomponents allows the Pepsi bottler to better assess customer profitability, design better marketing campaigns, and set more accurate prices. The first breakdown of the total variance is into price and quantity variances as introduced in Chapter 12. That is,

$$\text{Price variance} = (\text{Actual price} - \text{Standard price}) \times \text{Actual quantity}$$

$$\text{Quantity variance} = (\text{Actual quantity} - \text{Standard quantity}) \times \text{Standard price}$$

Table 13–7 presents the calculations of the price and quantity variances for the quarts and cans. Both quarts and cans had favorable total variances and most of the total favorable quantity variance of $3,051 at the Friendly Supermarket was due to the favorable quantity variance of $2,700 on cans. There were small price variances, but most of the favorable variances resulted from selling more units of both quarts and cans than were budgeted.

Suppose the sales manager sets the prices and the route salesperson stocks the shelves. The price variance can be used to evaluate the sales manager and the quantity variance can be used to measure the performance of the route

TABLE 13–6   Budgeted and Actual Sales of Quart and 12-Ounce Cans to the Friendly Supermarket, May (Cases)

	Quarts	12-Oz. Cans	Total
Standard sale price	$ 3.80	$ 5.40	
Standard quantity	6,000	4,000	10,000
Standard revenue	$22,800	$21,600	$44,400
Actual sales price	$ 3.81	$ 5.38	
Actual quantity	6,100	4,500	10,600
Actual revenue	$23,241	$24,210	$47,451

TABLE 13–7   Price and Quantity Variances of Quarts and 12-Ounce Cans, Friendly Supermarket, May

	Quarts	12-Oz. Cans	Total
Actual price	$3.81	$5.38	
Standard price	3.80	5.40	
Price difference	$0.01 (F)	$0.02 (U)	
Actual quantity	× 6,100	× 4,500	
Price variance	$61 (F)	$90 (U)	$29 (U)
Actual quantity	6,100	4,500	
Standard quantity	6,000	4,000	
Quantity difference	100 (F)	500 (F)	
Standard price	× $3.80	× $5.40	
Quantity variance	$380 (F)	$2,700 (F)	$3,080 (F)
Total variance	$441 (F)	$2,610 (F)	$3,051 (F)

salesperson. If the route salesperson gets more shelf space or sets up special display racks in the store, then the quantity variance reflects the route salesperson's efforts.

Instead of reporting price and quantity variances, contribution margins can be used. Price less variable costs can be substituted for price in the preceding calculations. Using contribution margin indicates the additional profits instead of additional sales that result from the route salesperson's efforts. Using price simplifies the example.

2. Mix and Sales Variances

Based on the data in Table 13–7, the question arises as to what caused the favorable quantity variances. Two things happened: More total units of Pepsi (both quarts and cans) were sold and a higher fraction of cans were sold than projected. People bought more Pepsi and they increased their purchase of cans relative to quarts. Quarts and cans of Pepsi are substitutes. The bottler projected that quarts would be 60 percent of total cases (6,000 ÷ 10,000) and cans 40 percent. However, quarts were actually 57.55 percent (6,100 ÷ 10,600) of total cases.

TABLE 13–8   **Mix and Sales Variances of Quarts and 12-Ounce Cans, Friendly Supermarket, May**

	Quarts	12-Oz. Cans	Total
Actual mix %	57.55%	42.45%	
Standard mix %	60.00%	40.00%	
% difference	2.45% (U)	2.45% (F)	
Actual units of all products sold	10,600	10,600	
Change in units	260 (U)	260 (F)	
Standard price	$ 3.80	$ 5.40	
Mix variance	$ 988 (U)	$1,404 (F)	$416 (F)
Actual units of all products sold	10,600	10,600	
Standard units of all products sold	10,000	10,000	
Difference in units sold	600 (F)	600 (F)	
Standard mix %	60%	40%	
Additional sales	360	240	
Standard price	$ 3.80	$ 5.40	
Sales variance	$1,368 (F)	$1,296 (F)	$2,664 (F)
Quantity variance	$ 380 (F)	$2,700 (F)	$3,080 (F)

Table 13–8 displays a further breakdown of the quantity variances of $380 for quarts and $2,700 for cans into two additional variances: mix variance and sales variance. The formulas for these variances are

Mix variance = (Actual mix % − Standard mix %) × Actual units of all products sold × Standard price

Sales variance = (Actual units of all products sold − Standard units of all products sold) × Standard mix % × Standard price

Mix and sales variances are particularly useful when a company sells multiple products that tend to be substitutes. The mix variance captures the effect of substitution among the products, whereas the sales variance measures the effect of differences between actual and standard quantities sold.

The mix variances in Table 13–8 show how much of the quantity variance is due to the change in product mix, holding constant the number of units sold. The higher percentage of cans sold generated $1,404 of additional can sales but reduced quart sales by $988.

The sales variances show that holding the mix constant at the standard mix percentages (60 percent and 40 percent) generated additional sales of both quarts and cans of $1,368 and $1,296, respectively. Therefore, most of the favorable quantity variance of $3,080 resulted from the 600 additional cases sold, not from the shift in consumer purchases from quarts to cans. The analysis in Table 13–8 indicates that consumer demand for Pepsi products increased—not that consumers shifted their demand for cans relative to quarts.

If a company sells products that are viewed as substitutes, the mix variance is a useful way to isolate the dollar magnitude of the substitutions. There are other ways to calculate mix and sales variances. The formulas presented above illustrate just one particular way to calculate the variances. Marketing organizations will tailor their variance reports to provide the most meaningful data for their particular circumstances.

Concept Questions		
	Q13–6	Define four different marketing variances.
	Q13–7	Describe what the mix and sales variances measure.

D. Summary

This chapter extends the discussion in Chapter 12 on standard costs by describing overhead and marketing variances. Chapter 9 introduced over- or underabsorbed overhead as the difference between the total overhead actually incurred and the amount of overhead absorbed. Over- or underabsorbed overhead, which represents the total overhead variance, can be disaggregated into three variances that help identify the reasons for the total overhead variance. The overhead efficiency variance is the amount of overhead that results from actual volume differing from standard volume. The overhead volume variance is the amount of unused or overused fixed capacity. Finally, the overhead spending variance measures the difference between how much overhead was actually incurred versus how much should have been incurred for the actual volume worked.

Marketing variances identify why budgeted revenues differ from actual revenues. Price variances calculate the effect of actual prices differing from standard prices. Quantity variances calculate the effect of actual quantities differing from budgeted quantities. Quantity variances can be further disaggregated into mix variances that show how total revenues changed because customers substituted one product for another and into sales variances that show how total revenues changed because actual units sold differed from standard. These marketing variances illustrate how variance analysis can be used in nonmanufacturing settings.

Self-Study Problem

Injection Molding Department (Continued from Chapter 12)

The injection molding department has the following standards for materials, direct labor, and overhead:

		Per Finished Lot
Materials	10 pounds @ $3.00/pound	$30.00
Direct labor	0.5 hour @ $20.00/hour	10.00
Variable overhead	0.5 hour @ $30.00/hour	15.00
Fixed overhead	0.5 hour @ $54.00/hour	27.00
Total cost per lot		$82.00

Overhead is assigned to products based on standard direct labor hours. The number of finished lots budgeted for the period was 10,000, but 9,810 lots were actually produced. Actual overhead was $425,000 and actual direct labor hours were 3,950.

There were no beginning inventories. All variances were written off to cost of goods sold.

Required:
Calculate all overhead variances.

Solution:
The first step is to construct the flexible overhead budget:

$$(\$27/\text{lot} \times 10,000 \text{ lots}) + \$30/\text{hour} = \$270,000 + \$30/\text{hour}$$

Since 10,000 lots are budgeted and each lot requires one-half hour of direct labor, then 5,000 direct labor hours are budgeted. Also, note that the overhead rate is $84 per direct labor hour ($30 variable + $54 fixed). The overhead rate can be computed directly as

$$\text{Overhead rate} = [(\$270,000 + \$30/\text{hour}) \times 5,000 \text{ hours}] \div 5,000 \text{ hours}$$

$$= \$84/\text{hour}$$

At the end of the year, standard volume is computed as

$$\text{Standard volume} = \text{Actual lots} \times \text{Standard direct labor hours per lot}$$

$$= 9,810 \text{ lots} \times 0.50 \text{ standard labor hours per lot}$$

$$= 4,905 \text{ standard labor hours}$$

Given the flexible overhead budget and standard volume, the three overhead variances can be calculated:

$$\text{Spending variance} = \text{Actual overhead incurred} - \text{Flexible budget @ actual volume}$$

$$= \$425,000 - [(\$270,000 + \$30) \times 3,950]$$

$$= \$425,000 - \$388,500$$

$$= \$36,500U$$

$$\text{Efficiency variance} = \text{Flexible budget @ actual volume} - \text{Flexible budget @ standard volume}$$

$$= \$30 \times (3,950 - 4,905)$$

$$= \$28,650F$$

$$\text{Volume variance} = \text{Flexible budget @ standard volume} - \text{Overhead absorbed @ standard volume}$$

$$= [(\$270,000 + \$30) \times 4,905] - \$84 \times 4,905$$

$$= \$417,150 - \$412,020$$

$$= \$5,130U$$

690   *Chapter 13*

Summary of variances:	
Spending variance	$36,500 U
Efficiency variance	28,650 F
Volume variance	5,130 U
Total underabsorbed overhead	$12,980 U

Problems

P 13–1:   On-Call

You work in the Strategy Analysis department of On-Call, a worldwide paging firm offering satellite-based digital communications through sophisticated pagers. On-Call is analyzing the possibility of acquiring AtlantiCom, an East Coast paging firm in Maine.

AtlantiCom's latest quarterly report disclosed an unfavorable volume variance of $1.3 million. The engineering staff of On-Call, familiar with AtlantiCom's network, estimates that AtlantiCom has quarterly fixed overhead costs of $6.5 million that can deliver 800,000 message packets per quarter. A message packet is the industry standard of delivering a fixed amount of digital information within a given time period.

In valuing AtlantiCom, senior management at On-Call wants to know whether AtlantiCom has excess capacity, and, if so, how much.

Required:

As a percentage of AtlantiCom's current capacity of 800,000 message packets, estimate AtlantiCom's over- or undercapacity last quarter. Assume that the quarterly fixed overhead costs of $6.5 million approximate budgeted fixed overhead and that actual and standard volumes are the same.

P 13–2:   Milling Department

The milling department uses standard machine hours to allocate overhead to products. Budgeted volume for the year was 36,000 machine hours. A flexible budget is used to set the overhead rate. Fixed overhead is budgeted to be $720,000 and variable overhead is estimated to be $10 per machine hour.

During the year, two products are milled. The following table summarizes operations:

	Product 1	*Product 2*
Units milled	10,500	12,000
Standard machine hours per unit	2	1
Actual machine hours used	23,000	13,000

Actual overhead incurred during the year was $1.1 million.

Required:

Calculate all the relevant overhead variances for the department and write a memo that describes what each one means.

P 13–3:   Derf Company

Derf Company applies overhead on the basis of direct labor hours. Two direct labor hours are required for each unit produced. Planned production for the period is set at 9,000 units. Manufacturing overhead for the period is budgeted at $135,000, of which 20 percent is fixed. The 17,200 hours worked during the period result in production of 8,500 units. Manufacturing overhead cost incurred is $136,500.

Required:
Calculate the following three overhead variances:
   a. Overhead volume variance.
   b. Overhead efficiency variance.
   c. Overhead spending variance.
Source: CMA adapted.

P 13–4:   Purchasing Department

The purchasing department of Bradley Inc. is responsible for companywide purchasing. Its total costs are assigned to each division based on the number of purchase orders the purchasing department processes for each division. The purchasing department's fixed costs are $300,000 per year and it expects to process 15,000 purchase orders (POs) at a variable cost of $50 per purchase order. Purchasing costs do not include the cost of the items purchased.

Purchasing processed 16,000 POs during the year and incurred total costs (excluding the cost of the items purchased) of $1,180,000.

Required:
   a. Design a performance evaluation report for the purchasing department.
   b. Describe what each item in the report measures.
   c. Evaluate the performance of the purchasing department.
   d. What other performance measures would you want to collect and report for the purchasing department?

P 13–5:   Spectra Inc.

Spectra Inc. produces color monitors for personal computers. The firm makes 19-inch monitors with the following cost structure:

Direct materials	$220
Direct labor	$150

Because of the rapidly changing market for computer monitors, standard costs, overhead rates, and prices are revised quarterly. While the direct labor component of standard cost has been relatively constant over time, direct materials costs, especially the cost of the circuit boards, fluctuate widely. Therefore, for pricing purposes, management reviews costs each quarter and forecasts next quarter's costs using the current quarter's cost structure. It also uses this method for revising overhead costs each quarter. Overhead is absorbed to products using direct labor cost. Fixed overhead is incurred fairly uniformly over the year. The overhead rate next quarter is the actual overhead costs incurred this quarter divided by this quarter's direct labor cost. Data for the last six quarters are shown.

	2010				2011		
	Q1	Q2	Q3	Q4	Q1	Q2	Q3
Actual unit sales	200	200	190	180	190	250	
Total direct labor	$ 30,000	$ 30,000	$28,500	$27,000	$28,500	$ 37,500	
Actual overhead	$101,000	$102,000	$98,000	$95,000	$97,000	$118,000	
Overhead rate	$ 3.35	$ 3.37	$ 3.40	$ 3.43	$ 3.52	$ 3.40	$3.15

The president of the company, responding to the auditor's suggestion that Spectra set standard costs on an annual basis, replied, "Annual budgeting is fine for more static companies like automobiles. But the computer industry, especially peripherals, changes day by day. We have to be ahead of our competitors in terms of changing our product price in response to cost changes. If we waited eight months to react to cost changes, we'd be out of business."

Required:

Do you agree with the president or the auditor? Critically evaluate Spectra's costing system. What changes would you suggest, and how would you justify them to the president?

P 13–6:   Logical Solutions

Logical Solutions reports the following overhead variances for 2010:

Spending variance	$100,000 (F)
Efficiency variance	$100,000 (F)
Volume variance	$300,000 (F)

In addition, actual overhead incurred in 2010 was $1 million. Overhead is absorbed to products using standard direct labor hours. 2010 volume was budgeted to be 40,000 direct labor hours and fixed overhead was budgeted to be $600,000.

Required:

What were actual volume, standard volume, and budgeted variable overhead for 2010?

P 13–7:   Beanie Babies

The Ogden plant makes Beanie Babies, small stuffed toys in a variety of animal shapes. The toys are so popular that they have become collectors' items. The plant uses a flexible budget and predetermined overhead rates to assign overhead costs to the different Beanie Babies produced. Overhead costs are assigned using direct labor hours. Fixed overhead is budgeted at $2.3 million for the next year and variable overhead is predicted to be $3.50 per direct labor hour.

The plant was designed two years ago for 180 production employees (direct labor), each working 2,000 hours per year. With the high demand for Beanie Babies, 240 production workers are projected for next year, each expected to work 2,200 hours per year. At the end of the year, based on the actual number of Beanie Babies produced, standard volume was 480,000 direct labor hours.

Required:

    a. Calculate overhead rates using expected and normal volume. Round the overhead rates to two significant digits.

    b. Calculate the volume variance for the year assuming expected volume is used in setting the overhead rate.

    c. Calculate the volume variance for the year assuming normal volume is used in setting the overhead rate.

    d. Write a short memo that non-accounting senior managers can understand interpreting why the volume variance in part (*b*) differs from the volume variance in part (*c*). In other words, why do the numbers in parts (*b*) and (*c*) differ and why is this difference relevant to the managers?

P 13–8: Printers, Inc.

Printers, Inc., manufactures and sells a midvolume color printer (MC) and a high-volume color printer (HC). Each MC requires 100 direct labor hours to manufacture and each HC requires 150 direct labor hours. At the beginning of the year, 700 MCs are scheduled for production and 500 HCs are scheduled. At the end of the year, 720 MCs and 510 HCs were produced. Fourteen hundred hours too many were used in producing MCs and 3,000 hours fewer than standard were used to manufacture HCs. The flexible overhead budget is $2.9 million of fixed costs and $10 per direct labor hour.

Required:

    a. Calculate budgeted volume.

    b. Calculate standard volume.

    c. Calculate actual volume.

    d. Calculate the overhead rate.

    e. Calculate the overhead volume variance and discuss its meaning.

P 13–9: Galt Electric Motors

Galt Electric Motors (GEM) produces two types of motors, small and large. Standard machine time to make one small motor is 20 minutes; standard machine time to make one large motor is 30 minutes. GEM plans to make 30,000 small motors and 20,000 large motors during the year. Budgeted manufacturing overhead (fixed and variable) for GEM is $1,800,000. During the year, Galt used 21,600 machine hours to make 27,000 small motors and 24,000 large motors. Actual overhead incurred during the year was $1,900,000.

    a. What is GEM's standard overhead rate per machine hour? How much overhead is reflected in the standard cost of each type of motor?

    b. Use your answers in part (*a*) to verify that GEM's total overhead variance during the year was $10,000. Is this variance favorable or unfavorable?

    c. The table below decomposes the $10,000 overhead variance into spending, efficiency, and volume variances assuming that (1) all overhead is variable and (2) all overhead is fixed. Verify the variances and determine which variances are favorable and which are unfavorable.

Variance	(1) Overhead is Variable	(2) Overhead is Fixed
Spending	$44,000	$100,000
Efficiency	54,000	0
Volume	0	90,000
Total	$10,000	$ 10,000

d. Explain the economic intuition behind these variances. In particular, explain why even though in each case the expenditures, inputs, and outputs are the same, (1) the spending variances are different, (2) there is no efficiency variance in the "fixed overhead" case, and (3) there is no volume variance in the "variable overhead" case.

Source: R Sansing.

P 13–10:   Western Sugar

Western Sugar processes sugar beets into granulated sugar that is sold to food companies. It uses a standard cost system to aid in cost control and performance evaluation. To compute the standards for next year, the actual expense incurred by expense category is divided by the bushels of sugar beets processed to arrive at a standard cost per bushel. These per-bushel standards are then increased by the expected amount of inflation forecast for that expense category. This year, Western Sugar processed 63 million bushels of beets. The accompanying table calculates next year's standard costs.

WESTERN SUGAR
Standard Costs
Next Year
($000s)

	This Year's Cost	Cost per Bushel	Inflation Adjustment	Standard Cost per Bushel
Direct labor	$ 33,000	$0.524	4.0%	$0.544
Sugar beets	58,000	0.921	3.5	0.953
Variable overhead	24,000	0.381	5.0	0.400
Fixed overhead	43,000	0.683	2.0	0.696
Total	$158,000	$2.509		$2.593

Next year, actual production is 68 million bushels. At the end of next year, the following report is prepared:

WESTERN SUGAR
Actual Results Compared with Standard
Next Year
($000s)

	Actual Cost	Standard Cost per Bushel	Standard Cost	Variance
Direct labor	$ 38,100	$0.544	$ 36,992	$1,108 U
Sugar beets	64,829	0.953	64,804	25 U
Variable overhead	28,211	0.400	27,200	1,011 U
Fixed overhead	45,227	0.696	47,328	2,101 F
Total	$176,367	$2.593	$176,324	$ 43 U

Senior management was not surprised at the small variances for labor and sugar beets. The processing plant has very good operating controls and there had been no surprises in the sugar beet market or in the labor market. Initial forecasts proved to be good. Management was delighted to see the favorable total overhead variance ($1,090F = $1,011U + $2,101F). Although variable overhead was over budget, fixed overhead more than offset it. There was no major change in the plant's production technology to explain this shift (such as increased automation), so senior management was prepared to attribute the favorable total overhead variance to better internal control by the plant manager.

Required:

a. What do you think is the reason for the overhead variances?

b. Is it appropriate to base next year's standards on last year's costs?

P 13–11: Rett Publishing

Rett Publishing has a standard wage rate of $23 per hour. Direct labor hours are used to allocate overhead to various publishing jobs. Fixed overhead is budgeted at $2.8 million and variable overhead is $19 per direct labor hour. The following data summarize the results of operations for March:

Materials price variance	$12,350 F
Materials quantity variance	$ 6,430 U
Wage rate variance	$ 3,200 F
Labor efficiency variance	$19,550 U
Actual direct labor hours	12,500
Overhead volume variance	$ 9,130 F
Overhead spending variance	$ 3,175 U

Required:

a. Calculate the overhead efficiency variance for March.

b. What was the total number of standard direct labor hours for March?

P 13–12: Gear Cutting Department

The gear cutting department of Universal Transmissions cuts the teeth into gears. These gears are then finished in other departments and assembled into farm and construction equipment transmissions (tractors, combines, bulldozers). The department contains three identical cutting machines that were purchased two years ago. Projected usage of each machine is 2,400 hours a year. The production budget for the year follows.

GEAR CUTTING DEPARTMENT
Budgeted Production
1/1/10–12/31/10

Gear Type	Budgeted Production (Number of Gears)	Standard Minutes per Gear	Budgeted Minutes
A7474	965	36	34,740
B7682	290	21	6,090
C4983	993	24	23,832
D7575	514	44	22,616
F8390	733	39	28,587
H6363	547	54	29,538
H8983	989	32	31,648
J3839	354	33	11,682
K9828	546	52	28,392
L2738	922	48	44,256
L7378	494	26	12,844
L9383	313	11	3,443
M7483	199	52	10,348
M8992	950	50	47,500
Q2839	423	52	21,996
R093	588	37	21,756
S2829	719	45	32,355
S2882	488	25	12,200
T8390	373	57	21,261
U1920	185	34	6,290
Y7382	647	37	23,939
Total			475,313

The operating budget for the gear cutting department for 2010 follows.

GEAR CUTTING DEPARTMENT
Operating Budget
1/1/10–12/31/10

	Fixed Costs	Variable Cost per Machine Hour
Cutting oil		$ 3.21
Depreciation	$ 632,000	
Engineering	232,890	
Maintenance	69,840	4.56
Operators	25,400	36.34
Plant overhead	124,400	1.20
Utilities	26,800	2.21
Total	$1,111,330	$47.52

Costs in the gear cutting department are assigned to gears based on standard gear cutting machine minutes. At the beginning of the year, the manager sets the cost per minute on the gear cutting machines by dividing budgeted costs in the department (budgeted fixed costs plus budgeted variable costs per machine minute times projected minutes for the year) by projected minutes for the year. The following table summarizes actual operations by gear type.

GEAR CUTTING DEPARTMENT
Summary of Operations
1/1/10–12/31/10

Gear	Actual Production	Standard Minutes per Gear	Standard Minutes of Volume	Actual Minutes of Volume	Percentage Variance of Actual from Standard
A7474	1,041	36	37,476	41,528	11%
B7682	304	21	6,384	6,160	−4
C4983	937	24	22,488	24,671	10
D7575	543	44	23,892	26,359	10
F8390	724	39	28,236	29,546	5
H6363	544	54	29,376	26,970	−8
H8983	958	32	30,656	29,631	−3
J3839	331	33	10,923	10,142	−7
K9828	596	52	30,992	28,823	−7
L2738	1,007	48	48,336	49,494	2
L7378	536	26	13,936	14,484	4
L9383	335	11	3,685	3,936	7
M7483	208	52	10,816	10,657	−1
M8992	1,020	50	51,000	55,543	9
Q2839	462	52	24,024	23,125	−4
R093	603	37	22,311	22,761	2
S2829	675	45	30,375	28,110	−7
S2882	447	25	11,175	12,371	11
T8390	351	57	20,007	19,989	0
U1920	191	34	6,494	6,332	−2
Y7382	585	37	21,645	20,167	−7
Total			484,227	490,799	

Required:

a. Identify all the various measures of volume (e.g., actual volume) that can be used in the gear cutting department for 2010. For each volume measure identified, provide the 2010 empirical magnitude.

b. Prior to the beginning of 2010, estimate the cost per minute in the gear cutting department.

c. An outside company offers to provide cutting for gear #A7474 for $63 per gear. This includes pickup and delivery, and the company guarantees the same quality and timeliness as the gear cutting department. Analyze the outside offer and recommend whether or not the offer should be accepted. Be sure to identify any assumptions underlying your recommendation.

P 13–13:   Soldering Department

The soldering department of Xtel Circuits solders integrated circuits onto circuit boards. The department is highly automated. The existing machinery is state of the art, having been installed only 15 months ago.

Overhead in the department is allocated based on machine hours. Normal volume is 2,000 machine hours per month. Fixed overhead averages $160,000 per month, and variable overhead is $110 per machine hour. Actual volume for the month of March (which just ended) was 2,400 machine hours, and standard volume was 2,200 machine hours.

The accompanying table summarizes the overhead efficiency and volume variances in the soldering department for the last 14 months since the new equipment was installed:

	Standard Volume (Machine Hours)	Overhead Variances	
		Efficiency	Volume
Last Year			
January	800	$42,000 U	$96,000 U
February	1,200	26,000 U	64,000 U
March	1,300	21,000 U	56,000 U
April	1,100	22,000 U	72,000 U
May	1,600	3,000 U	32,000 U
June	1,900	2,500 F	8,000 U
July	2,100	3,000 U	8,000 F
August	1,700	1,800 F	24,000 U
September	1,050	900 F	76,000 U
October	2,300	14,000 U	32,000 F
November	2,150	5,000 U	8,000 F
December	2,000	740 F	0
This Year			
January	1,900	1,200 F	8,000 U
February	2,000	870 U	0

Required:

a. Calculate the overhead rate in the soldering department.

b. Calculate the overhead efficiency and volume variances in the soldering department for March of this year.

c. Comment on any apparent patterns in the overhead variances in the soldering department. What might be causing the patterns?

P 13–14:   Commando Force

Commando Force is a new set of children's action toys consisting of three separately sold pieces: Matt, Kim, and the multi-terrain vehicle (MTV). The MTV can be used by itself or it can hold either Matt or Kim or both. With male and female action figures, Commando Force toys are targeted at both boys and girls aged 7 to 11. Commando Force is sold to wholesalers who sell to toy stores, chains, and discount stores.

The first calendar quarter (January–March) tends to be very slow because it follows the holidays. Here are budgeted and actual sales data for the first quarter.

COMMANDO FORCE
Budgeted and Actual Sales Data
First Quarter

	Matt	Kim	MTV
Standard sales price	$8.00	$8.00	$12.00
Standard quantity	24,000	20,000	6,000
Actual sale price	$7.50	$8.20	$11.80
Actual quantity	23,000	22,000	7,000

Required:

a. Calculate the price and quantity variances for each separately sold toy and all the toys.

b. Calculate the mix and sales variances for each separately sold toy and all the toys.

c. Write a short memo interpreting to management the variances in (*a*) and (*b*).

P 13–15: Wine Distributors

Wine Distributors is a wholesaler of wine, buying from wineries and selling to wine stores. Three different white wines are sold: Chablis, Chardonnay, and Riesling. Here are budgeted and actual sales data for the month of April.

WINE DISTRIBUTORS
Budgeted and Actual Sales Data
April

	Chablis	Chardonnay	Riesling	Total
Standard sales price	$7.00	$8.25	$6.75	
Standard quantity	10,000	4,000	12,000	26,000
Actual sale price	$7.25	$8.10	$7.10	
Actual quantity	8,000	6,000	11,000	25,000

Required:

Write a short memo to management analyzing the operating performance for April.

P 13–16: Auden Manufacturing

Auden Manufacturing produces a single product with the following standards:

Standard direct labor cost per unit	$2.00
Standard direct materials per unit	$3.00
Flexible overhead budget	$60,000 + $4 per direct labor dollar
Normal production	10,000 units

FIFO inventory costing is used. Normal volume is used as budgeted volume. Actual production, sales, and costs for the year were as follows:

Sales	11,000 units @ $20 per unit
Production	9,000 units
Beginning inventory (composed of $5 variable cost per unit and $14 fixed costs per unit)	2,000 units @ $38,000
Direct labor cost of units produced	$18,000
Direct materials cost of units produced	$27,000
Total overhead incurred (composed of $60,000 fixed and $75,000 variable overhead)	$135,000

Required:

a. Compute the overhead rate used to apply overhead to the product.
b. Calculate all variances.
c. Calculate net income under absorption costing. (All variances are taken to cost of goods sold.)
d. Calculate net income under variable costing. (All variances are taken to cost of goods sold.)
e. Reconcile the difference in income between variable costing and absorption costing.

P 13–17:   Turow Trailers

Turow Trailers assembles horse trailers. Two models are manufactured: G7 and V8. While labor-intensive, the production process is not very complicated. The single plant produces all the trailers with 48 work teams of two or three workers. Sixteen supervisors oversee the work teams. Materials handlers deliver all the parts needed for each trailer to the work team. Human resources, accounting, inspection, purchasing, and tools are the other major overhead departments. Some operating statistics for 2010 and 2011 follow.

	2010	2011
Budgeted denominator volume (direct labor hours)	1 million	1 million
Flexible budget:		
Fixed overhead	$2.1 million	$2.2 million
Variable overhead per direct labor hour	$7	$8
Units produced:		
G7	11,000	8,000
V8	12,000	6,000
Standard direct labor hours per unit of:		
G7	40	40
V8	50	50
Actual overhead incurred	$9.0 million	$8.1 million
Actual direct labor hours	1 million	0.7 million

Required:

a. Calculate all the overhead variances for both 2010 and 2011.

   b. Discuss who in the plant should be held responsible for each overhead
      variance.

P 13–18:   Betterton Corporation

Betterton Corporation manufactures automobile headlight lenses and uses a standard cost system. At the beginning of the year, the following standards were established per 100 lenses (a single batch).

	Input	Amount
Direct materials	100 pounds @ $2.00/pound	$200
Direct labor	5 hours @ $18/hour	90
Factory overhead:		
Fixed overhead	$4 per direct labor hour	20
Variable overhead	$6 per direct labor hour	30
Total cost per batch of 100 headlight lenses		$340

Expected volume per month is 5,000 direct labor hours for January, and
105,000 headlight lenses were produced. There were no beginning inventories.
The following costs were incurred in January:

Total factory overhead incurred (Fixed + Variable)		$ 59,000
Direct labor	5,400 hours	$ 99,900
Direct materials used	102,000 pounds	
Direct materials purchased	110,000 pounds	$209,000

Required:

   a. Calculate the following variances:
      (i) Overhead spending variance.
      (ii) Volume variance.
      (iii) Over/underabsorbed overhead.
      (iv) Direct materials price variance at purchase.
      (v) Direct labor efficiency variance.
      (vi) Direct materials quantity variance.
   b. Discuss how the direct materials price variance computed at purchase
      differs from the direct materials price variance computed at use. What are
      the advantages and disadvantages of each?

P 13–19:   UOP

UOP is a manufacturing firm that has depreciation as its only overhead expense
(i.e., there is no indirect labor, indirect materials, property taxes, factory insurance, etc.). UOP uses a flexible budget at the beginning of the year to forecast
overhead in calculating the overhead rate. Overhead is assigned to products based
on machine hours.

UOP uses units-of-production depreciation to calculate depreciation. A single machine manufactures all products. Its original cost is $600,000 and it has an
estimated useful life of 10,000 machine hours.

UOP manufactures two products: A and B. Units-of-production depreciation is based on standard machine hours used. UOP assigns overhead to products based on standard machine hours, not actual machine hours.

The following budgeted data were produced at the beginning of the year:

	Products	
	A	B
Forecast production	100	200
Standard machine hours/unit	5	3.5

Actual operating data for the year are as follows:

	Products	
	A	B
Actual production	110	220
Actual machine hours	600	800

Required:

a. Calculate the overhead rate per machine hour and the amount of budgeted overhead for the year.

b. Calculate the total overhead absorbed to products during the year.

c. Calculate the over/underabsorbed overhead for the year.

d. Suppose UOP still assigns overhead to products based on standard machine hours, but now calculates units-of-production depreciation using actual machine hours. How much is the over/underabsorbed overhead?

e. Explain any difference between your answers to parts (c) and (d) above. What causes the difference? Why might UOP prefer the accounting treatment described in part (d) over that in part (c)?

P 13–20: Artco Planters

Artco manufactures fiberglass home and office planters in a variety of decorator colors. These planters, in three sizes, are used to hold indoor plants. Overhead is allocated based on the standard pounds of fiberglass per planter. Here are standards for the three planters:

Product	Standard Pounds/Planter	Expected Units
24" planter	2.3	1,200
30" planter	3.7	2,100
36" planter	4.6	1,400

Artco uses a flexible budget to calculate overhead rates at the beginning of the year. Fixed overhead for the year is budgeted at $593,950, and variable overhead is budgeted at $2.10 per pound of fiberglass. Actual overhead incurred is $633,805. The accompanying table summarizes the actual results for the year.

Product	Units Produced	Pounds of Fiberglass Used
24" planter	1,400	3,570
30" planter	2,000	7,040
36" planter	1,500	7,120

Required:

    a. Calculate the total variance (over/underabsorbed) if standard pounds are used to assign overhead to products.

    b. Calculate the total overhead variance (over/underabsorbed) if actual pounds are used to assign overhead to products.

    c. Explain why the answers differ in parts (*a*) and (*b*).

P 13–21: Shady Tree Manufacturing

Shady Tree produces two products: M1 and M2. There are no beginning inventories or ending work-in-process inventories of either M1 or M2. A single plantwide overhead rate is used to allocate overhead to products using standard direct labor hours. This overhead rate is set at the beginning of the year based on the following flexible budget: Fixed factory overhead is forecast to be $3 million and variable overhead is projected to be $20 per direct labor hour. Management expects plant volume to be 200,000 standard direct labor hours. Here are the standard direct labor hours for each product:

	M1	M2
Standard direct labor hours per unit	3	5

The efficiency and spending overhead variances for the year were zero. The following table summarizes operations for the year.

	M1	M2
Units produced	30,000	12,000
Units sold	20,000	10,000

Required:

    a. Calculate the plantwide overhead rate computed at the beginning of the year.

    b. Calculate the volume variance for the year.

    c. What is the dollar impact on accounting earnings if the volume variance is written off to cost of goods sold?

d. What is the dollar impact on accounting earnings of prorating the volume variance to inventories and cost of goods sold compared with writing it off to cost of sales?

P 13–22: Megan Corp.

The following data are available for the Megan Corp. finishing department for the current year. The department makes a single product that requires three hours of labor per unit of finished product. Budgeted volume for the year was 30,000 direct labor hours.

Overhead efficiency variance	$4,000 U
Budgeted fixed overhead	$900,000
Number of units produced	11,000 units
Standard direct labor wage rate	$15 per direct labor hour
Total overabsorbed overhead variance	$92,000 F
Direct labor efficiency variance	$15,000 U

Required:

a. Calculate

   (i) Actual overhead incurred.

   (ii) Overhead spending variance.

   (iii) Actual number of direct labor hours.

   (iv) Budgeted variable overhead rate per direct labor hour.

   (v) Overhead rate per direct labor hour.

   (vi) Overhead volume variance.

   (vii) Actual direct labor wage rate.

b. Write a one-paragraph report summarizing the results of operations.

P 13–23: Anpax, Inc.

Anpax, Inc., manufactures two products: L7 and Q2. Overhead is allocated to products based on machine hours. Management uses a flexible budget to forecast overhead. For the current year, fixed factory overhead is projected to be $2.75 million and variable factory overhead is budgeted at $20 per machine hour. At the beginning of the year, management developed the following standards for each product and made the following production forecasts for the year:

ANPAX, INC.
Current Year Standards and
Production Forecasts

	Products			
	L7		Q2	
Budgeted number of units to produce	25,000		35,000	
Production standards:				
Direct labor per unit	10 hours	$15/hour	12 hours	$15/hour
Direct materials per unit	85 pounds	$1/pound	95 pounds	$1/pound
Machine hours per unit	4 hours		5 hours	

There were no beginning or ending inventories. Actual production for the year was 20,000 units of L7 and 40,000 units of Q2. Other data summarizing actual operations for the year are:

Direct labor	700,000 hours	$9.8 million
Direct materials	5.0 million pounds	$5.5 million
Machine hours	270,000 hours	
Overhead (both fixed and variable)		$8.4 million

Required:

    a. Calculate the overhead rate for the current year.

    b. Calculate materials and labor variances. Report quantity (efficiency) variances and price variances.

    c. Calculate the volume, spending, and efficiency overhead variances.

    d. Your boss (a nonaccountant) asks you to explain in nontechnical terms the meaning of each overhead variance.

P 13–24: Maidwell Company

Maidwell Company manufactures washers and dryers on a single assembly line in its main factory. The market has deteriorated over the last five years and competition has made cost control very important. Management has been concerned about the materials costs of both washers and dryers. There have been no model changes in the past two years, and economic conditions have allowed the company to negotiate price reductions for many key parts.

Maidwell uses a standard cost system in accounting for materials. Purchases are charged to inventory at a standard price, and purchase discounts are considered an administrative cost reduction. Production is charged at the standard price of the materials used. Thus, the price variance is isolated at time of purchase as the difference between gross contract price and standard price multiplied by the quantity purchased. When a substitute part is used in production, a price variance equal to the difference in the standard prices of the materials is recognized at the time of substitution. The quantity variance is the actual quantity used compared with the standard quantity allowed, with the difference multiplied by the standard price.

The materials variances for several of the parts Maidwell uses are unfavorable. Part #4121 is one item that has an unfavorable variance. Maidwell knows that some of these parts are defective and will fail. The failure is discovered during production. The normal defective rate is 5 percent of normal input. The original contract price of this part was $0.285 per unit; thus, Maidwell set the standard unit price at $0.285. The unit contract purchase price of Part #4121 was increased to $0.325 from the original $0.285 due to a parts specification change. Maidwell chose not to change the standard; it treated the increase in price as a price variance. In addition, the contract terms were changed from payment due in 30 days to a 4 percent discount if paid in 10 days or full payment due in 30 days. These new contractual terms were the consequence of negotiations resulting from changes in the economy.

Data regarding the use of Part #4121 during December are as follows:

Purchases of Part #4121	150,000 units
Unit price paid for purchases of Part #4121	$0.325

Requisitions of Part #4121 from stores for use in products	134,000 units
Substitution of Part #5125 for Part #4121 to use obsolete stock (standard unit price of Part #5125 is $0.35)	24,000 units
Units of Part #4121 and its substitute (Part #5125) identified as defective	9,665 units
Standard allowed usage (including normal defective units) of Part #4121 and its substitute based on output for the month	153,300 units

Maidwell's materials variances related to Part #4121 for December were reported as follows:

Price variance	$7,560.00 U
Quantity variance	1,339.50 U
Total materials variances for Part #4121	$8,899.50 U

Bob Speck, the purchasing director, claims that the unfavorable price variance is misleading. Speck says that his department has worked hard to obtain price concessions and purchase discounts from suppliers. In addition, Speck says engineering changes in several parts have increased their prices, even though the part identification has not changed. The price increases are not his department's responsibility. Speck declares that price variances no longer measure purchasing's performance.

Jim Buddle, the manufacturing manager, thinks the responsibility for the quantity variance should be shared. Buddle states that manufacturing cannot control quality associated with less expensive parts, substitutions of material to use up otherwise obsolete stock, or engineering changes that increase the quantity of materials used.

The accounting manager, Mike Kohl, suggests that the computation of variances be changed to identify variations from standard with the causes and functional areas responsible for the variances. Kohl recommends the following system of materials variances and the method of computation for each:

Variance	Method of Calculation
Economics variance	Quantity purchased times the changes made after standards were set. Standards were the result of negotiations based on changes in the general economy.
Engineering change variance	Quantity purchased times change in price due to part specifications changes.
Purchase price variance	Quantity purchased times change in contract price due to changes other than part specifications or the general economy.
Substitutions variance	Quantity substituted times the difference in standard price between original part and part substituted.
Excess usage variance	Standard price times the difference between the standard quantity allowed for production minus actual parts used (reduced for abnormal scrap).
Abnormal failure rate variance	Abnormal scrap times standard price.

Required:

a. Discuss the appropriateness of Maidwell Company's current method of variance analysis for materials and indicate whether the claims of Bob Speck and Jim Buddle are valid.

b. Compute the materials variances for Part #4121 for December using the system recommended by Mike Kohl.

c. Who would be responsible for each of the variances in Mike Kohl's system of variance analysis for materials?

SOURCE: CMA adapted.

P 13–25:   Mopart Division

The Mopart Division produces a single product. Its standard cost system uses a flexible budget to assign indirect costs on the basis of standard direct labor hours. At the budgeted volume of 4,000 direct labor hours, the standard cost per unit is as follows:

Selling price	$38.00
Direct materials, 3 pounds @ $5	$15.00
Direct labor, 0.4 hour @ $20	8.00
Variable indirect costs, 0.4 hour @ $6	2.40
Fixed indirect costs, 0.4 hour @ $4	1.60
Total cost	$27.00

For the month of March, the following actual data were reported:

Units produced	9,000
Number of direct labor hours	3,800
Actual wage rate	$20.50
Direct materials used (pounds)	28,000
Average price of materials used	$5.50
Average selling price	$38.75
Number of units sold	8,800
Variable indirect costs	$21,500
Fixed indirect costs	$15,800
Variable selling and administrative costs	$34,500
Fixed selling and administrative costs	$28,000

There was no beginning inventory.

Required:

a. Analyze the results of operations for March. Support your analysis.

b. Present two income statements in good format using absorption costing and variable costing net income.

c. Reconcile any difference in net income between the two statements.

d. What is the opportunity cost of the unused normal capacity?

P 13–26: Butler Products

A manufacturing company produces a large variety of products within the Butler family of products. They are produced in three finishing departments (A, B, and C), which have identical assembly operations but package the products differently for different lines of business.

Each finishing line packages units as either single units or multiple units per package. For allocating overhead, volume is defined in terms of machine hours. Each department can package 1,140 single units per hour.

Department A has the oldest equipment, which is in the last year of its depreciable life. Department B's equipment is about half depreciated. Department C's equipment is in the second year of its life.

The budget prepared for each department in 2010 included the following costs, volumes, and overhead rates (M denotes millions):

	A	B	C
Expected number of units	73 M	73 M	55 M
Fixed overhead			
General expense	$1.5 M	$2.0 M	$1.25 M
Rent	$1.5 M	$2.0 M	$1.75 M
Depreciation	$0.5 M	$2.0 M	$5.0 M
Variable overhead	$150/machine hour	$131/machine hour	$150/machine hour
Machine rate	1,140 units/hour	1,140 units/hour	1,140 units/hour
Direct materials	$0.50/unit	$0.52/unit	$0.55/unit
Direct labor	$0.15/unit	$0.15/unit	$0.135/unit

The general expense portion of the overhead is set by each department at the beginning of the year for training, capital items under $2,500, and other department needs. The rent charged to each department is determined by the age and the structure of the building in which the department operates. In general, machines that are shut down because of volume decreases are not removed, so rent charges do not decrease with volume.

The company currently determines unit manufacturing cost (UMC) charges on a department basis, with one UMC for all types of products finished in that department. Under- or overabsorbed overhead is aggregated over the entire division and distributed to the departments based on normal volume.

The packaging machines in each department require different amounts of maintenance (variable overhead). In department A, the maintenance is higher because of older drive and logic systems. In department C, it is higher due to start-up costs that should decrease with time.

Direct materials costs depend on the products each department has been designated to run and the age of the equipment. They are outside the control of the department.

In 2010 Butler sales softened and not all of the capacity in departments A, B, and C is needed in 2011. Some capacity will be eliminated in one of the departments.

The UMCs for 2010 were as follows:

	A	B	C
Actual units packaged	67 M	73 M	49 M
Direct labor per unit	$0.15	$0.15	$0.135
Direct materials per unit	$0.50	$0.52	$0.55
Actual overhead charge	$12.7 M	$14.7 M	$14.3 M
Actual machine hours	58,772	64,035	42,982

Required:

a. Calculate all variances. Which department best manages the overhead that is within its control?

b. How would you recommend that the division distribute the fixed overhead that is not controllable by the departments?

c. Given the reduced demand, which department should reduce volume? Why?

SOURCE: G Butler, E Rubiano, S Tedesco, and B Watkins.

Cases

Case 13–1: Allglow Company

Allglow Company is a cosmetics manufacturer specializing in stage makeup. The company's best-selling product is SkinKlear, a protective cream used under stage makeup to protect the skin. SkinKlear is packaged in three sizes—eight ounces, one pound, and three pounds—and regularly sells for $21 per pound. The standard cost of SkinKlear, based on Allglow's normal monthly production of 8,000 pounds, is as follows:

Cost Item	Quantity	Standard Cost	Total Cost
Direct materials			
Cream base	9.0 ounces	$0.05/ounce	$0.45
Moisturizer	6.5 ounces	0.10/ounce	0.65
Fragrance	0.5 ounces	1.00/ounce	0.50
			$1.60
Direct labor*			
Mixing	0.5 hour	$4.00/hour	$2.00
Compounding	1.0 hour	5.00/hour	5.00	7.00
Variable overhead†	1.5 hours	$2.10/hour		3.15
Total standard cost per pound			$11.75

*Direct labor dollars include employee benefits.
†Absorbed on the basis of direct labor hours.

Based on these standard costs, Allglow prepares monthly budgets. Here are the budgeted performance and the actual performance for May, when the company produced and sold 9,000 pounds of SkinKlear.

ALLGLOW COMPANY
SkinKlear
Contribution Report
May

	Budget	Actual	Variance
Units	8,000	9,000	1,000 F
Revenue	$168,000	$180,000	$12,000 F
Direct materials	12,800	16,200	3,400 U
Direct labor	56,000	62,500	6,500 U
Variable overhead	25,200	30,900	5,700 U
Total variable costs	$ 94,000	$109,600	$15,600 U
Contribution margin	$ 74,000	$ 70,400	$ 3,600 U

Barbara Simmons, Allglow's president, was not pleased with these results. Despite a sizable increase in the sales of SkinKlear, there was a decrease in the product's contribution to the overall profitability of the firm. Simmons has asked Allglow's cost accountant, Brian Jackson, to prepare a report that identifies the reasons why the contribution margin for SkinKlear has decreased. Jackson has gathered this information to help in preparing the report:

ALLGLOW COMPANY
SkinKlear
Usage Report
May

Cost Item	Quantity	Actual Cost
Direct materials		
Cream base	84,000 ounces	$ 4,200
Moisturizer	60,000 ounces	7,200
Fragrance	4,800 ounces	4,800
Direct labor		
Mixing	4,500 hours	18,000
Compounding, manual	5,300 hours	26,500
Compounding, mechanized	2,700 hours	13,500
Compounding, idle	900 hours	4,500
Variable overhead		30,900
Total variable cost		$109,600

While doing his research, Jackson discovered that the manufacturing department had mechanized one of the manual operations in the compounding process on an experimental basis. The mechanized operation replaced manual operations that represented 40 percent of the compounding process.

The employees' inexperience with the mechanized operation caused increased usage of both the cream base and the moisturizer; however, Jackson believed that these inefficiencies would be negligible if mechanization became a permanent part of the process and the employees' skills improved. The idle time in compounding was traceable to the fact that fewer employees were required for the mechanized process. During this experimental period, the idle time was charged to direct labor rather than overhead. The excess employees could be either reassigned or laid off in the future. Jackson was also able to determine that all of the variable manufacturing overhead costs over standard could be traced directly to the mechanization process. These additional overhead costs are expected to persist if mechanization of the compounding process is continued.

Required:

a. Prepare an explanation of the $3,600 unfavorable variance between the budgeted and actual contribution margins for SkinKlear during May by calculating the following variances:

   (i)   Sales price variance.

   (ii) Materials price variance.

   (iii) Materials quantity variance.

   (iv) Labor efficiency variance.

   (v)   Overhead efficiency variance.

   (vi) Overhead spending variance.

   (vii) Contribution margin (CM) volume variance. Note that CM volume variance = Budgeted unit CM(Actual units − Budgeted units).

b. Allglow Company must decide whether or not the compounding operation that was mechanized on an experimental basis should continue to be mechanized. Calculate the variable cost savings that can be expected to arise in the future from the mechanization. Assume that 40 percent of the compounding process is mechanized. Explain your answer.

SOURCE: CMA adapted.

Case 13–2: Lancaster Chamber Orchestra

The Lancaster Chamber Orchestra is a small community orchestra that offers two distinct concert series for its patrons. Series A is devoted entirely to the performance of a classical repertoire and offers 10 concerts throughout the year, while Series B consists of six pops concerts and serves to broaden the audience base of the ensemble.

Since programming needs change from concert to concert, musicians are hired on a per-service basis. (A service is either a rehearsal or a concert.) They are paid at differential average rates due to instrumental doubling requirements and also due to solo pay for woodwinds, percussion, and brass players. After the budget has been set, variances in musician costs are the result of changes in programming and rehearsal scheduling. Programming changes can cause different numbers of musicians to be needed for a particular series of rehearsals and concerts or can change the doubling requirements. Changes in rehearsal scheduling can alter needs for certain families of instruments at some rehearsals. For example, one Series A concert usually consists of six services, but not all instruments are required at each service. Programming and rehearsal scheduling are decided by the music director, Maestro Fritz Junger, but musician cost constraints are imposed by the director of production, Candice Wrightway. Budgeted and actual musician costs for the 2010–2011 season follow.

LANCASTER CHAMBER ORCHESTRA
Musicians' Budget
2010–2011

Series A

		Budget		Actual	
Instrument Family	Average Rate	Number of Musicians	Services per Musician	Number of Musicians	Services per Musician
Woodwinds	$65/hour	11	60	10	56
Brass	$62/hour	10	55	12	53
Percussion	$58/hour	3	50	3	52
Strings	$55/hour	25	60	28	59

Series B

		Budget		Actual	
Instrument Family	Average Rate	Number of Musicians	Services per Musician	Number of Musicians	Services per Musician
Woodwinds	$65/hour	8	21	10	23
Brass	$62/hour	14	24	12	24
Percussion	$58/hour	5	24	3	24
Strings	$55/hour	22	21	28	19

When the budget was prepared at the beginning of the year, Alan Voit, director of marketing, admitted that projected ticket sales for the two series were optimistic, but he believed that his innovative advertising campaign would help the orchestra meet its goal. Although pops sales came in almost exactly on target, a devastating ice storm caused the cancellation of one of the classical concerts. Unfortunately, rehearsals had already been held and the musicians had been paid for their services. Series sales figures for the three levels of ticket prices follow.

LANCASTER CHAMBER ORCHESTRA
Revenue Budget
2010–2011

Series A

		Budget (10 Concerts)		Actual (9 Concerts)	
Price	Capacity per Concert	Attendance	Revenue	Attendance	Revenue
$12	800	7,500	$90,000	6,030	$72,360
15	300	2,800	42,000	2,475	37,125
20	150	1,300	26,000	1,260	25,200

Series B

		Budget (6 Concerts)		Actual (6 Concerts)	
Price	Capacity per Concert	Attendance	Revenue	Attendance	Revenue
$14	800	4,680	$65,520	4,734	$66,276
16	300	1,680	26,880	1,704	27,264
25	150	900	22,500	852	21,300

As with any orchestra, ticket sales alone are never enough to totally cover expenses, so the director of development, Lydia Givme, is responsible for the coordination of fundraising in the community. Unfortunately, the goals set at the beginning of the year did not anticipate an extended recession, with potential private, corporate, and government contributors tightening their fiscal belts.

Additional expenses include a long-term rental agreement for the hall, a permanent conductor, guest artists, music rental and advertising costs, and variable production costs based on total services. Music rental and advertising are treated as fixed expenses even though their cost may vary during the course of the season. Here are budgeted fixed and variable expenses for 2010–2011.

LANCASTER CHAMBER ORCHESTRA
Budgeted Fixed and Variable Expenses
2010–2011

	Series A	Series B
Rent	$ 8,000	$ 4,800
Conductors	30,000	12,200
Guest artists	18,000	6,000
Music rental	450	800
Advertising	10,000	6,000
Variable production	$15/musician service	$15/musician service

The income statement for 2010–2011 follows.

LANCASTER CHAMBER ORCHESTRA
Income Statement
2010–2011

	Budget	Actual
Earned income		
Ticket revenue	$ 272,900	$ 249,525
Operating expenses		
Musicians	232,322	241,982
Hall rental	12,800	12,800
Conductors	42,200	42,200
Guest artists	24,000	24,000
Music rental	1,250	1,100
Advertising	16,000	16,200
Variable production	59,190	63,953
Total expenses	$ 387,762	$ 402,235
Operating income	$(114,862)	$(152,710)
Other income		
Private and corporate contributions	100,000	95,000
Public funding	25,000	20,000
Total other income	$ 125,000	$ 115,000
Net surplus/(deficit)	$ 10,138	$ (37,710)

Required:

a. Calculate a flexible budget for the Lancaster Chamber Orchestra's 2010–2011 season.

b. After calculating the flexible budget, Randall Nobucs, director of finance, found a total unfavorable variance in net income of $53,158. Account for this unfavorable variance by calculating

   (i) Revenue variances.

  (ii) Labor efficiency variances.

 (iii) Overhead efficiency and overhead spending variances.

c. Nobucs is concerned that if the orchestra faces similar problems in the next season, the accumulated deficit will cause bankruptcy. He argues with Alan Voit that a 15 percent increase in ticket prices would ensure a balanced budget for the 2010–2011 season. Discuss the feasibility of this strategy.

d. In examining the income statement, CEO Peter Morris is puzzled. He believes that all of his senior staff members are superb and is not sure where to lay the blame for the orchestra's dismal financial performance. Discuss the areas of specialized knowledge involved in the operation. Which person should be held accountable for each variance?

SOURCE: M Ames, J Dallas, R Krebs, W Perdue, and J Ricker.

Chapter Fourteen

Management Accounting in a Changing Environment

The business sections of bookstores contain a variety of works describing how to make organizations function better. They speak of organizational innovations such as *benchmarking, empowerment, Total Quality Management, reengineering, teaming, the virtual corporation, downsizing, just-in-time,* and *corporate culture*. Most of these prescriptions are not directed specifically at improving firms' internal accounting systems. However, if implemented, most of these organizational changes require significant changes in the accounting system because the accounting system is an integral part of most firms' organizational architecture.

This chapter expands on the framework first introduced in Chapter 1 (section E), in which those forces that motivate changes in accounting and organizational architecture were identified. Such a framework is useful for understanding when a particular organizational innovation, such as Total Quality Management (TQM), should be introduced and the accounting implications of such a change.

Previous chapters of this book described and analyzed management accounting systems. Besides being used for both decision making and control, these accounting systems support external reporting for shareholders, taxes, and government regulations. Thus, one of the central themes of this text is that trade-offs arise when the accounting system is designed for multiple purposes. In addition to providing a better understanding of the internal uses of the accounting system, this book reinforces the importance of viewing the accounting system as part of the firm's organizational architecture. This analytic structure will help readers better understand, use, and design future accounting systems as well as other systems that evaluate and reward performance and partition decision rights.

SAP

A very popular software program, supplied by the German firm SAP, is an integrative suite of applications: financial accounting, production planning, sales and distribution, cost accounting, order costing, materials management, quality assurance, and human resources. Several thousand clients, including Dow Chemical, Du Pont, Chevron, and Exxon, use this software because of its flexibility and power. It has nine foreign languages and multiple currencies, supporting global operations. A complete, large-company SAP installation can cost from $20 to $200 million and take up to five years.

This software allows users on-line access to data in other operating divisions. While the software modules are functionally oriented (e.g., accounting, marketing, human resources), because they are integrated, data can be transferred easily among modules. This helps companies to change their organizational architectures from being functional to being process-oriented.

SAP software allows firms to automate many formerly manual administrative processes. Kodak installed SAP software to reengineer its order-taking business process. Order takers can now make immediate decisions about granting customers credit and the software lets them access on-line production data so customers can be told when their order will be shipped. The time to deliver products was cut 70 percent and telephone response time to customers fell 50 percent.

SOURCE: J Xenakis, "Taming SAP," *CFO*, March 1996, pp. 23–30.

This final chapter summarizes the text and applies the analysis in the previous chapters to some recent internal accounting system innovations. Section A reviews many of the key points raised in earlier chapters and expands Chapter 1's integrative framework in which accounting is an integral part of the firm's organizational architecture. This framework is used in section B to analyze recent organizational innovations (Total Quality Management, just-in-time production, and the balanced scorecard) and how accounting systems have responded to them. Section C discusses when accounting systems should be changed. Finally, section D offers a few concluding thoughts.

Over the course of your career, you will see numerous proposals to modify your firm's internal accounting system. Successful managers are those who can identify and implement firm-value-increasing proposals and avoid value-destroying changes. The three organizational innovations discussed in section B are good case studies for applying what has been learned thus far. They also help review the strengths and weaknesses of the traditional accounting systems studied earlier.

A. Integrative Framework

As described in Chapter 4, firms arise because they can produce goods and services more cheaply than single proprietors transferring intermediate products in market transactions. But with firms come agency problems because the employees tend to care more about their own personal welfare than about the owners' welfare. Organizational architectures arise to control these agency costs: Decision rights are partitioned and performance is evaluated and rewarded. A critical task is linking the decision rights with the knowledge required to make the decision. It may be easier to transfer the decision rights to the person with the knowledge than to transfer knowledge to the person with the decision rights.

Figure 14–1 expands Chapter 1's integrative framework for understanding how the accounting system is used in the firm's organizational architecture. Starting at the top, two external factors (technological innovation and market conditions) affect the firm's business strategy (described below). The business strategy then interacts with the firm's organizational architecture to provide incentives for managers and employees. These incentives affect the actions taken, which in turn affect the value of the firm. Thus, Figure 14–1 emphasizes that external factors like technology and market conditions affect investments, organizational architecture, incentives, actions, and ultimately the value of the firm.

1. Organizational Architecture

The box labeled organizational architecture in Figure 14–1 outlines the three major elements of the firm's organizational architecture described in Chapter 4. The first element, decision rights partitioning, consists in part of separating decision management from control. In particular, each decision is decomposed into the following sequence of requests and approvals:

Decision Step	Control or Management
1. Decision initiation	Management
2. Decision ratification	Control
3. Decision implementation	Management
4. Decision monitoring	Control

FIGURE 14–1

The determinants of business strategy, organizational architecture, and firm value

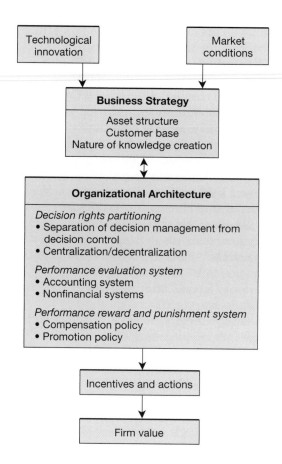

The individual with the decision rights for decision management usually does not have the decision rights for control. This separation of decision management from control reduces the agency problem in organizations. For example, as described in Chapter 12, standard-setting usually requires input from individuals who will have their performance judged, at least in part, by these standards. Therefore, the decision rights to set or change the standards are not all vested in the same people who will be judged by the standards. The cost accounting department, industrial engineering, and senior management retain the decision control rights to ratify and monitor the standard costs.

In order to make decisions (for either decision management or control), managers require information. One would expect the information used for ratifying and monitoring (control) to be qualitatively different from the information used in initiation and implementation (management). Decision control information is likely to be more aggregate, less detailed, less timely, and less under the control of the manager being monitored than is decision management information. In particular, the manager being monitored should have less discretion to alter the information system being used for control than the manager using the information for decision management.

Another aspect of decision rights partitioning is deciding what part of the organization should be able to make a particular decision; this is often referred to as the centralization–decentralization question. The location of decision rights affects the structure of the firm—whether the firm is organized functionally by

The Value Chain	The *value chain* is defined as those processes from research and development, design and engineering, production, and distribution through customer service that are critical to satisfying the customer and hence add value. Managing the firm's value chain involves a series of integrated applications designed to promote collaboration across all aspects of the supply chain. These include demand planning, inventory planning, supply chain planning, and other capabilities that increase customer responsiveness, reduce cycle time, and control costs. Value chain management often extends to electronically linking suppliers, customers, distributors, or other trading partners to share forecast, inventory, and replenishment plans easily and inexpensively. Technological innovations that have lowered telecommunication costs have spawned electronic data interchange (EDI) and vendor managed inventory (VMI) systems—computer-linked systems designed to allow firms to better manage their value chains.

marketing, manufacturing, and distribution or else by lines of business. In all cases, decision rights must be linked with the knowledge needed for decision making.

The second component of a firm's organizational architecture in Figure 14–1 is the performance evaluation system, which includes the accounting system. Besides using accounting-based measures of performance, we have seen firms also develop nonaccounting-based measures: the firm's stock price, customer complaints, quality, and percentage of deliveries on time.

The third component of a firm's organizational architecture is the performance reward system. This consists of the firm's compensation and promotion policies. If performance can be measured easily and with little error, such as by counting the number of units produced by the employee, then more of the employee's pay varies directly with performance (piece rate). Otherwise, more of the employee's compensation is relatively fixed and is not tied directly to measured performance.

2. Business Strategy

Why do firms have different organizational architectures, including different accounting systems? What factors cause firms to modify their organizational architectures? The top three boxes in Figure 14–1, labeled technological innovation, market conditions, and business strategy, provide a rudimentary outline of the factors affecting a firm's organizational architecture.

Each firm faces different investment opportunities, which are the investment projects available to the firm today and in the future.[1] The investment projects available to and selected by the firm comprise its **business strategy**. Some firms, such as consumer electronics firms, have large R&D programs that create many

---

[1] The following papers present evidence regarding the interdependencies among organizational architecture, capital structure, and accounting choice outlined in this section and summarized in Figure 14–1: A Christie, M Joye, and R Watts, "Decentralization of the Firm: Theory and Evidence," *Journal of Corporate Finance* 8 (2002); C Smith and R Watts, "The Investment Opportunity Set and Corporate Financing, Dividend, and Compensation Policies," *Journal of Financial Economics* 32 (1992); and J Gaver and K Gaver, "Additional Evidence on the Association between the Investment Opportunity Set and Corporate Financing, Dividend, and Compensation Policy," *Journal of Accounting and Economics* 16 (1993), pp. 125–60. Also see J Brickley, C Smith, and J Zimmerman, *Managerial Economics and Organizational (Architecture)* 3rd ed. (New York: McGraw-Hill/Irwin, 2004).

Business Strategy and Customer Base at Xerox

Xerox's traditional customer was the manager of the client's central reprographics department (CRD). Most large firms have CRDs with high-volume, light-lens copiers. CRDs were fairly similar, with operators feeding hard-copy originals and producing large volumes of copies. But new digital technology allows users to network computers directly to copiers. The customers of this new digital technology are no longer CRD managers, but computer center (information management) managers. Xerox sales representatives now must have more technical expertise in computer systems and networking and more specialized knowledge of the customer's business and document-processing needs. This has necessitated a change in how Xerox's sales force is organized. Instead of being organized geographically and by size of customer, the sales force is being organized more along industry lines.

new product ideas, some of which are profitable. Other firms, such as utilities, have very few new investment projects; regulatory agencies limit the types of services they can provide, and their investment opportunities consist of maintaining their current power-generating capacity. Public utilities rely on increases in consumer demand for electricity and heat to grow the utility's business, and most of their value derives from their existing assets in place (power plants and distribution systems). Firms such as consumer electronics firms and pharmaceuticals, however, have significant amounts of future growth options because of their R&D investments.

One important existing asset that generates future investment opportunities is the firm's *brand-name capital*, which provides consumer name recognition that lowers the information costs of introducing new products. Pepsi is recognized worldwide. When Pepsi introduced Diet Pepsi, consumers already had an expectation of taste and quality before sampling the new product. Its existing brand-name capital gives Pepsi a cost advantage that new entrants do not have when introducing a new product. Thus, brand-name capital affects the types of new investments a firm will undertake.

Business strategy affects the firm's organizational architecture because it determines the firm's asset structure, its customer base, and how knowledge is created and disseminated within the firm. Each of these in turn affects and is affected by the firm's organizational architecture. (Notice the two-way arrow in Figure 14–1.) That is, not only does the firm's business strategy affect how the firm is organized, the organizational architecture affects the ability of the firm to generate and implement new profitable investment opportunities and hence new business strategies. For example, Corning, a glass company primarily making dishes and glassware (Corning Ware and Pyrex) invented fiber optic cable and glass-based substrate for automobile catalytic converters. Both of these innovations caused significant changes in Corning's organizational architecture. Likewise, successful organizational architecture generates new investment opportunities that can be commercially exploited.

Business strategy consists of the following:

1. *Asset structure*. The firm's business strategy determines its asset structure. Pharmaceutical company assets are primarily drug patents and brand-name drugs, whereas telephone company assets are primarily telephone lines and switching equipment. If the firm's assets are in the form of buildings and machinery, the performance evaluation systems are more likely based on accounting measures. If the

Technology and Banking

Reliable high-speed phone lines and computers have made possible automated teller machines (ATMs). ATM networks have reduced the need for numerous local branch banks. Economies of scale in ATM networks and hence the need for fewer branch banks were one of the reasons for the many U.S. bank mergers in the 1990s. A corporate merger is an example of how companies change their organizational architecture.

firm's assets are in the form of future growth options, as in an oil and gas exploration firm, the firm is more likely to tie executives' compensation to market-based performance such as stock and stock options.

2. *Customer base.* The business strategy determines the type of customer and the geographic dispersion of customers, which in turn affect how the firm is organized to service the customer base. For example, franchised retail stores like fast-food outlets are an alternative to company-owned stores when the customer base is geographically dispersed. The franchised store is operated by an independent owner who has more incentive to acquire specialized knowledge of the local market and to maximize profits than would an employee of the parent company. But to monitor the quality of the franchised outlets, the franchiser requires a field organization to inspect the outlets, which in turn dictates how the franchiser is organized (including performance evaluation and reward systems for the field group).

3. *Knowledge creation.* The nature of knowledge creation is determined by the business strategy selected. If the firm is in very stable markets in which knowledge is not created quickly, a more centralized organizational architecture can be adopted. Certain kinds of knowledge (like sales figures) can be converted to numerical representation that can easily be communicated to others in the firm. But other types of knowledge, such as customer preferences in particular markets, are more difficult to write down and convey to others. Easily communicated knowledge allows decision rights to be vested higher in the firm, meaning that lower-level performance evaluation and reward systems can be simpler. Therefore, the investments chosen by the firm determine how and where knowledge is generated, which affects the partitioning of decision rights. At Xerox, understanding the customer's document processing needs is much more important with a digital, networked copier than with the older, light-lens technology.

3. Environmental and Competitive Forces Affecting Organizations

The top two boxes in Figure 14–1 indicate that the firm's business strategy depends on technological innovations and changes in market conditions. New technology such as fiber optics causes relative prices of competing technologies to change, which in turn causes some investment projects to become more valuable and others less valuable. For example, fiber optics helped to create the Internet, which allows e-mail. E-mail, in turn, reduces the demand for fax and regular postage services (snail mail). Technological change affects the costs of transmitting knowledge and monitoring performance. Manufacturing plants use beepers and cellular phones to monitor maintenance personnel. Restaurants use vibrating beepers to alert wait staff that orders are ready and to let customers know that their table is available. Technological change sets off a chain reaction that causes

Changes at US West	US West (later renamed Qwest) was a regional telephone company based in Denver. In September 1993, management announced that it was laying off 9,000 employees (15 percent of its work force), consolidating 560 service centers into 26, and streamlining the customer-order system. Also announced were plans to convert its network covering 14 states into a broadband system for high-speed data transfer and video on demand. US West invested $2.5 billion in Time Warner Entertainment. These moves were seen as competing with cable companies and other carriers in the new telecommunications era.

US West (later renamed Qwest) was a regional telephone company based in Denver. In September 1993, management announced that it was laying off 9,000 employees (15 percent of its work force), consolidating 560 service centers into 26, and streamlining the customer-order system. Also announced were plans to convert its network covering 14 states into a broadband system for high-speed data transfer and video on demand. US West invested $2.5 billion in Time Warner Entertainment. These moves were seen as competing with cable companies and other carriers in the new telecommunications era.

In addition to announcing the strategy and organizational changes, US West announced it was changing from straight-line depreciation to accelerated depreciation. The one-time accounting change reduced assets by $3.2 billion. The reason for the change was that new technology causes telephone assets to be replaced more often. "[Telephone companies'] assets aren't lasting as long as they thought, and need to be replaced."

These announcements by US West in one day illustrate how accounting choices (depreciation methods), organizational architecture (consolidating service centers), the opportunity set (video on demand), strategy (providing a broadband system), technology, and competition are all intertwined.

SOURCE: *The Wall Street Journal*, September 30 1993, pp. A3–4.

not only the investment opportunities but also the firm's knowledge base, asset structure, customer base, and organizational architecture (including its internal accounting systems) to change.

A similar chain reaction is set off when market conditions change. Increased global competition has forced many firms that once enjoyed protected domestic markets to become more cost competitive. Instead of making products domestically, firms now source parts and subcomponents globally, causing organizational changes. Market conditions change for a variety of reasons, including changes in government regulations and taxation policies. Changes in tax rates cause the profitability (after taxes) of investment opportunities to change, thus affecting which projects are accepted. The North American Free Trade Agreement (NAFTA) reduced tariffs among Canada, Mexico, and the United States. As a result of NAFTA, companies relocated production sites in search of lower costs. Not only has the flow of trade increased among the three countries, but the geographic dispersion of company operations has changed. Emerging markets in the People's Republic of China and the former Soviet Union also have set off chain reactions within firms seeking to expand into these markets. Their investment opportunities (business strategies) have changed, prompting modifications in organizational architecture.

It is important to emphasize that the preceding discussion and Figure 14–1 do not represent a complete overview of a very complex set of interactions. Many other important corporate policies such as capital structure, information management, and marketing strategy have been excluded to simplify the discussion. However, the important point should not be missed—the internal accounting system is related to a larger set of other corporate policies.

4. Implications

Successful firms (and managers) will be those who adapt quickly to changing markets and technologies. New profitable investments will appear and some previously profitable investments will become unprofitable. Successfully implementing profitable projects requires organizational architectures that link decision rights and knowledge and that create incentives for managers to use their knowledge to take actions that capture the value in the investments undertaken.

While this book has focused on the firm's internal accounting system, it is important to understand the larger setting into which the accounting system fits. Figure 14–1 gives the big picture and highlights how external shocks to the firm from technological innovation and changing market conditions affect its value by working through the interdependencies between organizational architecture (including the choice of accounting systems) and the firm's business strategy. Senior managers are constantly trying to adapt to these external shocks by modifying their business strategy and organizational architecture. Figure 14–1 provides two important observations:

1. Changes in the accounting system rarely occur in a vacuum. Accounting system changes generally occur at the same time as changes in the firm's business strategy and other organizational changes, particularly with regard to the partitioning of decision rights and the performance evaluation and reward systems.

2. Alterations in the firm's organizational architecture, including changes in the accounting system, are likely to occur in response to changes in the firm's business strategy caused by external shocks from technology and shifting market conditions.

Three significant managerial implications are derived from these two observations. First, before implementing an accounting or other organizational change, it is important to understand what is driving the change. Second, a new accounting system should not be adopted merely because other firms are doing so; they may be reacting to a different set of external shocks. Third, an accounting system should not be changed without concurrent, consistent changes in the way decision rights are partitioned as well as in the performance reward systems. All three parts of the organization's architecture must be internally consistent and coordinated.

In a study of 40 randomly selected manufacturing plants in the United States, the researchers report that changes in manufacturing practices cause changes in the performance reporting and control systems. They document that implementation of just-in-time manufacturing and total quality programs is positively correlated with the amount of information being provided to lower-level managers on the shop floor.[2] This study supports the earlier claim that accounting system changes often occur in conjunction with other changes in a firm's organizational architecture.

Concept Questions	Q14–1	Define the firm's business strategy.
	Q14–2	Describe how the firm's business strategy affects its organizational architecture.
	Q14–3	Describe why technological innovation and changes in market structure cause firms to change their organizational architecture.
	Q14–4	Is it a good idea for managers to copy organizational changes adopted by other firms?

---

[2] R Banker, G Porter, and R Schroeder, "Reporting Manufacturing Performance Measures to Workers: An Empirical Study," *Journal of Management Accounting Research* 5 (Fall 1993), pp. 33–55.

B. Organizational Innovations and Management Accounting

A number of organizational innovations have been proposed: Total Quality Management, just-in-time production, and the balanced scorecard. This section first describes these innovations and their effect on management accounting and then illustrates how to apply the framework presented in Figure 14–1 to better understand the innovations in terms of what causes firms to adopt them and whether they will be successful.

1. Total Quality Management (TQM)

Quality is a major issue in both the profit and nonprofit sectors of the economy. In attempting to improve quality, managers have had to grapple with what it means. There is considerable debate surrounding what constitutes Total Quality Management (TQM) and how to define quality. Nonetheless, to most experts, TQM encompasses both improving the tangible aspects of product quality (performance, reliability, conformance to specification, durability, serviceability, and perceived quality) and enhancing the efficiency of the organization (lowering costs and increasing productivity). TQM seeks to improve all aspects of the company: its products, processes, and services. Managers must also design measurement systems to report improvements in quality. This section describes various definitions of quality, discusses some quality measurement systems, and analyzes these systems within the framework presented in Figure 14–1.

While quality can be measured in many ways, the two most common methods involve meeting customer expectations and reducing defects.

Customers have expectations with respect to all of a product's attributes, including delivery schedules, downtime, operating characteristics, and service. These expectations include means, variances, and options. For example, a customer might expect a service technician to arrive on average within two hours of making the service call with a standard deviation of one hour. If the service representative arrives within one and a half hours on average but with a standard deviation of two hours, the firm has met one customer expectation (mean time for arrival) but has not met another expectation (arriving dependably within two hours).

Quality is often measured in terms of defects. For example, a component part must be within 0.001 millimeters of standard or else it is termed defective. If changing the machine producing the part reduces the defect rate from five per thousand to three per thousand, then quality is said to have increased. This concept of quality is lower variance. One problem of defining quality in terms of defect rates is that opportunistic employees can appear to improve quality if they have the decision rights to redefine the standard used as the benchmark for determining defects. For example, suppose defects are defined as being in excess of 0.001 millimeters from standard and a given part has a defect rate of five per thousand. By redefining defects as being in excess of 0.0015 millimeters, only two per thousand defects occur. "Quality" appears to have increased. Therefore, when installing quality improvement programs, one must be on guard that the definition of defects is held constant.

The term *Total Quality Management* (TQM) includes involved leadership, employee participation, empowerment, teamwork, customer satisfaction, and continual improvement. Most TQM programs contain the following elements:

- *Quality is a firmwide process.* Every employee, from the senior managers to the factory floor employees, must understand the quality work processes. Quality links customers to suppliers. The pursuit of excellence is a prime motivator in the company.

- *Quality is defined by the customer.*
- *Quality requires organizational changes.* The organization's architecture (performance measurement and reward and decision rights partitioning) must encourage mutual cooperation and create incentives to improve quality. Senior managers should develop hands-on, specialized knowledge of how to improve quality. Workers are empowered (i.e., given decision rights) to make changes that increase quality.
- *Quality is designed into the product.* Quality must be designed into the product and processes from the very beginning of manufacturing through delivery of a quality product to the consumer.

Defining quality as meeting customer expectations requires knowledge of the entire set of customer expectations, the actual realized values, and the importance customers attach to particular expectations. Each customer views deviations from some expectations to be more important than deviations from other expectations. For example, missed delivery schedules might be more important than missed service times for some customers. Preferences over product attributes vary across customers. Understanding customer preferences for product attributes is important specialized knowledge to acquire. Customers include external customers for the firm's products and services as well as internal customers. For example, the maintenance department might not have external customers, but it has internal customers.

The traditional approach to ensuring product quality was extensive inspection of raw materials, purchases, and manufactured products. Inspection stations and quality assurance inspectors were added along the production line to weed out inferior products. Statistical sampling methods were used to draw random samples from a batch and reject the entire batch if a statistically large number of bad units was detected in the sample. Notice that this process implicitly defines quality as low variance—meeting a certain set of specifications, which might or might not be of interest to the consumer. Sections of the factory stored defects waiting to be reworked or scrapped. Firms built into their operating budgets and standard costs a normal allowance for scrap and rework. In some cases, if market demand exceeded production in a period, marginally defective products were released. Defective products reaching the market were corrected by the field service

---

ISO 9000

The International Organization of Standards (ISO) is a European community body that establishes quality standards. The ISO 9000 standard has different levels of certification depending on the complexity of the manufacturer's operations. To become ISO 9000–certified, a manufacturer must document that it relies on written policies, procedures, and quality methods. Independent external registrars then visit the plant requesting ISO 9000 certification to ensure that the applicant has the necessary documentation, quality manuals, and procedures in place. Semiannual reviews and reaudits every three to four years are necessary to maintain certification.

ISO 9000 does not guarantee that quality products are being manufactured. It certifies that policies exist that allow quality products to be manufactured.

IBM's Quality Management Program

In the 1990s, IBM redefined its goal as total customer satisfaction, guided by the following four market-driven principles:

- Understand our markets.
- Commit to leadership in the markets we choose to serve.
- Execute with excellence across our enterprise.
- Make customer satisfaction the final arbiter.

To implement these principles, the following initiatives were implemented:

- Research, understand, and segment total potential market needs. Commit to market leadership and deliver the right solutions at the right time.
- Remove defects in everything we do to achieve market-driven quality.
- Reduce the total time between determining customer wants/needs and fulfilling those needs to the customer's total satisfaction.
- Give employees the authority and information they need to make timely decisions and carry out the activities necessary to ensure total customer satisfaction.
- Establish achievable business targets with a particular focus on quality and customer satisfaction.

organization under warranty arrangements. Most firm's accounting systems ignored the opportunity cost of inferior quality.

By the 1980s, two key factors combined to change the traditional approach to quality in many industries. First, the cost of detecting problems and monitoring production via computer instrumentation fell relative to the cost of maintaining quality via inspectors. The cost of inspectors (including health care benefits) made the cost of manually detecting and correcting error more expensive relative to performing these tasks electronically. Instead of manually detecting and correcting defects after production, improved instrumentation allowed earlier detection and correction of problems, often while the product was in production. Second, worldwide competition expanded to such nonprice forms of competition as quality. Once the Japanese automobile companies gained price competitiveness against the American automakers, they turned their attention to achieving quality advantages. Both the lower cost of detecting defects and increased global competition fostered quality improvements. Notice that in terms of Figure 14–1, both technological innovation and changed market conditions created the TQM movement.

To reduce defects, companies redesigned their products to require fewer different parts, making it easier to maintain tighter controls on the quality of their suppliers. Product designers redesigned parts that failed. Production processes were redesigned to reduce defects. Robots and more instrumentation were built into manufacturing to ensure more uniform production. Firms adopted TQM programs. While many TQM programs were initially started to improve the tangible aspects of product and service quality, TQM programs have evolved to enhance products, prices, and services for both internal and external customers. Major changes in the organization's architecture also occurred, including modifying the performance evaluation and reward systems and the partitioning of decision rights. Decision rights were pushed down lower in the firm, where the knowledge of customer preferences and the production process often resides.

As world markets become more competitive, companies now must compete not only on price but also on delivery schedules, service, and quality, where quality means higher mean, lower variance, and more options. Not only must fax machines produce exact reproductions with few smudges, but all the copies must be the same, the machines must be highly reliable and easy to operate and service, and the waits for service calls must be short. In general, quality has come to mean giving customers what they want. Notice that when firms compete on quality, many different dimensions of quality come into play. TQM programs emphasize the multidimensional aspects of quality.

In terms of Figure 14–1, both technological innovations (computer instrumentation) and market conditions have forced companies to change both their business strategy and their organizational architecture. Central to TQM programs is knowing what the customer wants and how to produce it at lower cost. If knowledge of customer preferences and production processes resides lower down in the organization with the people who have direct contact with customers, then the theory in Chapter 4 says to place the decision rights with those employees. Most TQM programs argue for empowering employees to improve quality. Empowerment is another way of saying that decision rights are transferred to people with the specialized knowledge of customer preferences. Therefore, an important component of TQM is changing the firm's organizational architecture by decentralizing certain decision rights to lower-level managers. Of course, if decision rights are repartitioned, then performance evaluation and reward systems also must change.

TQM programs also require accounting systems. Defect rates, on-time delivery, and customer complaints are easy for managers to understand and easy to measure. Without a corresponding accounting system, however, these diverse measures are difficult to aggregate. Managers do not know how to make trade-offs among quality decisions. For example, is it more costly to design and manufacture a product without defects or to focus on inspection and correcting defects from initial production? Is it cheaper to buy a scanning machine for more accurate inspections or stay with manual inspections? Managers require cost data to make these comparisons for decision management purposes.

Part of the TQM philosophy is that improved quality can actually be less costly to the organization. The opportunity cost of selling defective products and not satisfying customers can be very high. Errors must be corrected and disgruntled customers mollified. Dissatisfied customers will seek other suppliers of the service or product. A reputation for shoddy workmanship is often the death knell for organizations. Even if a defect is discovered before being sent to a customer, the cost of handling and fixing the problem can be quite high. In many cases, the defective product cannot be fixed and must be junked. However, as discussed a bit later, "Quality is not free." Improving the quality of the firm's products or services requires resources; hence enhancing quality is costly.

TQM programs start by redesigning the products so that there are fewer parts per product (fewer parts that can fail) in order to make manufacturing and assembly easier, and to make the product easier to service in the field. These total quality programs then define a series of quality measures, including product design (number of new parts, total number of parts), vendor rating systems (number of defects, on-time delivery), manufacturing (defect rates, scrap, rework, on-time delivery), and customer satisfaction (surveys, warranty expense). The framework in Figure 14–1 predicts that if other parts of the organization's architecture are being modified, the accounting system will be too. This is the case in TQM. Besides tracking the nonfinancial measures of quality listed above, some firms report the cost of quality. Quality costs can be categorized into four groups:

1. Prevention costs incurred to eliminate defective units before they are produced (reengineering products or production processes and employee training).
2. Appraisal costs incurred to eliminate defective units before they are shipped (inspecting and testing both raw material and work in process).
3. Internal failure costs (the costs of defective units in manufacturing).
4. External failure costs, including the cost of returns, warranty work, and product liability claims as well as the opportunity cost of lost sales from reputation effects.[3]

These various costs are dispersed throughout the firm, usually in numerous overhead accounts. The purpose of reorganizing and aggregating these costs into a single cost-of-quality report is to bring them to the attention of senior managers. However, the largest costs of quality are often the opportunity costs of forgone sales caused by a reputation for low-quality products. These opportunity costs are not captured by the accounting system.

As mentioned earlier, quality is not free. The question is, "Do the benefits of improving quality exceed the costs?" Figure 14–2 illustrates how quality costs likely behave as the firm seeks to improve quality. As the percentage of defects increases, the costs of internal and external failure also increase. However, higher defect rates usually result from low appraisal and prevention costs. Total quality costs will exhibit the usual U-shape, indicating that there is an optimum quality level. Trying to further reduce defect rates below this optimum costs more in prevention and appraisal costs than can be saved by lower internal and external failure costs.

While numerous firms have initiated quality improvement programs, not all have achieved their objectives. A *Wall Street Journal* report (October 4, 1990, p. B1) of a Gallup poll of 1,237 corporate employees notes that over half say that quality is top priority. But only one-third say that their company programs are effective. One major complaint is that employee participation is limited. A *Newsweek* article (September 7, 1992, pp. 48–49) reports that a number of companies, including McDonnell Douglas aircraft and Florida Power & Light, have abandoned their TQM programs. Wallace Co. won the prestigious U.S. Baldrige award in 1990 and filed for bankruptcy in 1992. Finally, a 1991 study of 584 U.S., Canadian, German, and Japanese firms concluded that "many businesses may waste millions of dollars a year on quality-improvement strategies that don't improve their performance and may even hamper it."[4] This evidence supports the notion of an optimum level of investment in quality, as depicted in Figure 14–2. Firms can over- or underinvest in quality.

---

[3] See W Morse and K Posten, "Accounting for Quality Costs in CIM," *Journal of Cost Management for the Manufacturing Industry*, Fall 1987, pp. 5–11.

[4] *The Wall Street Journal*, October 1, 1992, p. B7.

FIGURE 14–2
Optimum quality cost

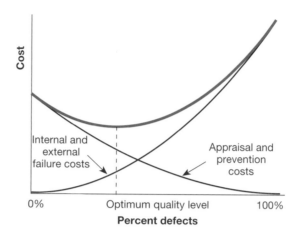

2. Just-in-Time (JIT) Production

The next organizational innovation is just-in-time (JIT) production. In a JIT plant, production and demand are synchronized because production does not start until an order is received. Products are *pulled* through the plant by customer orders, rather than *pushed* through by a master production schedule designed to keep the plant operating at full capacity. The goal of a JIT plant manager is to reduce the time the product spends in the plant. If total production time falls, presumably costs will also fall because fewer inventories have to be financed, stored, managed, and secured. To accomplish these goals, the plant is reorganized so that raw materials and purchased parts are delivered to the factory right before they are entered into the production process; therefore, there are no intermediate work-in-process inventories. Units flow from one production cell to another with no interruptions and all work is processed continually. Units spend time in the factory only when actual work is being expended on them. Of course, this describes an ideal JIT installation. Few actual JIT plants achieve the ideal.

Throughput time is the total time from when a product starts the production process until it is ready for sale. Throughput is the sum of processing time, time waiting to be moved or worked on, time spent in transit, and inspection time. The goal of JIT is to drive the last three items (waiting, transit, and inspection time) to zero. The sum of the last three items is referred to as *wasted* or *non-value-added time*. The benefits of reducing throughput time include smaller in-process inventories, leading to

- Lower capital costs of holding inventories.
- Factory and warehouse space and cost savings.
- Reduced overhead costs for material movers and expediters.
- Reduced risk of obsolescence.
- Faster response time to customers and reduced delivery times.

Achieving reduced throughput time requires the following changes:

1. Increase quality. To prevent production downtime, the quality of raw materials and the quality of the manufacturing process must be improved. Increased material and process quality eliminates the need to stop processing because of defects.

2. Reduce setup times. If machines can be set up for a new production run very quickly (or instantaneously), then parts do not have to wait for processing to begin. Moreover, inventories do not accumulate in front of the machine while it is being set up.

3. Balance flow rates. The rate of production in the various manufacturing cells must be the same or else work-in-process inventories will build up after the cells with the faster flow rates.

4. Improve factory layout. Redesign the factory to reduce travel time. Do not group machines that perform the same function in one department. Instead, organize machines by how the products are sequenced through them. The factory becomes organized around dedicated JIT production lines producing a single type of product, sometimes called **dedicated flow lines.**

5. Change performance measurement and reward systems. No longer must employees be evaluated and rewarded on efficiency measures such as the number of units produced or whether they keep machines busy. Individual work cells are no longer rewarded for maximizing flow rates. Such efficiency measures encourage workers to build inventories and to have inventories in front of their station as buffer stocks. The performance measure in a JIT system is throughput time divided by process time. As this ratio approaches 1, non-value-added time decreases.

One important aspect of JIT involves redesigning the firm's relationship with its suppliers. In the past, managers believed that having several suppliers of each input increased competition and kept prices down. Firms had policies of dividing total purchases among several sources, which required each arriving order to be inspected to ensure quality. Having multiple suppliers made it more difficult to coordinate timely delivery of supplies. In a JIT environment, firms have drastically reduced the number of suppliers, often going to long-term sole-sourcing contracts whereby a single supplier provides all of the firm's demand for a given input. The purchasing firm benefits from lower prices due to volume discounts, lower ordering costs (since only a single-relationship contract is required), and higher quality ensured by audits of the supplier's process rather than inspection of each shipment. Transportation costs are usually lower because suppliers can use long-term contracts with shippers. Through electronic data interchange (EDI), buyers and sellers integrate their computer systems so that orders are also received JIT.

However, sole-sourcing is not a universal panacea. Sourcing from a single supplier and specializing purchases from a single supplier create incentives for the parties to the contract to behave opportunistically.[5] For example, in the early days of General Motors, GM bought all of its auto bodies from the independent firm of Fisher Body. GM frames and Fisher bodies were specialized to each other and there were incentives for one party to try to extract gains from the other. The solution was for GM to buy Fisher Body.

Accounting in a JIT production environment becomes much simpler. It takes on many aspects of a process costing system such as described in Chapter 9. In a JIT organization, job order costing, in which costs are accumulated for each job or batch, is no longer desirable. Having production employees fill out job order

---

[5] B Klein, R Crawford, and A Alchain, "Vertical Integration, Appropriable Rents, and the Competitive Contracting Process," *Journal of Law & Economics*, October 1978, pp. 297–326.

Does JIT Work?	A study of 46 companies adopting JIT found some surprising results. Inventory turnover ratios increased following JIT adoption. However, not all the firms increased their profitability as measured by return on assets. The 15 JIT firms that had a major customer showed a decline in ROA following JIT adoption, whereas those without a major customer reported the same ROA. A major customer is likely to demand price concessions from its dedicated suppliers. Compaq Computers, Ford, and Chrysler demanded large price concessions from their suppliers. General Motors helped its suppliers reduce their costs and their prices by reducing inventory levels. Thus, it appears that much of the cost savings from JIT, especially for firms with major customers, pass through to their customers via lower prices. SOURCE: R Balakrishnan, T Linsmeier, and M Venkatachalam, "Financial Benefits from Improved Inventory Utilization: Effects of Customer Concentration and Cost Structure," *Accounting Review*, April 1996, pp. 183–205.

sheets as they work on a product is non-value-added time. Also, because inventory is in the form of work in process for such a short time, there is less need to worry about valuing partially completed products. In JIT accounting systems,

- Labor and overhead are combined into a single account (conversion costs).
- As much as possible, general factory overhead is traced directly to dedicated JIT lines (e.g., utilities, machine depreciation, and maintenance are metered directly for each JIT line).
- Material costs are charged directly to products.
- Conversion costs are assigned based on machine (or cell) time.
- Detailed work-in-process accounting is eliminated because WIP inventories vanish.
- A single inventory account, raw and in-process materials (RIP), is used.
- All raw materials and purchases issued to production are charged to RIP.
- As units are finished, RIP is reduced by the materials costs and finished goods inventory is charged for the materials. Reducing RIP for the materials costs when units are completed is called *backflushing*.
- Conversion costs are charged directly to finished goods (not RIP).

Figure 14–3 is a schematic drawing of a JIT accounting system. Unlike the traditional absorption costing systems described in Figure 9–1, JIT systems do not have a work-in-process inventory account. All conversion costs for the JIT line, such as direct and indirect labor, depreciation, and other overhead items, are first accumulated in an overhead account and then charged to finished goods based on machine time or total throughput time using a predetermined overhead rate.

To illustrate JIT accounting, consider the following example. Ryan Inc. manufactures a windshield-wiper control assembly for Ford Motor cars' steering columns. Ryan uses a JIT production system. Total manufacturing overhead is budgeted for the year at $8.8 million. Ryan expects to produce 2.2 million wiper assemblies this year. Each assembly has standard overhead of $4 per unit. Last week factory labor was $38,000 and $59,000 of materials were purchased and used to produce 10,000 wiper control assemblies. These units were shipped and billed to Ford. The following summarizes the financial entries:

FIGURE 14–3

Schematic of a just-in-time cost system

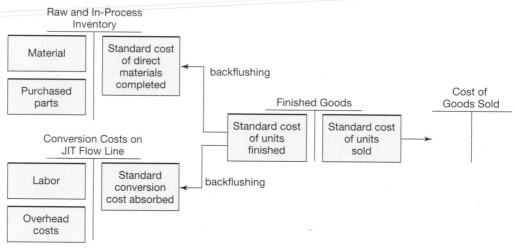

	$
Change in materials inventory	$ 0
Total conversion costs incurred (labor and overhead)	$ 78,000*
Change in finished goods inventory	$ 0
Cost of goods sold	$137,000†

*$38,000 + $4 × 10,000 units
†$78,000 + $59,000

Firms adopting these RIP accounting systems have significantly reduced the number of accounting transactions. Some firms have reduced their journal entry volume twentyfold because detailed payroll posting to jobs has been eliminated and jobs no longer need to be tracked through the work-in-process accounts as they move from department to department.

However, JIT also has drawbacks. Holding everything else constant, decreasing throughput time (like increasing quality or productivity) is unambiguously good because it increases firm value. However, everything else is not usually held constant. Redesigning the factory layout, reducing setup times, and requiring suppliers to increase quality and provide JIT deliveries can potentially increase costs. A sole supplier of a specialized input has some monopoly power and can use this position to extract higher prices. Accounting systems that measure throughput time without charging managers for the costs of improving throughput will cause throughput time to fall, but other costs might rise.

Moreover, firms hold inventories to smooth out fluctuations in supply or demand. If there is a labor strike, or bad weather prevents delivery of raw materials, or demand increases unexpectedly, inventories allow the firm to avoid the opportunity cost of lost sales. Reorganizing the factory, improving product and process quality, and changing purchasing relationships with suppliers can smooth out some of the fluctuations in production but cannot eliminate all the shocks to the system. Random fluctuations outside management's control, such as weather-related and demand-related shocks, will cause the firm to carry some inventories somewhere as a buffer against losing sales. An example of a demand-

Harley-Davidson and JIT 	Harley-Davidson manufactures motorcycles. Over the years direct labor has shrunk to about 10 percent of a motorcycle's product cost. In the past, each employee had to keep track of every product worked on in the course of the day. For an average employee, this meant about 20 bikes. Each day the accounting system had to record 10,000 entries. However, management was not using this information for any decision making. When direct labor was a larger fraction of product costs, managers tracked direct labor variances more carefully. After introducing JIT, Harley-Davidson changed the accounting system. Direct labor was no longer treated as a direct cost but rather it and overhead were treated as conversion costs. Conversion costs were assigned to individual products based on how many hours the product was in the manufacturing process. This change greatly simplified the accounting process because all the individual labor transactions were no longer entered daily. SOURCE: W Turk, "Management Accounting Revitalized: The Harley-Davidson Experience," in *Emerging Practices in Cost Management*, ed. B Brinker (Boston: Warren, Gorham & Lamont, 1990), pp. 155–66.

JIT in Japan 	In a survey of 198 Japanese companies in four industries, only 20 percent of the firms report using JIT. Thirty percent of the firms in electronic equipment and transportation equipment use JIT and 7 percent of the firms in chemical products and iron and steel manufacturing use JIT. The authors conclude, "This result belies the popular misconception that *all* Japanese manufacturers are JIT producers." SOURCE: P Scarbough, A Nanni, Jr, and M Sakurai, "Japanese Management Accounting Practices and the Effects of Assembly and Process Automation," *Management Accounting Research* 2 (March 1991), pp. 27–46.

related shock is a government agency with a lapsing budget. At the end of the fiscal year, the agency has unspent funds. To spend the money, it requires immediate delivery of the purchases. Only a supplier carrying inventories can make the sale.

While much has been written extolling the virtues of JIT and backflushing accounting, other commentators warn of the system's weaknesses. Few firms have been able to completely eliminate raw materials inventory. After JIT was installed at one Hewlett-Packard plant, raw materials inventory ranged from a two-day to a five-day supply on hand and finished inventory on hand fell from a 2.8-month supply to a 1.3-month supply. But since production tripled, the actual dollar value of inventory on hand increased. Backflushing at this plant drastically reduced the number of accounting entries. However, the accounting system was no longer able to track inventory levels, which meant that physical counts of inventory (some every six weeks) were required to supply managers with information on specific inventory levels. Inconsistent with the basic JIT philosophy, these inventory counts are non-value-added activities that disrupt the production process by forcing employees to stop producing and count the inventory.[6]

---

[6]R Calvasina, E Calvasina, and G Calvasina, "Beware of Accounting Myths," *Management Accounting*, December 1989, pp. 41–45.

Adopting JIT causes the plant to change its organizational and even physical structure. The organizational changes require changes in performance measurement systems, including the internal accounting systems. Thus, accounting system changes follow and support changes in the physical and organizational structure of the plant.

In terms of Figure 14–1, technological advances in instrumentation, computers, and telecommunications (computer-aided manufacturing) have been one impetus allowing factories to be redesigned along continuous flow JIT lines. Suppliers' computers are now linked electronically to their customers' computers, and electronic order processing is commonplace. These technological advances have made JIT production possible. Likewise, market conditions are changing. Customers are demanding that their purchases be delivered in continuous, small-order lot sizes, providing further incentives for manufacturers to adopt JIT techniques. Thus, two shocks to the firm's business strategy have caused changes in the physical and organizational architecture of plants. Accounting systems, as part of the organizational architecture, are not exempt from these changes and have also been modified, as evidenced by the RIP account and backflushing techniques described here.

3. Balanced Scorecard

Beginning in the 1990s many large firms, such as AT&T, KPMG, Bank of Montreal, Allstate, Tenneco, Mobil, and Citicorp, adopted a **balanced scorecard.** In Figure 14–1, successful firms develop a strategy that delivers goods or services to their customers at prices that exceed the costs of providing these products. The strategy of an organization provides a direction for the organization, such as goals for the introduction of new products, customer satisfaction, market share in specific areas, and efficiencies in production. Some companies, such as Dell Inc. and McDonald's, have chosen *operational excellence*. Others have chosen *customer intimacy* (Home Depot) or *product leadership* (Intel and Sony). Highly successful firms excel at one while maintaining high standards on the other two.

A strategy, however, is seldom specific enough to describe the steps necessary to achieve the goals. A more detailed plan identifying the inputs necessary to implement the strategy is required. A balanced scorecard translates the strategy into a plan of action that identifies specific objectives and performance drivers to help determine if the organization is moving in the right direction.

Kaplan and Norton suggest using a balanced scorecard that links the firm's strategy to performance drivers that provide a comprehensive view of the organization.[7] A balanced scorecard relates key performance indicators, such as on-time deliveries, to those actions required of employees to successfully achieve the firm's strategy and hence maximize firm value. In terms of Figure 14–1, the balanced scorecard is designed to identify those **key performance indicators** used to focus on actions required to implement the firm's strategy.

Most balanced scorecards combine both decision management and decision control. Decision management is provided by identifying the sequence of objectives and the key performance indicators that allow the organization to achieve

---

[7] R Kaplan and D Norton, "The Balanced Scorecard—Measures That Drive Performance," *Harvard Business Review*, January–February 1992. Also see R Kaplan and D Norton, "Transforming the Balanced Scorecard from Performance Measurement to Strategic Management: Parts I and II," *Accounting Horizons*, March and June 2004, pp 87–104 and 147–60.

its goals. The balanced scorecard also provides decision control by establishing performance measures and targets for each objective. It articulates the strategy of the organization and communicates this strategy in a commonly understood language.

The balanced scorecard derives its name from the balance it attempts to achieve among the firm's strategy (objectives) and key performance indicators. Many observers of corporate culture lament the emphasis on short-term performance measures in corporations. Quarterly earnings announcements appear to have undue influence on the actions of the managers of a corporation. Focusing on short-term performance measures can reduce the value of the organization because of a reluctance to invest in activities that benefit the organization in the long run. Research and development, plant maintenance, and employee training are examples of expenditures that harm the short-term financial measures, but benefit the organization in the long run. Balanced scorecards tend to include both short- and long-term performance indicators.

The ultimate objective of profit organizations is to generate value for the owners of the organization. But value for owners is the outcome of satisfying customers, operating efficiently, and having the infrastructure necessary to accomplish all of those activities. Therefore, most firms do not rely solely on financial performance indicators. Financial performance indicators occur periodically and may not be very timely. Clearly, nonfinancial performance indicators such as customer satisfaction and employee turnover are also important performance indicators.

Balanced scorecard's four perspectives

Advocates of the balanced scorecard argue that it recognizes the multiple stakeholders of an organization. These stakeholders include the shareholders or owners, customers, suppliers, employees, and society. Balanced scorecard proponents contend that the organization's objectives should reflect the interests of these stakeholders. Many corporate mission statements mention these stakeholders. Objectives related to the stakeholders are captured in the balanced scorecard through four perspectives: financial, customer, internal business processes, and innovation and learning. Each of these perspectives has objectives, performance indicators, targets, and initiatives.

The Balanced Scorecard at AT&T

AT&T's Universal Card Services, a credit card company, uses the balanced score-card to measure performance and to link various operations to economic value added (EVA). More than 100 internal process quality measures, such as phone-hold times and number of abandoned calls, are tracked daily. Each measure is chosen because it is a driver of economic value added. For example, to maximize the number of creditworthy cardholders, receivables are monitored very carefully. Teams are formed to solve problems as they arise.

Customer satisfaction is usually a key value driver in most firms. The office that handles customer telephone complaints can affect customer satisfaction. Therefore, one measure of performance for this subunit is how long callers have to wait before they speak to a representative. Another measure is how many callers hang up before their call is answered.

SOURCE: B Birchard, "How Innovative Companies Use the New Metrics," *CFO*, October 1995, p. 50.

FIGURE 14–4

The Balanced Scorecard's Four Perspectives

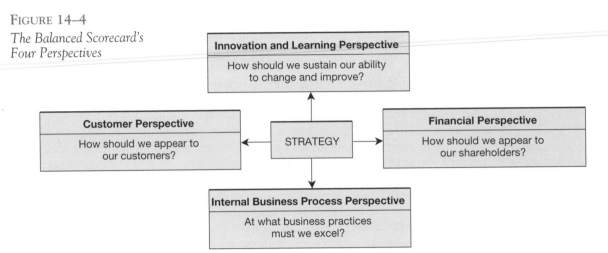

Figure 14–4 illustrates these four perspectives:

Financial perspective.   The financial perspective of the balanced scorecard represents the shareholders/owners of the organization. The objectives from the financial perspective in a profit organization are oriented toward providing shareholders a return on their investment. Typical performance indicators include profit, sales growth, and measures of risk. Nonprofit organizations would also have financial objective indicators such as balancing revenues and expenditures.

The objectives of the financial perspective in the balanced scorecard coincide with creating firm value in the framework of Figure 14–1. Increases in firm value come from the other perspectives: customers, internal business processes, and learning and growth.

Customer perspective.   The customer perspective of the balanced scorecard is concerned with adding customer value. Customer value can be achieved through innovative and high quality products and services and low prices. The balanced scorecard should highlight the organization's strategy for adding customer value. Typical performance indicators for the customer perspective include customer satisfaction surveys and market share, on-time delivery, and reduced defects.

Internal business process perspective.   The objectives of the internal business process perspective deal with issues of efficiency and quality. TQM, information technology, and JIT are processes that support this perspective. Activities should be analyzed to determine whether they add value and how they can be most efficiently performed. For example, supplier relations are critically important to the success of retail and manufacturing firms. Using business-to-business Internet transactions to speed purchases from suppliers increases on-time deliveries to customers and improves quality. Typical performance indicators for the internal business process perspective include number of defects, throughput time, and on-time delivery.

Innovation and learning perspective.   The innovation and learning perspective focuses on the infrastructure of the organization. To achieve its goals an organization requires the right people and systems as well as facilities to support them. Without learning and innovation in the organization, the organization will not be able to adapt to a dynamic environment. To adapt, an organization must have ongoing training of employees, requisite technology and information systems, and the

TABLE 14–1   An Insurance Company's Balanced Scorecard

Objective	Performance Indicators	Targets
Financial Perspective		
Efficient use of assets	Return on assets	17% per year
Grow underwriting	Premium growth	4% per year
Innovation and Learning Perspective		
Employee training	Percent of employee hours spent in training	5% per year
Employee retention	Percent employee turnover	6% per year
Internal Business Process Perspective		
Reduce error rates	Percent of time employees spend correcting errors	2% per year
Automate customer inquiries	Growth in percent of customers logging on to company Web site	18% per year
Customer Perspective		
Grow market share	Increase in number of under-35 insurance buyers	3% per year
Customer satisfaction	Percent of customers saying they are "very satisfied" on customer surveys	80%
Fast response to loss claims	Days to process loss claims	95% of all claims processed within three days

facilities to meet new customer demands. Performance indicators include employee training efforts, information system implementations, and equipment and facility purchases.

Table 14–1 presents an example of a balanced scorecard for an entire insurance company. For each of the four perspectives, objectives, performance indicators, and targets are specified. Each responsibility center in the organization then derives its own balanced scorecard.

Relations among perspectives.   The four perspectives of the balanced scorecard should be directly or indirectly related to each other. The strategy of the organization is the starting point and dictates the financial perspective objectives. To achieve the financial perspective objectives, the organization must look at its relations with its customers and determine how it can add value to its customers. Adding value to customers comes from efficient and quality operations of internal processes. But processes cannot operate efficiently without the appropriate learning and innovation within the organization. Identifying these links is critical to implementing a successful balanced scorecard. For example, an insurance company might determine that improving its information systems and training employees leads to faster insurance claims processing for its policyholders. This leads to increased customer satisfaction, more loyal customers, and eventually, better financial results.

The Balanced Scorecard at Philips Electronics

Philips Electronics, with more than 250,000 employees in 150 countries adopted the balanced scorecard at the direction of corporate management as a way to communicate the firm's business strategy and vision throughout the firm. Four critical success factors were identified: competence (knowledge, technology, leadership, and teamwork); processes (drivers for performance); customers (value propositions); and financial (value, growth, and productivity). At Philips, the balanced scorecard starts at the corporate level and then cascades down to the divisions and the business units. At the corporate level is the strategy scorecard. The divisions have operations-review scorecards, and the business units have their own scorecards. Each lower-level scorecard must articulate with the next higher-level card in the sense that when the lower-level unit achieves its scorecard targets this furthers the next higher-level unit's targets. A typical business-unit scorecard contains the following:

- Financial: Economic profit realized, income from operations, working capital, operational cash flow, inventory turns.
- Customers: Rank in customer survey, market share, repeat order rate, complaints.
- Processes: Percentage reduction in process cycle time, number of engineering changes, capacity utilization, order response time, process capability.
- Competence: Leadership, percentage of patent-protect turnover, training days per employee, quality improvement team participation.

SOURCE: A Gumbus and B Lyons, "The Balanced Scorecard at Philips Electronics," *Strategic Finance*, November 2002, pp. 45–49.

Assessing the balanced scorecard

The balanced scorecard is consistent with Figure 14–1 to the extent that it links the firm's strategy with the cause-and-effect relationships among the various performance indicators. However, many balanced scorecard implementations focus only on identifying the various key performance indicators and are silent about which of these are then linked to compensation. Moreover, balanced scorecard advocates do not address changing other parts of the organizational architecture in response to the new strategy. Thus, decision rights assignments and compensation plan changes are often ignored. While many firms are embracing this approach, there are several conceptual and practical problems with balanced scorecards.

Telling managers to maximize firm value is like telling a sports team to win. More concrete strategies and objectives are required. Balanced scorecards help communicate to managers how to implement value-maximizing strategies. Problems arise when the scorecards are used as performance measures.[8] As performance measurement systems, balanced scorecards produce dysfunctional behaviors. Suppose a football quarterback has a very simple balanced scorecard consisting of number of completed passes, yards gained by running, and games won. Suppose the quarterback is paid on each measure. Clearly, the objective of the team is to

---

[8] M Jensen, "Value Maximization, Stakeholder Theory, and the Corporate Objective Function," *Business Ethics Quarterly* 12, January 2001.

FIGURE 14–5

*Relation between
customer satisfaction
and firm value*

win. Passing and running contribute to winning. But, if the quarterback thinks that a passing play has a greater chance of succeeding than a running play, even though the latter might win the game, the quarterback will in some circumstances choose the passing play.

Similarly, customer satisfaction is usually related to firm value. More satisfied customers are more loyal and willing to pay higher prices for the firm's goods and services. However, how far should managers go in maximizing customer satisfaction? Figure 14–5 illustrates the typical relationship between firm value and customer satisfaction. Firm value increases up to customer satisfaction level C*. But customer satisfaction levels beyond C* reduce firm value because it costs more to increase customer satisfaction than these more satisfied customers return in additional revenues. Giving managers balanced scorecards that include customer satisfaction (or employee turnover, market share, product quality, and so forth) can cause managers to reduce firm value.

Balanced scorecards often contain 10 to 30 performance indicators. However, you can only maximize one variable at a time. Telling managers to simultaneously maximize 20 balanced scorecard indicators provides that manager with no guidance as to the relative trade-off among the indicators. It is an impossible task. Suppose you are told to maximize your grade in managerial accounting and to maximize your physical fitness. You can't do both simultaneously. Because there are only 24 hours in a day, you must make trade-offs.

If managers receive compensation based on numerous balanced scorecard performance measures, they will choose those measures easiest to achieve and ignore more difficult tasks.[9] Firm value will almost certainly suffer. Balanced scorecards are not balanced in the sense of specifying how managers should make trade-offs between the various performance indicators. They do not tell managers when to stop producing more customer satisfaction because firm value falls beyond that point. Most balanced scorecards suggest that more of each performance indicator is preferred to less. Moreover, balanced scorecards are not scorecards in the usual sense of indicating who is winning and losing. They are statistical summaries of the game. They do not provide a single comprehensive measure of performance like, say, EVA.

One critic claims that many managers embrace the balanced scorecard concept because "it is easier for people to engage in intense value claiming activities

---

[9] See Brickley, Smith, and Zimmerman, 2001, p. 403.

A Balanced Scorecard Failure[*]

The U.S. retail banking operations of a leading international financial services provider adopted a balanced scorecard in 1995 and abandoned it in 1998. What went wrong?

To maintain confidentiality, the identity of the firm was not disclosed by the researchers. However, the firm has hundreds of branches located throughout North America. Prior to installing the balanced scorecard in the North American Division, each branch manager was evaluated according to a formula-based compensation system that awarded a bonus based on achieving specific performance objectives. For example, a bonus of 2 percent of the manager's salary was awarded if the branch achieved a prespecified targeted growth in households banking at that branch. This bonus system had grown so complex that it took a 78-page manual to describe it. Upper-level managers were frustrated with the system because branch managers were gaming the system to earn bonuses without delivering financial results.

In 1995 a balanced scorecard was introduced with five corporate imperatives: achieving good financial results, delivering for customers, managing costs strategically, managing risk, and having the right people in the right jobs. Extensive training programs accompanied the rollout of the scorecard system. Each branch was measured on about 40 different metrics such as customer attrition, customer satisfaction, assets under management, training and staff development, and so forth. But unlike the earlier formula-based bonus system, branch managers under the balanced scorecard received *subjective* performance measures. Proponents of the balanced scorecard provide little guidance on how each metric in the scorecard should be linked to compensation. However, they usually conjecture that subjective, rather than objective, compensation should be used because it is "easier and more defensible to administer . . . and also less susceptible to game playing."[†]

Under the new subjective performance evaluation scheme introduced as part of the balanced scorecard, each branch manager reports directly to an area director who assesses the branch manager's quarterly performance as being "below par," "at par," or "above par." No specific formulas were used to tie the scorecard metrics to the "par" ratings. Area directors were allowed to incorporate whatever factors they thought were important into the managers' performance "par" ratings. The "par" ratings were used to award the quarterly bonuses after the area directors' recommendations were discussed among all the region's area directors and approved by the region's president.

After a statistical analysis of the ratings, the research team concluded that subjectivity in weighting the measures in a balanced scorecard bonus plan allowed supervisors to ignore many performance measures, change criteria from quarter to quarter, ignore measures that predicted future financial performance, and weight measures that were not predictive of desired results.

Each year after implementing the balanced scorecard, the branch managers were surveyed. These surveys revealed that the scorecard brought little change in the branch managers' understanding of the firm's strategic goals or their connections to the managers' actions. Only 32 percent were satisfied with the scorecard process, while 45 percent were dissatisfied. Many branch managers

continued

A Balanced Scorecard Failure*

felt the process was unfair and did not cover all of the important aspects of their job and that their bonuses did not accurately reflect their performance. One branch manager wrote, "I hate the new process. Favoritism comes too much into play." At the end of 1998, the balanced scorecard was abandoned in favor of a more objective, commission-style system based on the branch revenues.

One must be careful not to generalize the results of this single balanced scorecard failure to other settings. This firm might have implemented the scorecard poorly, in the sense of not choosing the appropriate performance indicators. Alternatively, failure might be due to bad employee training, or to the use of subjective, rather than more objective, compensation schemes. Maybe the area directors were not adequately trained in assessing "par" performance. Perhaps the regional presidents did not supervise their area directors. What is clear from this case study is the close linkage between performance evaluation (the balanced scorecard) and performance reward (subjective evaluation by the area directors) as depicted in Figure 14–1. This international financial services firm rolled out a balanced scorecard that included both new performance metrics and a new bonus system. The combined system failed and was replaced. We cannot establish which piece caused the failure. However, we see that the two pieces are really inseparable and that each must be internally consistent and coordinated with both the decision rights assignment and the firm's strategy.

*Based on C Ittner, D Larcker, and M Meyer, "Subjectivity and the Weighting of Performance Measures: Evidence from a Balanced Scorecard," *Accounting Review* 78, July 2003, pp 725–58.

†R Kaplan and D Norton, *The Balanced Scorecard: Translating Strategy into Action* (Boston: Harvard Business School Press, 1996), p. 220.

at the expense of value creation."[10] The balanced scorecard gives managers multiple criteria for measuring their success and thus reduces their accountability for destroying shareholder value. Some reduction in shareholder value becomes acceptable if some other stakeholder is shown to have benefited.

Concept Questions		
	Q14–5	Describe four different definitions of *quality*.
	Q14–6	If *quality* is defined as meeting customer expectations, what does measuring quality require?
	Q14–7	Total quality costs can be categorized into four groups. What are they?
	Q14–8	How does cost accounting become easier in a just-in-time environment?
	Q14–9	What are some of the problematic aspects of a JIT environment?
	Q14-10	Describe which parts of Figure 14–1 are affected by a firm's adoption of a balanced scorecard approach.
	Q14-11	Describe two criticisms of the balanced scorecard.

[10] Jensen, 2001.

| National Financial Services (NFS) | NFS, with $58.3 million in assets, provides long-term savings and retirement products. In 1997, NFS faced a changing environment: increased competition and customers demanding individualized financial solutions. To respond, NFS went public, changed its strategy, overhauled its compensation plans, and installed a balanced scorecard. The balanced scorecard allowed NFS to link its performance measures to the new strategy. Fourteen measures were chosen, including net operating income, return on equity, customer retention, and back-office productivity. NFS's CFO explains that the new measures "often give a better and faster insight into what's happening and where your business is going." NFS illustrates how environmental changes cause firms to reevaluate their business strategies and revise their organizational architecture, including their performance measures. It is another example of the framework in Figure 14–1.

SOURCE: C Lazere, "All Together Now," CFO, February 1998, pp. 28–36. |

C. When Should the Internal Accounting System Be Changed?

There is no such thing as the ideal management accounting system. Each organization has different circumstances that lead to different management accounting systems. Also, accounting must continually deal with trade-offs among external users wanting information describing firm performance and internal users wanting information for decision making and control. Surviving organizations must meet the demands of changing technologies and markets by revising their business strategies and organizational architectures (Figure 14–1). Because organizations are in a constant state of flux, the accounting system must regularly adapt.

Certain signs indicate that the internal accounting system is not working well. One sign is dysfunctional behavior on the part of managers because of poorly chosen performance measures. Managers will make decisions to positively influence performance measures. If those performance measures are not consistent with the goals of the organization, management will make decisions that do not coincide with the organization's goals. Another sign of problems with the accounting system is poor operating decisions. If product mix and pricing decisions based on management accounting are not adding to firm value, then the accounting system is either providing inaccurate estimates of opportunity costs and/or creating dysfunctional incentives.

Often changes in customers' organizational architectures cause suppliers to change their architecture (and accounting systems). For example, when the large automakers switched to JIT, firms supplying auto parts such as windshield wiper motors switched to JIT. If your major customers are modifying their organizational architectures, they are likely responding to technological and market conditions. The way in which knowledge is generated and disseminated has probably changed. These changes are likely affecting your firm's organizational architecture.

Organizations should not necessarily look to the latest management accounting fads to give them direction in changing their management accounting systems. Activity-based costing (ABC), for example, is only appropriate for certain types of organizations. Each organization must continually evaluate and improve its management accounting system to meet the challenges of a changing environment and a changing organization.

D. Summary

The preceding section analyzed three organizational innovations. These innovations illustrate that internal accounting systems are an integral part of the organization's architecture. When managers change the architecture of their organization by decentralizing decision rights and empowering employees via TQM programs because the firm's business strategy changes, accounting systems are likewise modified. Similarly, when JIT production systems are installed, accounting system changes follow. Firms adopt balanced scorecards to better link performance measures to their business strategy.

This text has emphasized the dual role of internal accounting systems for decision making and control. Because the internal accounting system is performing two separate roles (it is also being used for taxes and financial reporting), trade-offs between these roles must be made. In its decision-making role, the accounting system is the first place managers turn to help them estimate opportunity costs. However, accounting numbers are not forward-looking opportunity costs. Accounting systems record historical costs, which are backward looking. Therefore, accounting numbers are useful for decision making only under very strong assumptions, primarily that the future will look like the past.

A similar separation of decision making and control exists in budgeting systems (Chapter 6). Budgets not only help assemble specialized knowledge (useful for decision making), but they also provide incentives as part of the performance evaluation system (useful for control). The fact that budgets are used for both decision making and control requires a trade-off between the two that can reduce a budget's effectiveness to serve each role. This trade-off involves not giving managers sole decision rights to set their budgets. Higher-level managers ratify and monitor lower-level managers' budgets. Separating decision rights reduces the tendency of lower-level managers to exaggerate their forecasts.

Because the same system is being used for decision-making and control functions, it is not surprising that if the accounting system is used primarily for decision control, operating managers seeking information for decision making will find the accounting data deficient. Likewise, if the accounting system is being used primarily for decision making (e.g., pricing), then it is likely under greater control by the manager and will not prove very useful for control (performance evaluation).

As industries restructure in reaction to technological change and changing market conditions via downsizing, mergers, leveraged buyouts (LBOs), spinoffs, and recapitalizations, alternative organizational architectures such as outsourcing are being used to control agency problems. If agency problems are being reduced by these alternative organizational architectures, then internal accounting systems should move from a decision control function to a decision management function. Because changing the organization's architecture has reduced the agency costs, the internal accounting system becomes more oriented toward decision making. This may explain why certain firms adopt activity-based costing systems, which are designed primarily to improve decision making, not control. In fact, the analysis in this text predicts that firms changing to agency-cost–reducing organizational architectures such as LBOs are more likely to emphasize decision management rather than decision control in their management accounting systems.

Self-Study Problems

Self-Study Problem 1:   Gilbert Foods

Gilbert Foods manufactures food seasonings and packaged dry sauce mixes for sales in grocery stores. Gilbert started a quality improvement program in 2008. It expanded its training and quality assurance programs and began monitoring employee satisfaction and estimating lost sales due to quality problems. The data in the following table summarize the quarterly results of operating its TQM program over the last two years.

GILBERT FOODS
Quality Costs
2008–2009
(Millions)

	2008				2009			
	Q1	Q2	Q3	Q4	Q1	Q2	Q3	Q4
Customer complaint dept.	$ 3.90	$ 3.45	$ 3.03	$ 2.76	$ 2.50	$ 2.27	$ 2.14	$ 2.01
Inspection	1.40	1.56	1.75	1.95	2.39	2.96	3.63	4.46
Lost sales	49.20	40.31	33.11	28.42	24.45	21.08	19.20	17.44
Process engineering	2.20	2.46	2.76	3.11	3.87	4.86	6.13	7.58
Quality assurance administration	6.20	6.52	6.86	7.19	7.93	8.74	9.61	10.53
Returns	26.90	21.09	16.35	13.53	11.32	9.50	8.43	7.52
Rework	15.80	12.65	10.03	8.49	7.25	6.16	5.56	5.00
Scrap	17.60	14.48	11.92	10.32	8.92	7.72	7.00	6.34
Testing	1.60	1.72	1.85	1.99	2.29	2.62	3.01	3.45
Training	13.10	14.39	15.90	17.46	21.12	25.50	30.37	36.35

Required:

a. Prepare a cost-of-quality report that classifies each expense as being in one of four categories: appraisal, prevention, internal failure, or external failure.

b. What conclusions can you draw from the data presented about Gilbert Foods's TQM program?

Solution:

    a. The following table reclassified the cost-of-quality expenses:

GILBERT FOODS
Quality Costs
2008–2009
(Millions)

	2008				2009			
	Q1	*Q2*	*Q3*	*Q4*	*Q1*	*Q2*	*Q3*	*Q4*
Quality assurance administration	$ 6.20	$ 6.52	$ 6.86	$ 7.19	$ 7.93	$ 8.74	$ 9.61	$ 10.53
Training	13.10	14.39	15.90	17.46	21.12	25.50	30.37	36.35
Process engineering	2.20	2.46	2.76	3.11	3.87	4.86	6.13	7.58
Prevention	$ 21.50	$ 23.37	$ 25.52	$ 27.76	$ 32.92	$ 39.10	$ 46.11	$ 54.46
Inspection	$ 1.40	$ 1.56	$ 1.75	$ 1.95	$ 2.39	$ 2.96	$ 3.63	$ 4.46
Testing	1.60	1.72	1.85	1.99	2.29	2.62	3.01	3.45
Appraisal	$ 3.00	$ 3.28	$ 3.60	$ 3.94	$ 4.68	$ 5.58	$ 6.64	$ 7.91
Rework	$ 15.80	$ 12.65	$ 10.03	$ 8.49	$ 7.25	$ 6.16	$ 5.56	$ 5.00
Scrap	17.60	14.48	11.92	10.32	8.92	7.72	7.00	6.34
Internal failure	$ 33.40	$ 27.13	$ 21.95	$ 18.81	$ 16.17	$ 13.88	$ 12.56	$ 11.34
Returns	$ 26.90	$ 21.09	$ 16.35	$ 13.53	$ 11.32	$ 9.50	$ 8.43	$ 7.52
Customer complaint dept.	3.90	3.45	3.03	2.76	2.50	2.27	2.14	2.01
Lost sales	49.20	40.31	33.11	28.42	24.45	21.08	19.20	17.44
External failure	$ 80.00	$ 64.85	$ 52.49	$ 44.71	$ 38.27	$ 32.85	$ 29.77	$ 26.97
Total costs	$137.90	$118.63	$103.56	$ 95.22	$ 92.04	$ 91.41	$ 95.08	$100.68

    b. From the preceding data we see that prevention and appraisal costs are increasing while internal and external failure costs have been decreasing. The following graph plots three series: prevention and appraisal costs, failure costs, and total quality costs.

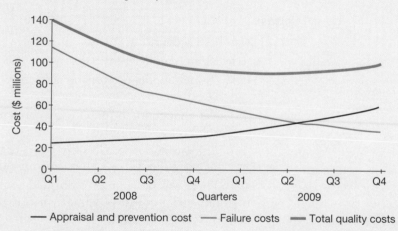

A preliminary conclusion from the graph is that Gilbert Foods is probably now spending too much on trying to improve quality. Assuming that the underlying production processes have not changed over time, quality costs were minimized in the second quarter of 2009. Since then, the additional money spent on appraisal and prevention has yielded smaller internal- and external-failure cost savings.

Self-Study Problem 2:   Abco

Abco manufactures car radio antennas. It produces the retractable wand that other firms assemble with a motor, wiring, housing, and switch for sale to the automakers. Abco receives deliveries of steel rod and tubing each day. These are cut, threaded, crimped, and assembled into final wands on continuous flow production lines. It produces four different models on dedicated flow lines. Twice a day finished wands are shipped to customers who assemble the complete antenna unit.

On March 16, $2,040 of rod and tubing were delivered for the 28-inch antenna model. These materials were converted into wands and shipped out:

Completed units shipped in the morning	160
Completed units shipped in the afternoon	180

Labor and overhead incurred on March 16 were $980. Each completed 28-inch wand has a standard conversion cost of $4.80. Abco uses JIT accounting and backflushes RIP and conversion costs directly to cost of goods sold when the units are shipped because wands are not started until Abco receives an order.

At the end of the year, total 28-inch antenna conversion costs incurred were $3,285,080, and 702,100 28-inch wands were completed. Any over- or underabsorbed conversion costs are charged to cost of goods sold.

Required:

    a. What accounting entries are made on March 16 for the 28-inch wands?

    b. What accounting entries are needed at the end of the year for the 28-inch-antenna conversion cost account?

Solution:

    a. March 16 accounting entries:

      (i) 28-inch model conversion account is increased by $980.

      (ii) 28-inch model conversion account is decreased by $1,632 (or 340 × $4.80).

      (iii) Net change in 28-inch model conversion account is a decrease of $652 (or $980 − $1,632).

      (iv) The raw and in-process inventory account was both increased and decreased by $2,040, thus showing no change.

      (v) There was no change to finished goods. Rather, all the costs of finished products of $3,672 (or $1,632 + $2,040) were charged directly to cost of goods sold.

b. The entry for the 28-inch-antenna conversion cost account at year-end was

Conversion costs applied (702,100 × $4.80)	$3,370,080
Total 28-inch model conversion cost incurred	3,285,080
Overabsorbed conversion costs	$ 85,000

The conversion cost account is decreased by $85,000 to produce a zero balance; cost of goods sold is decreased by $85,000.

Problems

P 14–1: British Airways

British Airways (BA) has implemented the balanced scorecard. Match the following performance indicators:

Return on invested capital	On-time arrivals
Earnings growth	Percent empty seats
Lost baggage	Employee turnover
Employee training hours	Number of frequent flyers (25,000 miles on BA)

to these four balanced scorecard perspectives:

Financial	Innovation and learning
Customer	Internal business processes

Note: Performance indicators may be used for more than one perspective.

P 14–2: Bay Street Bank

Commenting on the following six-month operating statement, the president of the Bay Street Bank reports to the board of directors, "The bank has a six-month operating loss of $90.6 million compared with a budgeted loss of $13.7 million. In the annual budget for 2009, we planned on covering the budgeted six-month operating loss ($13.7 million) with projected surpluses in the second half of the year. Thus, unless we have a better-than-expected second six months, we are projecting an operating shortfall of $76.9 million for 2009. The problem has been almost entirely on the revenue side of the budget. The extremely weak economy the last six months caused us to make fewer new loans and charge lower interest rates than we projected. Interest rates are substantially lower than when the budget was prepared. This has forced us to invest our funds in lower-yielding investments than we planned. Revenues were $70.7 million under budget, but expenses were only $6.2 million over budget. Much of the expense increase was the result of higher unexpected costs for CDs (certificates of deposit). We have done a good job controlling costs; now if only we could control the general economy and interest rates."

BAY STREET BANK
Operating Results
Six Months Ending June 2009
($000s)

	Actual 6 Months	Budget 6 Months	Fav. (Unfav.) 6 Months	Last Year 6 Months
Revenue				
Interest income:				
Home mortgages	$431,000	$443,000	$(12,000)	$420,000
Car loans	330,000	375,000	(45,000)	345,000
Government securities	9,000	14,500	(5,500)	45,000
Service charges	19,000	28,000	(9,000)	25,000
Miscellaneous	1,600	800	800	1,700
Total income	$790,600	$861,300	$(70,700)	$836,700
Expenses				
Interest on savings accounts	$380,000	$376,500	$ (3,500)	$370,000
Interest on CDs*	175,000	168,000	(7,000)	160,000
Interest on bonds	275,200	279,500	4,300	270,000
Administration	51,000	51,000	0	52,000
Total expenses	$881,200	$875,000	$ (6,200)	$852,000
Net operating surplus (deficit)	$(90,600)	$(13,700)	$(76,900)	$(15,300)

*CDs are savings accounts that pay higher interest rates when held for a specific length of time. Penalties for early withdrawal apply.

Required:

Critically analyze the bank president's comments.

P 14–3:   Vail

Vail operates a JIT plant assembling ceiling fans. The Sunset Model ceiling fan has a standard material cost of $28.40, a standard direct labor cost of $14.80, and overhead (fixed and variable) of $16.10. On Monday, a batch of 100 Sunset fans is completed. All of the materials for the 100 fans were on hand prior to Monday and had been previously recorded in the raw and in-process inventory account.

Required:

a. Describe the accounting entries that are made at the end of Monday to record the assembly of the batch of 100 Sunset fans.

b. In analyzing the financial statements of a firm using JIT and another firm in the same industry not using JIT, what differences would you expect to observe?

P 14-4:   Fiedler International

You work on a team that reports to the chief financial officer of Fiedler International, a consumer products company that manages a variety of consumer beauty brands (shampoos, facial soaps, deodorants). Your team evaluates possible acquisitions. You are currently analyzing the possible purchase of Lush, a manufacturer of face moisturizers with UV sun blockers. Lush is a small, publicly traded company that has no single large shareholder. Most of the stock is held by institutional investors and Lush managers hold a small percentage of the stock.

The materials you have received from Lush include information about its senior management performance evaluation and incentive compensation plans. Lush uses a balanced scorecard to evaluate and reward senior managers. Managers can earn up to 50 percent of their salary as a bonus depending on four balanced scorecard metrics: customer service, human resources and innovation, operational efficiency, and financial performance. Each of the four metrics is scaled between 0–1. Senior managers receive up to 25 percent of their bonus for each metric. If the customer service metric is 0.67, and a particular manager's salary is $400,000, then for customer service, that manager receives $33,500 (50% × $400,000 × 0.67 × 25%). The compensation committee of Lush's board of directors sets the scale for each of the four metrics. For example, the financial performance metric is economic value added, or EVA. Last year's EVA was $13 million. The compensation committee sets the lower and upper bound of EVA as $12 million and $16 million. Hence, if the current year's EVA is $12 million, the financial performance metric is 0. If EVA is $15 million, the metric is 0.75 [($15 − $12)/($16 − 12)], and the manager earning the $400,000 salary would receive a bonus of $37,500 (50% × $400,000 × 0.75 × 25%).

Fourteen separate metrics are used to compute the four metrics. The following metrics are computed and then aggregated to form the four metrics:

Customer Service	Human Resources and Innovation	Operational Efficiency	Financial Performance
Returns	New products	On-time production	EVA
Customer complaints	Percent of new products developed on time and on budget	Unit manufacturing cost	
On-site customer training seminars	Employee satisfaction	Safety accidents	
Shipping errors	Employee turnover	Dollars of scrap	
	Employee training		

Lush has been using the balanced scorecard for three years and the achieved levels of each metric for the last three years are:

	Customer Service	Human Resources and Innovation	Operational Efficiency	Financial Performance
2009	0.86	0.77	0.76	0.79
2010	0.92	0.91	0.82	0.73
2011	0.95	0.94	0.94	0.69

Required:

Write a memo to your acquisition team describing balanced scorecards and the primary reasons they are used, and the likely affect of Lush's use of the balanced scorecard in terms of how Fiedler should be evaluating Lush. Specifically: (*a*) briefly describe balanced scorecards and why firms use them and (*b*) analyze Lush's use of the balanced scorecard and how this might affect Fiedler's evaluation of Lush as a possible takeover target.

P 14–5:   Curtis on Corporate Performance

Donald Curtis, in "The Modern American Accounting System: Does It Really Measure Corporate Performance?" in *The Financial Executive* (January/February 1985, pp. 58–62), criticized corporate accounting systems by arguing:

> The SEC, the stock market, and the corporate compensation committees all seem to focus on accrual earnings as the only reliable and fair measure of corporate performance. . . . What's wrong is that the modern American accounting system is a very imperfect measure of corporate performance (whether publicly held or not). The plain fact is that it cannot *technically* do what we are asking it to do with anything like the precision we are expecting. A failure to adequately understand the system's limitations—combined with our penchant for treating things which seem to be quantifiable (such as profit) as more real than things which are difficult to quantify (such as quality of a company's [product])—has, in my view, contributed to serious mismanagement of American business during the last several years.

Required:

Critically evaluate this statement.

P 14–6:   Guest Watches

Guest Watches is a division of Guest Fashions, a large, international fashion designer. Guest Watches manufactures highly stylish watches for young adults (age 18 to 30) who are fashion conscious. It is a profit center and its senior management's compensation is tied closely to the reported profits. While Guest Watches has succeeded in capturing the fashion market, product dependability is eroding these gains. A number of retailers have dropped or are threatening to drop the Guest watch line because of customer returns. Guest watches carry a one-year warranty and 12 percent are returned, compared with an industry average of 4 percent. Besides high warranty costs and lost sales due to reputation, Guest Watches has higher-than-industry-average manufacturing scrap and rework costs.

Senior management, worried about these trends and the possible erosion of its market dominance, hired a consulting firm to study the problem and make recommendations for reversing the situation. After a thorough analysis of Guest Watches's customers, suppliers, and manufacturing facilities, the consultants recommended five possible actions ranging from the status quo to a complete Total Quality Management, Zero Defects program (level IV). The accompanying table outlines the various alternatives for Guest Watches. (Dollar figures are in thousands.)

	Additional Training Cost[*]	*Additional Prevention/ Compliance*[†]
Status quo	$ 0	$ 0
Level I	80	180
Level II	200	240
Level III	350	340
Level IV	550	490

[*]Includes the annual costs of training employees in TQM methods.
[†]All annual costs including certifying suppliers, redesigning the product, and inspection costs to reduce defects.

The consultants emphasized that while first-year startup costs are slightly higher than in subsequent years, management must really view the above cost estimates as annual, ongoing costs. Given employee turnover and supplier changes, training, prevention, and compliance costs are not likely to decline over time.

The consulting firm and the newly appointed vice president for quality programs estimated that under level IV, rework and scrap would be $25,000 and warranty costs zero. Level IV was needed to get the firm to zero defects. A task force was convened and after several meetings generated the following estimates of rework/scrap and warranty costs for the various levels of firm commitment:

	Total Rework/ Scrap Cost[*]	*Total Warranty Costs*[†]
Status quo	$500	$350
Level I	300	280
Level II	150	140
Level III	75	80
Level IV	25	0

[*]The costs of manufacturing scrap and rework.
[†]The costs of repairing and replacing products that fail in the hands of customers.

There was considerable discussion and debate about the quantitative impact of increased quality on additional sales. While no hard and fast numbers could be derived, the consensus view was that the total net cash flows (contribution margin) from additional sales as retailers and customers learn of the reduced defect rate would be

	Contribution Margin on Additional Sales
Status quo	$ 0
Level I	600
Level II	1,000
Level III	1,200
Level IV	1,300

Required:

a. Assuming that the data as presented are reasonably accurate, what should Guest Watches do about its deteriorating quality situation? Should it maintain the status quo or should it adopt the consultants' recommendation and implement level I, II, III, or IV?

b. Evaluate the analysis underlying your policy recommendation in (*a*). Will the senior management of the Watch Division make the same decision as the senior management of Guest Fashions?

P 14–7: Applying TQM in Manufacturing versus Administration

One large company that has been successful in applying Total Quality Management (TQM) principles in manufacturing reports that it has had less success in applying the same techniques in improving administrative functions such as order taking, distribution, and human resources. This company (which has won several quality awards and has significantly improved its product quality) used state-of-the-art TQM methods to train all of its employees in how to apply TQM. However, the company has not been able to achieve the same cost reductions and service quality enhancements in administrative areas as it has in the manufacturing area. Assuming that this phenomenon extends to other companies, why do you think that TQM works better in manufacturing than in nonmanufacturing/service areas?

P 14–8: Old Town Roasters

Old Town Roasters (OTR) owns and operates a chain of 12 coffee shops around town. OTR's strategy is to provide the highest-quality coffee and baked goods in a warm, friendly environment. Each OTR provides its customers Internet access and current newspapers. Some shops are open 24 hours a day, especially those located around college campuses. Each shop manager is responsible for deciding the hours that the store is open, the selection of baked goods to stock, and the number of Internet terminals to provide in the store.

Required:

Design a balanced scorecard to evaluate and reward the manager of each shop.

P 14–9: The Pottery Store

The Pottery Store is a chain of retail stores in upscale malls that sells pottery, woodcarvings, and other craft items. The typical customer is shopping for a gift and spends between $50 and $200. Buyers in the corporate office contact artists around the country and buy inventory for the stores. Corporate headquarters sets the final selling price for each item and determines when to mark them down for sales. Each store manager is responsible for store staffing and layout. Store managers do not have responsibility for choosing the merchandise, store hours (set by the mall), or pricing decisions.

Required:

    a. Design a balanced scorecard for the store managers.

    b. How would your answer to (*a*) change if the store managers also had decision-making responsibilities for both selecting the merchandise to carry in the store and pricing?

P 14–10:   Software Development Inc.

Software Development Inc. (SDI) produces and markets software for personal computers, including spreadsheet, word processing, desktop publishing, and database management programs. SDI has annual sales of $800 million.

Producing software is a time-consuming, labor-intensive process. Software quality is an extremely important aspect of success in computer software markets. One aspect of quality is program reliability. Does the software perform as expected? Does it work with other software in terms of data transfers and interfaces? Does it terminate abnormally? In spite of extensive testing of the software, programs always contain some bugs. Once the software is released, SDI stands behind the product with phone-in customer service consultants who answer questions and help the customer work around problems in the software. SDI's software maintenance group fixes bugs and sends out revised versions of the programs to customers.

SDI tracks the relation between quality costs and quality. The quality measure it uses is the number of documented bugs in a software package. These bugs are counted when a customer calls in with a complaint and the SDI customer service representative determines that this is a new problem. The software maintenance programmers then attempt to fix the program and eliminate the bug. To manage quality, SDI tracks quality costs. It has released 38 new packages or major revisions in existing packages in the last three years. The accompanying table reports the number of defects (bugs) documented in the first six months following release. Also listed in the table are total product cost and quality cost per software package release.

Product costs include all the costs incurred to produce and market the software, excluding the quality costs in the table. Quality costs consist of three components: training, prevention, and software maintenance and customer service costs. Training costs are expenditures for educating the programmers and updating their training. Better-educated programmers produce fewer bugs. Prevention costs include expenditures for testing the software before it is released. Maintenance and customer service costs include (1) the programmers charged with fixing the bugs and reissuing the revised software and (2) the customer service representatives answering phone questions. The training and prevention costs are measured over the period the software was being developed. The number of defects and maintenance and service costs are measured in the first six months following release.

SDI Defects and Quality Costs by Program Release[*]

Program Release	Number of Defects	Product Cost	Training Cost	Prevention Cost	Software Maintenance and Customer Service Cost	Total Costs
1	66	$3,455	$442	$ 770	$2,160	$6,827
2	86	3,959	428	447	2,658	7,492
3	14	3,609	417	1,167	687	5,880
4	73	3,948	211	655	2,334	7,148
5	17	3,104	290	1,013	544	4,951
6	48	3,179	253	547	1,556	5,535
7	80	3,112	392	508	2,633	6,645
8	41	3,529	276	577	1,563	5,945
9	50	3,796	557	634	1,666	6,653
10	67	3,444	365	947	2,140	6,896
11	42	3,922	453	869	1,444	6,688
12	64	3,846	378	1,108	1,942	7,274
13	71	3,014	555	762	2,384	6,715
14	1	3,884	301	773	423	5,381
15	18	3,183	378	1,080	857	5,498
16	85	3,475	528	1,010	2,572	7,585
17	17	3,445	357	666	631	5,099
18	50	3,203	285	427	1,546	5,461
19	22	3,839	239	1,080	891	6,049
20	73	3,060	540	1,054	2,309	6,963
21	52	3,182	329	1,079	1,867	6,457
22	75	3,075	395	832	2,697	6,999
23	35	3,456	447	969	1,518	6,390
24	53	3,987	355	651	2,042	7,035
25	25	3,836	309	1,160	1,036	6,341
26	6	3,886	234	794	252	5,166
27	78	3,846	418	833	2,800	7,897
28	82	3,106	409	1,092	2,871	7,478
29	39	3,506	448	899	1,342	6,195
30	47	3,545	450	442	1,450	5,887
31	30	3,376	456	784	1,260	5,876
32	17	3,740	542	420	607	5,309
33	67	3,479	411	821	2,018	6,729
34	51	3,773	351	1,145	1,873	7,142
35	74	3,034	497	671	2,389	6,591
36	25	3,768	268	887	1,094	6,017
37	14	3,168	356	645	837	5,006
38	77	3,561	492	1,167	2,597	7,817
Average	48	$3,509	$390	$ 826	$1,671	$6,395

[*]Per 100,000 lines of computer code.

All the numbers in the table have been divided by lines of computer code in the particular program release. Programs with more lines of code cost more and also have more bugs. Prior studies find that using lines of code is an acceptable way to control for program complexity. Thus, the numbers in the table are stated in terms of defects and cost per 100,000 lines of code.

The figure below plots the relation between total cost and number of defects. The vice president of quality of SDI likes to use it to emphasize that costs and quality are inversely related. She is fond of saying, "Quality pays! Our total costs fall as the number of defects declines. The more we spend on quality, the lower our costs."

SDI total costs by defects

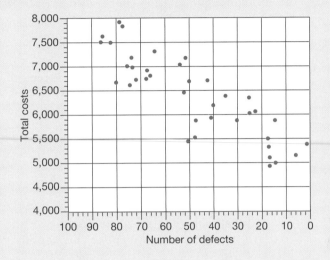

Required:

Critically evaluate the vice president's analysis.

P 14–11: Stirling Acquisition

You are working for an investment banking firm. One of your clients is examining the possibility of purchasing Stirling Manufacturing, a parts supplier (specifically, tail-light assemblies) to the automobile industry. Stirling has sales of $130 million and assets of $93 million.

Your client has asked your firm to evaluate Stirling (a privately held company) and indicate how much should be paid for Stirling. Stirling has a batch-manufacturing process. Raw materials inventories are held until they are placed into production. Batches of between 2,000 and 2,500 tail-light assemblies are manufactured. These are then delivered daily, 100 to 150 at a time, to satisfy Stirling's customers' demand for just-in-time (JIT) deliveries. Your client is considering installing JIT production methods at Stirling if the acquisition is completed.

Your boss asks you to write a memo that outlines the various likely results if Stirling adopts JIT production techniques and the likely impact on Stirling's cash flows and eventual market value. Your memo will provide background information for your colleagues who are actually estimating Stirling's current price and future value after acquisition. Your client is planning on making a number of changes at Stirling. JIT is just one of them. Your memo will assist the analysts in your firm and should direct them in their data gathering and valuation efforts. Your memo should describe specifically what additional data your colleagues should collect in order to estimate JIT's cash flow effects.

P 14–12:   TQM at the Stowbridge Division

The Stowbridge Division is analyzing expanding its Total Quality Management program. It already has a TQM program in place. However, one of its customers, Amlan Equipment, is asking all suppliers to become ISO 9000–qualified, a process that certifies that the firm meets various standards. Once suppliers are ISO 9000–qualified, Amlan can reduce its inspection costs. Not all of the suppliers will be certified, and those that are will receive more business from Amlan.

Amlan purchases a stainless steel rotor from Stowbridge. After earning ISO 9000 certification, Stowbridge estimates that it will have to incur the following annual incremental costs as long as it wants to maintain its certification:

Annual Incremental Costs to be ISO 9000–Certified	
Training	$74,000
Inspection	$96,000
Prevention	$62,000
Direct materials	+10%
Direct labor	+15%

To manufacture the current quality of the rotors (before ISO 9000 certification), the budgeted selling price and standard cost data per rotor follow.

Selling price	$14.00
Less standard costs:	
Direct materials	$ 4.30
Direct labor	2.40
Manufacturing overhead (all fixed)	2.05
Selling and administrative (all variable)	1.60
Unit cost	$10.35
Unit profit	$ 3.65

Unless Stowbridge receives ISO 9000 certification, it will lose Amlan's business of 120,000 units per year. Management estimates that the higher quality of the rotor that meets quality criteria will allow Stowbridge to add 14,000 rotors to its existing sales from new and continuing customers. Stowbridge is currently selling 480,000 rotors per year, including the Amlan sales. The 480,000 current sales amount to 63 percent of plant capacity. The additional 14,000 units sold can be manufactured without exceeding plant capacity. The higher-quality process after ISO 9000 certification is received would apply to all the rotors produced.

Required:

Should Stowbridge seek ISO 9000 certification? Support your recommendation with an analysis of the costs and benefits of certification.

P 14–13: Home Lending Inc.

Home Lending Inc. (HLI) is a mortgage application service company. It is a subsidiary of Relocation Realty, a large real estate sales firm. Real estate agents working for Relocation Realty refer their clients to HLI to arrange financing. Instead of contacting several banks to compare mortgage rates, home buyers use HLI as an intermediary. HLI maintains a current list of all of the various mortgage terms at all area banks (fixed and adjustable rates, terms, balloon payments, points, etc.). Home buyers in one place can then select the mortgage parameters that best fit their situation. Because all banks use a common mortgage application form, HLI can fill out and file the necessary application for its client. Banks and HLI charge one point (1 percent of the requested loan amount) for filing the application if it is approved. (In the rare event that a bank denies an application, the loan applicant is not charged any fee.) Consumers are indifferent between filing an application directly with the bank versus using HLI.

HLI employs mortgage processors who meet with the home buyers, go over the various loan options, file the applications, and represent the borrower when the loan is consummated. Each processor can file a maximum of 120 mortgages per year. HLI owns and maintains a mainframe computer system that automates the loan application process. In addition to the mortgage processors, HLI employs secretaries who function as receptionists, computer data entry clerks, and office supply managers. The president of HLI, Linda Jeter, oversees the office, hires (and fires) office staff, and helps with difficult loan applications. She reports to the owner of Relocation Realty.

The housing market is in a recession. Two years ago HLI processed 580 mortgages with an average mortgage of $80,000 and employed five processors and two secretaries. This year Jeter projects only 280 mortgage filings with an average mortgage of $70,000. She laid off two processors and a secretary last year.

The following data summarize operations two years ago and the projections for this year:

	Two Years Ago	Projected for This Year
Number of mortgages	580	280
Average revenue per mortgage	$ 800	$ 700
Revenue	$464,000	$196,000
Mortgage processors	(125,000)	(90,000)
Secretaries	(34,000)	(20,000)
Computer maintenance	(30,000)	(30,000)
L. Jeter's salary	(55,000)	(55,000)
Depreciation on computer	(40,000)	(40,000)
Office rent	(36,000)	(36,000)
Supplies, utilities, phones, etc.	(12,000)	(14,000)
Profit/loss	$132,000	$(89,000)

HLI has noncancelable five-year contracts for office rent and computer maintenance, with one more year to run on each contract. The computer system and office equipment have no salvage values. Jeter has been told to cut the losses or else Relocation Realty will close the subsidiary. She is considering two possibilities: further layoffs of mortgage processors or cutting the price charged for mortgage processing to ¾ of 1 percent. She thinks such a price cut will not be met immediately by the competition and in the meantime will increase the quantity demanded by 30 percent. Ignoring taxes, evaluate the various proposals and recommend a course of action for Jeter. Justify your recommendation with a clearly presented financial analysis.

P 14–14:   Warm Glo Furnaces

Warm Glo manufactures gas furnaces for residential use. It uses a standard cost system that isolates all variances at purchase so that all product costs are stated at standard cost. All variances are included as part of cost of goods sold. Overhead is allocated based on direct labor hours. Standard cost for the basic economy model furnace follows:

Standard Cost Sheet for Basic Economy Furnace

Raw materials and purchased parts	$193
Direct labor (8 hours at $21/hour)	168
Overhead (8 hours at $20/hour)	160
Standard cost	$521

Warm Glo manufactures the basic economy furnace in a dedicated flow line using just-in-time production principles. All raw materials and purchased parts needed to assemble a complete furnace are delivered to the plant by 8:00 a.m. of the day the furnace begins production. While each furnace requires eight direct labor hours, total throughput time for each furnace is two working days (16 hours). The difference between total throughput time and the eight direct labor hours is waiting time. Furnaces that are started in production one day are finished the next day. Four hours of direct labor are used the first day and four hours of direct labor are worked the second day. All production for the week is accumulated and shipped out to the distributor by train on Saturday.

Warm Glo maintains a finished-goods inventory account for basic economy furnaces that reflects the standard cost of furnaces not yet shipped out. Warm Glo uses a raw and in-process materials account (RIP) and JIT backflushing accounting. All accounts are updated at the end of each day for all production and transactions occurring that day. Conversion costs are charged directly to the finished-goods inventory account as work is performed on furnaces. Through the end of Thursday of the current week, the following table contains information about the plant's production of basic economy furnaces:

Basic Economy Furnace—Daily Production Flows

	Mon.	Tues.	Wed.	Thurs.
Units started	17	18	19	16
Units finished	20	17	18	19

Required:

    a. What is the balance in the RIP account for the basic economy model at the end of Thursday?

    b. What is the balance in the finished-goods account (basic economy model) at the end of Thursday?

P 14–15:   Winter Games

Winter Games manufactures a competitive line of skis and sells its skis to retailers at a price of $225 per pair. Based on an annual volume of 5,000 pairs, the cost per pair is $185:

Direct labor ($75 per pair)		$375,000
Direct materials ($60 per pair)		300,000
Overhead		
Fixed*	$100,000	
Variable ($0.40 per direct labor dollar)	150,000	250,000
Total costs		$925,000
Annual volume (pairs)		÷ 5,000
Cost per pair		$ 185

*Composed of depreciation, property taxes, charitable contributions, insurance, and so on.

    Sports Palace, a discount sporting goods store, currently purchases 500 pairs of skis from Winter Games. Sports Palace has asked to purchase 1,000 pairs of skis under a private brand label, at a price of $200 per pair. The skis would be identical to those normally sold for $225.

    Winter Games believes that if it accepts the order, Sports Palace will cancel its usual order of 500 pairs. These sales cannot be recouped elsewhere. If this special order is accepted, the direct labor hours for the additional 500 skis would have to be compensated at overtime rates (at 1½ times the base rate). Analysis shows that variable overhead varies with total direct labor dollars at the rate of $0.40 per direct labor dollar.

    Should Winter Games accept the special order from Sports Palace?

P 14–16:   Warren City Parts Manufacturing

Warren City, with sales of $2 billion, produces and sells farm equipment. The manufacturing division produces some parts internally and purchases other parts from external suppliers and assembles farm equipment including tractors, combines, and plows. Within the manufacturing division is parts manufacturing, which fabricates a large variety of parts. Parts manufacturing is further subdivided into 12 departments, including screw products, metal stamping and fabrication, plastic injection molding, and steel castings. Each of these parts departments is headed by a department manager whose performance is evaluated along several dimensions: meeting budgeted costs, meeting delivery schedules, improving quality, achieving affirmative action and employee satisfaction goals, and minimizing inventory adjustments.

    Inventory adjustments occur twice a year after internal auditors conduct a physical inventory of the parts department's work in process and compare it with the amount of inventory as reported in the work-in-process (WIP) account. For example, if on June 30 the auditors take a physical inventory count and find $130,000 of physical WIP inventory in the steel castings department but the WIP account reports an inventory balance of $143,000, then a negative inventory adjustment of −9.1 percent (−$13,000 ÷ $143,000) is made. Any inventory adjustment, positive or negative, reflects unfavorably on the parts department manager's performance and results in a reduction in the manager's bonus. The parts department manager is expected to maintain a tight control of WIP inventories, including ensuring the integrity of his or her department's accounting reports of WIP. Large inventory adjustments indicate that the manager does not have good control of WIP.

Four years ago Warren City adopted JIT production procedures. The result has been a drastic reduction of WIP inventories. For example, the following data illustrate the steel castings department's WIP account balance before adjustments, inventory adjustment, and throughput for the last seven years.

Warren City Steel Castings Department

Year	WIP (as of 12/31)	Inventory Adjustment*	Throughput
2002	$1,920,000	12.0%	$76,550,000
2003	1,780,000	−12.9	82,130,000
2004	1,690,000	13.2	69,780,000
2005	1,550,000	13.6	73,290,000
2006	1,480,000	17.9	88,360,000
2007	1,430,000	−17.8	91,080,000
2008	1,390,000	19.5	93,960,000

*Deflated by 12/31 WIP.

Throughput is the total dollar cost of parts manufactured in the year. It is the sum of the beginning inventory plus direct labor and materials and overhead, less ending inventory. Warren City uses a standard cost system and all inventories are valued at standard cost. When a batch of parts completes production, the WIP inventory is reduced by the standard cost of the part times the standard number of parts in the batch. Each part is manufactured in standard lot sizes.

Inventory adjustments can result for a number of reasons:

1. *Different batch sizes.* The department manager decides to deviate from standard batch sizes. Unless a special entry is recorded, the accounting system assumes that the number of units in the batch is the standard number. Sometimes the manager has some excess production capacity and decides to increase the standard batch size. In some cases, the manager produces fewer parts than called for by the standard lot size because of machine breakdowns or bottlenecks. For example, suppose a certain part calls for a standard batch size of 150 but the manager decides to produce 200 parts, keeps 50 as spares, but fails to update the WIP account for the additional 50 units. The WIP account contains only 150 at standard cost but the auditors count 200, causing a positive inventory adjustment.

2. *Timing differences.* The accounting system charges some expenses in a different time period than the department manager expects. This causes the dollar amount of the WIP balance to differ from standard cost.

3. *Standard cost revisions.* The standard cost of a part is revised and the auditors use a different standard cost in valuing the ending WIP inventory than was used in the WIP account.

4. *Audit mistakes.* The internal auditors make mistakes in counting the final physical WIP inventory.

The first two reasons are by far the most prevalent causes of inventory adjustments.

Required:

a. Management is concerned that the magnitude of the inventory adjustment has increased over time. What are some likely reasons that the absolute value of the inventory adjustment has grown?

b. Evaluate the use of the inventory adjustment described above to measure a parts department manager's performance.

P 14–17: Kollel Hospital

Kollel is a private hospital that operates in a large metropolitan area. The hospital admits "regular" patients and "private" patients. Regular patients are admitted and treated by staff doctors who are full-time employees of Kollel Hospital. Private patients are admitted and treated by private physicians (physicians in private practice who have admitting privileges to Kollel). To maintain its leadership role in the community, Kollel is deeply committed to its Total Quality Management program. Management and staff form multidisciplinary teams to study various hospital functions. This year, one team reviewed a hospital unit that exclusively treated a particular type of medical admittance. (All patients of this type of admittance were treated in this unit.) The team found that patients preferred to be discharged sooner rather than later and that, overall, the patients felt that they were kept in the hospital too long.

The specific unit under review consists of 16 beds. Last year the unit treated 300 patients. The patients were heterogeneous with respect to their level of illness. Properly diagnosed and treated, patients should have been discharged in an average of 16 days. Nevertheless, the TQM study showed that patients remain in the hospital an average of 19 days. Furthermore, research showed that the average stay of regular patients was shorter than the average stay of private patients, even though the private physicians did not handle more difficult cases at the time of admission. The study found that private doctors took longer to diagnose their patients and spent less time with them during treatment. As a result, these doctors did not promptly recognize whether a treatment was working or whether the patient was ready to be discharged.

In order to increase the quality of care, hospital management is studying plans to lower the average stay of these patients. One alternative being considered is preventing the private doctors, who are keeping their patients in the unit the longest, from admitting patients into the unit. Some, but not all, of these patients can be replaced by patients admitted by staff doctors. The trade-off between the number of patients admitted and the length of a patient's stay is shown in the following table. Last year 150 regular and 150 private patients were admitted. The average stay was 16 days for regular patients and 22 days for private patients, making an overall average of 19 days per patient.

Admissions as a Function of Reducing Length of Stay

	Status Quo	1 Day	2 Days	3 Days	4 Days
Regular patients' stays (days)	16	16	16	16	16
Regular patients admitted	150	153	160	173	185
Private patients' stays (days)	22	21	20	19	18
Private patients admitted	150	145	135	117	95

For this specific type of admittance, the hospital collects $10,000 per stay from the insurance companies, regardless of whether the patient is admitted regularly or privately. This amount is used to cover the unit's fixed cost of $1,752,000 per year (365 days) and a variable cost of $150 per patient per day. Note that the charges for the doctor's services are handled separately and are not considered for purposes of this analysis.

Required:

a. Calculate the average hospital stay for all patients under each scenario listed in the table. Also, for each case calculate the occupancy rate (percentage of beds filled on average). Discuss the relation between the average length of stay and the occupancy rate.

b. Prepare an income statement showing the net income for each scenario, separating the margin earned on regular and private patients. Where is profit maximized? What are the components of the change in net income?

P 14–18: Tagway 4000

Tagway 4000 is a computer manufacturer based in Montana. One component of the computer is an internal battery that keeps track of the time and date while the computer is turned off. Tagway produces the batteries in-house. The division that produces the batteries (one million each year) is treated as a cost center. The manager of the division is compensated based on her ability to keep total costs low and meet quality control measures of numbers of defects and delivery time. She has a base salary of $144,000. She is eligible for a $34,000 bonus if total costs do not exceed $2 million, not including her compensation. She is eligible for a $40,000 bonus if there are 32 or fewer defects per one million units produced. Finally, she is eligible for a $22,000 bonus if she delivers batteries on time. *On time* is defined as averaging two days between the order from the assembly department and delivery to the assembly department.

The basic cost of producing a battery is $1.55. However, current methods have an inherent defect rate of 1,032 defects per million (approximately four standard deviations or 4 sigma). The cost of improving the defect rate involves using higher-quality materials and more experienced labor. Down to 32 defects per million (approximately 5 sigma) the costs are linear. (Based on currently available inputs, improving the defect rate below 32 per million is impossible.) For every additional $450, one defect per million can be removed. In other words, the cost to reduce defects to the desired level of 32 per million is $450,000.

The current production method delivers the batteries in an average of four days. The cost of overtime necessary to lower the average to three days is $90,000. The cost of speeding up delivery another day is $95,000, making the cumulative cost of lowering the average to two days $185,000. The marginal cost of reducing the average delivery a third day is $115,000, making the total cost of reducing the average delivery time to one day $300,000.

Required:

a. Create a table showing the production costs for defect rates of 1,032; 500; 100; 50; and 32 per million and average delivery times of one to four days. Do not include the manager's salary. Note the minimum cost.

b. Create a table showing the manager's compensation for defect rates of 1,032; 500; 100; 50; and 32 and average delivery times of one to four days. Note the maximum compensation level.

c. Comment on the ideal number of defects and delivery times necessary to achieve the minimum costs and the maximum compensation level.

d. Assume that the company as a whole can measure the financial losses related to defects and late deliveries. The costs would include warranty costs, express delivery charges, lost sales, and lost goodwill. These costs do not affect the manager's compensation. The cost for each defect is $460. The cost for each day above one-day average delivery is $500,000 per day late. That is $0 for one-day average delivery, $500,000 for two days, and so on. Create a table showing the firm's total costs—including production costs, costs of defects, costs of delays, and the cost of the manager's compensation (including applicable bonus)—for defect rates of 1,032; 500; 100; 50; and 32 per million and average delivery times of one to four days. Note the minimum cost.

e. Comment on the optimum delivery times and number of defects necessary to achieve the minimum costs to the firm and the maximum compensation level now that the firm's total costs are considered.

Cases

Case 14–1:   Global Oil[11]

In 1995 Global Oil Corporation's Marketing and Refining (M&R) Division was the fifth largest U.S. refiner with 7,700 Global-branded service stations selling about 23 million gallons per day, or 7 percent of the nation's gasoline. All the service stations are company owned. In 1990, M&R ranked last among its peers in profitability and was annually draining $500 million of cash from the corporation.

In 1993, M&R reorganized from a centralized functional organization (Refineries, Transportation, Warehousing, Retail, and Marketing) into 17 geographic business units (sales and distribution) and 14 service companies. The functional organization was slow to react to changing market conditions and the special customer needs that differed across the country. The new decentralized organization was designed to better focus on the customer. New marketing strategies could

---

[11] This case is based on R Kaplan, "Mobil USM&R(A): Linking the Balanced Scorecard," Harvard Business School Case 9–197–025 (May 7, 1997).

be better tailored to local markets by giving local managers more decision-making authority.

A new corporate strategy to focus on the less price-sensitive customer who would not only buy Global gas but also shop in its convenience gas-store outlets was implemented simultaneously with the reorganization. Global's new strategy was to redesign its convenience stores so they would become a "destination stop," offering one-stop shopping for gas and snacks.

The old organization used a variety of functional measures: manufacturing cost, sales margins and volumes, and health and safety metrics. After changing its corporate strategy and organizational structure, M&R decided to change its performance metrics and began investigating the balanced scorecard.

Balanced scorecard (BSC) at M&R

M&R formed project teams of managers to design performance metrics for its operations. Thirty-two different metrics were identified. These included Financial (ROA, cash flow, volume growth, etc.), Customer (share of segment, mystery shopper, etc.), Internal (safety incidents, refinery ROA, inventory level, etc.), and Learning (strategic skills accumulation, quality of information system, etc.). The "mystery shopper" is a third-party vendor who purchases gas and snacks at each station monthly. During each visit, the mystery shopper rates the station on 23 items related to external appearance, rest rooms, and so forth. A brochure describing the BSC was prepared and distributed to M&R's 11,000 employees in August of 1994. Extensive meetings with employees explained the new metrics and the BSC concept.

Compensation plans

All salaried employees of M&R received up to a 10 percent bonus if Global ranked first among its seven competitors on ROA and earnings per share (EPS) growth. In addition to this existing plan, a new program was added that awarded bonuses up to 20 percent to managers. The size of the bonus depends on the average performance of three factors:

- Global's competitive ranking on ROA and EPS growth.
- M&R's balanced scorecard metrics.
- Own business unit's balanced scorecard.

In 1995, M&R generated more income per barrel of oil than the industry average, and its ROA exceeded the industry's average.

Required:

a. Critically evaluate M&R's implementation of the balanced scorecard. Identify any strengths and weaknesses of the program.

b. Was the adoption of the balanced scorecard at M&R responsible for the turnaround in its financial performance?

Case 14–2:   Inorganics, Inc.

At the monthly managers' meeting, the vice president of marketing, Fred Rooks, pointed out that based on the new IMPACT (Incentive Motivation Plan Act), only 4 of the 19 general line salespeople qualified for the annual bonus. (Table 1 explains IMPACT and shows sample salesperson performance.) He believed that these bonus results were too low since 12 salespeople had received bonuses the previous year. Furthermore, he was concerned over the increasing number of cus-

TABLE 1   Sample of Salesperson Performance for Current Year Based on IMPACT*

Sales Rep	Business Area	Current Year Sales $	Contribution $	Contribution %	Prior Year Sales $	Prior Year Contribution %
Rob B.	Photo	$1,000,000	$ 480,000	48%	$ 800,000	45%
	Water	2,500,000	1,000,000	40	2,000,000	39
	Electronics	150,000	(22,000)	−15	180,000	−17
	CaCl	700,000	300,000	43	600,000	33
	Soda ash	3,000,000	1,000,000	33	2,900,000	50
	Sulfuric acid	2,000,000	10,000	1	2,400,000	−16
		$9,350,000	$2,768,000	30%	$8,880,000	27%
Jane R.	Photo	$ 300,000	$ 180,000	60%	$ 200,000	59%
	Water	650,000	300,000	46	450,000	44
	Electronics	75,000	1,000	1	250,000	9
	CaCl	75,000	25,000	33	50,000	34
	Soda ash	1,000,000	575,000	58	1,050,000	57
	Sulfuric acid	150,000	(40,000)	−27	200,000	−26
		$2,250,000	$1,041,000	46%	$2,200,000	41%
Jack B.	Photo	$1,600,000	$1,100,000	69%	$1,200,000	65%
	Water	790,000	350,000	44	750,000	42
	Electronics	0			100,000	−5
	CaCl	900,000	320,000	36	850,000	34
	Soda ash	3,000,000	1,725,000	58	2,000,000	57
	Sulfuric acid	1,750,000	(700,000)	−40	2,000,000	−39
		$8,040,000	$2,795,000	35%	$6,900,000	25%

*IMPACT is the Incentive Motivation Plan Act, created for general line salespeople to promote product sales across all business areas. Bonus is based on four criteria, with the amount of bonus directly proportional to the degree of criteria satisfaction. (CM is contribution margin.) The four criteria are

1. Show positive CM > 35 percent in at least four business areas.
2. Overall CM > 31 percent.
3. Show increase in sales dollars over prior year.
4. Show increase in CM over prior year in at least four areas.

tomer and distributor accounts with low or negative contribution margins. (Table 2 gives sample accounts with low contribution margins.) He explained, "The state of the economy is uncertain. A recession would force us to tighten our credit policy to control the accounts receivable outstanding. This might mean dropping marginal accounts. These low contribution margins are unprofitable for us."

Company background

Inorganics is a closely held company that manufactures and distributes industrial and specialty chemicals. The company requires a contribution margin of 30 percent across all products and business areas to obtain a required rate of return. (Table 3 lists the standard contribution margins.) Inorganics's management is evaluated on its ability to meet the corporatewide profit objectives. Among its portfolio of chemical businesses, Inorganics's revenues are derived from the soda ash unit, the water chemicals division, the electronic chemicals unit, photo and specialty chemicals, calcium chloride, and the sulfuric acid business. These chemicals are manufactured at various plant locations across North America. In addition, Inorganics distributes imported methanol and other chemicals purchased from outside manufacturers.

TABLE 2   Sample Customer Accounts with Low Contribution Margins (Year to Date)

Customer Number	Product*	Quantity	Sales $	Contribution $	Contribution %
4582	001001	100 tons	$ 90,000	$ 60,000	66.67%
	006002	1,800 tons	792,000	(200,000)	−25.25
	004002	10,000 pounds	230,000	100,000	43.48
			$1,112,000	$ (40,000)	−3.60%
6528	002002	2,000 tons	$ 60,000	$ 21,000	35.00%
	004003	10,000 tons	240,000	80,000	33.33
	003005	450 tons	16,650	3,200	19.22
	003003	1,300 tons	357,500	(70,000)	−19.58
	003002	100 tons	20,000	1,000	5.00
	006002	200 tons	$ 8,800	(2,150)	−24.43
			$ 702,950	$ 33,050	4.70%
5724	006002	40,000 tons	$1,880,000	$(450,000)	−23.94%
5364	001003	1,000 tons	$ 478,000	$ 375,000	78.45%
	003001	20,000 tons	3,900,000	(400,000)	−10.26
			$4,378,000	$ (25,000)	−0.57%
3645	003003	2 tons	$ 550	$ (80)	−14.55%
6512	005001	20 tons	$ 1,000	$ 600	60.00%
	006002	3,000 tons	144,000	(38,000)	−26.39
	001006	75 tons	34,350	14,000	40.76
			$ 179,350	$ (23,400)	−13.05%
5987	006002	1,800 tons	$ 75,600	$ (20,000)	−26.46%
	006002	2,600 tons	120,900	(32,000)	−26.47
	002001	1,000 tons	35,000	13,000	37.14
			$ 231,500	$ (39,000)	−16.85%
3258	004002	35 pounds	$ 805	$ (600)	−74.53%

*Table 3 lists the product descriptions.

Electronic chemicals division

The electronic chemicals division is a low-volume order business. The division has not been profitable for 10 years. The firm has not made any capital expenditures in this division and is seeking to divest this unit. However, management has been unable to find a buyer. Shutdown of this unit would require cleanup to meet EPA regulations. The cost of this cleanup is estimated to be $50 to $100 million. Inorganics's management does not feel it can afford the costs associated with this cleanup and hence has not shut down the division. Electronic Chemicals is the only unprofitable division of Inorganics.

Sulfuric acid division

The sulfuric acid business is specific to the oil and petrochemical industry. Pipelines from customer refineries bring in spent acid for regeneration. This is a very profitable core activity of the sulfuric acid business. This business is a service provided to the oil refineries to refurbish spent acid from the refinery alkylation or detergent manufacturing processes. If these customers choose to replace their used

TABLE 3   Standard Contribution Margins[*]

Product Number	Product Description	Contribution Margin (CM)
	Photo and Specialty Chemicals	
001001	Sodium nitrite, bulk	65%
001002	Sodium nitrite, food group	60
001003	Sodium nitrite, photo group	60
001004	Sodium bisulfite	45
001005	Sodium metabisulfite, bulk	55
001006	Sodium metabisulfite, food group	40
	Water Chemicals	
002001	Aluminum sulfate, standard	45%
002002	Aluminum, bulk	35
002003	Aluminum, T/T	30
	Electronic Chemicals	
003001	Etchants	−10%
003002	Fluborates	5
003003	Fluborates, 99%	−20
003004	Silicone dioxide	−2
003005	Hydrofluoric acid, standard	20
003006	HFL, bulk	22
	Calcium Chloride	
004001	CaCl pellets	45%
004002	CaCl powder	40
004003	CaCl liquid	30
	Soda Ash	
005001	Sodium carbonate, bulk	60%
005002	Sodium carbonate, bag pound	59
	Sulfuric Acid	
006001	Sulfuric, regenerated	81%
006002	Sulfuric, virgin	−25

[*]Standard CMs are established from the sales data of the prior and current years, based on total dollar sales and corresponding dollar contribution. $CM = \dfrac{Price - Variable\ cost}{Price}$

acid with a new supply, they bear a significant cost in disposing their spent acid to meet EPA regulations.

The regeneration process of the recovered spent acid produces one ton of the regenerated acid (which is piped back to the customer refinery) and two tons of virgin acid for every one ton of spent acid input. There is a negligible cost attached to further process this virgin acid to meet marketable standards. The price for the regenerated acid is set through negotiations with the customer. The average price for the regenerated acid is $260 per ton. The market for the virgin acid is highly competitive and Inorganics is a price taker for this commodity. The average price is $40 per ton for the virgin acid. If Inorganics chooses not to compete in the virgin acid market, it bears a cost of $20 per ton to dispose of this acid per EPA regulations. Both products are costed using fully absorbed costing. The comptroller mentioned that all costs were allocated equally to the three-ton output to reflect the costs of product sold. The cost of goods sold for the sulfuric acid business has been averaged out equally over the total production output.

Marketing manager Ray Bash, whose primary responsibility is to manage the virgin acid business, complained, "Boy, are they unfair! They give you a low contribution product and then evaluate you on profitability. They don't respect the efforts and results that I have obtained in increasing our market share."

Required:

Evaluate the issues raised at the managers' meeting and make recommendations. The issues raised include whether unprofitable customer accounts should be discontinued and how sales performance should be evaluated.

SOURCE: B Dembla, T Hollenbeck, C Keegan, E Nordhoy, and M Quercia.

Case 14–3:   Telephone Computer Corporation (TCC)

Telephone Computer Corporation (TCC) manufactures and sells two computerized directory assistance computers to telephone companies. The firm has its own sales force that sells directly to the phone companies. TCC currently sells two computer systems: the Alpha and the Beta. TCC has 90 percent of the high-end market (Beta) and 50 percent of the low-end market (Alpha). The Alpha sells for $100,000. The Beta sells for $200,000 but has three times the capacity of the Alpha.

TCC has developed a new high-volume machine, Zeta, that has four times the capacity of the Beta and lower operating costs, but a price of $300,000. The unit manufacturing cost is $170,000. Users can connect the Zeta directly to mainframe computers for customer billing as well as to future expected telecommunications advancements. If the Zeta is introduced, management expects that its closest competition will be from the Beta, so most initial sales of the Zeta will come at the expense of Beta sales.

Senior management has invested considerable resources in Zeta. It believes that the future of the company is tied closely to the success of this project. Next year's operations of TCC (if the Zeta is not introduced) are:

Next Year's Projected Profits by Product without Zeta

	Alpha	*Beta*	*Total*
Sales in units	100	50	
Selling price	$ 100,000	$ 200,000	
Revenue	$10,000,000	$10,000,000	$20,000,000
Cost per unit	50,000	80,000	
Cost of units sold	5,000,000	4,000,000	9,000,000
Sales force salaries*	2,000,000	2,000,000	4,000,000
Commissions (10% of revenue)	1,000,000	1,000,000	2,000,000
Product-line profits	$ 2,000,000	$ 3,000,000	$ 5,000,000

*Assigned based on commissions.

The existing sales force will sell all three types of machines. Salespeople are paid a salary plus 10 percent of sales. To sell the Zeta, salespeople with more knowledge of telecommunications and computer systems will be hired. The additional salary cost of these new employees will be $500,000. The existing sales force will still sell the Zeta but will call in these system experts to assist with the sale. The

Zeta system experts are paid a flat salary, and the existing sales force's 10 percent commission incentive will not change with the introduction of the Zeta.

If the Zeta is not introduced, Alpha unit sales are projected to grow at 5 percent per year and Beta unit sales are projected to grow at 10 percent per year. Selling prices will remain constant in real terms. (Prices and salaries will grow at the inflation rate. To keep the analysis simple, all numbers should be projected in real, not nominal, terms. That is, do not adjust the numbers for inflation.)

If the Zeta is introduced, Alpha unit sales will not be affected. But Beta unit sales *will* be affected: All the Zeta sales will come from the Beta sales in the first year and then Beta unit sales will grow only 2 percent per year. Zeta sales will grow at 9 percent per year from an initial base of 25 machines.

Required:

Management wants to see how the preceding table on product-line profitability will appear when the Zeta model is added. In particular, management asks you to project profits for the Alpha, Beta, and Zeta for the next five years and to make a recommendation on this project. Discuss how the five-year product-line profitability projections should be presented to senior management.

Case 14–4 Productivity Measures

Background

Economists and managers have long recognized the importance of productivity in determining an organization's success. Productivity is the relation between the firm's output of goods and services and the inputs necessary to produce that output. If a firm is able to produce more output with the same inputs, we say it has improved its productivity. Likewise, if two firms produce the same quantity of goods and services but one firm uses less input, that firm is called more productive. Countries that produce more output per person generate more consumable wealth. Economists keep productivity statistics, and these numbers are reported in the financial press as measuring the competitiveness and well-being of that country.

In the 1970s many of the largest U.S. firms became interested in productivity and better ways to measure and improve their firms' productivity. Largely driven by foreign competition, these American firms were losing market share to Japanese and European rivals. Japanese auto companies were producing cars with fewer employee hours per car than American companies, thus offering lower-priced and often higher-quality cars than U.S. automakers. Foreign steel producers were more productive than their U.S. counterparts. Concerned about their declining relative productivity in 1977, large U.S. firms financed the formation of the American Productivity Center (later the American Productivity and Quality Center). To become more productive, some firms experimented with various productivity measures.

In its most basic form, productivity is defined as:

$$\text{Productivity} = \frac{\text{Output}}{\text{Input}}$$

If the firm uses a single input (steel) to produce a single homogeneous product (horseshoes) that never changes over time, then the measure of productivity is the units of output per quantity of input, or the number of horseshoes per pound of steel. If steel waste is reduced, more horseshoes can be produced with the same amount of steel. One measure of productivity is the ratio of horseshoes to steel, in terms of physical volume. Steel is not the only input to making horseshoes. Labor is also an input, and labor is usually the input of most interest to managers. Productivity is usually thought of as the amount of output per unit of labor. Most managers want to know the number of horseshoes produced per person and how this number changes over time and compares to the competition.

Proponents of productivity measurement systems argue that managers should focus on productivity instead of accounting profits. A firm can appear profitable but can be experiencing declining productivity if selling prices are rising faster than input prices. Productivity measures help identify these cases. Managers control the physical aspects of the manufacturing process, such as the amount of steel scrap in making horseshoes, but they cannot control the price of steel or the price of horseshoes. For the most part, managers cannot influence prices but must take them as a given and try to produce more output from a given physical input or the same output using less physical input.

Proponents of productivity measures argue that basing managerial performance on productivity, which does not include uncontrollable price changes, yields a better indicator of the manager's performance. They argue that traditional accounting measures, such as net income, include many factors that managers cannot control and do not focus enough attention on factors that managers can control such as labor productivity. The following example illustrates productivity measurement systems in more detail.

Measuring productivity

If the firm produces several types of outputs (large and small horseshoes) and the mix of output varies over time, then the productivity measure must somehow aggregate the quantities of outputs into a single aggregate quantity. Likewise, several inputs must be aggregated to derive a homogeneous input measure. The measure of productivity (outputs/inputs) must aggregate the multiple inputs and the multiple outputs.

To measure firmwide productivity when multiple inputs and outputs exist, prices are used as the weighting factors. The productivity measure with two outputs and three inputs becomes:

$$\text{Productivity} = \frac{\text{Output}_1 \times \text{Price}_1 + \text{Output}_2 \times \text{Price}_2}{\text{Input}_1 \times \text{Cost}_1 + \text{Input}_2 \times \text{Cost}_2 + \text{Input}_3 \times \text{Cost}_3}$$

Output_i ($i = 1$ or 2) and input_j ($j = 1, 2,$ or 3) denote the physical quantities of the ith output and the jth input. Price_i and cost_j are the corresponding output prices and input costs. If one then compares how productivity changes over time, this aggregate measure of productivity will vary with changes in both physical quantities and relative prices. But productivity measures should exclude noncontrollable price and cost changes, thereby focusing managers' attention on physical quantities.

To exclude price and cost changes from the performance measure, yet still have a way to aggregate multiple inputs and outputs, the following scheme is used:

1. Choose a base period year and use that year's prices and costs as the weights for future years. The base year should be one of high production, and a new base year should be chosen about every five years as the structures of production and prices change.
2. Weight the physical quantity of each input and output using the base period cost or price for that input or output.
3. Divide the weighted outputs by weighted inputs to compute the productivity index for the year.

4. Divide this year's productivity index by last year's to get the change in productivity.[12]

A simple example with two inputs (steel and labor) and two outputs (small and large horseshoes) illustrates the mechanics of the computations.[13] The following data summarize operations for the last two years:

TABLE 1   **Physical Quantities**

Inputs/Outputs	Base Year Prices	Last Year	This Year
Outputs:			
Small horseshoes	$2	500	600
Large horseshoes	$3	500	550
Inputs:			
Steel	$1	1,000	1,200
Labor	$4	300	320

Based on these data, the productivity measures are calculated as:

TABLE 2

Inputs/Outputs	Last Year	This Year
Outputs:		
Small horseshoes	$1,000	$1,200
Large horseshoes	1,500	1,650
Total outputs	$2,500	$2,850
Inputs:		
Steel	$1,000	$1,200
Labor	1,200	1,280
Total inputs	$2,200	$2,480
	$2,500	$2,850
Productivity	$\frac{\$2,500}{\$2,200}$ = 1.136	$\frac{\$2,850}{\$2,480}$ = 1.149
Increase in productivity	$\frac{1.149 - 1.136}{1.136} = 1.1\%$	

Total productivity increased from 1.136 last year to 1.149 this year, or a 1.1 percent increase. Using base period prices, the productivity measure indicates that more output was produced using relatively less input.

---

[12] J Kendrick and D Creamer, *Measuring Company Productivity,* Conference Board (1969). For an alternative scheme to measure productivity within a more usual standard cost system, see R Banker, S Datar, and R Kaplan, "Productivity Analysis and Management Accounting," *Journal of Accounting, Auditing and Finance,* 1989. Also see E Adam, J Hershauer, and W Ruch, *Productivity and Quality: Measurement as a Basis for Improvement* (Englewood Cliffs, NJ: Prentice-Hall, 1981) and B Gold, *Productivity, Technology, and Capital: Economic Analysis, Managerial Strategies, and Government Policies* (New York: Lexington Books, 1979).

[13] The example and discussion gloss over the thorny issue of including capital as an input. See Kendrick and Creamer (1969) for one possible treatment.

In a study of productivity systems in Canada, few firms were found to measure aggregate firmwide productivity as the ratio of firm outputs to firm inputs.[14] Instead, firms develop a few distinct nonfinancial measures that capture the essential strategic elements of their business. For example, a steel company tracks tons of steel shipped divided by tons of iron purchased and tons of steel shipped divided by number of employees. In an insurance company, the number of policies processed per employee in a particular department is reported. Other companies measure yield rates, defect rates, and production rates. The study concludes (p. 132), "We believe that productivity measures are *operational aids* in the strategic process that helps organization members keep track of what is required for the organization to achieve its long-run goals."

Required:

a. Critically analyze the productivity calculations in Table 2. Did the managers of the firm perform better this year compared with last year, as the productivity measures indicate?

b. Discuss some plausible reasons why comprehensive productivity systems have not been widely adopted by organizations.

c. Consider the situation of Burk Wheels. Burk Wheels manufactures aluminum automobile wheels (onto which rubber tires are mounted). The owner, Gerry Burk, is worried about increased competition from foreign countries (with lower labor costs) and is seeking to increase the productivity of her workers. She decides to implement a bonus system for direct line supervisors and department managers to reward them for improving labor productivity. In particular, supervisors will receive bonuses if they improve their department's labor productivity, defined as Output ÷ Labor hours. The casting department is the primary production process whereby molten aluminum is poured into molds, cooled, and then removed to form the wheels. Operating data for the casting department for the last two months prior to announcing the labor productivity incentive program are:

	March	April
Wheels cast	1,680	1,710
Direct labor hours	722	701
Aluminum used (pounds)	14,616	15,219
Direct labor wages/hour	$23.10	$23.75
Price of aluminum/pound	$ 0.92	$ 0.91

Calculate the productivity of direct labor for March and April and discuss how labor productivity changed between March and April. Gerry Burk asks your opinion of her proposal to increase productivity by rewarding production supervisors and plant departmental managers for increasing labor productivity. Write Ms. Burk a memo outlining your views of her plan.

[14] H Armitage and A Atkinson, *The Choice of Productivity Measures in Organizations: A Field Study of Practice in Seven Canadian Firms* (Hamilton, Ontario: Society of Management Accountants of Canada, 1990). A Study of U.S. firms reported that fewer than 15 percent used or planned to use total productivity measures (J Kraus, *How U.S. Firms Measure Productivity* [New York: National Association of Accountants, 1984]).

Solutions to Concept Questions

Q1–1: One system cannot be designed to maximize two conflicting objectives better than two systems each maximizing one objective. If a single system is used for both decision management and decision control, trade-offs must be made to create a balanced system that maximizes profits for the firm.

Q1–2: An internal accounting system provides managers and executives with key cost information regarding their business. Examples include financial budgets, inventory costs, product costs, factory costs, and overhead costs.

Q1–3:

i. External reports (taxes, financial statements).

ii. Performance evaluations. (How well did a manager meet profit expectations for a given year?)

iii. Decision making. (Does it make sense to continue to produce a given product line?)

Q1–4: An internal accounting system should have the following characteristics:

i. It should provide information necessary to identify the most profitable products and at what volumes they should be produced.

ii. It should provide information in such a way that production inefficiencies are detected.

iii. In combination with the performance evaluation and reward systems, the internal accounting system should create incentives for managers to maximize firm value.

iv. It must support the financial and tax accounting functions.

v. Its cost-to-benefit ratio must be less than 1.

Q1–5: Few firms have multiple systems. The typical reasons are

i. There are additional costs required to maintain multiple systems, including additional data processing and bookkeeping costs.

ii. There is confusion surrounding different measures. Managers wonder which system has the "right" number. The natural tendency is to reconcile the difference. Reconciliation is costly in terms of time.

iii. With one system, the external auditor can also be used to monitor and control the internal reporting system at no additional cost.

Q1–6: Surviving firms in competitive industries tend to use administrative procedures whose benefits net of costs are at least as high as their competitors'. In a competitive world, if surviving organizations are using some operating procedure over long periods of time, then it is likely that this procedure is yielding benefits in excess of costs.

Q1–7: The chief financial officer's major responsibilities involve providing all the accounting reports for both external parties and management, tax administration, budgeting, treasury including financing, investments, and internal audit.

Q2–1: The opportunity cost consists of the receipts from the most valuable forgone alternative when making a decision or choice among many options.

Q2–2:

i. Opportunity costs are not necessarily the same as payments.

ii. Opportunity costs are forward-looking.

iii. Opportunity costs can be dated at the moment of final decision.

Q2–3: The $8,325 is an accurate estimate of the opportunity cost if we can resell the material for that amount or we can replace the material and the future price is expected to be $8,325. In general, historical costs can be reasonably accurate estimates of opportunity costs if the current market price has not changed and there is a ready market to buy and sell the material.

Q2–4: Sunk costs are costs incurred in the past that cannot be recovered and are therefore irrelevant for future decision making. An example of a sunk cost is as follows. A firm purchases 100 pounds of a material required in a one-time project. Sixty pounds are used in this project. The remaining 40 pounds have no market value. Using the opportunity cost concept, the historical cost of the remaining 40 pounds is sunk and irrelevant for future uses of this material.

Q2–5: Avoidable costs are those costs that will not be incurred if an existing operation is closed or changed. Avoidable costs are the opportunity costs. Unavoidable costs are costs that will continue to be incurred regardless of the decision.

Q2–6: Mixed costs are cost categories that cannot be classified as being purely fixed or purely variable. An example is utilities.

Q2–7: A step cost is a cost that is fixed over a given range of output level. For example, supervisory personnel cost is a step cost.

Q2–8: A fixed cost is a cost that does not vary with the number of units produced. Although fixed with respect to volume changes, fixed costs can still be managed and reduced.

Q2–9: A variable cost is the additional cost incurred when output is expanded. Labor and materials are usually the two costs classified as variable. A variable cost is not necessarily a marginal cost. A marginal cost is the cost of the last unit produced, while variable cost is the portion of the total cost that varies with the quantity produced. If the variable cost is linear, then marginal cost per unit equals variable cost per unit and is constant as volume changes. If variable cost is not linear, marginal cost will be nonconstant.

Q2–10:

  i. Price and variable cost per unit must not vary with volume.
  ii. It is a single-period analysis.
  iii. It assumes a single-product firm.

Q2–11: The major benefit of CVP analysis is that it forces managers to understand how costs and revenues vary with changes in output. Its limitations include

  i. Price and variable cost must not vary with volume.
  ii. It is a single-period analysis (no time value of money).
  iii. It assumes a single-product firm.

Q2–12: Estimating opportunity costs requires the decision maker to formulate all possible alternative actions and the forgone net receipts from those actions. This is a costly and time-consuming process. Furthermore, the opportunity cost changes as the set of alternative actions changes.

Q2–13: Direct costs are those costs that are worthwhile tracing to the unit being costed. Cost/benefit analysis requires one to determine whether tracing the cost has a benefit greater than its costs.

Q2–14: Overhead costs include indirect labor and materials and other general manufacturing costs that cannot be directly traced to the units produced. Overhead costs are usually allocated using a base that most closely approximates those factors that cause overhead to vary in the long run.

Q2–15: Period costs consist of all nonmanufacturing costs, including selling, distribution, general, and administrative costs. Period costs are not included in the cost of the products that are in inventory. Period costs are written off to the income statement when incurred.

Q2–16: Motion and time studies break each labor task down to its basic movements and then time each movement. These studies have two objectives: (1) to estimate direct labor costs of a particular job and (2) to reduce these costs by redesigning the way employees perform or redesigning the product to reduce labor input.

Q2–17: Fixed costs do not directly enter the pricing decision. Fixed costs (if not incurred yet) only enter the decision to produce or not produce the good or service.

Q2–18: Most firms produce a set of heterogeneous products and thus a single measure of output does not exist. Even with those firms for which it is possible (e.g., steel), there are other problems. Accounting costs are noisy measures. The cost structure of the firm changes over time as does the underlying production process. As a result there is a reduction in the number of observations of the production process while it is stationary that are available for analysis. If interim (quarterly) data are used, seasonal patterns must be removed. It is doubtful, therefore, that very precise fixed and variable costs can be estimated from regression analysis.

Q3–1: Even for riskless investments, a dollar today can be deposited in the bank and start earning interest so that in the future it will have grown to more than a dollar.

Q3–2: If expenses are paid after they are deducted for accounting purposes, then the present value of the expenses is smaller than the cost recognized on the income statement causing an accounting loss. However, if the discounted expenses are less than the revenue, then there is an economic profit. For example, suppose a product is sold for $10, costs $9 to manufacture, and has a three-year warranty. The expected warranty cost is $1.10, which is expected to be paid at the end of three years. The accounting loss is $0.10 because the warranty expense is recognized when the product is sold, not when the warranty cost is paid. If the interest rate is 12 percent, then the present value of the warranty expense is $1.10 ÷ $(1.12)^3$ = $0.78 and the economic profit is $0.22 (or $10.00 − 9.00 − $0.78).

Q3–3: Present value is the amount of money needed today that, when invested at the prevailing interest rate, will grow to the future amount.

Q3–4: Future value is the amount of money available at a future date by taking the present amount and investing it at the prevailing interest rate.

Q3–5: Compound interest is the interest earned on money invested including principal and reinvested interest.

Q3–6: Perpetuities are infinite streams of equal payments while annuities are finite streams of equal payments.

Q3–7: Net present value is the discounted value of future cash flows minus initial investment.

Q3–8: Savers must be indifferent between the two. Since the monthly account compounds interest more frequently, the monthly interest rate must be smaller.

Q3–9: Accounting depreciation is an allowable deduction in calculating taxable income and taxes payable. Being able to depreciate fixed assets reduces taxes and increases net cash flows after taxes.

Q3–10: The real interest rate is composed of the risk-free rate and a risk premium.

Q3–11: The nominal interest rate is composed of the risk-free rate, a risk premium, and an inflation rate.

Q3–12: Three flaws with IRR are that (1) it does not take into account the magnitude of investment (a larger dollar amount earning a lower return may be worth more than a smaller dollar amount earning a higher return), (2) some projects result in multiple IRRs, making investment decisions unclear, and (3) the IRR method incorrectly assumes that intermediate cash flows are reinvested at the project's internal rate of return.

Q3–13: The dollar invested in the building can be depreciated, and thereby lowers taxes and increases cash flows. However, a dollar invested in land or working capital cannot be depreciated and provides no tax shield.

Q3–14: Accounting earnings contain accruals and deferrals and as such are not the same as cash flows. Only cash flows can be invested and earn interest; earnings cannot be invested until cash is realized.

Q4–1: Agency costs are the decline in value resulting from agents pursuing their own interests instead of the principal's interests. Differences between risk tolerances, working horizons, and excessive job perquisites all contribute to agency costs. Agency costs also arise when agents seek to manage larger organizations, to increase either their job security or their pay.

Q4–2: Agency costs are reduced by monitoring and bonding activities. Agency costs are limited by the existence of a labor market for managers, competition from other firms, and the market for corporate control.

Q4–3: Goal incongruence means simply that agents and principals have different utility functions.

Q4–4: By restructuring the agent's incentive scheme, the agent's and principal's objectives can be made more congruent.

Q4–5: Because knowledge is valuable in decision making, the right to make a decision should reside with the person who has the specific knowledge for the decision.

Q4–6:
  i. Measuring performance.
  ii. Rewarding and punishing performance.
  iii. Partitioning decision rights to their highest-valued use.

Q4–7: Influence costs consist of the forgone opportunities arising from employees trying to affect decisions by politicking and other potentially nonproductive influence activities. Influence costs arise when employees waste valuable time trying to influence decisions.

Q4–8: The firm, defined as a locus of contracts, exists because each resource owner is better off contracting with the firm than either contracting separately with all the resource owners individually or not contracting at all. Each resource owner, by contracting with the firm, is implicitly contracting with all others contracted with the firm. The firm economizes on repetitive contracting and transaction costs are reduced.

Q4–9: *Decision management* refers to those aspects of the decision process whereby the manager either initiates or implements a decision (e.g., a supervisor requesting an additional employee to make her department run more efficiently).

Decision control refers to those aspects of the decision process whereby managers either ratify or monitor decisions (e.g., the supervisor's boss ratifying the decision and allowing her to hire an additional employee).

Q4–10: All organizations must construct
  i. Systems that partition decision rights. Decision rights lie initially with the board of directors. The rights are then assigned throughout the organization.
  ii. Systems that measure performance. The system developed must measure the performance of variables over which the agent has been given decision rights.
  iii. Systems that reward and punish performance. The system must be matched to the performance variables being measured.

Q4–11: The four steps in the decision process are
  Decision initiation—the beginning of the decision process. This step is usually performed by the person with the specific knowledge; a decision management function.
  Decision ratification—reviewing and approving the request; a decision control function.
  Decision implementation—usually associated with the individual(s) who initiated the process; a decision management function.
  Decision monitoring—evaluating the implementation; a decision control function.

The separation of management and control helps reduce agency costs. The separation is structured so that the decision makers do not measure their own performance.

Q5–1: Responsibility accounting dictates that decision rights are linked with the specialized knowledge necessary to exercise the decision rights and that the performance measurement system (e.g., the accounting system) measures the performance of outcomes that depend on the decision rights assigned to agents.

Q5–2: The internal accounting system is most useful in decision monitoring and is an important part of the separation of decision management and control. Accounting departments, being independent of operating management, are part of the firm's internal contracting system designed to reduce agency costs. Accounting reports are one measure of an agent's performance.

Q5–3: Responsibility centers differ in their assigned decision rights and their performance management system.
  • *Cost center.* This center's goal is either to maximize output given a fixed amount of resources or to

minimize input costs given a fixed output. The performance measures are (1) actual versus budgeted output and (2) actual versus budgeted cost. If measured on total cost, the quality of the output may be a problem. If measured on average cost, the incentive to increase inventory exists.

- *Profit center.* Profit centers are given a fixed amount of capital; they control pricing and the input mix. The performance measure is the center's budgeted versus actual profit. Managers have the incentive to build inventories and request more capital assets as long as they are not charged the opportunity cost of the assets.

- *Investment center.* Investment centers have all the decision rights of profit centers plus some control over the amount of capital invested. The performance measure is either ROI or residual income. There are two problems with ROI. First, ROI is not a measure of the center's economic rate of return, creating a potential horizon problem. Second, managers have the incentive to reject profitable projects if the expected ROI is less than the mean ROI for the center. Residual income also has its shortcomings. Primarily, it too suffers from the horizon problem. Residual income is an absolute number and cannot be used to compare centers of different size.

Q5–4: EVA and residual income are based on the same formula. EVA might adjust accounting earnings, uses weighted-average cost of capital, and links performance measurement (EVA) to compensation.

Q5–5: The controllability principle holds managers responsible for only those decisions they have the authority to affect. One limitation is that while managers may have little control over the likelihood of some event, if they can influence the costs (or benefits) of the event, they should still be held accountable. The second limitation is that the performance of managers can often be better gauged by comparing it with the performance of others (relative performance evaluation) even though the managers being evaluated may have no control over others' performance.

Q5–6: All performance measurement schemes, including accounting-based schemes, are likely to produce misleading results and induce dysfunctional behavior if used mechanically and in isolation from other measures. The second point is that no system is perfect. The question to ask is this: Is the proposed system better than the next best alternative?

Q5–7:
  i. International taxation.
  ii. Incentives and performance measurement of profit or investment centers.

Q5–8:
  i. Market price: Given a competitive external market for the good, the transfer price is determined by the external market price.
  ii. Variable cost: Transfer price is determined by the variable cost of manufacturing the good.
  iii. Full cost: Transfer price is determined by the full (fixed and variable) cost of manufacturing the good.
  iv. Negotiated price: A negotiated price is determined by negotiations between the purchasing and selling divisions.

Q5–9: No. Changing transfer pricing methods does more than shift income among divisions. The method used can change the profitability of the firm as a whole because the buying/selling division changes its scale of operations in response to the transfer price.

Q6–1: Budgets are developed using "key planning assumptions" or "basic estimating factors."

Q6–2: Key planning assumptions represent those factors that are to some extent beyond management control and that set a limit on the overall activities of the firm. They must be forecast based on past experience, field estimates, and/or statistical analysis.

Q6–3: A budget variance occurs when actual expenses do not match budgeted expenses exactly or when budgeted revenues do not match actual revenues exactly.

Q6–4: Budgets are part of both. Most managers are evaluated in part on how well they are able to meet the budgeted expectations of their department, division, and so on. Budget variances are indicators of whether managers are meeting expectations. A large unfavorable variance may cause a manager to be demoted or lose his job.

Q6–5: Budgets provide
  i. A communication device involving both vertical and horizontal information transfers.
  ii. A negotiation and internal contracting procedure.
  iii. A role in the performance evaluation and reward system.
  iv. A role in partitioning decision rights.

Q6–6: Budgets separate decision management from decision control. Managers have the decision management rights (i.e., budget preparation and operating decisions). The board of directors has the decision control rights (i.e., budget review and approval and financial statement review).

Q6–7: The budgeting process serves as a communication device in a large firm. The process gives managers incentives to share their specific knowledge, thus transmitting this knowledge vertically and horizontally throughout the firm. Key planning assumptions are shared and developed in this process as well. The information-sharing process also serves as a negotiation and contracting procedure between different subunits within the firm. Review of the prior year's budget is a part of this process, and therefore budgeting is part of the performance evaluation and reward and punishment system. These processes partition decision rights within the firm.

Q6–8: This is just another example of the trade-off between decision making and control. The budget system transfers specialized knowledge about key planning assumptions. However, if the budget is also used for control and provides incentives for meeting the budget, then managers will "shade" their forecasts to enhance their performance whenever performance is measured by comparing actual results with budget.

Q6–9: A bottom-up budgeting system means that lower levels in the organization prepare the initial budgets because they have the specialized knowledge, and as the budget winds its way through the decision ratification process, higher levels in the organization review the budget and bring to bear additional knowledge.

Q6–10: The *ratchet effect* refers to basing next year's budget on this year's actual performance if this year's actual performance exceeds this year's budget. If, in this year actual performance falls short of budget, next year's budget is not reduced. Budget ratcheting causes employees to reduce output this year to avoid being held to a higher standard in future periods.

Q6–11: Participative budgeting occurs when the person ultimately held responsible for meeting the target makes the initial budget forecast.

Q6–12: A short-run budget is a one-year budget. Like all budgets, it forces managers with specific knowledge to communicate their forecasts and becomes the internal contract between the manager and the firm. A long-run budget projects from 2 to 10 years into the future and is a key part of a firm's strategic planning process. A short-run budget involves both decision management and decision control, while a long-run budget is primarily for decision management.

Q6–13: Line-item budgets authorize a manager to spend only up to a specific amount on each line item. These budgets are an extreme form of control; decision rights to substitute resources are denied. The benefit of such control is a reduction of agency costs. The disadvantage of these budgets is that managers are disinclined to look for savings because they cannot transfer the savings to another line item. If coming in under budget reduces the next year's budget for that line item, then the manager has no incentive to search for savings.

Q6–14: Budget lapsing provides tighter controls on managers than budgets that do not lapse. The primary purpose is to prevent certain agency problems from occurring. The opportunity cost of lapsing budgets is usually less efficient operations. Managers will devote time at year-end to ensure that the budget is fully spent, thereby protecting future budget levels.

Q6–15: A static budget is a budget that does not change with volume, while a flexible budget changes with volume. The major reason for using flexible budgets is to better measure the actual performance of a person or entity after controlling for volume effects, assuming that the person/entity being evaluated cannot control the volume changes. However, if a manager can influence the effect of the volume change, then it is unwise to shield the manager from the volume changes.

Q6–16: With incremental budgeting, each lower-level manager submits a budget by making incremental changes to each line item. Detailed explanations justifying the incremental changes are submitted and reviewed by the organization. Base budgets are taken as given.

Zero-based budgeting (ZBB) resets each line item in the budget to zero and the entire amount must be justified. ZBB, in principle, maximizes firm value by identifying and eliminating expenditures whose total costs are greater than total benefits, whereas inefficient base budgets can still exist with incremental budgeting. However, ZBB often degenerates to incremental budgeting. The same justifications are submitted to support the incremental changes. The volume of reports under ZBB is larger than under incremental budgeting, causing senior managers to focus on changes.

Q7–1: Some of the reasons for allocating costs are taxes, external financial reporting, third-party reimbursement, and solving the organizational problem.

Q7–2: Cost allocations can affect cash flows if the firm has contracts tied to reported costs (e.g., defense contractors using cost-plus contracts). Cost allocations can also affect taxes and thus cash flows. For example, allocating costs can affect product costs and thus the amount of cost of goods sold.

Q7–3: Allocating costs causes an increase in the reported costs of using the resource being allocated. For example, if property taxes are allocated using square footage, then floor space becomes taxed. These cost allocations are like taxes on these resources. Like all taxes on consumption items, the tax discourages use of the item levied with the tax.

Q7–4: Externalities are costs or benefits imposed on other individuals without their participation in the decision-making process and without compensation for the cost or benefits imposed on them. An example is air pollution.

Q7–5: A negative externality causes others to bear some cost as the result of a decision made that is beyond their control. A positive externality causes others to receive some benefit as the result of a decision made that is out of their control.

Q7–6: One way to reduce an externality is to impose a tax on the use of the resource or the decision that creates the externality.

Q7–7:

   i. R_a, the overhead rate at volume level a, is greater than MC_a, the marginal cost at a. Under this condition, the cost allocation overstates the marginal cost of the externality. Therefore, taxing might cause more harm than good.

   ii. $R_b = MC_b$. Under this condition, the cost allocation and the marginal cost are equal. In this case the cost allocation perfectly reflects the amount of tax to apply.

   iii. $R_c < MC_c$. Under this condition, the cost allocation rate is less than the marginal cost of the externality. Taxing under this condition is better than no tax.

Q7–8: If common costs are not allocated, managers have less incentive to invest in the specialized knowledge necessary to determine the optimal level of the common costs. Furthermore, if the decision rights over the level of the common costs do not reside with a manager and are not allocated back to the manager's department, the manager will always demand more common costs.

Q7–9: A noninsulating allocation method causes the performance measure (e.g., divisional profits) to depend on the performance of another division. If other divisions improve their performance, your division bears fewer allocated costs and hence will show better performance (after receiving allocated costs). Noninsulating allocation methods create incentives for managers to cooperate and mutually monitor each other to protect their interest.

Q7–10: Factor prices do not represent the total cost to the firm of the input factor. "Distorted" factor prices represent an attempt by senior managers to proxy the total cost.

Q8–1: The death spiral can result whenever transfer prices include fixed costs and users shift away from the internal common resource. This further increases the full cost transfer price, causing further users to reduce their demand. Death spirals can be avoided by using variable cost transfer pricing and cost allocations.

Q8–2:

   i. To tax the users with some positive price that causes them to reduce their consumption from what it would be under a zero price (no allocation).

   ii. By allocating the costs, senior management gets information about the total demand for the service at the allocated cost.

   iii. By comparing the internally allocated cost with the external market price of comparable services,

senior management is able to assess the operating efficiency of the service department.

   iv. Taxing the internal service helps allocate a scarce resource. At a zero price, demand will almost always exceed supply. In the absence of a price mechanism to allocate department services, senior management will be confronted with complaints to increase the amount of service via larger budgets and must devise nonprice priority schemes to manage the queue waiting for service.

Q8–3: Step-down allocation is an allocation method that recognizes that service departments use each other's services. The process begins by choosing one service department and allocating its cost to the remaining services and operating departments. The process is repeated for each of the remaining service departments. A major criticism of the step-down method is that the sequence is arbitrary and large differences in the cost per unit of service across different sequences are possible. The step-down method also ignores the fact that departments earlier in the sequence use service departments later in the sequence.

Q8–4: The direct allocation method ignores service departments using each other's services in allocating costs. The step-down method allocates service department costs to other service departments later in the sequence.

Q8–5: The first service department in the step-down sequence has a smaller cost per unit than if it is the last department in the sequence. The reason is twofold: (1) there are fewer costs to allocate, and (2) there are more users over which to allocate the costs.

Q8–6: Joint costs are costs incurred in the production of two or more outputs from the same production process in fixed proportion. Joint products are produced in fixed proportions. Common costs arise in production settings where there can be substitution among outputs. More of one output can be produced by reducing the output of another product.

   Joint costs are associated with disassembly processes where a joint input is disassembled into several products. Common costs usually describe assembly processes where numerous inputs including some common resources are assembled to form the output.

Q8–7: Three common methods to allocate joint costs are (1) physical measures, (2) relative sales value method, and (3) net realizable value method. The fundamental point to remember when analyzing situations involving joint costs is that any joint cost allocated to final products is meaningless for assessing product-line profitability.

Q8–8: The advantage of NRV is that it does not distort the relative profitability of product-line costs and hence is better for decision making. The disadvantage of NRV is that it is costly to collect selling prices and costs beyond the split-off point.

Q9–1:

　i. Job order costing.

　ii. Process costing.

Q9–2:

　i. Direct labor, direct materials, and overhead allocations are charged to "work in process" while the job remains in process.

　ii. When a job is finished, the total cost of the job is transferred from "work in process" to "finished goods inventory."

　iii. When the goods are sold, the total cost of the job is transferred from "finished goods inventory" to "cost of goods sold."

Q9–3: The $2,750 cost of materials should be charged to the overhead account as indirect materials. Machines occasionally malfunction and destroy raw materials. This is not unusual and is a normal part of the manufacturing process. To charge the current job that happens to be in production at the time overstates the cost of this job. Charging the $2,750 to overhead and then allocating it to all jobs does not misrepresent the cost of the current job in production.

Q9–4: Using a prospective overhead rate allows more timely reporting of total costs since actual total overhead costs cannot be determined until the end of the year.

Q9–5: Overabsorbed overhead can be the result of higher volume produced during the year than budgeted. Overabsorbed overhead also can result if less overhead cost was incurred than budgeted.

Q9–6:

　i. Charge it off to cost of goods sold.

　ii. Allocate it among work in process, finished goods, and cost of goods sold based on the amount of overhead in these categories.

　iii. Recalculate the cost of each job using actual overhead incurred and actual volume to compute a revised overhead rate.

Q9–7: Manufacturing plants produce a wide variety of products that are measured in different units. Input measures, however, are common to any product. Therefore, an input measure that is common to all manufacturing units and has the greatest association with the overhead is used to calculate the prospective overhead rate.

Q9–8: Flexible budgets split overhead into fixed and variable components as in the formula

$$Budgeted\ OH = Fixed\ OH + Variable\ OH \times EV$$

Using a flexible formula allows a firm to derive an estimate of the total overhead that varies with volume.

Q9–9: Absorption costs represent average costs and are often used in the pricing decision. Fluctuations in sales volume may or may not cause marginal costs to change. Overhead rates based on normal volumes prevent incorrect pricing decisions based on temporary volume fluctuations.

Q9–10: Unforeseen circumstances that lower volume do not increase unit costs. To increase unit costs will give a misleading signal to raise prices. Managers make capital investments using assumptions of normal volume. Unit costs are also developed using these assumptions. If these assumptions are incorrect, then the capital investment should be written off as a period expense and the unit costs recalculated using the new estimate of normal volume.

Q9–11: Multiple overhead rates do not necessarily always produce more accurate estimates of product costs. It often depends on the particular decision context. For some decisions using multiple overhead rates for different classes of overhead costs, each overhead item can be analyzed and the most representative cost driver for each overhead category can be identified and used as the allocation base.

Q9–12:

　i. Single factorywide overhead rate. This method is useful when the plant has a single homogeneous production process.

　ii. Separate overhead rate for each indirect cost item. This method is useful when different products consume varying amounts of indirect costs but the plant is not organized into production departments.

　iii. Separate overhead rate for each department. This method is useful when different products consume varying amounts of indirect costs and the plant is organized into production departments.

Q9–13: Process costing is used in continuous flow production processes. Costs are averaged because there are no discrete batches. Information is aggregate in form and therefore not very useful in decision making.

Q10–1: Viewing unit costs as variable costs implies that there is causality between unit cost figures and volume produced. In many cases unit costs are mixtures of variable and fixed costs and thus do not represent the incremental cost of producing one more unit.

Q10–2: By producing more units than are sold, some of the fixed costs are inventoried instead of being assigned to the income statement.

Q10–3:

　i. Charge inventory holding costs against profits or adopt variable costing.

　ii. Implement rules against adding to or building inventories.

　iii. Use stock-price-based incentives for managers instead of accounting numbers for compensation. This will only work in a single-plant, publicly traded firm.

　iv. Use JIT production systems.

Q10–4: The major difference is how they treat fixed manufacturing overhead. Under absorption costing, overhead is treated as part of the product costs. Using variable costing, fixed overhead is written off as a period expense.

Q10–5: Two claimed advantages of variable costing are

i. It eliminates the distortions to income and product costs when volume changes.

ii. It reduces the dysfunctional incentives to overproduce.

Two potential problems with using variable costing are

i. Determining which costs are fixed and which are variable.

ii. It produces unit cost figures that contain no estimate of the opportunity cost of capacity.

Q11–1: Traditional absorption costing can lead to inaccurate product costs if the allocation bases chosen do not capture the underlying overhead cost drivers. In other words, the allocation bases used to allocate overhead to products do not accurately reflect the factors that cause overhead to vary.

Q11–2: Complex products are usually undercosted by absorption cost systems because the factors that cause one product to be more complex than another are not used to allocate overhead. Unless the more complex products use proportionately more direct labor than less complex products, then too little overhead is allocated to the more complex products.

Q11–3:

i. Unit level.

ii. Batch level.

iii. Product level.

iv. Production-sustaining level.

Q11–4: Both allocate the same total costs to products.

Q11–5:

i. To develop more "accurate" product or product-line costs.

ii. To change incentives of operating managers.

Q11–6:

i. An increase in the percentage of product costs directly traced to individual products.

ii. A better understanding of how costs are consumed by individual products and what activities are required to produce individual products.

iii. A better understanding of the direct and indirect costs in the various activity centers.

iv. A better understanding of how indirect costs are generated by the cost drivers.

Q11–7: The physical activities that consume resources and generate costs are not tracked through historical costs; the cost drivers cannot be discerned from the accounting numbers. Managers must be able to identify and manage the cost drivers to successfully control costs.

Q11–8: The form of an absorption system is audience dependent. If the collected information is to be used for decision management, then the form of the absorption system will lean toward an ABC system where the under-lying drivers can be measured. If the information is primarily for decision control, then ABC is less useful. Multiple systems are costly; therefore, in choosing a system, trade-offs between decision management and decision control usually must be made.

Q11–9: High-volume products tend to be overcosted in unit-based absorption costing because much of the factory overhead is due to managing the number of products and batches in the plant. The low-volume products cause just as many transactions to occur in the plant (such as purchase orders and setups).

Q12–1: Standard costs are a set of benchmarks used to measure the performance of the firm with respect to controlling costs and for internal repetitive contracting.

Q12–2:

i. Product pricing decisions.

ii. Make-versus-buy decisions.

iii. Plant resource allocation decisions.

Q12–3: Yes. For example, the standard cost of an hour of machine time in the lathe department is a proxy for the opportunity cost of using one hour of lathe time. This standard cost conveys to other managers throughout the firm the opportunity cost of using lathes.

Q12–4: If managers with the specific knowledge for updating the standard have part of their performance evaluation based on the difference between actual performance and the standard, this creates an incentive for them to update standards to levels that they feel are achievable.

Q12–5: Target costing is a top-down approach. It begins with a target price established by marketing. The firm's required return on investment is subtracted from the target price to derive the target product cost. This cost is then exploded into its subcomponents, which become the standards to be met if the firm is to meet its desired market penetration and required return. Traditional standard costing is a bottom-up approach and is less product/market driven.

Q12–6:

i. Direct labor variances.

ii. Direct materials variances.

iii. Overhead variances.

Q12–7:

i. Wage variance.

ii. Efficiency variance.

Q12–8: Large favorable variances could be the result of replacing the standard-quality material with substandard-quality material, yielding a favorable price variance.

Q12–9:

i. Price variance.

ii. Quantity variance.

Q12–10:

i. Incentive to build inventories and/or lower quality.

ii. Externalities.

iii. Discourage cooperation.

iv. Mutual monitoring incentives.

v. Satisficing behavior.

Q12–11: In seeking favorable price variances, the purchasing department has incentives to buy materials in large lot sizes to secure quantity discounts.

Q12–12: The purchasing department can impose costs on manufacturing by purchasing low-quality materials. Manufacturing can impose costs on the purchasing department by requesting rush deliveries or by changing the specifications of purchased parts.

Q12–13: There are two organizational reasons for writing variances off to cost of goods sold. First, prorating the variances creates incentives for managers to manipulate reported income. Second, prorating variances back to inventories will change the product costs incurred by the manager responsible for selling these inventories. The first reaction will be to change prices, an action he or she should not take. Of course, marginal costs can and do change, and standards must be updated to correctly reflect any changes.

Q12–14: Standard cost systems are expensive in terms of the opportunity cost of a manager's time to investigate cost variances and to oversee the development and maintenance of the standards. The benefit of standard costs comes from the development of specialized knowledge created by the manager in his or her investigations.

Q12–15: Many cost systems were developed as a means to measure and control direct labor costs. The fraction of direct labor in modern factories has decreased, thus lowering the benefits of a standard cost system. Also, modern factories have "flexible manufacturing systems" in which there are numerous changes in products and/or processes. Numerous changes cause the costs of maintaining a standard cost system to increase while the benefit decreases.

Q13–1:

i. *Budgeted volume.* The production volume used in calculating the overhead rate.

ii. *Standard volume.* The production of volume that the plant would have generated if each unit of product manufactured used precisely the standard unit of volume allowed.

iii. *Actual volume.* The actual production volume incurred.

Q13–2: *Budgeted volume* can be estimated using either the projected number of units times their standard volume per unit (*expected volume*) or the long-run average units of volume (*normal volume*). Expected volume more accurately estimates next year's actual volume, but it causes overhead rates to vary inversely with volume. Normal volume is likely to cause larger over- or underabsorbed overhead, but overhead rates do not vary with volume.

Q13–3:

i. At the beginning of the year, estimate the flexible budget for the year.

ii. Convert expected overhead into an overhead absorption rate.

iii. Apply overhead to production using standard volume.

iv. At the end of the year, compute overhead variances.

Q13–4:

i. *Overhead efficiency variance.* The difference in flexible budgets using actual volume and standard volume.

ii. *Overhead volume variance.* The difference between the flexible budget at standard volume and overhead applied.

iii. *Overhead spending variance.* The difference between how much overhead was actually incurred versus how much overhead should have been incurred for the actual volume worked.

Q13–5:

i. Unexpected changes in prices of variable overhead items.

ii. Unexpected changes in fixed costs.

iii. Unexpected changes in the plant's production technology cause costs to vary in ways different from those captured by the flexible budget.

Q13–6: The difference between budgeted revenues and actual revenues can be disaggregated into a *price variance* and a *quantity variance*. The quantity variance can be further disaggregated into *mix* and *sales variances*.

Q13–7: The *mix variance* reports how much of the *quantity variance* is due to the change in product mix because of substitution across products, holding constant the number of units sold. The *sales variance* reports how much of the *quantity variance* is due to actual quantity sold differing from budget, holding the mix constant.

Q14–1: The firm's business strategy is all the investment projects available to the firm today and into the future. The business strategy arises from the nature of the business the firm is in and the amount and type of spending on R&D.

Q14–2: Business strategy affects the organizational structure in three ways. The types of investments affect the way specialized knowledge is created and thus how decision rights are partitioned. The investments affect the physical asset structure and how the firm must be organized for decision making and control of these assets. Finally, the investments affect the type and nature of the customer base, which again causes the firm to adopt organizational structures to service this customer base.

The organizational structure in turn affects the business strategy. The ability of the firm to generate profitable investment ideas and implement them requires an organizational structure with incentives and controls conducive to maximizing firm value.

Q14–3: Technological and market structure changes cause firms' investment opportunities (business strategy) to change. Some previously profitable projects disappear and new profitable projects emerge. These changes in investment opportunities prompt changes in organizational architecture.

Q14–4: Maybe. Other firms adopting organizational changes are often reacting to a change in either technology or market conditions. Such changes should cause management to reexamine its firm's policies. But to simply mimic the other changes is not a good idea. Other firms have different investment opportunities and different organizational architectures. They may be changing organizational policies not because of some change in technology or market condition but because they realized their old system could be improved. Also, sometimes managers make mistakes and adopt value-reducing organizational changes, which should certainly not be mimicked.

Q14–5:

   i. High mean (e.g., Rolls-Royce versus Toyota).

   ii. Low variance (McDonald's hamburgers versus local diner).

   iii. Larger number of options.

   iv. Meeting customer expectations.

Q14–6:

   i. Knowledge of customer expectations.

   ii. Measures of actual realized value.

   iii. Weights to combine the various deviations from expectations.

Q14–7:

   i. Prevention costs—incurred to eliminate defective units before they are produced.

   ii. Inspection costs—incurred to eliminate defective units before they are shipped.

   iii. Scrap/waste costs—the costs of defective units in manufacturing.

   iv. Failure costs—costs of returns, costs of warranty work, and opportunity cost of lost sales from reputation effects.

Q14–8: JIT takes on many aspects of a process costing system; there are no batches or discrete jobs. Instead, separate accounts, labor, and overhead are charged to a conversion costs account, and materials costs are charged to products. Finished goods inventory is charged for conversion costs and for materials as units are completed. The materials charge for completed units is backflushed, reducing the raw and in-process inventory account.

Q14–9: Decreasing throughputs has some dysfunctional aspects. Increased costs are incurred in factory redesign, setup time reduction, and JIT delivery of raw material. Accounting systems focused on throughput time do not charge managers for these costs. Consequently, managers measured on throughput will do things that may decrease throughput but at the expense of firm profits.

Q14–10: The balanced scorecard seeks to better link the boxes in Figure 14–1 on business strategy and the performance evaluation system. A balanced scorecard translates the strategy into a plan of action that identifies specific objectives and performance drivers to help determine if the organization is moving in the right direction.

Q14–11: Balanced scorecards can be useful if they cause managers to identify the underlying value drivers that create firm value and communicate these inside the firm. However, balanced scorecards have several drawbacks. First, balanced scorecards ignore changes in other parts of the firm's organizational architecture, such as decision rights assignments and compensation plans. Changing just one leg of the three-legged stool can create dysfunctional results. Second, telling managers to simultaneously maximize 20 balanced scorecard indicators provides no guidance as to the relative trade-off among the indicators. It is an impossible task. You can only maximize one variable at a time. Third, if their pay is based on multiple metrics, managers will choose those measures that are easiest to achieve and ignore more difficult tasks. Fourth, by giving managers multiple criteria for measuring their success, the balanced scorecard reduces their accountability for destroying shareholder value.

Glossary

Absorbed Overhead. See *Applied Overhead*.

Absorption Cost System. A cost system designed to allocate all manufacturing costs into product costs. All direct and indirect manufacturing costs, including overheads incurred in the period, are assigned to products produced or still in progress.

Accelerated Depreciation. Any depreciation method that depreciates an asset faster than the straight-line depreciation method. See *Double-Declining-Balance Depreciation as an example*.

Activity Base. See *Cost Driver*.

Activity-Based Costing. A process of identifying activities that cause indirect costs and choosing cost drivers to apply those indirect costs to different products and services.

Activity-Based Management. The management processes that use activity-based costing information to improve firm performance by eliminating non-value-added activities, making better pricing and product-mix decisions, improving manufacturing and administrative processes, and designing better products.

Actual Expenses. The expenses incurred during a given budget period.

Actual Overhead Costs. Indirect costs incurred by the organization.

Actual Revenue. The revenue generated during a given budget period.

Actual Usage. The number of times an allocation base is used during the period.

Actual Volume. The amount of the volume produced during a period of time.

Agency Cost. The cost of agents pursuing their own interests instead of the principal's. Cost includes the reduction in the value of the firm and all resources expended to reduce the divergence of interest.

Alienability. The right to sell something and receive the proceeds from the sale.

Alienable Right. The right of an individual or a firm to take an action with a specific object, including selling the object.

Allocation Base. The unit of measure used to allocate costs. For example, direct machine hours would be an allocation base used for distributing indirect manufacturing costs.

Annuity. A stream of equal cash flows for a fixed number of periods.

Applied Overhead. Overhead costs allocated to products based on an overhead absorption rate. Also called absorbed overhead.

Appraisal Costs. Costs related to identifying defective units before they are shipped to customers.

Asset Structure. The nature and geographic dispersion of assets held by the organization.

Average Cost. The total costs of production divided by the number of units produced.

Avoidable Product and Service Costs. Those costs that are no longer incurred if a product or service is dropped.

Balanced Scorecard. A set of performance measures that provide a comprehensive view of the organization by recognizing the goals of shareholders and the satisfaction of customers.

Basic Estimating Factors. Forecasts of strategic elements faced by the firm, such as selling prices and input costs.

Batch-Level Costs. Indirect costs that are associated with the number of batches of a particular product or service.

Benchmarking. Comparison of an organization's processes, products, or services with those of a top competitor.

Benefit. Aspects of a decision that help the organization achieve its goals.

Benefit-Cost Ratio. The ratio of benefits divided by costs of a project, program, or decision. If the ratio is greater than 1, the benefits outweigh the costs. If the ratio is less than 1, costs outweigh the benefits. If the ratio equals 1, costs and benefits are equal.

Beta. The systematic (nondiversifiable) risk of a firm's stock. Beta is an estimate of the sensitivity of the firm's stock in relation to the market. If a firm's beta is greater than 1, the firm's stock varies more than the average stock in the market. If a firm's beta is less than one, it is less risky than the average stock in the market. A stock with a beta equal to 1 is of average riskiness. Beta is estimated as the slope coefficient from regressing a firm's stock returns on the market returns.

Book Value. Purchase price minus accumulated depreciation for a depreciable asset.

Bottleneck. The process of an organization that has the least capacity.

Break-Even Analysis. The process of identifying the number of units that must be sold to achieve zero profit.

Break-Even Point. The number of units needed to sell in order for total revenues to equal both fixed and variable costs.

Budget. A forecast of the revenues and/or expenses expected to occur within a future time period. Budgets are an integral part of the organization's performance evaluation and decision rights partitioning system.

Budget Lapsing. A type of budgeting that does not allow managers to carry over budget surpluses from one year into the next year. Under a budget lapsing system, funds not spent are lost at the end of the budget period.

Budget Variance. A budget variance occurs when actual expenses differ from budgeted expenses or when budgeted revenues differ from actual revenues.

Budgeted Expenses. The forecast of expenses expected to be incurred in a given time period.

Budgeted Overhead. Total overhead predicted to be incurred during a period, including fixed and variable overhead at budgeted volume.

Budgeted Overhead Costs. The expected indirect costs used to establish overhead rates.

Budgeted Revenue. The forecast of revenue expected to be generated in a given time period.

Budgeted Volume. The amount of production expected to occur during the year, usually stated in terms of a common input measure such as direct labor hours. Budgeted volume can be estimated as expected volume for next year or normal volume over the long run.

Budgeting. Process of gathering information to assist in making forecasts.

Business Strategy. How the firm creates value in terms of products offered, markets served, technology utilized, and the nature of the firm's asset structure, including the investment projects available today and in the future.

By-Product. A joint product of a manufacturing process that has either little commercial value or is not of sufficient interest to management to maintain separate cost and revenue reports.

Capacity. Measure of constraints on the operation of an organization.

Capital Budgeting. The process of choosing an investment project by comparing the future cash flows from the project with its investment.

Carrying Costs. See *Holding Costs*.

Common Cost. A cost that is shared by two or more products or users.

Compound Interest. Interest earned on money invested, including principal and reinvested interest.

Computer-Aided Manufacturing (CAM). Use of programmable robots and other programmable devices to assist in the manufacturing of products.

Contribution Margin. Revenues less all variable costs.

Contribution Margin per Unit. The sales price minus the variable cost per unit.

Control. Use of procedures which help ensure that self-interested agents of the organization maximize the value of the organization.

Controllability Principle. Holding managers responsible for only those decisions for which they are given authority.

Controllable Costs. Costs that are affected by a particular manager's decisions.

Controller. The person in charge of both management accounting and financial accounting in an organization; usually the chief accountant. Also called comptroller.

Conversion Costs. All manufacturing costs other than direct material costs.

Cost. Cash or other assets that must be surrendered or future claims that must be given in order to achieve a specific goal.

Cost Accounting. Section of managerial accounting that involves the calculation and reporting of actual or predicted costs of products, services, or processes.

Cost Allocation. The distribution or assignment of indirect, common, or joint costs to different departments, processes, or products within an organization.

Cost Application. The distribution (or assignment) of indirect, common, or joint costs to different products, as distinguished from cost allocation, which broadly covers departments, activities, or products.

Cost/Benefit Analysis. The process of making decisions by comparing the costs and benefits of alternative choices.

Cost Center. A type of organizational subunit in which managers have decision rights over a set of costs and are evaluated in part on achieving cost targets.

Cost Driver. The physical measure of activity, such as machine setups or number of purchase orders, that is most highly associated with total costs in the activity center.

Cost Object. A product, process, department, or program that the organization wishes to cost.

Cost of Capital. The opportunity cost of funds invested in a particular project, or the minimum required rate of return necessary for a potential project to be considered.

Cost of Goods Sold. The historical cost of products sold as reported in the income statement.

Cost of Quality. Cost of preventing, identifying, and correcting quality problems. Also includes external costs such as the cost of lost sales and lost goodwill due to failing to prevent or correct quality problems.

Cost Pools. The accumulation of costs related to an indirect activity.

Cost–Volume–Profit (CVP) Analysis. The process of estimating profit assuming fixed and variable costs and a constant price over all rates of output.

Current Cost. The cost of replacing current resources using the prices of identical or similar resources available in the market.

Customer Base. The type and geographical location of customers.

Death Spiral. A situation occurring when transfer prices include fixed costs and users reduce their use of the internal product or service. This further increases the transfer price (based on average cost) and more users reduce their demand.

Decentralization. Assignment of decision-making rights to lower operating levels of an organization. Decreases cost of transferring specific knowledge needed to make decisions, but increases the cost of controlling behavior.

Decision Control. Those aspects of the decision process in which managers either ratify or monitor decisions.

Decision Management. Those aspects of the decision process where managers either initiate or implement decisions.

Decision Model. Methodical routine, such as a mathematical formula, for comparing alternative actions.

Decision Rights. The duties that a particular individual in an organization is expected to perform.

Dedicated Flow Line. The factory is organized by product line, and workers and machines are arranged to produce a single type of product. Products are not produced in batches but rather in single units.

Denominator Volume. The production level used to determine the budgeted overhead absorption rate.

Depreciation. The reduction in the historical cost of a fixed asset over time.

Depreciation Tax Shield. The reduction in taxes due to depreciation's reducing taxable income.

Differential Cost. See *Incremental Cost.*

Direct Allocation Method. A method of allocating service department costs directly to operating departments. This method ignores service departments providing services to other service departments.

Direct Costing. A cost system that values products based on only their variable costs and writes off all fixed costs against income in the year that the fixed costs are incurred. Also called *Variable Costing.*

Direct Costs. Costs that can be easily traced or metered directly to a product or service.

Direct Labor. Labor costs that can be identified with a specific product or service.

Direct Labor Variance. Difference between actual labor cost incurred and standard labor cost; a variance that occurs as the result of a combination of two variances: wage variance and efficiency variance. The wage variance is the difference between the actual and standard wage multiplied by the actual number of hours worked. The efficiency variance is the difference between the actual and standard number of hours worked multiplied by the standard wage rate.

Direct Materials. Parts and raw materials of a product.

Direct Materials Variance. Difference between actual materials cost incurred and standard labor cost; a variance that occurs as the result of a combination of two variances: price variance and quantity variance. The materials price variance is the difference between the actual and standard materials price multiplied by the actual quantity of materials. The materials quantity variance is the difference between the actual and standard materials quantity multiplied by the standard price.

Discount Factor $[1/(1 + r)^t]$. r is the discount rate and t is the number of years until the cash flow is received. The present value of \$1 received at a future date.

Discount Rate (r). Interest rate used to calculate the present or future value of cash flows. See *Cost of Capital.*

Discounted Cash Flow. Multiplying future cash flows by discount factors to obtain a present value.

Double-Declining-Balance Depreciation. Form of accelerated depreciation in which the depreciation rate $(2/n$, where n is the useful life) on the book value in each year is equal to double what the first year's depreciation rate would be under straight-line depreciation.

Dysfunctional Decision Making. When the benefits from a decision are smaller than the costs for the firm as a whole.

Economic Darwinism. Differential variations among firms' organizational architectures, decision processes, or technologies that affect firms' chances of survival in a competitive environment. Natural selection is the process whereby those differential variations that increase an organization's chances of survival will tend to be imitated and become more prevalent in other firms. Managers will not imitate management practices of failing firms but those of successful firms.

Economic Order Quantity. The order size that minimizes inventory ordering and holding costs.

Economic Value Added (EVA®). A performance measure calculated by taking adjusted accounting earnings and subtracting the weighted-average cost of capital times total capital employed. Similar to **Residual Income.**

Electronic Data Interchange (EDI). The direct exchange of data such as purchase orders and invoices between organizations via computer networks.

Employee Empowerment. The delegation of greater decision rights to members of the organization.

Encumbrance Accounting. Adding outstanding purchase orders to expenditures to help ensure that line-item spending authority is maintained.

Engineered Costs. Costs that result as a direct technological relation between inputs and outputs.

Enterprise Resource Planning (ERP). An integrated, automated, computer-based system that tracks production by job, work center, and activity and then shares the information enterprisewide in real time.

Equivalent Units. The amount of output stated in terms of complete units. For example, if 200 units of product are in work-in-process at the end of the month and these units are 75 percent complete, then these 200 units represent 150 equivalent units ($200 \times 75\%$).

Ethics. The process of determining standards and procedures for dealing with judgmental decisions affecting other people.

Expected Overhead. The fixed overhead plus the variable overhead multiplied by the expected volume.

Expected Volume. The amount of production expected to occur during the period, usually stated in terms of a common input measure such as direct labor hours.

Experience Curve. Theory that production costs per unit decrease as output increases because workers learn how to make the product more efficiently.

External Failure Costs. Costs incurred when a customer receives a defective product.

Externality. Costs or benefits imposed on other individuals without their participation in the decision-making process and without compensation for the cost or benefits imposed on them.

Facility-Related Costs. Indirect costs that are common to multiple products and services.

Failure Costs. The costs of returns, warranty work, and opportunity cost of lost sales from reputation effects when the product fails to meet customer expectations.

Favorable Variances. The amount that budgeted costs are greater than actual costs or budgeted revenues are less than actual revenues.

Financial Accounting. Accounting for the revenues, expenses, assets, liabilities, and equities of an organization, concentrating on external users (shareholders, lenders, and government). Constrained by FASB rulings and other generally accepted accounting principles.

Financial Accounting Standards Board (FASB). An independent board that is responsible for the establishment of *generally accepted accounting principles* (GAAP) used in external reporting.

Financial Leverage. The amount of debt in the firm's capital structure. Measured as the ratio of debt to equity or debt to total assets. The greater the firm's financial leverage, the more variable are the firm's profits and the more likely the firm will be forced into bankruptcy for a given downturn in sales.

Firm. A locus of contracts between individuals and resource owners.

First-In, First-Out (FIFO). An inventory flow that assumes that the oldest units in inventory are sold first.

Fixed Cost. The cost of initiating production, which does not vary with the number of units produced.

Flexible Budget. A budget that is stated as a function of some volume measure, such as units produced. Flexible budgets adjust for changes in volume.

Flexible Overhead Budget. The flexible overhead budget consists of fixed overhead plus variable overhead multiplied by volume.

Full Cost. The sum of all costs incurred in the production of a product or service.

Future Value. Value of cash flows at a future date, taking into account interest accumulated between when the cash flow occurred and the future date.

Goal Incongruence. When agents of the firm maximize their personal utility, not the principal's. See *Agency Cost*.

Gross Margin. Sales less cost of goods sold.

Historical Costs. The actual costs incurred to acquire resources. Accounting systems measure historical costs, not opportunity costs.

Holding Costs. Costs including insurance, labor, interest on capital investment, and storage space necessitated by storing inventory.

Implementation. The step in the decision process to carry out the plans of the organization.

Incremental Analysis. Basing a decision on changes in cash flows that result from that decision. Also called *incremental approach*.

Incremental Budgeting. A system whereby only the anticipated change in expenditures or revenues over last year must be justified to senior management.

Incremental Cost. The cost difference between two viable alternatives.

Indirect Cost Pool. All costs that cannot be directly traced to the product and that are similar are combined into a single amount and allocated to products or processes using a single allocation base.

Indirect Costs. Costs that are shared by two or more products or users.

Inflation. Decline in the purchasing power of money due to the average increase in prices.

Information System. A network, usually within an organization, by which information is generated and circulated. This network involves computer systems as well as other mechanisms, such as payroll records, purchasing documents, and managers' impressions and specific knowledge.

Initiation. The step in the decision process to identify areas of improvement within the organization.

Inspection Cost. Cost incurred to eliminate defective units before they are shipped; for example, testing costs.

Insulating Allocation. A method allocating costs in such a way that the performance of one division or subunit of the organization is unaffected by the performance of others. See *Noninsulating Allocation*.

Intermediate Product. Product passed from one segment of an organization to another for further work before it is ready for sale. May require transfer price.

Internal Accounting System. The accounting system that collects, aggregates, and generates and distributes budgeted and actual financial and cost information within the firm for use by executives and managers for both decision making and control.

Internal Auditor. A person within the organization who monitors various divisions and departments of the organization to determine whether prescribed operational procedures are being followed.

Internal Control System. A system of checks and balances within the organization that help the organization achieve its goals.

Internal Failure Costs. Costs incurred when a defect is discovered before being received by a customer.

Internal Rate of Return (IRR). Interest rate that equates the present value of future cash flows to the current outlay, or the discount rate that produces a zero net present value.

Internal Revenue Service (IRS). An agency of the U.S. government responsible for administering and collecting taxes.

Inventoriable Costs. See *Product Costs*.

Inventory. Depending on classification, direct materials, work in process, or finished goods, includes cost of materials, costs of producing incomplete units, or costs of producing complete, unsold units.

Inventory Ordering Costs. Handling costs, including the purchasing department and inspection costs resulting from ordering inventory.

Investment Center. A subunit of the firm that has decision rights over the amount of capital to be invested, the prices of its products, and the manufacturing process and is usually composed of several profit centers.

Investment Opportunities. All the investment projects available to the firm now and in the foreseeable future.

Job Order Costing. Products are produced in distinct batches or jobs and the costs of each specific batch are tracked separately using a Job Order Cost Sheet.

Job Order System. A system of recording costs for a particular job, which could be a single unit or a batch.

Joint Cost. The cost of the input and process that yields two or more products in fixed proportions as a result. For example, the cost of the barrel of oil and of splitting it into gasoline and motor oil is a joint cost.

Joint Products. Products generated from the splitting of a single material input.

Just-in-Time Production. A production system in which each item on the production line is produced immediately as needed by the next step in the process, thereby reducing raw materials and in-process inventories.

Just-in-Time Purchasing. The purchasing department can only order materials as they are needed for production. Usually, the purchasing department has a blanket purchase order with the vendor calling for daily deliveries.

Key Performance Indicators. Those actions and activities required for the firm to achieve its strategy and hence maximize its value.

Key Planning Assumptions. Those factors that are to some extent beyond management control and that set a limit on the overall activities of the firm. See *Basic Estimating Factors*.

Labor Efficiency Variance. The actual number of hours worked minus the standard number of hours, multiplied by the standard wage rate.

Last-In, First-Out (LIFO). An inventory flow that assumes that the newest units in inventory are sold first.

Line Item Budget. A budget that authorizes the manager to spend only up to the specified amount budgeted for each particular expense item listed in the budget.

Line Personnel. Production supervisors, workers, and other employees with direct responsibility for manufacturing (or for another firm objective).

Linear Programming. A mathematical technique for finding the optimal decision given a linear objective function and multiple linear constraints.

Management Accounting. The accounting system used within the organization to help the organization achieve its goals.

Management by Exception.   The practice of focusing on operating activities that show results that significantly differ from expected standard results.

Managerial (Management) Accounting.   The internal use by managers of the accounting system for decision making and control. Also called *Internal Accounting*.

Marginal Cost.   The incremental cost of the last unit produced, which in most cases varies as volume changes.

Marginal Revenue.   The incremental revenue added by the last unit sold, which in most cases varies as volume changes.

Market Price.   The price or value of a good or service received in an exchange between two independent parties.

Master Budget.   A document that integrates all the estimates from the different departments to establish guidelines and benchmarks for the whole organization.

Materials Price Variance.   The difference between the actual price and standard price of raw materials times the actual quantity used or purchased.

Materials Quantity Variance.   The difference between the actual and standard quantity of materials used times the standard price.

Materials Requirement Planning (MRP).   Computer programs that allow organizations to quickly ascertain resource requirements to make a product.

Microeconomics.   The study of the behavior of consumers and firms in competitive, oligopolistic, and monopolistic markets using the underlying theories of supply and demand.

Mix Variance.   Captures the effect of substitution among the products, holding constant the number of units sold.

Mixed Cost.   Cost that cannot be classified as being purely fixed or purely variable; for example, utilities.

Modified Accelerated Cost Recovery System (MACRS).   Allowed depreciation expense for tax purposes based on tax regulation that classifies depreciable assets into different recovery periods that have various patterns of depreciation.

Monitoring.   The step in the decision process to make sure that plans are implemented as designed.

Monitoring Cost.   The cost of observing members of the organization directly or indirectly.

Multistage Cost Allocation.   The process of allocating costs to cost objects followed by the allocation of costs from those cost objects to other cost objects.

Mutual Monitoring.   When one agent observes and reports on dysfunctional/nonoptimal decisions made by another agent.

Negative Externality.   A cost imposed on individuals that is the result of a decision that took place without their participation in the decision-making process and without compensation.

Negotiated Price.   A transfer pricing method whereby the transfer price is determined through negotiations between the purchasing and selling division managers.

Net Income.   The excess of all revenues and gains over all expenses and losses for a specific period of time.

Net Present Value (NPV).   Discounted value of future cash flows less initial investment. Method for evaluating capital investment projects.

Net Realizable Value.   Revenues less direct and separable costs for each product.

Nominal Interest Rate.   Interest rate observed in the market, composed of two elements: the real interest rate and expected inflation.

Noninsulating Allocation.   A noninsulating method bases cost allocations on the performance of all divisions' actual performance in aggregate. Therefore, the cost allocated to a division is, in part, dependent on the performance of the remaining divisions. See *Insulating Allocation*.

Non-Value-Added Cost.   Cost of an activity that does not improve a product or process and may be eliminated without changing the level of function, form, or volume of the product or process. See *Value-Added Cost*.

Normal Costing.   In setting overhead rates, expected volume is set at long-run average volume to prevent product costs from rising in downturns and falling in upswings.

Normal Volume.   The long-run average production volume of a plant or department.

Operating Leverage.   The ratio of fixed costs to total costs. The higher a firm's operating leverage, the greater will be the variability of profits for a given change in sales.

Opportunity Cost.   The receipts from the most valuable forgone alternative when making a decision or choice among many options.

Opportunity Cost of Capital.   The forgone opportunity of using cash for another purpose such as earning interest in a bank account.

Organizational Architecture.   The structure of an organization. Consists of (1) the assignment of decision rights within the organization; (2) the methods of rewarding individuals; and (3) the systems to evaluate the performance of both individuals and business units.

Outlay Cost.   A cost that requires a cash disbursement. Also called *out-of-pocket cost*.

Outsourcing.   Choosing to have an outside supplier rather than an internal subunit of the organization provide a product or service.

Overabsorbed Overhead.   The amount of overhead applied is greater than actual overhead cost incurred.

Overhead. All manufacturing costs that cannot be directly traced to a product. Overhead includes indirect labor and materials, plant depreciation, insurance and property taxes, plant management salaries, and so forth. See *Indirect Cost Pool*.

Overhead Absorbed. The overhead rate multiplied by standard units of volume.

Overhead Absorption Rate. Budgeted overhead divided by budgeted volume. Also called overhead application rate.

Overhead Costs. Indirect costs of products or services.

Overhead Efficiency Variance. The difference between flexible budgets using actual volume and standard volume. It is an estimate of the additional overhead incurred or saved as a result of the inefficient or efficient use of the plant or department.

Overhead Spending Variance. Actual overhead cost incurred less the flexible budget at actual volume. It is an estimate of how much actual overhead incurred differs from the amount of overhead that should have been incurred given the actual volume in the plant or department.

Overhead Volume Variance. The flexible budget at standard volume less the overhead applied. It is an estimate of the unused or overused fixed plant capacity.

Participative Budgeting. Eliciting opinions from affected managers in establishing a budget.

Payback Method. Method of evaluating a project by measuring the time until the investment is recovered. Although very easy to compute, this method ignores time value of money and cash flows after payback, making it a poor measure of profitability.

Payback Period. The time required to generate cash inflows equal to the initial investment.

Performance Measure. Direct or indirect measures of actions of individuals or groups of individuals within the organization.

Performance Reports. Evaluation tool used for comparing budgeted and actual performance.

Period Costs. Costs that are expensed in the period in which they are incurred because they are not part of the product's costs. Includes interest expense, advertising, selling, administrative, and distribution expenses, and research and development costs.

Perpetuity. An infinite stream of equal payments received each period and invested at a given discount rate.

Physical Measure Method. A procedure of dividing joint costs based on a physical characteristic of the joint products.

Planning. Establishing goals and preparing possible budgets to achieve those goals.

Positive Externality. A benefit seen by individuals that is the result of a decision that took place without their participation in the decision-making process and for which they do not pay.

Practical Capacity. The highest rate at which an organization can operate without a rise in congestion.

Present Value. The amount of money that, if invested today, would grow to a designated future amount. Discounted value of future cash flows.

Prevention Costs. Costs incurred to prevent defective units before they are produced. For example, reengineering products or production processes.

Pricing Decision. The choice of a price for a product or service.

Prime Cost. Direct materials plus direct labor costs.

Process Costing. A method of costing products produced in a continuous process in which costs cannot be accumulated by the batch or job.

Product Costs. All costs incurred in the manufacturing process that can be traced or allocated to a given product and inventoried. Unlike period costs, product costs are accrued to the period in which they are sold.

Product-Level Costs. Costs associated with a product, but not with a particular unit or batch of the product.

Product Mix Decision. A decision on the types and proportions of products and services to offer.

Product or Service Cost. The forgone opportunity of using resources to provide a product or service.

Production-Sustaining Costs. Costs that arise from sustaining the overall operation of the factory.

Profit Center. A subunit of the firm with the decision rights over prices and manufacturing processes to maximize profit. Profit centers are evaluated on meeting target profits and are composed of several cost centers.

Pro-Forma Financial Statements. Financial statements based on forecasted data.

Projected Costs. Costs forecasted for a future time period.

Proration. The process of dividing over- or underabsorbed overhead into finished inventory, cost of goods sold, and work in process.

Qualitative Factors. Elements that are not measurable using numerical means.

Quality. Measure of a product's conformance to prespecified standards for both qualitative and quantitative factors as perceived by the customer.

Ratification. The step in the decision process to determine whether a proposal is consistent with the goals of the organization.

Real Interest Rate.   Interest rate that would occur with no inflation. The real interest rate is composed of a risk-free interest rate plus a risk premium.

Reciprocal Allocation Method.   A method of allocating service costs that explicitly recognizes all interactions among the service departments.

Relative Performance Evaluation.   Instead of basing performance on absolute performance, performance is judged relative to some benchmark, usually other individuals' performance as a group, to help control for random events outside the control of the manager being evaluated.

Relative Sales Value Method.   A procedure of dividing joint costs based on the gross sales value of the joint products.

Relevant Range.   The range of output levels over which variable costs are reasonable approximations of opportunity costs.

Required Rate of Return.   See *Cost of Capital*.

Residual Income.   A performance measure for investment centers that subtracts the opportunity cost of the investment from the income generated by the assets of the investment.

Responsibility Accounting.   The process of recognizing subunits within the organization, assigning decision rights to managers in those subunits, and evaluating the performance of those managers.

Return on Investment (ROI).   A performance measure calculated by dividing the income from an investment by the size of the investment.

Risk Premium.   Expected additional return that compensates for the uncertainty involved with an investment.

Risk-Free Interest Rate.   The guaranteed interest rate that can be earned loaning money to the federal government. Government securities define the risk-free rate since they are the only investments considered to be free of default risk.

Robinson-Patman Act.   A federal law that prohibits charging customers different prices if it is injurious to competition in the market.

Sales Variance.   Captures the effect of quantity sold holding the mix of products sold constant.

Satisficing Behavior.   Employees seeking to achieve satisfactory levels of performance, but not trying to excel.

Securities and Exchange Commission (SEC).   A federal commission, established through the Securities Exchange Act of 1934, which administers the securities laws and regulates purchases and sales of securities, including financial disclosure.

Segment.   Any part of an organization that can be separated out for purposes of investment, profit, and/or cost

evaluation. See also *Cost Center, Investment Center*, and *Profit Center*.

Semivariable Cost.   See *Mixed Cost*.

Separable Costs.   Separable costs are not part of the joint production process but rather are beyond the point at which the joint costs are incurred. Separable costs can be directly traced to individual products.

Setup Costs.   Costs, including labor and materials, necessary to prepare a machine to begin a production run.

Shutdown Costs.   Costs incurred in shutting down a division or product line. These costs are only incurred if the shutdown decision is made.

Split-Off Point.   The point in processing at which all joint costs have been incurred.

Staff Personnel.   The employees of an organization who provide services such as purchasing, sales, and maintenance to support line personnel.

Stakeholders.   Parties that are affected by an organization.

Standard Costs.   Costs that are predetermined on a per-unit basis. Standard costs are used as a benchmark for evaluating performance. These costs are often used in or are the output from the budgeting process.

Standard Volume.   The amount of volume the plant would have generated if each unit of product manufactured used precisely the standard unit of volume allowed.

Static Budgets.   Budgets that don't adjust for volume.

Step Cost.   A cost that is constant over ranges of production and increases by discrete amounts as volume increases from one interval to the next.

Step-Down Method.   A method of allocating costs whereby one service department's cost is allocated to all remaining service departments and operating departments, and so on, until all service department costs are allocated to final products.

Straight-Line Depreciation.   Depreciation method in which the amount taken to depreciation expense each year is constant and equal to $1/n$ times the depreciable amount, where n is the depreciable life of the asset.

Strategic Planning.   The process whereby managers select the firm's overall objectives and the tactics to achieve those objectives.

Suboptimal Decision Making.   See *Dysfunctional Decision Making*.

Sunk Cost.   Costs that were incurred in the past, cannot be recovered, and are therefore irrelevant for decision making.

Target Costing.   The process of designing a quality product at a sufficiently low cost to be able to sell the product at a competitive price and still yield a sufficient profit.

Tax Accounting. The accounting system used to calculate taxable income and report to government taxing authorities.

Theory of Constraints. A process of identifying and managing constraints in the making of products or in the provision of services.

Throughput Time. The total time from when a product starts the production process until it is ready for sale, including processing time, time waiting to be moved or worked on, time spent in transit, and inspection time. Also called *cycle time*.

Total Overhead Variance. The difference between total actual and applied overhead.

Total Quality Management (TQM). A philosophy of continually lowering costs and improving the provision of services and products to customers.

Transfer Price. The cost charged by one segment of an organization for a product or service supplied to another segment of the same organization.

Transferred-In-Cost. The total cost of production from previous processing that is transferred to the next department in which the product is scheduled for processing.

Treasurer. Manager or officer responsible for cash management.

Tubs on Their Own Bottoms. An expression used to refer to operating units in a nonprofit organization in order to avoid the term "profit center."

Underabsorbed Overhead. When actual overhead incurred is higher than overhead assigned to products during the year.

Unfavorable Variances. The amount by which budgeted costs are less than actual costs or by which budgeted revenues are greater than actual revenues.

Unit-Level Costs. Costs that arise from activities that are performed at least once for each unit of product. Direct labor and materials are unit-level costs.

Value Chain. Flow of business functions where value (function, form, or volume) is increased at each stage. Examples would be R&D, Manufacturing, Marketing, Sales, Distribution, and Service.

Value-Added Activities. Activities that provide value to the customer.

Value-Added Cost. Cost related to an activity that improves the function, form, or volume of a product or process, and may not be eliminated without changing the product or process. See *Non-Value-Added Cost*.

Variable Costing. A cost system that excludes fixed costs from product costs and writes off all fixed costs against income in the year that the costs are incurred. Also called *Direct Costing*.

Variable Costs. Additional costs incurred when unit production increases. Variable costs per unit usually are assumed not to vary with volume.

Variance. The difference between budgeted and actual costs or standard and actual costs. May relate to price or quantity for labor, materials, or overhead.

Wage Variance. The actual wage per hour minus the standard wage multiplied by the actual number of hours worked.

Waste Costs. The costs of defective units in manufacturing.

Weighted-Average Cost. A per-unit product cost determined by taking the weighted average of the cost of all units in inventory.

Zero-Based Budgeting. A system in which each budgeted line item must be justified and reviewed in total each year. That is, each year the budget for each line item is set to zero and the total has to be justified to senior management before the budget is approved.

Index